IPOMADON

EARLY ENGLISH TEXT SOCIETY
No. 316
2001

Here begynneth a good tale of

Ipomydon Ipomadon

Of love were lykynge of to lere
And joye tille alle that wol here
That wote what loue may mene
But who so hath gretto haste to lose
And may not com to his Aboue
That poynts dothe loners tene

Fayrs speche brekyth neuer bone
That makythe these loners ilkone
Ay hape of better to wone
And gyue theym selfe to grete trauayle
Wheddyr it helpe or not Auayle
Ofte sythes theyr hartes be sore
Be this poynts Avell may I preue
That of his loue Avas lothe to leue
Tho tyme that he be gran
Therefore in þe worlde where and he went
In Iustys or in turnamente
And more the pryce he wan
But A straunge louer he Avas one
I hope ye haue harde speke of non
That euer god made to be man
So lother knowen for to be
No wheduie a better knyght þan he
Was no lewarde than
In Cessyle sumtyme wonys A kyng
That holden Avas Wt olde and ynge
Off poyntis wythe outen pere
he Avas Worthy were p Wyse

IPOMADON

EDITED BY

RHIANNON PURDIE

Published for
THE EARLY ENGLISH TEXT SOCIETY
by the
OXFORD UNIVERSITY PRESS
2001

OXFORD
UNIVERSITY PRESS

Great Clarendon Street, Oxford OX2 6DP

Oxford University Press is a department of the University of Oxford.
It furthers the University's objective of excellence in research, scholarship,
and education by publishing worldwide in

Oxford New York

Athens Auckland Bangkok Bogotá Buenos Aires Cape Town
Chennai Dar es Salaam Delhi Florence Hong Kong Istanbul Karachi
Kolkata Kuala Lumpur Madrid Melbourne Mexico City Mumbai Nairobi
Paris São Paulo Shanghai Singapore Taipei Tokyo Toronto Warsaw

with associated companies in Berlin Ibadan

Oxford is a registered trade mark of Oxford University Press
in the UK and in certain other countries

Published in the United States
by Oxford University Press Inc., New York

British Library Cataloguing in Publication Data

Data available

Library of Congress Cataloging in Publication Data

Data applied for

ISBN 0-19-722319-2

1 3 5 7 9 10 8 6 4 2

Typeset by Joshua Associates Ltd., Oxford
Printed in Great Britain
on acid-free paper by
Print Wright Ltd., Ipswich

PREFACE

I wish to thank Chetham's Library, Manchester, for permission to print the text of *Ipomadon* from MS Chetham 8009, and to include a plate as the frontispiece. This edition originated as a PhD thesis at the University of Bristol, and was completed during my time as a British Academy postdoctoral research fellow in the School of English at the University of St Andrews: I would like to acknowledge my gratitude to both of these institutions and to the British Academy. For advice and assistance in preparing this edition I am particularly indebted to George Jack, Ad Putter (who supervised the thesis), and John Burrow. In addition I must thank Priscilla Bawcutt, Judith Jefferson, Myra Stokes, Tony Lodge and Alison Williams for various individual contributions and last-minute rescues from error. The extraordinary efficiency of the Early English Text Society's editorial secretary, Dr. Helen Spencer, should also be recorded here for posterity. And finally I must thank Neale, who now knows more about *Ipomadon* than he could ever have wished to but still manages to express encouragement and even enthusiasm for my work. For this partisan blindness I am deeply grateful.

CONTENTS

ABBREVIATIONS

A:	Anglian
AN:	Anglo-Norman
Andersen:	D. M. Andersen, 'An Edition of the Middle English *Ipomadon*' (unpubl. Ph. D. thesis, University of California at Davis, 1968).
Campbell:	A. Campbell, *Old English Grammar* (Oxford, 1959).
Chaucer:	All citations from *The Riverside Chaucer*, 3rd edn., ed. Larry D. Benson *et al.* (Oxford, 1988).
EETS (ES):	Early English Text Society (Extra Series).
EETS (OS):	Early English Text Society (Original Series).
Holden:	A. J. Holden, ed., *Ipomédon: poème de Hue de Rotelande (fin du XIIe siècle)* (Paris, 1979).
Jordan:	Richard Jordan's *Handbook of Middle English Grammar: Phonology*, trans. and revised by Eugene Crook (The Hague, 1974).
K.:	Eugen Kölbing, ed., *Ipomedon in drei Englischen Bearbeitungen* (Breslau, 1889).
Ka.:	Max Kaluza, review of Kölbing's *Ipomedon. Englische Studien* XIII (1889), 482–93.
Ki.:	G. L. Kittredge, 'Anmerkungen zum me. *Ipomadon A.*' *Englische Studien* XIV (1890), 386–91.
Kp.:	Emil Köppel, 'Zur Textkritik des Ipomadon'. *Englische Studien* XIV (1890), 371–86.
LALME:	A. McIntosh, M. L. Samuels, M. Benskin. *A Linguistic Atlas of Late Medieval English.* 4 vols. (Aberdeen, 1986).
Manual:	J. Burke Severs, ed., *A Manual of the Writings in Middle English 1050–1500*, Fascicule 1: Romances (New Haven, 1967).
MdnE:	Modern English
ME:	Middle English
MED:	*Middle English Dictionary* (Ann Arbor, 1954–).
Mustanoja:	Tauno F. Mustanoja, *A Middle English Syntax*, Part 1. Mémoires de la Société Néophilologique (Helsinki, 1960).
Nth.:	Northern
OE:	Old English

OED: *New English Dictionary* (Oxford, 1888–1928).

OF: Old French

ON: Old Norse

PMLA: *Publications of the Modern Language Association of America.*

S&J: A. V. C. Schmidt and N. Jacobs, eds. *Medieval English Romances* (London, 1980). (Extracts from *Ipomadon A* pp. 40–9; 196–239; 273–81).

SGGK: *Sir Gawain and the Green Knight*, eds. J. R. R. Tolkien & E. V. Gordon; 2nd edition ed. Norman Davis (Oxford, 1972).

Whiting: B. J. Whiting, *Proverbs, Sentences and Proverbial Phrases from English Writings Mainly Before 1500* (Cambridge, Mass. & London, 1968).

INTRODUCTION

GENERAL INTRODUCTION

IPOMADON A

Ipomadon A is an anonymous Middle English rendition, dating from anywhere between the last decade of the fourteenth century and the middle of the fifteenth century, of the twelfth-century Anglo-Norman romance *Ipomedon* by Hue de Rotelande.[1] It is written in tail-rhyme stanzas of twelve lines each, 8,890 lines in total, and is extant in a single manuscript, MS Chetham 8009 (Manchester). It was first edited, along with the two other Middle English versions of *Ipomedon*, by Eugen Kölbing in his *Ipomedon in drei Englischen Bearbeitungen* (Breslau, 1889), where he labelled them *Ipomadon A*, *Ipomydon B* and *Ipomedon C*. [2] Since, however, the different spellings of the eponymous hero's name are sufficient to distinguish between the Middle English texts, the version edited here will be referred to simply as *Ipomadon* from this point on. It has also been edited in full by D. M. Andersen as an unpublished dissertation for Davis University, California,[3] and selections have been published in the collections of Middle English romances by French and Hale and, most recently, Schmidt and Jacobs.[4] Despite the fact that it only survives in one manuscript, Severs describes the poem as 'one of the most notable in Middle English',[5] and there are several good reasons for this: it is the longest continuous example of tail-rhyme verse in Middle English; it is elegantly written—nothing like the kind of verse parodied in Chaucer's *Sir Thopas*—and finally, it is unusual

---

[1] The most recent edition is by A. J. Holden, *Ipomedon: poème de Hue de Rotelande (fin du XIIᵉsiècle)*, (Paris, 1979): all references to the Anglo-Norman text are to this edition.

[2] All subsequent references to Kölbing are to this edition unless otherwise indicated.

[3] D. M. Andersen, 'An Edition of the Middle English *Ipomadon*', (unpubl. PhD thesis, University of California at Davis, 1968). Contains an interesting general introduction but only twenty-eight pages of explanatory notes in total and no glossary. The discussion of authorial dialect places the text on the West Midland/East Midland border: it includes misleading comments on Kölbing's far more comprehensive analysis, and the criteria used to evaluate the linguistic evidence are in some cases completely erroneous.

[4] *Middle English Metrical Romances*, eds. W. H. French and C. B. Hale (New York, 1964), originally published in 2 vols. in 1930, pp. 649–67; *Medieval English Romances*, 2 vols., eds. A. V. C. Schmidt with Nicholas Jacobs (London, 1980), pp. 40–49, 196–239, 273–81.

[5] *Manual*, p. 155.

among Middle English translations for its faithfulness to its source, a copy of which the translator almost certainly had before him (see below, 'The Translator and his Source'). It is unfortunate that much of the English author's skill has been marred by the copying process. The scribe of MS Chetham 8009 seems to have been a careful enough copyist himself, but his predecessors were rather less so: several lines or passages are garbled beyond recovery; the names of people and places are frequently confused or mistaken, and rhyme and rhythm have been spoilt everywhere.[6] An exasperated Kölbing wrote grimly, 'sie stellt . . . eine der nachlässigsten und sorglosesten abschriften dar, die mir in der mittelenglischen litteratur vorgekommen sind' ('it represents one of the most slipshod and careless copies that I have ever encountered in Middle English literature').[7]

PLOT SUMMARY

The beautiful young heiress of Calabria makes a public vow to marry only the best knight in the world: for this and for her pride in general she is known as 'The Fere' ('Proud One'). Ipomadon, son of the King of Apulia, falls in love with her on the strength of her reputation and comes to her court to serve her, where he is known only as 'the straunge valett'. He devotes himself to hunting but refuses to bear arms, for which the Fere, who has secretly fallen in love with him, severely chides him.

Ashamed, he returns to Apulia and is knighted by his father. He then travels the world tourneying and winning *losse and pryce*. The Fere, meanwhile, is under severe pressure from her barons to marry. Hoping to lure back her 'straunge valett', she agrees to set a three-day tournament, the champion of which she will marry. Upon hearing of the tournament, Ipomadon returns to the neighbouring court of her uncle Mellyagere, The King of Sicily, where he goes by the name of 'Drew-le-reine'—the queen's special servant and something of a fool. At court he shows interest in nothing but hunting, but in secret he goes to the Fere's tournament each day and wins the *pryce* in successive disguises of white, red and black armour. At the end of this he has won the tournament and the Fere, but instead of

---

[6] See below, 'Language of the Text, Part I—Rhyming Practice'. Among the names of people and places, Jason is rechristened 'Josane' at l. 3143 and remains so for almost every subsequent citation; Imayne is rendered variously as 'aglyne', 'a maydon', and 'I maye' (ll. 831, 2147, 2160, 6541), and Canders is also called 'Tynders' (l. 2031).

[7] Kölbing, *op.cit.* p. xi.

claiming her he disappears once more, sending messages to her and the Sicilian court to say that her 'straunge valett', 'Drew-le-reine' (with whom the Sicilian queen is now also in love) and the three triumphant knights were all one and the same person. Upon the death of his father, Ipomadon becomes King of Apulia, but he leaves again to earn renown in the wars in France. When he hears that the Fere is besieged by the hideous Sir Lyolyne from 'Ynde Mayore', he hurries back to Mellyagere's court in Sicily disguised as a fool so as not to be recognised from his previous stay there as 'Drew-le-reine'. When the Fere's lady Imayne arrives to petition for a champion, she is horrified to find that the fool is the only one who offers.

On the journey back, Ipomadon-as-fool rescues her from various evil-intentioned knights, for which she too falls in love with him. Upon reaching Calabria, he defeats Lyolyne, but since they are both armed in black, no one knows who has won. Ipomadon pretends to be Lyolyne and prepares to disappear once again, but Cabanus, the Fere's cousin and his erstwhile companion at the Sicilian court, arrives just in time to rescue her from, as he thinks, the triumphant Lyolyne. In the ensuing battle Ipomadon's gauntlet flies off to reveal a ring, given to him by his mother, that identifies him to be Cabanus's long-lost half-brother. The half-brothers are joyfully reconciled; the lovers are at last united and married.

IPOMEDON IN MIDDLE ENGLISH

There are two other versions of the *Ipomedon*-story in Middle English, both apparently written in the fifteenth century. The first is a 2,346–line couplet version known as *The Lyfe of Ipomydon*, and the second is a prose rendition, unfinished in the only extant copy, which Kölbing called *Ipomedon C* and which shall be referred to here as 'the prose *Ipomedon*'.[8]

At least three Middle English copies of the couplet *Lyfe of Ipomydon* have survived in complete or fragmentary form. The complete text appears in British Library MS Harley 2252, ff. 54a-84a. A nearly complete version printed by Wynkyn de Worde appears in Pierpont

---

[8] The prose version has so far only been edited by Kölbing in his edition of all three Middle English versions. *The Lyfe of Ipomydon* was also published by H. W. Weber in *English Metrical Romances of the Thirteenth, Fourteenth and Fifteenth Centuries* (Edinburgh, 1810), and was edited most recently by Tadahiro Ikegami, *The Lyfe of Ipomydon*, 2 vols. (Tokyo, 1983). The three versions are described briefly in the *Manual*, pp. 153–5.

Morgan Library MS 20896 (ff. B.i.ᵃ-I.v.ᵇ, corresponding to l. 193 ff. of the Harley text), and a single folio of a second Wynkyn de Worde edition now forms item 18 of the British Museum's Bagford Ballads collection (corresponding to ll. 261–320 of the Harley text).[9] Ikegami, its most recent editor, dates its composition to the second half of the fifteenth century.[10] The prose *Ipomedon* survives in only one manuscript, the fifteenth-century vellum MS Longleat 257, and is missing its conclusion. The *Manual of the Writings in Middle English* dates the manuscript as c.1460: that *Ipomedon* at least was copied before 1483 is indicated by the intriguing fact that f. 98b of this text is inscribed with the motto *tant le desieree* and name of Richard, Duke of Gloucester.[11]

It seems that all three Middle English versions of *Ipomedon* were translated independently from the Anglo-Norman (this is unquestionable in the case of the tail-rhyme *Ipomadon*—see below, 'The Translator and his Source'). The most obvious indication of this is in the names of some of the characters. The correspondences are best explained in tabular form:

AN *Ipomedon* (all MS variants)	*Ipomadon*	*Lyfe of Ipomydon*	*Ipomedon C*
Capaneus, Capenaus, Kapeneus	Cabanus, Gabanus	Capanyus, Campaynus, Camp(p)anus	Capaneus, Ca(m)panius
Caemius, Kaemius, Kaenneus, Kamius, Kaeminus, Caeninus	Cananeus, Canoneus, Gananeus	Caymys, Caymes	Kanius, Kaenius
Leonin(s), Lionin(s)	Lyolyne, Lyelyne	(Geron)	Leonyn

---

[9] On the relationships between these, see Carol M. Meale, 'Wynkyn de Worde's Setting-copy for *Ipomydon*', *Studies in Bibliography*, 35 (1982), 156–71.

[10] Ikegami, *op.cit.*, pp. lxiii–iv.

[11] See the *Manual*, p. 154; Carol M. Meale hazards a dating in the third quarter of the fifteenth century in 'The Middle English Romance of *Ipomedon*: a Late Medieval "Mirror" for Princes and Merchants', *Reading Medieval Studies*, 10 (1984), 136–79 (p. 137). On the connection with Richard III, see Meale, *ibid.*, pp. 138–41, and Anne F. Sutton and Livia Visser-Fuchs, 'Richard III's Books: II. A Collection of Romances and Old Testament Stories: 1 *Ipomedon*', *The Ricardian*, Vol. 7 No. 95 (Dec. 1986), 327–32 (pp. 331–2).

The Lyfe of Ipomydon is so different in style, focus and content from either the Anglo-Norman or the other two Middle English versions that it would be impossible to tell from these criteria alone which version it might stem from.[12] The prose *Ipomedon* presents the opposite difficulty in that the text follows the Anglo-Norman narration very closely in those sections where it has not either been pruned or embellished, but this closeness could at first glance have been drawn from the Middle English tail-rhyme *Ipomadon*, which is likewise extremely faithful to the Anglo-Norman in the relevant sections. The evidence of the names noted above, however, suggests immediately that neither *The Lyfe of Ipomydon* nor the prose *Ipomedon* derives from the tail-rhyme *Ipomadon*. While the name *Capanyus* might have been known to the authors independently through some version of the well-known legend of the 'Seven Against Thebes', from which Hue took many of his characters' names, the steward's name *Caymys* (in *The Lyfe of Ipomydon*) or *Ka(e)nius* (in the prose *Ipomedon*) can only have come from some version of the *Ipomedon*-story, and both of these forms of the name are far more similar to the Anglo-Norman variations than to the *Cananeus* used exclusively in the tail-rhyme *Ipomadon*.[13] Likewise, the form *Leonyn* in the prose text echoes the Anglo-Norman but differs appreciably from the tail-rhyme version's *Lyolyne*. It is not impossible that the forms in the extant version of *Ipomadon* are the result of scribal corruption—the text is certainly rife with it—but their consistent and frequent use would seem to argue against this.

Other indications that the prose *Ipomedon* was translated directly from the Anglo-Norman can be found in the dozens of occasions on which small details in the Anglo-Norman appear in the prose version, but not in *Ipomadon*. An example is the scene in which La Fière's barons are persuaded to grant her eight days' respite before naming a husband, and her defender Drias argues that *a theif or a manys mortherrere, that were appelled of fellony by the law of the land, shuld haue eight dayes of respite* (p. 331, ll. 43–45). This

---

[12] Kölbing could find no conclusive evidence for the dependence of *The Lyfe of Ipomydon* on either the Anglo-Norman text or the Middle English tail-rhyme text (pp. lix-lxv).

[13] The name of the hero, spelt *Ypomedoun* and *Ipomedon*, also appears in Chaucer's *Troilus and Criseyde* (Bk. V, l. 1502) and *Anelida and Arcite* (l. 58), but there it seems to have been derived from Statius's *Thebiad*. See notes to ll. 1485–1510 of Chaucer's *Troilus and Criseyde* in *The Riverside Chaucer*, 3rd Ed., ed. Larry D. Benson et al. (Oxford, 1988), pp. 1054–5.

corresponds to AN ll. 1879–82 *Se ço fu un de voz veisins, / De murdres u de larecins, / Kar par dreit l'esgardereit, / Al meins vint* [var. *owyt] jurz de terme avreit,* 'if one of your neighbours were to be investigated by law for murder or theft, he would have at least twenty [var. 'eight'] days respite', but the tail-rhyme *Ipomadon* has no mention of murderers: *The strengythe theeff þat euer my3te leve / Be the lawe ye muste hym gyffe / Respytte VIII dayes* (ll. 1808–10). Another example of wording that follows the Anglo–Norman version while differing from the tail-rhyme *Ipomadon* occurs after the first day of the tournament, when the courtiers say of Ipomedon's disguised combat, *it was double knighthode* (p. 340, l. 43). This translates unmistakably the Anglo–Norman narrator's praise for his hero at the same point in the narrative, *ço fu duble chevalrie* (l. 4270), as opposed to the *Ipomadon* version, *They sett all opur off worthynes / But at a chery stone* (ll. 3439–40).[14] Since there is no reason to suspect major scribal corruption in the two passages of tail-rhyme text quoted above (or in most of Kölbing's ninety-three other such examples), we must conclude that they approximate to the original text, and therefore that the wording of the prose *Ipomedon* is not derived from an earlier, slightly different version of the tail-rhyme text, but was translated directly from the Anglo-Norman.

IPOMEDON AND MIDDLE ENGLISH LITERATURE

The three different Middle English versions of the Anglo–Norman *Ipomedon* attest to the popularity of this text in England, as do the mentions of 'Ipomedon' in the fourteenth-century Middle English poems *Richard Coeur de Lion* and *The Parlement of the Thre Ages*.[15] Gavin Douglas, meanwhile, included *the secrete wyse hardy Ipomedon* in a list of noble lovers in his Middle Scots *The Palis of Honoure* (completed in 1500 or 1501), the adjective *secrete* indicating that he had the publicity-shy romance character in mind rather than the warrior in the legend of 'Seven against Thebes'.[16] This casual

---

[14] Kölbing gives a comprehensive list of ninety-five examples of this kind, pp. xlvi-li.

[15] For further discussion of these, see 'Date of Composition' below.

[16] Gavin Douglas, *The Palis of Honoure*, ed. David Parkinson (Kalamazoo, 1995), l. 578 (see p. 2 for date of poem). Ipomedon's bizarre love of secrecy is much remarked upon in the Anglo-Norman, and the adjectives *secrete* (or *prevy*), *wyse* and *hardy* are often applied to the hero in the tail-rhyme and prose Middle English versions, suggesting that Douglas had one of these three versions in mind rather than the couplet *Lyfe of Ipomydon*, in which the hero is not described thus and the secrecy theme is much diminished.

reference relies on the audience's recognition of the characters listed:
since the *Palis* was addressed to James IV of Scotland, this gives us
some idea of the social circles in which *Ipomedon* was moving by
1500, as does the fact that the prose *Ipomedon* appears in a manuscript that seems to have been autographed by the future king
Richard III of England.[17] It was clearly still being read in the
middle of the sixteenth century in Scotland, where it is cited in a
lengthy list of tales in the c.1549 *Complaynt of Scotland*.[18] The
influence of some version of *Ipomedon* may also be traceable in the
plots of Malory's tale of *Sir Gareth*, and in the fifteenth-century
Middle English romances of *Generydes* and *Roswall and Lillian*,
although Holden dismisses all but the last of these.[19]

The closest parallel is undoubtedly with *Roswall and Lillian*,
which presents a telescoped version of the first two episodes in
which Ipomedon appears in court in disguise—the first as the
'strange valet' at La Fière's court, and the second as Drew-le-
reine at the Sicilian court. The youthful hero Roswall arrives
incognito at the court of Bealm, where the princess Lillian makes
him her cup-bearer and falls in love with him. However, she is
betrothed to a man who is, as it happens, masquerading as Roswall,
and who has earlier extracted from Roswall a promise not to reveal
his identity. A three-day tournament is staged to celebrate the
forthcoming marriage, but Roswall goes out hunting instead. There
he meets a stranger who presents him with white armour and a
white steed, and Roswall, thus doubly disguised, is victorious at the
tournament. The pattern of *Ipomedon*'s tournament episode is
followed, with successive strangers presenting Roswall with red
and gold (rather than black) armour, and Lillian praising the
unknown knights while privately lamenting the fact that her beloved
valet refuses to engage in the tournament.[20] The parallels with
Ipomedon are too specific to doubt its influence.

[17] See above for discussion of the other Middle English versions of *Ipomedon*: see
Parkinson, *ibid.*, p. 2 on the dedication to James IV.

[18] *The Complaynt of Scotland*, ed. A. M. Stewart, Scottish Text Society, 4th Series,
vol. 11 (1979), p. 50 (f. 50v).

[19] Holden, *op.cit.*, p. 59. The case for *Ipomedon*'s influence on *Sir Gareth* has been
set out most thoroughly by Larry D. Benson in *Malory's Morte Darthur* (Cambridge,
Mass. & London, 1976), pp. 94–106. The connection with *Roswall and Lillian* is noted
in the *Manual*, pp. 152–3, and the parallels with characters and incidents in *Generydes*
are discussed by Kölbing, pp. xxxii–xxxiii. See also 'The Translator and his Source'
below.

[20] *Manual*, pp. 152–3.

THE MANUSCRIPT

The sole extant version of *Ipomadon* appears in MS Chetham 8009, a miscellany of fourteen religious and secular items copied in the last quarter of the fifteenth century, most likely in London, and now held in Chetham's Library, Manchester. A London provenance is suggested by Item 13, a list of the 'wardeyns and balyffys' of London. The dating is indicated by two factors: the paperstocks, which at their very widest range date from between 1423–93 (see below), and Item 12, which describes a meeting that took place between Charles the Bold of Burgundy and the emperor Frederick III at Trier in 1473 (this item was copied by a scribe who is also responsible for several other items in the manuscript, including *Ipomadon*). The manuscript has been described by Kölbing, N. R. Ker, Gisela Guddat-Figge, and Carol M. Meale.[21] All items are in English except Item 5, in which English alternates with Latin. The contents are as follows, with manuscript titles between quotation marks and editorial titles in italics:

1. *Life of St. Dorothy*; ff. 1a–2b. Prose, incomplete. Begins abruptly, 'The right glorious virgyn seint Dorothea . . . by all þe worlde of worldes Amen.'

2. 'Assvmpcio Sancte Marie', ff. 3a–17b. Verse. 'A merye tale tell I may . . . That lastithe evire wᵗ owte end . . . Explicit Assumpcio Sancte Marie Amen.'

3. 'Lyff of Seynt Anne'; ff. 18a–29b. Verse. 'O blessed Ihesu that arte full of myght . . . Here endyth the lyff of Seynt Anne.'

4. 'Lyf of Seynt Katerin'; ff. 30a–47b. Prose. 'Here begynnyth the lyf of Seynt Katerin and how she was maried to oure lord . . . Here endyth the lyf of Seynt Katerin And the maryage to oure lorde.'

5. 'Liber Catonis'; ff. 48a–75b. Verse (Latin and English). 'Cum anima aduerterem . . . Explicit liber Catonis . . . Quod non p ire ad 1 nisi S me.'

[21] N. R. Ker, *Medieval Manuscripts in British Libraries, vol. III* (Oxford, 1983), p. 361–4; Gisela Guddat-Figge, *Catalogue of Manuscripts Containing Middle English Romances* (München, 1976), pp. 238–40; Eugen Kölbing, 'Vier romanzen-handschriften', *Englische Studien*, 7 (1884), 195–201; Carol M. Meale, 'The Middle English Romance of *Ipomedon*', *op. cit.*, pp. 137–8, pp. 144–6, and notes 8, 47, 58, 59. On the probability of London provenance, see Meale, *ibid.*, p. 138. For further discussion of this and of themes evident in the organisation of the contents, see Rhiannon Purdie, 'Sexing the Manuscript: the evidence for female ownership of MS Chetham 8009', *Neophilologus*, 82 (1998), 139–48.

6. *Torrent of Portyngale*; ff. 76a-119a. Verse. 'Here begynnyth a good tale of Torrence of Portyngale. God that ys worthy and Bold . . . Oute of this world whan we shall wend Amen. Explicit Torent of Portyngale.'

7. *A Lamentation of Oure Lady*; ff. 119b-121a. Verse. 'Of all women that euer were born . . . Wnto the blis where is my son dere.'

8. 'A Prayar of Oure Lady'; ff. 121a-121b. Verse. 'Mary moder well thou be . . . To heuyn blis that I may wend Amen.'

9. *Beues of Hamtoun*; ff. 122a-190b. Verse. 'Here begynnyth a good tale of Bevys of Hamton A good werriour. Lystenythe lordinges . . . That for vs died vppon a tree Amen. Here endyth a good tale of Beuis of hamton that good verriour.'

10. *Ipomadon*; ff. 191a-335b. Verse. 'Here begynnyth a good tale of Ipomadon. Off love were lykynge . . . To brynge vs to the blysse that lestis aye Amen ffor Charyte.'

11. 'A Good Boke of Kervyng and Nortur'; ff. 337a-355a (with f. 336 as title page). Verse. 'A good boke of kervyng and Nortur. In nomine patris god kep me . . . þᵗ neveʳ shall haue endynge Amen. Explicit the boke of nvture and of kervynge quod Ego.'

12. *The Book of the Duke and the Emperor*; ff. 357a-366b. Prose. 'The Lady of Comynes the best and the derrest of my spirituelle Doughters . . . Writen at þe sayd Saint Maximien beside Tresues the xxviiᵗʰ day Octobr.'

13. 'The Namys of Wardeyns and Balyffys' of London, from 1189 to 1217, ff. 367b-368b.

14. *Ballad of a Tyrannical Husband*; ff. 370a-372a. Verse. 'Ihesu that arte Ientyll ffor Ioye of they dam . . . Here begennethe anoder fytte yᵉ sothe for to sey' (nothing follows).

It is a fairly substantial paper manuscript with 372 leaves plus three flyleaves at each end, and measuring approximately 265mm by 190mm. Its present binding—done in 1921—is half-vellum with *Early English Poetry / Fifteenth Century* on its spine, and is too tight to allow one to see the original gatherings. There is some water-damage throughout to the top quarter of the pages, especially at the beginning where some parts of *St. Dorothy* are illegible, and the bottom right corners of f. 163 and f. 272 have been torn off, but it is otherwise in good condition and easily legible.

There are two systems of foliation: an early one in ink (which Kölbing follows) and a later one in pencil, followed in the present edition.[22] Four intersecting lines in pencil with frequent prick-marks at the intersections mark out the writing-space, which is approximately 190mm high; all items are in single columns of 28–34 lines. At two points in the manuscript there are random lines of pricking as if someone had idly run a pricking-wheel across a stack of paper: from f. 129b (the sheet the wheel was run across) back through to about f. 117b, and from f. 166b back to about f. 164b. The section containing *Ipomadon* has catchwords on ff. 204b, 218b, 232b, 245b, 257b, 271b, 284b, 297b, 311b, 325b, 334b. Partially cropped but still visible at the bottoms of the pages are roman numerals, starting on f. 232 with XXII.

The manuscript is the work of probably nine contemporary hands according to Ker (Guddat-Figge suggests ten; Meale possibly eleven) although roughly three quarters of it, including *Ipomadon*, was written by Ker's Hand 5. The hands are mostly secretary script with varying admixtures of anglicana forms except for Hand 3 (Item 2) which is mainly anglicana. All items are written in black or brown ink with sections marked off by red capital letters; for Item 5 the English lines are in black ink and the Latin in red. 'Seynt Katerin', 'A Good Boke of Kervyng and Nortur', and *Beues of Hamtoun* also have some blue capitals, and many texts have strap-work flourishes on their incipits.

Written on the third front fly-leaf (v) in ink faded by water-damage is: 'This booke I founde ymoungest my fatherry[s] 20 Januarie 1595 [or 1598]. [?]oger Hanwood'. Written below and over the water-damage is: 'written in ye Regn^e of Rich. 2^d. or [v]er ne[r]'. Below this appear successive scholars' opinions as to the manuscript's date. J. Hardres in 1732 thinks the reign of Richard II; Br. Taussett suggests the end of the reign of Henry III or the beginning of Edward I, and J. O. Halliwell the reign of Edward IV. There are few scribbles within the MS, the most interesting of which is a shakily-written 'Elysabet' on f. 334b of *Ipomadon*.[23]

---

[22] The pencil foliation runs from f. 1 to 372 and was clearly added to correct the ink numbering, which begins after the fly-leaves at 2; skips 51 but then repeats 52; misses a leaf between 59 and 60 (pencil f. 59); skips 86; repeats 91, and misses the leaves counted in pencil as f. 156, f. 176, f. 183 and f. 353 to reach a total of 368 numbered leaves.

[23] The other elements of marginalia are: at the foot of f. 22b, 'Itm ffurst ffor a M^ll of ffaggot'; on f. 141a, 'fothe [?r m m] ym'; on f. 178a, 'father m'; on f. 209a, 'And Joseph

At least ten different paperstocks are attested to by watermarks. The list of contents, folios, hands, and paperstocks can be presented most usefully in tabular form:[24]

Item	Folios	Watermark (see below)	Hand
1. *Life of St. Dorothy*	ff. 1a–2b *(both worn)*	*a*	1
2. 'Assvmptio Sancte Marie'	ff. 3a–17b *(both worn)*	*b*	2, 3
3. 'Lyff of Seynt Anne'	ff. 18a–29b *(both worn)*	*c*	4
4. 'Lyf of Seynt Katerin'	ff. 30a–47b *(both worn)*	*d*	5
5. 'Liber Catonis'	ff. 48a–75b *(both worn)*	*e*6	
6. *Torrent of Portyngale*	ff. 76a–119a *(f. 76a worn)*	*c, d*	7, 5
7. *A Lamentation of Oure Lady*	ff. 119b–121a	*c*	5
8. 'A Prayar of Oure Lady'	ff. 121a–121b *(f. 121b worn)*	(none)	5
9. *Beues of Hamtoun*	ff. 122a–190b *(both worn)*	*d, f, g*	5
10. *Ipomadon*	ff. 191a–335b *(f. 191a worn)*	*g, d*	5
title page for following item	f. 336	*d*	
11. 'A Good Boke of Kervyng and Nortur'	ff. 337a–355a	*d*	8
f. 356 blank		*h*	
12. *The Book of the Duke and the Emperor*	ff. 357a–366b	*j*	5
13. 'The Namys of Wardeyns and Balyffys'	ff. 367b–368b	*j, k*	8 (Ker); 9, 10 (Meale)
f. 369 blank	*(f. 369b worn)*	(none)	
14. *Ballad of a Tyrannical Husband*	ff. 370a–372a *(all worn)*	*k*	9 (Ker); 11 (Meale)

Asone as he awoke' and two further trials of 'and Joseph' scrawled in the right-hand margin; f. 252a has some barely visible writing in what looks like the same pencil that did the ruling, perhaps reading 'Fory[sh]-'.

[24] The hand numbers are Ker's: Meale agrees except where noted. Guddat-Figge differs with both writers and assigns scribal hands as follows: Hand I—f. 1; II—f. 2; III—items 2, 3; IV—item 4; V—item 5; VI—items 6–10; VII—item 11; VIII—item 12, also titles, side titles and large explicits; IX—item 13; X—item 14 (Guddat-Figge, *op.cit.*, p. 238). First and last folios which are noticeably worn have been noted to make it clear which sections seem to have existed as separate booklets before being bound together in their present form.

KEY TO WATERMARKS[25]

(*a*) long thin watermark, too obscured by the dense prose of the text to be any more distinguishable

(*b*) sun with face inside (also otherwise unidentified)

(*c*) bull's head topped with star on a stalk : similar to Briquet no. 14908 (Gênes 1475–84)

(*d*) a variation of the French coat of arms crowned, with pendant *i* or *j*, very similar to Briquet's no.1741 (Troyes 1470)

(*e*) leafy crown : similar to Briquet's nos. 4636–48 (various continental origins, 1423–91) and identical to Heawood's no. 986, occurring in an English heraldic manuscript of 1463[26]

(*f*) a fleur-de-lys shield mounted with a cross : similar to Briquet's *fleur-de-lys sommée d'un lambel* no. 1557 (Chartres 1476, with variations 1476–90)

(*g*) a short-tailed unicorn not especially similar to anything among Briquet's hundreds of unicorns: the closest is the group nos. 9991–9—found in manuscripts from Lorraine, Belgium, the Rhineland and the Netherlands 1463–1492—with no. 9999 (Lubeck, 1492) perhaps the closest. More distantly, there is 10178 (Châteaudun 1474). An altogether closer set of unicorn watermarks can be seen in Piccard, nos. 2168–72: nos. 2169–72 all hail from Köln, 1484–6, and all show the short tail, the raised and flexed off-side foreleg, the well-separated flexed hind legs, and the striped horn of the Chetham unicorn.[27]

(*h*) diamond-shaped bunch of grapes with pendant crescent and 'E C II' written above it. Meale notes that '*raisins* with pendant designs . . . seem to date from the late fifteenth and early sixteenth centuries'[28]

(*j*) tear-shaped ring with square cross above its jewel : similar to Briquet no. 694 (Palermo 1479)

(*k*) bull's head topped with St. Andrews cross on a stalk : similar to Briquet's *tête de boeuf* nos. 14232–43 (various continental origins, 1440–93)

---

[25] References are to C. M. Briquet, *Les Filigranes*, Jubilee Edition, revised Allan Stevenson, 4 vols. (Amsterdam, 1968).

[26] Edward Heawood, *Watermarks: mainly of the seventeenth and eighteenth centuries* (Hilversum, 1950).

[27] Gerhard Piccard, *Wasserzeichen Fabeltiere: Greif, Drache, Einhorn* (Stuttgart, 1980).

[28] Meale, 'The Middle English Romance *Ipomedon*', *op. cit.*, p. 159, note 8.

When the evidence from watermarks, hands, and worn pages is assembled, it becomes apparent that the bulk of this manuscript collection must have been put together at the same time and place. Those few items which do not share either scribal hands or paper-stocks with the main group (i.e. Items 1, 2, 5, 13 and 14) may have been added later. Among these texts, the *Life of St. Dorothy*, the 'Assvmptio Sancte Marie' and the 'Liber Catonis' (Items 1, 2 and 5) are each in their own hand, with their own paper, and have worn front and back pages as if they had existed for a time as loose booklets. 'The Namys of Wardeyns and Balyffys' and the *Ballad of a Tyrannical Husband* are likewise copied mainly on their own (shared) paper in hands not seen in the rest of the collection. However, the 'Namys' begins on the final verso leaf of the gathering containing the *Book of the Duke*, continues onto the first leaf of the watermark-*k* paper (f. 368), and neither of the leaves from these different paperstocks is rubbed. As Meale points out, this 'suggests that the latter [pages] were added soon after the former was acquired by an owner—perhaps with the immediate purpose of copying the *Annals* ['Namys']'.[29] Since this is the same paper onto which the *Ballad* is copied (ff. 368, 370, 372 all bear watermark *k*), it looks as though both of these items were added soon after the bulk of the collection had been put together.

The 'main group' is formed by the other nine items in the manuscript: these are linked by shared paperstocks, scribal hands, or both. The biggest single group is that formed by the seven items copied by Ker's hand 5: 'Seynt Katerin', *Torrent*, the two Marian lyrics (items 7 and 8), *Beues*, *Ipomadon*, and *The Book of the Duke*. The 'Boke of Kervyng' and 'Seynt Anne' are in different hands from the rest, but the former is copied on the watermark-*d* paper also used for *Ipomadon*, *Beues*, 'Seynt Katerin', and *Torrent*, while the latter shares watermark-*c* paper with *Torrent* and the first Marian lyric. The asssociation of *The Book of the Duke*, which shares the copyist but none of the paperstocks of this main group, with the 'Namys' and the *Ballad* has been discussed above.

---

[29] Meale, *ibid.*, p. 145.

LANGUAGE OF THE TEXT
PART I: DESCRIPTION

This section is a catalogue of the significant linguistic features of the extant text, covering authorial features as well as those for which later copyists are responsible. It has not proved practical to make separate catalogues for authorial and scribal language, different though they clearly are, because while the forms indicated by rhyme are usually authorial (except perhaps in some of the more corrupt passages), there are many more forms in non-rhyming position that may either be authorial or relics from one of any number of copying layers. All forms that are confirmed by rhyme, and therefore probably indicate the author's usage, are given here with their rhyme-pairs: any form listed without a rhyme-pair is not in rhyme-position and consequently may or may not represent the original author's dialect. All words are spelt as they appear in the manuscript unless otherwise marked. Examples of short and long vowels from the text have not always been rigorously distinguished, since it is clear that the poet often rhymed etymologically short and long vowels together (see 'Rhyming Practice' later in this section).

SPELLINGS AND SOUNDS

Vowels

1. (a) The reflex of OE *ā* is spelt as, and rhymes on, both *a* and *o* : *oke* n. (: *wake, make, sake*) l. 3616; *rade* pa.t. (: *hade* pa.t.) l. 3727; *brayde* 'broad' (: *fade* v., *hadde* pa.t., *mayde* pa.t.) l. 4366—while the spelling *brayde* might be derived from ON *breiðr*, the rhymes require the form descended from OE *brād*; *rowe* n. (: *sawe* pa.t.) l. 7510; *hame* n. (: *madame*) l. 3564; *home* n. (: *same*) l. 6948 against *sore* adv. (: *Mayore, fore* prep.) l. 6501; *roos* 'roes' (: *sopposse* v.) l. 3029; *stone* n. (: *Egyon*) l. 3440. The inexact rhyme *home* n.: *downe* adv. (from OE *dūne*), l. 4537, only makes sense if *home* is assumed to have some form of /oː/, enabling assonance with the /uː/ of *downe*.

   (b) The reflex of OE *ǽ* has frequently been replaced by *a, o* where there was an ON cognate form with *ā*: parallel forms with *e* from OE *ǽ* are also found, but the vast majority of rhymes show the ON-derived *a, o* : (1) pa.t. *ware* 'were' [ON *váru*] (: *fare*) l. 1044; *wore* (: *whereffore*) l. 1113; *were* (: *nere, her* pron.) l. 174. (2) *heyre* 'hair' [ON *hár*] (: *care*) l. 4473; *heyre* (: *before*) l. 6226. (3) *ere* 'before' [ON

ár] : *are* (: *bare, were, lare* n.) l. 739; *are* (: *fore*) l. 1370; *ore* conj..
l. 7556 (no forms in *e* confirmed by rhyme). (4) *sloo* 'slay' [ON *slá*]
(: *too*) l. 7009; *slone* pp.(: *Ipomadon*) ll. 3250, 5891. (6) *thare* 'there'
[ON *þar*] (: *care, sore, fare*) l. 3625; *thore* (: *before*) l. 4027 rhymes
overwhelmingly on *-a-* or *-o-* against occasional rhymes on *e* such as
there (: *nere*) l. 7887.

2. The reflex of OE *ā* + w or *g* (representing [ɣ]) is usually spelt *o*,
occasionally *a*, but rhymed most often on *a* : the spelling *awne* adj.
l. 4984 once against usual *owne* ll. 357, 711 etc.. Rhymes on *a* : *lowe*
(: *sawe* n.) l. 7719 (showing lOE *ā* < ON *lágr*); *blowe* (: *thrawe*) l. 673;
blowe, snowe (: *dawe* 'dawn') ll. 3092, 3095. *Know* is always spelt thus
(ll. 548, 695 etc.), but rhyme-evidence shows *-a-*, e.g. *know(e)*
(: *wythdrawe, awe, sawe* n.) l. 8158; (: *sawe* pa.t.) l. 8476.
3. The reflex of OE *a/o* + *n* is spelt with, and rhymed on, both *a* and
o:[30] *can, man* (: *thanne, began*) l. 448, (: *banne* v., *thanne*) l. 1306; *man*
(: *Iurdanne, thanne*) l. 3212; usual spelling *many(e)* against only six
mony(e) (ll. 1801, 2080, 2657, 2906, 4015, 4765). The pairing of *conn*
(: *wonne* 'live', OE *wunian*) l. 212 and *con* (: *sonne*, OE *sunne*) l. 222
only makes sense if assonance is assumed between /o:/ and /u:/,
while *man* (: *Ipomadon*) l. 1743 shows a straightforward rhyme on *-o-*
since *Ipomadon* is never otherwise rhymed on *-a-*. *Tane* pp. 'taken',
with *ā* after loss of intevocalic *-k-*, is always spelt thus, but the fact
that it, along with *gone, gane* pp., is often paired with *vppon* or
Ipomadon in rhyme (e.g. l. 817) indicates that its vowel was at least
sometimes rounded to *o*.

4. The reflex of OE *a/o* + *nd* is spelt with either *a* or *o*, but there is
no conclusive evidence for rhymes on *o*: *rennande : hande* l. 1597 ff.;
londe, fonde, hande : groande l. 4663 ff..

5. The reflex of OE *a/o* + *ng* is usually spelt with *o*, but sometimes
with *a*: where rhymes are not self-rhymes, they are almost always on
a : *longe* (: *gange*) ll. 215,1513, 8169; *lange* (: *gange*) l. 1151; *lange :
wrange* ll. 7638–9; but *stronge, longe* (: *ronge* pp.) l. 2981 ff.

6. OE *ǣ* (a) The reflex of *ǣ*[1] (A, Kt. *ē*) is spelt as *e* or *a*, but only
rhymes as *e*: *adrade* (: *wedde* inf.) l. 5055; *adred* pp.(: *flede* pa.t.)

---

[30] The *a/o* variation was much more widespread in OE than the predominantly WML
distribution in ME would suggest. It seems to have represented a sound between the two
vowels, and the same situation may prevail here. See Campbell §32, §130.

l. 5923; *dede* n. (: *yede* pa.t.) l. 77, (: *spede* pr.subj.) l. 485, (: *redde* adj.) l. 1477.

(b) The reflex of *ǣ²* appears as *e* or *a* in both spelling and rhyme: rhymed with OE *ē* in *clene* (: *quene*) l. 2606, (: *kene* adj., *bedene*) l. 4279, (: *sene* pp.) l. 4929; rhymed with OE *e*(in *lede* pa.t. (: *wede* pa.t. 'wed') l. 74; *ledde* pa.t. (: *bedde* n.) l. 3003; rhymed with ME *ē* from other sources in *deale* n. (: *well* adv.) l. 1074; *leyste* 'least' (: *feeste* n.) l. 172. Rhymes indicate a shortening to *a* in *lefte* pa.t. (: *crafte* n., *rafte* pa.t., *shafte* n.) l. 5402; *ledde* pa.t. (: *had* pa.t.) l. 3588, *ladde* pa.t. (: *had, stadde* pp.) l. 1048.

7. The reflex of OE *æ̆* rhymes on, and is spelt as, *a* : *bare* pa.t.sg. (: *more*, where the original rhyme was on a lengthened /*a:*/) l. 1738; *was* (: *place*) l. 2068.

8. ME *ai, ei* sometimes rhymes on *a* : *seyde* (: *hade*) l. 1481,[31] *orfrayes* (: *place*) l. 2699, and possibly *harnes* (: *rose, mase, goothe*) l. 4169, (: *Dreas*) l. 4447, (: *was*) ll. 1280, 7692. The normal rhyme for *harne(i)s* is on *-ey-/-ay-* (e.g. *harnes : palffreys* l. 2375; *harnays : dayes* l. 2493), but the form *harnas* also existed in OF.
Cf. also the spelling *mayde* pa.t. l. 4369, rhyming with *hadde* pa.t., *fade* inf..
The unusual rhyme *clene* (: *ageyne*) l. 5972, where *clene* usually rhymes on *-e-* (see above, 6(b)), may illustrate the beginnings of a tendency sometimes visible in eMdnE pronunciation for ME *ei* to be equated with ME *ē*.[32]

9. OE *ea* before lengthening groups such as *-ld-* spelt and rhymed as *e, o*. Both the forms with *e*, deriving from Saxon *ea* > *ǣ* > e, and those with *o*, deriving from Anglian *a* > *ā* > a/o, appear in rhyming position despite the apparent southerly origin of the *e*-forms. (Since all examples are necessarily self-rhymes, it is impossible to know whether the original rhyme of those spelt with *o* was on /*o:*/ or

---

[31] Pa.t. *sayde* also appears spelt as *sade* in the North-West Midland *Pearl*: Gordon's note to l. 532 of this text observes that there are sporadic other occurrences of this verb spelt with *-a-* in the *Pearl*-manuscript as well as in other North-Western texts such as the *Stanzaic Life of Christ* and *Audelay's Poems*: he speculates that the lack of diphthong derives from an unstressed pronunciation of this common word. E. V. Gordon, ed., *Pearl* (London, 1953).

[32] On the complicated relationships between ME *ei, ai, ā;* and *ē* generally, see §225 ff. in E. J. Dobson, *English Pronunciation 1500–1700*, 2nd edn, 2 vols. (Oxford, 1968), II: on monophthongization, see §228, especially note 4.

/a:/). The forms in -e- might have originated through a combination of the knowledge of their currency further south, and analogical
extension from other parts of the words, i.e. the pa.t. *held*, the comp.
elder, the inf. *tell* (see Jordan §61 Remark 2) : *holde* inf. (: *felde* n.,
shelde n.) l. 117, (: *bold*) l. 5694, (: *colde*) l. 7711; *tolde* pp. (: *dwellyd*,
feellyd) l. 144; *olde* adj. (: *wolde* pa.t. ll. 1933, 1980, 5206) but *old*
(: *shyld* n., with original rhyme on -e-) l. 2524.

10. The reflex of OE *ēa* + palatal *g* or *h* is normally spelt *i/y*, but
rhymes as either *e* or *i* : *hy* adj. (: *lewte* n.) l. 4994 against *hye*
(: *Normandye, why, forthy*) l. 3790. 'Eye' only rhymes on *e* : *eye* n.
(: *bee*) l. 984; *iȝe* (: *be, mee, the*) l. 2665, (: *kne, lewte, see*) l. 4755. The
reflexes of 'die' v. are a special case in that they may represent OE *
dēgan or ON *deyja*: *dye* v. (: *se, be, me*) l. 1191 and *dye* (: *crye, securlye,
I*) l. 7418.

11. The reflex of OE *ēo* is usually *e*, although some words show
variants with both *e* and *o* : *deyre* n. (: *swere* v., *here* adv., *spere* n.)
l. 1120; *tene* (: *wene* v.) l. 1082. Words with two forms are *yede*
(: *mode, good*) l. 3712 against *youde* (: *hede* 'heed') l. 774; *trewe*
(: *Thalamewe*) ll. 206, 1245 against *trowe* (: *alowe, thou, you*) l. 3155
(note that for this word, the *o*-forms are used for the verb, while the
e-forms are used for the adj.).
ME /e:/ from OE *ēo*, as from other sources, also sometimes rhymes
on *i* (see (13) below): *tene* n.(: *Lyolyne*) l. 8561.

12. The reflex of OE *eo* + *r* + cons. is spelt as *e, a, o, (u)* : OE *weorc-*,
A *werc-* is spelt twice as *wark-* (e.g. *warkys* l. 1234), six times as *work-*
(e.g. *worke* l. 2324), and eleven times as *werk-* (e.g. *werke* l. 1798). In
rhyme it shows *e* or possibly *a* : *worke* : *shorte* l. 7075 and *werke* :
shyrte l. 8003, where *shorte, shyrte* must represent either *serk* or *sark*
(with ME *er* > *ar*) from OE *serc*. Note also the spellings of 'worse' (A
wersa) as *wars* ll. 4222, 6192, *wers* l. 3910 and *wors* l. 1357, and the
single occurrence of *hurt* 'heart' at l. 4737.

13. The reflex of OE *e, ē* is usually spelt *e*, sometimes *ey* or *ea* for the
long vowel. ME *e*, from this and other sources, also sometimes
appears as *i* in both spelling and rhyme before dentals:
    (a) OE /e/ > *e, i* : *dwell* v. (: *hill*) l. 3961 against *dwell* (: *hell, fell*
adj., *bell* n.) l. 4791; *dwell* (: *damysell, mell, telle* inf.) l. 1188 etc.
    (b) OE /e/ before lengthening groups spelt and rhymed as *e* or *i* :
felde n. (: *mylde* adj., *smylyde, begylyde*) ll. 2728, 6672; *feld* (: *shelde*)

l. 1971; *weynde* v. (: *behynde*) l. 331; *wynde* v. (: *behynde*) l. 5081; *wende* : *lende* ll. 226–7; *ende* (: *frende*) l. 347; *yelde* v. (: *welde*, *feld* n., *beheld*) l. 4306.

(c) OE /e:/ spelt and rhymed as *e*, occasionally *i* (with or without shortening): *yete* adv. (: *ete* inf.) l. 782; *beyre* n. (: *clere* adj., *Fere*, *yere* n.) l. 1937; *wille* adv. ll. 1794, 1869 etc.. With shortening : *yett* (: *hit* pron.) l. 3525

(d) ME /e:/ spelt as *e*, rhymed as *e* or *i* : *ben* pp. (: *Lyolyne*) l. 8561; *sene* pp. (: *ermyne*, *wyne*, *fyne* v.) l. 2701 against *bene* (: *wene* n.) l. 255; *sene* (: *bedene*) l. 914.

14. The reflex of OE *i* is spelt as both *i* and *e*: in the latter case this represents either lME *ĭ* > *ĕ*, or Nth. *ĭ* > *ē* in open syllables : *begge* adj. l. 52 against *bigge* l. 1887; *wen* 'win' l. 1129; *wynne* (: *in*, *synne*) l. 535; *wheche* pron. l. 2142; *whiche* l. 218; usual spelling *mekyll* adj. & adv.; *reden* pp. : *byden* pp. ll. 4192–3; *thekyste* super. l. 4377.
OE *y* > *i* > *e* : *denne* n. 'din' (: *wythinne*) l. 7626.
Nth. *i* > *ē* in open syllables is certain in *onskylle* n. (: *wele* adv., *dele* n., *damysell* n.) l. 1408, *skylle* (: *deyle* n.) l. 1070 against *skylle* (: *tille* prep.) l. 277.

15. The reflex of OE *ō* appears as *o* in spelling and rhyme, and occasionally as *ou* in spelling; it rhymes with itself or with lengthened OE *ŭ* (see below, (17)) : *goode* adj. : *blode* n. ll. 52–3; *hode* n., *good* adj. (: *blode* n., *youde* pa.t.) l. 2590 ff.; *loke* inf. : *toke* pa.t. ll. 4251–2; *floure* 'floor' (: *dore* n.) l. 6451.

16. The reflex of OE *ō* + g, h appears as *ow*, *ogh*, *ew* in spelling; in rhyme it is either self-rhymed, or rhymed with OE *ū* or OF *u/ eu* : *i-nowe* adv. (OE *genōh*) (: *thou* pron.) l. 2768; *lough* pa.t. : *i-nowgh* adv. : *bovgh* n.: *drewe* pa.t. l. 5154 ff.; *drowgh* pa.t. : *i-nowgh* adv. ll. 5542–3; *drowe* pa.t. (:*Thelamewe*) l. 1255; *i-nowe* : *slowe* pa.t. ll. 5783–4. Pa.t. 'laughed' is usually spelt *lowʒe*, *lough(e)*, *louʒth*, *louthe*, but occasionally *lewʒ(e)* ll. 3579, 3582, 6332, *lewgh* l. 3609: rhymes are *lowgh* (: *rewe* n.) l. 121; *lough*, *lowʒ* (: *drewe* n.) ll. 3012, 3602; (: *blew* pa.t.) l. 3460; *lewʒe* (: *i-nowthe*) l. 6335.

17. The reflex of lengthened OE *ŭ* is normally spelt *o* (rarely *u*), and rhymes with itself or OF and OE *ō* : *dore* n. (: *floure* (OE *flōr*)) ll. 6452, 6556; *love* n. (: *hove* inf.) l. 3126; (: *reprove* n. (OF *reprove*)) ll. 941, 951, 1040; (: *behove* n. (OE *behōf*)) ll. 859, 5339; *woode* n.

(: *goode* adj., *stoode* pa.t., *blode* n.) l. 3077; but see spellings *durre* n.
l. 4739, *luffe* v. l. 926.

18. The reflex of OE *ū* is spelt as *ow*, *ou*, and normally rhymed with
OF *ou* or other OE *ū*, but also occasionally with OF *u/ eu* : *nowe* adv.
(: *avowe* n.) l. 6536; *towne* n. : *adowne* prep. ll. 307–8; *nowe* adv. :
yowe pron.: *cowe* n. l. 6372 ff.; against *howse* n. (: *Cananeus*) l. 3867
and *nowe* adv. (: *drewe* n. (OF *dru, dreu*)) l. 3049.

19. The reflex of OE *y* is usually spelt *i/y*, and there is no evidence
for anything else in rhyme except where the *i* appears to have been
lowered to *ē* (see (14)): *kys* v. (: *blis* n., *i-wis* adv., *this* dem.adj.)
l. 7972; usual spelling *littill, lyttill* adj. against single spelling of *lutill*
l. 2778; *muche* adj. occurs 7 times, starting from l. 6544; *moche* occurs
3 times, ll. 2801, 6440, 8522 (normal form *mekyll*).

20. Development of a glide before initial *e* or *o*, and between initial *h*
and *o*:

　　(a) *e > ye* : *yerlye* 'early' l. 1346; *yere* adv. 'ere' l. 7246; *yes* pr.3 sg.
'is' ll. 1364, 4428.

　　(b) *(h)o > w(h)o* : *whome* n. 'home' ll. 2596, 4729, 5559, 7494;
perhaps MS *wold* adj. 'old' l. 1933, but see note to this line.

21. Loss of unstressed *e* : see adjectives and verbs below for evidence.

Consonants

22. ME *ch* from either OE or OF is occasionally spelt *sh* or *sch*:
schastyse l. 825; *shyld* l. 2412 and *sheld* l. 3912 for 'child'; *schosyn*
'chosen' l. 3361.[33]

23. The reflex of OE voiced *f* often appears to have been unvoiced in
final position: *luffe* v. l. 926 (also *lufflye*, l. 2374). For the verb 'give',
the inf. and pres. form appears as *gyf(fe)* 24 times against 12
occurrences of *geve*; pa.t., *gaf(fe)* occurs 25 times against 3
occurrences of *gave*.

24. The reflexes of both palatal and velar OE initial *g* are present,
though the palatal variants are rare: *yattis* n.pl. l. 4026; *yaffe* pa.t.
l. 4507 against regular *gatys* l. 3459 etc.; *gaffe* l. 492 etc..

---

[33] The *OED* records *s(c)h-* as a minor spelling variant for /*ch-*/ in the fourteenth and
fifteenth centuries for several other words, e.g. *cheer* n., *cheese* n., *chew* v., *chicken* n..

25. Although the fricative [x] is normally spelt *gh* in final position and normally rhymes with itself, it is sometimes lost in both spelling and rhyme : *hygh* adj. (: *wee* pron.) l. 6385; *hye* n. (: *why* interr., *Normandye*) l. 3790 etc.; *drowe* pa.t.(: *Thelamewe*) l. 1255, *lough* pa.t. (: *drew* n.) l. 3013,: *drewe* pa.t. (: *bovgh* n., *lough* pa.t.) l. 5163; *drowgh* pa.t.(: *inowgh* adv.) l. 5542. (All of these cases may have arisen from analogy with the inflected forms, where medial [ɣ] was already lost—see Jordan §198: he describes this as a northern development of the early fourteenth century in §101.)

26. [ɣ], [x] + *t* (normally spelt *-ght, -ʒt*) : There are no examples of [ɣ] or [x] + *t* either spelt or rhymed without medial *gh/ʒ* except in the case of 'not', which is often spelt *not*, but still only rhymes with other words that historically bore the fricative: *not* (: *thoughte* pa.t.) l. 191; *nought* : *wrought* pa.t. ll. 1019–20; *bovghte* pp.: *nowght* ll. 6876–7 etc..

(a) Very occasionally this consonant group is spelt *-(g)th* : *knygth* n. 'knight' : *fygth* v. 'fight' ll. 6168–69; *mowthe* v. 'might' (: *brought* pp.) l. 7304.

(b) Late ME [ɣ] > [f] is indicated by the spelling *ofte* 'aught' l. 1365 and the reversed spellings *fyghtte* 'fifty' l. 2507; *lyght* adj. 'left' l. 3899.

27. Loss or addition of *h* : loss is shown in *helper* 'help her' l. 6485, *gyffner* 'given her' l. 6868; addition is shown in *heft* 'eft' l. 6805; *hellys* 'else' l. 4076. Jordan (§293) lists this under fifteenth-century traits, and notes that the addition of *h* is a phenomenon associated with the loss of aspirated pronunciation in words with etymological *h-*. It has no dialectal significance.

28. False juncture with *n* is seen once in *myne noune bane* l. 4477.

29. OE *s* is occasionally spelt *c(e)* : *wyce* adj. l. 348, *alce* 'als' l. 2433; *cecurly* l. 3952.

30. OE medial *-sc-* seems to have developed to *-ss-* in pr. and pa.t. forms of the verb 'ask' : *asse, aske* (: *was, passe, alas*) ll. 946, 1666; *axte* (: *paste*) l. 68; *axid* (: *caste* pp., *blaste* n., *faste* adv.) l. 1282.

31. ME */v/* spelt as *w*: *welvet* n. l. 367, *wovche-saffe* v. l. 5168, *wovche-save* v. l. 4988, *lewand* pr.p. 'living' l. 548, *awove* n. 'avow' l. 833; *newov* n. 'nephew' l. 36 (the *ov* spelling in these last two examples represents the vowel).

ACCIDENCE

Nouns

(a) Plural: The usual ending is *-s* with its variants *-es, is/ys, us*: occasionally this is confirmed by rhyme, e.g. *foos* (: *losse* n., *sopose* v.) l. 1137; *wayes* (: *harneys* n.) l. 6598. The OE wk. pl. *-n* survives for 'eyes' *eyne* l. 1627, *ynne* l. 1835, *yȝen* l. 4315. Some nouns occasionally have no pl. suffix in rhyme: *pavelyon* (: *towne*) l. 2943; (: *downe* prep., *renowne* n., *Iasone*) l. 3933; *dedis* (: *blede* v., *spede* v.) l. 3014. *yere* often rhymes without *-s* though it is otherwise spelt *yer(e)s*, e.g. l. 79: (: *clere* adj., *beyre* n., *Fere*) l. 1943; (: *Fere*) l. 6802.

(b) Genitive: The usual form is with *-s*, e.g. *his faders hall* l. 161. Occasionally there is no ending: *a brother son* l. 35; *the quene chambyr* l. 278; *his syster doghttur* l. 2372; *the quene leman* l. 4178; *Lyolyne brothere dere* l. 7508. Occasionally also a 'detached' genitive marker is used: *his brothere is sake* l. 57; *Syr Amfyon is men* l. 3237; *Cananeus his own* l. 5066; *Cabanus ys stede* l. 5142; *Ipomadon his stede* l. 7902.

Pronouns

(a) The 1 sg. nom. is *I* (l. 13 etc.), rarely *Y* (l. 229 etc.); oblique *me(e)* (ll. 117, 432 etc.); poss. *myn(e)* (ll. 3036, 3121 etc.). The poss. adj. is usually *my* (l. 49 etc.), although sometimes *myn(e)* occurs before a vowel, e.g. *myn avowe* l. 549, and even more rarely before a consonant, e.g. *myn lewte* l. 4312.

(b) The 2 sg. nom. is *thou, thow(e)* (ll. 205, 398, 1985 etc.), oblique *the(e)* (ll. 920, 3959 etc.). The 2 pl. nom. is normally *ye(e)* (ll. 20, 1430 etc.), occasionally *you, yow* (ll. 1587, 2229 etc.); oblique form *you, yow(e)* (ll. 223, 834, 5150 etc.). In the extant text, the sg. and pl. forms are sometimes used interchangeably in address, e.g. ll. 3959–60 *My ladye dyes for love of the / And you will fro her fare.*

(c) The 3 sg. masc. nom. is *he(e)* (ll. 15, 35 etc.); oblique form normally *hym* (l. 30 etc.) but occasionally *hem*, e.g. ll. 4988, 5134, 6434. The poss. adj. is usually *hys/his*, but occasionally *ys/is*, e.g. ll. 290, 656 etc.; once *hes* l. 425.

(d) The 3 sg. fem. nom. is usually spelt *she(e)* or *sche* (ll. 83, 811, 8662 etc.), twice *sho(o)* (ll. 4116, 6946): however, it only rhymes on *-o-* (: *doo* v. l. 6805, 6946, 8174, : *rowe* l. 7210). The most common oblique forms are *her* (l. 68 etc.) and *hur* (l. 90 etc.), although *here, hure, hyr(e), hir* also occur (ll. 68, 503, 1780, 3721, 4810 etc.).

(e) The 3 nom. pl. is usually spelt *they* (l. 79 etc.), once *thay* l. 6469. Since *ey* and *ay* normally represent alternative spellings for a single diphthong by the fourteenth century, no further information about authorial forms is to be gained from rhyme. Oblique *them(e)* (ll. 69, 5365 etc.; once *theym* l. 7838) is about five times as common as *hem* (l. 346 etc.); *tham* occurs twice (ll. 50, 8609). The poss. adj. is usually *ther(e)* (l. 82, 87 etc.) against occasional *her* (ll. 3238, 8609 etc.).

(f) The demonstratives are *this* (ll. 12, 39 etc.), *thes(e)* (ll. 8, 354 etc.), *that* (ll. 6, 4853 etc.), and *þo* (l. 2492 etc.; rhymed once with *forgoo*, l. 4367); *those* does not occur.

Articles

The definite article is *the(e)* (ll. 18, 618 etc.). The indefinite article is *a* or *an* (l. 19, 345 etc.), with *an* sometimes occurring before consonants as well as vowels; e.g. *an lawghyng herte* l. 1022; *an churche* l. 4491.

Adjectives

There is no evidence of any distinction between sg., pl., weak or strong forms of adjectives in the extant text.
The superlative ending is spelt four times without final -*t*: *hottys* l. 1103; *whyghttys* l. 2411; *grettys* l. 3159, l. 7227.

Adverbs

The adverbial ending is normally spelt and rhymed as -*ly(e)*: *worthely* (: *curtessye*) l. 320, *veralye* (: *crye*) l. 610, *angurlye* (: *forthy*) l. 1101.

Verbs

(a) Infinitive: This has usually lost final -*n*, but verbs with a vocalic stem may retain it: *sey* (: *day*) l. 3445 against *sayne* (:*layne*) l. 43, (: *agayne, payne*) l. 2347.

(b) Present Indicative: In the extant text, 1 sg. has no ending; 2 sg. often has -*st* beside -*s*, but only rhymes on -*s*; 3 sg. sometimes has -*th(e)* next to -*s*, but only rhymes on -*s*; pl. sometimes has -*the* next to -*s* or no suffix, but it rhymes either with -*s* or without suffix. The pl.,

2 sg. and 3 sg. are rhymed together in ll. 7918 ff. (*lenys* pl., *demenyste*
2 sg., *conteynes* 2 sg., *raynes* 3 sg.), confirming that all three persons
could take the pr. suffix -*s* in dialect of the original.

Examples:
pr.2 sg.:
    non-rhymed: *yrkys* l. 1934, *kythes* l. 1974; *knowest* l. 3220; *comyste*
      l. 862
    in rhyme: *goos* : MS *losythes* ll. 3231–2; *haste* (: *face, grace*) l. 7751
pr.3 sg.:
    non-rhymed: *comethe* l. 3605, *hyes* l. 3613
    in rhyme: *lyethe* (: *wyce* adj.) l. 352, *bryngys* (: *kyngys* pl.) l. 3465;
      MS *hathe* (: *gos*) l. 7182. Twice the ending is absorbed by the -*s*
      of the stem: MS *losythes* for *los* (: *goos* pr.3 sg.) l. 3231; MS *rysis*
      for *rys* (: *lyes* pr.3 sg.) l. 6985.
pr.pl.:
    non-rhymed: *foundes* l. 605; *gedyrs* l. 1775; *makythe* ll. 6338, 7026;
      levythe l. 2025.
    in rhyme: *fynde* (: *behynde*) l. 1881; *have* (: *face*) l. 3023; *tellis*
      (: *ellys*) l. 7146.

(c) Past Indicative:

(1) There is usually no distinction between sg. and pl.: the vowels of
strong verbs have generally been levelled to the sg. forms, but very
occasionally the vowel from the plural is found. Pa.t.pl. forms of
strong verbs occasionally have the ending -*n*, but this is never
confirmed by rhyme. Occasionally the pa.t.2 sg. (weak or strong)
has -*este*, but again, not in rhyme.

Examples:
3 sg. *ryse* l. 4221; *rede* 'rode' l. 3807; *ryde* (: *abyde* n.) l. 3624
2 sg.(wk, str.)
    non-rhymed: *hadeste* l. 5414; *þou dyd* ll. 1021, 1064 against *dydyste*
      thou l. 7268.
    in rhyme: *gartte* (: *herte* n.) l. 1023; *lefte* (: *crafte* n.) l. 5402:
      showing vowel from 3 sg.; *thou badde* (: *thou hadde* pa.t.) l. 8713.
pl. (str.)
    non-rhymed: *sayden* l. 1880, *sawyn* l. 8259 against *sawe* l. 1945.
    in rhyme: showing vowel of sg. form: *beganne* (: *þanne* adv.) l. 5606;
      sange (: *longe* adv., *wronge* n., *hange* subj.) l. 7265; *ranne* (:*man*
      n.) l. 3780.

(2) The weak pa.t. and pp. ending does not seem to have been syllabic, though it is spelt variously as *-ed*, *-yd/id*, *-ud*, *-d*, *-t* in the text (but once *calde*, l. 7585): *dwellyd, feellyd* (: *helde* pa.t., *tolde* pp.*)* l. 138 ff.; *callyd* (: *fold* n., *wold* v., *told* pa.t.) l. 2147; *sparyd* (: *Lyard*) l. 4128; *begillyd* (: *wyld* adj.) l. 4818; *sterde* 'stirred' (: *swerd* n.) l. 8420. Where the stem ends in a dental, the ending is often absorbed: *davnte, graunte* (: *havnte* v., *seruante* n.) l. 802; pp. adj. *wounde* (: *rownde* adv., *stovnde* n.) l. 6926. There is no evidence from rhymes of the West Midland unvoicing of final *-d* after *n*, *l*, *r*, although the spelling *fellt* 'felled' appears at l. 4385.

(d) Imperative : The sg. has no ending, e.g. *goo* l. 2513, *lede* l. 4825 (it never appears in rhyme-position). The pl. often has *-s*, but in its one occurrence in rhyme it has no ending: *wend* (: *ende* n.) l. 2009; *gravnte* l. 275; *telles* l. 4748; *abydes* l. 3630; *leppis* l. 7260.

(e) Present Participle: Always rhymes on *-and*, though occasional *-yng* spellings occur: *waginge* l. 5567 against *rennande* (: *hande* n.) l. 1597; *groande* (: *londe* n., *fonde* pa.t., *hande* n.) l. 4666. *Lauȝhyng* (: *tydyngys*) l. 2319 probably rhymed as *lauȝhand : tythand*.

(f) Past Participle: The pp. of strong verbs almost always has *-(e)n* in rhyme as well as spelling. As pp. adj., it occasionally has the prefix *i-*: *done* (: *sone* adv.) l. 884; *drawen* (: *agayne*) l. 4523; *sene* (: *bedene*) l. 914, but *se* l. 8234; *beholde* (: *bold* adj., *olde* adj.) l. 1896. Pp.adj. with with *i-*: *ibete* l. 368, *isete* l. 726, *iwroughte* l. 7073, *idyght* l. 7078.

(g) Verbal Noun: Always ends with, and rhymes on, *-ing*: *blowyng* (: *yong* for *ying*) l. 4008; *byddyng* (: *kyng* n.) l. 5425; *stodeynge* (: *ring* n.) l. 8488; *sighand* l. 7853 occurs once, but it is mid-line and may be an error.

(h) OE weak class II verbs: very rarely, the verb 'to love' retains its OE wk. class II *-y-* between stem and ending: pr.1 sg. *louye* l. 6316; pa.t. *lovyed* l. 56, *louyed* l. 168.

(i) Preterite-present Verbs: pr.2 sg. has either *-st* or no ending, but it always rhymes without suffix. Pa.t. 2 sg. occasionally has *-ys* or *-(e/i)st*, though this is unconfirmed by rhyme. All other forms have no suffix and sg. and pl. are not distinguished.

Examples:
pr.2 sg.: *shall* l. 1990 etc. against *shalte* l. 444 etc.; *wilte* l. 406 etc. against *will* l. 5050 etc.; *can* (: *man* n.) l. 1306; *maye* (: *saye* v.) l. 7375.

pr. pl.: *we shall* l. 448; *ye schall* (: *all* adj.) l. 8526; *ye will* (: *þertille* prep.) l. 6927, 8087; *ye may* (: *lay* pr.1 sg., *they*) l. 3425.

pa.t. 2 sg.: *shuldys* l. 1932; *myghttys* l. 1067; *woldyste* l. 1981.

pa.t. 'might' appears usually as *myght*, from the forms with OE i-mutation, but in rhyme the non-mutated reflex *mowȝte* also occurs (rhymed with *nouȝte* l. 7251; *thought* pp. l. 7359).

ON. pres.1 sg. *mvn* l. 724, *mon* l. 1199.

(j) The verb 'to be':

inf. *been* (: *bedene* adv., *kene* adj., *wene* pr.1 sg.) l. 6450, against *been* (: *degre* n., *lewte* n., *se* v.) l. 8839.

pr.1 sg. *am(e)* l. 1011, 7719 etc.; (: *whome* pron.) l. 962.

pr.2 sg. *art(e)* ll. 245, 1142 etc. (does not appear in rhyme).

pr.3 sg. almost always spelt *is/ys* (ll. 116, 122 etc.) but rhymes as *es*, e.g. *is* (: *worthynes* n.) l. 1580, twice spelt *yes* ll. 1364, 4428; once *bees* mid-line, ll. 6732.

pr.pl. Three forms: (1) the usual spelling is *ar*, sometimes *are* (ll. 935, 1233 etc.), although it actually rhymes as *er(e)* (: *nere* 'never', *geyre* n.) l. 6246, (: *swere* v.) ll. 7965, 8719: while *swere* could conceivably have been lowered to *sware*, it seems to rhyme elsewhere only on -*e*- (ll. 1123, 3530, 4313, 5227, 5421, 5984, 8114). (2) *ys* ll. 887, 3099, (: *worthynes* n.) l. 1580. (3) One occurrence of *bene* l. 6352: *bene* l. 7843 (: *seene* pp., *betwene* prep.).

pa.t.sg. *was* (: *asse* v., *passe* v., *alas*) ll. 943, 1673; (: *Dryas*) l. 1803.

pa.t.pl. Two forms: (1) Normally *were* or *ware*: *were* (: *clere* adj.) l. 4434, (: *more* comp.) l. 6256; *ware* (: *yare* adv.) l. 4222. (2) Sometimes *was* l. 558, (: *place* n., *face* n.) l. 2081, (: *Dryas*) l. 2236 etc..

pr.subj.sg. and pl. *be* l. 387 (sg.); *be* l. 238 (pl.).

pa.t.subj.sg.: *wore* (: *whereffore*) l. 1113; *were* (: *bare* adj., *þare* adv., *yare* adv.) l. 2201.

pp. Usually *bene*, but also *be*: *byen* (: *quene*, *bedene*) l. 162; (: *mene* v., *wene* n., *sene* pp.) l. 255 etc.; *be* l. 12 etc., though no examples in rhyme.

(k) the verbs 'to go', 'to make', 'to take'. *Go* often rhymes on Nth. -*a*-; 'make' and 'take' often use the Nth. shortened stems *ma*- and *ta*- in rhyme-position, and all three are found together in rhyme-position.

Examples:

pr.3 sg. *tas* : *gas* ll. 1694–5; *taas* (: MS *hath* for original *has*) l. 3777; MS *take* inf. (: *forgoo* v.) l. 2152 (but *take* (: *sake* n., *spake* pa.t.)

ll. 51, 1942); *tane* : *gonne* ll. 1049–50; MS *made* (: MS *goothe, rose* pa.t., *harnes*) l. 4175; *mase* : *gos* ll. 4029–30; *masse* : *gos* l. 6981–2.

(l) The pa.t. of 'come' rhymes either on *o* (from OE *cōm*) or on *a*, perhaps by analogy with ON pa.t. *kvam*:[34] *come* (: *home* n.) l. 302; (: *sum* pron.) l. 1880; (: *towne* n.) l. 7325, against *came* (: *name* n.) l. 1748, (: *same* adj.) l. 6819.

(m) Mixed verb endings: there is a small but steady stream of what look to be misplaced southern verb endings throughout the text: 3 sg. *hym besyest* l. 612; *hathe thou* l. 1066; *hath þou* l. 1401; *who so losythes* (: *gos*) l. 3231 (this is a curious amalgam of northerly *loses* or *los* and southerly *losythe*: the *-es* is not an abbreviation in the MS, so it is not the result of an absent-minded twirl of the quill); *thou levythe* l. 3302; *thou . . . hathe sene* l. 4926; *he dedyst* pa.t. l. 5153; *thou . . . vnderstondythe* l. 7941.

RHYMING PRACTICE

The poem is written in twelve-line tail-rhyme verses, rhyming aabccbddbeeb. The English poet is generally very careful with his rhymes: occasionally he resorts to *m*/*n* assonance (only twice does he rely on assonance involving other consonants). Long and short vowels may be rhymed together, although it is not always possible to predict the ME vowel-length simply from the OE form of a word. Occasionally a rhyme-word is re-used within a stanza, or a couplet will rhyme with the tail-rhymes of that verse. However, the vast majority of the rhymes are perfect and without repetition in individual stanzas. The bedraggled state of the extant text does no justice to the elegant workmanship of the original poet, and it is safe to assume that the original rhythm and stress were also considerably smoother than this version would lead one to believe.

Examples of variations on normal rhyming practice:
short vowels rhymed with long: e.g. *her* : *Fere, nere* l. 180; *hade* pa.t. : *rade* pa.t. l. 3733; *hadde* : *fade* v., *brayde* adj., *mayde* v. l. 4363; *blake* adj. : *take* l. 4916; *wedde* inf. : *lede* inf. l. 5049; MS *hathe* for 'has' : *grace* n., *tras*, n. *goothe* l. 5363; *thanne* : *Loreayne* l. 5660; *Ipomadon* : *stone* n. l. 7705 etc.
assonance (ten occurrences): *home* : *moone* v. ll. 1068–9; *raunsome* :

---

[34] See entry for *come* in *The Oxford Dictionary of English Etymology*, ed. C. T. Onions (Oxford, 1966).

towne ll. 4307–8; *ravnsum, home* : *downe, presone* l. 4534 ff.; *lyne* v. :
tyme n. ll. 6178–9; *come* : *towne* ll. 7325–6; *theym* : *men* ll. 7838–9;
white : *hyde* l. 3955–56; *togeddur* : *stakyre* v. ll. 7827–8; *merthe* n. :
wrethe n. ll. 6352–3; *dowte* : *novght* l. 7665–6.

couplets rhyming with tail-rhyme: ll. 4463–4 *face, Dreas* with *was*
   pa.t., *alas*, MS *axe* v., *passe* v.; ll. 8364–5 *pas, was* with *hathe, toke,*
   goothe (for original *has, tas, gas*)

repeated words: K. lists 21 examples of 'rhyme riche' (usually
   involving words functioning as different parts of speech), 6
   instances of a compound word rhyming with its final element,
   and 21 examples of the same word simply repeated:

   rhyme riche: e.g. *more* adj. and adv. ll. 1054, 1060; *not* adv. and
   nought pron. ll. 1322–3; *wyld* adj. 'wild', v. 'wield' ll. 4824, 4827;
   hee pron. and MS *hye* adj. 'high' ll. 8339, 8342; *spede* n. and v.
   ll. 8624, 8630;

   compound words: e.g. *wythinne* : *inne* ll. 4744–5; *glade* : *vnglad*
   ll. 5734, 5740; *before* : *therefore* l. 482–3;

   same words: e.g. *wende* ll. 1006, 1009; *me(e)* ll. 2148–9; *youde,*
   yede ll. 3329, 3335; *had(de)* ll. 5297, 5303; *witte* ll. 6884, 6890;
   wrothe ll. 8753, 8759.

If the practice of rhyming short and long vowels together is excluded
(vowel-length being highly unstable and often unpredictable in the
northern dialects as a result of, among other factors, the early loss of
unstressed final *e*), this gives an approximate total of a mere sixty
anomalies over the course of 8,890 lines. With the amount of scribal
corruption in the extant text, this can only ever be a rough estimate,
but it still demonstrates beyond any doubt that the author of
Ipomadon was extremely consistent with his chosen rhyming pattern
and careful with his rhymes, the vast majority of which were perfect.

LANGUAGE OF THE TEXT
PART II: DISCUSSION

References in wavy brackets {   } are to sections in Part I.

(1) DIALECT OF THE ORIGINAL

The principal aim of this study of the language of the text is to
establish the dialect, and thus the place, of composition of the poem.

Naturally, it is possible that the author moved from the place where he acquired his dialect before composing the poem, but for the sake of convenience, the place of composition and the geographic source of the author's dialect are here referred to as if they were one and the same thing. The main source of information about the author's dialect must be the rhymes, since the mere spelling of any given word in the manuscript may be scribal rather than authorial. In a poem of nearly 9,000 lines, with a rhyme-scheme rigid enough to show where lines have been accidentally omitted and an author who was evidently careful to use exact rhymes in the vast majority of cases (see {Rhyming Practice}), this furnishes us with a surprisingly large amount of detail with which to determine the author's dialect. Once the approximate area of composition has been thus established, additional supporting evidence can sometimes be drawn from non-rhymed forms that can be shown to belong to the same general area.

Despite the multiple layers of copying, it is clear from even a cursory reading of *Ipomadon* that this is a North Midland composition.[35] This is demonstrated by a host of phonological, morphological and lexical features, the first two categories of which have been set out in detail in the preceding section. The following discussion is arranged in such a way as to narrow down gradually the possible area of origin: first, features restricting us to the northern area generally, followed by features that indicate the northern half of the North Midlands (the area shown in Fig. 1), and finally to the small combination of features that indicates the West Riding—and the north-west part of it in particular—as the most probable source for the dialect in which *Ipomadon* was composed.

(*a*) *Evidence for northern provenance*

Morphological features that virtually rule out composition anywhere outside the northern area are the pr.ind.2 and 3 sg. suffix -*s*, and either -*s* or nothing at all as the pr.pl. suffix: these are frequently shown in the extant text and are the only forms confirmed by rhyme (see {Verbs} for examples and *LALME* 1, maps 645 and 653 for

[35] The 'North Midlands' refers in this discussion to the area comprising Lancashire, the West Riding of Yorkshire, North Lincolnshire, and the parts of those counties to the south of these which lie north of a line drawn roughly from the Mersey to the Wash, i.e. Cheshire, Derbyshire, Nottinghamshire and South Lincolnshire. The 'North' refers to the North and East Ridings of Yorkshire, Durham, Northumberland, Cumberland, Westmoreland, and Scotland. Uncapitalised 'northern' is used to refer to the entire area.

distribution). The fact that the pr.pl. never rhymes on -en, the suffix that dominates the Midlands, suggests composition in either the North Midlands or the North proper (*LALME* 1, map 652). Other verb-forms that are more clearly confined to the northern area are the forms *bus* for ME *behoves* (*LALME* 1, map 698), *mas* 'makes', *tas*, pp. *tane* from 'take' ({Verbs (k)}; Jordan §178, remark 4), and the ON pr. sg. *mon*, *mvn* ({Verbs (i)}; *LALME* 1, map 831). The use of *es* and *er* for the pr.3 sg. and pl. forms of 'to be' {Verbs (j)} is discussed in more detail below under 'Evidence for the West Riding of Yorkshire', but it may be observed here that both are restricted to a band stretching diagonally from the Scottish border to South Lincolnshire, but avoiding Lancashire and Derbyshire (*LALME* 1, maps 134, 121). The use of the present participle suffix -*and* has often been taken as a clear marker of northern provenance, although pockets of it can in fact be found further south ({Verbs (e)}; *LALME* 1, maps 345–6). The greater significance of the lack of pr.p. -*ing* in the rhymes is discussed below under 'Evidence for the West Riding of Yorkshire'. The form *scho* for the pronoun 'she' is the only one to be confirmed by rhyme {Pronouns}, and this too is largely restricted to the northern area (*LALME* 1, map 13; *LALME* 2, maps 4 and 7).

One phonological feature that has largely been obscured by the spelling of the present text is the predominance of -*aw*- in such words as 'know', 'blow', 'low' and 'snow' beside -*ow*- forms {2}: this virtually eliminates the possibility of composition outside the northern area (*LALME* 1, map 813 for 'know').

A second phonological feature which, when it appears as frequently as it does in *Ipomadon*, indicates the northern area is shown in certain words which had *ǣ* in Old English. As a result of the influence of Old Norse cognate forms with *ā*, these have *a* or *o* beside the *e* to which OE *ǣ* normally developed {1(b),Verbs (j) pa.t.pl. and subj.}. Examples are the words for 'hair' (rhymed with *care* or *before*), pa.t. *ware* or *wore* (the former is far more common in rhyme than *were*), the adv. 'ere' (never rhymed on *e*), and the forms of the verb 'slay', the pp. of which rhymes as either the OE-derived *slayne* or the ON-derived *slan*, *slon*. The main concentration of these forms is in the North and the North-East Midlands, where Scandinavian influence was heaviest (see *LALME* 1, map 131, 'were' as *war*-, and note how all but the northern part of Lancashire is excluded).

There are many other phonological features evident in the text which were either not restricted to the northern area, or did not remain thus restricted for the whole of the Middle English period. They therefore cannot be viewed as proof of northern provenance, but they are certainly consistent with it:

- A general Midland feature, derived from the Anglian dialect of Old English, is the development of words with OE *$\bar{æ}^1$* (*adrede* adj., *dede* n.), which in Anglian had *$\bar{e}$* instead of West Saxon *$\bar{æ}$*. When these vowels were shortened, the West Saxon-derived words would generally show *a* while Anglian-derived forms would show *e*: the examples of shortened *$\bar{æ}^1$* in *Ipomadon* show *e* {6}.

- The reflexes of OE *ea* (e.g. *helde* inf., *olde* adj., *welde* inf.) show *e* and *o*, a mixture that is difficult to explain on purely philological grounds {9}, but which Kölbing (p. CLXXIII) also finds in the Northern or North Midland poems *Sir Gawain and the Green Knight*, *Sir Tristrem* and *Percevall of Galles*.

- The reflexes of OE *$\bar{e}a$* + *h*, e.g. 'high' {10}, show both the *e* characteristic of the North-West Midlands and Yorkshire (from A *hēh*), and the more widespread *i* (Jordan §101; for 'high' see *LALME* 2, map 149, 1–3). The reflexes of 'die' show either this development to *e* beside *i* from OE **dēgan*, or influence of ON *deyja*, either of which indicates the Midlands or the North (*LALME* 1, maps 393–5 and *LALME* 2, map 103, 1–3). The distribution of 'eye' differs slightly in that the *i*-forms do not penetrate very far into the North Midlands, and no *i*-forms appear in rhyme in *Ipomadon* (*LALME* 1, maps 750–2).

- The intermittent raising of OE *ĕ* > *ĭ* {13(a)} is a phenomenon found throughout Middle English, but Dobson and Jordan note that it seems to have been especially common in Northern English (Dobson §76 note 4, Jordan §34, but see *LALME* 1, map 915 for 'well' adv. spelt *wil-*, which shows specific concentrations in East Anglia and the West Midlands).

- The Middle English sound-changes OE *ĭ* > *$\bar{e}$* and OE *ŭ* > *$\bar{o}$* in open syllables are represented in such rhymes as *onskylle*: *dele* n. and *dore* n. : *floure* n. {14, 17}. Jordan (§36) notes that these first became apparent in northerly dialects in the thirteenth century and spread southwards. Their presence here simply agrees with a northern provenance.

- The appearance of OE *y* as *i* can also do no more than agree with a northern provenance, since the only areas where *i* would not be the normal reflex are the West Midlands, the South-West and Kent.

- The spelling of 'worse' as *wars* is significant despite only being recorded mid-line because although *wars* and *wers* were equally common in the North and North Midlands, and *wors* reaches as far north as Lancashire and South Yorkshire, the spelling *wars* is extremely rare outside the North Midlands, so the two mid-line occurrences of it here may be authorial, or at least from an early northerly layer of copying ({12} and *LALME* 1, maps 393–5). Related is the appearance of *warkys* from A *werc-*, which Jordan describes as a Northern product of the lME change of *er* > *ar* (§270, remark 1, §66 remark 3; Campbell §222).

Northern Vocabulary

In this first section must be included most of the lexical evidence. Many words seem to be indicative of northern provenance, but it is notoriously difficult to determine the past geographic ranges of words. Modern English dialectal evidence is of limited use, since geographic ranges may expand or contract over time, and there is often no way to determine which, if either, has happened. Rolf Kaiser attempted to define the range at least some Middle English words by compiling two lists, one Northern and one Southern, from texts about whose geographic origin there was little doubt. Dunlap subsequently conducted a more specific study on the vocabulary of the tail-rhyme romances based on Kaiser, and Frances McSparran, in her edition of Northern *Octovian,* has similarly refined some of Kaiser's designations.[36] Words in this text corresponding to Kaiser's list of northernisms as filtered through Dunlap's list of tail-rhyme romance words are: *ado* n. 'trouble', *belde* n. 'happiness' (emended form), *brathe* 'eager' (emended form), *brond/ brand* n. 'sword', *byrde/ berde* n. 'noble lady', *carpynge* vbl.n. 'gossiping', *farand* adj. 'fitting', *gang* v. 'go', *gar* v. 'make, do' (and see *LALME* 1, map 790), *gayne* adj. 'quick', *grete* n. 'ground', *lythe* n. 'estate', *in mell* prep. 'between', ON pret.pr. *mon, mvn* 'must' (and see *LALME* 1, map 831), *nerehand* adv. 'almost', *rose* v. 'praise', *rose* n. 'boast', *spere* v. 'enquire', *swime* n. 'unconsciousness', *tene* adj. 'angry', *tyne* v. 'lose', *wande* n. 'slim

---

[36] See R. Kaiser, *Zur Geographie des mittelenglischen Wortschatzes, Palaestra,* 205 (1937); A. R. Dunlap, 'The Vocabulary of the Middle English Romances in Tail-Rhyme Stanza', *Delaware Notes,* 14 (1941), 1–42; *Octovian,* ed. Frances McSparran, EETS os 289 (1986), p. 27.

branch', *wathe* n. 'harm' (emended form), *yene* adj. 'yon' (see also *OED* entry), *yrkys* v. 'be weary of'.[37] McSparran would add the following words she notes to be 'chiefly, if not exclusively, northern or North Midland in distribution': *abowne* prep. 'from above', *till* conj. and prep. 'to', and northern or North Midland forms of such words as *dede* n. 'death' (and see *LALME* 1, maps 728–9), *mekyll* n. and adj., *ilke* adj., and the plural form *brether*, 'brothers'.[38] This last form, which occurs here once at l. 8697, derives from Northumbrian OE *bræþre* and thus may suggest a slightly narrower northern range (Campbell §630). The form *ying* for 'young' should also be included here as it is found mainly in either East Anglia or Yorkshire: in the latter case, it would be reasonable to assume that it derives from Northumbrian OE *ging* rather than simply through analogy with the comparative forms (*LALME* 1, map 926). Of similar distribution is *ferde* for 'fourth' (MS *fovrthe* l. 8423 rhymed with *sterde, swerde*), which occurs in the North Midlands, in Scotland, and in a pocket in the East Midlands (*LALME* 1, map 780). A similar distribution exists for the form *emonge*, 'among', which occurs once at the beginning of l. 87 (*LALME* 1, map 682).

(b) The northern part of the North Midlands

The North proper is ruled out as a place of composition by the fact that words with OE *ā* can rhyme on either *-o-* or *-a-* {1}: the southern limit of OE *ā* remaining as *a* is traditionally given as the boundary between the North proper and the North Midlands. If the variation between *o* and *a* in our text is indeed a reflection of the author's own dialect, then he must be from somewhere at the southern limit of the Northern dialect area. Kristensson has been able to define this boundary fairly accurately from the abundant place-name evidence:[39] it is represented in Fig. 1 as **Line A**. (The *ā/ ō* boundary continues south of the area illustrated to bisect Lincoln-shire, but all but the North-Western tip of Lincolnshire is ruled out by other factors discussed below.) Connected to the development of OE *ā* are the reflexes of OE *ă* before lengthening groups, e.g. OE *hand, lang*, which also appear as both *o* and *a* {4, 5}. Although spellings of OE *-and* as *-and* extend to the South Midlands, the *-ond*

---

[37] He also lists *cayre* v., which however has a wider distribution: see *MED*.

[38] McSparran, *op.cit.*, p. 27.

[39] Gillis Kristensson, *A Survey of Middle English Dialects 1290–1359* (Lund, 1967), p. 283.

reflexes do not occur north of the $\bar{a}/\bar{o}$ boundary described above, once again eliminating the North proper (*LALME* 1, maps 936–7). Meanwhile, the distribution of OE *-ang* spelt as *-ang* is principally a North Midland feature, although it too can be found as far south as the South Midlands (*LALME* 1, maps 938–9).

A Northern feature that is partially obscured in the present text is the reflex of OE $\bar{o}$ + *h*, as in the OE preterites *hlōh* 'laughed' and *drōh* 'drew': these are both sometimes found with the spellings *lewgh*, *lewȝ* and *drew*, and rhymes with OF *u/eu* confirm these forms as original {16}. This diphthong arose from the peculiarly Northern development of OE $\bar{o}$ to a fronted sound [øː], similar to Modern German *ö*: when, in inflected forms, the fricative [ɣ] was vocalized to /u/, the spelling *-ew-* was used to represent the resulting diphthong. The form *lewgh* is a result of this new diphthong being imported into the non-inflected form (Jordan §119, §128). Since the southern limit of OE $\bar{o}$ > [øː] is roughly the same as that for OE $\bar{a}$ > *a* (shown as **Line A** on Fig. 1), these are clearly Northern forms (Jordan §54) and demonstrate yet again that the author of *Ipomadon* was probably from somewhere along the linguistic boundary between the North Midlands and the North proper.

There is sporadic evidence for a development of Middle English *ei*, *ai* > $\bar{a}$ in such rhymes as *orfrayes* : *place* {8}. This is described by Jordan as a change of the second half of the fourteenth century which took place in most areas of Scotland and in the south of Yorkshire (§132), and it is the root of the later northern use of the *ai*-spelling to represent /aː/.

Perhaps also to be included in this section is the form *asse*, pa.t. *aste*, for 'ask': it appears in rhyme several times and indeed is the only form of 'ask' to do so {30}. The *MED* citations for this form all refer to Northern texts dating from the last quarter of the fourteenth century at the earliest, and Jordan also notes that this form appears first in the North, citing such sources as the *Towneley Plays* and the Thornton manuscript (§182).

(c) Evidence for the West Riding of Yorkshire

Since this section depends for its arguments on certain assumptions about the nature of the rhyme-evidence in this text, these should be outlined first before specific features are discussed. The tail-rhyme stanza in which the entire poem is written is a relatively demanding form: each stanza requires four rhyming words—preferably all different—for the tail-rhyme, on top of four couplets, also preferably all different. It follows that an author writing in tail-rhyme will need as many types and combinations of rhymes as possible, and that words for which more than one pronunciation is available, such as *yede/yode* pa.t., are especially desirable. Under these circumstances it becomes significant when, for example, the author never rhymes 'she' on *-e* although it appears in rhyme-position five times, each time rhymed on *-o* and occasionally spelt *sho(o)*—see {Pronouns (d)}. The form *she* is widespread in the northern area from which we know the poet hails; it rhymes conveniently with a host of other words including the pronouns *he, the, ye* and *me* and all words ending with OF *é*, and furthermore the author is obliged to use 'she' continually on account of the number of female characters. But the versatile form *she* is not used once in rhyme over the entire 8,890 lines. Such avoidance *must* be deliberate. We already know that our author was not careless with his rhymes (see {Rhyming Practice}). It would appear from his treatment of the variants of 'she' that he was also anxious to be dialectally consistent, because the only reasonable explanation for his avoidance of the versatile and widespread *she* is that it was not part of the dialect of his immediate area. This dialectal consistency incidentally argues that source of the author's dialect and the place of composition were indeed one and the same: there would be little point in conforming so consistently to the characteristics of one particular local dialect if dialectal consistency were not expected by the audience.

Having established that the author of *Ipomadon* avoided borrowing forms from outside his dialect to satisfy rhyme, we can then assert more confidently that the *a* and *o* reflexes of OE *ā* are indeed the result of composition near this isogloss (**Line A** on Fig. 1). When this is added to the fact that 'she' is never rhymed on *-e*, we can eliminate Lincolnshire as a possible source of the author's dialect, since *sche* is the main form throughout this county while *sho* only ever appears as a secondary variant if at all (*LALME* 2, map 4). This leaves us with Lancashire, the West and perhaps East Ridings of Yorkshire, and the very north of Nottinghamshire.

A second common word for which only one variant can be proved in rhyme is the pr.3 sg. of 'to be' {Verbs (j)}: in *Ipomadon* the rhymes only show *es*. As with *she,* the more widespread variant *is/ys* would have been extremely useful for rhyme, and its absence is similarly significant. The *es*-form appears through most of the

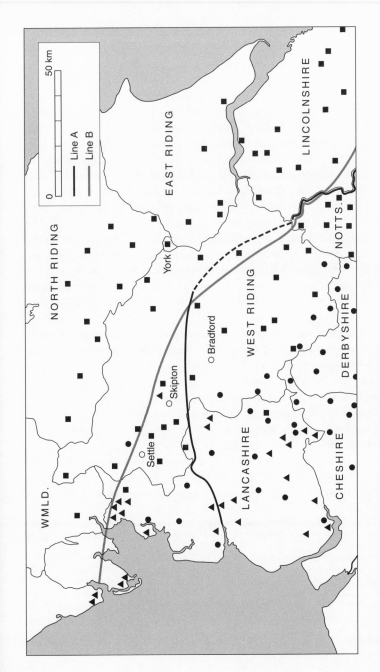

Figure 1: Distribution of Forms in the North Midlands

northern area down to South Lincolnshire, but is almost entirely excluded from Lancashire, where the normal form is *ys/is*: the occurrences of *es* are marked on Fig. 1 as ■ (from *LALME* 4, p. 35).

The preceding feature would, by apparently eliminating Lancashire, seem to place us very firmly in Yorkshire, but there is another linguistic feature which almost contradicts this finding. This is the occurrence in rhyme of such words as the auxiliary verb 'can' or the noun 'man' with *o* as well as *a* {3}. This feature is generally regarded as a clear West Midland trait, and indeed it is not found in the East Midlands at all. In Fig. 1, ● marks the occurrence of *o*-forms in manuscripts surveyed by *LALME*,[40] and ▲ marks place-names with *-mon-* as mapped by Kristensson.[41] The respective areas of distribution of *es* and *o* + *n* meet, but barely overlap, along the western and south-western borders of the West Riding. The area of greatest interpenetration seems to be the top northwest corner of the county, and this agrees with the necessity of staying close to the $\bar{a}/\bar{o}$ isogloss in this search for the *Ipomadon*-poet's origins.

The final feature of the language whose distribution is shown in Fig. 1 is the pr.3 pl. of 'to be': although it only appears in rhyme three times, it rhymes as *er* in all three cases {Verbs (j)}. The area in which the Scandinavian-influenced *er* occurs is narrower than, though parallel to, the distribution of the singular form *es*.[42] **Line B** represents the approximate boundary below which *er(e)* is no longer the dominant form (*LALME* 2, map 17): the absence of the far more widespread North Midland form *ar(e)* in rhyme suggests, as do *es* and *sho*, that the poem was composed in an area where the easily-rhymed *ar(e)* was not a local variant. Even at its widest extent, the distribution of *ere* shows only two occurrences as far west as

---

[40] *LALME* 4. The distribution shown in Fig. 1 was produced by mapping the locations for the *-o-* forms of these words, given in *LALME* 4, onto the 'key maps' at the back of that volume.

[41] Kristensson, *op.cit.*, p. 270.

[42] M. L. Samuels has discussed the geographic distribution of *er(e)* in the context of delimiting a narrow belt of especially strong Scandinavian influence on Middle English which stretches from Cumberland and Westmoreland in the west, to the North and East Ridings, and often North Lincolnshire, in the east. It would explain some of the differences apparent in the otherwise similar dialects of Yorkshire and North Lancashire, such as those discussed here in relation to *Ipomadon*. See M. L. Samuels, 'The Great Scandinavian Belt', in *Middle English Dialectology*, eds. A. McIntosh, M. L. Samuels and M. Laing (Aberdeen, 1989), pp. 106–15 (p. 107).

North Lancashire, and one in the extreme North-East of Cheshire, against a swathe of occurrences through Yorkshire, Lincolnshire, and the borders of Nottinghamshire. These last two counties have already been ruled out of consideration by the lack of *o*-forms for OE *a/o* + *n*, as has all but the West Riding of Yorkshire, so we remain confined to the border between Lancashire and the West Riding as the only plausible source of the dialect of *Ipomadon*.

There is one more feature of the language of the text that can be used to help pinpoint the area of composition. This is the fact that the only ending for the present participle to be used in rhyme is *-and*. The use of the ending *-and* is itself unremarkable—there is no part of the northern area that does not use this form—but the absence of the main Middle English form *-ing* is, by contrast, very revealing (*LALME* 1, maps 345–6). Since the form *-ing* carries such a wealth of rhyme-possibilities, the only explanation for its absence from the thousands of rhymes in *Ipomadon* is, again, deliberate avoidance. As it happens, the only visible area of the country where this form does *not* occur according to the *LALME* maps is precisely that northwest portion of the West Riding which other linguistic features have already indicated to be the most likely place of composition of *Ipomadon A*.

The Gough Map, c.1360, illustrates many of the travel routes used in the North of England.[43] In the north-western area of the West Riding, it marks a road that runs north-west from Doncaster through Wakefield, Bradford (passing on the way the little town of 'Ledes'), Skipton, Settle, and finally connecting with the Lancaster-Carlisle road at Kirkby Lonsdale in Westmoreland: it follows the route of the modern A65. This road passes neatly through the area which linguistic features of the text show to be the most likely source of our author's dialect: Skipton perhaps fulfills these criteria best. Of course, this is a highly speculative placing, and it is not impossible that future research on Middle English dialects may result in the repositioning of some of the isoglosses used in this study. Even at the most conservative estimate though, it would be very difficult to argue for anywhere beyond the borders of the West Riding of Yorkshire as the place of composition of *Ipomadon*.

---

[43] E. J. S. Parsons, *The Map of Great Britain circa A.D. 1360 known as The Gough Map: An Introduction to the Facsimile* (London, 1958). This is essentially a road-map of Great Britain, marking the common travelling routes, the towns through which roads pass, and occasionally the distances between them.

(2) THE DIALECTS OF LATER COPYISTS

There are several intervening layers of copying between the original product of the author and the extant copy in MS Chetham 8009. We know now that the poem was originally composed in the West Riding of Yorkshire, and we also know that the manuscript is probably of London provenance. In situations such as this, where the origins of both original and final 'linguistic layers' have been identified, it is theoretically possible to peel these off to reveal the fainter impressions left by intervening layers of copying. In practice, however, this is very difficult to do, especially with later fifteenth-century copies such as MS Chetham 8009. Benskin and Laing, who explain the technique, caution that linguistically mixed texts 'arising from contact with the written standard of the Central Midlands, and later of the Chancery, present frequently intractable problems'.[44] Nevertheless, a certain amount can still be learned about both the scribe responsible for copying *Ipomadon* in MS Chetham 8009—Ker's Hand 5—and some of his predecessors.

(a) The Chetham Scribe

When a scribe has copied more than one text, as has the scribe represented by Hand 5, it should be possible to learn something of his own language through a detailed comparison of the language of the different texts he has copied.[45] Where a single item shows a variety of forms, the one (or ones) common to all texts can be attributed to that scribe. In MS Chetham 8009, the scribe responsible for *Ipomadon* also copied the two Marian lyrics, the 'Lyf of Seynt Katerin', *Beues of Hamtoun*, l. 1050 ff. of *Torrent of Portyngale*, *The Book of the Duke and the Emperor*, and the 'Good Boke of Kervyng and Nortur'.

Fig. 2 shows a selection of linguistic items whose forms vary amongst at least some of the texts copied by our scribe.[46] There are two columns for *Torrent*—the first is Ker's Hand 7, who copied ll. 1–

---

[44] M. Benskin and M. Laing, 'Translations and Mischsprachen in Middle English', in *So meny people longages and tonges*, eds. M. Benskin and M. L. Samuels (Edinburgh, 1981), pp. 55–106 (p. 57).

[45] Benskin and Laing recommend looking at at least a hundred linguistic features, including elements of vocabulary, grammatical endings, phonological variants, and even orthographical details such as the use of thorns or doubled consonants, *ibid.*, p. 57.

[46] The sections analysed are as follows: 'Seynt Katerin'—all; *Beues*—ll. 1–504 (p), ll. 2000–3000 (m); *Torrent* Hand 7—ll. 1–407, 903–1049; *Torrent* Hand 5—ll. 1050–1400, 2353–2668; *Book of the Duke*—ff. 357a–363b; *Ipomadon*—all.

1049, and the second is our scribe, who copied the rest (since there is no change of paper-stock, it is likely that the scribes were working together and therefore from the same exemplar). The Chetham copy of *Beues* is unique in that it is derived partly from the printed, and partly from the manuscript tradition: it would appear that the Chetham scribe filled the gaps in one exemplar with passages from another.[47] Where the forms of an item differ between the sections derived from the print or manuscript traditions, they are marked as (p) or (m). The relative frequency of each form of an item is indicated by brackets: where a form is not bracketted, it is the main or sole form; single brackets enclose forms which occur roughly between one-third and two-thirds as frequently as the main form, and double brackets enclose forms occurring less than a third as frequently as the main form. For the text of *Ipomadon*, the exact number of occurrences is sometimes also given in brackets.[48]

The first thing that becomes apparent upon looking through this chart is that there is very little consistency from one text to the next: there is no form of items such as 'again', 'many', 'much', 'said' and 'when' that can be found in every text where that word is used. This suggests that the *Ipomadon*-scribe is copying what lies before him, rather than substituting his own preferred forms. The fact that there are differences between those sections of *Beues* derived from either printed or manuscript exemplars supports this hypothesis. The forms in *Torrent* also lead to the same conclusion. All the Hand 7 forms apparently rejected by the *Ipomadon*-scribe have in fact been used elsewhere by him, so they cannot have been in what we are presuming was their common exemplar (see above). There is no way to know whether the *Ipomadon*-scribe had such a broad linguistic repertoire that everything he came across in these texts belonged to it, or if he were simply determined to copy his exemplars to the letter. All that we can conclude from this analysis is that the *Ipomadon*-scribe, for whatever reason, left almost no discernible linguistic layer on the texts he copied.

(b) Intermediate layers of copying

This is the area for which we, inevitably, have the least evidence to work with, and it is also potentially the most complex: we have no idea how many, or how many varieties, of dialectal layers may be

---

[47] Jennifer Fellows, '*Sir Beves of Hampton*: Study and Edition' (unpubl. Ph.D. thesis, University of Cambridge, 1980), pp. 37, 40.

[48] This system is taken from *LALME*, where it is set out in vol. 4, p. ix.

ITEM	Katerin	Bevys	Torrent, Hand 7	Torrent, Hand 5	Book of the Duke . . .	Ipomadon
AGAIN	ageyn	ageyn	ageyn	agayne, ageyn	ayen	agayne, (ageyne)
EACH	o	yche, (eche), (euerych), (euerychone),	eche	echone, euerych, eueriche, ech	o	ilka, ilkone, (euerychone), ((eche)), ((eche chone)) , ((ilke))
MANY	meny, ((many))	meny, (many, mony)	o	meny	many	many, ((mony, monye))
MUCH	moche	p = mekyll, (moche), ((muche)) m = moche ((mekylle))	meche, ((mekyll, mykyll))	moche, (moch)	muche, (miche), ((moche))	mekyll (70 ×), mekill (20 ×), muche (7 ×), moche (3 ×), mekell (1 ×)
SAID	said, ((sayd))	said, ((seid))	seyd, (sayd)	said, ((sayd))	said ((sayd))	sayd ((seyd))

SHOULD	shold	shold	schuld, ((schold))	shold	shold(e), ((shuld(e)))	shuld (147×), shold(5×), schuld (3×), schold (1×)
THEM	hem, ((them, ham))	ham, (hem), ((them))	them	hem, ((them))	theim, (theym, þem, them)	them(e) (128×), hem (17×), þem (6×), tham (2×), theym (1×)
THEY	they	they	they ((thay, thei))	they, ((thay))	they, (þey), ((thay))	they, thay (1×)
WHEN	whan, ((when 1×))	whan	when	whan	whanne, ((whan, whenne))	when ((whan, whanne))
WK. PA.T. SUFFIX	-ud, -id, -yd, -ed	**p** = -id, (-yd), ((-ed, -ud)); **m** = -yd, -ud, (-ed), ((-id))	-yd, ((-d, -ed,- t))	-yd, -id, -ed	-yd, -ed, ((-t))	-yd, ((-ed)), ((-ud)), ((-id))

Fig. 2: Linguistic forms copied by the *Ipomadon*-scribe (Ker's Hand 5)

sandwiched between the Yorkshire original and the extant London copy. One consequence of this is that only those features which represent the same dialect-area may be examined together: it is not possible to use the overlap between the geographic range of different features as it was in analysing the original dialect, because there is no way to tell whether, for example, a characteristically southern and a characteristically western feature belong to a single southwestern layer of copying, or two separate layers from the South and the West. Rather surprisingly however, there is enough evidence to demonstrate beyond reasonable doubt that there is at least one southwestern layer of copying.[49]

Two features that could be found throughout the South, but were particularly prevalent in the South-West, are occasionally illustrated in the extant text. One is the sporadic development of an initial glide shown in such words as *whome* 'home' and *yerlye* 'early' {20}: Jordan (§283) records this as beginning in Middle English 'toward 1400 predominantly in the more western parts of the South'.[50] The second is the rare retention of the OE weak verb class II stem with *-y-* in *louye* 'love' {Verbs (h)}: this occurs throughout the South but has its greatest concentration in the South-West and South-West Midlands (*LALME* 1, map 193).

A general Western feature is the rare *-u-* spelling for OE *eo* and *y* in *hurt* and *lutill* {12, 19}.[51] To this it is tempting to add the occurrence of the unstressed endings *-us, -ur, -ud,* which are consistent minor variants throughout this text. Serjeantson notes that *-us, -ud* are common in the works of West Midland writers Myrc and Audelay (both from Shropshire), but are not found in East Midland texts of the thirteenth and fourteenth centuries. However, she adds that 'they are . . . found occasionally in non-West Midland documents of the fifteenth century, e.g. Lincoln Diocesan documents and the later London documents', so these are

---

[49] The term 'southwestern' refers to both the South-West proper—Cornwall, Devon, Dorset, Hampshire, Wiltshire and Somerset—and the South-West Midlands—Gloucestershire, Herefordshire, and Worcestershire.

[50] See also *LALME* 1, map 235 for *yere* as a spelling for conj. 'ere': the few mapped points are all Western, with a small clump of them at the borders of Shropshire, Worcestershire and Herefordshire.

[51] See Jordan §66 for quick reference: for fuller evidence of this feature's West Midland (and Southwestern) distribution see Mary Serjeantson, 'The Dialects of the West Midlands in Middle English', *Review of English Studies*, 3 (1927), i. 54–67; ii. 186–203; iii. 319–331 (pp. 190–1).

of dubious significance in our late-fifteenth-century copy of *Ipomadon*.[52]

One unusual feature of the extant text of *Ipomadon* is the interchangeability of the spellings *this* and *thus* throughout the text. This is not authorial: where the words appear in rhyme, as they do several times, 'thus' always rhymes on *-us* and 'this' on *-is*.[53] Nor is it attributable to the Chetham scribe, who never confuses them in his other texts. This proves incontrovertibly that there is at least one intermediate layer of copying between the original and extant versions, but more importantly, *LALME* locates such reversed spellings almost exclusively in the southwestern area of the country.[54] To be precise, it records 'this' spelt *thus* once each in Devon and Wiltshire (but also once in Suffolk); 'thus' spelt *this* in Wiltshire, Somerset (twice), Herefordshire, and Gloucestershire (and once in Essex), but the combination of the two only three times— twice in Worcestershire and once in Somerset. (*LALME 4*, pp. 315– 6). Given the regular confusion between the two forms in *Ipomadon*, it is these latter localisations that are most significant.

This suggestion of a specifically southwestern layer of copying is supported by several occurrences in the text of a detached genitive ending, e.g. *Cananeus his own* {Nouns (b)}. Ronald Waldron, writing on the distinctively southwestern nature of Trevisa's language, notes his regular use of the detached genitive, and observes that in Middle English this trait is found only in the South West and in Trevisa's Gloucestershire-based writings (Trevisa himself was originally Cornish).[55] The single spelling of 'age' as *eolde* at l. 114 may be yet

---

[52] Serjeantson, *ibid.*, p. 61. See also Jordan §135. The single occurrence of pp. *fallon* with unstressed *-o-* (l. 4303) is a related, characteristically Western feature.

[53] E.g. *this* for 'thus': (: *Cabanus, vs*) l. 39; (: *Cabanus*) l. 3855. *Thus* for 'this': (: *his, i-wys, blis*) l. 1372; (: *kys, i-wys, blis*) l. 2746; (: *i-wis, blis, yeis*) l. 6396.

[54] Other minor features that prove the existence of at least one intermediate layer of copying are: (1) the MS spelling of Jason's name: it is *Iason(e)* 21 times up until his disappearance from the narrative at l. 1552, but he reappears at l. 3143 with his name spelt *Iosane*, and continues to be thus misspelt 36 times against only 4 correct spellings. The most likely explanation is that an exemplar copied by two different scribes lies somewhere in the text's line of transmission. (2) In the five times where 'should' appears in rhyme with *-old* (ll. 742, 2268, 2661, 2831, 7546) and where the author would presumably have written *shold*, it is spelt here as *shuld*: it is unlikely that *shuld* is the Chetham scribe's own substitution since he is happy to use *shold* as the sole form in some of his other texts, so it must be from an intermediate layer.

[55] Ronald Waldron, 'Dialect Aspects of Manuscripts of Trevisa's Translation of the *Polychronicon*', in *Regionalism in Late Medieval Manuscripts and Texts*, ed. Felicity Riddy (Woodbridge, 1991), pp. 67–87 (pp. 67–8). *LALME* records the detached genitive once

another small indication of southwestern copying, since *LALME* only records it (for late Middle English) in Gloucestershire (twice), Herefordshire and Wiltshire (*LALME* 4, p. 319).

These apparently southwestern features may or may not be related to the more generally southern and western traits noted earlier. In all probability, the text went through several stages of copying before coming into the hands of the Chetham scribe: at least one of these stages looks to have been southwestern, but there may be other layers that originated from elsewhere within the southern and western dialect areas.

DATE OF COMPOSITION

The evidence for the date of composition of *Ipomadon* is varied but inconclusive. There is convincing evidence (see below) for a date after c.1390, but the upper limit cannot be set more firmly than the first half of the fifteenth century, despite several ultimately unprovable details that would indicate a narrower dating of c.1390–1400. The original spelling, which might have been helpful in establishing date, is impossible to recover. One datable sound-change that is illustrated sporadically in the rhymes is the Northern development of ME *ai* to *ā*, a development of the second half of the fourteenth century which is not yet provable in, for example, the mid-fourteenth century Yorkshire text *Ywain and Gawain*.[56] Other datable sound-changes that have taken place in the author's dialect are: the loss of a fricative resulting in spellings such as *he* for 'high', which Jordan dates from the early fourteenth century,[57] and the *ass-* forms of 'ask', citations of which date from the last quarter of the fourteenth century.[58] The loss of the vowel in the pa.t. suffix of weak verbs, illustrated by such rhymes as *dwellyd : helde*, may also indicate a dating in or after the later fourteenth century at the earliest, since Jordan does not find it spreading to non-northern English until the fifteenth century.[59] The end of the fourteenth century at the earliest is also suggested by the

each in Cornwall, Dorset, Hampshire and Wiltshire, and three times each in Somerset and Devon (*LALME* 4, p. 322).

[56] See *Ywain and Gawain*, eds. Albert Friedman and Norman T. Harrington, EETS 254 (1964), pp. 39–40; Jordan §132, and 'Language of the Text: Part I', {8}.

[57] See 'Language of the Text: Part I', {25} and Part II, 1(a).

[58] See 'Language of the Text: Part I', {30} and Part II, 1(b).

[59] See Jordan §291, and 'Language of the Text: Part I', {Verbs (c) 2}.

use of the phrase *a littill tyne*, 'a little bit', at l. 3909. The *OED* dates its usage from 'about or soon after 1400', but its appearance at l. 59 of *Patience* pushes this back to c.1390, the approximate date currently agreed upon by critics for the works of the *Gawain*-poet. On the other hand, there is no evidence in *Ipomadon* of such later sound-changes as the Great Vowel Shift, which scholars now agree was firmly underway in the North by the fifteenth century.[60]

The remaining potentially datable elements in the poem consist of descriptions of, and terms for, clothing, and an arresting reference to *Sir Ypomadonn de Poele and the Fere de Calabre* in the Middle English alliterative poem *The Parlement of the Thre Ages*.[61]

COSTUME

The well-known propensity of medieval scribes to substitute a more familiar word for a strange one would seem to cast doubt on the reliability of dating texts by the vocabulary of costume: since medieval translators clearly felt free to alter and modernise their texts (at least in vernacular translation), one may suspect that scribes would have felt equally free to revise. In the case of descriptions of costume, however, this is less likely to have taken place than it may first appear. The author's own vocabulary is generally assured in rhyme-position, where any scribal changes are immediately apparent. Words that form part of an alliterating phrase are also more likely to be original. The status of individual words found outside rhyme-position is less certain, but the terms used for costume were relatively long-lived (although the appearance of the items they referred to altered over the course of years), so it is unlikely that later scribes would have encountered any unfamiliar words that they would have felt moved to change. Any differences between the Anglo-Norman and Middle English costumes are therefore more likely to be attributable to the author of the Middle English text than to a later scribe.

When the Anglo-Norman Ipomedon first arrives at the Fere's court, he is dressed in purple cendal, his *bliaut* (a type of tunic) is unlined for the heat, and his mantle is lined with ermine and inlaid with red cendal (ll. 377–89). In the English version, Ipomadon's

---

[60] See Jeremy J. Smith, 'The Great Vowel Shift in the North of England, and some forms in Chaucer's *Reeve's Tale*', *Neuphilologische Mitteilungen*, 95 (1994), 433–6.

[61] *The Parlement of the Thre Ages*, ed. M. Y. Offord, EETS 246 (1959), l. 618. See below, 'External References', for a discussion of the date of this text.

bliaut has been replaced by a *dobelett . . . of red melvet, / Of bryght gold botuns ibete* (ll. 367–8); otherwise he retains the Anglo-Norman mantle furred with ermine and bordered with red cendal.[62] The first appearance of doublet-like garments that are done up with, or at least conspicuously ornamented with, buttons is datable to around 1340, when curved seams first came to be used for armholes instead of simple T-junctions: the much tighter-fitting garments which could then be designed necessitated the more elaborate buttoned fastenings.[63] If such fastenings are what is indicated by Ipomadon's *bryght gold botuns*, then the text must have been written some time after 1340, but of course the linguistic features mentioned above have already demonstrated this. Interestingly though, the use of the actual word 'doublet' in reference to a man's close-fitting outer-garment does not seem to have been current in England much before 1400, although it is increasingly common afterwards. Costume historians seem to agree that, in England at least, the term 'doublet' does not become current until the fifteenth century.[64] The *MED* has three citations of the word before 1400 (and several immediately after it), but the first one to refer to the cloth garment that we now associate with the word (rather than an armoured jacket) is once again from the poems in the c.1400 MS Cotton Nero A. x, where the Green Knight in *SGGK* sports a *dublet of a dere tars* (l. 571).[65]

   Other words used in the poem to describe items of clothing are of more uncertain dating, or merely indicate a date no earlier than the fourteenth century. Margaret Scott observes that the term 'kirtle' for

---

[62] V. A. B. Bjorklund notes that the Middle English translator of the Old French *Partenopeu of Blois* (c.1450?) also transforms a French *bliaut* into a *doublette*; OF ll. 6300–4, ME ll. 7707–8; 'The Art of Translation in *Ipomadon*: from Anglo-Norman to Middle English' (unpubl. D. Phil. thesis, Yale University, 1977), p. 155.

[63] Stella Mary Newton, *Fashion in the Age of the Black Prince: A study of the years 1340–1365* (Woodbridge, 1980), p. 4. She notes further that buttons first appear in accounts of the king's wardrobe from 1337–38 (p. 15).

[64] See Margaret Scott, *A Visual History of Costume: The Fourteenth and Fifteenth Centuries* (London, 1986), p. 142, and the entry for 'doublet' in C. W. and Phyllis Cunnington and Charles Beard, *A Dictionary of English Costume* (London, 1976). This latter text explains that, although the term was used from the fourteenth until the later seventeenth centuries, it was not commonly used to refer to civilian wear until the fifteenth century in England, despite the existence in the mid-fourteenth century of items which we would now describe as doublets.

[65] The first *MED* citation is from 1355 in the records of Norwich militia, where it refers to an armoured jacket, as does the citation from a 1391 expediture account for the Earl of Derby. Scott (*ibid.*, p. 142) notes that the future Henry IV had one of red satin made in 1391 for use with armour.

an inner garment worn over the shirt, 'seems to replace "tunic" about the turn of the fourteenth and fifteenth centuries'.[66] Ipomadon is twice described as wearing one of these, and on both occasions the word alliterates: *a kyrtyll and a crochett fyne* (l. 7078), and *his kyrtell covyrd not his kne* (l. 660). This would be more promising for establishing date if the word 'kirtle' were not derived from Old English *cyrtel*, but as it is, it seems inherently improbable that the word could have fallen out of use entirely between the Old English period and that indicated by Scott, although its popularity may of course have waxed and waned.

The *gyte*—apparently a type of gown—worn by Imayne at l. 6460 is of more certain dating, but *MED* citations of this term appear too early, and continue too late, for it to be of use in dating *Ipomadon*. Stella Mary Newton notes the appearance of these otherwise unidentified garments in the 1340's,[67] and the *MED* and *OED* combine to give citations of this garment from c.1349 onwards. The *velvet* of which her *gyte* (and Ipomadon's doublet) is made is likewise something that became common from the mid-fourteenth century onwards—Daniel Rock observes that 'velvet is for the first time mentioned at Exeter in 1327 . . . . From the middle of the fourteenth century velvet is of common occurrence'.[68] Imayne is also wearing a *syrcote* over her *gyte* (l. 6461): this term referred to an overgarment worn by both sexes in the fourteenth century, but Scott writes that women developed a sleeveless, open-sided version of it over the course of the century, 'and it was in this form, the "surcote ouverte", that the garment and its name survived into the fifteenth century'.[69] If the term 'surcote' had indeed become restricted to items of female attire by the fifteenth century, then the fact that Ipomadon is still described as being *clothed in a syrket of palle* (l. 2697) would suggest a date of composition of not much after 1400, but there is not the same weight of evidence for this usage as for that of the word 'doublet'.

Descriptions of armour are another potential source of datable material, but *Ipomadon* unfortunately contains very few of these. The knight Cavder is at one point described as wearing a *basnette* (l. 4460)—the 'basinet' helmet that was common throughout the

---

[66] Scott, *ibid.*, p. 142.
[67] Newton, *op.cit.*, pp. 21–2.
[68] Daniel Rock, *Textile Fabrics* (London, 1876), p. 31, quoted in Andersen, p. xxiii.
[69] Scott, *op.cit.*, p. 143.

fourteenth and fifteenth centuries. Later, Cabanus fights with
Ipomadon and strikes off *the halfe of his glove of plate* (l. 8470):
plate gloves—initially leather gloves with plates stitched on—also
date from the end of the thirteenth century.[70] Several references to
mayle, such as the description of Ipomadon as *a man cled in mayle* at
l. 6950, appear to suggest a date before the mid-fifteenth century
when full-body plate armour became available, but in the later
fifteenth-century romance *Capystranus*, which recounts the 1456
siege of Belgrade, the Turks are still described as *clene clad in
plate and male*.[71] Mail evidently continued to be used both as actual
armour and as a convenient word in rhyme (pairing with such words
as *batayle, fayle, assayle, avayle*) well into the fifteenth century, and it
cannot be used to help date a text.

There is one piece of armour which initially promises to be more
informative as regards the date of composition. This is the *gorgede*
worn by Cananeus at l. 5496.[72] The 'gorget' was a piece of neck
armour about which G. C. Stone writes, 'the earliest gorgets of
which we have definite knowledge were made of mail and worn in
the fifteenth century. Before these were abandoned plate gorgets
were also in use'.[73] The *MED* agrees with this date for the first
appearance of gorgets: its earliest citations of the word are from
Ipomadon, the *Laud Troy Book* (c.1400), and Lovelich's *Merlin*
(c.1410), while the *OED* has nothing before c.1470. The narrator
of *Ipomadon* does not specify whether this *gorgede* is an early model
of mail, or a later one of plate, but he does relate that *were his gorgede
neuer so good, / The* [spear-] *hedde thorowe the hawbreke yede* (ll. 5496–
7). The image is clearly one of Ipomadon's spear piercing both the
gorget and the *hawbreke*, 'mail shirt', beneath it (in the Anglo-
Norman ll. 7102–3, Ipomadon's spear instead pierces shield and
hauberk). Since it is hard to imagine even Ipomadon's spear

---

[70] See for example Richard Barber, *The Knight and Chivalry*, revised edn. (Woodbridge, 1995), p. 231.

[71] *Capystranus*, in *Middle English Romances*, ed. S. H. A. Shepherd (New York &
London, 1995), l. 430. *Mayle* is also mentioned at ll. 3320, 7046, 7815, 7988, 8447, in
Ipomadon, three times in rhyme. On the dating of full-body plate armour, see Barber,
op.cit., p. 232.

[72] The *gorget* described on Lyolyne at l. 6158 may refer to the same item—see note to
this line.

[73] George Cameron Stone, *A Glossary of the Construction, Decoration and Use of Arms
and Armor: in all countries and in all times* (New York, 1934), p. 250. David Edge and John
Miles Paddock also date the appearance of 'gorgets' to the fifteenth century in *Arms and
Armour of the Medieval Knight* (London, 1988 repr. 1994), p. 183.

punching through solid plate armour, the poet appears to have had a
chainmail gorget in mind. There is, however, a problem with the use
of this term to establish a date of composition in or near the early
fifteenth century for *Ipomadon*: a very similar word *gorgere* was used
throughout the fourteenth century to refer to a (presumably similar)
piece of neck armour—it occurs for example at l. 1618 in the Cotton
copy of *Lybeaus Desconus*, where it is confirmed by its rhyme with
fer.[74] Since *Lybeaus Desconus* is clearly a fourteenth-century text
(Mills argues that it antedates Chaucer's *Sir Thopas*)[75] the almost
identical term *gorget* cannot after all be used to prove a date shortly
after 1400 for *Ipomadon*. In the end, the only conclusion that can be
drawn with any certainty is that Cananeus's armour was conceived
before the mid-fifteenth century availability of full plate-armour.[76]

EXTERNAL REFERENCES

The final item of interest in this attempt to establish the date of
composition of *Ipomadon* comes from another text altogether. This is
the reference in the alliterative poem *The Parlement of the Thre Ages*
to *Sir Ipomadonn de Poele* and *þe faire Fere de Calabre* (ll. 618–9). The
first problem is to establish which version of *Ipomedon* is being
referred to. One might suppose that a poem written in English would
be more likely to refer to other English poems, but this is not
necessarily the case: the reference to an Ipomedon in the early
fourteenth-century Middle English romance *Richard Coeur de Lion*—
I wole reden romaunces non / Off Paris [or *Pertonape*] *ne off
Ypomodone*—was written far too early for it to be referring to any
known Middle English version of either romance, and probably
refers to the Anglo-Norman version.[77] Nevertheless, the reference to
Sir Ipomadonn in the *Parlement* is striking—particularly so because
the dialect of the *Parlement* is so similar to that of *Ipomadon*, and

---

[74] *Lybeaus Desconus*, ed. Maldwyn Mills, EETS 261 (1969): l. 1680 of the Lambeth
copy rhymes *gorger : clere*. In *An Historical Guide to Arms & Armour* (London, 1991),
Stephen Bull calls the fourteenth-century chainmail skirts around the neck 'gorgets'—but
this may be through confusion with the earlier term *gorgere* (pp. 63, 67). The *MED* has
citations of *gorgere* from c.1312 onwards.

[75] Mills, *ibid.*, pp. 66–7.

[76] See Barber, *op. cit.*, p. 232.

[77] Cited in Kölbing's introduction, p. xi, from Weber's edition of *Richard Coeur de Lion*
in *Metrical Romances* (1810), vol. II, pp. 3–278; l. 6659 ff.. Hornstein dates this poem as
'soon after 1300', although its earliest extant copy is that in the c.1330–40 Auchinleck
manuscript: *Manual*, p. 158–9.

indeed was tentatively placed in the West Riding of Yorkshire by one of its most recent editors.[78] *Sir Ypomadonn* is part of a list of heroes and heroines including Sampson and Delilah, Generides and Clarionas, Sir Eglamour of Artois and Cristabelle, Tristan and Isolde, Dido, Candace, Penelope and Guinevere. All of these characters were well known from Old French (and also Middle English) texts except for *Sir Eglamour of Artas* (l. 622). Sir Eglamour's story may also be based on an Old French text, but none is extant: this hero is only known to us through the various extant versions of a fourteenth-century Middle English tail-rhyme poem which was, once again, composed in the North Midlands, possibly Yorkshire.[79] Offord dates the *Parlement* between c.1353 'and about 1390', although both manuscripts are fifteenth century, while Turville-Petre calls a late fourteenth-century date 'likely enough, but the evidence is inconclusive'.[80] Offord goes on to mention the *Parlement*'s connections to other late fourteenth-century northern alliterative poems such as the *Siege of Jerusalem* (dated after 1385), the alliterative *Morte Arthure,* and *Death and Liffe.* The upper limit of c.1390 for the *Parlement*'s date of composition is fixed only by the apparent indebtedness to it of *Death and Liffe*, and some verbal parallels with the *Siege of Jerusalem.* Since both of these poems are dated from the end of the century at the earliest, the *Parlement* could well have been written during the 1390's.[81] And if both *Ipomadon* and the *Parlement* were written in the West Riding, as is probable, one need not assume a large gap between the composition of the one and a reference to it in the other. It is consequently quite possible that both *Ipomadon* and the *Parlement* were written in the 1390's. At best, however, this citation demonstrates the possibility that the author of the *Parlement* knew the English tail-rhyme *Ipomadon.* It does not constitute proof, and the *Parlement* must reluctantly be discounted as part of the evidence for the date of *Ipomadon*'s composition.

---

[78] Offord, *op.cit.*, p. xxvi. Its other recent editor, Thorlac Turville-Petre, more cautiously describes it as 'North Midland' in *Alliterative Poetry of the Later Middle Ages* (London, 1989), p. 67.

[79] *Sir Eglamour of Artois*, ed. Frances E. Richardson. EETS 256 (1965), p. xxx.

[80] Offord, *op.cit.*, p. xxxvi, and Turville-Petre, *op.cit.*, p. 67.

[81] Offord, *op.cit.*, p. xxxvii.

THE TRANSLATOR AND HIS SOURCE

THE ANGLO-NORMAN SOURCE

The source of all three Middle English versions of *Ipomedon* is the twelfth-century Anglo-Norman romance *Ipomedon* by Hue de Rotelande, of which *Ipomadon* is by far the most faithful rendition. *Ipomedon*'s most recent editor, A. J. Holden, dates the composition of the poem as 'not long after 1180', using as reference points the mention in the text of the 1174 siege of Rouen (ll. 5531–2), and the statement in its sequel, *Protheselaus*, that this latter poem was written for one Gilbert Fitz-Baderon, lord of Monmouth 1176–7 to 1191.[82] Rotelande's audience was formed from the Anglo-Norman society of the Welsh Marches: Rotelande himself probably took his name from the town of Rhuddlan, just inside the Welsh border, and at l. 10,571 of *Ipomedon* he gives his residence as Credenhill in Herefordshire.[83]

The text survives in five manuscripts altogether, although only one is complete and two consist of single leaves. The following summaries, to which reference will be made in later discussions, are taken from Holden:[84]

A   London, British Library MS Cotton Vespasian A VII. (complete text, and Holden's base manuscript)
- small vellum manuscript of the mid-thirteenth century; 107 ff.; 230 × 190mm; written in two columns of thirty-eight lines per column;
- *Ipomedon* is preceded by Guillaume le Clerc's *Bestiaire*, the *Vision de Saint Paul* (both texts illustrated and illuminated, though *Ipomedon* is not), and the (presumably later) additions of a list of nobles present at the ratification of the 1360 treaty of Calais, as well as a list of towns then ceded to Edward III.

B   London, British Library MS Egerton 2515 (contains all but ll. 1–149)
- small vellum manuscript of the early fourteenth century; 197 ff.; 265 × 175mm; written in two columns of forty-one lines per column; there are some decorated or illuminated initials, and the scribe signs himself 'Johan de Dorkingge';
- *Ipomedon* is the first text, followed by *Protheselaus* and a prose *Lancelot*.

[82] Holden, *op.cit.*, p. 11.
[83] Holden, *ibid.*, pp. 7–11.
[84] Holden, *ibid.*, pp. 16–20.

C Oxford, Bodleian Library MS Rawlinson Miscellanea D 913
(ll. 10171–10330)
– contains a single fourteenth-century leaf of *Ipomedon*.
D Dublin, MS Trinity College 523 (ll. 1–6164 and ll. 7485–7700)
– small vellum manuscript of the fourteenth century; 31 ff.;
265 × 160mm; written in two columns of fifty-four lines per
column and decorated with red and blue initials; *Ipomedon* is
the only text.
E a manuscript that had belonged to C. H. Livingston and was
described by him in *Modern Philology* XL (1942–3) (contains
ll. 8504–8675 and 9362–9533)
– Holden was unable to see this manuscript, but reports from
Livingston's article that it dates from the mid-fourteenth
century, measures 378 × 308mm, was written in two columns
of forty-three lines per column, and is the only manuscript of
the poem whose language is *not* markedly Anglo-Norman in
character.

Hue's own sources and influences are less obvious than those of
his Middle English translator. Certain elements of the story appear
in several other texts written both before and after *Ipomedon*, such as
the three-day tournament or the motif of a heroine being rescued by
a hero disguised as a fool. Holden lists Chrétien's *Cligès* (before
1170), *Partenopeus de Blois* (perhaps 1182–5), the prose *Lancelot*
(before 1230), *Robert le Diable*, the German *Lanzelet* of Ulrich von
Zatzikhoven and the Middle English romances *Sir Gowther*, *Richard
Coeur de Lion* and *Roswall and Lillian* as examples of texts containing
the three-day tournament motif (or four-day in the case of *Cligès*).
The hero disguised as a fool is a feature of texts based on a 'Fair
Unknown' theme, the earliest known example of which is Renaut de
Beaujeu's eponymous *Le bel Inconnu* (1190–1200).[85] It is difficult to
say which, if any, of the French texts Hue might have known, since
these elements are probably folkloric in origin.

On the other hand, it is fairly certain that Hue knew and used the
mid-twelfth-century *Roman de Thèbes*, from which he drew many of
his characters' names, the *Roman d'Eneas*, and probably Thomas's
Tristan and a version of the *Fabulae* of Hyginus. Of the few names
that do not derive from the *Roman de Thèbes*, most can be found in

---

[85] Holden, *ibid.*, pp. 46–51. On the 'Fair Unknown' in medieval literature generally, see
Mills, *op.cit.* pp. 42–68.

the *Fabulae*: Atreus, Jason, Nisus (not in the Middle English version), Parseus (ME 'Pryncyus'), and Thoas all appear there. The name of the sarcastic steward Caemius may also have derived from a 'Caeneus' in Hyginus, who was supposed to have been invulnerable to steel, and of whom Hyginus remarks enigmatically, 'some say he was once a woman': one can imagine how Hue might have delighted in assigning this name to his hapless steward.[86] The *Roman d'Eneas* is the source of the stammering scene between La Fière and Ismeine (see note to ll. 1439–40). The Tristan legend might have suggested such elements as Ipomedon's much-lauded skill in hunting, and his role as the comical *dru* of the Sicilian queen (recalling Tristan's sojourn disguised as a fool at King Mark's court), although these could simply derive from a common source. The same might be said of similar complaints in each text on the changeability of women (see for example l. 7088 ff. of *Ipomadon*). However, the parallels between Hue's more unusual, and outrageous, epilogue and the epilogue of Thomas's *Tristan* are so close as to make it hard to believe Hue's version is not a direct parody.[87]

Whether or not Hue knew the works of Chrétien, the parallels between the court of Meleager and that of Arthur suggest very strongly that Hue knew some version of the Arthurian legend. There is the beneficent king, bold and hardy in theory but never seen in military action (Meleager/Arthur); the king's heroic nephew (Capaneus/Gawain); the sarcastic steward (Kaemius/Kay, where even the names are suspiciously similar); secondary characters such as the impetuous Sicanius, or Segamus in the Middle English (Sagremor); and of course the manipulative and desirable queen (Meleager's queen/Guinevere).[88]

Much has been written on Hue's skilful poetry, topical allusions, wit, and the attitude he evinces towards women, which is ambiguous at the very least. There is an on-going critical debate as to whether *Ipomedon* constitutes an early parody of the romance form, or is essentially a serious romance with humorous and self-conscious elements. Holden describes it as having a spirit 'foncièrement parodique',[89] differing from Philippe Ménard, who feels that it was

[86] Holden, *ibid.*, note to l. 5017. Translation of Hyginus from *The Myths of Hyginus*, trans. & ed. by Mary Grant (Lawrence, 1960), p. 34.

[87] Discussed further under 'The Remodelling Process' below.

[88] Holden, *ibid.* p. 52, except for Guinevere.

[89] Holden, *ibid.* p. 55.

composed too early for an author to be taking an ironic view of the genre.[90] M. Dominica Legge says that the text was designed as a 'burlesque', although she adds cuttingly—and inexplicably—that 'when all is said, however, the most interesting point about Hue de Rotelande is his topical allusions'.[91] Susan Crane takes the measured approach of understanding Hue's work as 'juxtaposing serious treatment and parodic inversion'.[92] Schmidt and Jacobs seem, on the other hand, to reject the idea that *Ipomedon* is at all parodic when they play down Hue's flagrant obscenity and antifeminism as 'refined sensuality', and find 'cynicism . . . too strong a word to apply to his realistic worldly wisdom, which in some ways anticipates Chaucer'.[93] Whatever the exact nature of Rotelande's comedy, however, it is clear that his Middle English translator did not mean to reproduce it.

STYLE AND TECHNIQUE

The two aspects of the Middle English *Ipomadon* that have been most remarked on by critics are its length, which tends to be quoted in discussions even where those of other romances are not, and its faithfulness to the Anglo-Norman original.[94] The length of *Ipomadon* is unusual among Middle English romances, but it is not unique: *Guy of Warwick*, the couplet *Generydes* and *Partonope of Blois* are among those that are even longer (although only *Guy* contains any tail-rhyme, and that a relatively meagre 6,000 lines' worth).[95] The 8,890 extant lines of the Middle English *Ipomadon* correspond to 10,580 lines in Holden's edition of the Anglo-Norman text, or approximately 84% of its length. In fact, the original Middle English composition must have been even closer to the length of its source. The sizes of the lacunae in this text are relatively easy to gauge thanks to the closeness of the translation and the recognisable blocks

---

[90] Philippe Ménard, *Le rire et le sourire dans le roman courtois en France au moyen âge* (Genève, 1969), pp. 513–5.

[91] M. Dominica Legge, *Anglo-Norman Literature and its Background* (London, 1963), p. 85 and p. 94.

[92] Susan Crane, *Insular Romance: Politics, Faith and Culture in Anglo-Norman and Middle English Literature* (Berkeley and Los Angeles, 1986), p. 159.

[93] Schmidt and Jacobs, *op.cit.*, p. 41.

[94] See for example the *Manual*, p. 155, and Brenda Thaon, 'La Fiere: the Career of Hue de Rotelande's Heroine in England', *Reading Medieval Studies*, 9 (1983) 56–69 (p. 56).

[95] The *Manual* gives the lengths of the longest versions of these texts as follows: *Guy*, 12,000 lines; *Generydes*, 10,086 lines; *Partonope*, 12,195 lines (pp. 28, 149–50).

of twelve linked lines into which the tail-rhyme stanza divides the text. The total number of missing lines thus exposed is either 202 or 214, depending on whether one or two whole stanzas have been lost between ll. 3547–8.[96] When the five extant lines that seem to be superfluous (i.e. those printed between double brackets in this edition) are subtracted from this total, this gives an original line-count of either 9,087 or 9,101 lines, or 86% of the length of the Anglo-Norman. And the difference may have been smaller again from the translator's point of view, since neither of the 'complete' Anglo-Norman manuscripts on which Holden's edition is primarily based contains all of Holden's 10,580 lines, so there is no reason to suppose that the translator's copy was any fuller.

The nearness in size of the Middle English translation to its source suggests in itself that its author was working from a manu-script rather than memory. This hypothesis is immediately con-firmed by a comparison of the texts themselves. Many lines can be matched almost word for word, rhetorical devices are borrowed (anaphora, or the repetition of a set phrase, is a particular favour-ite),[97] vocabulary is transferred verbatim, and occasionally even the same rhyme-pairs are used. The two texts often correspond so closely that not only can the Anglo-Norman be used to emend the Middle English, but the Middle English can occasionally be used to correct or clarify lines in the Anglo-Norman.[98] A typical example of the almost literal translation, sustained over several lines, that abounds in the text is:

[96] The lacunae, with the number of missing lines in brackets, occur after the following lines: ll. 274 (3), 631 (3), 729 (1), 748 (3), 1081 (3), 1127 (1), 1258 (3), 1339 (3), 1768 (3), 1824 (1), 1848 (3), 1906 (1), 2000 (3), 2252 (1), 2797 (1), 2886 (60), 3545 ff. (22 or 36), 3910 (1), 3977 (1), 4263 (1), 4378 (1), 4437 (3), 4454 (2), 4622 (1), 4645 (2), 4724 (1), 5243 (1), 5326 (4), 5330 (5), (5548 (1), 5914 (3), 5995 (3), 6054 (1), 6073 (1), 6486 (3), 6808 (1), 7077 (1), 7142 (8), 7324 (4), 7330 (6), 7333 (9), 7393 (2), 7685 (3), 7831 (1), 8282 (2), 8462 (3), 8771 (3), 8777 (3), 8814 (1). Lines that may be later additions but are still printed here are ll. 2833, 6177, 7133–5.

[97] See for example ME l. 2564 ff., where the Anglo-Norman usage is expanded upon. The translator adds it of his own accord in the *as folis* . . . passage at ME l. 7376 ff. (AN l. 8806 ff.), but this is in imitation of an earlier Anglo-Norman usage of *cum fous* . . . at AN l. 8785 ff., which was itself retained at ME l. 6981 ff.. Anglo-Norman anaphora is ignored in translations of the battle-scenes at AN l. 3903 ff., l. 4033 ff., l. 9577 ff.; the scene in which the lovesick Imayne drifts helplessly back and forth between her bed and that of the sleeping Ipomadon (AN l. 8743 ff. and l. 8786 ff.; ME l. 7124 ff.), and the description of the people's distress when they believe that Lyolyne has been victorious (AN l. 9331 ff.; ME l. 7608 ff.).

[98] See Holden's notes to ll. 571, 771–2, 964, 2295–7, 2932, 5667, 6858, 7049–50, 7872, 8346, 8962.

The lady callyd hur botelere;
'This cupe of gold þou shalte take here
And gyff hit to younde man;
To buttrey dore lede hym wyth the,
Therwyth of wyne to serue me;
We shall see yf he can.'
(ll. 443–8)

La Fiere dit al botiller:
'Ma demeine cope de or fin
Baillez a l'estrange meschin,

Si me servira al mangier;
Verrom s'il siet de tel mester.'⁹⁹
(478–82)

or with a borrowed rhyme-pair;¹⁰⁰

Iason wepte and fro her turnyd,
And sche into her tente and mornyd
(ll. 1397–8)

Jasun atant d'iloc s'en turne,
E la Fiere s'en reveit murne
(ll. 1461–2)

This kind of close translation from the French is, again, not unique to *Ipomadon* among the Middle English romances: *Guy of Warwick*, the Auchinleck version of *Beues of Hamtoun, Partonope of Blois, Sir Ferumbras* and *Kyng Alisaunder* are among the texts which contain passages of close correspondence with extant Old French versions, and the haphazard nature of the survival of medieval texts has probably obscured several more.¹⁰¹

Where *Ipomadon* is unique is in the way the correspondence with its Anglo-Norman source has been maintained throughout. The Middle English text is not a faithful translation in the way the term might be understood today: its author has rearranged, expanded, truncated or omitted some sections (usually battle-scenes, narratorial descants on the wiles of women, and some descriptive scenes).¹⁰² He has brought the theme of love into much

---

⁹⁹ 'La Fière said to the butler, "Take my own cup of pure gold to the strange youth, and he will serve me at dinner; let us see if he knows this art."'

¹⁰⁰ Other examples are: *turn-* : *morn-* at ll. 1397–8 (AN ll. 1461–2) and ll. 1526–7 (AN ll. 1563–4); *artte* : *parte* ll. 1532–3 (AN ll. 1565–6).

¹⁰¹ *Guy of Warwick* is discussed by Maldwyn Mills, 'Techniques of translation in the Middle English versions of *Guy of Warwick*', in *The Medieval Translator II*, ed. Roger Ellis (London, 1991), pp. 200–9, and also A. C. Baugh, 'Improvisation in the Middle English Romances', *Proceedings of the American Philosophical Society*, 103 (1959), pp. 418–54 (pp. 433–4, 437–9). On *Beues*, see Baugh, *ibid.*, pp. 431–2, 435–7. On *Partonope*, see Brenda Hosington, '*Partenopeu de Blois* and its fifteenth-century English translation: a medieval translator at work', in Ellis ed., *op.cit.* (1991), pp. 231–52; on *Sir Ferumbras*, see S. H. A. Shepherd, 'The Ashmole *Sir Ferumbras*: translation in holograph', in Roger Ellis ed., *The Medieval Translator* (Cambridge, 1989), pp. 103–21; on *Kyng Alisaunder* see pp. 44–6 of J. D. Burnley, 'Late medieval English translation: types and reflections' in Ellis ed., *ibid.* (1989), pp. 37–53.

¹⁰² E.g. The first day's action at the tournament is described in 227 lines in the Middle

sharper focus, painted some characters differently, removed both Hue's narratorial character and his bantering sarcasm from the narrative, and generally made his own distinct version of the Anglo-Norman original. Nevertheless, it is very recognisably a version of the Anglo-Norman text—however retouched—rather than a new narrative based upon it, and the near-literal translation of so many lines means that Hue's text remains a constant presence throughout.

The lesser length of the Middle English text overall is not the result of continuous condensation, or even just of selective pruning. Many dramatised scenes in the Middle English text are actually longer than their Anglo-Norman counterparts as a result of the translator's penchant for assigning a series of small courteous speeches to his characters, even where his source had favoured indirect narration. For example, the scene at the Fere's court in which the newly-arrived Ipomadon serves the wine (quoted in part above) occupies fifty-nine lines of Middle English verse as opposed to only thirty-five lines of Anglo-Norman (ME l. 443 ff.; AN l. 477 ff.). This kind of selective expansion ensures that the final text is nearly the same length as its source, despite the heavy pruning of battle-scenes and narratorial asides remarked upon earlier.

The mechanics of transforming couplets into tail-rhyme verse will not be discussed in detail here, since the translator follows patterns described sufficiently in existing literature on the subject. Techniques employed range from simply inserting tail-rhymes between translated couplets, to using translated lines from the source-text in a different order, to translating the sense of a passage without following its actual wording at all.[103] This latter route is the one that the translator most often adopts: the impression of extreme faithfulness to the Anglo-Norman is often the result of the direct

English (ll. 3114–3341) against 531 lines in the Anglo-Norman (l. 3609–4140)—a combination of lengthier laments by La Fière and longer and more rhetorical descriptions of the fighting itself. The description of Ipomadon on his entry to the Fere's court fills 21 lines of Middle English (l. 361 ff.) but 68 of Anglo-Norman (l. 377 ff.). For examples of less drastic but more significant shortenings, see the comments on l. 2021 ff. and ll. 2055–66 under 'The Remodelling Process'.

[103] See the works cited in note 101 above. The classic piece on couplet to tail-rhyme conversion, though it refers only to Middle English, is A. J. Bliss's introduction to his edition of *Sir Launfal* (London, 1960). On *Ipomadon* specifically see also Brenda Hosington, 'The Englishing of the Comic Technique in Hue de Rotelande's *Ipomédon*', in *Medieval Translators and Their Craft*, ed. Jeannette Beer (Kalamazoo, 1989), pp. 247–64 (pp. 247–8).

translation of a few select lines with the rest of the narrative built around them in his own words, as in this passage describing the power of love:

Whate myghte þat be but derne love	*Qe porra ceo estre for d'amer?*
That allways wyll be above	
To them that shall it havnte?	
All othere thyngys men d[avn]te may,	*Tote autre rien puet hom danter,*
But sertenly be no waye	
Love wille not be davnte.	*Mes amour n'ert ja mes dauntee*
(ll. 797–802)	(ll. 763–65)

Kölbing breaks the style of translation seen in *Ipomadon* down into five main techniques (with numerous additional minor variations on each):[104]

1. A passage is translated initially from the Anglo-Norman and re-used, in full or part, elsewhere in the Middle English where there may or may not be something similar in the corresponding Anglo-Norman lines;[105]
2. A Middle English passage is more similar to a later Anglo-Norman passage than to the one to which it corresponds directly, while there is nothing equivalent at the later point in the Middle English narrative which *should* correspond to the Anglo-Norman passage in question;[106]
3. Two passages which are almost identical in the Middle English are a conflation of two slightly different Anglo-Norman passages;[107]
4. An Anglo-Norman passage is translated, but moved to another part of the Middle English;[108]

[104] Kölbing, pp. lxv–cxviii.

[105] E.g. ME ll. 3551–3 translates AN ll. 4425–6, *Mut ad ui ben curu Nublet, / E Ridel e tuit mi brachet*: ME ll. 4152–4 repeats ME ll. 3551–3 almost verbatim although it corresponds to AN l. 5501, *E cum unt ben curu si chen*. ME ll. 3063–5 roughly translates the corresponding AN ll. 3550–2, *A Tholomeu prent a parler, / 'Beaus duz amis, en bois alez / E de ben fere vus penez'*; the lines are repeated at ME ll. 4188–90 although there is nothing equivalent in the corresponding AN l. 5548 ff..

[106] E.g. ME ll. 3018–21 echoes AN l. 4307 ff., but the latter's corresponding Middle English passage, ll. 3471–3, is slightly different.

[107] E.g. ME l. 2531 ff. and l. 2678 ff., which are almost identical, but represent a conflation of the two corresponding Anglo-Norman lines, l. 2806 *Pur quant mut bel les salua* and l. 2948 *Mut l'en mercie bonement*.

[108] E.g. ME ll. 1198–1200 echoes the earlier AN ll. 1046–8, *Oïl, vers, tot halegre e sein, / E vus remeindrez com cheitive, / Morne, desheité e pensive*. See also AN ll. 6362–3, *Il me amout quant jo ne voleie, / Or revoil jo e il ne volt*, the sense and syntax of which was moved back to ll. 4694–5 in the Middle English.

5. The translator re-uses passages of his own that have no Anglo–Norman equivalent.[109]

Such divergences from strictly literal translation demonstrate the translator's confidence in remodelling his source. The stylistic habits described above under 1, 3 and 5 give the Middle English poem a more repetitive and formulaic air than that of the Anglo–Norman, and this impression is reinforced by the translator's habit of circling or repeating points which he either had difficulty explaining clearly, or seemed to feel were particularly important. A typical illustration of this is ME ll. 5143–8, which six lines manage to contain far less information than the four Anglo–Norman lines (ll. 6767–70) to which they correspond:

To you herttly he besovghte,	*Il li mande mut ben par mei*
Witnes wyth hym he stale hym novght	*Ke il le guaaigna al turnei,*
But wan [hym] be dovȝtty dede.	*Si ne li chaut ke nuls en die,*
Ye witte well he hym wanne;	*Il fut cler jur, ne l'embla mie.*[110]
Wheþer that ye blys or banne,	
Wyth hym he will hym lede.	

The same sort of lumbering repetition can be seen on a larger scale in the speech of the Fere after the burgess has revealed the single identity of the tournament's three champions, in which she declares that she can accept no one but the mysterious man who won her thus. The single Anglo–Norman speech at l. 6883 ff. is translated in abbreviated form at the corresponding point in the Middle English narrative, l. 5253 ff., but then repeated redundantly, and at greater length, at l. 5289 ff.. Similarly, the scene in which Imayne greets with angry contempt the fool-knight Ipomadon's insistence that he is loved by the Fere lasts for ten lines in the Anglo–Norman (ll. 8162–71), but thirty in the Middle English, where Ipomadon claims the Fere loves him; Imayne expresses contempt; the dwarf observes that great men do sometimes fight in disguise; Imayne repeats her contempt for the fool; Ipomadon claims once again that the Fere loves him; she challenges him; and he finally becomes coy on the subject (ll. 6640–69). There are other points in the text where the

---

[109] E.g. ME ll. 3354–5, 3391–2, 4637–8, 5008–10 and 5243 are all very similar, but none correspond to any Anglo-Norman line in the relevant passages, AN ll. 4152 ff., 4207 ff., 6305 ff., 6686 ff., 6838 ff..

[110] 'Through me he makes it known clearly that he won it at the tournament, so it doesn't matter to him what anyone says: it was broad daylight, he didn't steal it at all.'

much more direct Anglo-Norman is needed to clarify the convoluted Middle English, and the confusion is not always attributable to the interference of a later scribe.[111]

THE REMODELLING PROCESS

This section deals with how the translator remodels the Anglo-Norman text as a whole. Slight differences in the perceived theme of the story are accompanied by a comprehensive effort to make the Middle English version more of an exemplary tale. The background against which the story is played out is more idealised, with wars being reduced to disputes and bloody battles to games; the character's (noble) motivations are explained; morals are more firmly drawn from actions; and anything that might detract overly from the hero or heroine's dignity, such as Hue's mocking sexual innuendo, the apparent fickleness of the heroine, or the occasional wilful cruelty of Ipomadon, is generally removed.[112] As Susan Crane writes, 'the adapter conducts a rescue operation, freeing characters from Hue's manifold ironies and restoring integrity to their actions and motivations'.[113]

The consistent impression we get of the world of Hue's romance is one of instability and violence, where for example the qualities required of a good king are of a more shrewd and practical nature than the mere good breeding recommended by the English poet. In describing the Sicilian king Meleager, the Anglo-Norman devotes twenty lines to detailing his admirable qualities: he is an excellent knight; he holds his kingdom in peace; there are no neighbours anywhere around him who would dare to start a war against him because he is noble and influential and of sufficiently great wealth to

[111] The inconsistencies in the Middle English version of the *v-alet* stammer scene are scribal—see notes to ll. 1439–40, 1445, 1455—but the author himself seems to be responsible for the lack of clarity at l. 5490 ff., l. 6487 ff. and the confusing repetition at l. 8239 ff. (see notes to these lines).

[112] Some elements evidently proved harder to remove than others: the translator seems to have been sufficiently anxious to retain the dramatic irony in scenes where Ipomadon acts *incognito* that he allows the occasional attendant cruelty to remain, e.g. Ipomadon's message to the Fere on the second day of the tournament, when he insists she be informed that the vanquished red knight was her beloved champion of the day before (l. 4337 ff., and see note to these lines), or later when he taunts her by pretending to be the victorious Lyolyne (ll. 8147 ff.).

[113] Crane, *op. cit.*, p. 207. A brief summary of the translator's main changes is offered by Rosalind Field in '*Ipomedon* to *Ipomadon A*: Two Views of Courtliness' in Ellis ed. *op.cit.* (1989), pp. 135–42.

be generous in gifts; he maintains laws and rights carefully, and he is not foolish, for he has conquered all the lands about him so that there is no duke, count or marquis who has not become his vassal— whether rightly or wrongly, Hue adds dryly (AN ll. 49–68). This is a world where a ruler needs all his wits about him to hold on to his lands and subjects. The English text, by contrast, devotes a mere nine lines to Mellyagere's virtues: once upon a time in Sicily there lived a king called Mellyagere who was held by all to be peerless; *He was worthy, were and wyse, / Ouer all he wan losse and pryce*; and *He had bovnden to his hande, / In Fraunce and many other lande, / Douȝty dukys and dere* (from ll. 25–33). The vague statement *ouer all he wan losse and pryce* seems to relate more to chivalric tournaments than territorial battles, especially when compared to his very specific achievements in the Anglo-Norman, and this impression is reinforced by the fact that the *douȝty dukys* who owe him loyalty seem to be a random assortment from *Fraunce and many other lande* rather than immediate neighbours who might otherwise pose a threat. The English Mellyagere simply collects honour like any other knight, rather than establishing and holding a recognisable kingdom.

The one curious exception to this trend is on the subject of inheritance and the reign of minors. The arrangements for the Fere's minority, detailed at ME ll. 85–93, are entirely absent from the Anglo-Norman, where the only comment is *la meschine ot le heritage / Ke a merveille devint sage*, 'the girl, who became extremely wise, gained the inheritance' (ll. 103–4). Later, the Fere settles a dispute between dukes *for holdynge of an ayre*, 'over the preventing of an heir's succession', where the only information given in the Anglo-Norman is that two barons *esteient entré en grant guerre* 'had begun a great war' (l. 372). It is tempting to speculate on historical reasons for the English poet's apparent interest in the problems of succession, and especially that of minors, but the evidence for this and for the precise date of *Ipomadon* is too slim to allow any sensible conclusions to be drawn.

In the descriptions of battles and tournaments, Hue is also uncomfortably realistic in comparison to the English poet. Where the English tends to state blandly that *x* struck *y* and *y* fell, Hue not only goes into more detail on the various strokes given, wounds received and deaths dealt, but is also at pains to depict the general chaos and destruction of a tournament. After one lengthy and alarming description of fighting, in which he notes among other things how *meint la boïlle i traïne, / E meint la cervele i espant*, 'the entrails hang from many, and many brains are scattered' (ll. 3894–5), he observes caustically that *Unc mes ne fut pur une femme / Si fere bataille en nul regne*, 'never before in any kingdom has there been such a fierce battle for a woman', and *Tel i quidout venir ke sage / Ke mut mar vit le mariage*—'such as came there thinking they were acting wisely regarded the marriage to be much cursed' (ll. 3887–3914). None of this appears in the Middle English. The English poet is dealing with unambiguous ideals, so the world in which he sets his story is correspondingly idealistic.

This difference in the attitude of the two writers to the wider effects of romantic love is highlighted again in La Fière's / the Fere's despairing monologue on the second day of the tournament, when the white knight whom she knows to have been her beloved fails to appear (AN ll. 4584–4614; ME ll. 3677–3700). Although the Middle English goes so far as to borrow the repeated construction *par mun orgoil . . . (thrugh pryde . . . , be my pryde . . .)* and the comparison of this pride to that of Lucifer (AN l. 4597; ME l. 3693), the Middle English Fere's complaints are all about her own personal loss and the flaw in her character that occasioned it: *pryde bryngys me vnder and not above* (l. 3681); *I haue byn ay ouer-proude in hertt . . . And now full lowe I lyghte, / Myselff till ouer-mekyll shame* (ll. 3695–8). While this regret is also present in the Anglo-Norman, it appears alongside the social consequences: *Par mun orgoil oi primes guerre . . . pert ceste terre . . . pert mes amis . . . sui desherite*, 'by my pride I experienced war . . I will lose this land . . . lose my friends . . . will be disinherited' (ll. 4589–95). Love, for Hue, is not something that operates in idealised isolation, but a dangerous force with the potential to harm all who are associated with the lovers.

Overall, the changes made to the story by the English poet reflect his impulse to create an exemplary tale of noble love and courtesy from what, for Hue, was a far more problematic presentation of romantic love.[114] The desire to illustrate the conventions of courtesy probably lies behind the translator's fondness for expanding dialogues, or adding them where the Anglo-Norman has only narration. The translator's changes goes far beyond such details of narrative technique, however. From the very beginning, he tightens and makes

---

[114] See Crane, *op.cit.*, pp. 198–215 for the most insightful discussion of this process, its social background, and literary parallels.

explicit its theme of the relationship between chivalry and love.[115]
This theme underlies the Anglo-Norman text as well, but there the
reader can be distracted by Hue's ambiguous approach, not to
mention his other pet subjects such as the irrational nature of
women or local Herefordshire gossip. Both texts begin with the
offer of a useful lesson for the reader: *Off love were lykyng of to lere*
(l. 1), and *Qui a bons countes voet entendre, / Souvent il poet grans biens
aprendre*, 'Anyone who is willing to heed a good story may often
derive great benefit from it' (ll. 1–2), but only the Middle English
makes explicit that this lesson is to be about love. The two-stanza
Middle English introduction is direct, clear and succinct: the first
stanza introduces the theme of the tale as romantic love, and the
second introduces the exemplary hero (not yet named) and his
extraordinary modesty, on which much of the plot will turn. The
Anglo-Norman introduction is exactly twice as long as this—forty-
eight lines—but is far more coy about the story's content. Much of it
is a self-conscious imitation of a twelfth-century historical prologue:
Hue expresses amazement that other wise clerks have neglected to
pass on this marvellous tale (l. 21 ff.), humbly offers himself as the
transmitter (l. 30 ff.), and promises to tell it truthfully and briefly
(l. 41 ff.).[116] There has been no mention of love at all.

The subject and didactic purpose declared, the translator consistently tries to explain (and occasionally invent) the significance of
actions and events throughout the story, and to illustrate contemporary chivalric or courtly practice wherever an opportunity presents
itself. Thus the knighting scenes of both Ipomadon and Jason are
expanded to include the ceremony of girding of the sword, not
mentioned at all in the Anglo-Norman, and Ipomadon takes *the order
of his fader* (l. 1694),[117] a detail that seems to refer to such knightly
confraternities or orders of chivalry as developed over the fourteenth
and fifteenth centuries.[118] In the scene where Ipomadon serves wine
at the Fere's court and is ridiculed by the courtiers for keeping his

---

[115] See Schmidt and Jacobs, *op. cit.*, p. 45.

[116] For a summary of the characteristics of such prologues, see Antonia Gransden,
'Prologues in the Historiography of Twelfth-Century England', in *Legends, Traditions and
History in Medieval England* (London, 1992), pp. 125–51 (pp. 125–6).

[117] In the Anglo-Norman, Hue writes only that Ipomedon, *A sun pere armes demanda; /
E il li dunat volenters, / Mut ert de lui privez e chiers,* 'he asked for arms from his father
[indicating passage to knighthood], and he gave them to him willingly, he was very dear
and close to him' (ll. 1740–2). See ll. 4278–82 for Jason's knighting.

[118] See Chapter 4 of Maurice Keen, *Chivalry* (New Haven & London, 1984).

mantle on, the Middle English narrative interrupts an otherwise extremely close rendering of the Anglo-Norman to have the courtiers explain pedantically, *'Yff that he shuld serue one, / It were semande,'* *they sayd ilkone, / 'Away his mantell were'* (ll. 461–3). At a banquet some time later, a cutting speech made by the Fere to quell Ipomadon's loving looks is partially excused by the practical consideration, added only by the translator, that *She drede that it shuld ryse þorow chaunse / Sum slavnder thorow countenavnce* (ll. 818–9). Similar are the sections where the translator assigns acceptable motives to Ipomadon's curious behaviour. When Ipomadon as Drew-le-reine presents the Sicilian queen with three hart's heads, suppo-sedly hunted while everyone else was at the tournament, the court ladies jeer: in the Anglo-Norman, the narrator simply says that *Ipomedon ben l'aperçut, / Mes il unkes semblant ne fist / Ne il de ço garde n'en prist,* 'Ipomedon was well aware of this, but he did not show it, and he paid it no attention' (ll. 4322–4). The Middle English, however, first makes clear how noble his behaviour is in suffering their scorn: *There is now but knyghttys fo[n]e / That hathe so douȝtty dedys done / That wold so lyght his lose have lefte,* and continues to explain, *But he dyd, for he thought eft / To wynne more worthynes* (ll. 3477–82). This anxiety to justify and explain runs throughout the text: when Ipomedon tells the burgess that he will not marry yet because it is bad for knights to marry too young (AN ll. 6647–52), only the Middle English version has him add that he intends to win more worship so that he might *a wyff wyth worshipe wedde* (ME ll. 5038–49), a sentiment that is also inserted at ll. 5098–5100, *But euer more in his herte he þought, / Yet till her avow cordede he nowght, / Her husbond for to bee.* When Ipomadon dresses in black to fight the similarly clad Lyolyne, the English translator explains that this is to spare the Fere potential trauma of seeing him in jeopardy (ll. 7684–5, 7689–7700). His attempt to flee afterwards is justified at ll. 8158–61 as anxiety that he might still be unworthy, although Hue states bluntly that he *recomença estrange ovre,* 'started to behave strangely again' (l. 9919). These and other examples of the translator's dogged determination to assign clear and noble motives to every aspect of his hero's and heroine's behaviour remove every trace of the ambiguity in the Anglo-Norman text's attitude towards the value of courtly love.[119]

[119] Further examples of explanations helpfully inserted by the Middle English

Another method the Middle English narrator employs to add both cohesiveness and a certain amount of humour to the tale is a greater use of foreshadowing and dramatic irony. When we are first introduced to Cabanus, it is only the Middle English narrator who adds slyly, *How he was gotton I can not sayne; / Yff ye wille witte, wythoute layne, / Further spyre ye [bus]* (ll. 43–5—Cabanus will turn out to be Ipomadon's half-brother). Though the dramatic irony can be a little heavy-handed at times, it is difficult not to share some of the author's glee when, for example, Ipomadon nonchalantly recounts the noble exploits of a hound who just happens to be the same colour as that day's winner at the tournament, or when, still disguised as the tournament-shy Drew-le-reine, he sweetly instructs the chamberlain to tell King Mellyagere that the latter would not have lost his horse to the mysterious red knight had he remained at home with him, Drew-le-reine.[120] The audience is thus continually reminded of what has gone before and what is to come: whether or not the audience needs such reminders, their purpose is clear enough, and they work to give the narrative a clearer sense of purpose and direction, while providing a little amusement along the way.

It was clearly the translator's intent to insure that the serious didactic purpose of the text as a whole did not prevent it from being entertaining. Apart from increasing dramatic irony in such scenes as those described above, the translator has added or expanded upon other sections purely for the comedy. The description of the hideous Lyolyne is made longer and more hideous by such additions as lips that *hyngyth like a blode puddynge* (l. 6152). Imayne's outrage at being followed by the embarrassing fool-knight is exaggerated by her exclamation, *'I wold be drowned in a pole / Or I ouer land shuld ledde a fole!* (ll. 6652–3), where the Anglo-Norman Ismeine was merely *irez*, 'furious' (l. 8176). When the proud steward Cananeus rides home from his encounter with Ipomadon, the translator pens an entire new vignette of his sorry return:

translator are: ME ll. 6646–8, where the dwarf observes that wise men sometimes disguise themselves as fools to gain greater honour (missing from AN l. 8172 ff.), and Ipomadon's insistence on trying to conform to the Fere's vow at ME ll. 8541–3 and 8565–7 (absent from AN l. 10253 ff.).

[120] ME ll. 4125–33; missing from AN l. 4419 ff. On the colour-coded hounds, see note to l. 3555 ff.. Another example of helpful narratorial links appears at ll. 2853–4 (see note to these lines).

> *His arme hyng waginge be his syde,*
> *The blod ranne down fro his wondys wyde*
> *As hit was droppus of rayne.*
> *'What, how now ser!' quod the quene,*
> *'Be your semblant it is sene*
> *Ye haue mett wyth Drew-le-rayne!'*
> (ll. 5567–72)

As with the heightening of the dramatic irony discussed earlier, the comedy in this little scene encourages the reader to delight in the hero's matchless prowess.

This kind of humour goes some way to replacing Hue's more sardonic wit, and his sometimes outrageous sensuality. The infatuation of La Fière, Meleager's queen, and Ismeine with Ipomedon is retained in the Middle English, but nearly all improper suggestions of lust have been excised. The chaste Middle English comment on the queen's love for Ipomadon, *Thowe she wold þat no man wyst, / She louythe hym neuer þe lesse* (ll. 3472–3) replaces Hue's gleefully lascivious observation that love's main goal is always *le juster enz el lit,* 'the jousting in bed' (l. 4314). The information that the newly-married hero and heroine *se entrefoutent tute jur,* 'copulate all day long' (l. 10516) is likewise absent from the Middle English (as it is from the B manuscript of the Anglo-Norman).

It is not difficult to see why such commentary was removed by the translator: it cannot but detract from the dignity of the characters involved, and the value of the text as a serious exemplary tale of courtly love. The most celebrated example of Hue's flagrant obscenity is his epilogue (described thrillingly by Legge as 'too shameless to be quoted here'),[121] in which he states that through him, Ipomedon instructs everyone to love loyally and unreservedly. He further claims to possess a pardon for all over-timid lovers, which he offers to show any *dame u pucele, u riche vedve u dameisele* ('lady, virgin, fine widow or maiden'), and before they leave his house *ço n'ert pas trop grant damages / Se li seaus li pent as nages,* 'it would be no great harm if the seal should hang from her arse' (AN ll. 10573–80). If one imagines a pardon as a document rolled into a tube, with a large round wax seal dangling from a ribbon at one end of it, the image is embarrassingly clear.[122]

---

[121] Legge, *op.cit.,* p. 93.

[122] Nicholas Jacobs points out that an almost identical image is used by the thirteenth-century troubadour Peire Cardenal, and suspects the image may have a common source in medieval Latin puns on the word *testes*: 'Une allusion impudique chez Hue de Rotelande: *se li seaus li pent as nages*', *Neuphilologische Mitteilungen,* 96 (1995), 223–4.

Unsurprisingly, the translator cuts all but Ipomedon's injunction to lovers that they should love loyally, and replaces the rest with the advice that the only medicine which should be applied to *lovys wounde* is *poynttis of grette pette* (ll. 8880–1). The poem then concludes with a prayer. The transformation of this epilogue is particularly interesting in that Hue's scurrilous version was itself almost certainly a parody of the epilogue to Thomas's *Tristan*, as was noted earlier.[123] This more sober text concluded with the hope that it might offer comfort to lovers *encuntre change, encuntre tort, / Encuntre paine, encuntre dolur, / Encuntre tuiz engins d'amur!*, 'against change, against wrong, against pain, against misery, against all the trickery of love!'[124] It is impossible to say whether the translator knew Thomas's text, but it is interesting nonetheless that the ending of the Middle English Ipomadon should recall the text which Hue had originally set out to parody.

Whether or not Hue's ultimate aim was to question the value of courtly love, the immediate objects of his mockery were often women. The 'rescue operation' that Crane describes the translator as mounting on the text is more than anything else on behalf of the dignity of the heroine and of women in general. Hue's misogynistic banter has been much remarked upon, as has the translator's systematic removal of it.[125] However, the translator's 'rescue operation' goes much further than the mere removal of lewd or openly derogatory commentary that might have offended members of the audience, either male or female. Such elements were removed partly, no doubt, to avoid mocking the concept of courtly love, but this does not fully explain the lengths to which he goes to praise women, to drum up more sympathy for the heroine, and to stress the dignity and equality of the relationships between even such minor characters as the Fere's parents.[126]

---

[123] Holden, *op. cit.*, p. 51.

[124] ll. 837–9 of the Sneyd fragment in Thomas, *Les Fragments du Roman de Tristan*, ed. Bartina H. Wind, Textes littéraires français 92 (Paris & Genève, 1960).

[125] It is most comprehensively analysed by Roberta Krueger, 'Misogyny, Manipulation and the Female Reader in Hue de Rotelande's *Ipomédon*', in *Courtly Literature: Culture and Context: selected papers from the 5th Triennial conference of the International Courtly Literature Society, Dalfsen, The Netherlands, 9–16 August, 1986*, eds. Keith Busby and Erik Kooper (Amsterdam & Philadelphia, 1990), pp. 395–409, and again in her *Women Readers and the ideology of gender in Old French verse romance* (Cambridge, 1993), pp. 73–82. On the translator's handling of it, see Thaon, *op.cit.* and Crane, *op.cit..*

[126] In the Anglo-Norman, Meleager gave his sister to the duke of Calabria to settle a war between them (AN ll. 87–96). In the more idealistic Middle English, Mellyagere's sister is beautiful and wooed by many, until finally the duke of Calabria offers to become Mellyagere's vassal in return for being permitted to marry her (ll. 60–72).

A clear illustration of this aim is the reworking of the section in which Ipomedon attracts the scorn of La Fière's courtiers for refusing to display any prowess (ME ll. 533–62; AN ll. 530–50). The Anglo-Norman narrator laments the fact that his beloved hero should be denied La Fière's love because of this single flaw (AN ll. 541–49), attracting the readers' sympathy to the distressed narrator and perhaps also to the young Ipomedon, with his touching ignorance of the rules of the game of love. Most of this aside is retained in the Middle English, but instead of being delivered by the anonymous narratorial voice that replaces Hue's, it is put into the mouth of the Fere. After lamenting his lack of prowess, she says:

> For were he a man of hardynes,
> As bovnte semys and bewte ys
> Be God and be my lewte,
> On lyve I know non lewand nowe
> That cordys so well to myn avowe
> In all this world as hee! (ll. 545–50)

The reference to her vow is the translator's own addition: the Fere is clearly only too aware of Ipomadon's virtues, but feels helpless in the face of the painful conflict between Ipomadon's lack of prowess and her obligation to uphold a very public vow. The Anglo-Norman narrator's distress has been transferred to her, and the readers' sympathies along with it. A similar transformation has been effected on the commentary to the scene in which Ismeine finally becomes infatuated with the fool-knight she had previously scorned (ME ll. 7088–96; AN ll. 8656–66). The Anglo-Norman narrator produces yet another tirade against the senseless fickleness of women—something the translator might more easily have cut, as he does many other such passages.[127] Instead, he reworks it into a very different passage in which women are actively praised for withholding favour from those who pursue them too eagerly, thereby teaching men a

---

[127] At AN l. 9095 ff., Hue illustrates the power of love by listing a number of men, such as Adam and Samson, who have been betrayed by the women they loved; the ME ll. 7346–54 merely observes that love has power over everyone. In the tournament scenes earlier on, every suggestion that La Fière's loyalty is wavering has been firmly excluded, e.g. AN ll. 4804–6, as have the attempts by Jason and Ismeine to interest her in other knights, e.g. AN ll. 5264–6, AN ll. 5909–74. Assurances of the Fere's unwavering loyalty are added at ME ll. 1763–5 and 3107–10 (see notes to this lines). Where La Fière declares that the red knight has fought better than either Capaneus or her love (AN ll. 4813–6), the Middle English instead has her declare that he is better than all *except* Cabanus and her love (ME l. 3852 ff.; see note to this line).

vital lesson in moderation: *Godys dere blessyng and myne / Muste they have therefore,* he concludes enthusiastically (ll. 7095–6).

Possibly the most memorable example of how the translator rewrites the female characters of his text is the section in which the Fere/La Fière is first described in detail, ME ll. 2055–66 and AN ll. 2214–70. In the Anglo-Norman, Hue describes her fashionable twelfth-century clothes and the arrangement of her hair, then launches into an ordered catalogue of her physical attractions: forehead, eyes, nose, mouth and lips (about which he makes suggestive comments), shoulders, sides, hips, arms, hands. He pauses here to note how *chescuns pur s'amur fremist,* 'everyone trembled for love', before continuing down to *cel desuz / Ke nus apelum le cunet,* 'that below, which we call the cunt', and carrying on through the hissed intake of breath this comment may be imagined to have caused with *Je quit qe asez fut petitet,* 'I believe it was small enough' (ll. 2268–70). Philippe Ménard notes that this is the first occurrence of the word *cunet* in French courtly literature, so it is probably safe to assume that this was designed to shock.[128] Some critics have taken the English poet's exclusion of such passages from his translation as evidence for his relative prudery (and by extension the relative prudery of Middle English romances in general), but it should be pointed out that the B and D manuscripts of the Anglo-Norman text are also missing these three lines. It is more to the point to note that this disrespectfully prurient description of La Fière's charms is replaced by a little dramatisation in which *kyng, baron and knyghte* decide that someone as beautiful as the Fere is, after all, entirely justified in being *daungerus / To take an onworthy spowsse* (ll. 2058–9), a justification of her behaviour that is entirely absent from the Anglo-Norman romance. It is through omissions, additions and alterations such as these that the translator manages to create a view of women entirely at variance with the one expressed by the Anglo-Norman text he otherwise follows quite faithfully.

None of the various differences between translation and source noted above should obscure the fact that the Middle English *Ipomadon* is on the whole a close and accurate rendition of the Anglo-Norman *Ipomedon*. The original is recognisable all the way through, and some scenes seem to be reproduced exactly, but slight alterations of focus and narrative style have resulted in small,

---

[128] Ménard, *op. cit.,* p. 693, n. 108.

systematic differences all the way through, and these are clearly visible to anyone who sets the Middle English text next to the original. The translator himself must certainly have been conscious of offering a new and updated version of *Ipomedon*.

THE TRANSLATOR'S ANGLO-NORMAN COMPETENCE

There are very few signs that the translator had any difficulty with Anglo-Norman: for the most part the translation is smooth, and often word-for-word. There are only five points in the whole of the text where he may have mistranslated, and even here, the disparity between the Anglo-Norman and the English can be explained satisfactorily by other means in all but the first and third instances.

(1) l. 941–3, *It hathe byn sayd in lest of love / That aftur pryde comythe grette* reprove: based on *Mes cil dit bien* en reprover, 'it is said proverbially' (AN l. 971)

(2) l. 1103–4 *Of helle yt is th[e] hottys payne / To love and be not lovyd agayne*, may stem from a misreading of *Pasma s'en e revent a payne*, 'he fainted and comes round only *with difficulty*' (AN l. 1170), but the Anglo-Norman and English narratives are sufficiently different at this point that the translator may not have intended to follow his source at all here[129]

(3) l. 1230–1 *Me thought my fader had loste a syde, / My moder another also* mistakes the Adam's rib metaphor when the Anglo-Norman Ipomedon fears that his father *une des costes out perdue*, 'had lost one of his ribs' (AN l. 1279)

(4) l. 2868 *Tomorowe shall þis tur[na]ment be*, for AN l. 3196 *li turneiz ert þus demain*, 'the tournament will be *the day after tomorrow*'

(5) At ll. 7992–3, the unexpected image in the extant text of helms being strewn *as flowres in feld* could represent a misunderstanding of the Anglo-Norman image employed elsewhere of ornaments—*flurs*—from helms being knocked to the ground (AN ll. 9843–4), but a simple emendation to the English would give it the same sense as the Anglo-Norman, so the translator may not have been responsible for the lines as they stand (see note to these lines)

---

[129] Bjorklund, *op. cit.*, pp. 17–44, assumes this is a mistranslation.

EVIDENCE FOR THE TRANSLATOR'S EXEMPLAR

Various minor disagreements between the extant manuscripts of the Anglo-Norman text and the Middle English text indicate that none of them could have been the Middle English translator's actual exemplar:

1. The candidacy of MS A is weakened by the fact that it says La Fière's parents lived together for two years (l. 101) where the Middle English and MS D read ten (ME l. 79: MS B is missing the page that would have contained this line).
2. MS D is ruled out by the fact that it mistakenly reads *hernez* at l. 2003, where MSS A and B have the *fius* that is confirmed by rhyme and translated as *feys* (MS *foys*) at the corresponding ME l. 1940.
3. A few details of MS B do correspond to the Middle English text, but others prove that it, too, could not have been the translator's exemplar. It seems to agree with the Middle English at ME l. 540, where the rhyme calls for *cowardise*: this corresponds to B's *cuardise* at l. 549, but not the *cowardie* of MSS A and D (although of course the translator need not necessarily have had this form of the word in front of him to complete his rhyme thus). MS B also corresponds most closely in the number of days' respite granted to the Fere when she is pressed for a decision on a husband: the Middle English has her ask for eighteen days, be granted eight, and they all reconvene on the eighteenth day (ll. 1797, 1808–10, 1864). MS A has twenty days, twenty days, and no day mentioned; MS D has ten and eight days; MS B has eight and eight days (AN ll. 1848, 1880–2, 1951). Since the Middle English numbers are written in roman numerals, to which single letters like *x* may be added, MS B might be the closest of the three. At ME l. 7009, Ipomadon claims that Imayne wants to kill him: in the corresponding line in MSS A and D, he says rather that *La putain me volt fere oscire*, 'the whore wants to get me killed', but B is missing the crucial verb *fere*, and thus reads the same as the Middle English. However, there are two other passages which demonstrate conclusively that B could not have been the translator's exemplar. Firstly, ME ll. 800–2 translate more or less literally AN ll. 764–5, but B is missing l. 765. Secondly, the section ME l. 8000 ff., in which Ipomadon is badly wounded but fortunately remembers his mother's magic ring, corresponds to AN ll. 9743–82, but these lines are missing from B.

Thus, none of the extant Anglo–Norman manuscripts could have been the translator's actual exemplar. MS B remains important, however, because in it the text of *Ipomedon* is immediately followed by Hue's even longer sequel, *Protheselaus*, and it can be demonstrated that our translator also had access to a copy of this text.

PROTHESELAUS

The ending of the Middle English *Ipomadon* contains information about Ipomadon's sons and his death that is not present in the Anglo–Norman *Ipomedon*. Hue does not mention the deaths of Ipomadon and Cabanus together at Thebes (recorded at ll. 8859–60 and ll. 8874–5 in the Middle English); he refers his audience instead to the story of *Thebes*, and claims incidentally that this text was taken from his own. (The reference is probably to the anonymous mid twelfth-century *Roman de Thèbes*, from which Hue has drawn the majority of his characters' names.) The Middle English translator could of course have known of Ipomadon's and Cabanus's deaths from elsewhere, since the legend of the 'Seven against Thebes' was well known (it is alluded to, for example, in Book V of Chaucer's *Troilus and Criseyde*, where the immediate source was Statius's *Thebaid*).[130] However, the information about Ipomadon's sons can only have come from *Protheselaus*. As with *Ipomedon*, it is the literal translation of several lines from this text which indicates that the translator must have been working from manuscript rather than memory. What follows are the relevant passages from the beginning of *Protheselaus* with the corresponding Middle English lines:[131]

Dous fiz urent e neent plus,	*In hyr tyme she bare hym sonys two,*
Unc si bels enfanz ne vit nuls;	*The fayrest that on ground my3t goo,*
Andui esteient chevalers	*No godelyer myght non been.* (8837–39)
Pruz e hardiz, jofne e legers.	
Daunus aveit nun li einznez,	*Cawnus was the oldest brothere* (8840)
De Poille fu rei coronez.	*Of Poyle was Cawnus crownyd kyng* (8844)
La Fiere, quant el devia,	*And Portusalus of Calabere* (8846)
A sun fiz pusnee devisa	*Was crownyd, for why it come of hyr* (8847)
Tote Calabre en eritage	*She toke hit hym be heritage,*
Kar ç'ot esté son mariage.	*For hit was hyr in mariage* (8849–50)
Protheselaüs fu nomez,	
Plus bels hom ne fu nez,	

[130] Benson *et al.*, ed., *The Riverside Chaucer*, l. 1502 ff. and notes on p. 1055.

[131] From Hue de Rotelande, *Protheselaus*, 3 vols, ed. A. J. Holden, Anglo–Norman Text Society, 47, 48, 49 (1991, 1993).

Kar en totes rens resembla	*Lyke to his fader in all thynge,*
Le bon pere qui l'engendra,	*That was so wonder wighte,*
En sens, en belté, en vesdie,	*Of kyndnes and of curtessye,*
En pruësce e en curteisie,	*Off armvre and of chevalrye,*
En totes teches de bonté.	*Off semelynes be sight.* (8853–7)
(*Protheselaus*, ll. 53–69)[132]	(*Ipomadon*, ll. 8837 ff.)
Quant el de Ipomedon oï	*There dyed that nobull knyght.*
La nuvele qu'il esteit mort,	*And when that to the Fere was told,*
Al quer li prist en doel si fort	
Que unc pus ne manga ne but,	*Neuer after ette ne drynke she wold,*
En bref terme aprés morut	*For pure love dyed that wight.*
(ll. 47–50)[133]	(ll. 8860–3)

The slight differences between the AN and ME versions of the names for the sons of Ipomedon indicate, however, that neither of the two manuscripts containing this section of *Protheselaus* can have been the translator's actual exemplar, since both agree on the form of these names against the Middle English.

---

[132] 'Two sons they had and no more. Such beautiful children had never been seen; both were bold and hardy knights, youthful and gentle. The eldest was called Daunus, he was crowned king of Apulia. La Fière, when she died, bequeathed her younger son all of Calabria as heritage, for it was her dowry. He was called Protheselaus—a more handsome man had never been born, since he resembled in every way the good father who had begotten him; in sense, in beauty, in intelligence, in prowess and in courtesy, in all aspects of excellence.'

[133] 'When she heard the news that Ipomedon was dead, she had such misery in her heart that she did not eat or drink again, [and] died a short time after.'

SELECT BIBLIOGRAPHY

Full and Partial Editions

Andersen, D. M., 'An Edition of the Middle English *Ipomadon*' (unpubl. Ph.D. thesis, University of California at Davis, 1968).

French, W. H. and Hale, C. B., eds., *Middle English Metrical Romances* (New York, 1964), originally published in 2 vols. in 1930.

Hue de Rotelande, *Ipomédon*, ed. A. J. Holden (Paris, 1979).

—— *Protheselaus*, 3 vols., ed. A. J. Holden, The Anglo-Norman Text Society 47, 48, 49 (1991, 1993).

Ikegami, Tadahiro, ed., *The Lyfe of Ipomydon*, 2 vols. (Tokyo, 1983).

Kölbing, Eugen, ed., *Ipomedon in Drei Englischen Bearbeitung* (Breslau, 1889).

Schmidt, A. V. C., with Jacobs, N., eds., *Medieval English Romances*, 2 vols. (London, 1980).

Reference

Guddat-Figge, Gisela, *Catalogue of Manuscripts Containing Middle English Romances*, (München, 1976).

Ker, N. R., *Medieval Manuscripts in British Libraries*, Vol. III (Oxford, 1983).

Mehl, Dieter, *The Middle English Romances of the Thirteenth and Fourteenth Centuries* (London, 1969).

Severs, J. Burke, ed., *A Manual of the Writings in Middle English 1050–1500*, Fascicule 1: Romances (New Haven, 1967).

Specific discussion of Ipomedon

Bjorklund, Victoria Ann Baum, 'The Art of Translation in *Ipomadon*: from Anglo-Norman to Middle English' (unpubl. D. Phil thesis, Yale University, 1977).

Burrow, J. A., 'The Uses of Incognito: *Ipomadon A*', in *Readings in Medieval English Romance*, ed. Carol M. Meale (Cambridge, 1994), pp. 25–34.

Calin, William, 'The Exaltation and Undermining of Romance: *Ipomedon*', in *The Legacy of Chrétien de Troyes*, vol. II, eds. Norris J. Lacy, Douglas Kelly and Keith Busby (Amsterdam, 1988), pp. 111–24.

Crane, Susan, *Insular Romance: Politics, Faith and Culture in Anglo-Norman and Middle English Literature* (Berkeley and Los Angeles, 1986).

Field, Rosalind, '*Ipomedon* to *Ipomadon A*: Two Views of Courtliness', in *The Medieval Translator*, ed. Roger Ellis (Cambridge, 1989), pp. 135–142.

Gay, Lucy M., 'Hue de Rotelande's *Ipomedon* and Chrétien de Troyes', *PMLA*, 32 (1917), 468–91.

Holthausen, F., 'Zu me. Romanzen: VI *Ipomadon*', *Anglia*, 41 (1917), 463–97.

Hosington, Brenda, 'The Englishing of the Comic Technique in Hue de

Rotelande's *Ipomédon*', in *Medieval Translators and Their Craft*, ed. Jeannette Beer (Kalamazoo, 1989), pp. 247–64.

Jacobs, Nicholas, 'Une allusion impudique chez Hue de Rotelande: *se li seaus li pent as nages*', *Neuphilologische Mitteilungen*, 96 (1995), 223–4.

Kaluza, Max, Review of Kölbing's *Ipomedon*, *Englische Studien* 13 (1889), 482–93.

Kellner, Leon, 'Syntaktische Bemerkungen zu *Ipomadon*', *Englische Studien*, 18 (1893), 282–93.

Kittredge, G. L, 'Anmerkungen zum me. *Ipomadon A*', *Englische Studien*, 14 (1890), 386–91.

Kölbing, Eugen, 'Vier romanzen-handschriften', *Englische Studien*, 7 (1884), 195–201.

Köppel, Emil, 'Zur Textkritik des *Ipomadon*', *Englische Studien*, 14 (1890), 371–86.

Krueger, Roberta, 'Misogyny, Manipulation and the Female Reader in Hue de Rotelande's *Ipomédon*', in *Courtly Literature*, ed. Keith Busby and Erik Kooper (Amsterdam & Philadelphia, 1990), pp. 395–409.

—— *Women Readers and the ideology of gender in Old French verse romance* (Cambridge, 1993).

Legge, M. Dominica, *Anglo-Norman Literature and its Background* (London, 1963).

Meale, Carol M., 'The Middle English Romance of *Ipomedon*: A Late Medieval "Mirror" for Princes and Merchants', *Reading Medieval Studies*, 10 (1984), 136–79.

Thaon, Brenda, 'La Fière: The Career of Hue de Rotelande's Heroine in England', *Reading Medieval Studies*, 9 (1983), 56–69.

Willert, H., 'Zum ME. *Ipomadon*', *Englische Studien*, 38 (1907), 131–32.

Medieval Romance

Baugh, A. C., 'The Authorship of the Middle English Romances', *Bulletin of the Modern Humanities Research Association*, 22, (1950), 13–28.

—— 'Improvisation in the Middle English Romances', *Proceedings of the American Philosophical Society*, 103 (1959), 418–54.

—— 'The Middle English Romance: Some Questions of Creation, Presentation and Preservation', *Speculum*, 42 (1967), 1–31.

—— 'Convention and Individuality in Middle English Romance', in *Medieval Literature and Folklore Studies*, ed. J. Mandel and B. Rosenberg (New Brunswick, 1970), pp. 122–46.

Burnley, David, *Courtliness and Literature in Medieval England* (London & New York, 1998).

Burrow, J. A., *Ricardian Poetry* (London, 1971).

Everett, Dorothy, 'A Characterization of the English Medieval Romances', in *Essays on Middle English Literature*, ed. Patricia Kean (Oxford, 1955), pp. 1–22.

Fewster, Carol, *Traditionality and Genre in Middle English Romance* (Cambridge, 1987).

Finlayson, John, 'Definitions of Middle English Romance', *Chaucer Review*, 15 (1980), Part 1, 44–62; Part 2, 168–81.

Hume, Kathryn, 'The Formal Nature of Middle English Romance', *Philological Quarterly*, 53 (1974), 158–80.

Gaunt, Simon, *Gender and Genre in Medieval French Literature* (Cambridge, 1995).

Jackson, W. T. H., 'The Nature of Romance', *Yale French Studies*, 51 (1974), 12–25.

Knight, Stephen, 'The Social Function of the Middle English Romances', in *Medieval Literature*, ed. David Aers (Brighton, 1986), pp. 99–122.

Leyerle, John, 'The Major Themes of Chivalric Literature', in *Chivalric Literature: essays on relations between literature and life in the later Middle Ages*, eds. Larry D. Benson and John Leyerle (Kalamazoo, 1980), pp. 131–46.

Ménard, Philippe, *Le rire et le sourire dans le roman courtois en France au moyen âge* (Genève, 1969).

Orme, Nicholas, *From Childhood to Chivalry: The Education of the English Kings and Aristocracy, 1066–1530* (London & New York, 1984).

Pearsall, Derek, 'The Development of Middle English Romance (1240–1400)', *Mediaeval Studies*, 27 (1965), 91–116.

—— 'The English Romance in the Fifteenth Century', *Essays and Studies*, NS 29 (1976), 56–83.

Reiss, Edmund, 'Romance', in *The Popular Literature of Medieval England*, ed. Thomas J. Heffernan (Knoxville, 1985), pp. 108–30.

Stanesco, Michel, 'Le secret de 'l'estrange' chevalier: Notes sur la motivation contradictoire dans le roman médiéval', in *The Spirit of the Court: selected proceedings of the Fourth Congress of the International Courtly Literature Society (Toronto 1983)*, eds. G. S. Burgess and R. A. Taylor (Cambridge, 1985), pp. 339–49.

Strohm, Paul, 'The Origin and Meaning of Middle English "Romaunce"', *Genre*, 10 (1977), 1–28.

Trounce, A. McI., 'The English Tail-Rhyme Romances', *Medium Aevum*, 1 (1932), 87–108 and 168–82; 2 (1933), 34–57 and 189–98; 3 (1934), 30–50.

Windeatt, Barry. 'Troilus' and the Disenchantment of Romance.' *Studies in Medieval English Romances*. Ed. D. S. Brewer. Cambridge: D. S. Brewer, 1988. 129–147.

EDITORIAL POLICY

The question of how much to emend is problematic with this text since it was composed in a northerly dialect very different from that of at least some of its later copyists. Rhymes have frequently been spoilt by the substitution of more southerly forms, although northern forms have also survived haphazardly in both rhyme-position and elsewhere. The extant text is thus an amalgam of several quite different Middle English dialects. It is very tempting to restore those parts of the original that can be recovered through rhyme evidence, and this is the route Kölbing takes in his edition. Unfortunately, the text that this method produces is no more consistent than the manuscript version. It is simply a new artificial mixture of dialects, with some lines beginning in one dialect and ending in another, and others remaining as they stand in the manuscript because they are too obscure, or our knowledge of Middle English is too incomplete, to allow such straightforward conversion.

There are cases where the author's own form seems obvious: 'young' for example only ever rhymes with words whose main vowel is *i/y*, such as *kynge, brynge, þinge*, and it is indeed once spelt *ynge* and once *yenge*. Kölbing emends these instances of *yo(u)ng* and *yenge* to *yinge* but leaves *yo(u)ng* where it appears mid-line, so the text is still inconsistent as a whole. An editor could emend all instances of *yo(u)ng* to *yinge*, but unfortunately there is no way of knowing whether the original writer used the *i*-form exclusively, or whether he did in fact vary and the *i*-form just happened to be more convenient for rhyme: there is no known dialect-area where *yinge* is the sole variant. One is faced with the possibility on the one hand of showing two variants where the original only had one, or on the other hand of allowing only one variant where the original had two after all. Even if this question could be settled, the rhyme-pair of a word can only ever indicate the approximate pronunciation of that part of the word on which the rhyme depends. It cannot indicate, for example, the initial consonant, the original spelling, or anything about other syllables not participating in the rhyme, although such things too have dialectal significance. Kölbing spells his line-end emendations for 'young' as *yinge*, but it may equally well have been *yhing(e), ynge, ȝyng(e), ȝing(e)*. This objection may seem trivial, but when such differences can have dialectal significance, it is misleading to select a written form on the limited basis of what rhyme can indicate about the pronunciation of the original word. And pronunciation, as illustrated by rhyme, is usually the only evidence we have. Then there are all the words that never appear in rhyme-position—does one alter them to some more Northern variant where such is known? This is fairly clearly stepping beyond the bounds of the editor's job, but it is the logical follow-on from the less drastic emendation-by-rhyme described above: if one is going to try to recover the original form of the text at all, one should be consistent about it. Since, however, consistency is impossible, I have decided for the most part to leave the copyist's forms as they stand. This applies to morphological variants, such as the copyist's frequent pr.3 sg. ending *-th* for original *-s* (or *-es*, or *-is*/*-ys*), as well as to phonological variants. Occasionally the variant employed by the copyist may not be immediately recognisable as the same word as that required by rhyme, for example MS *fovrthe* at l. 8423 where rhyme calls for the Northern variant *ferde*: such instances are signalled in the Explanatory Notes. Where, however, the copyist's alterations have affected the tense of a verb and thus the meaning, I do emend. For example, the original rhymes of the couplet ll. 7337–38 must have been pr.3 sg. *tas* : *mas*: since the copyist's *toke* : *made* are pa.t., I have emended to the original pr. forms.

Periodically the copyist goes beyond merely altering the form of the original to substituting an entirely different word. These substantive variants, whether motivated by dialectal differences (as often seems to be the case) or by simple misunderstanding, I have emended. I include in this category not only the obvious substitutions of dissimilar words, such as MS *byddynge* for the *prayere* demanded by rhyme at l. 452, but also such cases as where *gange* has been replaced by *goone* 'go'—the two words look similar and are used interchangeably, but one derives from OE *gangan* and the other from OE *gān*, so these instances have been emended. Most importantly, I have attempted to emend where the sense of the text seems to have been lost, even though the uncertainty involved often relegates the more tentative emendations to the Explanatory Notes.

I have been equally conservative as regards metre: since we have no evidence for the degree of our author's attention to metre beyond this (very corrupt) version of this text, I have emended nothing on purely metrical grounds. The poem is skilfully written, but is not so extraordinary as to justify an assumption that the metre was always regular.

All additions and emendations to the manuscript text appear in square brackets, while abbreviations have been silently expanded. Punctuation and stanza-division are modern since the manuscript contains neither. Double round brackets enclose manuscript lines which appear to be superfluous, e.g. l. 6177. Word-division has been modernised without comment except in the case of such archaic words as *i-wis, i-noghe, lang-ere, be-lyve, all-way(es)*—written variously as one word or two in the manuscript—which I have hyphenated where they are found as two words in the manuscript. The occasional doubled final *ee* has been removed in cases where it is unaccented (and probably unpronounced), such as in MS *godee* 'good' at l. 212, but left in words where it is part of the sole accented vowel, such as in *hee* at l. 35. Capitalisation is modern. Capital *I* has been retained where it stands for modern 'j'; the distribution of *u, v* and *w* has not been regularised; and *þ* and *ȝ* have been retained. Doubled consonants have been retained except in the case of initial *ff*, which has been treated as the capital form. The foliation given is the more recent series, added to correct the occasional errors of the older series followed by Kölbing in his edition.

IPOMADON

Here begynnyth a good tale of Ipomadon

Off love were lykynge of to lere,
    And Ioye tille all that wol here,
    That wote what love may meane;
But who so have grette haste to love,
And may not com to his above,   5
That poynte dothe louers tene.
Fayre speche brekyth never bone;
That makythe these lovers ilkone
Ay hope of better w[e]ne,
And put themselffe to grete travayle   10
Wheddyr it helpe or not avayle:
Ofte sythes this hathe be sene.

Be this poynte well may I pre[f]e
That of his love was lothe to le[f]e
Fro tyme that he began.   15
Thereffore in þe world where euer he went,
In Iustys or in tur[na]mente,
Euer more the pryce he wan.
But a stravnge lover he was one;
I hope ye haue harde speke of non   20
That euer God made to be man,
Ne lother knowen for to be,
No whedure a better knyght þan he
Was no levand than.

In Cessyle sumtyme wonyd a kyng,   25
That holden was wyth old and ynge
Off poynttys wythe owten pere.
He was worthy, were and wyse,
Ouer all he wan losse and pryce: f. 191^v
Men callyd hym Mellyagere.   30
He had bovnden to his hande,
In Fraunce and many other lande,
Dou3ty dukys and dere.
He gatte neuer chyld his eyre to be,

9 wene] K.; MS wone   13 prefe] prese   14 lefe] lese
17 turnamente] K.; MS turaemente

But a brother son had hee   35
That was his newov nere.

That chyld he þouȝte to make his eyre,
In all this world was non so fayre,
I darre welle wittnes thys;
Large he was of leme and lethe,   40
And wonder well he wex there wyth:
Men callyd hym Cabanus.
How he was gotton I can not sayne;
Yff ye wille witte, wythoute layne,
Further spyre ye [bus].   45
His brother to the kyng hym sent,
And prayed hym ofte wyth goode intente,
'For the love he owe tyll vs,

'That he wille kepe well my son':
He sayd, 'fro tyme he kepe tham can,   50
My landys I shall hym take.'
Begge [he] wex of bonne and blode,
Therewyth so handsum and so goode
That all men hym worshipe spake.
He was a derlynge to the kynge;   55
Hym lovyed above all oþer þinge
For his brothere is sake.
Whanne Cabanus was co[myn] to elde
That he cowde ryde and armus welde,
f. 192ʳ   Knyghte he gan hym make.   60

A systur hadde kynge Melyagere,
That was chaste and mylde of chere,
The feyrest that on fote myght goo.
The[re] come many a ryall kynge
For to wowe that lady yonge,   65
And other prynces moo.
The kyng of Calabrye thedur paste,
And at her brother he here axte
And sayd betwene them tow,
His systur gyffe hym yf he wolde,   70

40 he] he he   45 bus] K.; MS mvste   47 And] nd *interlined, caret after A*
52 he] K.; MS of   58 comyn] K.; MS conym   64 There] K.; MS The

Of hym shold he his landys holde,
And in acorde made soo.

Wyth worshipe he that lady wede,
And to Calabur he her lede,
Wyth game and grette lykynge.   75
He made his omage or he yede
Tyll hym that douȝty was in dede,
Syr Mellyager the kynge.
They levyd togeddur but yers ten;
A chyld they gatte betwene them þan,   80
A doughtter fayre and younge
That aftur them ther ayre shuld be;
The elevenyth yere bothe she and he
Dyede wythoute lesynge.

The may was younge and tender of age,   85
And therefore all her baronage
Emonge them toke there rede:
The moste worthely man and wyse
Shuld kepe this lady mekyll of pryse,
And teche hur womanhoode.   90
Off bewte and of grette bovnte,   f. 192ᵛ
She was the beste in all degre
That euer on erthe myghte trede:
Be that she was xv yere of elde,
She toke hyrselffe her londys to welde   95
To gouerene in that stede.

She was blyth and bryȝte of hewe;
All men callyd her that her knewe
Of Calabere the F[e]re.
Visibyll and vertuyvs,   100
Meke, mylde and mervelys,
Chaste and fayre of chere;
Fro she come to here above,
That may wax so provde of love,
Her thought no prynce her pere.   105
Yf she were semelyeste vnder schrovde

99 Fere] *K.; MS* fayre

Of other poyntys, she was namyd prowde
But of love to lere.

She sayd the fyrste day, I vnderstonde,
That she toke sesyn in her lande,   110
That fayre as flowre in felde,
'Now here to God a vowe I make:
I shall never man for riches take
I' youthe ne in eolde.
For welle or woo whether it be,   115
Man that is of lowe degre
Shall never to wyffe me holde
But yf he be the best knyghte
Of all this world in armus bryghte
Assayde vnder his shelde.'   120

f. 193ʳ
Thereat all her lordys lowgh
And sayd, 'This vowe ys grette rewe
For anny that euer were borne!'
Than spake as has don other moo
Some of them saye not so   125
Though it were a skorne. †
[N]owghte she covthe of love amowre
And held hur howse wyth so grette honoure
Of welthe of wyne and corne,
And dyd so worthely and so well,   130
All prayd God gyffe her happe and sell
That come that fre beforne.

In Brettayne, Fraunce and Lvmbardy,
The word sprange in to Araby
What howse that laydy helde,   135
In Cypres and in many a soyle.
The same tyme in the lond of Poyle,
A noble kynge ther dwellyd
That was callyd Ermagynes:
Yf anny man wold agayne hym ryse,   140
Euer more his foos he feellyd.
A worthy wyghte he had to wyffe;

127 Nowghte] *K.; MS* owghte

A sone she bare hym in her lyffe,
As I haue harde be tolde.

Men keppyd hym tille he reasone knewe,   145
And they betoke hym to Talamewe,
That worthy was all-waye:
In the world was emperoure ne kynge
But he cowde in all thynge
Have seruyd hym well to paye.   150
Fyrste he leryd the chylde curtessye,
And sethe [of] chasse [the] chevalrye,   f. 193ᵛ
To weld in armys gaye.
He waxed worthely, ware and wyse,
Of hvntynge also he bare the pryce,   155
The sertayne sothe to saye.

This was he holdyn in his dayes
Comely, kynde and curtayes,
Bothe wyth kynge and quene;
Hende and happy ther wythall,   160
He seruyd in his faders hall,
And had never forther byen.
His name was Ipomadon;
A fayre chyld he was one,
Ye haue but selden sayne.   165
Of all ken fetowre and of face
Therwyth God gyaff hym grace;
They louyed hym all bedene.

His fader was a noble man,
Well his landys he governyd than,   170
Bothe fare and nere;
His meyne louyd hym moste and leyste,
And on a tyme he made a feeste
To men that worthy were.
When they wer set and seruyd all,   175
The worde spronge in the hall

147 worthy] r *written in above* o   152 of . . . the] *K.; MS* the . . . of

Of Calabrye the F[e]re:
Than sayd a knyghte of bewte,
So fayre, so good at all degre
Was non levand to her.   180

f. 194ʳ

'A[s] worthy a corte she holdys on,
As ys fro Ynde to þe o[cc]yane;
This darre I warande welle!'
Ipomadon servyd in the hall,
And herde the knyghttys wordys all   185
Of that damysell.
So grette good of her he spake,
Hym thoughte [hys] hertte asvunder brake
Wyth syghynge and vnsyle.
No thyng he sayd what so he thoughte,   190
But stode stille and answeryd not,
But thynkyd ylk a dell.

Whene he to his mette was sett,
He myghtte nother drynke ne ete,
So mekyll on her he thoughte.   195
He wax wan and pale off hewe;
That sawe his maystur Talamewe,
And he parsayuyd yt not.
Hym þouȝte full longe þat þey had ettyn;
Talamewe had not forgetton,   200
But to the chyld he [soughte]:
He sayd, 'Sone, me mervayls mekyll of þat
So thoughtfull at your mette ye sate;
Ys anny þinge myssewroghtte?'

He sayd, 'Dere maystur Thalamewe,   205
Ye haue byn to me trusty and trewe
Sethe fyrste your faythe was [fest].
Here I lye as bere in denne,
And come neuer amonge no men,
Nother este ne weste: 210

177 Fere] K.; MS fayre   181 As] K.; MS A   182 occyane] Kp.; MS
oxylane   188 hys] K.; MS om.   201 soughte] K.; MS gothe
206 haue] haue haue   207 fest] K.; MS sett

Who lovys ay at home to wonne,
Lyttill gode shall he conn
Of bewete whan he ys beste.   f. 194ᵛ
To seke my seruys will I gange,
Here me thynke I dwell ouer longe;   215
It rewys me ro and reste.

'I haue harde speke of contreys straunge,
The whiche it makyth my hertte to cha[un]ge:
Mekell more it mone.
The wyse man and the boke seys,   220
"In a cowrte who so dwell alweys,
Full littill good shall he con."
I will you swere, mayster ya,
I trowe ye will wyth me ga,
Suche frenshipe in you I fynde;   225
Me alone forther yf I wende
Here I woll not lengur lende
As se I syghtte of sonne.

'And therfor, mayster, Y you praye
That ye will to my fader saye,   230
And to my moder fre;
Me were full lothe I shuld them greue,
Therefore I praye you axe them leve,
Grythe for you and me.
And yf they will not lett me goo,   235
Myselffe at mydnyght leve shall take,
Thowȝ I sh[u]lde barfote bee.
Whethur they be foo or frend,
Tyll vncovth contreys will I wende;
The maner wille I see.'   240

And when he had þis tale tolde,
His mayster stode and hym behylde,
Awonderd as he were:
'Dere sone Ipomadon,

212 gode] godee   218 chaunge] chamge   237 shulde] K. shullde; MS
shallde

Syn thou arte purposyde here vpon,   245
Wheddur wille ye fare?'
'Maystur,' he sayd, 'Ye harde full wele
Of that dereworthy damysell
The knyght spake of lang-ere,
The semely Fere of Calabyre: 250
The way thethur will I spere
To se the maner there.

'And sertys yf ye will helpe me nowe,
For euer I shall be holden to you
As I haue euer mekyll bene;   255
But maystur and ye leve behynde,
I not where I sholde frenshipe fynde,
Ne to home I myghte me mene.'
His maystur stode and lowde gan lowȝe,
And sayd, 'Sone, þis ples me well i-nowe   260
To wette wythowten wene.
To leve behynde me were full lothe:
I shall aske leve for vs both,
And that [shall] sone be sene.'

His mayster made no tarynge,   265
But sought tille he fande the kynge,
And thus to hym sayd thanne:
'In a courtte who ay soioyrons so,
And se the maner of no moo,
Of no mo they can: 270
Leve I rede that ye hym geve,
For yf God will lett hym leve,
He will be a noble man . . .

'Syr a poynte I you praye:
Gravnte me leve as I saye,   275
For wyth hym wynde I wol[d]e.'
The kynge þought he sayd but skylle;
The quene chambyr he went tille
And here thus purpos tolde.

262 full] *Followed by crossed-out* s   264 shall] *K.; MS om.*   276 wolde] *K.;*
MS wole

His moder had full mekyll care 280
Her sone so fere shuld fro her fare,
And she ne wyste whedder he shulde:
She graunte hym leffe at the laste,
And wyth a sorowfull hert he axte
Her blessynge vppon molde. 285

When they had getton leve to goo,
In hertt full Ioyfull were they tow;
They made no tarrynge.
The kynge to Thalamew bek[e]nde
Gold and syluer i-nowghe to spende, 290
For ys sone so yonge:
Ayther hade a palffraye,
Tow somers for the chyldys araye,
And eke for his spendynge;
Tow men and no mo meny, 295
That chyldys currure for to be,
Tythandys to bere and brynge.

His leve he toke at kyng and quene,
And sethen at all the courte bedene;
His moder sighed sore. 300
They travayllyd day be day fro home,
Into Calabyre that they come,
They wold no spendynge spare.
They speryd aftur that bryght of ble;
Men tolde them, 'in a ryche citte', 305
And thedyr can they fare.
Att the beste ynne of all the towne   f. 196ʳ
Talamewe is lyght adowne,
And toke then herbowre there.

In the world was kynge ne emperour 310
That he [ne] myghte wyth grette honoure
Have holden his howse wythynne:
Wyth bankers brodyrd all abowte,
The dosers steynyd wythoute dowte
Wyth fowle and fyshe well fyne. 315

289 bekende] K.; MS be kynde   311 ne] K.; MS om.

His oste vpon the chylde gan loke,
And in his cuntenavnce vndertoke
He was full hye of kynne:
The burgays cowth of curtessye,
And at his w[i]lle full worthely   320
He purveyd hym that inne.

Talamewe sayd, 'I the praye,
Ordayne for vs corne and heye,
And loke that we well fare,
Off mette and drynke grette plente,   325
The beste wyne of thus contre
Fayne wold I wette where were.
Thou artte wythe thy neybors kynde,
Brynge it in; we haue i-now to spende,
And God shall send vs more.   330
But maystur to the covrtte wille weynde:
To make you mery that levys behynde,
Godys forb[o]de that ye spare.'

The chyld wolde no lengur to abyde
But arayde hym ryally to ryde   335
And to the courte gan [cayre];
Talamewe wyth hym gan fare.

f. 196ᵛ   Allsone as they come thare,
They were resseuyd full fayre.
The courte was plenere all that day   340
Off worthy lordys, the sothe to say,
And other grette repeyre:
A duke had doone another wronge,
Att grette debatte had byn longe
For holdynge of an ayre.   345

That day the Fere hade made hem frende
And broughte that grette debate to ende,
So ys she ware and wyce;
Ladyes wille that she not wote †

---

320 wille] wolle   333 forbode] forbede   336 cayre] K.; MS carye
346 day] d corr. from b

Abowtte hur suffyr no debatte: 350
So grette goodenes in her lyethe,
Her [m]eyny lovyd her euer ilke one.
Into the hall comys Ipomadon
Amonge thes lordys of price;
An ewen pase forthe he paste,   355
Nother to softe ne to faste
But at his owne devyce.

Lordys, laydys in the hall
Lokys on hym, men and all,
And grette mervaylle they þought: 360
He was large of lyme and lythe
And made so wonder the[m] wythe,
Of fetter faylyd hym not.
A llyttell wax he rede for shame,
Full welle that coloure hym became,   365
Before that high he sowghtte.
His dobelett was of red welvet,
Off bryght golde botuns ibete
That worthely was wrovghte.   f. 197ʳ

His mantell was of skarlett fyne,   370
Furryd wyth good armyne,
Ther myght no better been;
The bordoure all of red sendell,
That araye became hym wele
To wete wythouten wene.   375
A noble countenavnce he hade;
A blyther and a better made
Before they had not sayne.
Also bryght his coloure shone
All hym lovyd that lokyd hym one,   380
Bothe lord and lady shene.

And longe h[ym] beheldys the Fere
But no thynge chaunges her chere
For carpynge of the crowde.
[Her] hertte is sett so mekyll of wyte,   385

52 meyny] *K.; MS* neyny   362 them] *K.; MS* then   382 hym] *K.; MS* he
385 Her] *K.; MS om.*

Wyth love it is not daun[t]yd yte
Thowȝe she be shene in scherovde,
But aftur sore it bande the fre,
And so I wold that all ye shuld be
That is of love so prowde!   390
The chyld before her knelys than,
And to the lady he began
To tell his tale on lowde.

He sayd, 'Dereworthy damysell,
Grette God kepe the in hele   395
And all thy fayre menye;
Vnder heyvyn is holdyn none
So worthy a lady as thow arte on,
Ne of so grette bewete;

f. 197ᵛ   Ofte sythes this haue I harde saye,   400
A noble[r] courte then thyne allwaye
There may non holdyn bee.
The to serve haue I thowghte,
Thereffore haue I hedyr sought
Oute of farre contraye.   405

'What as thou wilte put me tow
That longys a gentill man to doo,
Gladlye [wille] I [do].
Thereffore I praye the me tell
Whedur thow [will] I wyth the dwell,   410
Or wynde thedyr I come froo.
On asay now shall I see
Yff it be as men say of the
In countreys many and [moo].'
The lady satt and hym behylde   415
And lykyd full wele the tale he tolde.
When she hym hard say soo,

That he wold hur servand be,
She behyldys his grette bewte

386 dauntyd] K.; MS daunnyd   388 fre] r corr. from e   401 nobler] K.;
MS noble   408 wille I do] K.; MS do I wille   410 will] K.; MS om.
414 moo] K.; MS fell

And in her hertt she thought   420
That he myghte wyth grette honoure
Haue seruyd kynge or emperoure,
He was so worthy wroughte.
A thynge in her hert gan ryse
That she shuld lyke wele hes seruyce;   425
Forgoo hym wold she note.
She answeryd hym full curtesly,
'Thou arte welcome, belamye,
I thanke hym that the browghte.

'Syn thou to seruys will be sett,   430
What ys thy name, þou stravnge valete?   f. 198ʳ
Anon that thou tell mee.'
'I was callyd at home by the same name
And borne I was in ferre contre
Forther wotte ye not for me   435
Wheddyr ye blysse or blame.'
The lady att his wordys lough;
She sayd sone, 'This holde I good i-nowe;
It is a noble name,
And thou artte welcome securly.'   440
His mayster sayd, that stode hym by,
'Gravnte mercy, madame.'

The lady callyd hur botelere;
'This cupe of gold þou shalte take here
And gyff hit to younde man;   445
To buttrey dore lede hym wyth the,
Therwyth of wyne to serue me;
We shall se yf he can.'
The butteler hym the cuppe betoke
And he was fayne and not foresoke,   450
To the chylde sayd he thanne,
'It ys my ladyes [prayere]
That thou off wyne shall serue here.'
In covrte thus he began.

425 hes] s *corr. from* r   452 prayere] *K.; MS* byddynge

Rightte in his mantell as he stode,   455
Wyth the botteler forthe he youde,
The cupe on hande he bare:
All that lovyd þat chyld beforne
For that dede lovghe hym to skorne,
Bothe the lesse and the more.   460
'Yff that he shuld serue one,
It were semande,' they sayd ilkone,
'Away his mantell were.'
But littill knewe þey his entente;
To the buttery dore he went   465
And offe he caste hit yare.

To the boteler than went hee;
'Syr, this mantell gyff I the:
As I haue happe or sele,
And thow wilte take þis sympull gyfte,   470
It shall be mendyd be my thryfte
Wyth efte so good a wille.'
The butteler thankyd hym curtesly
And sayd, 'Gentyll syr, gramercy
Off this frenshipe I felle,   475
An[d] in owght þat I can do or saye
Be grette God that oweth this day
It shall be quytte full wele;

'For this VII yere, be my thryfte,
Was not gevyne me suche a gyfte!'   480
The mantyll he toke hym tille.
All them that thowght skorne before
Thought themselfe folys therefore;
They satt and held them stille,
And sayden, 'It was a gentill dede;   485
There may no man, so God vs spede,
Otherwyse say be skylle.'
All they spake in prevyte;
'A hundyrd men may a man se
Yet wott not one his wille.'   490

f. 198ᵛ

470 sympull] p *corr. from* s   476 And] *K.; MS* An

This dede saw the lady clere,
How he gaffe to the butelere   f. 199^r
That gyfte of grette bewete.
Tille herselffe she sayd forthy,
'Younde dede ys doon full gentilly,   495
Be God and be my lewte;
When[s] he euer come or what he is,
I wot he cam of conuyence; †
Be younde full wele I see!'
She sayd to hem þat by her stode,   500
'This chyld is comyn of gentille blode;
It may no nother weye bee.'

The cope he brought before hyr syne,
And seruyd the fre wyth the wyne
So worthely alweys.   505
Tille iii yere ende were comyn and gon,
The lady she thought she saw neuer one
So mekyll to holde to prayse,
And in the courtte now he is
Louyd bothe wyth more and lesse,   510
So gydyde hym in his dayes.
But a condycyon havys he
That I shall say sore rewys me,
All layde to love it ys. †

C[o]varde be countennaunce hym semyd;   515
To hardenes nothynge he yemyde
To melle hym there wyth all:
When knyghttys yede to turnement
Thereto wold he take no tente,
Nother grette ne smalle.   520
Of dedes of armus when they spake,
Ipomadon wolde turne his bake   f. 199^v
And hye oute of the hall.
He wold here of no cheva[l]rye;
Prowde men of the cowrte forthy   525
'Cowarde' gan hym call.

497 Whens] When   515 Covarde] K.; MS cavarde   517 To] K.; MS To te
524 chevalrye] chevarye

Bysyde ther was a fayre foreste;
Huntynge lovyd [he] alder beste
To see his grehoundys renne.
Gamen of houndys was all his thought,   530
Be dede of armys sett he noughte;
That was parsauyd hym in.
Of chevalry wold he not here;
Grettly that myslyke[d] the Fere,
He wold no worshippe wynne.   535
'Allas,' she sayd, 'So mekyll fayrenes
Ys loste on hym wythouten proves;
Yt is a sory synne!

'Allas that euer so grette gentryse
Ys loste on hym for coward[ise].   540
Woo worthe destonye,
Syn he is so fayre of face,
That God had not gevyn hym that grace
Of hertt hardy to bee:
For were he a man of hardynes,   545
As bovnte semys and bewte ys
Be God and be my lewte,
On lyve I know non lewand nowe
That cordys so well to myn avowe
In all this world as hee.'   550

Thus she monys the stravnge valete:
To love hym yf her hertte be sett,
It makys here lekyng leke
That he sett be no chevallrye;
To euery he spendys so largely   555
That all good of hym spake,
Then sum men hem to huntyng louthe,
Sum therefore was wrothe i-now
That harde behynde his bake.
Thow the lady hym wolde not chyde,   560
For hym in herte many a tyde
Here thovght asunder wold breke.

f. 200ʳ

528 he] K.; MS om.   532 in] Otiose flourish on n   534 myslyked] K.; MS
myslyke   540 cowardise] K.; MS cowardenes   559 harde] Otiose stroke
through d   561 For] followed by in

In somer seson it befell
When flovrys were sprong swete of smell
And fowlys songe bedene,   565
The fre bethought her at þat tyde
That she wold of huntyng ryde
Into the foreste grene.
She bad her men, the sothe to saye,
They shuld be redy the VIII day   570
Amonge the schawes schene:
'Into the foreste wyll we fare,
To hunte at the herte full yare
That longe has soveryd been.'

Her meyne made them redy faste;   575
On the VIII day to wood they paste
As was her comaundemente.
Vppon a lavnde fayre and wyde
Be a rennande reuer syde
They sett that ladyes tente.   580
There was the dere won
When they were wery for-rwne
Wythe baynge on the bente;   f. 200ᵛ
Or any reysyd oute of araye,
Grette herttys to byde the bay   585
To the watter wente.

Logys and pavelons they pyghte
For erle, baron and for knyghte
That huntyd in that foreste.
Ipomadon was not the laste,   590
His horne abowte his halse he caste
And went in to the weste
Into the depe foreste.
How so he dothe of other thynge,
Of Iustus or of tvrnaynge,   595
Huntynge lovyde hee beste;
Thowȝe he set be no chevalrye,
Moste he couthe of venarye,
Thereon his hert was feste.

581 the] there *with re crossed out*   594 he] they

For she schuld moste of solas see,   600
On the lavnde they set þat bryght of ble
And many a man her wythe.
Hunters blewe there hornys þat stovnde,
Caste of and oncowpelyd ther hounde,
Foundes into the frethe.   605
Dyueres weys went her men
To reyse the dere oute of there denne
Lyght of ly[m]e and lythe;
For bugelys blaste and brachys crye
Wyth oppon mowthe full veralye   610
There myght no best haue gryethe.

Hym besyest faste Ipomadon
For why he cowthe i-nowgh þerone,
Lowde his horne he blewe.
Wyth hym he toke a lytill rache,   615
The dere oute of there kyth to cache,
The coste full wele he knewe;
That was a brachet of thee beste
That euer wold trewly queste
And securly pursewe.   620
He hyes hym oute of all the prece,
Thre greyhoundys he lade in lese
His maystur Tholamewe.

Hornys blewe and houndus ranne
Wyth oppyn mowthe full mery than   625
And many bugels blaste.
A noble noye it was to here;
In hertte full wele yt lykyd the Fere,
There houndys fell to so faste.
Ipomadon a hertte he chase,   630
His hounde so gladely to hym gos . . .
This grette hertte at the laste,

So wery was for-ron that day
That on the bent to byde the bay

608 lyme] *K.; MS* lynne

f. 201ʳ

To the watter he made hym bone.   635
The littell hounde nyghed hym so nere,
In myddys of the lavnde before the Fere
For feyntys fell he downe;
Forther myghte he go no foote
So had þis hertt be holdyn hoote   640
Wyth that brache browne.
The hounde also myghte renne no more;
For fey[n]tenes fell downe before
That lady fayre off facyon.   f. 201ᵛ

So wery for-renne wer they tow,   645
A foote further myghtte noþer goo,
But fell before the F[e]re.
A littill fro hym þis hounde lay
Att the grette hertte questyde aye;
That saw that lady clere.   650
Att the brachet lowde she lowȝe;
'Now sertys he can of fete i-nowȝe
That þus his hounde gan lere;
Hymselffe comys sone, he is not ferre.'
Ipomadon drawythe nere   655
Where he is hounde gan here.

As a hunter all in grene
He come before that bryght and shene
And on his foote he lyghte;
His kyrtell covyrd not his kne.   660
To that grette hertte [gon] is hee,
And seruyd hym full right:
He lacys the s[l]owche to fede the hounde,
Then sayd the lady in the stovnde
Tille her maydens bryghte;   665
'Folowe me, for I wille wende
To se younder curteys chyld and hende
How he younder dere gan dyghte.

'More helpe ne hade he note
But the hounde that hym to bay brouȝte.'   670
When he this hertte hade slayne,
Ipomadon in a thrawe
Aftur his maystur he wendys to blowe
Welle forthe on the playne.
The brachett by the hertte lay stylle,   675
He wold not let no man come hym tille,
The sothe ys not to layne;
Ne sertys he wold not takyne be,
This hounde, of no man till he se
His maystur was comyn agayne.   680

And when he sawe his maystur thore
He dyd his besynes the more,
It shulde the better bee:
The hedde he co[r]vde wonder well,
And sethe vndyd euery deyle   685
Full fayre before that fre.
All that she sawe of oþur men
Tille hym she held but fablis then,
So deyntely dede hee.
Agayne into her tent she turnys;   690
In hertte for hym full mekyll she mornys
And cursyd his destonye,

That in so mekyll fayrenes forȝete,
That ne hade poynte of p[r]owes sete:
'For suche anoþer know I none   695
So fayre, so curteys as he is,'
But for he louyd no hardenes
The lady was full woo.
She thynkys to haue Ipomadon,
And thought agayne, 'Thynke not the[re]on,'   700
Thus turnythe she tow and fro.
Att the laste, of love drewry
Dystrwes defawte of chevallrye:
'Alas why [ys] [it] so?

f. 202ʳ

684 corvde] K.; MS covde   694 hade] Followed by crossed-out a   prowes] K.;
MS powes   700 there] K.; MS then   704 ys it] K.; MS it ys

'For hym to love yf I had thoughte   705
To myne avowe acordys he not;   f. 202ᵛ
That makyth myne hertte vnblythe.
That prowde sory vowe that I
Made be my grette folye
Now makyth m[e] wrynge and wry[t]he.'   710
Wyth hur owne he[r]te thus she thowght
That amys that she wroughte,
And sykynge sayde sythe;
'I shall love neuer no knyghte
But he be man of myghte   715
His costes for too kythe:

'For louyde I hym sekyrlye,
All men therof wold haue envy
And praye God shuld them wreke.
They wold saye, 'Be our lady nowe,   720
She hathe well sett her grette avowe
On a febyll freke'.
I trowe that tyme shall com above
That [I] mvn fynde a knyght to love
That wele a schafte gan breke;   725
But se[r]tys my love is so isete
That hym to love I may no lette
What so euer they speke.'

Ipomadon hym bysyes faste . . .
Wondere wele hym bare;   730
That day he brought to quary tenne
Moo than dyde all other men,
Of noble herttys that were.
The sonne beganne to drawe downe;
They hyed them to pavelyon   735
Before þat wyse off lare.   f. 203ʳ
Ipomadon lowde blewe;
Full well that Fere his horne knewe
That she hade herde it are.

710 me] *K.; MS* my   wrythe] *K.; MS* wrynche   711 herte] *S&J; MS* hete
719 And] n *corrected from* r   724 I] *K.; MS om.*   726 sertys] *K.; MS* seytys

His maystur Thalamewe and he   740
Blowes aftur mo meneye,
Semble where they shulde.
Sevyn heddys he brought to present;
She rose and gayne hym wente
Vppon them to beholde.   745
So grette heddys as they were,
The lady thoughte she sawe neuer ere
That made were on molde . . .

In a stody full stylle she stode:
I hope here lokynge dyd here goode,   750
Be God and my lewte;
The righte I trowe who vndertake,
She had more luste on hym to loke
Then any herttys hedde to see.
Whenne erlys and barnys asemblyde wer,   755
All they gaffe, bothe l[e]sse and more,
Before that bryghte of ble,
The pryce to that straunge valet
That came alone wyth his brachet
And sayd, 'Beste worthy ys he.'   760

A cosyn had that lady bryghte,
A noble chyld that Iason highte,
Ryghtte bygge of bone and blode,
And fro he had Ipomadon sene
They lovyd as they had brethryn been;   765
Togedder ay they youde.
In a swtte they bothe were clade,
Grette Ioye of them the ladye hadde,
They were so fayre and goode;
So semely chyldern as they tow   770
In all the curte was no moo,
Ne mylder of there mode.

The tow wyshe and to supper youde;
Ipomadon toke good hede,

f. 203ᵛ

756 lesse] *K*. lasse; *MS* losse

His cope forgate he note. 775
To the bottry went he syne
And made hit there be fyllyd wyth wyne
And to the borde it browghte.
Here lokynge hade she not forgetton;
'Say valett,' she sayd, 'As thow etton? 780
Today thou haste welle wroughte.'
'Damysell,' he sayd, 'Not yete
Drynke I dranke ne mete I ete,
Fro bale as I be broughte.'

'Syr that ys to longe, be skyll; 785
My cosyn Iason call the tille,
For suppud I wold ye hadde.
In the flore before me sett ye adowne.'
They bothe were att her byddyng bown
And dyd as she them badde: 790
There was berlyde at þat suppere
Drynke that sethyn was bought full dere
Wyth many a syghyng sade;
And lyke brethryne they toke them there
That aftur rewyde sum full sore, 795
Ofte sythes to gamen onglade.

Whate myghte þat be but derne love, f. 204^r
That allways wyll be above
To them that shall it havnte?
All othere thyngys men d[avn]te may, 800
But sertenly be no waye
Love wille not be davnte.
Who presus ofte to serue hytte,
Worse schall have his gurdovn quyte
For he be loves seruante; 805
Who entrys into lovys scolys
The wyseste is holdyn moste foolys
Fro that they haue graunte.

How so it be, this lady yenge
Makythe many a love lokynge, 810

799 that] *Written above line*   800 davnte] *K.; MS* dowte

But foly thoughte sche non,
And yet she thought it dyd here good;
That full wele vnderstode
The chyld Ipomadon.
He caste her many a lovely loke;   815
Full well that lady vndertoke
That he wyth love was tane.
She drede that it shuld ryse þorow chaunse
Sum slavnder thorow countenavnce,
He lokyd so here vppon.   820

For in a stodye styll he sate,
That mete and drynke clene he forg[a]te,
So mekyll on hur he þoughtte.
Thereatt the Fere began to smyle,
And bethought hur on a wyle   825
How sche hym schastys myghtte.
In hertte sche thynkys so to devyce,
Be hyr owne cosyn hym to chastyce;
f. 204ᵛ   That other parcevyde yt note.
'Iason,' sche sayd, 'for Goddys pyne,   830
Why lokys thow so vpon [Imayne]?
What has my mayden myswroghte?

'What ayles the man, for God a[v]o[w]e?
Say damysell, ys this for yowe
That Iason lovys so hoote?'   835
Rede for shame wexyd [that may],
And sayd, 'Certys, madame naye;
Not that I of wotte!'
Iason [e]fte she turnyd vntille
'Whate, wene thou, fole, þat ladyes wille   840
Her love be on the latte,
On the to lay for curtesye? †
Nay, i' feythe sekyrlye
Then loste they there estate.

817 wyth] *corr. from* was   822 forgate] *K.; MS* for gete   825 hur]
Followed by crossed-out a   831 Imayne] *K.; MS* aglyne   833 avowe] *K.;*
MS awove   836 that may] *K.; MS* for shame   839 efte] *K.; MS* ofte

'Be thou neuer of so grette bewte,   845
Trowes thou this lady bryght of ble
Here loue on the to laye
For fayrehedde [o]r for any largenesse?
But thow were man of proves,
I say the shortely naye!   850
Yf thou wylte love of laydes wynne,
On othere wysse þou mvste begynne:
Syr, for thy good I saye,
Gyff the to Iustys or to turnaynge
Or els lett be thy nyce lokynge,   855
For helpe the not maye.

'These brethellys now, the soth to tell,
Be they be crepte oute of the schell,
Yet mvste they laydys love,
Yff they cowthe neuer of chevalrye.   860   f. 205ʳ
Nay syr, I say the securly
Thou comyste not so above!'
Iason in a stody he sate
That mete and drynke he forgatte,
So drede hym that reprove;   865
Hym thought for tene his hert wold brest:
Ipomadon full wele wyste
She sayd for his behove.

He sayd, 'Iason, broþer, be þou stylle,
And that thou take it at no ille   870
I praye the specyallye.
Yff she haue gevyn the þis vmbrayde,
It ys for good that she hathe sayde;
Greve the not forthy.'
But welle wyst Ipomadon   875
The wordys were sayd for hym ychone,
Spokyne of that ladye,
And therefore was he shamyd full sore
That on hur durste he loke no more;
She toke good hede therby.   880

845 neuer] *Followed by crossed-out* so   847 to] *interlined, with caret after* the
848 or] *K.; MS* ar   862 above] *K.; MS* abovte   865 that] *Followed by
crossed-out* p

All dropyng downe held he his hedde,
All lykynge love fro hym is reued,
So herde his hertte was sette.
When the sopper was all done
To chambyr went that lady sone;   885
Her lordys, wythovten lette,
Toke leve and to there innys ys goone.
Before hyr knelyd Ypomadon
And hur full godely grette;

f. 205ᵛ   'Have good nyghte damysell, for I mvst wende.'   890
'What meanys this?' þought þe lady hende;
This dyde her meche yll. †

But neuer the lesse for parseyvyng sake,
Countenaunce of love she wolde non make,
But gravntyd hym leve to goo,   895
And that repent her syth full ille.
The dore tille he was comyn tille
Here eye come never hym fro.
For love she myghte stonde þer no lenger;
The lady thought for pure angur   900
Here herte wold braste in tow.
To her chambyr sche her spede,
Tomblyd downe vpon her bede
And wrythyng and wyth woo,

She callyd Imayne, here mayden fre,   905
And bade hyr [bed] shuld redy be
That sche myght bye there[inne].
No thynge sche slepyd all the nyght,
But ofte tymes turnyd and sadely syte;
Her gerdyll waxit thyn,   910
And [sayd], 'Dere God, wherefore and why
And wethyr thou thus sodaynly
To love hym schall begynne?
So worthy lordys as þou haste sene,
Pryncys and many dukys bedene,   915
And kynggys of noble [kinne];

906 bed] K.; MS sche   907 inne] inme   911 sayd] K.; MS om.
916 kinne] K.; MS lenage

'Never the les yt saw I neuer none
So godely, so fayre of flesche and bonne,
So kynde ne so curtays—
A fole so thynkys thee!   920   f. 206ʳ
Trowyste thou þat þer any oþer bee
Here loue so one hym l[ayes]?
Nay, I trowe serttys thus,
Ellys were þey ill avysed i-wys,
He ys so good all-wayes.   925
Luffe hym mvste I nedys doo,
Syn thou, hertte, ledys [me] theretoo
What so any man sayes.

'I may not do; sertys I maye
Be grette God that made me; nay,   930
I may not do thertoo!
For thou, hertte, ys so on hym sett
That hym to love þou wylt not lette
For oughte that I may doo.
Are they not sorow-worthy be lawe   935
That willfuly will ouer hem sorow drawe?'
Thus tyll herselffe sayd sche.
'Cursyd pryde, woo mot thou be;
Thou bryngys me to lowe degre
And rewes me reste and rowe.   940

'It hathe byn sayd in lest of love †
That aftur pryde comythe grette reprove
Of the wysest yet that was:
Prowde in hertte ay haue I been,
Therefore I haue a falle, I wene,   945
It nedys no helpe to asse.
Euer more worthe [ys] sempylte
Then ouerprovde or fers to be
For ay that poynte wille passe.
Had never man so grette reprove   950
As I gaffe hym this nyght fore love;   f. 206ᵛ
Why dyd I so alas?

922 Here] *followed by crossed-out* so   layes] *K.* layese; *MS* lyse   927 me] *K.;*
MS in   947 ys] *K.; MS om.*

'I myghte haue had hym when I wolde,
And all my purpos to hym tolde:
A, wetles wreche, lett bee!   955
Alas, foule, what haste thou sayde?
Reson wolde þat thou were prayde;
Thou shuld not praye parde.
A, Lord, what I haue ben fers:
I thought no [k]ynge ne prynse my perys,   960
Ne no man in no degre.
And now thys lythe be-lefte I am
Of love, and I wott not wyth whome
Ne wott not what ys hee.

'Ne sertys his name know I not,   965
Ne in what londe he shuld be sought
And he were fro me goone.
Me nedyd not to love forthy
The kyng of Pers or of Araby,
And now my hert ys tane,   970
Yet me mvst love att lowere degre.
But sertus a fayre one than hee
Was neuer of blode ne bone,
A kyndere nor a curtysure,
Thorow this world thowȝ men shuld spere;   975
That makys me make this mone.

'So fayre, so good in all thynge:
He come neuer lowere than of a kynge,
This dare I savely saye,
Who so thynkys the foll and no moo.   980
Hopys thou þat all other thynke hym soo?
I say the securly, naye.
Trowes thou any other ther bee
That lokys on hym wyth suche an eye
As thou haste done all-waye?   985
Nay I hope, as I haue roo;
Yes, i' faythe I hope ther doo,
Ellys ille avyssud were they!

f. 207ʳ

960 no kynge] *K.; MS* nothynge   963 whome] w *corr. from* h

'For there ys nother old ne yo[n]ge
But they mvst love hym ouer all thynge,   990
He ys so fayre and goode.
Yestur nyghte, settynge by Iason,
Full swettely lokyd he me vppon
That myngys thus all my mode:
But more of huntynge I hope he thoughte   995
Thenne a[n]ye loue in hertte was wroghte,
That blythe of bon and blode.
Nay, that trowe I not parde;
Why lokyd he so faste on mee
But he love vnderstoode?   1000

'He toke his leve when he shuld fare,
And sertys so dydde he neuer are
Syn fyrste that I hym [kende].
That was to his inn to goo;
Nay, in faythe I trowe not soo;   1005
It was his weye to wende!
Nay, I hope—yes, in faythe!
Yestur nyght thou lokyd on hym so lothe,
No wonder thow3 he wold wende.
Yf he goo then mvste I dye,   1010
Or els in care be-lefte am I
Foreuer wythowtyne ende!   f. 207ᵛ

'Alas, wy[ll] he þus parte awey?
Be God of hevyn, I hope naye;
Yes, in fayth he will!   1015
Thou cowde not hold thy peas, but chyde;
He were a foule and he wold byde,
Me thynkys be prove and skylle.
Yf he goo, wonder the nought;
Yestur nyght so grette shame þou hym wrought—   1020
Alas, þou dyd full ylle!
He may goo wyth an lawghyng herte,
And thou—thyselffe hit gartte—
Shalte leve in mornynge [sti]lle.

989 yonge] yomge   996 anye] amye   1003 kende] K.; MS knewe
1013 wyll] K.; MS whye   1021 Alas] Followed by crossed-out d   1024 stille]
K.; MS falle

'But yf he tomorow abyde   1025
I shall hym shewe [no] poynte of pride
Yff God will geve me grace:
Curtesly I wyll hym call,
And wyth good wille tell hym all
My covncell of þus casse.   1030
Ressone wille, it is not to layne,
He shuld not love but he be lovyd agayne;
He ys so fayre of face.
Bettur were me suche ane to haue
Then anny tow, so God me save,   1035
Me thynkys on ground þat goothe.'

Wyth hyr owne hertt þis she strave,
That rest that nyght she cowde non haue;
That for hurselffe was [bad].
That she shuld entur so farre in love,   1040
Hit shuld hur doo sum grett reprove,
She was so streytly stadde.
Wyste she on morowe how it shuld fare,
Her grette sorowe doblyde ware
And yet i-nowgh she had: 1045
Her mynde was not but for to morne.
Agayne to hym will I retorne
That nyght what lyffe he ladde.

When the chyld his leve had tane,
To his in he is gonne   1050
Wyth sorowys and sykynge sare;
He saw right nought þat was hym leffe,
All thynge he þought dyd hym greffe
In ye, bothe lesse and more.
His maystur Thelamewe he prayed   1055
That his bedde were redy arayde;
'Therein I wold I were.'
Off all the nyght he slepyd no þinge,
But lay wyth many a sore sykynge
And mornyethe aye more and more.   1060

f. 208ʳ

1026 no] *K.; MS* a   1039 bad] *K.; MS* good

'Alas foule, what alysse the,
Soo farre oute of thy owne contre
Heddur for to come?
Thou dyd as many haue done are;
Come to seke sorye care,   1065
And therof hathe þou sum.
Thou myghttys no man but þiselffe blame;
Thyne owne wille made þe come fro home,
Thereffore no man wille the moone.
As euer haue I happe or skylle,   1070
That makys þou, lady, euer[y] deyle,
Yet love makys me so d[o]me!

'Be God of hevyn, now I wott well
That she parcevys hit euery deale
How I wyth love was tane,   1075
And thoo she gyffe me wyth vpbrayde,   f. 208ᵛ
Hit was for gode þat she me sayde
Thowȝe I toke hit wyth none.
Therefore spake she all þat þing
To make me leve my long lokynge   1080
That I caste hur vppon . . .

'Thereatt I wotte welle she gave tene,
Yet be hur owne cosyn as I wene
She blamyd me forthye,
And sayd it was a skorne, parde,   1085
That anny suche brothels as we
Anny ladyes love shuld th[ye],
That nought þinkyth for to thryve,
Nor neuer gyffys in oure lyve
To no chevalrye.   1090
But ther was anoþur þinge:
On me she cast an longe lokynge;
I toke good hede therebye.

1064 are] K.; MS ayre   1071 euery] K.; MS euer   1072 dome] K.; MS
deme   1073 of] Followed by crossed-out I   1074 deale] dealee
1083 owne] Followed by crossed-out s   1087 thye] K.; MS they

'A, dere God what myghte þat meane?
I shall the tell all bedene: 1095
Younde lady ys so whyce,
In fayth she holdythe me but a foole
That shuld me melle of lovys scole
That neuer wanne losse ne price.
Now sertys þat trowe I well forthy;   1100
She lokyd and spake so angurlye,
And callyd vs euer full nyce.
Of helle yt is th[e] hottys payne
To love and be not lovyd agayne;
Thereon no wysdome lyethe!   1105

'Now hertte I praye the, lett hur be:
f. 209ʳ   Nay, þat maye I not parde
Yf thow wylte I were slayne.
Yes—nay—in faythe I!
For thou hertte artte sett so sodenly,   1110
Thou wilte not turne agayne.
Why, I wotte neuer whereffore,
But dede I had leuer I wore
Than longe to dryve this payne.
Dyd neuer love man so deyre: 1115
Had she parte yet rovghte I neyre;
In faythe then were I fayne.

'We, leef, what dyd thou in this londe?
I came to seke and I hur favnde;
That aye wille do me deyre.   1120
He fallythe that puttys hymselfe so farre
That all his lyffe louythe to warre,
Thus darre I savely swere.
Yet is ther non that wotte that,
Ne whens [I] come ne what [I] hatte   1125
So prevely I am here.
Shalte thou tell them? Sertys naye . . .
And gette the schyld and spere,

1103 the] tho   1105 on] *Followed by crossed-out* an   1123 swere] w *written in over* y   1124 Yet] e *interlined before* t   1125 I . . . I] *K.; MS* he . . . he

'And wen the pryce and þen may þou
Acordynge be to her avowe,   1130
For thou have gotton losse.
Yet in her cowrte there ys none
That so mekyll of bowrdyng can
Ne of all gamus that goothe,
Bothe wyth schyld and schafte to ryde,   1135
But so that love ys all thy pryde
Thereffore all men be thy foos: f. 209ᵛ
In erthe ys none so worthy a knyght
But yf his dede be shewyde in syght
Men will no good sopose.   1140

'And vnder pryde so arte thow hyde
That for a cowarde art thou kyde
Bothe wyth lesse and more.
And yf thou now thyselfe schuld rose,
Men wold say, "All this he dos   1145
His spendyng for to spare:
Of suche dedys have we not se[n]e
As [he] awauntys hym of, bedene;
Hym semes of bownte bare!"
Therefore thy way I rede the gange;   1150
In faythe, and thou dwell here lange
It moo the sorow full sore.

'Foole, wille thou lyghttly goo
Fro thy love, and lovys [her] soo?
Be God I may not byde.   1155
May thou goo? Sertys naye;
Yes, in faythe I hoope I maye,
Suche harmys in hertte I [hyde]!
Tomorowe thou goos yf þou haue quarte;
Yea, and thou haue anny hertte   1160
Thou turnys not that tyde.
Here has thou take thy leve for aye
That nedys behovys the love all-way,
Where thou shalte goo or ryede.

1147 sene] *K.; MS* sere   1148 he] *K.; MS om.*   1154 her] *K.; MS* the
1158 hyde] *K.; MS* take   1163 behovys] h *corr. from* b *or* v

'And here shall thou wynne no þinge   1165
But many a skorne of old and younge;
Lo, here this foole forthe.

Whoso maye be nere hys love
Su[m]tyme love it comys above,
Be they neuer so slye;   1170
And fere therefro yf he be browghte,
Then shall no man witte his thought
But his hertte and hee.
On thynge ys yf he take kepe
Sore is he bett that darre not wepe,   1175
Be God and be my lewte.

'He hathe no myghte þat mornynge gos,
Ne no ese that sorowe hathe,
This darre I trewly telle.'
Thus lythe he wrynggyng tow and fro   1180
Wyth many a sory syghyng so
And mewsus ay in mell.
A while to go he ys in wille,
Anoþur stovnde to hold hym stille
Wyth þat gay damysell.   1185
To hymselfe he told þis tale:
'Might I byde I were all hale;
Be God I may nought dwell!

'For love my herte hathe bovnde so faste
That euer more love will wyth me last   1190
To tyme that I shall dye.
It ys full swete to enter in [love],
But ay more and more it bryngys above
To sorowe, and that I se.
Whosoeuer ys takyne þerwyth   1195
Or wythe-inne hem he ly[th]e

Full sore schall bovnden be.
Wyth a sorovfull hertte I mon wende,
And sche in quarte mon leve behynde
And haue no maynde on me!'   1200

1169 sumtyme] K.; MS sunntyme   1174 take] followed by deleted hedee
1175 he] followed by crossed-out w   1192 love] K.; MS sele   1196 lythe] K.;
MS lyghte

Where he was well he ne wyste,
In towne or in wylde foreste,
So mekyll on her he þoughte:
But aye was the last ende,
He toke his purpose hole to wende   1205
And byde ne wold he noughte.
No thynge he slept of all þe nyght,
And when the day daved lyght
Vp fro his bede he soughte.
In come his maystur Thelamewe   1210
And sawe he was pale of hewe,
So grette wo love hym wroughte.

His maystur than began to spere,
And sayd, 'I praye you tell me sere,
Ayels you awoght but good?   1215
Of all this nyght ye had no reste,
But many a gresly grone [ye] vp caste
That grettly mengys my moode.'
'Thowȝe I myght for sorow synke,
Maystur, ye woll no wonder thynke   1220
And ye wyst how hit stode.'
The sothe to tell hym wold he not
For no thyng that he cowde owte,
But faynyd hym seke
That he nouȝte vnderyode.   1225

'Mayster, I schall tell þe now ryghte;   f. 211ʳ
A wonder dreme I dremed tonyghte,
Vnglade that gars me goo.
The sothe fro you I will not hyede:
Me thought my fader had loste a syde,   1230
My moder another also;
And therby darre I well warrande
They ar bothe dede or ellys ny-hande;
That warkys me all this woo.
In to my contre wille I ryde;   1235
Here wille I no lengur byde
For frenshipe nor for foo.

1217 ye] K.; MS he   1227 dremed] r corr. from e   1237 For] Corr. from Fro

'And maystur, me thynkys it were the beste
We wend into younder thyke foreste
And made vs redy there,   1240
For be God that ys but one,
Of oure wendyng he ys non
I wold the wyser were.'
Welle wend his maystur Thalamewe
The tale he told hym had byn trewe,   1245
And thedyr gan they fare:
Sone were chargyd the somors towe,
Wyth sorowfull hertt forthe they goo
And many a syghyng sore.

He for her love hymselffe lyste   1250
And she for hym, and no þing wyste
His maystur Thelamewe.
Yf they cowde neuer so mekyll of a[rt]e,
Love them betwene well ys parte,
For bothe one draught they drowe;   1255
Thowȝe grette loste of love hit garte,
f. 211ᵛ   Ayther of them hath oþers herte,
Ye trowe this tale for trewe . . .

Thowȝe this chyld his way gan fare,
His hertte he levys in ostage þere,   1260
So mekyll of hur he thought,
And hyrres away he beyrethe
That brethen hym full littill deryþe;
For why he knewe hit noughte.
He hathe the tonne and she þe tother   1265
But noþer of them comfortyd oþer,
So warely they wroughte.
Betwene them burgenyd such a bravnche,
That in þer lyves schall neuer stavnche
Tille they on bere be brought.   1270

1253 arte] *K.; MS* age   1256 loste] *Apparently written over* love

I pomadon went his waye;
 Sythen forther on the day
 Hovndys of hath he caste;
In the forest gan they fare
At the herttys to hounte þere   1275
Wyth many a bugell blaste.
A way travasyd come Iason,
And mett wyth Ipomadon
Hyinge wonder faste,
His hors trussud wyth his harnes.   1280
Iason grettly wonderd was
And of his purpos axid:

'Whedur broþer, whedder arte þou bovn?
Shall þu not wyth vs to the towne?'
'Sertys, Iason, nay: 1285
Suche a dreme I dremyd tonyght
That here to dwell I haue no myghte
For noughte þat I can saye;
Into my contre mvste m[e] goo.'   f. 212ʳ
'Then schall I wyth the wend also,   1290
Be God þat owth this day.'
'Nay brother, so may it not be,
But I schall come agayne to the
Hereafter while I may.'

'Hathe anny man for the mysdoone?'   1295
'Nay, be hym þat made the mone.'
'Why shuld thou wend thanne?
Ys none so grette in all this londe
That ye dyd greue, I vnderstonde,
That bargynne myght he banne.   1300
So grette right in my lady lyethe
And wyth her artte þou holdyn a pryce
Moste of anny man;
Therefore turne agayne wyth me,
Or sertys I shall wend wyth the   1305
For any crafte thou can.'

1282 purpos] _K.; MS_ purposud   1289 me] _K._ I; _MS_ m

'Iason, this ys not to tell,
Here may I no lenger dwell:
Tonyght so dremyd me,
That I mvst nede wend my waye.'   1310
'Be grette God that oweth þis day,
Then schall I wend wyth the.'
'Nay, turne agayne brother dere,
And on my behalve grette welle thy Fere
And serue to hande that free.   1315
Syn thou wold wynde wyth me so fayne,
Now in faythe I come agayne
When it may better bee.'

'Now syn I shall behynde þe dwelle,
Thy name I praye the thow me tell   1320
And where I may the fynde.'
'Nay Iason, that do I not
Be hym that made vs boþe of noughte,
All this world to wynne.'
'Alas brother, what may þis bee?   1325
Ye doo but skorne me now I see;
All frenshipe levythe behynde!
Be the grette God þat all hath wrought,
Now se I wele ye love me nought!'
Wyth that he waxyd nere blynde.   1330

Wythe a sorowfull hertte sayd he þan,
'Yt is full ille to know a mon;
For no thyng ye me l[o]ve.'
'Iason, brother wythoute blame,
Yf I shuld tell the my name   1335
Yt turnyd to no behove.
Kys me therefore and haue good day;
Be the grette God þat oweth þis day
I do it for no reproffe.' . . .

Ipomadon this is way is paste,   1340
And Iason thorow the forest faste

1333 love] *K.; MS* leve

f. 212ᵛ

He hyeth hym wyth good spede;
Wythe sorowfull herte and stille mornynge
He sawe right nought to his lykynge
But to the tentys he yede.   1345
In the mornyng yerlye þat lady rose,
Oute of her pavelyone on she goos,
Abowte her she toke good heede
Yf sche sawe oughte the straunge valet:
To love hym t[h]owgh hur hertte [b]e sette,   1350 f. 213ʳ
Euyre more has she dredde,

That he shuld be frome hur went.
So co[m]e her cosyne ouer the bent
And on his foote he lightte.
'What tydyngys Iasone, I the praye?'   1355
'Madame yf I the sothe schall saye,
No wors be they ne myghte.'
'How soo cosyne, be God alonne?'
'Your valette, damysell, ys agoone;
Ofte grette you wele that wyghte.'   1360
'Whiche?' sche sayd. 'þe valet straunge;
Ye of hym schall haue chalenge
Nether be day ne nyght.'

'Yes he goone?' 'Madame, yea.'
'Whotte thow o[gh]te why?' 'Madame nay,   1365
As haue I Ioye or blis.'
'Dyd anny man hym ought but righte?'
'Nay, but a dreme he dremyd to[n]yghte
Hathe made hym wend i-wys.'
She hard neuer tydyngys are   1370
That sche was halffe so sory fore,
But he pursevyd not thus.
She answeryd, thow sche were woo;
'Ye cosyne, lett hym goo;
Good aventure mut be his.   1375

1342 hyeth] *Followed by crossed-out* wyth   1350 thowgh] *K.; MS* towgh   be] *K.;*
MS he   1353 come] *K.; MS* conne, o *corr. from* a   1358 God] *Followed by*
deleted for   1362 schall] *Followed by* ye shalle   1365 oghte] *K.; MS* ofte
1368 nyghte] myghte

'But has he trussyd his harnys?'
'Ye, and his maystur also his.'
Then was sche woo allweye:
Thowʒe sche lett as sche [n]e rovghte,
The contrary in hur hertte sche þouʒte;   1380

For sorowe mornyd þat maye.
'Iason now thyselfe maye se
That þou wyth me, ne I wyth the
May not won allwaye.
And ofte ys sayd in old saw,   1385
"Lett hym goo—he was a felowe",
Good cosyn I the praye.'

Iason turnyd wyth mekyll payne;
The lady callyd hym efte agayne,
'Syr, spyrd thou not his name?'   1390
'Ye, but he wold not me tell.'
'Alas that ys a payne of helle!
Why dyd he so, for schame?'
'Thow my hertte wold barste in tow,
I [ne] myght of hym haue moo;   1395
I haue told you the same.'
Iason wepte and fro her turnyd,
And sche into her tente and mornyd
And faste herselffe gan blame:

'Lo foule, what sayd I the?   1400
Now hath þou lost thy love parde
Foreuer, that wotte I wele.
Fole, thou haste thy fayrehedde fylyd,
And wyth eye thyselffe haste gylyde;
Thou wotte hit ilke a dele.'   1405
She tomblyd downe vpon her bedde,
And sonyde thryse or sche myʒte steede
Wyth syghyng and onskylle.
Be that sche was in state comyn agayne,
Wyth that come hyr maydon Imayne   1410
[Vn]to that damysell,

1379 ne] *K.; MS* ye   1391 Ye] *written over 'ser' abb.*   1395 ne] *K.; MS om.*
1411 Vnto] And

And sayd, 'Damysell, for God avowe, f. 214ʳ
For Goddis loue, what aylys you
To make this grette mornynge?
Tell me, lady fayre and fre, 1415
Yf there myghte anny comforte be
Of thy sore syghynge.
Ofte sythe it dothe men good i-wis
To trewe felows a tale to rehersse,
For covnsell askyth suche a thynge.' 1420
'Alas Imayne that I was borne;
My pryde wille make me be forlorne
And to my dede me brynge.'

'Whate pryde, lady, for God avowe?
That hard I speke neuer or nowe 1425
Of no man leuynge are.'
'What pryde? Ye of love:
That bryngys me vnder and not above
Wyth many a syghyng sare.'
'Leve lady, whome loue yee?' 1430
'In faythe I can not tell thee,
Shuld I be dede þerfore,
Where he ys, ne ys name nat;
And wette thou well thyselfe, for þat
My mornynge is the more.' 1435

'I praye you tell me, good madame,
That ye so love, what ys his name?
Whennes he be here abovte?'
She sayd, 'It is the straunge va-'
But syghyng made þe word breke in tow, 1440
She myght not bryng it owtte;
And aftur that bydyng of þat brayde,
Another tyme efte sche sayde, f. 214ᵛ
It made her low to lowte:
'Ymayne, do thereto a 'lete', 1445
And sythyn the wordys together set,
And there ye have no dowte.'

1439 va-] valett

Ymayne sayd, 'Be my lewte,
To witte what his name myght be
I can no reason fynde, 1450
For att the fyrste word sayd ye "va",
A[nd] sethyn afturward "a",
A "let" ther come behynde;
And yf I them togeddur sett,
Then it was the straunge valet 1455
Or els ye wantyde wynde.'
'Ya systur, ther wantyd alacke;
For syghynge the word in sonder brake,
In bale me thought I br[yn]de.

'When I shuld althur beste have spokynne, 1460
Syghynge it hathe asonder brokyne
Thate oute it myghte not gette,
And therefore do as I the bydde:
Leve the syghyng in the myde
And them togeddur sett, 1465
And thare the not fayle of þat,
To wytte his righte name and whatte he hate,
That me wythe greve hathe grete.'
Ymayne parcevyd it euery deyell,
And sayd, 'Now lady, wot I wele 1470
That is the straunge valet.'

f. 215ʳ

'Yea Ymayne, he ys goone,
And I am lefte here alone
Wythe herte as hevy as ledde:
I se hym neuer, so wot I well, 1475
Therfore thys syghynge and vncell
Wille drawe me to my dede.
Yestur nyghte I ouer mekell toke on me
When I spake to you parde,
Thate garte you be so redde, 1480
And to Iason, that no cope hade,
I toke in good kepe what I seyde;
That made me efte sythe [grede].

1452 And] *K.; MS* A   1459 brynde] brede   1483 grede] *K.; MS* That
made me wayle efte sythe

'He lokyd on me full lovely;
Wyth wrong blamyd I you forthy;   1485
That made hym wende his way.'
Ymayne sayde, 'I toke goode tente,
But I wyste not what it ment,
Be God that owthe þis day.
Now I wot I am apayde;   1490
Well was euer that word sayde,
For savely I darre saye
Wythinne fortenyghte ye schall hym see,
The beste of all knyghttys þat may be;
My lyff þat darre I well lay.'   1495

'Why, dere systur, trows þou so?'
'Ye in fayth, þat made hym goo,
I darre welle warrand þus:
So fayre, so curtes as he ys,
Was neuer wythouten proves   1500
But hopyng ay was hys.
He corded not to your avowe: f. 215ᵛ
That wotte I welle hathe made hym now
Wende his way i-wys,
For to gette hym loos and pryce,   1505
So ys he worthy, ware and wysse,
As haue I Ioye and blysse.

'And forthe, lady fayre and fre,
For Goddis love, of better comforte be ye
And lette this greve ouer gange: 1510
When he haue provyd hymselffe a knyghte,
Of all other moste of myghte,
He dwellythe not fro you longe.'
Full welle þat lady vnderstoode
The worddus of Ymayne dyd her good;   1515
Syghynge sche sayd amonge,
'My dere syster, blessud mut thou be,
For righte wele haste þou comforte me
Of thoughttys þat on me thronge;

1508 forthe] o *mistakenly crossed out*   1513 fro] *Corr. from* for

'But Ymayne, be the heyvyn one,   1520
Lord but hym wille I haue none,
Emperoure nor kynge.'
This comfortyd hur þe lady gent.
Ipomadon his way ys went
Wyth many a sory syghyng;   1525
Stravngly in his herte he mornythe,
And full ofte sythes ageyne he tornyþe
Wyth full longe lokynge.
A while he is in wille to byde,
Another stovnde forthe to ryde,   1530
Suche þoughttys vppon hym thr[y]ngge.

Thus of love he lernythe the artte,

f. 216^r

And well I trowe he hathe his parte
Whereeuer he goo or ryde;
And hur suche dere it dothes,   1535
Her [th]ar not of her parte make no rows
Yf sche in bowre abyde.
His maystur Thalamewe vndertoke,
And hevely he sawe hym loke,
And mercy to hym he cryedde.   1540
He sayd, 'Tell me ilke a deyle,
For be your covntenavnce wotte I well
Grette hevynes ye hyde.'

'Maystur, so haue I nede of masse
For ouer mekyll love it ys,   1545
I may no lengur layne.'
'Whome love ye ser, be God avowe?'
'Therefore maystur I telle it you:
She dothe me all this payne.'
He tolde hym all her love lokyng,   1550
And how sche made hur chastenyng
Be Iason and Ymayne,
And all the purpose to the ende.
His maystur sayd, 'So God me mend
Sone, hereof am I fayne: 1555

1522 nor] *Preceded by crossed-out* or   1531 thryngge] *K.; MS* throngge
1536 thar] *K.; MS* far   1551 made] *Followed by* c

'Who so louythe schall lykynge haue
Worschipe to wynne, so God me saue,
And hit may moste avayle.
For ofte sythes pryde of paramowers
Makys men to payne them to grette honourys   1560
And hold them in battayle:
Lett them be never lengur badde
But knyghttys anon that they were made   f. 216ᵛ
And put you in travayle.
Wend euer more fro londe to londe   1565
To gette you pryce and loos wyth hande
Where knyghttys will oþur assayle.

'Ye wotte well sche hathe made a vowe;
[S]he may take no man for her prowe
But yf it be the beste.   1570
Soo wynne you pryce and then maye ye
To that avow acordyd bee,
That to weld wyth peas and reste:
Fro hit come to the ladyes eyre
In feld how boldely ye you bere,   1575
And holdyn be the worthyeste,
[I] darre say savely for her sake,
Lorde but you sche wille none take
Her fayethe vppon to reste.

'Syr, louers euer more besy is   1580
To gette them loos and worthynes,
Belouyd for they wolde bee.
Yf he before was neuer not worthe,
Fro tyme he louys, he puttys hymselffe forthe
And sythes [wax]ys he   1585
The wyser and the worthyer all-way.'
'Maystur, sothe ys that you say
Be God and by my lewte:
And he wille gyffe me grace þertoo,
My besynes schall I doo   1590
And that schall ye well se.'

1569 She] K.; MS he   1577 I] K.; MS A   1585 waxys] K.; MS puttys

He comforte hym and forth gan ryde,
But sone wythin a littill tyde
Come there new ty[thande]:
Welle forthe on the day   1595
Saw they come be the waye
A chylde full faste rennande.
A messyngere it semyd he were,
For be his syde a box he bare,
A schorte spere in his hande;   1600
And when they were togeddur mette,
The chyld them full gladlye grette;
Stone stille they st[an]de.

Ipomadon sayd, 'I praye the,
Fro when[s] come þou and what contre,   1605
And wheddur wilte þou fare?'
'Certys syr, I come oute of Poyll:
I have travelyd many a soyle
Wyth sorowys and syghynge sore.
Thes xii monthe oute but iii dayes   1610
I haue goone many dyueres wayes
Where þorowe I wery sore,
For to seke a straunge valett,
And for I haue not wyth hym mette,
My mornynge ys the more.'   1615

'What ys his name?' 'Ipomadon.'
'Syr, for God that is but one,
What were thy wille wyth hym?'
'In faythe syr, when I toke my waye,
Sore seke his modur lay   1620
Takynne in lyethe and lymme.'
'Lo maystur,' quod Ipomadon,
'Come never sorow be it one
But there come mo full gryme:
I wotte never what happe I hadde   1625
Off the dreme when I the lesynge made.'
Wythe that his eyne wax dymme.

1594 tythande] K.; MS tydynge   1603 stande] K.; MS stoode
1605 whens] when   1613 valett] Preceded by a   1623 one] onee

In sowunynge downe he tomblyd swythe;
Thereof his mayster was vnblythe
And fro his hors he lyghte. 1630
In armus he toke hym vp agayne
And comfortted hym wyth all his mayne,
But full sore he syghte.
'Now dere sone, lett thys gronyng ouer goo,
I wold not se the sowune soo 1635
Fore good men gyff me myghte.'
Whan he myghte of sorow slake,
The way into Poyle they toke:
Yet lyves his moder brightte.

To the citte of Barlett comyn ar they; 1640
There his moder seke laye
Wythe many a grevous peyne.
Downe before hyr gan he knele
And to comfortte her he thought full wele;
Thereof sche was full fayne. 1645
'Dere so[n]ne, welcome mot thou be.
A counsell wille I telle to thee,
No lengur I may it layne:
Of my fynger þou take a rynge,
And kepe it well for any þinge 1650
Wyth myghte and all thy mayne.

'Ipomadon, thou has a brother,
But loke thou telle it to no noþure,
I warne the welle off that;
For certys thy fader wot yt not, 1655
Ne none in erthe þat euer was wroughtte f. 218ʳ
Notte passynge thre.
Whate man in erthe þat euer he be
That knoweth þis ringe, thy broþer is he,
I do the welle to witte. 1660
Parte nott therwyth forthy;
Thy brother schall the know thereby
Yf ever God wolle þat ye mette.

1646 sonne] somne   1650 And] *Followed by crossed-out* A

'He gaffe hit me at our departyng,
Hit was our laste tokenynge;   1665
The tharre not farther aske.'
Then was Ipomadon glade,
And as grette sorowe in hertte hadde,
He syhyde and sayd 'alas';
Ioyefull he was that he had a broþur,   1670
And well more sory of that othere,
He wyste never where he was.
His moder gaffe hym hyr blessynge
And dyede wythoute more tareynge
And fro this world can passe.   1675

Ryghte sory was Ipomadon,
And so was all the courte eche-chone
For his moder was dede:
Women wepte and colovre caste,
They sayd for sothe sche was þe best   1680
That euer on erthe myghte trede;
All that hyr seruyde before
Grette gyftys sche gave bothe lasse and more
Of syluer and gold so redde.
More to say it is ryght noughte;   1685
To her beryinge they here broughte
Wyth hertte as hevy as lede.

Ipomadon wolde no lenger abyde,
But prayed his fader at that tyde
To graunt hym the order of knyght,   1690
And he assent wyth noble chere:
Abowte his sonne that hym [was] dere,
He gyrdythe a bronde full bryght.
The order of his fader he tas;
That kepes he welle were he gas,   1695
Ryghte yt wolde wyth all his myghte.
Thyrty chyldorne wythowten moo
He made knyghttys for his sonnus sake also
That worthy were and wyghte.

1692 was] K.; MS om.

Fayne wolde Ipomadone   1700
His maystur had the ordure tane:
He sayd schortely nay,
For he knew noþer be northe nor sowthe
Non so welle that hym serue covthe
As he dyd nyghte and day,   1705
And levere hym were his seruaunt be
Thanne to be made a knyghte of fee;
'So haue I louyd the aye.'
He sayd, '[I] haue byn [your] mayster,
And yf ye fynde any trestyer   1710
Then wille I wynd my waye.'

'Nay dere maystur Thalamewe;
Ye haue byn to me trusty and trewe
In all werkys that ye haue wroughte.
Therefore a gyfte I schall you gyffe: 1715
Whylys God send me grace to leve,   f. 219ʳ
Fayle you schall I not.
A, maystur, who seruys longe,
Me thynke men dyd hym mekyll wronge
When the laste to the ende were broughte,   1720
Yff he his seruys longe schold lose;
He myght thynke, as I sopose,
All to sone he thedyr sowghte.'

Ipomadon thus is a knyghte made;
All that he wold to wille he hadde   1725
Of hors and noble armowre.
There he wold no lengur byde,
But toke his leve and forthe gan ryde
Att kyng and berde in bowre.
He travellyd euer fro land to lande   1730
To wynne his los and price wyth hande
Where styff men were and st[owr]e;
In Brettayne, Fraunce and Lumbardy,
In Allmayne and in Arabye
The[y] hylde hym for the floure.   1735

1709 I...your] K.; MS ye...my   1710 trestyer] r corr. from e   1718 who] w
corr. from h   1732 stowre] K.; MS stronge   1735 They] K.; MS The

Whereeuer he came at any werre,
Euer more the price away he bere,
So boldely he hym bare:
He wex so worthy a man of hande,
Agayne his stroke myght no man stonde,   1740
He set them so sade and s[a]re.
But so prevyd was Ipomadon,
What he was there wyste no man
Nother lesse ne more,
And also his men comaundyd he   1745
They schuld tell no man of no degre
f. 219ᵛ   Off whens ne whatte they were.

Men covthe not calle hym there he came
But 'the worthy knyghte þat had no name'
In cuntres fere and nere.   1750
In suche londys where he come inne,
Bothe love and los he gan to wynne
Off lordys and ladys clere;
Los of lordys and love of ladyes,
Of gentille damysellys and curtays   1755
That grette and worthy were.
But euer more in his hert he þouȝte
That love be reson myghte he nowghte
No woman but the Fere.

But noþur wyste of othere wille   1760
But ovthere suffyrd grette ille.
Ryght longe this lyff they leede,
And also thynkys this bryght of ble,
Knyght in erthe but it were hee
Shuld neuer to wyff her wedde.   1765
Ipomadon now leve we here
And speke we of that lady clere
That is strangely stade . . .

Tow yere fel[l] yt after sete
That went was þat straunge valet—   1770

1741 sare] K.; MS sure   1751 inne] With redundant abb. for n/m   1769 fell]
Kp.; MS felt

The lady levyd stylle—
In Calabur grett warre þer rosse;
Eche man on othere gosse
And mekyll blod they spylle.
The grette them gedyrs on a day,   1775
Eche man to othere gan saye,
'Oure lady dothe full ylle
That she will not take a lord
To mayneteyme vs in good acord.   f. 220ʳ
We will goo witte hure wille,   1780

'For folly makythe she wyth her pride;
Oure lordys be storde on yche a syde,
Thereof she maye thynke synne.'
The[y] went to that lady hynde
And told hyr all the tale to þe ende   1785
What care that they were ynne;
They sayd, but she a lord take,
That they shuld þer omage make
To kyngys of other kynne.
Well more sorowe then she hadde;   1790
These tydyngys makythe here vnglad,
Here hertte for bale wold brenne.

She sayd, 'Lordys bothe more and lasse,
Wille I witte sothe it ys
This tale ye haue me told.   1795
But of o poynte I you praye:
Of respyte tille the xviii day;
Your will fayne werke I wold.'
Therewyth grochyees boþe old and younge
And sayd, 'In oure longe tareynge   1800
Comes greves monye a fold.'
Vp startte an er[l]e Ser Dryas,
A worthy man of warre he was,
And spekys wordys bolde.

1772 In] *Followed by crossed-out* cl   1784 They] There   1798 Your] *Otiose*
flourish on u   1800 tareynge] K.; *MS* tarerynge, *extra curl on* n   1802 erle]
K.; *MS* erke   Dryas] K.; *MS* adryas

He sayd, 'Be Gode that syttys above,   1805
Ye shew your lady lyttille love
That you so herttly preysse:
The strengythe theeff þat euer myȝte leve
Be the lawe ye muste hym gyffe
Respytte VIII dayes.'   1810
Yche man þouȝte he sayd but skylle,
'Lett this lady haue hure wille;
It was hyr woo all-wayes.'
To hyr chambure gan she g[ang]e
Wepyng, and hure handys wrange   1815
And on here bedde hur layes.

Wythe that come hyr mayde Ymayne
And sayd, 'Madame, hit is not to layne;
Ye can not haue your peasse.'
'Imayne, systur, woo ys me,   1820
My lordys will make me weddyd be;
That makes my sorowes incresse.
For me were better all to leesse,
Anoþur loue then I shuld chese . . .
Yf þou wylt, syster, that I leve,   1825
Sum good counsell þou mvste me geve,
How I may make them seasse.'

Imayne sayd, 'By my lewte,
And yff ye will do after me
It shall turne to no skathe;   1830
Suche rede I hope I shall you geve
That yt shuld be while we bothe leve
A lykynge for vs bothe.
Wyth fayre wordys ye shall them answere,
Therewyth all there ynne to blere;   1835
Yff they be neuer so w[ro]the,
And yff they all there lyff chyd,
Tille that ye wille, ye shall abyde,
Whethere they be leeffe ore lothe!

1814 gange] *K.; MS* goone   1818 layne] *Otiose flourish on* n   1824 shuld]
Followed by crossed-out leesse   1826 mvste] *Extra minim in* m   1834 them]
Corr. from then   1836 wrothe] *K.* wrathe; *MS* worthee

'The kyng of Sissille ys your eyme,   1840
And welle th[ey] wotte ye haue your reme
Off hym, bothe farre and nere.
Off the kyng of Sissille haue they drede:
Ageynste hym dare they not ryde
But yff they bydde warre.   1845
And yf they will haue it at a[n]nye ende,
Messengers behouythe them sende
To kynge Malengere . . .

'The wordyste of the barons sv[m] †
And yf the kyng will hedur come   1850
Then shall ye not wythstonde;
When he ys in [t]his contre,
At his will well ye maryede be,
Ellyes forfytte your londe;
And in that tyme ye maye gette   1855
Sum tydyngys of your straunge valette
Yff he be oughte nere-hande,
Or els caste anoþur wile
How ye maye farther them begyle
Thus to be taryande.'   1860

'Imayne, sister, wythoutyn fayle
Thus is a full good counsell,
Whereffore blessud mot þou bee.'
Here barons come the XVIII day
And sayd, 'Ladye, the sothe ye vs saye;   1865
Your will fayne wete wold wee
Whome ye wold to husbond haue.'
She sayd, 'Lordys, so God me save,
Alse wille as witte ye   f. 221ᵛ
That all my londys farre or nere   1870
I hold of kynge Melangere,
And also my eyme ys hee,

1840 eyme] *Corr. from* eme   1841 they] *K.; MS* thye   1846 annye] *K.;*
MS amnye   1849 svm] *Kp.; MS svn*   1852 this] *K.; MS* his
1861 sister] *Written above crossed-out* saythe, *with caret*

'And yf [I] werke agayne his wille,
He will take it to grette ille
And wherevpon me bynde;   1875
Therefore yf ye will wynd hym too,
R[i]ght as he byddythe me will I doo,
Be þe leeffe on the lynde.'
Therewyth grogydde boþe all and sum
And sayden, 'In long tarying will come   1880
Grette noyse, and that we fynde.'
Yff one or too þerof was payde,
Othere III or IIII sayd,
'Oure happe comythe euer behynde.'

A noble erle startte vp anon,   1885
His name was Ser Am[f]yon,
A bigge man and a bold,
And was wyse wythoute leasse;
He hatyd warre and louyde peasse,
For why he was full olde,   1890
Moste he cowthe of awncyente layes.
Wythe angrye hertte he sayes,
'Be hym that all shall wyld,
Vs may thynke it ille sett of ilke a syde
That [to] our lady wyth her pryde   1895
Thes be we hare beholde!

'Thus maye she dryve vs to delaye
This fyve yere euery daye
f. 222ʳ   While she full sone maye sete;
But sorowe haue [I], I saye for me,   1900
And hangyd by I on a tre
And I suffyre ite!
But she will a lord take
That maye peas amonge vs make
I do you welle to witte,   1905
Be the troughe of my right hand . . .
Right sone she shall be quyte.

1873 I] K.; MS om.   1877 Right] rght, with horizontal stroke above g
1886 Amfyon] Amyson   1895 to] om.   1900 I] K.; MS they

'More than I haue maye I not coste,
Nee lesse more then I haue loste;
My londys arre fro me tane.   1910
Full lykkely lordys she myghte haue had
That off her wold be full glad;
In Almayene mone one,
In Poyle, where noble kyngys ar kend.'
He sayd wel sother then he wend   1915
Be [God] þat ys but one;
Many doughtty wold her haue,
But none so fayne, so God me save,
As wold Ipomadon!

He sayd sothe and wyste it noughte,   1920
And, as the lady in her hertte þoughte,
She wold haue hym full fayne.
Amphyvn was grevyd full sore;
For angur he myghtte speke no more
But sette hym downe agayne.   1925
Syr Drias st[er]tte vp anone
And sayd, 'Me wondyrs, Ser Amphyvn,
As be I sauyd fro pyne,
That þou nedyste medull m[a]ste;
Syr, yff þou wilte vowe the chaste,   1930 f. 222ᵛ
Me thynkythe wyth all thy mayne

'Thou shuldys werke as thy lady wold.
But welle I wite þou artte so old,
Thou yrkys of armore clere.
Wythin this xxᵗⁱ yere and towe,   1935
Thou wold, or thou had sayd soo,
To haue byne layd one beyre.
Thou artte of old auncetrye,
And wythholdon, cecurlye,
Grette f[e]ys wyth the Fere: 1940
Thou ovghte to fyght for hyr sake
Yff she no husbond wold take
Off all this vii yere!'

1916 God] that   one] onee   1926 stertte] strette   1929 maste] mvste
1933 old] wold   1938 old] *Followed by* m   1940 Grette] *Kp.*; *MS preceded by* A
feys] *Kp.*; *MS* foys

Bothe eer[l]e and bold barone
Sawe she askyd but resone;   1945
'And sothe it is that she sayes:
Ageynste his wille and we haue done,
The kynge for ille wille take hit sone
And wherevpon vs reysse.
Thow shalte goo, Ser Amphyvn,   1950
And off thy felowes I shall be one
That shall passe on this weyes;
Lette se of all this comynte
Who shall wend wyth [thee] and mee.'
This word no thynge [hy]m payes.   1955

Amfyon waxyd nye wood for wrothe,
And to Dryas swore his othe:
'Bee God in maygeste,
Were I strenghe as I haue bene
Thy skornynge wordys all bedene   1960
Dere boughte sholde they bee:
In feythe, or I frome the youde
I shuld se thy hertte blod,
Elys I hange full hye!'
Dreas wax nere woode forthy   1965
And sayd, 'Old favelard, I the defye
That thou maye do to mee;

'Thow artte old and dotyste faste,
And welle I wotte þou artte agaste;
Thow lyste not to fyghtte,   1970
"Yett was þ[ere] neuer sete in feld
So harde ware I feld vnder shelde
No be day ne be nyghtte!"—
Ille thow kythes, and that is sene,
Off thy wordynes þat þou haste done,   1975
Be grette God moste off myghtte!
But wylle I wotte this is thy thoughte;
Thow wodeste haue vs þat know it nov3te
Wen thow hade ben lyghte.

f. 223ʳ

1944 eerle] Eerke   1953 comynte] K.; MS comynteys   1954 thee] K.:
MS om.   1955 hym] K.; MS them   1957 othe] othee   1958 maygeste]
ge written above   1971 þere] þou   1973 be¹] be be

'For wee ar younge and thow arte olde;   1980
Thou woldyste lede vs as thou wolde,
Than wold thou thynke it welle.
Att thy wille thou woldyste vs haue;
Nay, doter, or thow haue,
Sorowe shalte thowe feelle!   1985
Here ys none that onyes the þanke
Then the kyng had forf[e]te by brym and banke
Here landys euery deylle.
Yff thou goo waylond wood for woo,
On this message shall thow goo   1990
Be God and seynt Myghell.'

Full wele the barons vnderstode
Dryas reasone was trewe and goode,   f. 223ᵛ
For in ther hertte they þought,
Yff they wrought agaynste h[i]s wille   1995
The kyng wold grettly take it to ille.
Wherevpon they broughte
Syr Dryas and Ser Amfyon,
The thryd hight Ser Madon;
Thre better knewe they noughte . . .   2000

They trayveld so day by day
That into Sesille come they
To Melyaȝer the [hende].
They told there message all and sum,
Who his nece prayed hym to come   2005
Righte as hure faythefull frende,
And when the kynge wyst all togeder
Whereffore they were come thedyre,
He sayd, 'Serys, home ye wend;
I shall come be a sertayne day   2010
And helpe to bryng, yf þat I maye,
Your grette debate to ende.'

1987 the] *Followed by* e *written over* n; *both crossed out*   kyng] kyngys   forfete] *K.;*
MS forfote   1995 his] *K.; MS* hes, *with* s *corr. from* r   1997 they] *followed by*
otiose flourish   1998 Syr] *preceded by crossed-out* & *in margin*   2003 hende] *K.;*
MS kyng

The mensyngers were full glad
Of that answere that they had
To spede them home ageyne.   2015
Whanne þey come to þe lady clere,
Whateuer she þouȝte, she made good chere
And lete as she were fayne,
But she ne rekky[s]—wheder he come or not
Ageynste the tyme he come movȝte—   2020
To trappen hym wyth a trayne.

f. 224ʳ   Kyng Melyngere wold not foregeete;
The same day that he had sette
He came wyth all his meyne.

His young knyghttys all levythe at home;   2025
The oldyste wyth hym thedur come
That wyse were all-waye.
They trayueld so be see and sonde,
That into Calabur-londe
At the laste come they   2030
To [Ca]nders, that riche citte—
In erthe ther myghte no bettur be—
Ther that lady laye.
When she hard tell hyr eyme was come,
To welcome hym the waye she nome   2035
In a riche araye.

The lady of her eyme was glad;
Att there metynge grette myrthe þey made,
Into a towre they youde.
Ioyfull was that lady clere   2040
Off Syr Gabanus, hyr cosyn dere,
That he was stalleworthy on stede;
Wyth myrthe they draw to ende þat nyȝte.
On morowe, whane day was lyghte,
Kynge Melangere toke hede;   2045
Into an erber fayre and grene
The kynge youde wyth his knyghttys kene
That doughtty was off dede.

2019 rekkys] rekkyd   not] *Followed by otiose flourish*   2025 levythe] *Followed by*
crossed-out all   2031 Canders] *K.;MS* Tynders

There lighttys he downe kynge Melangere;
Sone aftur comythe that lady dere   2050
Wyth many a worthy wyghte;
xxx^{ti} maydons all bedene,
The sympelyste seme[d] to be a quene,   f. 224^v
Off ble they were so bryghte.
Formeste she hurselff was: 2055
Her beheld all in that place,
Kyng, baron and kn[y]ghte.
They sayd, 'No wo[n]dere yf she be daungerus
To take an onworthy spowsse,
Be grette God moste of my3te!'   2060

There was no man than on lyve
That myghtte he[r] bewte dyscryve;
So made off blode and bone.
Had Ipomadone þan here sene,
I trowe full lothe hym wold haue byne   2065
Hyr love to haue forgoone.
Also there was in place
A chyld that full witte was,
H[ys] cosyn [E]gyon,
That he hymselff had sent thedure   2070
To spere and to herkyne all togedyr
Whedur she had lord or none.

Hur eyme she full godely hym grette;
He roosse and by his syde hur sette,
That ferlye fayre off face.   2075
Bothe barons and bachelers,
And laydys and squyers,
They presyd in to place
[To witte] whome she wold to lord take,
That so mony hathe forsake   2080
Off worthy men that was.
Vp roosse Ser Amphivn

2053 semed] *K.*; *MS* seme   2057 knyghte] kynghte   2058 wondere]
womdere   2062 That] *corr. from* there   her] *K.*; *MS* he   2069 Hys] *K.*;
MS her   Egyon] *K.*; *MS* Sygyon   2079 To witte] *MS om.*

And spake before them euery chone,
Trewe in hertte [he was]:

'Syr kyng, all þ[i]s comente   2085
Be one assent sent after the
To witte þ[i]s ladyes wille,
Whome she wold take to husbonde
To maynteyme vs and hyr lond,
Our stryffe to stabull and stille.   2090
Righte godely she is benoyed,
On ilke syde her londys ar stroyed;
That maye vs lyke full ylle.
Many worthy wold here haue
But þer is non, so God me save,   2095
Yet þat she will corde t[ill]e.

'There is þe kyngys sonne of Spayne;
I wotte he wold haue hyr full fayne,
Right bold and full hardy.'
Vp the[n] stertte Ser Dryas,   2100
That rede for angur wax is face,
And sayd, 'Faylard, fye,
I praye to God ille mot þou lyke
For I am no eratyke,
I meyne for my ladye!   2105
Be the grette God þat all hathe wrouȝte,
All men maye see þou louyste her nouȝte;
Well I wotte therebye.

'There shall neuer eretyke, as I haue roo,
Worshipe to no woman doo,   2110
They are so wykkyd and ille;
For leuer th[ey] had wyth lassis to loure
Than to Ioye wyth byrdys in bowre—

That ladyes loue be skylle.
Bettur one that she chesse hureselff   2115
Than she shuld do off oþur twellffe

2084 he was] *K.*; *MS* ye is, *preceded by crossed-out* he   2085 þis] þs
2087 þis] þs   2089 maynteyme] *Followed by crossed-out* h   2096 tille] *K.*;
MS towe   2100 then] *K.*; *MS* them   2112 they had] *K.* they hadde; *MS*
thou haddyst

That men constrayns hyr tille.
Syr kynge, yff she a lord shall haue,
I rede she chesse hym, soo God me save,
Be hur owne good wille.'   2120

All this harde kynge Malengere;
He goos to that lady clere
And sayd, 'Nese, what seye ye?
Yff ye will acorde theretoo,
Me wold thynke hit were to doo;   2125
In peas the[n] myghte ye be.'
In a stody stille she satte,
And sayd a longe while after þat,
'Syr, be me lewte,
I wille werke after þe wille of yours,   2130
But for to loue paramowers
I haue chosyne thre:

'One is the kynge of [R]osy,
Another the dukys sonne of Normandy,
The thryd of Irelond he is.   2135
I wott neuer, by the holy goste,
Whiche of hem thre I loue moste
As I haue mede off me[sse];
Thereffore a poynte I you pray
Off ryspyte tille the morowe day   2140
That I in hertte maye gesse
Wheche of them thre I love beste.'
To gar them bydde this wile she keste;
They graunte bothe more and lesse.

Wythe myrthe þat day þey dreve to ende;   2145   f. 226ʳ
Into hyr chambyr þat lady wende
And [Imayne] to hur callyd:
'A dere systyr, wo ys mee;
How maye I now excuse me?
My care is many a fold,   2150

2126 then] *K.; MS* them   2132 thre] r *corr. from* e   2133 Rosy] *K.; MS*
Iosy   2134 the] *followed by crossed-out* kyng   2135 he is] *K.* he es; *MS* is he
2138 messe] mercye   2147 Imayne] *K.; MS* a maydon

For me had leuer all forgoo
Another love or I shuld t[a];
Right now dye I wold!
Be God þat ordeyned all þinge,
Lang-eyre I made a lowde lesynge,   2155
That tale that I them told,

'That I hadde chosyne thre.
There shall non haue my herte but hee,
Whatte that euer I sey.
But Imay[ne], wythouten fayle,   2160
Ye mvste geve me sum good counseyle
How I begyle them maye,
For me were leuer all forsake
Then oþur loue I shuld take,
Be hym that owethe þis daye.'   2165
'I not,' she sayd, 'be my lewte,
I [n]ot in erthe what best maye be,
My lyff yf I shuld laye.

'Synne ye hadde leuer all forgoo
Then lese your love, ye saye euer so   2170
I rede, so God me save.'
'Whate seyste þou syster? Alas, lett bee;
Then wold all men saye, parde,
I were in poynte to rave!

f. 226ᵛ   So proude a vowe as I haue made,   2175
Yll sett men wold saye I had
That now shuld loue a knave.
He dyd neuer prouys that men dyd se,
And I wott neuer of whens is hee
Ner where I shuld hym [crave].   2180

'But yf þu wilte acorde hit tille,
A bettur counsell say I wille
How I may garre hem byde:
I shall praye hem for my sake,

2152 ta] too   2155 lang-eyre] a corr. from o   2157 thre] there
2160 Imayne] K.; MS I maye   2163 me] written above with caret   2167 not]
K.; MS wot   2180 crave] K.; MS fynde

A turnament that he wold make   2185
Off knyghttys that wele gan ryde;
That it maye be lastynge dayes thre,
And what man on erthe that he be
In all þ[i]s world so wyde
That maye beyre the pryce awey   2190
Shall wyld me and my londys for aye,
To laye me by his syde.

'And yff my love be levande
And maye here tell, I understond,
Thus turnament yare,   2195
Yff he haue any þoughte on me,
Or anny provys in hym bee,
I hope he wille be þare.
Yff he love me, I suppose
Hee will his loue not lyghttly loose;   2200
Yff he doo, wronge it were!
Whedyr hit turne to wele or woo,
His loue and I shuld forgoo,
Off blis I were full bare.'

Then Ymayne lowde she loughe   2205
And sayd, 'Thus is good i-nowghe   f. 227ʳ
Be God that all hathe wroughte;
Myghte non in erthe haue better sayd,
Euyll or wele whedur he be payd;
This counsell nyghe ye noughte!'   2210
On the morowe when þe sonne was bryghte,
Kynge Melangere wyth many a knyghte
Into the erbere soughte.
Sone after come the lady gent;
The kyng by the hand hyr hent   2215
And tille a sete hyr broughte.

Beefore them all spake Amfyon:
'Syr kynge, your barons ychone

2189 þis] þs   2213 to] *Otiose curl on* o   2216 a sete] *K*.; *MS* assete
2217 spake] *Written above with caret*

Wille specially you praye;
As thou artte our faythefull frend,   2220
Brynge our grette bate to ende,
For best we trowe ye maye.'
The lady at his wordys wax tene
And sayd, 'Amphivn, yt is sene,
Be God that owe þ[i]s daye,   2225
That ye no þinge hold wyth mee,
But full ageynste me, ser, ye bee,
And so ye haue byne aye!

'Yow nede not hye you halff so faste;
For all the wyles that ye caste,   2230
In faythe ye gette me note.
I corde no thynge for your estate;
Love your makys, ser, not so hote,
For grette God that you wroughte!'
She callyd to hyr Ser Dryas,   2235
f. 227ᵛ   And other that nere of her counsell was
And told them all her thought.
She sayd, 'Lordyngys more and lasse,
A matter to meve there ys
That me in bale hathe brou3te;   2240

'Yff it were done be grette folye,
A vowe amys for sothe made I
A longe while here beforene,
That me shuld neuer wedde no wy3te
But yff he were the beste knyghte   2245
That in his tyme was borne.
And yff I shuld now that vow breke,
All that therof hard speke
Wold laughe me to skorne.
Take I anny but the beste,   2250
They myghte sey, so haue [I] reste,
My grette pryde were forlorne.

2221 our] *Written as* ou *plus the abb. for* ur   2225 þis] þs   2228 aye] ayee
2233 Love] *followed by* ser   2236 that] *followed by crossed-out* were   2251 I] K.;
MS om.   2252 were] w *corr. from* f

. . . . .
'Ye will lett sett a turnament
That myghte last dayes thre:
Whedyr he come frome est or weste,   2255
Man in erthe þat berythe hym beste
Shall wyld my londys and me.
Yff ye thynke I sey resone nowe,
Thus me thynke my riche avowe
Efte hit myghte holdyn be.'   2260
The yong knyghttys euerychone
Sayd, 'Be God þat is but one,
Hereoff full fayne ar wee.'

All men to the kyng in-soughte
That he shuld graunte and groche it noughte   2265   f. 228ʳ
To sette this turnament:
'Thus beste [he]r vow maye be hold.'
Yche man wen[d]e hymselff shuld
Wynne þat lady gente.
Manlengere wold not lette;   2270
Fowre monethes after þat day was sett
Be all the lordys assent.
Knyghttys that were off farre contre
Myghte here and come to þat semble
That wele durste byde ouer bente.   2275

Vnder Canders, that riche citte,
Men sayd this turnament shuld be
In a full fayre mede.
When this sertayne day was sett,
Euery man toke leve wythoute lette   2280
And to there contrey youde.
The lady to her bowre ys goon;
Full wondyr woo was Amfyon
That they had done this dede.
The damysell now leve we there   2285
And of hur louer speke we more
That leuythe in m[e]kyll drede.

2254 dayes] *Followed by crossed-out* f   2262 one] onee   2267 her] *K.; MS*
your   2268 wende] *K.; MS* wene   2287 mekyll] mkyll

A cosyn had Ipomadon,
A noble chyld Egyon
The same tyme in the place,   2290
That hard there wordys all bedene
And knewe ther purpose white and clene
But none wyste what he was.
He sogarende not nyghte ne daye,
But in to Poyle he toke the waye   2295
And to Barlet he goose,
And told Ipomadon the hende
Eche word to the ende;
Thereoff grette Ioye he ha[s].

He told hym also, so God me save,   2300
How they a lord wold make hur haue;
'Syr, this is there caste,
And she be hyr owne assent
Prayd hem of a turnament
That thre dayes oute myghte laste.   2305
The knyghttys þat were of huncouthe [londe]
Mighte redely them vnderstonde
And thedur myghte hye them faste.'
Ipomadon he was so glad,
Therefore grette Ioye he made,   2310
Off laughynge oute he breste.

His mayster Tholamewe he callyd
And all his purposse hym told;
Sayd, 'Ser, what ys your rede?
Be worthynes nowe mvste me chese,   2315
And mayster, or I my love shuld lese
In faythe I wille be dede.'
Whan Thalamewe hard þis tydyngys,
He sayd wyth hertte full well lauȝhyng,
'Now darre I lay my hedde   2320
That God will haue hit brouwghte above
That ye shall wyth worshipe wynne your love
Off stronge men in that stede.

f. 228ᵛ

2294 sogarende] a *corr. from* e   2299 has] K.; MS had   2306 londe] K.;
MS om.

'Now shall ye worke as dothe the wyse;
Hye you thereto and gette þe pryce   2325   f. 229ʳ
Be worthynes off hande.'
'Ye mayster, and I were there
So non wyste what I were
I wold be wel lycande.
Gyf I shuld presse to put me forthe,   2330
But I of dedys were holdyn worthe
[N]o love wyth hur I fonde. †
For euer more, mayster, thynkys mee
That louers shold l[aynand] be;
For mekyll I pre[f]e that wande   2335

'That brekys not, and will well bowe;
Righte so it farythe be them, I trowe,
That lovys and well can layne.
In few wordys ys curtesye;
Lette his dedys bere wittenes why   2340
He shuld be louyde agayne.
In suche place men may hym dyscure,
Hym were better to hold hym sure,
For ofte that poynte dothe payne.
In fele wordis be reson ys lyes   2345
And ay the moste man of price
The leyste of themselff wille saye.

'[I] wille wende into the pres
My love to wynne wythoute lesse,
Maystyr, so hastely   2350
To pasande poyntys that may say
That I am best worthy all-way
To weld that wyghte forthy.
Oute of this contre wynde I wille
To serue the kynge of Cesille,   2355
Ys eme to that fayre lady;
I wotte welle he wil be at hit,   f. 229ᵛ
And so shall I, that no man witte
Ne know þat it is I.

2325 Hye] *Kp.*; *MS* Hyue   2332 No] *Kp.*; *MS* For   2334 laynand] *K.*
wel leynand; *MS* lovers   2335 prefe] presse   2345 ys lyes] *K.*; *MS* ys no lyes
2348 I] *K.*; *MS om.*

'Lett God do wyth me what hym lyste,   2360
Were I there þat no man it wyste,
I gaff no fors in faye.
Therefore, mayster, for charyte,
That hors and harnes redy bee
For Goddys loue I you praye.'   2365
'Syr, I shall do your comaundement.'
Wyth good wille his mayster went
And ordeyned his araye.
His leve toke Ipomadon
Att fader and frendys ilkone.   2370
Wyth hym he ledde a maye;

His syster doghttur, sib full nere;
A maydon chaste and myld of chere,
Lufflye of chynne and cheke.
Grette hors many wyth his harnes,   2375
And also III spare palffreys
Toke he wyth hym eke;
Greyhondys wyghte wyth small brachettys,
Rei[a]ll hawkys and yonge valettys
That were bothe myld and meke.   2380
Wyth hem he ledde stedys thre,
In erthe þer myȝtte no better bee
Thorowe all þus world to seke;

An as white as anny mylke,
The sadull couered in white sylke   2385
Was neuer non better seene.
Thereon satte a chyld in white,
That syght to se was grette dylyghte
To them þat there had byn.
Abowte his neke a white scheld,   2390
A white spere in his hand he helde,
The pensell white I wene.
That was the [l]est stede of them thre;
Furþermoste on the grounde gothe he
And all was white bedene.   2395

f. 230ʳ

2365 praye] prayee   2374 chynne and cheke] *Reversed in MS*   2379 reiall]
revill   2384 An] *K.; MS* And   2393 lest] best

Efte came another stede,
On grounde neuer a better yede,
And that was rede sore;
Redde sadull, shyld and spere,
Redde was all his oþur geyre,   2400
And shone as gold y[co]re;
A chyld in rede theron sittande,
Wyth a rede spere in his hand,
The pensell red therefore;
As bryght as the sonne beame,   2405
Or lyghter then the s[terr]es leme
That stede was sum dele more.

A blake stede come after hym,
So well made of lythe and lym
That in hym was no lake.   2410
The whyghttys of hem all was þat,
And therevpon a shyld satte
Ryche and a mykyll make;
A blake sheld aboute his halsse,
Blake was all his armur alse   2415
That he bare on his bake;
Cole blake stede and conysau[nc]e;
The chyld bare on his launse
A pensell all off blake.

Was non off them oþur lyke,   2420
But in þat tyme þer were non syke,
This dare I savely saye.
Eyther before oþur goothe;   f. 230ᵛ
Syn after comen in rose
Wythe a littill way,   2425
Men wyth haukys and houndys harde;
Tholemewe come afterwarde
Righte in good aray,
Vppon a chesour noble and wyghte;
Lyke an hunter he was dyght,   2430
Ryght well to his paye.

2401 ycore] K.; MS fayre   2406 sterres] K.; MS sonnes
2417 conysaunce] K. conysance; MS conysaure   2418 launse] K.; MS launsere
2428 aray] K.; MS a rayse   2429 chesour] chesou + 'ur' abb.

A grette horne aboute his havls;
Behynde hym bowes and arrowes alce
He bare for drede of gille.
Sethen after come Ipomadon,   2435
The mayden þat he had wyth hym tane.
This rode they many a myle;
They held þem wele behynde þe rowte
For they durst not drawe aboute
Nere the dust, þere clothyng shuld fyle.   2440
So long the[y] rode in this araye
That at the last come they
Into þe lond of Cesille,

Into a foreste feyre and grene
Ther foulys song al bedene   2445
On bowes bothe lesse and more.
The frithe was full of swete flouris—
Who lyst to love paramowres
Grette lykyng had byn there.
Ipomadon forgettys nouȝte   2450
To haue his leman in his thoughte,
That made hym sigh full sore.

And also he rode in his thynkynge,
A songe of loue he gan to syng;
'For her ay mys I fare.'   2455

Lyghttly was he clade to ryde
In a mantell panyd wyth pryde
And semys sette grette plente.
He loysyd his mantell band for hete
And downe fro his neke he it lete,   2460
It covyrd ouer his kne.
Hose he had of clothe of Ynde,
Suche shull no man now fynde,
To seke all crystyante.
Spurrys of gold he had vpon;   2465
Was neuer kyng better weryd none
Ne no man in no degre.

2432 his] *followed by crossed-out* favls   2441 they] *K.*; *MS* the   2465 had] h
corr. from w

Rychely was that maydon clade,
And on his righte hond he here ledde.
Togeddyr forthe they rod   2470
Bothe þorow frythe and ferne;
Toward the sitte of Palerne
The way they toke þat tyde
There the kyng and þe quene lay.
The kyng huntyd all þat day   2475
In foreste there besyde.
His meyne had hym loste ychone,
All but Cabanus alonne,
In hert ys nouȝte to hyde.

They too parcevyd a grette hertte,   2480
A littill in the way yt starte,
A nobull dere at assaye.
They folowyd on the chasse so faste   f. 231ᵛ
Thate they were warre at the laste
Of men come by the waye   2485
Rydyng money wyth fayre [harn]es.
Thereof the kyng hymselff was
Right in a grette affraye:
He wend, for they come soo,
His londys they wold take hym fro   2490
And this he stode [in d]ismaye.

The custum was not in þo dayes
Knyghttys to ryde wyth suche harnays,
The more he was in dowte:
He that boldyste du[r]ste abyde   2495
Hym, a[lone] he was wont to ryde
And wyth hym lede no rowte.
To seke auntrys when knyȝttys youde
Hymselff was wonte his geyre to lede,
Were he neuer so stowte.   2500
Forthy the bokys tellyth ychone,
The fyrste man was Ipomadon
That harnes ledde aboughte.

2486 harnes] K.; MS arrowes   2491 in dismaye] K. dismayde; MS this mayde
2495 durste] K.; MS duste   2496 alone] K.; MS and

The kyng seyd to Cabanus,
'What meane þat these meyne come þus   2505
Wyth horsse and harnes bryghte?
This fy[f]tte wyntur and ıı monethe stille
Kyng haue I byn in Cesile,
I saw neuer suche a syghte;
So money stedys hernes beyre,   2510
Hit semeth as they come for werre
To robbe vs off our ryghte.
Cabanus, goo witte þer wille,

f. 232ʳ

Whethere they come for good or ille;
Younder semythe a knyghte.   2515

'I praye the spyrre on feyre manere,
Wyth suche araye what dothe they here
Wyth armoure, spere and shyld?'
Att his byddyng forthe he youde,
And in there waye stille he stode   2520
A longe while and behylde
Bothe stedys and palfrayes,
Grette horse and good harnes,
The chyldorne bothe yong and old,
The havkys and the houndys ychone;   2525
Fayrer saw he neuer none
Syn he is witte cowde wyld.

Ipomadon can after ryde,
His cosyn ledand by his syde
That he fro home had broughte.   2530
Cabanus wyth laughyng chere
Haylyd þem in fayre maynere
And sythe he the knyȝt besought;
'Syr, the kyng of Sissille huntythe here by
Wyth a ryall company   2535
Off knyghttys that wele hathe wrouȝte.
He send me for to witte your wille,
Whedur ye come for good or ille,
To warre yf ye th[ought].'

2507 fyftte] K.; MS fyghtte   2520 And] Followed by crossed-out looped stem
2539 thought] K.; MS thynke

'Nay ser,' quod Ipomadon,   2540
'Warre in þ[i]s lond ne seke I non
To do no man no deyre,
But as off kyng Melyngere,
Men speke of hym boþe farre and nere
Hy[s] worthynes of warre.'   2545 f. 232ᵛ
'Ye, in faythe,' quod Cabanus.
'Syr, for Goddis loue shewe ye vs
My eronde to hym here,
And say here is a knyghte sertayne
That will speke wyth hym right fayne—   2550
No þing me so [dere].

'Good ser, goo witte his wille
Whedur I shuld come hym tille
Or here hym to abyde;
To hym wyth you wold I fare   2555
Sothely, ne this maydon were
That houythe by my syde.'
Cabanus to the kyng is goone
And told hym all tho poyntys ychone,
And how ryally they ryde: 2560
'Ser, synne I was of my moder borne,
I sawe neuer suche a syghte beforen
In this world so wyde.

'So fayre stedys, so fayre palfreys,
So fayre hors, so fayre harnes,   2565
Wyth chyldur so fayre and yonge;
So fayre haukys, so fayre hovndys,
So fayre racchis goynge on groundys,
To se ys grette lykynge.
So fayre knyghttys, so fayre a maye,   2570
So fayre and so good araye
But yff it were a kynge.
Hit semyth he hath no wordys to waste;
To speke wyth you he co[v]y[t]s moste
Ouer all oþer thynge.   2575

2541 þis] þs   2545 Hys] K.; MS Hy   2551 dere] K.; MS leeff
2555 fare] r corr. from y   2574 covyts] Kp.; MS comys

'To yow had he comyn wyth me,
But a lady ledys hee
That hym is lothe to leve,
Thereffore he prayes you herttly
That ye wold come to hym forthy;   2580
He bydys you beyounde younder greve.'
The kyng sayd, 'Be my levte,
His riche araye will I see
Gyf it be so to pre[v]e.'
The kyng is to þe way goon;   2585
Then see hym come Ipomadon
And vp his hand gan heve;

He seyd, 'God loke þe, Melengere,
In all þ[i]s world farre and nere
Ys holdyn non so good   2590
Off kyndenes ne of curtessy,
In dede of armus of cheualrye,
So bigge of bone and blode.
Of[t] sythes thus haue I herde saye;
That made me hedyre take the waye   2595
Frome whome when I youde.
In erthe ys non in all degre
That at me deyne but it were ye,
Ne to serue, be my hode.

'So grett good men spekythe of the   2600
That I wold thy seruant be;
This made me hedyr to ryde.
Fro fere contreys I haue soughte,
My cosyn wyth me haue I brought
That hovis be me syde.   2605
In faythe she is a mayden clene,

And she I wold shuld dwell wyth þe quene,
In erthe is nouȝte to hyde.
But ser, yf þou my seruyce take,
A comnaunte wyth the must I make   2610
Ellys will I not byde.

2584 preve] *K.*; *MS* preysse   2589 þis] þs   2594 Oft] *K.*; *MS* Of

'Now shall I say in littill wayes
Yff it be of the as men sayes
In cuntreys here and there.'
The kyng lokythe on the knyght   2615
And sayd, 'Ser, all that is righte
Shall þou haue and more.'
He was full lothe to lese hym soo.
'Cabanus, wyth hym goo
And to the citte ye fare,   2620
To the beste inne þou hym lede;
Goo wyth hym so God þe spede
That þou no þing spare.'

Be þat his folke were comyn ychone,
Forthe togedder ar they goone   2625
To Palerne the riche citte,
And at the best innes of all þe towne
Cabanus lyght is adowne
And sayd, 'Ser, here shall we be.'
Wysse i-nowthe was Tholamewe,   2630
Full wele his mayster he knewe;
There dyner ordeyns hee.
Ipomadon sayd at þat tyde
To Cabanus, 'Ye shall abyde
Syr, and dyne wyth me.'   2635

He wyst the kyng it wolde
For after hym comen he nold,
Thereffore he dwellyþe stille.   f. 234ʳ
Ipomadon and Cabanus
On benche togeddur sett ar thus,   2640
And Tholamewe wyth good wille
Ryche mettys before hem brought.
Off all welthes they wantyd nouȝte,
Cuppis sythe gan they fylle
Off pyment and of riche wyne;   2645
In cuppis that were off gold fyne
On hand he browght them tille.

2630 was] *Followed by crossed-out* thalewe

At the laste was browght forthe for þe nonys
A cupe sett wyth precyous stonys,
Wyth cassadouns þat were clere.   2650
The cupe was good and precious,
The stonys good and vertuous
And dyamovndys þat were dere,
The [cr]apet and the sersolette,
The emeraud and the ametas,   2655
The ruby and the safure;
Perle, topyas and mony [I]aspys,
And fowre sydys were dyueres ha[s]pis
That queynte and sotell were;

Tweyne of syluer and twayn of gold,   2660
So prevy þat non them know shuld
Where the openyng myghte be;
In the pomell, a stone wythouten moo
That wold anny syluer sloo
That euer was sene wyth iȝe.   2665
The cuppe toke Ipomadon,
Cabanus he lokyd vppon
And sayd, 'Ser, herkyns mee;
The on halff herof shalt þou drynke,

f. 234ᵛ

The other deyle myselff; I thynke   2670
The cuppe to gyff to the,

'In the begynnyng of our company,
Thereffore I praye the specyally
Frendely it to fonge;
As I shall frenshipe fynde in þe,   2675
This sympull gyfte þou take of me;
I wille mend it or it be longe.'
Cabanus on fayre manere
Thankys hym wyth lauȝhand chere
And sayd wyth myrthe amonge;   2680
'Syn thou this cuppe haste gevyn to me,
Myselffe holly I gyff to the
Or els I dyd the wronge;

2654 crapet] S&J; MS tapet   2657 Iaspys] S&J; MS claspys
2658 haspis] S&J; MS happis   2660 Tweyne] w corr. from a   2672 our]
Written as ou plus abb. for ur

'In that þat I may, in my lyff,
Betwene vs too shall neuer be stryffe   2685
Yff God wille gyff me grace,'
Wyth myrthe they dreve to ende þat day;
At evyn the kyng, the sothe to saye,
Fro huntynge comen was.
Cabanus to the courte ys goone   2690
And wyth hym leydys Ipomadon,
That frely fayre of face.
So semely knyghttys as they were II,
In all the courte ys no moo
That þe kyng wyth hym hasse.   2695

Ipomadon comys in to þe hall
Clothed in a syrket off palle
Purfelyed wyth ermyne,
Bend abowte wyth orfrayes;
All the folke of that place   2700   f. 235ʳ
Hade neuer no bettur sene.
A visage he had bothe stoute and bold,
A godely countenavnce to behold,
Ther was Ioye off all wyne.
In handys togeddur com they twoo,   2705
Knyghttys gaffe them rome and lett them goo,
Cabanus wold not fyne.

To Melenger the kyng bothe ar goon:
'Syr kyng,' quod Ipomadon,
'Thy wille fayne witte I wold.   2710
But yf I shuld thy seruante be,
A comnavnte muste I make wyth the,
Lang-ere as I the told.
I do they welle to vnderstond,
But yf þou fullfyll my comnande   2715
I byde not, be þou bolde.
Yff it be so, now shall I see
As I haue herde speke of þe
In contreys many a fold.'

2686 grace] gracee   2707 fyne] *K.*; *MS* faynte

The kyng stoode in a stody stille   2720
And sayd, 'Ser, all þat thy reason wille
Thou shalte not be begylyde.
I hyre the: for syluer ne gold
Thy company forgoo I nolde,'
And ther wythall he smylyde.   2725
To þat answerd Ipomadon,
'Nay ser, gold ne syluer kepe I none
Nowhere in towne ne felde;
I haue i-novghe in my contrey,
I thanke grette God þat sent it mee   2730
f. 235ᵛ   That moste is meke and mylde.

'But and it be as men say of the,
Thou groge not, but graunt it me
That I shall to þe sey
My askyng, ser, al bedene: 2735
That I mvste dwell wyth þe quene
That worthy is all-way,
And also, ser, I say to you
I wille be callyd þe quenes drewe
Bothe wyth man and may;   2740
The therd poynt ys þat no man gon
After the quene but I alonne
To chambyr ilke a day.

'Tille her mette I wille her [f]ette
And serue her when she is set,   2745
Yet mvste thou graunt me thus;
That I maye lede hur vp agayne,
Beffore her bedes syde, sertayne,
Att eche a tyme her kys.
And yf thou graunte me as I saye,   2750
I shall serue hur well to paye
Worthely, i-wys,
Wyth huntynge and haukyng bothe,
But thou not drede þe for no skathe
As haue I Ioye and blis.   2755

2744 fette] sette   2753 haukyng] y *corrected from "ys" abb.*

'Syr kyng, now wot þou all my wille,
Whereffore and why I come þe tille;
Holdeste the þou hereof payde?'
The kyng at his wordys lovȝth;
'Me thynkys and mekyll were i-nowgh;   2760
Largely haste thow seyde.
Whate myster man arte thou?   f. 236ʳ
Thou haste me grevyd, for God avowe.'
There to God he leyde;
'Why, yf þou wilte not graunte it me,   2765
Have good day ser, I goo fro the;
I am no þinge dysmayde,

'That I shall gette lordys i-nowe
To serve, ser, as welle as thou.
Fare well, for now I goo.'   2770
Melengere waxt nere wrothe;
To leue the knyght he was full lothe
That he shuld parte frome hym soo.
'Alas ser,' quod Cabanus,
'Foreuer it is a shame to vs   2775
And he þus fro you goo.'
Then sayd bothe erle and barone,
'Syr, yede he for so lutill chesone
[W]e wold be full woo.'

The kyng saw it myght no better be;   2780
All the barons grauntyd hee
He shuld beleve there stille,
The knyght and the lady gente.
To the quene is he sente
To serue hyr att hyr wille;   2785
The quene lokyd on hym and þoughte
That message myslykis her not
For he was comen her tille.
He dyd his seruyce full diligentlye
And swythely kyste that lady,   2790
His forward to fullfyll.

2779 We] *K.*; *MS* he   2787 myslykis] *Followed by cancelled* thou
2790 kyste] *Corr. from* kys

She louyd hym wondur wele þerfore;
And he had axed her any more
I hope he myght haue bene.
But of foly he ne roughte;   2795
Another loue was in his [th]oughte
Than on that lady shene . . .
Yet is there no man þat wottist it
Off all the folke bedene.
Eche man callyd hym the Drew-le-r[a]yne;   2800
That ys as moche for to saye
As leman to the quene.

In the courte he hym so bare
That all men louyd hem les and more
Wythin a littill stounde.   2805
Two monethys thus led his lyff,
Cauȝtte dere and fovlys ryff
Bothe wyth hauke and hounde.
When kyngys spake of werryng,
Ipomadon spake of huntynge,   2810
How he in forest founde;
When euery knyght regyd hym to Iuste
To kepe there armowur fro the roste,
No thynge he hem bonde.

Whan barons in gay aray ȝede,   2815
Ipomadon to the foreste grede
To hunte and to haukynge;
Whan knyghtys spake of stedys rounde,
He spake of a fayre grayehounde
And of no nother thynge.   2820
Knyghttys of the courte boþe lesse and more
To skorne louȝhen hym þerfore;
That was his grette lykynge.

He parcevyd the warnyngys full well,
And lykyd the doyng ilk a dell   2825
Bothe of knight and kyng.

2796 thoughte] *K.*; *MS* soughte   2800 Drew-le-rayne] *K.*; *MS* drewlerengyne

So longe they levyd in þis talent,
The tyme is comyn of turnament
That they before had sett;
Kyng Melengere forgett it he nolde   2830
His promys to kepe that he shuld.
Betwene the II sees he [fet]t
((To hold that he had hyght))
Wyth II M^l knyghttys good
That were hy borne of blode,   2835
The best that he myght gette.
Thedere wyth hym went þe quene
And all his othere meyne bedene.
Thus many a myle they mett,

Tille they come in to Calabure,   2840
Mekyll folke wyth hem there
That wyse and worthy were.
They wold not to Candores goo,
But in a castell a myle þerfro
The quene shuld soioyrne there   2845
Whiles they were at the turnament,
And wyth hyr many a lady gent,
Hyr comeforte was the more.
That holde stode in the foreste
That Ipomadon knewe alþerbest;   2850
Full well hym lykyd therefore.

Many tymes he had huntyd þerin,
The fyrste was not then to begynne,
For there beganne his payne.
That thike foreste lastyd all-way   2855   f. 237^v
To Candires, there the lady lay;
Thereof he was full fayne.
Knyghttys dyd þer besynes
Horse and harnes for to dres;
All louȝhen at Drew-le-rayne.   2860
He did but as he was wonte;
On the mornynge erly went to hunte,
At eve come home agayne,

And grette wonder hade Cabanus
When he his felow saw thus,   2865
And lyghttly to hym yede:
'Syr,' he sayd, 'well wayte ye,
Tomorowe shall þis tur[na]ment be;
Why raye ye not [in] w[e]de?
Ye haue hors and noble harnes;   2870
Cast you to be there all-wayes
As God in heyvyn you spede.
Dresse you, ser, and go we thedyre;
We too shall all-way be togeddur
And ayther helpe o[the]re at nede.'   2875

When he off tur[na]ment spake so,
Hee lokyd hym right as he were woo
And sayde, 'So haue I seyle,
Now se I well I fynd it not
Full frenshipe in þe as I haue sought;   2880
For grette hevynes I fele.
Thou hard thyself, wythout lesyng,
I made a comnaunte wyth þe kyng
To serue my lady well:
It is noþur my wille ne myn entent   2885
Wyth Iustis ne wyth turnamente . . .

. . . .
f. 238^r   Ne boke to ende in all his lyff
The warkys that there were dyȝte;
And a bell stode þeron off gold
That was wysely made on mold.   2890
When wayttys shuld blow on nygtt,
It wold ringe a long while,
That men myȝte it here more þen a myle
To comfort kyng and knyght.

In this belle a stone stoode,   2895
A charebokyll riche and good;

2868 turnament] K.; MS turment   2869 in wede] K.; MS to wynde
2875 othere] K.; MS ore   2876 turnament] K.; MS turment   2891 nygtt]
K.; MS nygttys

Lyght as the mone it shone.
The tent was white as anny mylke,
The bordures all of clene sylke,
In þe world was bettur non.   2900
There Malengere abydythe stille
Wyth wyne and ale at all þer wille
And knyghttys as trewe as stone.
On ilke a syde they reysud þan,
For lordys and for gentilmen,   2905
Tenttys monye one.

By þat was sett come oþer grett plente,
Dyueresse lordys of ferre contreye
That worthy were and wyghte.
Syr Monestus, I understond,   2910
The kyngys sonne of Irelond
That now was dubbyd kny3te,
He had seruyd Malengere
In hope to ha[ve] þat lady clere
A longe while day and nyghte.   2915
Tow c knyghttys of hert thro
He browght hym wyth and many mo
In armure burneshed bryghte.

For all þe power that he brou3te,   f. 238ᵛ
I trowe that lady gettys he nou3te,   2920
So mot I euer thryve.
Then come the riche duke of Breytayne,
That also her wold haue full fayne,
Wyth fyftye skore knyghttys and fyve;
But he myght wynne þat lady hynde,   2925
He þought or all were brou3te to ende
Wyth stalworthy men to stryve.
All this travell lesythe hee:
While sum men on lyve is, parde,
He weldys her not to wyff.   2930

Then come the duke of Normandy
Wyth noble knyghttys a companye

2914 have] *K.*; *MS* had

Well L a skore,
To haue þat lady as he þought,
But in faythe he gettys her nouȝte;   2935
His name was Ser Astore.
The kyng of Denmarke come after thanne,
Wyth hym many a noble man
Right welle arayd þerffore.
Off Skottelond and off Norwaye,   2940
Off Irelond and of Orkeney,
Yet spede they neuer þe more.

The woode was full of pavelyon
Wythoute them that lay in the towne,
Ten thousand and moo.   2945
All that came oute of the west,
They harbured them in the foreste;
They wold no farthere goo.
Be than was come þe kyng of Spayne
Wyth II C knyghttys of mayne   2950

f. 239ʳ
That were of hertte full thro.
The lady a[n]es hathe hym forsakyn;
Amfyon hathe he wyth hym takyn
And thought to wa[r]kyn þem woo.

The better spede he not þerffore;   2955
His name was Ser Antymore,
A styffe man and a st[e]re.
Amfyon had provde pensell
That wrought was of a damsyll
Was in the Fers [chamb]ere,   2960
But þeroff wyst the lady nought;
Syr Ottymore to feld it brought—
That bought he sythe full dere.
Syr Dayres come after thenne,
The riche duke of Loreyn,   2965
He þought to wynne [Calabe]re;

2952 anes] *Ka.*; *MS* aves   2954 warkyn] wakyn   2957 stere] *K.*; *MS*
stowre   2960 chambere] *K.*; *MS* banere   2966 Calabere] *K.*; *MS* honoure

To haue that lady was his cast,
But yet he faylyd at the laste,
Were she neuer hym so dere.
The erle of Flaunders come in feld 2970
Wyth II C vnder sheld
Off worthy men that were;
He brought in his companye
Noble knyghttys oute off Russye
To wynne that lady clere. 2975
Syr Dryseus was his name;
Yet fayls he or he come home
To gett hur to his fere.

Provde [I]semyon of Almayne,
The emperour, was not to layne, 2980
A styff man and a stronge,
Cam dether wyth many a dou3tty knyghte; f. 239ᵛ
And yf he were neuer so wyghte
Yet fayls he hur to fonnge.
Many other come be than, 2985
Well more then I rekynne can
But I shuld byde ouer longe.
Some were wythoute and sum were wythin;
On the morowen the turnament shuld begyn
Whan that a bell had ronge. 2990

Leve we now this folke there
And off the knyght speke we more
That dwellys wyth the quene:
To serue hur welle he dyd his tente,
No semblaunte made he to turnament; 2995
There a[t] was ladyes tene.
The maydons hym to skorne lou3gh;
Thereoff had [h]e Ioye i-nowgh,
For he the sothe had sene.
The quene to hur mete he fett, 3000
And seruyd hyr when she was sett
Right worthely I wene,

2975 lady] *Followed by initial loop of* h *or* l   2979 Isemyon] Semyon
2980 emperour] emperours sone   2996 at] *K.; MS* as   2998 he] *K.; MS* þey

And sythen agayne vp her ledde
And kyssyd that lady before her bedde,
To speke he gan hym spede;   3005
'Madame, lett thy turnay to morn;
I will hunte wyth hounde and horne
And bryng vs home a brayd.
I hold it better amonge þe okys
Then in turnament to take strokys;   3010
I kepe no blod to blede.'
The maydons hym to skorne lough
f. 240ʳ   And seyd, 'Loo, madame, your drew
Spekys off doughtty dedis!'

The quene cursyd his desteny,   3015
Wythoute prowes þat he shuld be
That was so fayre off face;
But sothe ys sayd in olde sawe,
'Whedur þat euer love will drawe,
Lake n[o] lettyng mase'.   3020
She louyd hym well for his service,
But oþur damysels of pryse
Grette skorne at hym have.
To there skorne toke he no hede
But toke his leve and forth he yede;   3025
To the porter he goose.

He gaf the porter a grette gold rynge
And he sayd, 'Ser, I love huntyng
At raynedere and at roos,
And as well wott thow as I,   3030
He that ys not there erlye
His best tyde mvst he lose:
Therefore of o thyng I þe praye;
Lett me forthe before the daye.'
'In faythe ser, I sopposse   3035
Whyles this offyce shall be myn,
Entre and issue shall be thyne
For frenshipe or for foos.'

3008 bryng] *followed by cancelled* bryng   3012 skorne] *followed by crossed-out* s
3020 no] ne

Ipomadon to bede goos,
And in the mornyng erly he roosse   3040
Or day began to sprynge.
He ge[r]tte aray his why3te stede,
And all his armore that hym nede   f. 240ᵛ
Be-lyve he lett vp brynge.
Sonne was covpled all his houndys,   3045
Wyth lowde blowyng forthe he [fou]ndys
That wakyd ladys yonge.
They sayd, 'Lo, madame, your drewe
Wyth horne and hound se ye may now;
He hyes to turnayeng!'   3050

The quene þerto wold take no kepe,
But laye in bedde purposyd to slepe,
And sore for-thought þat tyde
That he ne was man of prowes.
Whedur she loved hym, neuer the lesse   3055
In hertt she it hyde.
In the thykest place of all þat woode
A ermytage he wyst þer stode,
And thedur gan he ryde.
There he g[er]t araye hym tyte   3060
His stede and hym all in white;
He wold no lengur byde.

'Mayster,' quod Ipomadon,
'Today on huntynge mvste ye goone,
For Goddis love I you praye.   3065
Yff God will send you any dere,
Agayne the nyght abyde me here;
I shall come while I maye.'
Fro then vnto the Iustyng plase
A full de[p]e dale ther was   3070
In a deerne waye:
Couyrd-heddyd myght men ryde;
No man myght se hym on no syde
Yf it were lyghte of day.   f. 241ʳ

3042 gertte] K.; MS gette   3046 foundys] K.; MS wendys   3048 They]
Large capital in MS   sayd] d written above with caret   3060 gert] K.; MS gret
3070 depe] K.; MS dede

His mayster dyd his comaundement;   3075
Ipomadon his waye is went
Thorow the thike woode.
No man take wyth hym he lyst
But a chyld þat he on tryste,
Whiche was bothe fayre and goode;   3080
Of his lond a barons sone
That wele hym serue con,
And ofte in stedde [by] hym stoode.
The semely chylde Egyon
Was cosyn to Ipomadon,   3085
Right nere sib of his blode.

In the mornynge erly
He passyd thorow the derne sty
Be þat the day gan dawe.
He hovis before that fayre castell;   3090
The wynd wavyd his whyght pensell,
And waytys began to blowe,
And ouer the walle þey behylde
And sawe hym hove in the feld,
As why3te as any snowe.   3095
He cryed, 'Wake, lady bryghte!
For sothe, younder hovis a knyghte
The feyrest that euer I [saw]e.

'His stede and he is all in why3te;
That syght to se is grette dely3te,   3100
Fro bale as I be broughte!'
The lady weyndis to a wyndowe
f. 241ᵛ   And saw hym hove as white as snowe;
In grette care is she broughte,
So ne she wyst at that day   3105
On whome she shuld her love laye,
For in hur h[e]rtte she thought
She wold not the valet [str]aunge
For emperoure nor for [k]yng [chau]nge,
Gette hym and she movghte.   3110

3083 by] K.; MS om.   3098 sawe] K.; MS the   3101 Fro] Corr. from For
3105 So ne] K.; MS Sone   3107 hertte] K.; MS hrtte   3108 straunge] Kp.;
MS chaunge   3109 kyng] lyng   chaunge] Kp.; MS stronge

She beholdys the knyght in whyte,
But what he was she wot but lite,
The more care had the maye.
The sonne was vp on lofte be thanne;
All the feld was full of men   3115
There armys to assaye.
The kynge of Spayne, Ser Ottynore,
Sawe the white knyght hove thore
In armys good and gaye.
To all his folke he sayde syne,   3120
'The fyrste Iuste to day is myne,
And I hold comnaunte aye!'

Wyth hym was Ser Amfyon;
The kyng comaundyd hys men ilkone
Stille they shuld abyde.   3125
He sayd, 'Younder is for the Fers love:
A kyng in white wele dothe hove,
And to hym will I ryde.'
A grette spere in honde he nome;
Ipomadon was ware he come   3130
And ble[nc]hyd on anoþur syde;
Ayther on other brake þer speris,
Ipomadon behynde hym beyris
Twenty foote þat tyde.   f. 242ʳ

The kyng laye waltrand in his wede;   3135
Egyon of his hors toke hede
And lyghttly lepte þerone:
For all the strengh þat he weldyþe,
The riche kyng of Spayne hym eldyþe
To Ipomadon.   3140
Ioyfull was þat lady clere;
How she ordayned now shall ye here,
Hyr owne cosyne I[aso]ne
That he shuld serue þer o[f] speyres
[To] what man that best hym beyres   3145
To the III dayes were goone;

3127 A] *Written in margin*   3131 blenchyd] *K.; MS* blemesshyd
3137 And] *Otiose curl above* n   3143 Iasone] Iosane   3144 þer of] *K.; MS*
þerfore   3145 To] *K.; MS* and

And þerfore trewly she hym highte,
The thryd day he shuld be knyghte,
His good dedys to alowe.
A spere to Ipomadon he bare: 3150
As he hadde neuer sene hym ayre
[He] sayd, 'Ser, what artt thou?'
'I am the laydys cosyn, Ser,
That thus is ordayned here be hur,
Trewly for to trowe,   3155
That I shall serue here of speris
To what man that hym best beris,
And sertus that I hold you,

'For the man that was of grettys boste,
And hym that my lady hatyd moste   3160
In feld here haue ye felde!'
For wele he wyst it was reson,
But he knewe not Ipomadon,
Togeddur that they had dwellyd,
But it was long beffore.   3165

f. 242ᵛ   Ipomadon likyd the more
The tale that he hym tolde,
And he sayd, 'Ser, so God me spede,
My presonere to thy lady lede;
I wold þat she hym hylde.   3170

'Thou shalt haue to þi lady gent
His hors, and saye þat I hit sent,
The kyng to hur presone!'
Syr Attynore than sorow hade,
But vp he wanne as he hym bade   3175
And rydythe forthe wyth Iasone.
Whan he come to þat lady bry3te,
'Madame,' he sayd, 'younde white kny3te
That berythe all oþur downe
The kyng off Spayne takyn hath he,   3180
And he send hym for to bee
Att your byddyng bowne.'

3149 alowe] alowee   3150 Ipomadon] *Followed by deleted* here   3152 He]
K.; MS and   3157 to] two   3165 But] *K.; MS preceded by* to gedyr
3174 Attynore] y *corr. from* o

Whereffore was þat lady fayne,
But eft she sayd to Imayne,
'For ought þat I gan see,   3185
Alas this is a grett myscheffe;
For welle I wott þat my leeff
Ys not in this contre.
Certenly, he had byn here,
I[aso]ne hym knewe þat was his fere;   3190
Now wotte I well, parde,
That othere [fayles] hym manhode
Or he is dede, so God me spede—
Thereffore full woo is me!

'Younde knyght to myne avowe will corde;   3195
And yff I take hym to my lorde,
I losse my love, alas!'
Wonder woo was Amfyon   f. 243ʳ
That Ser Attynore was tane,
Oute off the prece hym [gas],   3200
He thought to wyne that riche kyng;
Ipomadon saw his comynge,
His spere all redy was:
He sette Ser Amfyon so hard
That neuer afterward   3205
He nede neuer prest to aske.

His hors threwe þe mayster downe;
Wyth a spere come I[aso]ne
And lyghttly to hym wanne.
Before Ipomadon he gan hym lede,   3210
And sayd, 'Ser, loo, here a stede
That owethe a wykkyd man—
Was none my lady louyd lasse!
A better stede non þer is
Frome hethen to flem Iurdanne.   3215
Thus endyrs daye he hyght it me
Agayne that I shuld dubbyd bee,
I shuld haue had hym thanne.'

3190 Iasone] Iosane   3192 fayles] K. failes; MS om.   3200 gas] K.; MS
preste   3208 Iasone] Iosane

Ipomadon sayd wyth myld mode,
'Syr, syn thou knowest hym for so good,   3220
To stabull all our stryffe,
Off my myght thou hym take;
I witte-saff for my lady sake
Were he worthe suche fyve.'
I[aso]ne thankyd hym herttly   3225
And sayd, 'Ser, gramercye,'
And vp he hathe hym [gyve].
Hee ledde hym to þe lady bryght;
'I[aso]ne,' she sayd, 'be Goddis myȝte,
Ye begynne to thryue!   3230

'Who so wynnes and who so losythes,
Me thynke not wythout þou goos,
Be God and be my lewte!'
'Madame, þe knyght þat gaff me þ[i]s,
Wold God off heyven ye were his,   3235
For noble i-nowghe is hee.'
Syr Amfyon is men wer full woo
That her lord was slayne soo;
To hym come grett plente.
Tille a temple they hym bare   3240
And beryed hym, wythoute more;
Hit lykyd that lady fre,

For he had done her grette dyssesse,
And littill hym cast hur to please
The whilis he was on lyve.   3245
In world was neuer a curteyser knyght
Then he wold and he myghte
Have wedde hur to wyffe.
That knew not Ipomadon;
All woo was hym þat he was slone,   3250
But sonne was stynt þat stryffe.
I[aso]n in towre wold not abyde;
To the whyȝte knyȝt he hym hyde
Wyth shaftys iiii or fyve,

3225 Iasone] Iosane   3227 gyve] K.; MS nym   3229 Iasone] Iosane
3234 þis] þs   3250 All] Preceded by unfinished B   3252 Iason] Iosan

And serue[d] hym worthely off sperys.   3255
Many a bold man downe he beyrys
That p[r]ecys in to þe place:
There was non þat he hit
That lengur myȝte in sadull sitt,
But to the grounde he goos.   3260
Stronge waxid þat turnament,   f. 244ʳ
Ipomadon þer haubrakys rente
And brekys many a br[ac]e;
He hew in sounder helme and shyld
And feld many knyghttys in þe feld   3265
That wyght and worthy was.

Prowde Isomyon off Allmayne,
Mekill folke he put to payne
Be worthynes off werre;
He was holdyn moste of myghte   3270
Off all, next the whyte knyght,
So dyd hym mekill deyre.
That parceuyd Cabanus,
A kene knyght and a coryous;
[In] hand he hent a spere.   3275
To the emperoure he rode,
And [he] to hym wythoute bode,
Eyther oþur downe gan bere.

Lyghttly vp agayne he[m] stertte,
Pulde oute there swerdys wyth eygure hertt,   3280
To fyght they wold not fyne.
The emperoure wyth a brond full bright
Hit Cabanus on þe helme on hight
That nygh had done hym pynne:
Before his visage the dent yede downe,   3285
Nere-hand he had fallen in sowen.
The emperoure saw hym lyand syne:
'What, wenyst þou, prowde knyght, þou be
At Palerne now, thy riche citte,
Drynkand pyment or wyne?   3290

3255 serued] K.; MS serue   3257 precys] K.; MS specys   3261 turnament]
Otiose flourish on t   3263 brace] K.; MS browe   3275 In] K.; MS he
3277 he] K.; MS om.   3279 hem] K.; MS he   3280 hertt] herttys

'N[a]ye, thou art in turnamente!'

Cabanus þerto toke good entent
And was nere wood for wrothe:
Wyth a styff swerd in þat stoure
He smote of the eyre of þe emperoure   3295
And his lyfte arme bothe.
'In turnament I wene [I] be,
That sore I hope for-þynkys the;
Thy skor[nyng]e doth the skath!
Now may thou skorne wyne to drynke,   3300
But whereuer þou goo, here on thynke—
Thou levythe a wedde off w[a]the!'

Grette sorowe made the duke Dayres
For his cossyn [germayn], i-wis,
That was the emperoure.   3305
So hard Cabanus on the helme he [f]ett
That vnnethe a lof[t] he my3te [s]ett,
So stroke he in that stoure.
He was so stonyed þer wyth all,
Hus swerd oute of his hand gan fall,   3310
But sone come to hym succoure:
Ipomadon þerto toke heede,
To reskewe Cabanus he yede—
That bought þe duke full dere.

Ipomadon wyth a swerd thanne   3315
Stroke the duke off Lorayne
Thorowe oute the good ventayle,
That downe he fell as a stone;
Off þat stroke they wondyrd ychone,
So breste he many a mayll.   3320
On bothe sydys they turneyed faste,
Blode oute off the bre[nni]ys braste.

Be that the day gan fayle,
All praysud the whyte knyght moste,

3291 naye] K.; MS nye   3297 I be] K.; MS he be   3299 skornynge] K.;
MS skorynethe   3302 wathe] K.; MS worthe   3304 germayn] K.; MS
Elmany   3306 fett] sett   3307 loft] K.; MS loff   sett] fett
3313 he] h corr. from y   3322 brenniys] K.; MS bremmys

Wythouten dowte he toke a[n oste].   3325
One com hym to assayle

In a turnynge of his bake:
The duke off Breten a spere brake,
That all to pecys it youde.
Ipomadon turnethe hym agayne   3330
And stroke the duke off Breytene
Wyth a swerd full good;
On lofte myght he no lengur sitte,
On the shulder he hym hitte—
Benethe the ribbus it yede.   3335
His stede to the lady he sent;
That day it was the last present.
All that aboute hym stode

Sayd for sothe he was the best
Off knyʒtes þat come fro est or weste;   3340
Thus graunt they hym the gre.
Be þat the turnament gan twyn
Yche man drawethe to his inne
To towne and to citte.
To the towne lokys Ipomadon,   3345
Soo was he warre off I[aso]ne
And lowde on hym cryes he:
'A I[aso]ne, brother, I the praye,
Abyde swette Ser yf þou maye
A while, and speke wyth me.'   3350

The tothere sayd, 'Be goddys myghte,
Syr, how wiste ye how I highte?'
'Yes I[aso]ne, I the kenne.
Thynkyth þou not off the strange valett,   f. 245ᵛ
Att the super be the was sette?   3355
Thou wotte wele where and whanne.
That tyme I went of this contre,
I sayd I shuld come speke wyth the;

3325 an oste] a shafte   3328 Breten] *Preceded by crossed-out* bred
3337 was] s *corr. from* y   3346 Iasone] Iosane   3348 Iasone] Iosane
3353 Iasone] Iosane

Now I hold that I hight thanne.'
'A mercy Ser, for God avowe,   3360
My lady to love has schosyn you
Off all other men!'

'Nay I[aso]ne, þat may not be;
I mvste to my contre,
I maye no lengur abyde;   3365
But a thousand tymes þou her grette,
For efte synes maye we mete!'
And frome hym gan [h]e ryde.
Ipomadon prekyd in to the presse;
I[aso]ne hym loste, wythoute leasse,   3370
And sawe hym on no syde.
[Wyth] sorowffull hertt, the sothe to say,
He wyndythe home where þe lady laye,
Chaungynge hewe and hyde.

'I[aso]ne,' she sayd, 'what ayls the,   3375
Off so hevy chere to be?'
'Right so may ye, madame:
Today haue ye lorne
The best knyght þat euer was borne,
Yet know I not his name.'   3380
The lady sayd, 'For Goddis myghte,
What was he? The white knyght?'
'Ye, be God, the same.'
'Why, wyste þou, I[aso]ne, what he was?'
f. 246ʳ   'Ye, þerfore we may say 'alas',   3385
As God me spede fro blame!'

'Why, dere cosyn, know I hym ovght?'
He sayd, 'Lady, vyse ye not
Off þe straunge valet
That was my felow þ[i]s oþur yere?   3390
In þe foreste before you at suppere
Togeddur were we sett.

3363 Iasone] Iosane   3368 he] K.; MS we   3370 Iasone] Iosane
3372 Wyth] K.; MS My   3375 Iasone] Iosane   3384 Iasone] Iosane
3386 fro] Corr. from for   3390 þis] þs

When he went fro this contre,
That he shuld come and speke wyth me
Trewly he me hight.   3395
That is he þat Iuste so well þ[i]s day
In whyte, but he is goon for aye—
Me rewes that euer we mett!

'He ys goon now for euer;
Whedyr, I wot neuer,   3400
That sore for-thynkys me.
A M^l tymes he grettys you well,
But I hope, as I haue sell,
We shall hym neuer see.'
To chambyr went þat lady, I wene,   3405
And then she þought for pur tene
Her hert wold breke in thre.
I[aso]ne to her gan she calle:
'Loke hym, cossyn, ouer all,
Yff he may foundyn bee!'   3410

Then hur sorow dobelyd was;
The lady syȝhed and sayd 'alas',
And on hur bedde gan fall.
'Cursyd pryde, woo worthe þe aye!
Off all women so may I say,   3415 f. 246^v
And more I hope I shall.
Dothe he þus, he dothe grette synne!'
Imayne, that all hur trust is in,
To her gan she call.
'Dere systur, þat was [my] loue, I say,   3420
That Iusted so well in white to day,
And bare downe ouer all;

'But he is gone—wo ys me!'
Imayne sayd, 'Be me lewte,
Thanke God off heyven ye may!   3425
Now wott ye well he is alyve,
Yet shall he weld you to his wyff—
My lyff thereon I lay.

3396 þis] þs   3408 Iasone] Iosane   3420 my] K.; MS om.

Ye shall weld hym att your wille
Herafter, and ye will hold you stille,   3430
For this not helpe you maye.'
I[aso]ne sekyth hym farre and nere,
And so dyd kyng Melengere,
But fynd hym not can they.

They wythoute was full woo,   3435
And so was them wythin also
That he was forthe gone.
Euery man spake off his prowes;
They sett all oþur off worthynes
But at a chery stone.   3440
Ipomadon his way is rydden;
At the ermytage hathe hym bedyn
His cosyn Egyon.
His mayster had huntyd full well þat day
In the foreste, the sothe to sey;   3445
Th[r]e grette herttys hade he slon.

Ipomadon in his hert was fayne
That his mayster had this herttys slayne.
When he the sothe had sene,
Off he kyst his armore bright,   3450
And as an hunter he hym dyght
In a gowne off grene;
A grette horne aboute his halse,
His horse wyth his harnes alse
Lede Egyon, I wene.   3455
To the citte by anoþer way
Wyth lowde blowyng and grette bay
He rydythe home to the quene.

Before the gatys lowde he blew;
The maydens hym to skorne lowȝ,   3460
And to the quene þey sayde;
'Madam, now comyth your derlyng
Wyth hounde and horne fro turnaynge;
As swythe ye shall be payde

f. 247ʳ

3432 Iasone] Iosane   3446 Thre] K.; MS The

Off noble stedys þat he you bryngys,   3465
That he hathe wonne off riche kyngys
On grounde when he them layde.
Suche on is worthy þanne
To be a quenis leman!'
She bydythe all þat vnbrayde.   3470

She lett them say what þe[m] lyst;
Thowe she wold þat no man wyst,
She louythe hym neuer þe lesse.
The knyghte wendythe in to þe halle;
Thre hedys he present her wyth all   3475 f. 247ᵛ
That high and hat[hel] ys.
There is now but knyghttys fo[n]e
That hathe so douȝtty dedys done,
So haue I mede of messe,
That wold so lyght his lose have lefte;   3480
But he dyd, for he thought eft
To wynne more worthynes.

To þer skorne toke he no [hede];
The quene to hyr soper yede,
Ipomadon toke good tent   3485
To serue hur well wyth all his may[n]e.
Sone come the kyngys chamburlay[n]e
Fro the turnament.
Before the borde downe gan he knele:
'Madame, the kyng gretys you wele;   3490
He hathe me hedur sent.'
The quene sayd, 'Thoas, þou art welcome:
Syr, off thy tydandis tell vs sum—
Who durst best byde on bent?'

'In fayth, madame, þat can I not,   3495
To tell you who most worthy wrought
Off all that were comen thedur.'
The quene sayd, 'Fye, for shame!

3471 þem] *K.; MS* þer   3476 hathel] *K.; MS* hattred   3477 fone] *K.;*
MS foure   3483 toke] *Followed by deleted* they   hede] *K.; MS* kepe
3486 mayne] *K.; MS* maye   3487 chamburlayne] *K.; MS* chamburlaye

In faythe, ser, þou art to blame—
Whereffore come þou home hedur   3500
But þou sum tythyngys covth haue told?
Me had leuer that thou wolde
Ye had gon where þou neuer went.'
He sayde, 'Lady, be this daye

I shall as farforthe as I may   3505
Tell yow all togeddur.

'Madame, syn all þ[i]s world began,
That any tydyngys tell can
Noþur be frythe ne be feld,
Was neuer a fayrer turnament   3510
Off knyghttys þat wele durst byde on þe bent
Bothe wyth spere and shyld.
My lord hathe borne hym well today;
May non hym blame, þe soth to say,
That euer yet couthe weld.   3515
He feld downe knyȝttys in the [lee],
Me þought grette Ioye to see
As I hovyd and behylde.

'Certes, madam, Cabanus,
And off Irelond Manastus   3520
Full boldly þey gan hem bere,
So dyd Astore and Ser Dr[y]as;
But a knyght in white þer was
That welle couth weld geyre:
All þat we speke of yett   3525
Ys but fabuls to hit,
Be worthynes off werre.
Wonder [þ]e[y] karpe of hym is non,
So worthy a knyght as he is one,
This darre I savely swere.   3530

'The riche kyng of Spayne toke he,
And sent hym to the lady fre
To presoune at hur wille.
The emperoure, be dent off hand

3507 þis] þs   3516 lee] feld   3522 Dryas] K.; MS dras   3528 þey]
K.; MS ye

On the land he left hym lyand,   3535
Lykyd hym neuer so ille;   f. 248ᵛ
The duke of Lorayne has he slayn,
In feld the riche duke of Bratayn
Left he lyand still,
And the provde erle Amfyon   3540
He hath made to his bereyng to be bone
That hardy was on hill.

'Hade not the white knyghte þer be sene,
Cabanus had takyn bene,
The sothe is not to layne.   3545
To be wyth sheld or schaft spent
And brokyne arme ore they . . .'

. . . .

'Grette hym well, ser, I þe praye.
All my houndys, thou may hym say,
Today hathe done full well: 3550
Bothe Blokan and Nobillet
Hathe ronne a-right and gon wel bet,
And also dyd Redel.
Off all that I on cowpell keste,
Today the white hath borne hym best,   3555
As I haue happe or selle.'

Then lowȝe all, both lesse and more;
The quene off his wordys shamyd sore,
And þat was his lykyng.
The more off oþur þing she spake,   3560
That no man þerto tent shuld take,
Nother elde ne yonge.
He sayd, 'I praye you, good madame;
Off the venesone that we brouȝte hame,
Lett send parte to the kyng—   3565
Then may he se I s[er]ue you right
[Wyth] my power and my myȝte   f. 249ʳ
Right well in all kyne þinge!'

3541 bone] borne   3553 Redel] K.; MS redely   3566 serue] K.; MS sure
3567 Wyth] K.; MS That

Then lowde lawȝed þe chamburlayn,
To[k]e l[ev]e, and wyth hym leydys agayne   3570
A noble dere off gresse.
When he come into the hall,
The kyng he present þer wyth all
As he sett on the deysse.
Sethen he tellyd ilke a deyle   3575
Off Nobilled and off Rydell;
How they were lossyd off þe lesse,
And how the white hounde bare þe price.
The kyng lewȝ and held hym nyce,
And sayd, 'A noble folle he is!'   3580

When they all hard þus reasone,
Bothe lewȝe erle and barone
And all the folke bedene,
But no thyng lowȝ Cabanus;
Full woo hym was þat he wroȝte þis,   3585
To witte wythoutyn w[ene].
When the quene suppud had,
Hyr loue her to chamber ledde
And kyssud that lady shene.
He toke leve and to his in youde;   3590
To reste hymselff he had grett nede,
For sore bette had he been.

Ipomadon, the sothe to say,
Rosse before the spryng off day
And taryd not that tyde.   3595
His redde stede he dyd forthe take,
His redde armore redy make,
He wold no lengur abyde.
Wyth lowde blowyng forth he foundes,
His brachettys and his oþur houndys   3600
Cowpled by hys syde.
All that hym hard lowde lowȝ;
They sayd, 'þer is the [quen]ys drewe,
Will to the Iustyng ryde!'

f. 249ᵛ

3570 Toke leve] Ka.; MS To he lowe   3586 wene] K.; MS wynd
3603 quenys] K.; MS kyngys

When he comythe afore þe quenes castell,   3605
Then blewe he lowde and well,
That made the ladyes wake;
Att his noyese was full tene,
All they cryed on the quene
And a grette sportte gan make: 3610
'Low, madame, your love ys goone,
That rest for hym we may haue none,
So he hyes hym for your sake
To turnament; yff he may leve,
For you grett strokys will he geve   3615
In forest vnder an oke!'

The quene lay still as anny stone,
Word wold she speke none,
But had full mekyll care:
Syne he is so fayre all wyce,   3620
That no prowes on hym lysse
Thereffore she syghyd full sore.
Wytheovte any more abyde,
To the armetage he ryde,
And garte araye hym thare   3625
His stede and hym all in rede.
He sayd, 'Mayster, in that stede
On huntyng mvste ye fare.

'For Goddis loue do ye your myghte,
Abydes me here agayne the nyghte,   3630 f. 250ʳ
I pray you specyally.'
His mayster hies on huntyng faste;
Ipomadon his way is paste
Be that derne [st]ye.
The way prevely he nome   3635
As he had oute off the citte come,
That no man shuld hym spye.
As a worthy knyght he workys yare;
To helpe than, þat he hyede thare
Was his encheson whye.   3640

3620 wyce] *K.; MS* wayce   3634 stye] *K.; MS* waye

At the fyrst day wyth[inn] was he;
Wythoute thought he than to be,
For they dysconfyte were,
Wyth grette reddoure fled awaye
Off his strokys, the sothe to saye,   3645
So they were sad and sore.
The kyng was on the inner syde,
Thereffore wyth hym [n]old he abyde;
He þought non to spare
That day, noþur kyng ne knyght   3650
Ne no man, were he neuer so wyght
And bryme as any bore.

He hovis and heyes vp his lavnce,
Wyth the wynd wevys þe conisaunce.
Be that shewyd the day,   3655
The wayttys on the wallys were
And sawe the redde knyghte hove þere
In armoure good and gaye.
They cryed, 'Lady, awake, awake!
The turnamente for your sake   3660
f. 250ᵛ   Begennythe, the sothe to say.
Fyrste his power for to prove,
A knyght in rede younder I se hove
Righte in a good araye.'

'Waytys,' she sayd, 'for Goddys myght,   3665
Sees ye oughte the white knyght
That yesterday Iustyd here?'
'Nay madame, as ette I brede,
But younder hovys a knyght in rede
That semys off grette powere.'   3670
The lady wendys in to the wall
And lokys aboute here ouer all
Wyth a full sympull chere.
In agayne hur hedde she drewe,
To chambyr she went wyth sorowe i-nowȝe,   3675
Then sonyd that lady clere:

3641 wythinn] K.; MS wyth men   3644 fled] d corr. from b   3648 nold]
K.; MS wold

'Curst pryde and wykkyd vysse,
Woo worthe thy grette malesse,
I may so say hardely.
Thrugh pryde forsakys me now my love;   3680
Pryde bryngys me vnder and not above
Wyth many a carefull crye.
Be my pryde I am dystroyde,
And be my pryde grettly noyed;
He hathe e[n]chosone why.   3685
Wyse men saye be Sent Sykasbas,
"Who hes themselff þat be levyd islas"—†
In good faythe, that am I!

'My þought was euer so mekyll on pryde,
Myne owne worde me now ch[yde],   3690
And trewly that is right:
For he above as God wolde pere,
For his pryde fell Lusyfere   f. 251ʳ
To hell fro heyven on hy[ght]e.
I haue byn ay ouer-proude in hertt—   3695
Movnt ouer-hye that hathe me gerte
And now full lowe I lyghte,
Myselff till ouer mekyll shame;
Now forsakys me the same
That I to love had ty3te.'   3700

I[aso]ne went to the walle
And sawe the feld ouer all
Wher many a stander[d] stoode.
To the chamber sone he went
And bad come se þat lady gent   3705
The Iustys fayre and good.
'Doway I[aso]ne, for thy lewte;
Off that Iustyng nothyng ys me,
Be God so myld of mode,
For why my leman is not here!'   3710
So comforttys he þat lady clere;
To the wallys she yede.

3685 enchosone] K.; MS echosone   3690 chyde] K.; MS chastyse
3694 hyghte] K.; MS hye   3701 Iasone] Iosane   3703 standerd] K.; MS
stander   3704 chamber] r corr. from u   3707 Iasone] Iosane

Syr Manastus of Irelonde
Was newe dubbyd, I vnderstond;
He knelyd to Melengere   3715
And prayed hym worthely, i-wis,
The fyrst Iustys myght be his—
'Full Ioyfull þen I were.'
I can not tell you all bedene;
Sum men sayd he louyd the quene,   3720
For euer he was hir nere.
The kyng hathe grauntyd what he as[te],
He made his harnes redy faste;

f. 251ᵛ   He thynkys to wynne the Fere.

His conisaunce was so good and gay,   3725
He lepus on a stede baye,
Oute of the tent he rade.
Still stode Ipomadon;
Sembleant to Iustyng made he none,
But hovyd and abade.   3730
His eye to the wall he cast
And saw hur there þat louyd best;
To Iuste then Ioye he hade.
He stroke Ser Manastus so sore
That hors and man boþe downe he bare;   3735
The spers on sundyr [glade].

Or any succure was to hym come,
Ipomadon hath his sewrance nome
Betwene þem too alonne.
I[aso]ne come to feld be þanne   3740
Wyth noble sperys IX or X.
Hym knewe Ipomadon,
But he lette as he hym neuer see:
He sayd, 'Good ser, of whens ar ye?'
The tother answered anon,   3745
'A cosyne nere to the Fere.'
'Noble spere[s] haue ye here—
For Goddis loue lend me one.'

3722 aste] K.; MS askys   3726 stede] Followed by deleted gaye
3736 glade] K.; MS brest   3740 Iasone] Iosane   3747 Noble speres] K.; MS
a noble spere

He sayd, 'Ser, so God me save,
Off the best shall ye haue;   3750
Chosse at your owne avyce,
For worthely ye gan þem welde.
Here haue ye feld in the feld
A venture off ladyes:
Off the quene hathe he made mekill rose,   3755   f. 252ʳ
But love hym hope I not she dos,
That womon ys so wyse.
Yt has he nothyng þe bett for þat;
To rose hem of her thar he sat,
The more I hold hym nyce.'   3760

'Syr, synne he hath done þat dede,
To thy lady þou hym lede
Wythouten wordys moo,
And saye a ventures knyghte hym [w]endys,
Att hur will to make amendys   3765
That he hathe trespassid so.
He is wyse that workys þus.'
Sythe he sayd to Manastus,
'Syr, wyth hym muste ye goo.'
The knyght þerfore grette mornyng made,   3770
But wyth I[aso]ne forthe he rode,
Whedyr he were well or woo.

Blyth she was in blod and boone
That yong knyght was soget þan,
But woo was Cabanus   3775
That Manastas hym yeldun hath:
A grette spere in hand he taas
And rydythe to Ser Dreseus
The erle off Flaunders, a noble man;
These too on werre togeddur ranne   3780
For tene off Manastus.
The erle to þe ground he bare,
His hors by the brydull toke he þere
Away-ward ledys hym thus.

3764 wendys] K.; MS sendys   3770 knyghtt] K.; MS knyghttys
3771 Iasone] Iosane

The whiles was Ipomadon   3785
In a stronge stoure wyth on,
The duke off Normandye;
Ayþer on oþur the sperys had brokyn—
They þought þey shuld be better wrokyn—
They drew þer swerdys on hye.   3790
Ipomadon layd on so faste,
The duke yolde hym at þe last;
He hadde a cawce why,
For þorowe the sheld was he shent.
To the lady he hym sent;   3795
Ioyfull was she forthy.

Ipomadon saw in þat stonde
The erle off Flaunders ly on þe grounde;
Right wrothe he was þat tyde.
Cabanus awayward his hors lede;   3800
He thought ful welle he shuld hym stede
And lovde on hym he cryede:
'Lett goo that hors, ser, i[f] þat ye maye;
In faythe ye lede hym not away,
Well faster yff ye ryde!'   3805
Cabanus no worde answered,
But forthe he rede as he not herde;
Ipomadon after hym hyed.

When Cabanus saw hym come,
An hevy swerd in hond he nome,   3810
To fyght he made hym bowne.
Ipomadon his swerd drawen bare
And strake Cabanus so sore,
In swounyng fell he down.
More to hym wold he not do;   3815
His hors he broughte þe erle too
And sett hym in the arsoune.
Ilke a man to oþer sware,
Suche a dede saw they neuer ayre,
Bothe erle and bold baron;   3820

3803 if] *K.*; *MS* it

They sayd þer was non so mekyll off mayne.
When Cabanus was recouered ageyn,
Vppon his fote he stertte:
He sware be God and Sent Myghell,
'Thus dede shall be venged full wele   3825
Yff God will gyff me [querte]!'
Hee wyste not where þe rede knyȝt was;
Sone he metys w[yth] Ser Dreas
That herdy was off hertte.
The banere of wythovten he bare,   3830
Thereffore Cabanus wold not spare;
Wyth clene love he hy[m] gert;

He bare hym down wythoute lesse.
Ipomadon was in þe presse
And saw how he had done;   3835
All woo he was for Ser Dreas,
To rescew hym grette haste he has
And to hym wan full sone.
He horsyd hym eft for his sake,
And gaffe so many a sterne strake   3840
That byde hym durste but [fone]:
All seyd, that hys dedis myghte see,
A better knyght myȝte non be
[This day] vnder sonne.

His dedis sawe the lady clere;   3845   f. 253ᵛ
Imayne callyd to her the Fere
And told hyr ilke a dealle,
'Syster, sythe þou younde knyghte
In the rede harnes þat is dyghte,
How he hathe doone so well?   3850
Yesturday, so haue I blis,
Off dede was not a poynte to þis
Be ovght that I gan [tell];
But mi love and Cabanus,

3826 querte] K.; MS grace   3828 wyth] was   3832 hym] K.; MS hy
gert] with superscript e, corr. from gre   3836 Followed by two lines which are an exact
copy of ll. 3784-5   3841 fone] K.; MS sum   3844 This day] K.; MS omitted,
and vnder sonne written as part of l. 3843   3853 tell] K.; MS see

Me thought, dyd halff-dele this   3855
As haue I hape and sele.

'Were not for losynge off my love,
Younde knyght to love were not reprove,
Fro bale as I be broght!'
A spere be Iasone she hym sent;   3860
Wyth her owne fyngeris gent
The pensell had she wrou3te.
Off the spere fayne was hee,
And dyd hym well, þer herselff my3te see
How many to grounde he brought.   3865
That saw a knyght Cananeus,
Steward off the kyngys howse;
Oute off a syde he soughtte.

A nobull man off werre he was,
But a condycion he hase   3870
That mevis all my mode:
Was non that tyme so worthy wetyn
Than he covthe haue wyth hym fletyn,
Hadde he ben neuer so good.

f. 254ʳ   Some men sayd, as haue I sell,   3875
That he louyd the quene well,
But in no stede hit stoode.
A seker stede he rydethe vppon
That mekyll hathe covetyd Ipomadon,
And to hym sone he rode.   3880

He stroke Canoneus soo,
Tope ouer tayle he garte hym goo;
That bargyn myght he banne.
The stede be the brydull caught;
All men saw he stale hym nought,   3885
But worthely he hym wanne.
He lede hym syne to Egyon;
To the forest wyth hym is he gone,
O the fet full well he can.
Kyng Melengere all þ[i]s behyld;   3890

3863 the] thee *(second* e *smudged)*   3887 He] H *corr. from* E   3889 fet] feter
3890 þis] þs

Worthely he gan his wepons wyld,
On Lyard lepythe he þanne.

The kyng waxe nye woo[d] for tene
That he smot downe his kny3ttys kene,
And to hym rydis on werre.   3895
Emyddis the shyld he stroke hym so
That þorow the soket he gert goo
And braste his oþur geyre;
Vndernethe the ly[f]t pappe
The dent yede, because it was happe,   3900
And dyd but littill dere.
Ipomadon wex red for tene;
He stroke the kyng ageyne, I wene,
That downe he gan hym beyre.

His shild myght no lenger laste;   3905   f. 254ᵛ
The naylis off his haubreke berste
That worthely was wrou3te.
Be his nakyd syde þe soket glas;
A littill tyne hurte hym it hathe,
But the wers was he not. . . .   3910
Ipomadon [Ly]ard ledis awaye
And to his sheld hym brought,
And into þe forest he hym ledde.
Melengere was stretlye stede,
But sade men to hym soughte,   3915

And socurryd hym, wythoute w[e]ne,
Els had þe kyng takyne bene,
In hertte is not to hyde.
The vttereste syde was full fayne;
They sawe the kyng lye on þe playn   3920
And lowde þerfore they cryed.
Wyth the banner prekys into þe place
The noble erle Ser D[rea]s,
His folke to hym rel[ye]d.
Ipomadon full wele hym bare   3925

3893 wood] *K.; MS* woo   3899 lyft] lyght   3908 glas] *K.; MS* glaste
3911 Lyard] *K.; MS* hard   3916 wene] *K.; MS* wonde   3918 is] *K.; MS* this
3923 Dreas] Deras   3924 hym] *Followed by crossed-out* reve   relyed] releuyd

His strokys were full sad and sore
Durste non that day hym byde.

So longe laste the turnament,
The nyghte ys comyn, the day is went,
The sonne drawethe downe.　　　　　　　　　　3930
The inner syde wyth grett honoure
Was drevyne to dyscomfettour,
They toke þer pavelyons.
Bothe lord and lady brightte
Seyd for sothe the redde knyght　　　　　　　3935
f. 255ʳ　　Moste was off renowne.
The seconde day this is comen to ende
And as Ipomadon to the wood shuld wynde
So metis he wyth I[aso]ne:

'Iasone, broþur, [s]e here thy l[aunc]e—　　3940
Thereon is yet the conysaunce
As thou thyselff may see:
Grette that lady, as God me save,
And saye wyth me I will it haue
Into myn owne contre.　　　　　　　　　　　3945
For her sake I shall þis spere
In well sharpe stowrys bere—
Thou sey to the bryght of ble!'
I[aso]ne sayd, 'Ser, who is that
That wat so well what I hat?　　　　　　　　3950
Grettly it mervels mee!'

'Yes, I[aso]ne, cecurlye
I know well i-nowe forthy;
Felowes onys we were.
Yesturday Iuste I here in white,　　　　　　　3955
To day in rede, ys not to hyde;
So may I do no more.'
'A, mercy ser, for Crystys pitte;
My ladye dyes for love of the

3939 Iasone] Iosane　　　3940 se] be　　launce] K.; MS lewte　　3941 There]
Followed by crossed-out is　　　3949 Iasone] Iosane　　　3952 Iasone] Iosane
3957 do] *Followed by crossed-out* mo

And you will fro her fare!'   3960
'Nay I[aso]ne, I may not dwell;
All my folke vnder younde hill
Abydys me hoveand thare.

'Ryght now to me tydynge come
That [m]e behovys to go home,   3965
And þerfore, s[yr], good day!
A M^l tymes grette her well
And saye I shall, as I haue sell,   f. 255ᵛ
Speke wyth hur when I maye.'
Lowde mercy he hym cryede;   3970
'Fare well—I may no lenger byde!'
Wyth that he went his wey.
In the pres I[aso]ne loste hym has;
Wyth sorofull hertt home he goos,
Where that the lady laye.   3975

'I[aso]ne,' quod that lady clere,
'Tell me, what is thy chere? . . .'
'Madame wepe I mvste,
For today haue I loste
The best knyght þat euer was wroght.'   3980
'Whiche, cosyn? þat knyght in rede?'
'Yea, he dryues me to dede!'
'Why? What he was wyst ye oughte?'
'The same that yesterday [I] mett.'
'Whiche? He þat was the straunge valet?'   3985
'In faythe, the same [me] [thou]ght.'

'Alas,' quod the lady thanne,
'I trowe he be no erthely man,
Be God and Sent Myghell!'
'Why, what trow ye than þat he be?'   3990
'Sum off the fayre is he—
I' faythe that hope I wele!

3961 Iasone] Iosane   3965 me] K.; MS ne   behovys] Followed by me
3966 syr] K.; MS shey   3973 Iasone] Iosane   3976 Iasone] Iosane
3984 I] K.; MS omitted   3986 me thought] K.; MS wyght

Dye I wot welle I [b]vs;
Trewly, and he goo fro me þ[u]s,
My care will neuer kele!'   3995
The kyng and I[aso]ne both hym sought,
But all þer travell is noȝt,
So have I happe or sele.

To the ermytage anon
Comyn is Ipomadon   4000
That in his hert was fayne:
His mayster had huntyd of the best
That day in the thyke foreste;
The grette herttys had he slon.
Off he kest his armore shene,   4005
And as a hunter all in grene
He rays hymselff agayne.
Home he rydys wyth lowde blowyng;
Than lowȝe and seyd both old and yong,
'Now comythe the Drew-le-rayne   4010

'Wyth nobull stedys many one,
And ryall knyghttys þat he hath tane
In the turnamente:
He ha[s] gevyn amonge þe okys
Knyghttys so mony grette strokys   4015
That nygh hymselff is shent!'
Egyon by other weye[s]
Wyth his hors and his harnes
Ys to the citte wente,
And that noble stede also   4020
That he wanne Gananeus fro,
Wyth hym has he sente,

And also Lyard of the kyng.
Wythouten any pars[e]uynge
He broughte þem to þat citte.   4025
The yattis when he come before,

3993 bvs] K.; MS mvste   3994 þus] þs   3996 Iasone] Iosane
4009 Than] Followed by deleted lowde   4014 has] have   4017 weyes] weye
4023 kyng] kyngys   4024 parseuynge] K.; MS parsuynge

Lowde his horne blewe he thore,
His houndys questyd grette plente.
The knyght into the hall he gos,   f. 256ᵛ
And to þe quene a present mase   4030
Off herttys hedis thre.
The lady lokyd on þe hornes,
Maydons gaff hym many skornys;
Thereoff grette Ioye hadde hee.

To supper þey went after that;   4035
Her leff be her on the benke sat
As shuld hur own drew.
Full littill had he slept þat nyȝte;
The quene lokyd on the knyghte
And saw hym pale off hewe: 4040
'Syr,' she sayd, 'it is sene,
At ouer mekyll travell has þou bene;
Today erlye ye blewe.
Put your huntyng to respyte—
Therein ye haue ouer mekyll delyte,   4045
And thou thyselff it knewe!'

'The[r]to, madame, I darre not graunte;
Ou[er] mekyll than were I recreaunte.'
Then lowȝ the maydons on hye
And sayd, 'Whedur þou hunte or non,   4050
A coward we hold the euerychone,
And littill thanke-worthy!'
Thereoff had he Ioye i-nowgh
That they hym so to skorne lowȝe;
He toke no hedde þerbye.   4055
Sone come the kyngys chamburlayne
Wyth tydyngys to the quene agayne,
The turnament to dyscrye.

Hee knelys downe on his knee;
'Welcome, Tho[a]s, so mot thow bee,'   4060 f. 257ʳ

4033 maydons] a *written above word*   4047 Ther] *K.*; *MS* The   4048 Ouer
mekyll] ou mekyll   4060 Thoas] thomes

Quod that worthy in wede;
'Swette ser, who dyd best today?
What man hath borne þe price awey?'
'Madame, so God me spede,
Yesterday, as haue I blis,   4065
Off dedis were not a poynt to þis
Haundell, whoso take hede!
Today þer was a kny3te in rede
That sterd hym so in þe stede
That all off hym þey dred.   4070

'That knyght of worthynes of honde
Toke Manastus of Irelonde
And sent hym to the Fer holde;
Sethen he stroke downe Cabanus,
And rescued the erle Dre[se]us—   4075
Hellys had his care byn cold.
He vencust the erle of Normandy,
And reskewed D[rya]s, securly,
So was h[e] bryme and bold.
Syx dyd not yesterday I say,   4080
Ne x so mekill as he todaye,
And all the trewgh my3te be told!'

'Why ser, wherefore shuld ye spare?
I praye God gyff you sorow and care,
The sothe but yff ye saye!'   4085
'Madame, that doughtty vnder sheld
My lorde the kynge hathe feld in feld,
And Lyard ledde awaye.'
She axte that all my3te here
Yff þe kyng hurtte were,   4090
f. 257ᵛ   And he sayd shortely, 'Naye.'
Then sayd þe quene on her law3inge;
'Lord, ser—who durst fell þe kyng?'
'I not, be my faye.

4075 Dreseus] Dreus   4078 Dryas] Dares   4079 he] K.; MS hym
4080 syx] K.; MS syxt   4082 be] Followed by deleted hold

'Had hym not come better succoure,   4095
He had byn takyne in that stoure
Wyth that noble knyghte.
Cananeus, your owne steward,
He stroke downe off his horse bakewarde
That all men saye in sighte;   4100
His hors he hathe, þe sothe to saye.
Whan all was done he went his way
A littill before the nyght.
The kyng hathe sought hym farre and nere,
And so hathe done þat lady clere,   4105
But fynd hym can no wyghte.'

'Ys he goone?' 'Madame, y[e].'
'Wotte no man whether? I say shew me!'
'That can no man tell.'
'Syr, where is the white knyght   4110
That yesterday was so mekyll of myght?'
'As I be sauyd, madame, fro hell,
In the feld he was not sene;
Today the rede knyght best haþe ben,
So thyke he dyd them fell.'   4115
Shoo lokyd on hym þat be her satte;
The whyte and the rede boþe she forgatte,
The comelye vnder palle.

When they hadde spokyn of chevalrye,
Ipomadon spoke off his foly   4120
Hyly in that hall,
And sayd,'Younde knyʒttys be folys [i]ll   f. 258ʳ
To take suche strokys [at] [w]ille,
And rennes ay to þat þey [fall]!
Syr, say the kyng þus, I praye þe: 4125
He had byn better at home wyth me,
The sothe say yff I shall;
I trow the red knyght shuld have sparyd
To haue ledde away Lyard!'
Then lowʒ the maydons all.   4130

4107 ye] ya   4109 & 4112 *reversed in MS*   4122 ill] all   4123 at wille]
ille   4124 fall] *K.; MS* say

'Syr, grette hym wele and say hym ytt,
He myghte haue redden on hym yet
Hadde he byn wyth mee!'
The quene of his wordys shamed is,
But þerfore sayd he neuer the les   4135
But to her spekis he,
On benche be her þer he satt;
'Madame, off þe veneson þat we gatte,
A parte to the kyng send yee,
And ye may say, as I haue seall,   4140
Today my houndys hath renne right wele,
Be God and be my lewte.

'Rydell ran at devyse;
To day my red hounde berythe þe pryce
And þeroff am I glade.'   4145
Then lowȝe the chamburleyne,
He toke his leve and went agayne,
A grette hertte wyth hym ledde.

f. 258ᵛ   He made his present to the kynge
And told hym all, wythoute lesynge,   4150
The tale as he hym bade;
How that Bloncan and Nobilet
Hathe renne right and goon well bett
And how the price Rydall ha[d],

And how the rede knyȝt shuld haue sparyde   4155
To haue lede away Lyard
And [he] had wyth hym been.
There att all men lowȝ there fille,
But Cabanus lykyd full ille;
His hertte brest nere for tene.   4160
When the soper tyme was done,
Ipomadon after sone
To chambyr ledde þe quene,
Kyste her wyth mowthe still—
Full well he wyst þe quenes will—   4165
To reste she went, I wene.

4154 had] K.; MS hathe   4157 he] K.; MS om.

His leve toke Ipomadon,
To his inne is he goone.
Before the day he rose
Wythoute more tareynge;   4170
His blake stede he dyd forth brynge
And his blake harnes,
Sone was copled all his houndys.
As he þorowe þe citte foundys,
An hedeowes noyce he ma[s]e;   4175
Hit was non þat slept so faste,
That they ne wakyd at the laste
And sayd, 'Now the quene leman goothe!'   f. 259ʳ

When he come þer the quene laye,
He blowythe as lowde as euer he maye.   4180
Thereffore was ladyes wrothe;
They cursude and bannyde hym euerychone,
Seyd, 'Reste for hym we may haue none,
His blewyng is so br[ath]e!'
To the ermytage gan he fare,   4185
In blake he made hym redy thare
And his steede bothe.
Then Ipomadon gan saye,
'For Goddis [love], mayster, I you praye,
On huntynge high you rathe.'   4190

His mayster dothe as he hathe hym byden;
Ipomadon ys way ys reden,
His stede and he in blake.
The same tyme in Gresse-londe,
A duke ther wonnyde, I vnderstonde,   4195
That grett maystryes covde make.
His name was Ser Adry[u]s,
A bolde man and a bountevs,
Off dedys nothyng to lake.
A dyuynere wyth hym had hee   4200
That be the sterres grett plente
Cowde grette insamble take.

4175 mase] *K.; MS* made   4184 brathe] *K.; MS* brighte   4189 love] *K.;*
MS om.   4197 Adryus] Adryes

Hys name was Ser Anferas,
He told hym mekyll þat he [asse]
Off devynyte, that cowd he.   4205
The same nyghte [th]at þe turnament
Was sett be the comen assente,

He went the sterres to see,
And be the planettys well hath he founde
That þer shuld grette worshipe be wonne   4210
Off knyght of that asemble;
But off the best he was onwyse—
Off hym þat bare awey the pryce,
His termes wrong toke he!

He dyd his lord to vnderstonde   4215
What he be the sterres fonde;
He made hym redy faste.
Two hundyrd knyghttys off grette araye
Sayles on the flode so graye;
To semble was his caste.   4220
The thryd day he ryse yare;
Whedyr syde wars ware
A bachelere he axsyd.
All men tolde hym at þat tyde,
They on the inner syde   4225
Was dyscomfett laste.

He pyȝtte his pavelyon, þat stouȝte,
To helpe them þat were in douȝte
Wyth all the myghte he maye.
The riche duke sware, i-wis,   4230
That yff he myȝte, it shuld be his
The fyrste Iust þat daye.
Ipomadon wyste well all togeder
The riche duke was comyne thedyr
On a ryche araye,   4235
That on þe inner syde wold he bee;

4203 hys] *Written above deleted* Syr   4204 asse] *K.; MS* wold   4205 cowd
he] *Reversed in MS;* he *followed by crossed-out* coud   4206 that] at, *preceded by*
crossed-out that   4216 sterres] e *written above; second* r *corr. from* e
4221 thryd] d *written above line*   4232 Iust] Iustys

Thereffore wytho[u]ten bydythe hee—
That boughte he sothen, I saye!

Ipomadon hovyd before the towne,
The wayte hym sawe þat lokyd abowne
And he callyd on the Fere.
He sayd, 'Awake, lady bryghte!
Younder hoves a blake knyghte
In armys good and clere.'
'Wayte,' she sayd, 'for mannys dede,
Sees thou auȝte the knyght in rede
That yesterday Iustyd here?'
'Nay madame, but no lake;
Younder hoves a knyght in blake
Wyth a noble chere.'

The way to the walles she toke;
After the rede knyght gan she loke
And sawe hym on no syde.
In sonyng fell she downe agayne,
To chambur leydys hur Imayne
And her comforttys þat tyde.
The duke off Gresse, wyth grette boste,
Comaundythe swythe to all his ost
That none shuld to hym ryde
But yff they se abowte hym mo
Knyghttys þen oþer one or two
That bolddly durste abyde.

He rydes vpon a red stede . . .
Toward the blake knyght
In rede sadull, sheld and spere,
And red was all his oþur geyre,
Hit shone as beymes bryghte.
On the lady cryes Imayne,
'Madame, as I be kept frome payne,
Here may ye se wyth syght
Your avncyante knyght arayde in rede

4240

4245

4250

4255

4260

4265

4270

4237 wythouten] *K.; MS* wyth oten
4259 none] *Followed by crossed-out* to
4246 Sees] *Preceded by crossed-out* k
4271 knyght] *Followed by deleted* wyth syghte

Agayne the blake in that stede
And forses hym to fyghte!'

So Ioyfull was she neuer ayre;
She wend the knyght in red were   4275
Hee had her leman beane.
In the mornynge erly as she myghte,
I[aso]ne she dubbyd knyght
In armore good and clene;
She gyrdythe hym wyth a swerd above,   4280
And xxx^ti other for his love
That herdy were and kene.
A younge squyere gan she byde,
'Serue oure of speris as I[aso]ne dyd
The tother to dayes bedene.'   4285

For well wend þat lady bright
The redde had byn her own kny3te
When she saw hym thare.
Togedder are these knyghttys gone;
The duke strake Ipomadon   4290
Wyth a stallworthe spere,
That his shild flo fram his halse;
Nerehande had he falen alse
Be worthynes off werre.
Ipomadon fayled nott;   4295
He sawe here þer that he on þoughte,
The duke downe gan he beyre.

Egyon wyst what shuld be done,
On Adryus stede he lepus sone.
The lady hovis and beheld;   4300
In sonynge fell þat lady clere—
She went þat it hur leman were
That so was fallon in feld.
Thee duke full dulf[u]ly was dy3te
That vp to ryse he had no my3te,   4305

f. 261^r

4278 Iasone] Iosane   4281 And] A *corr. from* T   4284 Iasone] Iosane
4299 Adryus] r *written above* y   4301 lady] *Followed by crossed-out* f
4304 dulfuly] *K.; MS* dulfly

His swerd he gan hym yelde.
He proferd hym to his raunsome
Castellys riche and many a towne
And mekyll gold to welde.

'Nay ser,' quod Ipomadon;   4310
'Off thy castelles kepe I none,
Be God and myn lewte,
But on thy trewght here shall þou swere
Today þou shall no armys were
Wyth yȝen that men may see.'   4315
He cryed, 'Gentill ser, mercy!
To this turnament comyn am I
Oute off ferre contre;
Grettly thereon haue I c[o]ste,
And yff I thus my travell loste   4320
It were grette shame to me!'

'Syr, synne thou wylt Iuste nede,
Thou shalte caste off thy rede wede
And sythen goo, do thye beste!'
Trewly his trewgh þerto he plyȝte;   4325
To his tente youde the knyghte
And off that armore caste.
Ipomadon saw oute of the castell   f. 261ᵛ
A chyld come he knew full well
A littell þer be weste,   4330
But he knewe not Ipomadon.
A noble spere he brouȝte hym one;
To take hit he was full preste.

He sayd, 'Ser, take thus rede stede
And to thy lady thou hym lede,   4335
For no man that þou spare.
The whyȝte knyght, þou may her say,
Ne the rede had not goon awey
Hadde I come anny ayre,
And I trowe today to be sene   4340
Her leffe is strekyne down, I wene,

For all his freshe fare.
In h[er] presoune shall he not be,
Ne sertus she shall hym not see
Today Iuste no more!   4345

'Swythe shall he wend in to þe weste,
The man I trowe þat she louythe beste,
And also þou her saye,
Yff he beffore the gre haue wonne,
Here he hathe his felow founde;   4350
Yche myghte se where he laye.
I trowe her leman had a squate;
Goo be-lyve and tell hur that
Good ser, I the praye.'
The chyld dyd as he hym badde;   4355
So mekyll sorowe þen she made,
In sonyng fell þat maye:

'A, God þat made bothe old and younge,
Thus is no wonder þinge
That makythe me fowle to fade.   4360
On the fyrste day was sent to me
The riche kyng off Spayne, parde,
Suche happe my leman hadde;
Syne Manastus off Irelonde,
And many other weldande   4365
In feld wyth brondys brayde.
But what is me of all þo?
Righte nought, synne I my love forgoo,
Be grette God that me mayde!'

So faste she grett and gaff her ille   4370
That ner she is in poynte to spille,
And to hersellff gan saye,
'Loste thus and my leman be,
Shall þer neuer man haue of me
As farreforthe as I maye!'   4375

4343 her] K.; MS his   4349 beffore] be written above, with caret   4356 þen]
en written above line   4361 On] Preceded by crossed-out T   4374 þer] Followed by
crossed-out e

f. 262ʳ

The stoure wythouten waxed stronge.
Ipomadon into the thekyste thronge
And dyd full welle that day . . .
Men on horsse faste they wynne
And many on lond they laye.   4380

They wythoute gadyrd myghte,
Faste forses they to fyghte
Bothe wyth spere and shilde.
So harde ychone on oþer layde,
Stedys stode stakerand for stonyede,   4385
There maysturs fellt in feld.
Dreas lokyd hym aboute
And blewe and creyd after his rowte,
The banere vp he helde.
Ipomadon þere sone cryed,   4390   f. 262ᵛ
III C knyghttys to hym rel[ye]d
That cowde þer wepons welde.

Sone come the kyng off Skottelonde,
His swerd boldely in his hande,
And strykys Ipomadon,   4395
That nere-hand to þe grounde he youde.
He þought to yeld hym as good;
The kyng he lyghtt vpon,
His body evyn in to he cle[ve];
The noble swerd, or it wold leeffe,   4400
Ys þorow the sadull goone.
His stede and hym bothe hath he slayne
Wyth that stroke mekyll off mayne;
Men wonderd [ilkone].

Now off I[aso]ne shall ye here: 4405
The blake knyght he holdythe nere
In armore burneshede bright.
That lyked Ipomadon full well,

4390 Ipomadon] *Followed by deleted* vp they helde   4391 relyed] releuyd
4395 And] *Followed by crossed-out* 'ser' *abb.*   4398 The] *Followed by crossed-out* kny
4399 cleve] *K.; MS* cleiyys   4404 ilkone] ouer all; *K.* euery one
4405 Iasone] Iosane

And sayd, 'Ser, so haue I sell,
Younder comythe a knyght: 4410
Dought hym not þowȝ he be [grym],
Goo ryde and Iust wyth hym—
[Mek]ill thou artte off myghte!'
'Gramercy ser, so haue I roo,
As ye me bydde so shall I doo,   4415
Be he neuer so wyghte!'

I[aso]ne wold no lengur byde,
To the k[ny]ght can he ryde,
He knewe his conusaunce;
He strake hym so myde þe shyld   4420
f. 263ʳ
That flate he feld hym in þe feld,
To shevers went the lavnce.
Be the brydull he toke þe stede,
But þe knyght coueryd and away yede.
Ipomadon lykyd that chaunce;   4425
He sayd, 'Be God and my lewte,
A better knyght of his tyme þen he
Yes not froo hens to Fraunce.'

Now shall ye se a wonder c[as]
Off the noble erle Ser Dreas: 4430
He had a brother d[er]e
Wyth the kynge of Irelonde;
Now dubbyd I vnderstond
The tother day bothe they were,
For he was stalworthe vnder s[tel].   4435
[Th]e [st]ought kyng louyd hym wele
And gaff hym armys clere . . . .

Dreas was wythouten þat day,
And he wythin, the sothe to saye;
Many to grounde he brought.   4440
That saw Dreas, securly;

4411 grym] *K.*; *MS* wyȝte   4413 Mekill] littill   4417 Iasone] Iosane
4418 knyght] kynght   4419 conusaunce] con*uer*saunce   4429 a] *Written
above line, with caret*   cas] *K.*; *MS* chaunce   4431 dere] *K.*; *MS* drede
4435 stel] *K.*; *MS* shild   4436 The] *K.*; *MS* he   stought] *K.*; *MS* thought
kyng] *K.*; *MS* kyng*ys*

Off his dedis hadde grette envye,
Oute that syde he [sought].
Dryas rydes vnto his broþer,
Noþer knowlegge had of oþere,   4445
To Iuste they bothe had þoughte.
Cavder smote his broþer Dreas
Thorow shild of gold and his harnes,
Yet sertus he hurte hym not.

Dreas stroke his broþer Cavder   4450
Wyth a spere sadde and sore
Thorowoute all his armore;   f. 263ᵛ
In at his brest, out at his bake,
The chyne bone asonder brake . . .
Dede of his brothers hande,   4455
And that was grett doloure.
He gaff hym suche a spetuous falle,
In sunder brast the lachettys all
That shuld his helme socoure.

His basnette flew off þere;   4460
When Dreas sawe his visage bare,
Wonder woo he was.
When he sawe his broþeres face,
In sonynge fell Dreas,
Syghand and sayd, 'Alas   4465
Dere broþer, wo ys mee
That euer I thy bane shuld bee—
Mercy I the axe!'
He lokyd vpe and lokyd hye;
His eyne closude and gan to dye,   4470
His soule away gan passe.

Then hadde Dreas mekill care;
He rent his clothes and drewe his heyre
And oute a swerd drawethe he,
The hylte downeward, þe poynte vp stode;   4475
He swere by God that is good,
'Myne noune bane shall I bee!'

4443 sought] *K.*; *MS* goos   4470 dye] dyee

To hym prekkythe Ipomadon,
His swerd oute of his hond hathe tane
And sayd, 'Benedycyte!'　　　　　　　　　4480
'Alas ser, for sorowe and payne,
It is my broþer that haue I slayne,
Therefore full woo ys mee!'

'Ye ser, lette this greffe ouer goo,
For better is oo man dede þen tow—　　　　4485
This is þe sothe I saye.
Ye, so there is no more to [ke]pe,
Agayne ye vp your stede ye lepe
And for his soule do praye.'
Dreas dyd as he hym bade,　　　　　　　　4490
The body to an churche þey hade,
In beryall they hym laye,
Yff they hadde neuer so mekyll care,
Thus Dreas leves his broþer thare
And wendythe forthe on his waye.　　　　　4495

The stowre lettyd no þing for þ[i]s,
But many a worthy man, i-wis,
Was boldely borne downe.
Yche of them sheverd oþeres shyld,
And feld many a knyghte in feld　　　　　4500
That were of grette renoune.
On noþer syde was not to lake,
But euer more the knyght in blake
Euer to the beste is bowne.
So worthely wroght Ipomadon　　　　　　　4505
That the vtter syde ilkone
Yaffe hym thare benysone.

One Segamvs made afraye
And grette boste all þat daye,
A noble spere he bare;　　　　　　　　　　4510
A knyght of the kyngys mene,
He louyd the quene in parte
As I haue harde seyde yare.

Till Ipomadon he [hym] chese
And he to hym, wythouten leesse,   4515 f. 264ᵛ
Two nobull knyghttys þey were.
Eyther on oþur þer sperys brake,
But still on ther hors bake
They bothe heyld them thare.

Sygamus hys swerd hathe tane   4520
And stornely strykys Ipomadon
Vppon the stelyne hatte.
Ipomadon his [swerd] hathe drawen
And strake Segamus agayne
That to þe ground fell he flatte.   4525
His swerd he yeldys to hym þare;
Vpon his trought he made hym sure
He shuld not leve for that,
That he ne shuld ryde home to þe quene
And yeld hym to that lady shene   4530
In chambur where she satte;

'And say a knyght in armys blake
Has for that ladyes sake
Forgevyne the thy ravnsum.'
He rydys home to þat lady hende,   4535
And told hur his tale to ende
When he was come home.
Then lowȝe the quene in preuyte,
And sayd, 'Lord, what man was hee
That durste beyre you downe?'   4540
'A blake knyght, madame—þat I know—
But well I wott down he me [th]ro[w]
And sent me to your presone.'

Hit was neuer, syn God þis world began,
A fayrer turnament þen þat was one   4545
Off men that worthy were.   f. 265ʳ
The Fere all-way had in sighte

4514 hym] MS om.   4523 swerd] K.; MS hand, written above with caret
4538–40 Copied after 4541–43 in MS   4542 throw] K. slow; MS froo
4543 your] Written above crossed-out my, with caret   4547 The] Ther

The dedis off the blake knyghte,
How boldly he hym bare;
So doughtly he dang them abowte,　　　　　　　4550
That all men off his dentys had dowte,
So warre they bothe sadde and sore.
Hit drewe to the nyght faste;
The inner syde att the laste
Was ouercome thare.　　　　　　　　　　　　4555

On the chasse folowed Ipomadon,
Cabanus turrned and lokyd hym on,
Toward hym rydythe hee:
Was neuer knyghte sithe þus world began
Better belouyd thanne he was þanne　　　　　4560
Amonge the comynalte.
Ipomadon west full well
Cabanus was stallworthe vnder stele,
And lothe he was to flee,
And lothe he was his love forgoo　　　　　　4565
And his travell also
Off his dayes thre.

In feuter ayther castys a speyre,
Sethen togedder ryddes [the]re
Wyth all the myghte they maye.　　　　　　　4570
There sheldys all in sounder brake,
They bothe noþer were to lake,
Behynde þer horsse they laye.
Cabanus sett his strokys so faste,
Ipomadons sheld asunder breste,　　　　　　4575
　　The serten sothe to seye.
Vndernethe the lyfte pappe
Thorowe all his hernes, þis was his hape,
The sokett glasyd away.

Nere-ha[n]d breste his hertte for tene,　　　4580
He wend he shuld a knowen ben
Or he hadde paste that playne;
The blake stede toke Egyon

4556 the] *Followed by crossed-out* s　　　　4569 there] *K.; MS* owre
4580 nere-hand] *K.; MS* nere haid　　　4582 that] thuat

And broughte hym to Ipomadon
And horsud hym efte agayne,   4585
And sethyne to Cabanus stede he wan,
Into the foreste he ledys hym thane,
And off that freyght was fayne.
Then waxed Cabanus nere-hand wood,
And he sterte vp wyth egur mode   4590
As he wold hym asslayne.

He s[wo]re, 'Be God and my lewte,
This dede shall well avenged be
Yff God will gyff me quarte!'
Ipomadon will stryke hym no more,   4595
But wyth his hors breste down hym bare
And sore for-thought it in hertte,
Soo godde a knyght wold hym not yeld.
Kynge Mellengere all þis beheld
And on a stede he stertte;   4600
He prekys to Ipomadon,
A spytuos stroke he gaff hym one
That right sore dyd smarte.

On the righte arme, in þe braune I wene,
Full faste the blod ranne down, bedene,   4605
That many a man myghte it see.   f. 266ʳ
He says, 'Thus shall be vengyd well!'
And oute he takys a bronnde of stele
And lyfte hit vp on hye;
Thereto the kyng good hede toke;   4610
When he sawe hym so gremly loke,
Righte sore aferd was hee.
I darre not say the kyng fled þat tyde,
But for his dent he durst not byde,
Be God and be my lewte!   4615

The inner syde was sore agasste
The kyng awayward heed hym faste;

4589 waxed] x *corrected from* s   4592 swore] sowre   4613 fled] l *corrected*
from e

To fle they toke that tyde,
Some to towne and sum to tente;
Thus endyd the turnamente,   4620
In faythe it is not to hyde.
The blake knyght was off dedys beste . . .
And boldyste durste abyde.
Be that hit drew to þe ny3te,
To wodward hyed that blake knyght   4625
As faste as he my3te [r]yde.

Bysyde hym lokyd Ipomadon,
Soon was he warre of I[aso]ne;
On hym lowde gan he crye:
'Abyde, I[aso]ne, and speke wyth me!'   4630
The other sayd, 'How may þis be?
So grette mervell haue I
That ye so well woste what I high[t].'
'Yes I[aso]ne, be Goddys myghte,
I haue a grette cause whye: 4635

Fel[o]ws I wot well onys we were,
Att a supper, thou wotte well where,
When I was sett the by.

'Thus thre days I haue Iuste here,
And euery day, broþer dere,   4640
In dyueres colours sene.
I thanke hym that all made off noughte
That he soo fayre for me hathe wroghte
Amonge the knyghttys kene.
Grette well thy lady bright of ble . . .   4645
A gyfte I shall hur gyff
Euer more while I leeff,
Too wytte wythouten wene.

'Thus maye thou, þat wyth me spake
When I was whyte, rede and blake,   4650

4626 ryde] *K.*; *MS* hyde   4628 Iasone] Iosane   4630 Iasone] Iosane
4633 I hight] high I   4634 Iasone] Iosane   4636 felows] felews

For nedys mvste I wende.
A M¹ tymes I praye thee
Grette well that lady brighte of ble,
Righte as my faythefull frend;
I shall hereafter, when God will,   4655
Att leyser speke wyth her my fille—
So saye to that lady hende.'
He cryede lowde, 'Mercy ser!
Trewly, goo ye this fro her,
My lady herselff shal shend;   4660

'For you she suffyrs mekyll care!'
'Naye Iasone, lett be thy fare;
Me mvste into my londe.
Fare well till [eft]sones þat we mete,
And as oftyne tymes þou her grette   4665
As gresses þer be groande.'
Into the thykyste prese he paste,
And I[aso]ne loste hym att the laste,   f. 267ʳ
In no syde he hym fonde;
Wyth sorofull hertte and grette mornyng,   4670
Wepand he gothe home to þat lady yonge,
Sorowfull, and wrange his hande.

'I[aso]ne,' quod that lady thanne,
'Why makyste þou suche mornynge, man?
Who ha[s] g[r]evyd thee?'   4675
'Alas, madame, that I was borne,
For today haue we lorne
The beste knyghte that maye be!'
'Why, cosyn?' 'The knyght in blake;
He makyth me all þ[i]s mornynge make.'   4680
'Why? Wyste thou what he be?'
'He that will brynge me to my dede—
The same that Iuste in whyte and rede
Today in blake was hee!'

Then had she thrys so mekyll care,   4685
She tare hyr clothes and drewe hur heyr
Wyth many a carefull crye;
'Thow, Dethe, thou come to me [in] [f]ey
And helpe be-lyve that I were slaye,
I praye the specyallye!   4690
Wyth tene and t[vr]mente I am take,
And shamefully I am forsake;
He hathe a grette cause why.
Foole, when þou myghte, þou wold not;
Now thow wylt, now shalt þou not—   4695
In faythe, no fores forthy!

'A, thou Dethe, lett for no ryches,
For bewte or [for] worthynes,
f. 267ᵛ   But helpe that I were slayne!
In all this world, securly,   4700
Ys not so pore a wyghte as I,
The sothe is not to layne.
They ar riche att þer above
That at þer will may haue þer love;
Whedur he comythe neuer agayne!'   4705
In sonyng fell þat lady bright;
They comfortyd her wyth all þer myȝte
Bothe I[aso]ne and Imayne.

I[aso]ne sayd, 'Madame, be stille;
Wythin shorte tyme he comythe you tille,   4710
Lanyere as he me hight;
And trewly, comythe he not, þat hende,
Froo lond to lond shall I wend
To seke hym, day and nyghte,
Tille the tyme that he may founde be.'   4715
Tho wordys comfordyd þat lady fre,
But full sore she sehyde.
The kyng dyd seke hym fare or nere
And so dyd that lady clere,
But fynde hym can no wyghte.   4720

4688 in fey] merey   4691 tvrmente] ternvmente   4698 bewte] K.; MS
bewtenes   for] K.; MS om.   4708 Iasone] Iosane   4709 Iasone] Iosane
4716 Tho] Thow

Ipomadon in a littill stage
Comyn he is to the ermytage,
His mayster fyndythe he þere.
Off hys armore castys hee . . .
His wondys was wonder sore;   4725
His mayster stuppyd his hurtys, I wene,
And sythe aryesse hym all in grene,
A hunter as he were.
Whome he rydyþe wyth lowde blowynge;
To wyndowes rennythe boþe old and yonge,   4730   f. 268ʳ
They cursyd hym, bothe lesse and more.

When he come att the castell yate,
Lowde his horne he blewe þerate,
The houndys queyre þo he brought.
The maydons hym to skorne lowȝe;   4735
Thereffore the quene was wrothe i-nowȝe,
For in hurt she thoughte
That she louyd hym neuer the lesse.
To the durre ageyne hym comyn she is—
For lakkyng lett she not—   4740
The knyght be the honde she hent,
Into the hall wyth hym she went,
To supper sithe they [sought].

As they at supper sett wythinne,
The kyngys chamburleyne come inne   4745
And knelyd downe on his kne.
'Welcome Thoas,' quod the quene,
'Telles this day who best hathe byne.'
'Madame, be my lewte,
The tothere too dayes before be past   4750
Was not a poynte to this laste
Be oughte that I cowde see!
A knyght in blake þer was todaye
That paste all oþer, I darre welle saye,
Off any þat euer was sene wyth iȝe.'   4755

4734 queyre] *K.; MS* queyrted   4743 sought] *K.; MS* gothe

Segamvs be the quene satte;
'Madame, the same knyght was þat
That feld me in the fyghte;
That was no velony for mee,
For why, all oþer downe strake hee,   4760

So was he wondur whyӡte!'
The chamburley[n] sayd, '[I] darre wel saye,
Bettur then hee hath done today
I trowe dyd neuer non knyght;
Madame, he hathe so mony stedys,   4765
That all men wonders off his dedys
Be grette God moste off myghte!

'And euer more to þe lady he sent
Bothe hors and man to presente
Fro tyme he had them wonne.'   4770
'Syr, where is þe white knyght
And the rede, so mekyll of myghte?'
'The white wolle not be founde;
[A] [r]ede þer was today at morne
That sone oute of his sadell was borne   4775
At the rysyng off the sonne,
And sithe couthe no man hym se—
Dede full well I trowe he be
Or els in presone bounde.

'Madame, today was non to lake,   4780
But sekyrly a knyght in blake
Off bovnte bereth the bell:
The trought yf I shall tell in towne,
The fyrste off our syde bare he downe,
Soo was he fers and fell.'   4785
'Who whas þat? My lord þe kynge?'
'Ye madame, wythoute lesynge,
As I be savyd fro hell,
And also Cabanus the kene,
Thereoff þe kyng was so tene   4790
He wold no lenger dwell;

4759 velony] l corr. from n   4762 chamburleyn] chamburley   I] K.; MS om.
4769 man] Written above line, with caret   4774 A rede] K.; MS Mede
4786 My] miy

To rescewe Cabanus he youde   f. 269^r
And strake the kny3te; I sawe the blode
Renne downe be his syde.
He was wonder wrothe forthy;   4795
The kyng sawe hym loke so gremly,
He tornyde hym the bake þat tyde!'
'Why, fled the kyng?' 'Nay madame,
But as God sheld me fro shame,
Vnder his dent he durste not byde!   4800
Off all that come fro este or weste,
Today the blake hathe borne hym beste,
In erthe it is not to hyde.

'Madame, on the kyngys behalffe I saye
That tomorowe erlye as day   4805
Redy ye you make;
Com to Canders, þat riche citte,
There the grette semble shall be
For that ladyes sake,
To loke wyth myrthe who shall hyre mar[y]e.   4810
Here I maye no lengur tarye;
To God I you betake.'
Be the quene sittythe Ipomadon;
The chamburleyn he callys vpon
And off hys foly spake;   4815

'Syr, sey the kyng, I praye þe,
Off venysone this dayes thre
He hathe not ben begillyd:
He turne[y]d all þus day;
I haue had fayre game and playe,   4820
Bothe be frythe and felde.
Now hathe he tome at home to byde,
Hymselfe may on huntyng ryde   f. 269^v
Amonge the woddys wyld:
Lede hym venysone wyth þe,   4825
And say he gettys no more off [m]e,
Be grette God me can wyld.

4810 marye] *K.; MS* mare   4818 ben] *Followed by crossed-out* ge
4819 turneyd] *K.; MS* turned   4824 the] *Followed by crossed out* god
4826 me] *K.; MS* þe

'Thou maye say, so haue I sell,
Today my houndys hathe done full well,
The sothe is not to leyne.   4830
In Beymovnde cowde I fynde no lake;
Today hathe borne hym best þe blake,
And þeroff am I fayne.
Say hym ser, I praye thee,
As I haue huntyd, now hunte hee,   4835
For I haue done my payne
For venysone—tell hym well good [w]onne!'
The chamburlayne his leve hathe tane
And to the kyng wendys agayne.

He present hym wyth venesone,   4840
Sithe told hym all this nyce resone,
How the blake hounde beste hathe bene;
All lough save Cabanus þeratte.
The knyghtte that be the quene satte
Was were and woundyd, I wene;   4845
A shortte on sylke had on hee,
The knyghtte bled so grett plente,
He waxe bothe wanne and gre[ne].
The quene toke good hede þertille
And in hur hertte she mornyde stille   4850
Fro she the sothe had sene,

How pale and how wanne he satte.
Ipomadon parseuyd thate
f. 270ʳ   And he had full mekyll care;
He went he shuld haue knowen ben,   4855
For he trowed that the quene
Wyste that he was hurt sore,
And lyghttly he waxe red þanne.
Thus wounde strayned, þe blode out rane
Dowene evyn by his gore.   4860
He hyde hit be his manttell noke,
Thereto the quene good hede she toke
And sayd, 'For Goddys ore,

4828 Thou] *Followed by crossed-out* myg   4837 wonne] *Ka.; MS* onne
4843 lough] *Otiose curl on* g   save] *Followed by crossed-out* but   4848 grene] *K.;*
MS gre

'Whoo hurte you ser? I se you blede!'
'Madame, so God me spede,   4865
The sothe saye yf I shall;
As I rode after an hert today,
Me hors me gaff a stovde outeraye
And a full spetuous fall
On a sharpe stoke of a thorne,   4870
That thorow the arme hit hathe me borne.'
Then low3e the maydons all;
'That was a dede off chevallrye!
Ys he not beste worthye forthy
To haue yon hende in hall?'   4875

'Thus is a man off grette renovne,
Today he hathe strekyne downe
Knyghttys grette plente:
For [he] hathe hym so boldly borne,
He shall haue to mede to morne   4880
Yon lady fayre and free!'
When the quene supped had,
To hur chambyr he hur ladde
And kyste that bryghte off ble.
The lady to hym spekys þanne,   4885   f. 270ᵛ
She sayd, 'To-morne, my dere leman,
Erlye ryse mvste yee,

'To the citte of Ca[n]dres me to lede.'
'Madame, so God of heyven me spede,
Wythoute any tareynge,   4890
To-morne to hunte haue I þou3te;
Att the citte of Candres come I note
For lady ne for [my] lord the kyng.
Off my merthes will I not fayle—
Why, what ys me off þer sposayll?   4895
Be grette God, nothynge!'
Off them all his leve toke he;
The quene cursyd his destonye
Wyth sorowe and grette mornynge,

4870 stoke] k *corr. from* d   4879 he] *K.; MS om.*   boldly] d *corr. from* e
4881 free] r *corr. from* e   4888 Candres] cadres   4893 my] *K.; MS om.*
4897 Off] *Large initial capital*

For in hym was proves none.   4900
The knyghte is to his inne goone
As faste as he myghte hye.
Egyone to his nese sent hee
And sayd that she shuld redy bee
Att mydnyght prevelye.   4905
He sent hur word on all wyse,
She shuld take no leve off no ladyes,
Thus was the cause whye:
'My way at [n]yghte will I goo,
Wythouten knowlege off any moo';   4910
The mayde was all redye.

To bedde went Ipomadon,
But littill reste had he þer[o]nne;
Before þe day rosse hee,
All his stedys he dyd forthe take,   4915
f. 271ʳ   Bothe rede, whyte and blake,
Wyth oþur grette plente
That he be dede of armus wanne.
The burges calles to hym þanne,
All alonne in prevyte;   4920
'To the I will my counsell saye,
But þou moste sure me on thy faye
That hit shall counsell be.

'A long while haue I dwellyd here
And seruyd the quene, my lady clere,   4925
As thow thyselff hathe sene;
But what I am yet wot not one,
Ne no[n] ne shall till I be goone
Oute off this contre clene.'
The burges sayd, 'Ser, will ye goo?'   4930
'Ye certys frend, it muste be soo,
To wete wythoute wene.'
The burges sayd, 'Be my lewte,

4901 inne] *Followed by* is   4903 Egyone] *Preceded by* wyth Jo *(the latter crossed
out)*   sent] ssent, *with* ss *corr. from* w   4908 whye] h *corr. from* a
4909 nyghte] myghte   4913 þeronne] þer inne   4924 I] *Otiose stroke before*
4926 thow] *Corr. from* thou   4928 non] *K.; MS* not   4930 Ser] *Written above
line*

That ye will wynd forþinkys me,
For good frend haue ye been.   4935

'But what-sum-euer ye me tell,
I shall hit kepe all whiles ye wille,
And þerto here my hand.'
'Vpon yound stede[s] þat þou may see
I haue Iustyd this dayes thre,   4940
In dyvers colours fande:
The fyrste in whyte, in rede þe oþere,
The thryd in blake, it was no noþere;
Thow maye see where they stonde.
I kepe no rose þeroff to make—   4945
Alas off me that euer they spake!   f. 271ᵛ
I thanke God off his sonde,

'That he so fayre for me hathe wroȝte;
But what I am yet wotte they nouȝtte,
And theroff am I fayne.   4950
On the day I Iusted as a knyghte;
As a hunter I come home at nyghte
T[o] serue the quene agayne.'
The burges sayd, 'Was þat yee
That Iusted so well these days thre?'   4955
'Ye, serttys! But loke þou it layne.'
The burges lowgh and sayd sone,
'Syr, better myghtte no man haue done,
As I be savyd frome payne!'

'Thus turnamente is at ende,   4960
Thereffore my way will I wynde,
I kepe not yet to wyff:
I maye hereafter many a yere
All be tyme take a fere
To lede wyth all my lyff.   4965
Wynde I will to ferre contre,
Deddys off armus for to see,

And where stalleworthe men will stryff.
To the citte off Candres muste ye fare,
Mekely to do my message there   4970
Wyth stedys fowre or fyve.

'There shall you fynd my lord þe kyng,
The quene, and also the lady yonge
That all this fare is fore,
Worthy lordys off grette renowne,   4975
Duke, erle and barone,
Other bothe lesse and more.
To the kyng hymselff, i[t] i[s] not to nyte,
This stede thou shalt geve hym þat is white,
And syn this rede soure   4980
Present to my lady the quene—
For suche a frend as she hathe byn
Ys good to kepe in store.

'Her awne drewe, thow may her say,
Sendis her this red palfreye,   4985
And say, as haue I sell,
And he were chargyd wyth rede gold,
Wovche-save hem on hyr I wold
Be God and Seynt Mighell.
Thus blake stede þou shalt geve Cabanus—   4990
And I praye the do my message thus—
That in no feyntys f[el]le;
And say I know not, be my lewte,
No knyght vnder the hevyn so hy,
He myghte be set on so well.   4995

'Syr, here is Lyard, wythoute drede,
That was the kyngys owen stede;
Hym shall þou geve the Fere.
Praye the kyng wyth good wille
That he take hit to no ille;   5000
And he dyd, grette wronge it were:

f. 272ʳ

Well he wott how I hym [wanne],
A thousand on vs lokyd [thanne],
The sonne shone wo[nder clere].
Pray her take hym for my sake;   5005   f. 272ᵛ
Hereafter I shall amendys make
To that myld off chere.

'And thou may say þat þe straunge valet,
Onys att sopper that was sett
Before her in the foreste,   5010
He grettys her well a thousand fold,
And besekys her that she holde
The forward that she feste:
Off an vowe I harde her speke
And praye hur þat she neuer it breke   5015
Nother be est nor weste;
That she take no man off no degre
But off grette b[o]wntes þat he bee,
And holdyn the wortheeste.

'Amonge them tell thy tale on hight   5020
Tyll her that is off ble as bryght
As sonne that shynes þrow glasse.
But yet, ser, here is a stede
[That] ye muste to I[aso]ne lede;
[Of Caban]us he was.   5025
[They well] wot I stale hym not;
[I wanne] hym, thovgh he well wrought
[Wythout he t]here novght [g]as.
[Grette well Cabanu]s fro mee,
[A bettur knyghte] thare þere non be;   5030
[Myself away] mvste passe.'

'[Alas syr], what is thy thoughte,
[A man that these werkes hathe] wrouȝte?

5002–4 *Bottom corner of folio torn off*   5002 wanne] *K.*   5003 thanne] *K.*
5004 wonder clere] *K.*   5018 bowntes] *K.*; *MS* bewntenes   5024–33 *Bottom
corner of folio torn off*   5024 That] *K.*   Iasone] Iosane   5025 Of Cabanus]
To Cabanus *K.*   5026 They well] *K.*   5027 I wanne] *K.*
5028 Wythout he there] *K.*   gas] *K.*; *MS* says   5029 Grette well Cabanus] Grete
Cabanus *K.*   5030 a bettur knyghte] *K.*   5031 Myself away] *K.*
5032 Alas syr] *K.*   5033 A man that these werkes hathe] *K.*

For Goddys loue, dwell ye stille
And weddys to wyff younde lady clere;   5035
All Callabur fare and nere
Ye may weld att your will!'
He sayd, 'Ser, nay, so mot I thryve;
I kepe not yet so sone to wyffe—
I shall shew the skille: 5040
Yonge men ofte, I saye forthy,
That takys them wyffys so hastly,
Repentys it sithe full ill.

'And þerffor I will wend my way
To gette me more worshipe, yff I may,   5045
Where men in stowre be stadde.
I kepe not yet at home to leve;
I maye hereafter all be-[lyve]
A wyff wyth worshipe wedde.
As thou will euer haue frend off me,   5050
Done that my message bee
These stedys to Ca[ndres] lede:
Meke thy present plenerly;
They know the well I wott, for why
The thare not be adrade.'   5055

'That ye thus sodenly shall goo,'
The burgesse sayd, 'I am full woo,
Ellys byde I neuer daye!
Bee God and Seynt Myghell,
Your message shall be doone full well   5060
As fareforthe as I maye.'
'Syr, yet is here a stede
That thyselff shall have to mede;
Wythe that þou wend thy waye.
Anoþur will I haue wyth mee: 5065
Cananeus his own was hee,
And hereoff I the praye;

f. 273^v

5048 be-lyve] K.; MS be tyme   5052 Candres] Callabre   5054 They] e
corr. from y

'Bid hym take it to no ille
Thow3 it were ageynst his will;
He wot well þat I hym wanne.   5070
That I hym stale he may not saye;
I wanne hym on a clere day
A thousand lokyd on tha[nn]e.
Wythouten stede may I not goone;
Hym will I haue and no moo,   5075
Whedyr he blesse or banne.
To the grette God take I the!'
On his stede lepus hee;
To wepe the oste beganne.

The burges mvrnyd, lefte behynde;   5080
Ipomadon his way gan wynde,
His cosyne by his syde.
Many a thought on hym thronge,
Whedur that he were best to gange
Other still þere for to byde,   5085
But euer more was þe last thoughte,
Turne agayne wold he novght
For thyng that myghte betyde.
Yff that he goo, yt levys he thare
The [th]yng that he louyd nothyng more   5090
In all this world so wyde.

There is but fewe knyghttys now
That had done so mekyll, I trowe,
Be God and my lewtee,   f. 274ʳ
That fro so grette price wold haue gone   5095
So well as myghte Ipomadon
Have had that bright off ble;
But euer more in his herte he þought,
Yet till her avow cordede he nowght
Here husbond for to bee;   5100
That made hym oftyn tymes fro her fare.
Now off this burges speke we more
That went to that citte.

5073 thanne] thame   5084 to] *Followed by crossed-out* s   5090 thyng] *K.*;
MS kyng   5098 herte] *Followed by crossed-out* I

There the courte was ful plenere
Off lordys and off ladyes clere,   5105
The kyng and eke the quene,
The F[e]re that was full stravngely stede;
Yonge cheldorne the stedys ledde,
Arayd were wele and clene.
In herte grette mervayll had sum   5110
When they saw the burgays come
That they knewe all bedene;
The lady on the stedys gan loke,
For very feyre hur hert qwoke,
And tremelyd for very tene.   5115

A thousand tymes after that
She chaungyd colovres þer she satte
And on hur leman thoughte:
'There are the III stedys,' she say[s]
My love Iuste on these III dayes,   5120
Be God that all hathe wroughte!'
Grettly marvelyd was þe kynge
f. 274ᵛ   When he saw, wythoute lesynge,
The stedys that the burgays brought;
His owne and Cabanus well he knew,   5125
But yff ye thynke this tale be trewe,
The tother knewe he nowghte.

The burgays to hym gan he call;
'Syr, where had ye this stedys all?'
He knelys downe on his kne;   5130
'In faythe ser, I shall not layne,
He that was the Drew-la-rayn
Them heder sent be mee;
That man that [he] made hem was he novght,
I trowe [y]e knewe how he hathe wroght   5135
Befor on this dayes thre.'
When they t[h]o wordys vnderstode,
The maydons lowryd vnder þere hode
And sayd, 'Lord, wheyþer [þat] was he?'

5107 Fere] fayre   5119 says] sayd   5134 he] K.; MS om.
5135 ye] K.; MS he   5137 tho] K.; MS too   5139 þat] K.; MS om.

'Ye, in faythe,' the burgas says;   5140
'But this nyght ys he went his weye[s]
On Ca[nane]us ys stede.
To you herttly he besovghte,
Witnes wyth hym he stale hym novght
But wan [hym] be dov3tty dede.   5145
Ye witte well he hym wanne;
Wheþer that ye blys or banne,
Wyth hym he will hym lede.
Syr kyng, this trew tale to trowe,
Thus white stede he sendys yow   5150
As God off hevyn me spede;

'On hym he Iustyd the fyrste day,   f. 275ʳ
But how he dedyst, me thare not say!'
The kynge a lawghtter lough
And in a stody stille he satte   5155
And he sayd a long while after that,
'In faythe ser, well i-nowgh;
Better I trowe dyd neuer no man
That was borne sithe þis world beganne
Wyth blysse vnder this bovgh.'   5160
The burgays hade well nortouryd ben;
Boldely he turnethe hym to þe quene
And nere-hand her he drewe.

He sayd, 'Madame, your owne drewe
Thus redde stede he sendys yowe   5165
The he Iuste on the seconde day:
And he were chargyd wyth gold,
Wovche-saffe hym on you he wold,
Be God off heyvyn that all maye.
Ye have harde, me thare novght tell,   5170
Fayre or fowle whedyr hym befell,
So well he dyd, I hard saye
Wyttnes off my lord the kyng.'
He toke vp a lowde lavghynge;
'Yea, that felte I well, in faye!'   5175

5141 weyes] *Ka.*; *MS* weye   5142 Cananeus] Cabanus   5145 hym] *K.*;
MS the   5153 he] *Written above line; preceded by deleted* thou

The bvrgas turnyd to Cabanus
And sayd, 'Trewly ser, it is thus:
This blake stede send he you,
He Iusted on hym the thryd day.
How he dyd me thare not saye—   5180
Ye knewe what tyme I trowe!'
'Sertus ser, me owethe to wete,
For in faythe I fele yt yette,
That sore it dothe me s[o]we;
And we on þis wyse had be [l]orne,   5185
Right prevely he hathe hym borne—
That make I God a [v]o[w]e.

'But dere ser, speryd þou ovght þat,
Where he was borne and what he hatte,
Or whenne he comythe agayne?'   5190
'Ya ser, and more myghte I gette,
But he that was the straunge valet
That was the Drew-le-rayne.
He sayd, a better knyght than ye
Ys not vnder the heyvyn so hye—   5195
The sothe is not to layne.'
'Ya, what so I am, sekyrlye,
I-noughe he can off chevallrye,
And þeroff am I fayne.

'A wortheer knyght þen he is one,   5200
Vnder the cope of heyven is none,
Ne sekyrer at assaye.
Alas, foule, where was thy þought?
His dedys why parsevyd thou nought?
That shall thow rewe for aye!   5205
Be hym that made bothe yong and old,
I myght haue wyst yf I wold;
He was full wyse alwey:
So kynd, so curtes, so fayre, so free,
Myghte neuer wythoute proves be—   5210
Sertys, that is no nay!'

5184 sowe] K.; MS swe   5185 lorne] K.; MS borne   5187 vowe] wove
5208 alwey] alweys

The burgays, wyth an laughand chere,
Knelys downe to the Fere,
Be Mellengere þer she satte:
'This Lyard, lady, he sendys to you,   5215
He was the kyngys; he wot, I trowe,
On what wysse he hym gatte!'
The kyng þeratte lowde lovgh
And sayd, 'Ya in feythe, well i-novgh,
There helpud noþer helme noþere hatte;   5220
I hym loste and he hym wanne,
On the londe he lafte me lyande þanne;
I may not gaynsaye that!

'Good lord God, whether þat were hee?'
The burgayes sayde, 'Ser, ye parde,   5225
Now trewly he ys wyce;
There was neuer knyght, I darre savely swere,
That more prevely covthe hym beyre
That wanne so mekill pryce.'
All that euer to skorne hym lovgh   5230
Off themselff thought skorne i-novgh
And sayden on ther avyce:
'Off a straunge man in vncovthe place,
In them that moste skornyng makys,
Leste off norture [lyes].'   5235

The burgays covthe off curtasye;
He knelyd downe to that lady,
'Madame, be you blythe off chere;
A thousande tymes he well you grette,   f. 276ᵛ
And sayd he was the stravnge valett   5240
That gon full thre yere.
I trowe you mende yoursellff of that,
At sopper how that he satte . . . . . .
He harde you onys speke avowe,
And prayes you well to kepe it nowe,   5245
That nether farre ner nere,

5235 lyes] K.; MS kythe

'Ye take non but he be the beste.'
The lady satte and coloure kyste
And euer mornyd stille;
She fadyd ofte, [but] she her feyn[d]e   5250
[And] be resvn she constrenede
That none parcevyd her w[y]ll.
She sayd, 'Ser, as haue I sell,
Thereon I am avysud well,
Therefore I say be skille,   5255
I shall take non, [by my stevyn],
As ferre forthe as God in hevyn
Will graunt me grace þeretille,

'But I may weld hym þat me wanne!'
The burgays turnythe to I[aso]ne þan   5260
And sayd, 'Ser, securlye,
This stede to you hee sent by me;
Cabanus I trowe was hee;
Lordyngys, leve ye this forthy—
He stale hym novght, ye may be gra[y]the.   5265
Cabanus seyd, 'Ser, no in feythe,
That well wyttnes I;
f. 277ʳ   He lefte me þare, the sothe to saye,
On lond when he ledde hym away,
On fotte full verely!'   5270

The burgays this euery deall
Hathe done his message wonder well
Before all that there were;
'Lordynges, yet is here a stede
That gaff me to my mede   5275
That fre, when he shuld fare:
Wyth that [I] shuld do his messavge
Before all þis boronage
And laydes wyse of lore.'
The burgays toke his leve and yede;   5280
All men marveld of his dede,
Lordys bothe lesse and more.

5250 but] K.; MS yf   feynde] K.; MS feyne   5251 And] K.; MS But
5252 wyll] K.; MS well   5256 by my stevyn] I seyne   5260 Iasone] Iosane
5265 graythe] K.; MS grathe   5277 I] þat (K. þat I)

Thee kyng in a stody he satte,
The quene tremeld after þat
And to hyrselff she told;   5285
'I had leyser i-novgh to saye,
But they that woll not when þey maye,
They shall not when þey wolde!'
She sayd, 'Lordyngys lesse and more,
Ye wytte well i-now3e wherefore   5290
This turnament was holde.
To you I haue forward feste:
What man in erthe bare hym beste
My londys brode shuld weld.

'Now here you who moste worthely hathe wrought, 5295
But where is he yet wott ye novghte,
Thow3e he his happe hath hadde:
Fynde you hym, yff that ye may,
And I shall shure you be my faye—
There ys no lenger bode—   5300   f. 277ᵛ
That I shall take hym wyth good will.'
Euery man thought she sayd but skille
And for-thought þat þey sayd had,
That he was so his gatys goone;
They sayd, 'So worthy a knyght was non   5305
In all this world so brode.'

There was no man for her sake
Wold covnsaylle hyr oþur lord to take,
But bad that she shuld byde
Tille tyme that he myght fovnden be.   5310
Thus partyd that grett semble
And euery man gan home ryde.
The lady in Candres boode,
The kyng to the castell rode
And wyth went the quene þat tyde   5315
Wyth sorofull hertte makyng her moone:
That he was so his gatys goone
Hyr herte nere braste that tyde.

5294 *K.*; *MS* Shuld weld my londys brode   5295 you] *Followed by crossed-out* hav

To chambyr she went sore sighande,
And when she come þer, she fonde   5320
Away the maydon clene
That Ipomadon hade theder broughte.
In a stody she stode and thoughte
What waye beste myghte been,
That he to her wer brought agayne;   5325
Might no þing make her so fayne . . .

Thus dare I savely saye,
As women, what þey will haue wrought,
To do ther lykyng lett they noughte
Come after what–sum maye . . .   5330
'The knyght that all these dedys dydde
Ill his curtasy here has kyde;
My mayde he hath lede away

'Whiles I was at þe grette semble,
And but I þeron vengyd bee,   5335
Hard is my behove;
I maye in romaunce and in ryme
Ellys say in sorye tyme,
That I haue lorn my love
On many worthy bachelere   5340
That wonnand is wyth Mellengere
Yff I take this reprove.
Yll hathe he shewyd his curtasye
That he shuld doo me this velonye,
Be God that sitteth above!'   5345

Cananeus, wyth hardy hertte,
Before all oþur vp he startte
And sayd, 'Madame, be stille:
Gyff ye off longe tyme hathe lovyd me,
Now it shall well yeldone bee!'   5350
'Syr, God graunt the grace þertille,
The quene sayd, 'Ser steward, loo,
Thou haste matter good þertoo

5338 Ellys] *Followed by* I may   tyme] tymee   5353 haste] s *corr. from* r

Be many dyueres skille
Dovble quarell of the and mee,   5355
For why thy stede away ledys hee—
I trowe agayne thy wille!

'Thereffore ser, so God the spede
To feche my maydyn and thy stede,
Yff God will graunte þe grace.'   5360
So that he were to hur broughte,
On what wyse she ne rovght,   f. 278ᵛ
So grette desyr she hathe.
'Gyf I may, this is not to layne,
I shall bryng theme bothe agayne,'   5365
And to his inne he goothe.
He armys hym in noble wede,
Sithen he leppis vpon his stede
And folowed on the tras.

Ipomadon was wonder sore   5370
As he gan thorow the foreste fare,
He lyght vnder a tre
There flovris were spryngand, swete of smell;
For-wery on slepe he fell
On his cosyns knee.   5375
The maydon hard at the laste
Horsse come rennand wyth bryduls faste,
But no man covthe she see.
The damysell ful w[i]tty was;
A littill she tovchis his face   5380
And þerwyth wakyd hee.

Vp he lepe full lyuerlye
Armyde well and all redy,
On his helme he hente;
Wyth that he saw þe high steward   5385
In the way come prekand [hard]e
Wyth grette ire ouer the bent,
And when he saw hym hy so faste,
He thoughte hit was the quenes caste

5379 witty] wtty   5386 harde] K.; MS faste

That he was thedyr sent.   5390
When he saw hym come precande soo,

He wyste full wele þat he[r] was woo
That he was so awey went.

The steward to hym rydys þanne,
To speke spettuesly he began,   5395
And lenys hym on his shafte;
'Why haste thou done, belamye,
The quene so grette velonye,
Her maydone when þou her rafte?
Syr, I say the by my thryfte,   5400
My lady will the peche off thefte;
Thy nvrture þer thou lefte.
Goo, lede agayne that maydon gent,
Or thou shalt suffur Iugmente
That fallys for thevys crafte.   5405

'Ye bothe forgatte your curtasye
To stele away so prevelye
Agayne my ladyes wille,
And noþur off you toke no leve;
Ye myghte well witte it wold her greve   5410
Ouer-grettly be that skille;
And also, ser, myselff hath knowen
Thou toke wyth the more þan thyne owen
Or euer hadeste resone tille:
Thow ledys a stede that is not thyne;   5415
Thou shalt abyde and leve me myne,
Lyke thow neuer so ille!

'Thy dedis shall þou by full dere
But neuer the lesse, yf þou wilt here
Become my lege man,   5420
And sweftely on my swerd swere

Neuer me nere non off myn to dere,
Yet will I save the thanne.
I am strong wyth the kyng;
Knyghttys will do at my byddyng   5425

5392 her] *K.*; *MS* he   5410 witte] *Followed by crossed-out* henn

In all that euer they can,
And I shall praye my lady the quene,
She shall forgeve þe all quarels clene;
That bargayn myght I banne.'

'Syr,' quod Ipomadon,   5430
'Your wordys I vnderstond ichone
Thow ye speke angurlye;
To so worthy a knyghte as you
That says more thane he may avowe
Ys verry grett velanye,   5435
For ser, so God off heyven me spede,
Off this maydon that I lede
Off other thyngys know not I,
But ofte I haue hard saye, securly,
A woman to take hyr own wille be   5440
Ys thefte of curtessy,

'And ser, as I se sonne or mone,
That I haue to this maydon mysdone
Me thare neuer shewe in shryfte;
But be God and my lewte,   5445
Me thynkyth ille avysud be yee
That ye wold me peche of thefte:
That I haue to þe quene done wronge
[I will] amende it or owght longe
Right gl[a]dly, be my thryfte.   5450
Be God that all hathe wrought,
Thus stede noþere I ne boughte
Ne hadde hym off no gyfte.   f. 280ʳ

'I wanne hym of a noble knyght;
That saw a thousand men in sight   5455
And mo, yff mo myghte bee:
I know hym not, so haue I sell,
But be all tokens I may wit well
Sothely that it is yee!
I stale hym not, wythovten les;   5460
I wend I myght haue gone in peas

5440 hyr own wille be] be hyr own wille   5449 I will] K.; MS To
5450 gladly] glddly

To myne owne covntre.'
'Why, wylt þou do no more but soo?'
'No, not and ye will lett me goo.'
'In faythe, here covntre will wee!'   5465

'I graunt ser!' quod Ipomadon:
A good stedde he leppus vpone,
In hande he toke a spere.
The steward was a noble man,
Off dedys off armus right well he cane   5470
And he had full secur geyre.
Ipomadon was not to lake;
These too knyghttys on þe stedys bake
Togeddur they rydde on were.
The Iustes betwene them was full fayre;   5475
Cananeus wyth a grett eyre
A shafte to hym gan beyre.

He hit hym so the myddes the sheld,
A quarter fle in to the feld
Thow it were neuer so good;   5480
So stravnglye stroke he at þat tyde
Thorowe all his harnes be the syde,

f. 280ᵛ   Evyn the spere in youde
Vndernethe the lyfte pappe;
But, as God gaff hym happe,   5485
The spere it drew no blode.
Ipomadon was wrothe wyth þat;
Stone stille in his sadull satte
And was þerwythe nere woode.

He strake the steward so sore agayne,   5490
The [n]asell fley in to the playne,
He gaff hym suche a batte.
So sternly he gan hym stryke
That nose and cheke was bothe lyke,
So had he made hit flate.   5495
Were his gorgede neuer so good,
The hedde thorowe the hawbreke yede

5491 nasell] K.; MS vasell

In sadull were he satte:
He brake his right shulder bone,
That to the grounde is he goone   5500
Tope ouer tayle wyth that.

The stuard lyethe on the grounde,
Grevously lay gronande in þat stounde
And hathe full mekyll care:
His shulder bone was brokyne so,   5505
That dyd hym twys so mekyll woo
That he myght Iuste no more.
'Syr,' quod Ipomadon,
'Syr, ye myght a lette me goone
And byn in peas langeyre;   5510
He that hath moste ys manas[an]d
Hymselff hathe cause, I vnderstond,
Febly yf he fare.

'Now shall thou ryde home to þe quene   f. 281ʳ
And yeld the to the lady shene—   5515
I wott thou arte her dere;
But, a[s] God of heyven me spede,
Thus mayden wyth the shall þou not lede,
Ne noȝte ellys that ys here.
A stede I hadde of th[e], broþer;   5520
In fayth, now will I haue anoþur,
To kepe hem all this yere;
But say I lede no more off thyne!'
'Nay ser, be the trovthe off myne,
Dede I, wrong it were.   5525

'I wyght the nought yf it be þus,
Thus vnhape nedys haue me bus;
Thereffore wo worthe destonye!'
'Syr, thou shalt haue a littill hackeney
That shall the beyr be the way   5530
Twesse so essely:

5511 manasand] K.; MS manasyd   5515 shene] s corr. from c   5517 as]
K.; MS a   5520 the] Kp.; MS thy

I wotte well thou arte wondyd ille;
That hackeney, mayster, bryng hym tille—
This other y[s] ouer-hye
So for an hurte man þeron to ryde.   5535
And yf þou wilt thy lyff sheyde
The better gothe mee.'

'Certus ser, I wyte the note,
So worthy werkys as þou hathe wrought
Before this thre dayes;   5540
I myght haue witten well i-nowgh,
Wyth sory grace I hedur drowgh;
That poynte no þinge me pays.
I myghte haue byn in peas langeyre,

f. 281ᵛ   Now laydes love grevythe me sore;   5545
So dothe it hym þat on hem layes.
They love, and but they be louyd ageyne
My longe travayle is now in veyne . . .

'I haue boughte her loue to dere;
Me rewis the tyme þat I come here,   5550
So mot I borowed bene!'
Ipomadon sayd, 'Ser, I praye the,
A thousand tyme recomaunde me
When thou comyste [to] the quene,
And all that I haue done wyth ille,   5555
It shall be amendid at hur will—
Thou say so to þat lady shene!'
In his sadull they hym sett;
Whome he rode, wythouten lette,
There fewe men wold hym m[e]ne.   5560

The quene was euer more lokyng oute,
But in hure herte euer had she dowte
He shuld not come agayne.
So was she warre at the laste
Where the steward come rydyng faste   5565
Alone on the playne;

5534 ys] *Kp.*; *MS* you   5540 thre dayes] dayes thre   5544 langeyre] g
written above line   5554 to] *K.*; *MS om.*   5560 mene] *K.* meene; *MS* moone

His arme hyng waginge be his syde,
The blod ranne down fro his wondys wyde
As hit was droppus off rayne.
'What, how now ser!' quod the quene,   5570
'Be your semblant it is sene
Ye haue mett wyth Drew-le-rayne!'

He sayd, 'Certys, ye madame;
Mee had ben bytter byne at home,
That make I God avowe!   5575 f. 282ʳ
In a sory tyme for my behove
Youde I to Iuste for my ladyes love—
Euer more that will me rewe.
Fro me he ledus younder mayden bright;
So wold he do for any knyght   5580
That dwelland is wyth you.
So worthy a man as he is one,
Brokyne he hathe my shulder bone—
Full sore that greuythe me nowe!'

Grette worship spake he off hym þare;   5585
So dyd he neuer off no man eyre
Syne he was borne to man;
To his chambyr sithen he went.
The quene in herte her sore repent
And wordys she began to banne,   5590
Synne he was at her owne will
That she [ne] had shewed hym þanne here will
How will she louyd hym þanne;
Mornyng in hur hertte she bode.
Ipomadon his wa[y]s f[or]the rode   5595
Wyth the worship he wanne.

Home to Poylle he þynkys to ryde,
His cosyn ledynge be his syde,
Wythouten anny tareynge.
On a day, it is not to lett,   5600

5567 arme] *Followed by* harme   5570 ser] s *corr. from* q   5574 home]
homee   5592 ne] *K.; MS om.*   5595 ways] *K.* way; *MS* was   forthe] *K.;*
MS frothe

Fowre barons off his land he mett—
Yche was a grett lordyng—
That many a day had hym sought,
And stravnge tydyngys to hym brought
That lykyd hys hertte [no thyng].　　　　5605

f. 282ᵛ

A tale to hym they beganne
That dede was his fadur þanne,
Ermogynes thee kyng.

When they saw Ipomadon,
The barons were glad euerychone　　　　5610
And wyth hym turnes ageyne.
When he was comyn into his londe,
Men send hym many a fayre presand,
And of hym they were full fayne.
Att Barlett, that riche citte,　　　　5615
Men brought hym omage and fewte,
The sothe is not to layne;
Right as they shuld do to þer lord,
He and his barons were sone acorde,
Knyght, squere and swayne.　　　　5620

Ipomadon thynkys, it is no witte,
In worshipe is not he growen yet
Be aught that he couthe see:
Farther þinkys he for to goo,
Aventurs for to seke moo　　　　5625
In many dyueres contre.
He þought þat tyme shuld come above
That he [wyth] worshipe shuld wyne love
When it myght better bee.
Att home he wold no lengur abyde;　　　　5630
For to kepe his londys wyde,
A warden ordeyns hee.

In Fraunce hard he say was werre;
Ipomadon dyd make his geyre
Thedur for to wynde.　　　　5635
His mayster toke he wyth hym thanne;

5605 no thyng] *K.* right no thing; *MS* right noughte　　　5626 In] I *corr. from* A
5628 wyth] *K.*; *MS om.*

Was neuer knyght sithe þis world beganne   f. 283ʳ
A more faythefull frend.
He badde his cosyne Egyone
Into Callabre that he shuld goone   5640
To herkyne after that hynde:
'Into Fraunce will I fare;
Thus twelffemonythe shalt þou fynd me þere
Yff any man will her shend.'

Egyon wyndys to Callaber   5645
Prevely after the Fere to spere,
Ipomadon into Fraunce
Wythe hors and hernes grette plente,
And wyth hym went kny3ttes three;
He toke no more reten[aunce],   5650
Neyther lyke kyng ne emperoure,
But he rydythe lyke a sodyoure
Wyth armore, shyld and lavnce.
Where any dede off armys were,
The gre he wynnes euerywhere;   5655
Betyde hym many a chaunce.

Att home he wold no lengur abyde.
In Fraunce dwellyd a kyng that ty[d]e
That callyd was Catry[u]s.
A young broþer hadde he thanne   5660
That lord was off Loreayne,
The storye wettnes thus.
That tyme men callyd hym Kyng Dayre;
Off Loreayne he had weddyd the ayre,
The doughttur off Dryseus.   5665
Att hym his broþer hadde envye;
Grette werre betwene them was, trewlye;
Defende hym nedys he [b]vs.   f. 283ᵛ

She is dede that was his wyff,
Thereffore stabuld not þere stryffe   5670

5650 retenaunce] *K.*; *MS* retenewe   5658 tyde] *K.*; *MS* tyme
5659 Catryus] *K.*; *MS* Catryeis   5664 ayre] a *corr. from* e   5668 bvs] *K.*; *MS*
mvste

But gadurd grette powere.
This Dayere was a noble man
And well his landys he gouerend þanne,
Bothe farre and nere.
His broþer wrought hym mekyll woo,   5675
And grette parte off his landys also
Wyth warre he wanne þat yere,
And off his castels II or thre
He stu[ff]ud and held it wyth grett plente
Off men that worthy were.   5680

The kyng off Fraunce in Paris laye;
Ipomadon that hard saye
And thedur gan he ryde.
He made his dwellyng wyth þe kyng;
Gladder was he neuer of þinge   5685
In al thys world so wyde.
Wyth grette honoure [there] was hee,
The kyng beholdys his knyghttis thre
And a[ll] his folke that tyde;
Many off them h[ym] hadde sene before   5690
But [t]he[y] knewe [hy]m neuer þe more;
The glader he was to byde.

The kyng sent after his barons bold,
And bad them counsell to hold
To loke how beste myghte bee,   5695
For his brothere þat on hym warred
f. 284ʳ   And all hys londys grettly deyred
Wyth knyghttys off grette bovnte;
And as they at the covnsell stand[es],
To Catryus came new tydandys   5700
That chaungyd all his ble:
His brother wyth xxxᵗⁱ thousand knyghttys,
Welle armyd att all righttis,
Were come before the ryche citte.

5677 Wyth] *Preceded by crossed-out* Thi   5679 stuffud] *K*.; *MS* stuppud
5681 Paris] parishees   5687 there] *K*.; *MS om*.   5689 all] *K*.; *MS* att
5690 hym] he   5691 they] he   hym] them   5699 standes] *K*.; *MS* stand

The kyng had many a noble man, 5705
But not halff so many as he had þanne,
Therefore he was in dovte.
Euery man made hym redy faste,
Sethyne oute of the citte þey paste,
A full ryall rowte. 5710
Ipomadon was full glad and blythe,
Hymself dyd hym aray swythe
Vppon a stede full stovte;
He was the fyrste that toke feld,
Clenly couered vnder shyld, 5715
And bolde men hym abowte.

A nobull knyght, wythowten les,
To Ipomadon he hym chesse
That was on Dayres syde.
Wythe a spere he to hym sought; 5720
The sheld was good and faylyd novght;
Therein the soket plyde.
Ipomadon strake to hym so faste,
The spere thorowe the sheld paste,
Wyth a stroke was vnryde. 5725
The hawberke vnder was good and sovnde,
He bare hym streyte to the grovnde   f. 284ᵛ
Wyth manly herte that tyde.

Or any socur to hym comeyn,
Ipomadon had his suravns nomyn 5730
Thow he grette rewthe hade;
Wythowten reskew off any man,
The knyght to hym yeldis hym thanne,
Whereof he was full glade.
Ipomadon saythe to hym fayre, 5735
Sethen he sent hym to Kyng Dayre;
'Goo tell thy lord,' he bade,
'The blake knyght now he maye se here,
That Iustyd in Calabyre for the Fere,
That made hym onys vnglad!' 5740

5716 bolde] *Followed by crossed-out* h

The kyng off Fraunce and all his men
Trewly was a-wonderd þanne
When they had sene that sight,
He sent his presonere to his enmye;
Off tresone dred they them than forthy,   5745
Them thowght he ded not righte.
There was neuer knyghte sith þis world began
That better wrought then he dyd than,
He forsyd hym so to fyghte.
The kyng off Fraunce, in armys clere,   5750
Ipomadon he heldythe hym nere,
He saw he was so wyghte.

The kyng Dayre had mekill care
When he wyste the blake knyghte þare
Wyth sorow in hertte his he wovnde,   5755
For wele he thought and it be not for he,
He shuld off Fraunce have grette plente
f. 285ʳ   That day wyth sworde haue wonne.
Wonder stronge was þat stoure;
There dyed many a va[ntou]re   5760
Be rysynge of the sonne,
And gevyn was many a stroke vnryde;
What knyght off Dayres durste abyde,
He hathe his felowe founde.

Dayres was a noble man off werre,   5765
He dyght hym lyghttly in his geyre
And into the pres gan pryke,
And wyth hym many a well good knyght.
The Frenshe folke wyth mekyll myghte
In thwerte wyles they were wyke.   5770
Ipomadon so worthely wroughte
That bothe sydys grett wondur þought,
So styff men gan he stryke;
Where he went on any syde,
Was none that durst his dent abyde,   5775
So was he wonder wyke.

5760 vantoure] Kp.; MS vamsore

There was non that p[er]yd to Ipomadon;
In werre he was so wyce a man
To do hit euery deell;
His mayster had lornyd hym well þat were   5780
Bothe to ryde wyth shyld and spere
And to weld a swerde off stele.
So many off Dayres men he slowe
That the kyng wepte and had sorow i-nowe,
Wyth sykyng and vnsele.   5785
He layde on faste on euery syde;
All his folke had fled that tyde
But that he dyd so welle.

The kyng Dayre had þere besyde   f. 285ᵛ
A castell stovffed in Fraunce þat tyde,   5790
And thedur he can hym drawe.
Two hu[n]dyrd knyghttys there fovnde oute;
Ipomadon met so wyth that rowte
That many he layd full lowe.
This nobull knyght as he well covthe   5795
An olywhantys horne he sett to mowthe
And lowde began to blowe:
The knyghttys that were strowyd wyde
To hym drawes on euery syde,
Redy and on a rowe.   5800

Barons vnder stedys fett
Lay hevely gronynge on the grete
And many there lyvys had lorne;
Ryche hawberkys al to-rente,
Barnys bledand on the bente,   5805
There shuldurs on sovnder shorne.
They presud togedyr so grette repayre
That att the laste kyng Dayre
Vnto the erthe was borne:
His stede agayne was to hym [f]e[t]te   5810
Tho he was in the sadull sette
Wyght men hathe hym worne.

5777 peryd] K.; MS persyd   5792 hundyrd] huvdyrd   fovnde] K.; MS
yfovnde   5810 fette] K.; MS sente

Ipomadon wrothe full worthely;
Thereat Dayre had grett envye
And lyghttly to hym wanne;   5815
He stroke hym so the myddyst þe backe
That bothe plate and hawbrake brake.
By his syde the sokett ranne,
But no harme in the fleshe it dede—
God wold not that it betydde.   5820
So strettly he stroke hym þanne,
Ipomadon to the grounde hym bare
That wors h[a]p betyde hym neuer yare
Sethe he was fyrste a man.

That was no thynge long on hym,   5825
Vp he sterte wyth hertte grymme
And oute his swerd he drewe,
The to[n]e hand his brydull he toke,
And wyth the tother hand, as tellyþe the boke,
He fendyd hym well i-novghe.   5830
The prese aboute hym come so faste,
His horse brake fro hym at the laste
And goos vpon a clowgh.
The chyld that shuld hym serue there
Therefore he had so mekyll care   5835
That nere he fell in [sw]oughe.

Ipomadon favghte so faste,
The blode thorow the browes barste
Off all the riche raye;
Knyghttys full thyke abowte hym [wendes]   5840
And he grettly then defendy[s],
The sertayne sothe to say.
There was non þat he hitt
That longe myght in his sadull sitt,
He sterryd as bere at baye.   5845
He smote so steffly hym abowte,

f. 286ʳ

5823 wors hap] K.; MS worship   5828 tone] K.; MS tothere
5836 swoughe] K.; MS thoughte   5839 K.; MS Off the riche of all the raye
5840 wendes] K.; MS presus   5841 defendys] K. defendes; MS defendyd

Off his [s]trokys they hadde suche dowete
That many on fled away.   f. 286ᵛ

Grette sorow his chyld had
That his mayster on foote was stade   5850
Fyghttand wonder faste;
He hyed faste after his hors,
And in the feld wyth playne fors
He toke hym at the laste.
Glader was he neuer of dede,   5855
To his mayster he dyd hym lede,
A lowde crye vp he caste;
Ipomadon drawys to hym warde,
He hew on there helmes harde
That the blod thorowe the browes barste.   5860

I pomadon was neuer so fayne
  As when his stede was brought agayne;
  Lyghtly vp he lepe.
Fresly fendys [he] hym now,
Off his steropus, as I trowe,   5865
He toke but littull kepe.
Suche strokys þen he sette,
The moste myghtty as he mett
He made there wyffys to wepe;
Knyghttys in the feld lay strewed,   5870
There neke bonys in sundere hewed
Wyth many a wounde full depe.

His felowes was sory euerychone;
That tyme they wend Ipomadon
He hadde byn loste them froo;   5875
The presse aboute hym was so thyke,
There wend noo wyghte he had byn quyke;
Therefore they were full woo.   f. 287ʳ
The rowte to reskewe hym wolde ryde;
So stravnge was that stoure that tyde,   5880

5847 strokys] trokys   5861 Ipomadon] Ipomandon; *Large red initial capital*
5864 he] *MS om.*   5867 *This line copied between ll. 5863 and 5864 in MS*
5874 wend] *Followed by crossed-out* euery

They myghte not to hym goo.
When they saw hym fyrste agayne,
The kyng of Fraunce was full fayne,
And many othere moo.

Mervelys you not forthy,   5885
Thow Ipomadon was wery,
So harde he gan hym to melle;
Was neuer knyght borne of woman eere,
Harde[r] besette then he were thare,
That darre I trewly tell.   5890
Many a man in feld laye slone,
But off them all Ipomadon
Off bounte bare the bell.
Dayres blew an horne that tyde;
His knyghttys relevyd on euery syde,   5895
That were bothe fers and fell.

Thereat Ipomadon was wrothe;
Thow he [was] were, there he gothe
He crakys many a crowne.
The inner syde euery dell   5900
Was comfortyd of hym wonder well;
As bere ay was he boune.
He hewe in sunder helme and shelde,
And feld many w[or]thy knyghttys in feld
That were off grette renowne.   5905
Many swonyd and lay in sw[i]me,
Kynge Dayre hymselff that tyme
Efte sonys he was borne downe.

Knyghttys to reskew hym wold thye ryde,
They prekyd many a stede that tyde   5910
Spetowsly wyth sporys.
Ther is no other þing to ax
But he that moste worthy waxe
And moste off bounte beyres . . .
Wyth mekyll woo wele they wyste   5915

f. 287ᵛ

5889 harder] harde   5898 was] *MS om.*   5904 worthy] wrothy
5906 swime] sweme   5907 hymselff that tyme] *K.; MS* that tyme hym selff

To the kyng they socourde at þe laste
Wyth strokys that many a man deyris.

Dayres folke wyth grette doloure
Were turnyd to dyscomfetture;
Oute of the feld they flede.   5920
The kyng of Fraunce folowyd faste,
A made many a man full gaste,
Before that day wer neuer adred.
Or they into the castell wanne,
Slayne there was many a noble man   5925
That D[a]yr[e]s thedyr ledde.
They speryd the gatys þat were wythin,
To seg[e] wythoute they begynne;
Thus Dayres men bale they brede.

They pyght pavelyons off pryde   5930
To kepe that hold on euery syde
That non shuld essu oute.
Ipomadon wyth good chere
Sett his tent the kyng nere,
Well borderyd all abowte.   5935
So worthely wrought he þat daye,
Dayres, that wythin laye,   f. 288ʳ
Off hym hade mekill dowte.
Righte wyse he was, wythouten lesse;
To be his mesengere he chesse   5940
Stille men and not stovte,

Off his barons many one.
He sent them to Ipomadon
As he that wold be frende;
'And specyally ye shall hym praye   5945
Helpe to brynge, as he þat may,
This grette debate to ende,
And on that comnaunte I will hym gyff
Halff my kyngdome while I leve,

5926 Dayres] dyras   5928 To sege] K.; MS two segis   5929 brede] bredee
5946 Helpe] He helpe

My doughtter fayre and hynde.'   5950
The mesengers were full wyse;
They waytyd where the knyght lyse
And to his tent they wen[d]e.

They dyd there message welle and fayre,
They tolde hym all of the kyng Dayre   5955
That them thedyr sente;
They prayed hym that he wold be frend,
And sythen to the kyng of Fraunce wend
Be rightewos Iugemente,
And helpe to make a good acorde   5960
Betwene the kyng and þere lord,
That no men were shent:
'On that comnaunte he hight þe fayre
Here that he thynkys to make his ayre—
His doughtter bothe fayre and gent.'   5965

f. 288ᵛ

Right wyse was Ipomadon;
He sayd to the barons ychone,
'His doughtter were me dere:
Syr, to yowre lord graunt mercy
That he wold shewe me þat curtessy,   5970
Worthy yf that I were,
But never the lesse say hym ageyne,
All Fraunce yf he wille quyte clene,
Bothe towne and castell [in fere],
And to the kyng omage make,   5975
This message I vndertake
Wyth a noble chere.

'His doughttur gladly have I wold,
Grette good of her I haue hard told;
That is to me but a trayne!'   5980
'[Nay] ser,' sayd the mesenger,
'That dare we boldely hight you here,
As we be sauyd frome payne,

5952 the] *Followed by deleted* kyng   5953 wende] wente   5959 rightewos]
righte whos   5969 lord] lordys   5974 in fere] *K.; MS* bedene
5981 Nay] *K.; MS* Yes   mesenger] mesengers

On bookys and sawters for to swere
[N]euer after to do you deyre   5985
Fro that they be frendys agayne!'
Ipomadon to the kyng gan wend
And told hym all þat tale to ende;
Thereof was he full fayne.

The mesengers was full glad   5990
Off the answers that þey hadde;
They foundyd on the felde.
When they come to the castell
And to there lord this tale can tell,   f. 289ʳ
They sayd, 'Ser, this berys you b[e]lde. . . .'   5995
Kyng Da[y]re on the morne
The kyng of Fraunce he come beforne
And omage gan hym yelde.

Brode bokys were brought oute thanne;
To swere the kyng Dayre began   6000
Wyth many a barone bolde,
That he shuld neuer stere ne stryve.
No more he dyd in all his lyve,
For the trouthe had he tolde.
This acorde is made fayre;   6005
Ipomadon shuld wedde his eyre
Wyth halff his lond in wolde.
Ioyefull was that maydon fre,
But I trowe, b[y] my lewte,
That comnaunde will not holde.   6010

Off hym the damysell was glade,
For in the towre sene she hadde
How dowȝttly he dydde;
He gaff so many a grette stroke,
She went hit had byn for hyr sake   6015
That suche maystres [he] [k]yde;
Thereby she thought he louyd here well.
To wedde hyr thought he neuer a deall,

5985 Neuer] K.; MS Euer   5991 þey] Written above line; followed by crossed-out
she   5995 belde] K.; MS bolde   5996 Dayre] dare   6009 by] K.: MS
but   6012 in] Written above line   6016 he kyde] K.; MS dyde

For oftyne tymes ha[s] byn tydde
And sayd off long tyme agoone,   6020
That on the bushe bettys one,
Anothere man hathe the byrde.

Then the kyng of Fraunce thankyd hym than
Off the grette worshipe þat he hym wanne,
And sayd, 'Be God alonne,   6025
f. 289ᵛ   Better than ye dyd yestyrday
Dydde neuer no man, I dare wel say,
That was made of blode and bonne!
In the reame of Fraunce I will the geve
Lond i-nowȝe thereon to leve   6030
And castels styff [of] sto[n],
For, as I haue happe or sell,
Ye haue seruyd hit full wele.'
Hym thankyd Ipomadon.

Sethe after, when they suppud hade   6035
And euery man was blyth and glad,
The kyng began to spere
Where he was borne and what he hatte:
'I wold right gladly witte that—
I praye you tell me syr.'   6040
'Sertys, that may I not do yet,
But hereaftur shall you witte
Synne ye this matter stere.'
The kyng saw he began to layne,
He wold no farþer of hym frayne,   6045
He was the curtysoure.

Wha[n] that the lordys leve hathe tane,
Ipomadon to his inne is gone,
The nyght comythe nere.
His mayster Thalamewe he callyd   6050
And all his matter he hym tolde
Wyth a ful sympull chere;

6019 has] K.; MS hadde   6031 of ston] K.; MS and stowte   6047 Whan]
K.; MS what

'Mayster, I haue hight the [kyng] Dayre
To wedde his doughtter and his eyre . . .
Be grette God that hathe me wroughte,   6055   f. 290^r
Love be reysone may I noughte
No woman but the Fere,

'And þerfore what so euer any man says,
Hors and harnes makys redy all weys,
For Goddys love I you praye!   6060
My waye att mydny3te will I wynd;
Yff I shuld bryng þis to an ende,
Hit wold me rewe for aye.'
His mayster dyd his comaundement,
Ipomadon his way is went   6065
Beffore the sprynge of day.
The kyng [he left] and all his folke, bedene;
On the morowe when the maryage shuld bene,
The knyght was clene awaye.

When this was told to the kyng,   6070
So sorye was he neuer off thyng
Syne the tyme that he was borne.
The maydon setheed and sayd alas . . . .
That she so hyr love had lorne.
This long day no tome I had   6075
To tell the sorow that she made
When they hym myssyd on the morne;
Off all them, moste mornyd the maye
That Ipomadon was þus went away,
Bothe wyth hounde and wyth horne.   6080

Thus tede hym þare a sely chaunce;
Att the essuynge oute of Fraunce,
He mettys wythe Egyon
That come walkynge hym agayne.
His herte lepud vp for fayne   6085   f. 290^v
When he sawe Ipomadon;
Well he thought tydyngys he brought,
But what they were it wyst [he] nou3te.

6053 kyng] K.; MS om.   6061 att] Followed by deleted myghte   6067 he
left] K.; MS om.   6088 he] K.; MS þey

Euyne to hym is he goone,
His mayster fayre haylyd hee;   6090
'Welcome cosyne mot thou bee,
Be God þat is but one!'

'Egyone, what saye ye ser?
When come ye oute of Calebere,
There haue I byn to-yere?   6095
What tydyngys þere, so mot þou goo?'
'Sum ar good and sum not soo.'
'Why, how faris the Fere?
Telle me how it stondythe wyth here—
Hathe she an husbond?' 'Nay ser;   6100
And she had, wrong it were.'
'I trow she hathe!' 'I say you, nay!'
'How it is thanne?' 'I shall you saye—'
'Tell on, good, now lett here!'

'Off body she is in quarte,   6105
But grett sorowe she hathe in hertte,
I say you securlye.'
'Alas cosyn, why is it soo?'
'For one is comyne that werkys hir woo,
Wyth a rewde companye.   6110
Her barons grettly hathe byn noyede,
On euery syde her landys stroyede
Wythe warre and wyth grette envye.
He hathe suerly sworne his othe;
He wylle hyr wedde be leff or lothe   6115
And haue that fayre ladye.

'Before Candres, that riche towne,
There hathe he pyght his pavelyon,
And there he thynkys to byde
Tille he haue, wyth good or ille,   6120
Wonne that lady to his will
Or waste her [l]on[d]ys [wyde],

f. 291ʳ

6110 companye] companyee   6114 othe] othee   6115 wylle] l *corr.*
from f   6122 *K.* Or waste he wille her londys wyde; *MS* Or waste he wille her onys

Or whether he may take in hand,
Sone to conquere all her lande,
So is his rowte vnryde;   6125
But so mekyll he truste hymsel[f] yn
That man for man he will her wynne—
This is on lowde dyscryede.'

The knyght stode in a stody stille;
Men wyste nere-hand noþur good ne ille,   6130
So grette sygh on hym soughte.
A long while no worde he spake,
He thought hys herte asonder brake
For the tydyngys that were broughte.
Thow hit were wekely, at the laste   6135
Wyth a worde oute he braste;
'Fro whens he come, wot þou ought?'
'Certys ser, oute of Ynde Mayore;
He is the sonne of Alamadure
That wonderfull werkys hathe wroght.'   6140

'Egyon, hard thow ought be told
Whedur that he is young or old?'
'Nay ser, he is but yonge.'
'Ys he fayre?' 'Nay certys, he!
A fowler man ther may non be   6145   f. 291ᵛ
Ne more vncomely thyng!
Hys hed ys row wyth feltred here,
Blake bryste[l]d as a bore,
Hys browys full they hynge;
Wyth longe tethe, I warand yow,   6150
Euery lype, I dare avowe,
Hyngyth lyke a blode puddynge.

'This dare I sauerly make asethe;
His nose towchys on his tethe,
His mothe wrythis all way,   6155
Blake as any bleche hys face,

6123 whether] wherther   6126 hymself yn] hymselvyn   6133 brake] r
corr. from l   6148 brysteld] K.; MS brysted   6155 way] waysys

As two dobelers euery eye he hathe,
Wyth gorget gret and gray;
His berde as pyche ys blake,
His body hathe an euyll smake,   6160
The vesnamy fovle I saye;
Neke as an ape, nebe as an owle;
In all this worlde ys none so fovle,
This dare I sauerly s[ay]!

'Tyll he hyre haue he will not fyne.'   6165
'What is his name?' 'Ser Lyolyne:
No man of myȝte ys more.
In all Calabyre is not a knygth
That agayne hym onys dare fygth;
Grett sorow hathe sche therefore.   6170
He hathe sworryn, so God hym saue,
That ouer wyth hym he will here haue
Into Ynde Maiore.'
'I' faythe, than wolde I be full woo;
I truste to God þat he schall goo   6175
Bakkere more abore. †

f. 292ʳ
((Ded I, grette wronge it were.))

'But Egyon, may I come be tyme?'
'Ye ser, and ye wille nott lyne,
That wotte I well ye maye.'   6180
'Ye dere cosyn, trowyst thou so?'
'Ye ser, for betwene them twoo
Ys sett a sartayne daye,
That other she mvste fynde a knyght
To kepe hyr fro that cursyd wyght,   6185
Or wyth hym goo her waye.'
Ipomadon askyd wyth egur wille,
'How longe, Egyon, is þer tille?'
'A monethe, ser, I saye.'

He callyd his mayster Thalamewe,   6190
And told hym all his tale for trewe;

6164 say] *K.*; *MS* swere   6169 hym] *Written above line, with caret*

'Hit is wars thenne I wende—
Mayster, there is but one to chese:
My loue to wynne or to lesse
Foreuer wythouten ende!   6195
Glade be I neuer in my lyff
Yeff he shuld wedde hyr to wyff:
But I there that Fere defende,
Hit will turne me to ouer mekill care;
But well were me and I were thare   6200
That none in erthe me kend.

'Hit is not long sithe I there Iuste
And wynde I thethere, nedys I mvste
Be knowen wyth the Fere.
In Cesille there byn nobull knyghtys bek[e]nde;   6205
I wotte wele they will thedyr send   f. 292ᵛ
To kyng Mellengere
[For] sum man to do this rayne.
Might I hit gett, I wold be fayne
To saue that lady clere: 6210
Agayne I will into Cesille,
But we mvst cast vs of sum while
That we ne knowen were.'

'Syr, that were right good to doo.'
'Grette mystur of socoure hathe she,   6215
And I wold helpe hur fayne.'
Wythoute any more abode,
Into Cecille forthe þey rode
The gatys þat moste were gayne.
Wythoute the citte of Palerne,   6220
They lyght a-downe in a dale so derne,
The sothe is not to layne.
Ipomadon sayd, 'Be my lewte,
A fole may welle I be
To begile them wyth a trayne.'   6225

6202 long] *Written above line*   Iuste] Iustee   6205 bekende] be kynde
6208 For] *K.*; *MS* To

He made his mayster to cotte his heyre
Hye behynde and lowe before,
Wondyr ille faringlye.
A blake soty sheld he gate;
VII yere before, I wott well þat,   6230
Hit had hange vp to drye.
An old rustye swerd he hadde,
His spere was a plowgh gade,
A full vnbryght br[yni]e;
Vpon the to[n] legge a brokyn bote,   6235
A rente hose on the other foote,
f. 293ʳ   Two tatrys hangyng bye.

His helme was not worthe a bene,
His hors myght vnnethe goo for lene,
Hit was an old crokyd meyre;   6240
An vncomely sadull behynde, seker,
His brydull was a wrethe wekyr;
Off othere rekkes he nere.
'Mayster, ye muste to the citte fare
And prevely take youre inne thare   6245
That no man wit what ye are.'
Thalamewe dyd his comaundement,
Ipomadon to the courte is went;
Ille farand was hys geyre.

The kyng was newly sett to mette,   6250
The quene and other ladyes grette,
And knyghttys many one.
Ipomadon amonge them all
Come rydyng into the hall
His crokyd mere vppon;   6255
So shortte his storoppus leddurs were,
His knes stode halff a foote and more
Abovyn his horsis mane;
Crokand wyth his backe he roode,
Off his attyre wonder they had,   6260
Knyghttys bigge off bonne.

6230 VII] *Followed by crossed-out* b   6234 brynie] *K.*; *MS* brande
6235 ton] to   6239 hors] h *corr. from ?*   6258 mane] manee

His horsse was wondyr harde of s[t]ere,
Wyth sporres and wand he stroke the mere,
He beyttys on her bonys,
And euer the fastur that he dang,   6265
The more softlye wold she gange,
She wold not stere on the stonys.   f. 293ᵛ
There knyves oute of there handys gan fall,
Wyth so good will lowȝe they all
That were wythin that wonis.   6270
To lawȝing made he no semblande;
There was non a coppe myght hold in hand,
So lowȝe they all att onys.

Abowte hem he began to stare
In euery hyrone here and there,   6275
Halff wood as he were;
Knyghttys att his attyre lowȝe
And sum off them was ferd i-nowgh,
Ladyes chaungyd þere chere.
Thowȝ it were long, yet at þe laste   6280
A worde of fowl[i]e oute he caste;
'God loke the, Mellengere!
I am the best knyght vnder shild
There no man comythe in the feld—
That bought þou onys full dere!'   6285

'When was that?' quod the kyng.
'Wotte þou not?' 'Naye, no thynge!'
'Syr, no more wott I!'
Then all men vp a lavȝtter caste
That nere there herttys asounder breste,   6290
Bothe on benche and bye.
Ipomadon sayd after thate
To the quene there she satte,
'God loke you, fayre lady!
Madame, that haue ye sene,   6295
That ye wold full blyth haue byne
To kys vs curteslye.'

The quene wax rede for shame;
The kyng sayd, 'Is it thus madame?'
'Syr, I sawe hym neuer eyre!'   6300
'Foule,' quod Cananeus thanne,
'I praye the, were was þat and whanne?'
'A, ser, are ye thare?
I can nott tell verelye what day,
But on the lond I hope ye laye   6305
And loste your hors euery heyre.'
'When was that? [I] wott no why!'
'No, in faythe no more wott I!'
Then lewgh bothe lesse and more.

'Syr kyng, yff it be thy wille,   6310
I praye the make these folke be stille
That Ianglys this lyke a gaye.
So worthy as I am one,
Vnder heyven I trowe is none,
Where freke men fleys awaye.   6315
I hate pease and louye the werre,
Thou may see be my glyttrand geyre
And be my riche ar[a]ye.
So good as I maye no man bee,
And yff thou wylte wythhold mee,   6320
Herke whatt I shall seye.

'Iff I dwell, wythouten fayle,
Thow mvste graunte me the fyrste battayle
That is askyde off thee,
And yff me lykys, I will fighte,   6325
And yff me lykys not, be þus lyght,
But turne my bake and flee.'
The kynge to laughe myght not fayne;
'I shall the graunt the fyrste der[a]yne

6307 I] K.; MS om.   6311 folke] Followed by crossed-out good
6316 louye] K.; MS louythe   6318 araye] aryee   6321 seye] seyee
6325–27 l. 6327 originally copied between ll. 6325 and 6326, but the latter two lines labelled 'a'
and 'b' in margin to indicate mistake.   6329 derayne] Kp.; MS deryne

And thow wylte byde and bee.'   6330
Ipomadon sayd, 'Syr, it is but lave.'   f. 294ᵛ
Then all men lewȝ and sayd þer sawe;
'A noble foule is he!'

Hee faryd as he were wrothe i-nowthe
That they hym to skorne lewȝe,   6335
And he sayd in that halle,
'I praye God gyff you all myschaunce
When ye makythe any destaunce,
Or foule shuld me call,
But the kyng, wythouten dowte;   6340
In faythe I take no mo wythoute,
Not one among you all,
But yff it be my lady the quene,
For the grette love that betwen vs hath bene.'
Then lowȝe bothe grette and small.   6345

'Syr,' quod Canoneus thanne,
'I redde you wytthold this man,
I shall say you for why:
So noble a foule as þus
Among men dothe good, i-wys;   6350
When herttys byne ofte hevye,
Att there wordys bene mekyll myrthe,
Many tyme they slake the wr[e]the—
Wytthold hym, forthye!'
Ipomadon so[re] angurd was,   6355
But neuer the lesse he lett it passe
That none parsevyd therebye.

'Cananeus, att my skole,
In faythe, [y]e held me for no fole
When ye laye on the lande!'   6360
When was þat, I yow praye?'
'I can not verely tell the daye,
Whedur hit were pul or pande; †   f. 295ʳ
That tyme the quene louyd me wele,

6338 ye] *Followed by deleted* any   6353 wrethe] *K.*; *MS* wrathe
6355 sore] *K.*; *MS* so   6359 ye] *K.*; *MS* he

And I agayne her neuer a deyle,   6365
Faye yff she me faunde.'
The[n] lowȝe all, bothe lesse and more
They sayd, 'To wette when þat it were
Ys righte a good demaunde!'

Syr Segamus sayd, 'When was þat?'   6370
'A ser, when ye had a squate
I am avysud nowe;
What day it was I am not graythe.'
Segamus sayd, 'Ser, no in faythe,
No more am I, I trowe!'   6375
'Syr kyng, where is Cabanus?
Serttys, I were not taryd thus
Had he byn here wyth yowe;
And he wyste what I were,
I trowe it wold myrthe hym more   6380
Than oþere oxe or cowe,

'For onys I made hym adrad,
That fro my handys faste he fled,
But I wott neuer what daye.'
There all men lovghe on hygh   6385
And sayden, 'In faythe, no more wot wee,
Savely darre we saye!'
'Good ser, when?' quod Maunstas.
'Sen me nedis tell you [b]vs,
On the lande when ye laye   6390
And I mysellff downe you bare!'
Then lowȝe bothe lesse and more,
f. 295ᵛ   They sayd, 'That ys no naye!'

Cabanus, the sothe to sey,
Was on huntyng all that daye   6395
And wyste no thyng off thus.
'Have done ser kyng, I praye the
Yff thou wilt wythhold mee,

6367 Then] The   6373 was] Followed by it was   6375 trowe] trowee
6381 cowe] cowee   6382 hym] Followed by onys   6389 bvs] K.; MS mvste
6391 you] youre

Ellis I dwell not, i-wis!
Wyste þou what maystres I covthe make,   6400
My service wold thou not forsake,
As haue I Ioye and blis.
Lordys, knyghttys, praythe for me nowe;
What deell! Is þer no helpe at yowe?
Why sayes none off you yeis?'   6405

Lowde he cryde on the quene,
'In faythe, madame, that day hathe been,
Ye wold for me haue prayed,
And so I trow ye wold doo yett,
But all a f[er]rome am I flyte   6410
That makythe you all af[ray]de.'
At hym they all had Ioye i-now3e;
The quene at his wordys lough
And to the kynge she sayd,
'Syn I have louyd hym, nedys I mvste   6415
Praye for hym nedys coste,
Yff ye wold hold you payde.'

All men prayes for hym so faste,
The kyng hym grauntyd at þe laste.
Then at the fyrste he lyghte;   6420
'My hors mysellff kepe I will,'
He sayd, 'Come hedyr to me, Gille!'
Then loughe they all arighte.
He shovyd the waykyr wyth his [arm]e   f. 296ʳ
Euery man sayd, 'It were grett harme   6425
And we had forgone this sighte!'
Emydys the floure he made his sete;
Wyth trenchours and wyth brokyne mete
They sayd that noble knyghte.

Thus is he kept for his folye   6430
More then for his chevalrye,

6410 ferrome] *Ka.*; *MS* frome, *with* ro *corr. from* ar   6411 afrayde] *K.*; *MS*
aferde   6424 arme] *K.*; *MS* myghte   6429 noble] noblee

Thowe he were breme as bore.
Were he neuer off hertte so bold,
A foule amonge them [they] hem hold,
His plesure was the more: 6435
But ofte is sayd be men of skole,
Many man callys anoþer a foule,
Well sought yff it were,
Hymsellff in suche a chaunce myȝte be,
He is twys so moche foule as hee—   6440
In faythe, so fell it there.

Hee satte and fedde hym faste i-nowȝe,
Att his araye lowde they lowȝe
The knyghttys all bedene.
Syn that he was so noble a man,   6445
Wyth sobur hert [he] suffyrd thanne;
For loue hy[s] care ys kene.
Yff he shuld his love forgoone,
Me thynke men dyd hym mekill wronge,
So mot I borowed been.   6450
As he satte etand in the floure,
Come rydyng in at the dore
A worthy wyghte, I wene,

Apon a palfreye white as mylke,
In a sadull all off sylke,   6455
The sege off rewell bone,
The trapoure well ordayned þerefore,
Frette aboute wyth gold so dere;
In the world was better non.
Here gyte was velvet to her f[ee]te,   6460
Hyr syrkote syngell it was for heete,
Besett wyth many a stone;
Her mantell all of red sendell,
That araye become her well;
As the sonne hyr coloure shone.   6465

6432 breme] bremne   6434 they] K.; MS om.   6444 bedene] bee denee
6446 he] K.; MS om.   6447 hys] K.; MS thy   6460 feete] K.; MS foote
6464 araye] the second a written above line

They thought was non of ble so bryght;
Here beheld bothe kynge and knyght,
And in there herttys they þoughte
That thay myghte have slepte her bye
The wynturs nyghte vtterlye,   6470
Yff too in one were broughte!
The maydon wysse and witty was;
Before the hye lord she goos,
To othere lyght she noughte.
A yard of gold in hand she bare;   6475
As sone as she come thare,
Off socure she besoughte.

She sayd, 'þou worthy kyng of price
In whome grette witte and wysdome lythe,
Herkyne whate I shall saye: 6480
'Your nece off Calabyre, that lady clere,
Ys bovnden wyth a fendys fere
That wastythe all here wyte [away];
She besekys you off youre grace
That ye will helper in this casse   6485
Wythe sum man that maye . . .   f. 297ʳ

'Syr, she hathe not in her hand
Wythoute Candres a foote of land;
A fend it hathe dystroyed.
In all Calabere is knyght non   6490
That darre fyght wyth hym alonne,
So is the fende vnryde.
He hathe sworne, so God me save,
Till his wyff he will heere haue,
Soo hathe that sot porveyde.   6495
But she maye fynde a knyghte kynde
Fro that fende her to defende,
She is vtterly dystroyde.'

The kyng sayde to þat mayden syne,
'What is his name?' 'Ser Lyolyne,   6500

6481 off] f *corr. from* ?   6483 away] *K.*; *MS om.*

That sittys my lady sore,
For he hathe sworne, so God hym save,
That ou[er] wyth hym he will her haue
Into Ynde Mayore.
A fortenyght hens the day is sette   6505
That she mvste fynde, wythowten lette,
A man to fyghte here fore.'
Off all them that satt at the borde,
Was non that answerd a word,
Nothere lesse ne more.   6510

Thereoff the kyng asorowed was;
The maydon syghed and sayd, 'Alas!
Why says non off you novght?
So worthy knyghttys as here ben manye,
Syr, shall I haue helpe off anye?   6515
In bale ellys be we broughte!'
Was there none a worde answerde þertill;
The mayden wepte and gaff hyr ille,
She sayd, 'Nowe I se vnsoughte
My travayle hedyr is all in vayne!'   6520
Full well Ipomadon knew Imayne;
To helpe hur hathe he thoughte.

He stertte vp att the laste
And wordis off foly forthe he caste;
'In faythe now I am fayne!   6525
Syr kyng, as I haue happe or selle,
My comyng hedyr me lykythe well,
For this is my de[ray]ne.
Thow graunte me beforehande
The fyrste poynte that fell in þat londe,   6530
The sothe is not to layne,
And ser, yf thou saye I lye,
Have here my hand to fyght wyth þe!'
Hym beholdys Imayne.

'Do away, foole, for God avowe,   6535
It is no tyme to Iape nowe;

f. 297ᵛ (margin, beside line 6516)

Thereffore come I not hedyr!'
'No damysell, goo forthe thy waye—
In faythe I shall be there þat day,
How so euer I come thedur.'   6540
'Alas!' [sayd] Imay[n]e to Melengere,
'Sertys, and I gette no helpe here,
To goo I wot neuer whedyre!'
Thowȝe she made neuer so muche moo[ne],
They satte all stille as anny stone,   6545
The kynge and all togedur.

'Allas ser kyng, why do ye thus?   f. 298ʳ
Where is gentill Cabanus
That is so mekill a knyght?
Hadde he byn here, so God me save,   6550
Some helpe of hym yet shuld I have,
As he my lady hathe hight!'
There was non a worde answerd agayne.
Here hors hedde turned Imayne,
And wepand went þat wyght   6555
Streghte oute off the hall dore.
Ipomadon knelythe downe in the floure
Before them all in syght:

'Graunte me this reyne, I the praye!'
The kyng sayd, 'Foule, goo forthe thy waye—   6560
I se the holden no man!'
'Syr, haue her my hande, I will.'
He sayd, 'Come heder to me, Gyll!'
And lyghttly vpe he wanne.
To his inne is he goone,   6565
A better coote he dyd vpone
Thanne euer his dame hym spanne;
Better shyld and better spere,
An helme his hedde wyth to were;
A stede he lepe on thanne.   6570

A thredbare tabard full of raggis,
An old hoode revyn wyth Iaggys,

6541 sayd Imayne to] *Kp.* sayd Imayne tho to; *MS* I maye thow   6544 moone]
K.; *MS* moo   6559 praye] prayee   6560 thy] they

He on his armore caste,
For all men hym a fole shuld hold;
Thow he off hertt was neuer so bold,   6575
f. 298ᵛ   Hym thought hit was the best.
A sotye sheld on his shulder he bare,
His spere as a raste it were
Thereon a soket feste:
Vnder was he armyd well,   6580
Aboven ill farande euery deall,
As wyttenesse here be weste.

He sent his hors and harnes
To Calabyr another wayes,
His mayster and his page,   6585
His knyghttys, and all his oþer meyne;
'Goo byde me, mayster, for charyte,
Att the e[r]mytage.
So prevelye ye you beyre,
That non other witte whate ye were;   6590
I dwell but littull stage.'
Right as he bad, his mayster dyd;
Wythin the thyke wood they them hyde
Wythoute any more owterage.

So faste hyes Ipomadon,   6595
The maydon he hathe ouertane;
Mornand euer she rode.
A dwarffe kepythe her in þe wayes
Bothe hyr hors and hur harneys,
Att the towne end hur bade,   6600
And whan he saw she wept so faste,
Wyth sorofull countenaunce he her axte
What answere that she hadde.
'I' faythe ser, helpe gett wee none here—
Allas that euer kyng Mellengere   6605
f. 299ʳ   My ladye so mekyll of hathe made!

'When I had all my tale told,
There was non that anwere wold

6588 ermytage] emytage   6606 My] *Preceded by* That

Off his knyghttys bedene,
But an old naturall fole   6610
Sterte vp when he se me make suche dole,
And carpud wordys kene.
He sayd this battayle shuld be his;
So fayre a fole, so haue I blysse,
Haue I but seldone sene.   6615
Loo, where he comys now may ye see.'
The dwarff sayd, 'For [Goddis love], yound he be?'
'Ye, the same that I off mene;

'I praye the, byd hym turne agayne.'
'Nay, in trowthe Imayne;   6620
Than fayle I curtassye.
Thow he be not all the wyseste wyght,
I wold he myghte ouercome the knyght
Bee his grette folye.
Lett hym come and hold his cowrsse,   6625
The waye is his a[s] well as ours;
What grevythe vs he ryde vs bye?
Why shuld I lett hym of his gate?'
The maydone began to chyde þerat
And wendyth forthe forthy.   6630

Hur owne hors hedde agayne she drewe
And cryde on hym long i-nowȝe
Wyth a sterne stevyne;
'Turne agayne, þou belamye,
I kepe not of thy companye   6635
Nothere [on morn] nor [on evyn]!'   f. 299ᵛ
'Maydone,' quod Ipomadon,
'I praye þe lett thy wordys alonne
For [his] love that sittys [in hevyn],
For wele thou wottys, and þou wylt say,   6640
The Fere hathe louyd me many a day,
But that is not to [n]evyn!'

6611 Sterte] e *written above line*   6617 Goddis love] *MS om.*   6626 as
well] *K.; MS* awell   6635 kepe] *Followed by crossed-out* of   6636 on morn nor
on evyn] *K.; MS* for Evill nor for*e* good   6639 his] *K.; MS om.*   in hevyn] *K.; MS*
above   6642 nevyn] *K.; MS* evyn

Imayne to the dwarffe sayd,
'Now may thou see þou art payd
Wyth a nyce folys resone!'   6645
'Ye, for to gette the[m] losse and prise
Men make them folys that byn wyse
And off full grette renowene;
Lett hym come, he may do well!'
'Wyth me, be God and Sent Myghell,   6650
He shall not truse of towne;
I wold be drowned in a pole
Or I ouer land shuld ledde a fole,
Be God that sittis above[n]!'

'Well ye wot, damysell,   6655
The Fere of long hathe lovyd me well,
Thow it not knowen bee.'
'I praye God send me sorowe vnsought,
That wot whether she love þe or not!
Syr, I say for mee,   6660
Well I trowe, fro she þe knowe,
Lyttill love she will the shewe!'
'Yes damysell,' quod he,
'She lovythe me more, so mot I thryve,
Then all the men that ar on lyve,   6665
Synne the laste tyme she me see.'

f. 300ʳ

'When was that ser, I the praye?'
'I can not verely tell that day,
Madame meke and mylde.'
Wythoute any more abode,   6670
Togedyr [f]lytand forthe they rode
Bothe be fyrthe and feld,
Wounder hoote shonne þe sonne.
Imayne hathe an while fonne,
And thought hym to haue begylyd: 6675
Fro hur palfray she lyght downe,
The dwarff pyght hyr pavelyon.
Ipomadon hovyd and smyled,

6646 them] then   6654 aboven] above   6667 praye] prayee
6671 flytand] K.; MS slytand

Syne he lyght a littell þerbye.
The dwarffe cowthe of curtessye,   6680
And lyghttly to hym youde—
Therefore was Imayne wrothe i-nowthe.
A littell fro hym to a bovgh
He raynd his stede;
His helme of for heet he toke   6685
And as a fole his hedde he shoke
And sayd, 'So mot I spede,
Iff me be happe lyff to haue,
I shall the quyte, so God me save,
All this grette fore-dede.'   6690

The dwarff prayes the maydon bryght
That she wold to her calle the knyght
That semys bold to bene:
'I praye God, fowle mot me befall
Yf I a fole shuld to me calle—   6695
Whatte, we dotte I wene!'   f. 300ᵛ
Go we now to Lyelyne,
That hathe a knyght to his cosyn
That wyde is knowe for kene;
Many a tyme he gan hym payne   6700
To praye his lord for Imayne,
That maydon bright and shene.

He prayes so herttly and so faste
He graunt hym Imayn at the laste.
Thus man, that hight Mauges,   6705
Welle he wyste that maydon clere
Off messavge was to Mellengere;
Thereon he hade good spyes.
He watyd hyr homwardys the way,
And he come rydand, sothe to say,   6710
Evyn where Imayne lyes.
The maydon was wery and slept faste,
But wyth a grett noyse at the laste
She woke, and vp gan ryse.

6693 bold to] to bold   6700 payne] *K.*; *MS* prayne

'Well fovnde, mayde Imayne—   6715
Vpon your palffrey ye lepe agayne
Wythoute wordys moo,
For trewly, lady, ye are myne,
Gyvyn off my lord ser Lyolyne!'
Than was Imayne woo;   6720
'Syr, that were grett outerage
Gyff I were ma[r]d of my message;
For Goddys loue lette me goo!'
'It nedys not to make þis mone;
Whether ye lyke or none,   6725

In faythe it shall be soo!'

Then as an aspleff she quoke,
Vppon the dwarff gan she loke
Wyth angur and syghyng syne.
Ipomadon sittys and lokys them two;   6730
'Syr, what wylte thou wyth þat maydon doo?
In faythe, she bees not thyne!
Lette hyr sitte there bysyde,
And home agayne I rede the ryde
To Ser Lyolyne,   6735
And byde that lord in oþure wyse
Reward the for thy long seruyce,
For in faythe thou shall here tene!'

His brokyne wede behelde he faste,
And sayd full lyghttly at the laste,   6740
'Thou nyce fole, sitt stille!
Yff thou will foors her to defende,
Foreuer thou shalt fele my hande;
Have here my trough theretill!'
'Syr, off a cause I cowpe thee;   6745
A fole now thou calyste mee—
That shall thou lyke full ille!
The more foule of vs to shall
Wythin a shorte whyle have a falle!'
His helme he takyth hym tille.   6750

6722 mard] *K.*; *MS* mayd   6738 shall] *K.*; *MS followed by* not

His shylde in cavntell kyst he þan,
And lyghttly on his stede he wane,
In hande he toke a spere.
Wythoute any more abode,
Thus ɪɪ knyghttys togeddyr rode   6755
Be worthenes of werre.   f. 301ᵛ
Maugis sett his stroke so faste,
The spere þorow the shyld paste,
But vnder it dede no dere;
So sternely stroke Ipomadon,   6760
In two he stroke his shulder bone,
And downe he gan hym bere.

Ipomadon lefte not þat knyght
Tille he hadde trewly his trovthe plyght—
Though hym were lothe theretoo—   6765
That he shuld ryde home to Lyolyne,
'And say the mayden ys not thyne,
In peas forthe may she goo;
Wyth Ioye they heldyn forthe þer Iorneye!
And also, ser, thou shalt hym saye,   6770
As thow haue reste or roo,
The F[e]re wythoute grette battayle
Shall not come to his spousayle,
For nought that he can doo!

'But ser, so God of hevyn me spede,   6775
Behynde the thow shalt leve thy stede,
I wyll the say for why:
Wetly wondyd I trow thou bee,
But thou shall haue to bere the
This lyttill lowe [rouncy].'   6780
In his sadull they hym sett.
He rewes that euer he wyth hym mette,
His arme hynge babelyng bye;
Thus hath he toke his leve [and] gone.
To the dwarff sayd Ipomadon,   6785
'I haue made grette maystrye,   f. 302ʳ

6765 hym] y *corr. from* e   6772 Fere] *K.*; *MS* fayre   6780 This] Thuis
rouncy] *K.*; *MS* powyse   6782 he²] che   6784 and] *K.* and ys; *MS om.*

'Gevyn a way thy littill hors,
But neuer the lesse, þerof no fors,
For thow shalt haue this stede.
I praye the, thow be not stravnge—   6790
I gyff the this for the better chavnge,
So God of hevyn me spede.'
The dwarffe was neuer ere so fayne:
'Damysell,' he sayd to Imayne,
'Have ye not sene this dede?   6795
That man was neuer vnder þe mone
That more dowtly myghte have done.'
'Ye ser, well worthe mede!'

'Hade ye langeare agayn hym drevyn,
We shuld wyth this knyght have strevyn   6800
Right nowe, this ys no naye.
The[n] shulde ye not this VII yere
Have done this message to the Fere;
That wolde have greuyd vs aye!'
T[o] the dwarffe heft sonys say[d] she,   6805
'I se well gy[f]tys may mekyll doo,
Be hym that all welde maye!
He was full lyght, be me thryfte . . .
This dare I savely saye.

'Trowest thou be any grett prowes   6810
He brought the knyghte to this destres?
We nay, be God syr, he!
He dyd it be his grette folye,
And nothyng be his chevalrye,
Therefor this wordys lett bee!'   6815
Thee hette was well ouercome þanne
Agayn vpon þer hors they [w]a[nn]e
And forthe they rode all thre.
Att evyn till an inne they came,
Ipomadon harboryd at the same,   6820
[Fro] the mayde all awaye drew [he].

f. 302ᵛ

6802 then] K.; MS them   6805 To] K.; MS om.   sayd] K.; MS say
6806 gyftys] gystys   6817 wanne] Kp.; MS name   6821 Fro the mayde all
awaye drew he] K.; MS The mayde drew all awaye

The dwarffe hym seruyd to fote and hande;
Imayne was wrothe, I vnderstonde,
But therefore lett he novght.
Att morowe they rose and went þer way,   6825
There thorowe a forest þer way laye,
The mayde rode in a thoughte.
Att hye pryme they fonde a well;
Ioyefull was that damysell,
Downe fro her hors she sovghte.   6830
The dwarfe pyght her pavelyone,
Wyne and bakyne venysone
Before that berde he brought.

Ipomadon lyght a llytell her fro,
The dwarffe to his hors gan goo   6835
And raynd hym to a boughe,
And prayd the mayde wyth good will,
The knyght she wold calle here tille.
The[r]wyth she was wrothe i-nowgh;
'I praye God I bede neuer [y]ole   6840
That I to me shuld calle a foule!'
Ipomadon satte and lovgh,
He lykyd hur wordys full well;
He said, 'þat day hathe ben, damysell,
We fro youre dal[ia]ns drewe,   6845

'But I ne wotte what tyme, ne where!'
Imayne to the dwarff sayd there,   f. 303ʳ
'Now thou may here take hede
How younde foole begynnythe to rave,
And yet thou wold, so God me save,   6850
Ouer land I shuld hym lede!'
As they satte spekyng alther beste,
A knyght come rydyng thorowe the foreste,
[Sytt]and on a stede;
Imayne sa[w] and syghed sore,   6855
[And] th[ough]t the tother day before
How she hadde byn in drede.

6839 therwyth] *Kp.*; *MS* the wyth   6840 yole] *K.*; *MS* olde   6843 well]
K.; *MS followed by* i-nowgh   6844 þat day hathe ben, damysell] *K.*; *MS* damysell
þat day hathe ben   6845 dalians] *Kp. MS* dalentys   6854 Syttand] *K.*; *MS*
rydand   6855 saw] sayd   6856 And thought] *K.*; *MS* That

That knyght was cosyn to Mawgis;
He mekill hathe wonne of losse and prise
In Ynde and Palestyne;   6860
He was Lyolyne suster sonne.
When he had Imayne fovne,
He sayd, 'Dere leman myne,
Vppon your palffraye leppe ye,
For to reward hathe gevyn mee   6865
My cossyn Syr Lyolyne!'
Thereffore had Magis be full wrothe,
For he had gyffner to them bothe,
As fayre a gyfte they t[y]ne.

Toward the foole gan she loke,   6870
And as an aspenleff she shoke,
She was so sore aferde.
'Syr,' than quod Ipomadon,
'Goo forthe thy wey and lett hur goone,
Fro wyghter I haue here weryd: 6875
Be my faythe, thow getyste her nowght
f. 303ᵛ   But yff it be wyth bofetys bovghte,
Thowȝe thou byght on thy berde!'
His eye on his sheld he caste,
And sayd deynely at the laste,   6880
'Syt still, thow foole moserd!'

'Ye, yff I be a foole,' quod hee,
'The sadder shall my strokys bee,
Right sone þat maye ye witte;
A fooll wott neuer where he shall stryke,   6885
But euer more lay on thyke
Where he may lyg[h]ttly hytte.
So grette God of heyvyn me spede,
The mayde away thou shalt not lede—
I do the well to wytte—   6890
But yff thou her in werre may wyne!'
This battayle boldely to begynne
A cowenaunte have they knett.

6869 tyne] K.; MS tane   6874 forthe] o written above r   thy] K.; MS they
6887 lyghttly] lygttly

Ipomadon of his spere toke hede
And lyghttly gatte vppon his stede,   6895
In cantell kyst his shylde.
The knyghttys name was Greon,
A worthyer knyght then he was one
Nede neuer be sene in feld.
That tyme they wold no lengur byde;   6900
On werre togeddur gan they [ryde],
So worthely they them welde,
These knyghttys þat were conyng of craftys.
To shevers wente bothe þere shaftys;
Imayne satt and behelde.   6905

Ipomadon smot hym wyth his spere
Thurghe shylde and all his oþer geyre   f. 304ʳ
A lyttill above the thyy;
Thereffore was Greon wrothe i-novgh,
A noble swerd oute he drowgh   6910
And att his hedde lette flee.
In his hand hit turnyd wyth that,
And on his hedde hit fell all flatte,
Ellys hadde he slayne that fre.
Imayene had full mekyll care   6915
When she saw hym smytte so sore;
Nere swovned that lady fre.

Ipomadon was no thyng payde
That he was so sore stonyed;
He drew his swerd that stovnde.   6920
Soo wyghttly he weldys hym in his geyre
That off he smythe Ser Greon eyre,
Wyth that he fell to grounde.
'Longe have ye callyd me but a foole;
Leve ser, now how lyke ye my skole?   6925
I holde you wyghttly wounde;
Ye may be orderde when ye wille
Syr, have here my trowthe þertille—
Thow arte shavyne rownde!'

6901 ryde] *K.*; *MS* goo   6922 smythe] *K.*; *MS followed by* of

He bade the dwarff, 'Go take the stede,   6930
The maydons harnes thereon to leede;
Thy somere hors thow hym make.'
A chylde wyth hym Greon hade
That in the woodesyde hym abode,
Righte sorye for his sake.   6935

f. 304ᵛ
He saw his mayster woundyd ille,
Another hors he brought hym till,
Vp they gan hym take.
Alofte wettly wondyd was hee;
Ipomadon sayd, 'I hope ye be   6940
Ill stonyd off a stroke;

'Att this tyme [y]e gett not Imayne!
To Lyolyne ryde home agayne
And say wythouten fayle,
Ye, for ought that [h]e can doo,   6945
To his weddyng come not sho
Wythoute grette battayll!'
Wyth sorowe hertt he hyed hym home,
As Magis had told, he told the same;
How a man cled in mayle   6950
Had ouercome them bothe in fyghte;
'In all this world is non so wyghte,
Ne so sekyr to assayle!'

Imayne att hur deynere satt
And grettely mervelayd was off þat,   6955
That had done so dovghtly;
Her hertte a littill bowed is:
'Hade it be done be worthynes,
He were grette thanke-worthy;
There is no man fro hens to Roome   6960
Mighte have done better, be my doo[m]e,
Ne yett hens to Normandye;
And he ne were right mekyll of myghte,
He hadde neuer ouercome this knyghte,
I se full well therebye,   6965

6942 ye] K.; MS e   6944 fayle] faylee   6945 he] K.; MS ye
6949 Magis] Followed by crossed-out a   6956 dovghtly] t written above line
6961 doome] K.; MS doone

'In battell can he well endure,   f. 305^r
Bothe be witte and be mesure,
So haue I happe or seall.
How so he farithe wyth folye,
His dedis byn off grette chevalrye,   6970
Be God and Sent Myghell!
There is a M^l knyghttys of skole
That holdys this man but a fole
Wythin the land off Cesile,
That Mallenger fyndys wyth honoure,   6975
Halff so strong be not in stowre,
Cowde not haue done so well.

'For a fole they hold hym there,
And pure foly is all his fare,
But bold is his der[eyn]es;   6980
As fole he comys, as folle he gos,
As fole all his matters masse,
As a fole he hym demeynes,
As a fole he lawghis, as a fole he lyes,
As a fole he sittys, as a fole he rysis,   6985
As a fole all way h[e] conte[ynes]:
Be God and Sent Myghell,
He fyghttys so worthely and so well,
I hope he dothe but faynes!'

She bad the dwarrfe prevely,   6990
'Goo byd yound knyght come sit me by;
Loke yf hym lyste to dyne.
Sethe þou haste so faste for hym prayed,
Lett hym come, I hold me payde.'
Thereof they novghte [f]yne: 6995
The dwarffe was glad and to hym he goos,
And herttly prayed hym he has   f. 305^v
To come and drynke a draw3t of wyne;
'And ye shall dyne of the wylde,
And wyth you shall younde maydon mylde   7000
Make a sufficiante fyne.'

6980 dereynes] K.; MS deueres   6986 he conteynes] K.; MS is his covntenaunse
6992 lyste] Followed by ofte   6994 me] Written above line, and preceded by deleted the
6995 fyne] Kp.; MS tyne

As he were halff wood he faris,
And on the dwarff sternly he staris
That for feyre he quak[e]:
'Nay! I praye to God I lesse my witte,   7005
By none suche rapokys will I sett
For all the fare ye make.
For hyr prowde wordys too,
Now wott I well she will me sloo,
Downe for I theme strake!   7010
For all your trappyng and your trayne
Therewyth shull ye bothe agayne
The devyll off hell you take!'

Then had the dwarff sorow i-novgh,
Sorofully agayne he drowe,   7015
So sore aferde was hee.
Imayn harde euery deale;
She sayd, 'Ser, so haue I sell,
But thou trowest nouȝte me
Off the tale that I the tolde,   7020
Be the grette God, thyselff I hold
A more fole then hee:
Hit farythe by the as dothe be moo;
Ye know [not] that ye here also,
Ye beleve not that ye see.   7025

'Men makythe them folis þat ar wyse,
And witte, them þat non in lyethe—
So fayreth of the playne!'
The dwarff was angurd sore
And wrothely spake to hy[r] þerfore,   7030
'Lett be thy fare Imayne!
In poynte of dethe we bothe hathe byn;
He hathe vs savyd, and þat is sene,
The sothe is not to lay[n]e.
To spere hymself dyd hym orde; †   7035
Off you he myghte gette neuer a worde
For his godenes agayne!

7004 quake] K.; MS quakys   7015 drowe] drowee   7024 not] K.; MS om.
7028 the] K. MS them   7030 hyr] K.; MS hym   7034 layne] K.; MS laye

f. 306ʳ

'Syne the fyrste tyme þat ye mett,
A mery word myght he non gett,
Thereffore wythouten fayle,   7040
He that seruys thanke[les] aye,
May thynke [i]ll set, I darre well say,
Att the laste his longe travell.
Right as ye say hit farithe be you:
That ye se, ye will not [tro]we!   7045
This myghtty man vnder mayle
Full worthely wrought hathe hee,
And þerof ye will not knowe bee,
What so euer ye ayell!'

The dwarff mett to hym bare,   7050
Full egurly he ettys there;
Imayne on hym can loke.
When they had dyned, forthe they rode;
Right as a fole, wythouten bode
Euer more his hedde he shoke.   7055
Hit drew to the nyghte faste,
They saw a towne at the laste   f. 306ᵛ
Stondyng on the syde of a broke;
Hit was but a meane velage,
So littill was the harburage,   7060
That both one inne they toke.

The inne was so streyte, forthy,
They bothe mvst in a chambur lye;
Imayne grogyd noughte:
In her hertte she thynkys sone,   7065
Ouer mekyll amys has she done,
To amend it she hathe thought.
He put of his armore euery deyle,
The dwarffe hym seruyd wonder well,
A mantill to hym he broughte,   7070
Blake wythin and red wythoute.
He wrapud hym worthely abowte
That richely was iwroughte.

7041 thankeles] thanke   7042 ill] well   7045 trowe] K.; MS rewe
7051 egurly] Followed by crossed-out e

Off sylke he hade one a s[erk]e
Wrought of a wondyr worke   7075
Sowyde bothe well and clene;
A kyrtyll and a crochett fyne . . .
Full wele idyght all bedene.
Imayne hym behyldys on the face,
A fayrer knyght thanne he was   7080
Her thought she hade not sene;
'Ys this a fole? Nay certys, hee!
In hertte sore for-thynkys mee,
So str[a]unge that I have been.'

Imayne repentys that she hathe done,   7085
And in her hertte she thynkys sone
To amend hit mekyll more.

f. 307^r

A womon is bothe warre and wyse,
Grette loue and lykyng in them lythe,
Who lyste to lere at there lore;   7090
There they haue byn most straunge,
All att onys then will they chaunge,
Yff they be not sought ouer sore,
And love twyse so herttly syne—
Godys dere blessyng and myne   7095
Muste they have therefore.

Imayne sayd, 'So haue I blis,
That I so mekill have done amys,
Sore for-thynkys mee!
Syr, forgyff me that I haue done ille,   7100
And I shall amend me at your will,
Be God and be my lewte.'
The dwarff was neuer so glad [in hertte],
Then lyghttly vp he stertte
And sayd, 'Syr, for charyte,   7105
As ye be curtayse knyght and [hend],
Eysythe you and be this maydys frend
That desyrythe hit off thee,

7074 serke] K.; MS shorte   7078 idyght] Followed by well
7084 straunge] K.; MS strounge   7086 in] i corr. from h   7103 in hertte] K.;
MS om.   7106 hend] K.; MS fre

'And I shall be hyr borowe, ser,
That ye shall fynde no more in hyr   7110
Forfettynge vnto yowe.'
Ipomadon this sewraunce toke
And as a fole his hedde he shoke
And kest downe wyth the browe.
Syne they were to supper sett   7115
Imayne may not hyr hert lett
In love to dure nowe;
Th[e] more she lokys on þat knyght,   f. 307ᵛ
The more hyr loue is on hym ly3te;
This is she fayne to bowe.   7120

When they had suppud, they went to bede,
Imayne was so streytly stede
And prykyd wyth a payne.
Trobelyng too and fro she lyes,
Waltryng on a woofull wyse,   7125
All syghyng sayd Imayne,
'In a sory tyme [it] was,
Oute of Candres when [I] [did] pase,
The sothe is not to layne;
So wyse as [I] was holden þerin,   7130
Off me my lady shall haue synne
Gyff I come neuer agayne.

((How hit is I can not wytte,
But well I wott as yet
In faythe, I haue grette payne.))   7135

'Alas, folle, why seyste thou soo?
She is not cause off thy woo
That to bewitt, i-wys.
Yff she the sent on her message,
She bade the do no suche outerage   7140
Thy body to ly be his!
Thou haste thyne owne hert to constreyne . . .

7113 And] *corr. from* as   7118 The] *K.; MS* Than   7127 it] *K.; MS om.*
7128 Candres] *K.; MS* the chambyre   I did pase] *K.; MS* she paste   7130 I] *K.;*
MS om.   7140 no] *Written above line, with caret*

'The blame ys thyne owne, Imayne,
That love dothe the so mekyll payne,
Woundys wythouten spere.   7145
Nay, it is turment as men tellis!
Hit is love—what is hit ellys
That peas hathe turnyd to warre?'

Vp she ryses and downe she fallis,
And on love playnly she callys,   7150
'Why doste thou me this de[r]e?

'I wyght the it neuer a deall
Though my lady loue hyr lemon well
That is so good a knyght,
When I thus wyth a fole is taked,   7155
That among all lordys is lakyd
For on so vnresnable a wyght.
Nay, be my faythe he is no fole!
He is a noble knyght of skole,
Who so hade sene hym [f]yght.   7160
Thowgh [I] allther wyseste be,
His manlynes and gret bewte
Makyth my loue on hym to lyght.

'Ye, wheder it turne to well or woo,
To know his will I will goo!'   7165
Her mantell she toke her tille,
To his beddys syde she youde.
Anoþer while [there] she stode
In a stody full stylle.
She sayd, 'Alas, fole, what is thy þought?   7170
In bale foreuer thou haste [th]e broughte,
This foly yf thow fullfyll;
But yf thou of þis foly blynne,
Imayne, thou shamest all thy kynne,
In faythe, than dos thou ille!'   7175

7146 turment] *K.*; *MS* turnament   7151 dere] *K.*; *MS* dene   7160 fyght]
syght   7161 I] *K.*; *MS om.*   7168 there] *K.*; *MS* stile   7171 the] *K.*;
MS me

Stille lay Ipomadon,
And how she made þis mekill mone,
He hard euery deyll.
To hyr wordys he toke no kepe,
And lay right as he dyd slepe.   7180 f. 308ᵛ
What she mend he wyst full wele;
That love full sore hyr bovndyn hathe.
To his bedde syde she gos
Wyth sighyng and vncele;
Softely at his clothes she drewe   7185
And sayd, 'Ser, ye haue slept i-nowe,
Be God and Sent Myghell;

'Awake a while and speke wyth me!'
Grewosly vp starte hee
And sayd, 'What devill art þou?'   7190
In his mowthe her hande he gate,
Right as he wolde haue eyton þat;
'Mercy!' she cryed nowe,
'For love I maye no lengur layne,
And sertys, it is Imayne   7195
That is comyn to you,
Off all þat I haue done wyth ille
To make amendys at your wille,
Trewly ye may me trowe!

'Syr, I am a dukys doughttur dere,   7200
As grette a lady as the Fere,
But neuer the lesse, forthy,
Love will lett me haue no peas.
Syr, after my faders dyssece,
Off Burgayne ayre am I: 7205
Lett this alone and goo we theder,
Ye shall be lord off all togeddyre,
Bothe of bowre and bye.
I shall you make, so haue I rowe,
As grett a lord as euer myghte she,   7210
I say yow securlye!'

f. 309^r

Ipomadon stille lay,
And hard all þat she wold saye;
That she had care, he wyste:
'Damysell, so God me save,　　　　　　　　7215
Tomorow thy leyser þou may haue
To say what th[e] lyste;
Tonyght thou gettys no more of me,
Goo to thy bedde, I comaunde the,
And lett me haue my reste!'　　　　　　　7220
A, littill comforte þou haste Imayne!
Vnto hyr bedde she went agayne,
But no thynge slepe she lyst.

At morow they [rose] and went þer way;
There way thorow a forest lay　　　　　　7225
The fowlys song merely and swette.
Off love, that is the grettys payne,
Soo mekyll then had Imayne,
Hyr dynere she forgatte.
The dwarff sayd to the damysell,　　　　　7230
'Here besydys is a fayre well,
And þere I red you sitte—
A morsell to dyne I wold ye had.'
Thereof was the maydon glad
She lyght adowne on hyr fete.　　　　　　7235

Bysyd hyr lyght Ipomadon,
To hym streyght is Imayne gone
And sett her hym besyde.
Bakone venysone and wyne
The dwarff [brought] befor them fyne,　　7240
In erthe is not to hyde.
As they at þere dyner satt,
A knyght come rydyng after þat
As faste as he myghte ryde:

f. 309^v

Whan he saw the mayden there,　　　　　7245
So Ioyefull was he neuer yere
In all þis world so wyde.

7217 the] thy　　　7224 rose] K.; MS say　　　7230 damysell] *Preceded by crossed-
out* si　　　7237 Imayne gone] K.; *reversed in MS*　　　7240 brought] K.; MS *om.*

Ofte sy[th]es had he done his payne
To praye his lord for Imayne,
That maydyn fayre and clere;   7250
He graunte hym lyghtly, and so he mow3te
The thyng þat neuer coste hym nou3te
A farthyng in forty yere!
Duke he was of grett [T]esayle,
And Lyolynes broþer, wythouten fayle;   7255
His name was Leyvnder.
He rydythe streyght to the well
And sayd, 'Dereworthy damysell,
Well be you foundyn here!

'Leppis on youre palffray and comyþe wyth me,   7260
The duchesse of T[e]ssayle I shall make þe;
I have covetyd the longe!'
Ipomadon, wyth hardy hertte,
Lyghttly vpon his stede he sterte,
And sayd, 'Ser, [fals] ye sang   7265
Yff thou so large gyff thy gyft,
Thou gettys non here; be my thryfte,
Me thynkys than dydyste thou wronge!'
The tother sayd, 'What arte thou
That so nycely answeris nowe?   7270
Sitt down, the devill the hange;

'Hold thy peas!' quod Lyvnder,
'Or, fole, thow shalt abye full dere
Thy foley wordys fell!'
Ipomadon sayd, 'Be my lewte,   7275
The moste fole here hold I the—
I make that no counsell!'   f. 310ʳ
The knyght houys and lokys hym [on],
And wenys he is in poynte to fonne;
He sayd, 'So haue I seyle,   7280
Yf thou be the fole onwyse
That skomfyght Cryon and Magis,
Wyth the I have to deale!'

7248 sythes] *K.*; *MS* syces   7253 farthyng] fayre thyng   7254 Tesayle]
K.; *MS* cesayle   7260 youre] r *corr. from* n   7261 Tessayle] *K.*; *MS* turssayle
7265 fals] *K.*; *MS om.*   7266 gyft] *K.*; *MS* gyftys   7278 on] *K.*; *MS om.*

'Certys, ser, ye may asaye!'
In werre togeddyr ryde they;   7285
To lett them non they fynde.
Ipomadon through þe body hym bare
Byhy[n]de his bake a fote and more,
The hedde lokyd oute behynde.
'Off Imayne, ser, now may ye fayle   7290
To make hyr duchesse of T[e]ssayle,
Though ye be wrathe as wynde!'
When they had dynyd, forthe they rode;
The knyght on the lond abode
Dedde vnder the lyn[d]e.   7295

A squyer had Ser Leyvnder
That made grett sorowe and ill chere,
And lyghttly to hym he soughte.
'Alas,' he sayd, 'Woo is mee
That euer I shuld leve after the!'   7300
A bere he had to hym brought:
Lordyngys, beleve, it was no noþer,
They bare hym vnto his broþer;
He was wro[th]e as he mowthe.
The knyghttys wer[e] sory euerchone   7305
That Lyvnder was so slone;
They sayd, 'Good ser, who [thus wroughte]?'

f. 310ᵛ

'I wott neuer, so God me spede,
But to the place I can yow lede
There he was levand laste.   7310
A folelyche knyght had hym slayn
That ledys a mayde þat hat Imayne,
And forthe he is way is paste.'
Now Lyolyne sayd, 'I wott well
That is the Fer[e]s damysell.   7315
I know what is hi[r] caste;

7288 byhynde] by hyde
Preceded by crossed-out no
wrothe] Kp.; MS wroughte
K. has that wrought; MS waste
MS his

7291 Tessayle] K.; MS trussayle
7295 lynde] K.; MS lyne
7304 was] Followed by a
7305 were] K.; MS wery
7315 Feres] K.; MS fers

7294 lond]
7307 thus wroughte]
7316 hir] K. her;

'In massage I wot þat she hathe byne,
And wyth hyr bryngyth a knyght kene
Wyth me to do this rayne.
As a fole he is dyghte   7320
But he is a man of mekyll myght,
The sothe is not to layne;
He skomfett Magis and Cryon,
And now he hathe my brothere slone . . .

'In peas ye lett hym goo and come;   7325
I wold not for this towne
That no man [dere] hym dyde
In feld or wee come and [batayle] have!'
Leyvnder they leyd in grave
And for his soule dyd byde . . .   7330

She paste thorow a derne stye
Ipomadon folowes prevelye
That was so curteys and kynde . . .

Hit drew faste to the nyghte,
Wyth his swerd a logge he dyght,   7335
For forthere myght they nought.
The dwarff downe his harnes t[as]
And to eche of them a bede he ma[s]
Wyth the clothes that he had brought.
Onarmyd was Ipomadon,   7340 f. 311ʳ
And syne to supper ar they goone;
Imayne no davnger thoughte,
But wonder nere the knyȝte she satte,
Grette lyste of loue makys that
Whiche in hyr herte was wroughte.   7345

Love is so mekyll off myghte
That it will davnte bothe kyng and knyght,
Erle and bold barone;
They that wyseste is of witte,
Fro tyme they be takyne wyth it,   7350

7327 dere] *MS.* to; *K.* myschef to   7328 batayle] *K.*; *MS om.*   7337 tas]
K.; *MS* toke   7338 mas] *K.*; *MS* made

Hit takythe fro them there reasone.
Love may save, love may spille,
Love may do what þat he will,
And turne all vp and downe.
After, when they suppud had   7355
And they [were] all blythe and glad,
To bedde they made them bovne.

Imay[n]e hadde so mekyll thought,
That, for sothe, slepe she ne movȝte
For wrythyng and for woo;   7360
On her lessone she thynkys more
That she lernyd on the nyght before
When she was turmentyd soo.
Her mantell eft she toke [her] tille,
Another tyme to witte his will,   7365
She makys her redy to goo.
Vp she rosse and downe she sitt;
She sayd 'alas' that euer she wyth hym mett;
'A, Looffe, I praye the hoo!

f. 311ᵛ

'In faythe, Imayne, thou was a fole   7370
That euer this thou enterde in lovys skole,
This dare I savely saye;
Willfully thow lesis thy witte,
That euer thou shuld so medull wyth hit,
Full sore the tyme banne thou maye!   7375
As folis we mette, as folys we goo,
As folys we are bothe two,
And as folys we werke allwey;
Folys we are and folys we were,
Foly is owre bothes fare;   7380
Be God of heyven, naye!

'It is no folye; love it is
That bryngys me to this dystresse,
I darre it say hardely:
But I of love sum bravnche haue,   7385
Hit will me bryng into my grave,
I fele full wele therbye.

7356 were] K.; MS om.   7358 Imayne] I maye   7364 her] K.; MS om.

Love workis me ouer mekyll woo;
For love yf I myselff sloo,
The cause of my dethe am I.   7390
To me it were [a] grette reprove
Wythouten swettnes off my love
This sodenly to dye . . .

'Then in his armys two
And yff he [the] worove as-tyte,   7395
The thare not but thyselff it witt—
Serttys, Imayne, noo!
But fro he wet it a woman be,
Thane I hope right sone that we
Shall softely settyll soo!'   7400
Forthe she goos, and turnythe agayne,
And at the laste sittys hyr downe Imayne
His bedde a littill froo.

A lyttyll she tovchyd his face thore;   f. 312ʳ
He lep vp as bryme as any bore   7405
And drew his swerd so kene:
'Be hym that weldyth heyven on high[t],
What on erthe that euer there be wyght
That dothe me all this tene?
But yff thou hygh the hens tyt,   7410
Have here my trowthe, I shall smyte
Thy hedde off quyte and clene!'
The mone shone wonder lyght,
Away went that byrde so bryght
As she there neuer hadde byne.   7415

But so wyth love led ys Imayne
That nedys mvst she go ageyne,
Therfore yff she shuld dye;
But tovche she durst hym neuer more,
But sett hyr downe his bedde before   7420
And mercy can hym crye:

7391 a] K.; MS no   7395 the] K.; MS om.   as-tyte] a styte   7400 Shall]
Preceded by That   7407 hight] K.; MS high   7410 tyt] K.; MS tyght

'But yff thou wake and speke wyth me,
Dye I mvste for loue off thee,
I say the securlye!
My hertte ys euer in poynte to breke;   7425
But yf ye softlye wyth me speke
No lengur leve maye I!'

Ipomadon laye full still,
He wyste full well she grevyd yll,
That lygaunce mvste she have: 7430
'What art thow, for thy lewte,
That on this wyse turmentys me,
As God off heyvyne me save?'

f. 312ᵛ'A, syr, hit is Imayne,
That for the suffers muche payne,   7435
Nere-hand in poynt to rave;
I love the so, wythouten fayle,
That yff I lesse my travayle
I shall be layde in grave!

'To Burgone turnethe agayn wyth me   7440
And lett this grett battayle be
I rede the, so mot I spede:
It ys worthe two off Calabre,
My lande and me ye shall have, ser,
Wythoute battayle or dede!'   7445
Mekley he answers thereto;
'Imayne, that may I not doo
For all this world to mede:
Am I not comen hedyr to fyght?
And yf I leve, I nolde so lyght   7450
Thy lady were in drede:

'Then myght all men savely say
That I for ferde were fled away;
That wold me shame and shende.
VII yere after, be thow bolde,   7455
Thyselff wold me a coward holde,
When thou ovghte at me tened.'

7432 turmentys] *K.*; *MS* turnamentys   7446 thereto] there two

'Nay, so haue I mede off masse,
I shall love you neuer the lasse,
And be a faythefull frende!'   7460
'Well Imayne, syster, that were rewthe,
But I shulde swer the be my trovthe,
Fro this be broughte to ende,

'And grette God will me þat grace geve,
After this Iurnaye þat I may leve,   7465 f. 313ʳ
And I have don this fyghte,
And thou and she have ovght knoven me,
At your bothe willis will I be,
For ye will do but right.'
'Dere ser, may I truste theretoo?'   7470
'Ye, here my hand, loo,
To hold that I have hight.'
Twyse kyst hym Imayne,
And to hyr bede she gos agayne
Well comfortyd of that knyght.   7475

In the mornyng vp he rose,
Ipomadon to Ymayne goos,
The dwarff he callyd hym till;
'Ye two shall ryde home to the Fere
And I behynde will byde here.'   7480
Thane lykyd Imayne ill.
'Say no more when ye come thedyre,
But a fole folowyd you hydder;
He grettys you well, be skyll.
And yff hym lyste, fyght will he,   7485
And yff hym lyste not, turne will he,
For sertys, so I wille!'

Wyth his sporris he strake his stede,
Into the foreste fro hem he yede
And logys hym wyth a bovgh,   7490
Till he come to the ermytage,
There his mayster and his page
They were wyth blis i-nowȝe.

Imayne rydythe whome to the Fere
They mett hyr wyth a symple chere,   7495

Nothere no thyng they lovgh:
'What tydyngys Imayne?' 'Madame, full yll!'
'Why sendys myne eyme non helpe me till?'
'Me rewys now I thedyr drovgh!'

'How so systure?' 'I wott neuer.   7500
That I there come me rewys euer!'
Be allmyghtty God she swore.
'It was told me yesturday,
A knyght come wyth you be the way
That was off grett powere;   7505
He skomfyght Mawgis and Greon,
And Leyvnder he hathe slone,
Lyolyne brothere dere!'
'Madame, ɪɪ c knyghttys I sawe
And mo, I trowe, sett on a rowe   7510
In the howse of Mellengere.

'When I hadde off my battayle tolde,
Was non a word that anwerd wold
But an fole vnwyse.
He stert vp among the[m] all, i-wis,   7515
He sayd this battayle shuld be his
Before this knyghttys off pryce;
Was there [n]on a word answerd þertill.
He folowed forthe ageyne my wille
Ther no man was amys;   7520
He skomfete by his grette foly,
And no thyng by his chevalrye,
Bothe Greon and Mawgis;

'Be foly he slow Lyondyre!'
Then wept that fayre lady clere   7525

For that knyght so bolde;
'Where ys he, Imayne?' 'What wot I?
Madame, I saye you securlye,
Att hym is littill holde;

7499 thedyr] K.; MS theredyr   7515 them] K.; MS the   7518 non] K.; MS on

In the forest he is loste behynde,   7530
And sertys, when he fro vs twyned,
A nyce tale he vs tolde:
He bade, "Say to the Fere when ye come home,
Say a fole wyth you hedyr come
That a thousande folde   7535

'Grette well that lady bryght,
And yff he lyke than will he fyght,
And yff he wolle nott, he will fle!"'
'What wordys were this off chevalrye?'
'Madame, I saye yow sekerlye,   7540
No nothere wyse helpe will hee.'
'Allas, it is wors thane I wende—
Will my eme no socoure me sende?'
'No lady, be me lewte.'
'Have yene traytur or I sholde,   7545
Me hade leuer a M^l folde
Goo drowne me in the see!'

She bade her men shuld botys take,
And on the sesyde redy make
That Lyolyne not it wyste;   7550
'Put me forthe into the flode,
Lett God that ys of myghtys [gode]
Do wyth me what hym lyste;
He may send me lande and lythe.
So have I leuere a thousand sythe,   7555
His mowthe onys ore I it kyste!
Now wott I wele, so God me spede,   f. 314ᵛ
My love is dede, wythouten drede.
A, hartte, when wilte thou barste?

'Este and west, northe and sowthe,   7560
This werre is in euery mannys mowthe
As I here, be my hoode.
Hadde my leman byn alyve,
He [h]a[d] byn here, so mot I thryue,
Or all this to havoke youde.'   7565

7534 come] comee   7544 lewte] lewtee   7545-6 Reversed in MS
7552 gode] K.; MS moste   7564 He had] K.; MS here as

A c bottys, wythouten fayle,
They stuffyd well wyth good vetaylle
That yff hyr nede best[o]de,
Men that wer of semblent sade
Shuld her put, or he her had,   7570
Forthe into the flode.

After this the day was come
That Lyolyne had þe battayle nomme;
He wold no lengur byde,
But made araye hym all in blacke,   7575
A stede off the same he dyd take,
He taryd not that tyde.
Blake pendavnt, shyld and spere,
Blake was all his oþur geyre.
He rydes hym forthe in pryde   7580
Before the towne to saye his stede;
The lady of hym hade grette drede,
And lowde on hyr he cryede.

After this Ipomadon
Calde his cosyne Egyon;   7585
'Goo loke be-lyve,' he sayde,
f. 315ʳ   'Hyde the wyth the grene woode tre,
Lyolyne till thou may see,
Off what wysse he is arayde,
And whethur he be blake or white;   7590
Come agayne and tell me [tyte]!'
Thereon his lyff he layde.
Egyone forthe he went
To do his maysteris comaundement,
Then were he well payde.   7595

He hyde hym wyth the grene holyne,
And att the laste he see Lyolyne
Rydyng vp and downe
Before the citte boldly,
As all had byn his owne, forthy—   7600
Castell, towre and towne.

7568 bestode] be stedde   7589 is] *Written above line, with caret*   7591 tyte]
Ka.; *MS* lyght

The lady in a corner stode
And wept as faste as she were wood,
That fayre was of facyone.
Hit was grette dulle, sekyrlye,   7605
To here that hedovs noyse and crye
Off burgays and barone.

Wedovs wept þat men myght rewe,
Wyffys and maydons chavngyd þer hewe,
Laydes there coloure caste,   7610
And sayd, 'Yf we shuld sodaynly here
Yelde vs to younde fendys fere,
Foreuer oure Ioye is paste!'
They cursyd Lyolyne euerychone.
Grette sorow had Egyone,   7615
He hard men wepe so faste.
To his mayster hyed hee,
And as sone as he hym see,   f. 315ᵛ
Egyrly he hym axte.

'What tydyngys?' quod Ipomadon;   7620
'Full febull syr,' quod Egyon,
Be myghttifull God he swore,
'Syr Lyolyne rides vp and downe
Boldely before the towne,
As all his owne were.   7625
It is grette dull to here þat denne,
The hedovs noyse they make wythinne,
So ar they syghand sore.
The lady is in so grett dystresse,
That nere to yeld her in poynt she [e]s—   7630
God forbede it were!'

'Egyon, saw thou Lyolyne?'
'Ye syr, be the trowthe myne,
Well harnessyd in the feld.'
'How is he arayd?' 'All in blake.'   7635
'The same will I myselff take;
Pendavnte, spere and sheld.'

7623 Syr] *Written with large red capital*   7630 es] *K*.; *MS* was   7637 spere
and sheld] *K*.; *MS* sheld and spere

Ipomadon sayd, 'I worke wrange;
Here may I dwell no lange,
My leman may hur yelde!'   7640
In blake he arayde hym there;
'Glade shall I be neuer more
Yf he hur to wyff we[l]de!'

A blake spere takythe Ipomadon,
A blake stede he leppus vpon,   7645
To long he thynkys he byd[e];
He comaundyd all his men, forthy,
Shuld be hym nere prevely,
What happe so hym betyd[e].

f. 316ʳ   As he bade, his men dyde,   7650
In the woode they them hydde;
Hymselff frome them [dyd] ryde.
When they saw this knyght come,
Ioyefull they were all and sum;
All men prayed God hym spede.   7655

Wyste non what he was, sertayne,
Allone but the maydon Imay[n]e;
She knew hym by his stede
That he hadde wone of Lyonder,
But she wold not tell the Fere.   7660
The dwarff she gan forbede
What he was he shuld not tell;
The dwarff sayd, 'Nay, damysell!'
Off hur he hade suche drede,
And wyste not, wythoute dowte,   7665
To tell his name covde he novght,
The sothe to say in dede.

'Imayne,' sayd the lady bright,
'Syster, younder is a semely knyght,
Right bygge of blode and bone;   7670
This is the same, I trowe,

7643 welde] K.; MS wedde   7646 byde] K.; MS bydys   7649 betyde] K.;
MS betydys   7652 dyd ryde] K.; MS rydys   7657 Imayne] Imaye
7664 he] *Preceded by crossed-out* s

That yesterday folowyd you,
But no fole semys hym o[ne]!'
'Nay, madame, it is not hee,
For he, be God and my lewte,   7675
Suche armore hadde he none.'
Imayne was to blame therfore,
She made hyr lady morne the more
And terys to wepe goode woone.

Imayne parcevyd euery deyll   7680 f. 316ᵛ
That it was he, she wyst it wele,
Yet tolde she not the Fere.
He made hym aray all in blake
That she no hedde to hym shuld take
For chavngyng off no chere . . .   7685
That he wold kepe and say younde knyght
Be his owne will he comythe to fyght,
Fro harmes to kepe the Fere.

Thow he sufferd neuer so muche pyne,
He was lothe his love to tyne,   7690
And therefore dyd he soo.
He was armyd in blake harnes
As Lyolyne hymselff was,
Evyn fro tope to tow,
In feld togedur when they strafe   7695
That she shuld no knowlege haue
Whedyr of them were [h]ere foo.
Hit wold ouer mekill sorowe haue brede
And she sawe hym strayte stade;
He wyst she wold be woo.   7700

Full well Imayne knew þat dere,
But ȝet she wold not tell the Fere,
She was to blame the more.
Lyolyne hovyd as still as stone;
To hym rydes Ipomadon,   7705
As breme as any bore.

7673 one] K.; MS thoo   7681 he] Preceded by crossed-out s   7689 pyne]
K.; MS payne   7690 tyne] K.; MS tayne   7697 here] K.; MS þere

Lyolyne sayd, 'Thou, ser knyght,
Art thou come wyth me to fyghte?'
'Ya!' 'That shall thou sorow full sore:

f. 317ʳ   As I be kepte frome carys colde,   7710
Euer more I will the holde
The more fole [þer]fore!'

'What devill of hell reke I ?' quod he,
'The more fole tho[u] holdest me,
The sorer shalt thou sowe!'   7715
'Why, of my kynrede art þou novght?'
'No, be God that all hathe wrought,
Now sayste thou sothe I trowe!
I ame of hight and þou arte lowe!'
Lyolyne answerd to that sawe,   7720
'Why—off what kynne art thou?'
'My fadyr was a kyng, I saye.'
'Arte thou a bastarde?' 'I sey the nay,
But what were that for you?'

'For I wold witte all bedene!'   7725
'In faythe my moder was a quene,
In spousehode borne was I.'
'Ser, where had þou þat stede [I] see?'
'What devill off hell is þat for the?
How thynkys the thereby?'   7730
'He was my brothers, I dare lay.'
'In faythe, sothe is þat thou saye.'
Than hade he grette envye;
'Ouercome ye hym?' 'Sertys, ye,
But wyth o stroke I saw no moo,   7735
And kepe thyself forthy!'

'Why, what thynkys thou to do?'
Ipomadon sayd, 'Sertys, loo,
Nowe sone, ser, witte mowe ye,

f. 317ᵛ   For as the grette God me save,   7740
Hym that þou on settis, I thynke to haue!'
'Doway, for thy lewte!

7712 þerfore] K.; MS be fore   7714 thou] K.; MS tho   7728 I] K.; MS in

Thynkys thou to haue my nobull stede?'
'Ye, so God of hevyne me spede!'
'Thow dottyst, I trowe!' quod hee;   7745
'Ouer mekill ado shuld be thynne
Or thou gettys this stede of myne;
In fayth, that will not be!

'But one thyng shall I tell the, frend;
Home agayne I rede the wende   7750
Wyth that thou wonne haste,
For be God and me lewte,
To sle the it were grette pitte—
Thow art so fayre of face.
That thou hast wrought agayne skill,   7755
Slayne my brothere and done so ille,
Yet shall I graunte the grace.
Wette thou well that þe Fere
Hathe me louyd many a yere;
For me vnglad she goos.   7760

'Full ofte sythes she hath sent me till,
That I shuld come and have my will!'
'In faythe, that beleve I novght;
She hade wel leuer, as I the tell,
Se the at the devill of hell!'   7765
'A, man, what is thy thoughte?
I myghte haue hade her long or nowe,
But well I wyll she hold her [v]owe,
Therefore I hedyre soughte,
To loke yf any man durste so bold be   7770 f. 318ʳ
That wold come and fyght wyth mee,
In erthe that euer was wrovghte.

'Therefor a fole hold I the, ser;
Yff thou be come to fyght for hyr,
Thou art in poynte to rave!'   7775
Ipomadon sayd, 'Wele I fynde
That many wordys wastys wynde;
I-nowȝe of them I have!

7768 vowe] K.; MS nowe

Ye have hov[an]d youndere, I see,
Well too c knyghtys or thre,   7780
And ser, so God me save,
I am here al alonne:
What worship is to al yonne
To ber me to my grave?

'They will the helpe yf þou haue nede,   7785
And ser, soo God of heyuen me spede,
That is no curtessye,
For ofte ys sayd be wyse of warre,
"Tow ageynst one man here,
Therein lyethe no chevalrye!"'   7790
'Hangyd be I on a tree
Yff any man shall fyght wyth [þ]e
Of all my men but I!'
Wythoute any more abode,
To his men be-lyve he roode   7795
And comaundyd them forthy,

Ageyne to the wood they fare;
'Vpon lyffe and lyme ye hold you there,
Whedyr I fare well or ille!'
His knyghttis dyd as he h[e]m badde,   7800
f. 318ᵛ   To come ageyne grette haste he hadde.
Ipomadon spekys h[e] tille;
'I redde the ryde forth to the towne!'
'I was neuer at thy byddyng bowne,
Ne hope not yet I will!   7805
I say, ser, wythouten fayle,
Thow gettys not hyr wythouten battayle;
Eyrste shall thou fight thy fylle!'

Then euery knyght toke þer ranke,
The[y] maydon no semblent to blen[k]e,   7810
There sperys in fewter they caste;
There stedys so strak[e] them on the [groun]de,

7779 hovand] hovyd   7792 þe] K.; MS me   7799 fare] *Preceded by deleted*
falle   7800 hem] K.; MS hym   7802 he] K.; MS hym   7810 They]
K.; MS The   blenke] K.; MS blente   7812 strake] K.; MS strakys   grounde] K.;
MS borde

There speris in sheldys rebownde
And braste there they were feste.
Yff they were neuer so sekyr of mayle,   7815
Hedys made them breke and fayle
As wyttnes her be weste;
Thorowe all there harnes be þere syde,
Euyne bothe her sperys dyd glyde
And brake that sure was fest.   7820

Thowȝe they were neuer so strounge þat stounde,
Bothe they tombled on the grounde,
But nothere woondyd were.
This knyghtys, that hardy were of herte,
Agayne vp on there stedys they sterte,   7825
As bryme as any bore.
Wyth speris efte sonys they met togeddur,
There strokys made there stedys to stakyre,
So were they sad and sore.
There speris all to pecys breste,   7830
They swang togeddyrs at the laste . . .

So manly they togedyr fyghte,
That battayle to deskrye no man myȝte,   f. 319ʳ
The st[r]okys that were them betwene.
The sparkels frome the helmes flewe   7835
As f[y]r that lemys in lowe;
They share the gresse on the gr[en]e.
The folke sayd that beheld theym
A grette[r] fight betwayne men
Before was neuer seene;   7840
Might no man vnder the heyvyn lyght
Know whiche shuld the better [fyght],
So bygge men bothe they bene.

Lyolyne was a nobull man,
He strykis to Ipomadon   7845

7815 so] *Followed by crosssed-out* mekyll   7834 strokys] K.; MS stokys
7836 fyr] fer K.; MS for   7837 grene] K.; MS grounde   7839 gretter] K.;
MS grette   7842 fyght] K.; MS bee

That on his helmet hit lyght;
Nerehand he made hym fall.
His stede stakyrd there wythall;
Was he neuer so wyghte,
He was so stonyed in þat stounde,   7850
On knes he knelyd on the grounde.
Imayne cryed lowde on highte,
And sayd wyth many a sighand sore,
'Thou that has made bothe lesse and more,
Kepe and save younde knyghte!'   7855

The Fere Imayne can axe,
'Why, wot ye syster what he was?'
'I say you nay, madame;
I wott neuer what he is,
But younde strokys of dystresse   7860
Makys my herte full tame.'
Imayne wyste well it was hee,
That wold she not tell the fre,
The more she was to blame;
To love [hym] hath hyrse[l]ff thought,   7865
That, in trought, it avayles her nouȝte,
As God me kepe frome shame.

Full wele hard Ipomadone
How they dyd make þis mekill mone,
And to hym drewe hertte;   7870
Be that his stede wyth myght and mayne
Haue gotton his myghte right wele agayne,
Vpon his fete he sterte.
Grevessly in agayne he gett
And in that stowre so he hym [hit]   7875
Wyth sterne strokys and smarte,
All that lokyd on þought grette skathe;
Thorow helme and browe bothe
The blod oute braste he garte.

f. 319ᵛ

7863 fre] *K.; MS* fere   7864 blame] blamee   7865 hym] *K.; MS om.*
hyrselff] hyr seff   7875 hit] *K.* hitt; *MS* storyde

Ipomadon was a nobull knyght   7880
And mekyll he cowde of fyght,
He stroke the[n] Lyolyne
A quarter of his helme away;
Downe by his shulders, sothe to sey,
The nakyd swerd youde inne,   7885
But wold to God it had gone nere—
I trowe hit shuld a hit hym there!
The blo[w] he cowde not fyne
Tille hit had clovyn his sadull in two,
And of his noble stede also   7890
In sonder smote the chyne.

The[n] fell Lyolyne to the grounde;
He stert vp lyghttly in that stounde
And sawe his owne blode.
A swerd in hand hathe he tane,   7895
And rennethe toward Ipomadon
As he were nerehand wood;   f. 320ʳ
Ipomadon saw hym so fare,
And wyth his hors he hym downe bare,
Though he were neuer so wood.   7900
Vp he starte bothe pale and wanne,
To Ipomadon his stede thane
Eygurly he youde.

Betwene two rybbis he smote his stede,
The swerd into his body yede   7905
Evyn to his hertte;
There wythal to grounde he youde,
Ipomadon saw his stedis blode,
Oute of his sadull he sterte.
He swore, 'Be God and be Sent Myghell,   7910
My stede shall be venged well
And God will gyf me quarte!'
So strong betwene them was the stowre,
Hit was grette wondyr they my3t indewre,
Bothe þer strokys were so smarte.   7915

7882 then] the   7888 blow] blod   fyne] K.; MS fynde   7892 Then] the

The fyght betwene them was so long,
A while to rest bothe they gan[g]
And on there swerdys the[y] [l]enys.
Lyolyne crabbyd spekys nowe,
'Hye, devyll, what fole art thou 7920
That this thy dedys demenyste?
As fole thou comyst and fole þou goste,
As a fole all thy matters makyste,
As a fole thou conteynes;
Wyth me thou may not deyle, forthy! 7925
Where is so bold a body as I
In all the world þat raynes?

'So worthy a knyght as I am one,
I say to the that þere ys none
Wonnand in all this world, 7930
Off body grette, of lymmes lyghte,
That may thyselff say, ser knyght.
Thow knowest how I haue fard
Wyth many a knyght in dyueres lond,
A Mˡ haue I hewen wyth my hand 7935
That neuer worde after harde—
There is none of [them] that maye!
And sone so will thyselff saye
Fro thow my lawys haue harde.

'And thou art littill man above, 7940
And vnderstondythe no la[dyes] [love],
As I be sauyd frome payne.
In warre, thou art warre and wyse
And of bewte mekyll of price;
Thou aught to be full fayne 7945
To yeld the while thou may leve!
All thy gylte I shall forgeve
And be thy frend agayne,
And to the Ynde, ser, come wyth me;
Thre good castels I shall geve the, 7950
And to thy wyff Imayne.'

7917 gang] K.; MS gan   7918 they lenys] K.; MS the kenys   7937 them]
K.; MS om.   7939 Fro] Corr. from for   7941 ladyes love] Kp.; MS lawe

The other sayd, 'So mot I thryve,
I will non of thy gyf[t] to wyfe;
Thy castells I defye!
I sent the neuer for me to wowe—   7955
I cowde gette me wyff i-nowe
And thow were hangyd hye!
Yff thow in wronge be neuer so wyght,
God is euer more wyth the right,
I say the securlye.   7960
Thorowe helpe of hym þat made the mone,
That thow to younde lady [has] done,
Full dere thou shalt hit bye!   f. 321ʳ

'But syr, wythoutyn othe to swere,
Me thynkys in my herte ye are   7965
Right ille avysud off this,
That this dystrowys þis fayre contre,
And ye thynke to wyffe þat louys not the,
Ne neuer more will, i-wis!
Be my faythe, she louythe þe nought,   7970
She made no fors what werke she wrought,
Thy mowthe or she wold kys;
Yff thou were all the devill bek[e]nde,
Agayne the I shall hyr defende,
As I haue Ioye and blis!'   7975

Lyolyne then for angur shakys,
His swerd in hande he takys
And coveryd hym wyth his sheld;
Full wrothe was thanne Ipomadon,
His geyre to hym has he tane,   7980
Right well he cowde hit weld.
So hard they hewe on helmus bright,
The fyre flew oute as candyll lyght;
Folke houyd and behelde.
There wold noþere a foote frome thens,   7985
So harde asawte and grette defens
Was fowndyn in that feld.

7953 gyft] _K._ gyfft; _MS_ gyff   7962 has] _K._; _MS om._   7973 bekende] _K._;
_MS_ be kynde

The[y] crasse mayles thrugh þer caste,
Blode oute of there browes braste,
So harde on helmus they hewe[d];   7990
They shevyrd shaftys and sondurde shyldys,
The helmus that they on hedde weldythe
As flowres in feld they strowed.
So freshely they faught at þat tyde,
The blod ranne downe on euery syde;   7995
Then sayde bothe leryd and lewede,

f. 321ᵛ

There was neuer a better battayle sene.
To hymselff sayd Lyolyne,
'This is a skornyng shrewe[d]!'

A mastry he thought to make;   8000
Ipomadon on helme he strake
Away a quarter clene;
So well he did hym in that werke,
Thorow all his harnes by his s[erk]e
The stroke went downe bedene.   8005
On the arme he stroke hym to the bone,
But harme wythinne hit dyd hym none;
Godys forbode that it hade ben!
As God gaff hym grace that tyde,
The swerd in his hand turnethe [aside],   8010
Or els he had be slayne, I wene.

Ipomadone was angred sore,
He was as wode as any bore
When he had sene his blode.
On the ring can he loke   8015
That his moder hym toke,
To dede when she youde.
He towchyd the wounde wyth the ston;
Off bledyng was he stavnchyd sone,
So was the vertu good.   8020
The knyght was wonder glad forthy;
Lyolyne spekys full skornefullye,
'How lykys you your m[o]de?

7988 They] *K.*; *MS* The   7990 hewed] *K.*; *MS* hewe   7999 shrewed] *K.*;
MS shrewe   8004 serke] *K.*; *MS* shyrte   8010 aside] *K.* be syde; *MS om.*
8012 angred] *Followed by* was   8023 mode] *K.*; *MS* mede

'Ye ar wyttly wondyd: I trowe
That ye come her sore rewis yowe!   8025
Will ye haue any more?
Lokys on your arme and rede þat letter;
I trowe full well ye hade better
Haue byn in peas langere!
Thus grevos worde now shall þou graunt   8030
And to me yeld the creante,   f. 322ʳ
Thowe thow were wode as bore.
But yet in peas and thou wilt be,
And yeld the, I will rewe on the;
To sle the synne it were.   8035

'Thow haste noþer myght ne mayne
To fyght no more me ageyne,
Thyselff now well may wotte.'
Ipomadon sayd, 'In fayth, ser knyght,
For non that I se here in fight   8040
I will not yeld me yett!
As grette God of heyven me save,
For any hurte yet that I haue,
Shall stroke for stroke be hit;
Or I shall yeld me this to the,   8045
Slayne in the feld fyrste shall I be
And onys for aye be quyte!'

Ipomadon grette wondur hadde
That he shuld be so streyttly bestadde
Wyth o man euery dell,   8050
So hard asayd as he hathe byn,
That o man shuld do hym þat tene
Wyth a swerd off stele.
He bethoughte hym on the Fere,
How he had louyde hyr many a yere;   8055
He sayd, 'So haue I sele,
I slepe not or it youlden bee!'
His swerd in hand grypus hee,
And thynkythe to venge hym well.

8028 hade better] *K.*; *MS* hade byn better

Thowe he were sore woundyd, I wene   8060
That tyme hit was forgotton clene;
As a bere thane was he bowne.
His strokys was so sadde and many,

The tother wyst not when he myght gyf any,
So thyke came they downe.   8065
Lyolyne begynethe to chasse
Vp and downe in the place,
That sawe they in the towne;
But when they had slayne the stedys bo,
Wyst no man whiche was oþeres foo   8070
That made them all knele downe.

But neuer the lesse, Lyolyne ys
A man off grett worthynes,
And manly faught ageyne.
Bothe there strokys were so good,   8075
The erthe quakyd as they stode,
The sothe is not to layne.
Att the last Ipomadon wex kene,
He strykys to Ser Lyolyne
A stroke of muche mayne,   8080
His helme he clave in two;
Thrugh hate and heryne pan also
He slave hym to the brayne.

'Long, ser, haue ye skornyd me;
The worste I trowe your owne bee,   8085
For you be grettly woundyde!
A monke ye may be when ye will,
For ye be shavynne wile þertill,
And right wele be ye crownyde;
Goo take youre abbyte on be-tyme   8090
And helpe to syng bothe oure and pryme,
For ye be shavyne rownde!
But, be God and my lewte,
In erthe ther is no leche so sle
I hope maye make you sownde.'   8095

8069 bo] *K.*; *MS* bothe   8086 be] *Written above line, with caret*

'No, in faythe,' quod Lyolyne,
'All the moste greffe is myne,   f. 323^r
My owne witte I wyte;
Therefore my swerd I yeld to thee,
The Fere, and all this fayre contre,   8100
Here I make me quyte.
[You] now right wele may she hold
Wyth worshipe, and ye wowe her wold,
She myght haue grett delyte
To loue you wyth all hur myght;   8105
In erthe there is non suche a knyght.'
Wyth that he sonyd astyte.

When he had getton myght and mayn,
Whittly he gettys hym vp agayne
And syghyng hym besought,   8110
On lyve he wold lette hym goo,
And wyth hym haue his knyghttys also
That he hadde thedyr brought:
'And on this swerd I shall the swere
Neuer after this land to dere,   8115
Be hym that all hathe wrought.'
Ipomadon sayd, 'Ser, I assent,
And leve me no thyng but thy tent—
Off thyne, more kepe I noughte.'

Thereoff was Lyolyne fayne,   8120
To his men he went agayne
And toke shippus that tyde.
A myle wythin the grekys see
Swythely thane sweltys hee,
The sothe is not to hyde.   8125
On fervm hovyd Thalamewe;
Be tokyns well he hym knewe,
On foote he saw hym byde.
A good stede he brought hym tille,
Vp he lepe wyth egur wille,   8130 f. 323^v
To the tent gan he ryde.

Thalamewe had byn oftyn þat day
Glad and sorowe bothe, in faye,
For syghttys that he had sene,
For they wyste neuer whiche better was;   8135
Oute off the citte durste no man passe
For the knyght Ser Lyolyne.
Into the tent when they sawe hym ryde,
And no man trubled hym that tyde,
There herttys brest nere for tene.   8140
A blake baner forthe toke he there,
And there went both lesse and more
It had ther enemye been.

He wold no lengur byde,
To wallys gan he ryde   8145
And cryed lowde on hight;
'Haue done and dight you, damysell—
Now maye ye se yourselff full well
That Lyolyne ys wyght!
Wete ye well I am hee;   8150
Tomorowe into Yndde ye shall wyth me,
For I haue slayne youre knyght!'
All that wythin the citte were
Wrang there handys and sighed sore,
Bothe lordys and ladyes brighte.   8155

Ipomadon thynkys aye
Prevely to wynd his waye,
That no man shuld hym knowe,
Fore euer more in his hert he thought,
'Till her vowe [c]o[r]de I novght,   8160
Therefore I will wythdrawe.'
f. 324ʳ   Lordys hade care and many a knyght,
In sownyng fell that layde bright,
So stode they in mekyll awe
Off hym that made wythoute the crye;   8165
To God she playns hyr petteweslye
Wyth many a syghyng sawe;

8141 A] *Written in margin*   8160 vowe] v *corr. from* n   corde] *K*.; *MS* woyde
8164 in] *Written above line, with caret*   awe] awee

'Wyth Lyolyne yf I gange,
And loos that I haue louyd so longe,
That wold me lyke full ille;   8170
Then myghte I sighe and savely saye
That I haue louyd many a day,
Were I in poynt to spyll!'
To hir burges sayd she,
'Syr, that shall I neuer doo,   8175
Haue here my trowth þertill!
I se it may no better bee;
Make vs redy to the see,
Lett God do what he will!'

Barons and burges were full woo,   8180
Wyffys, weddows and maydons also
Wept as they were woo[de];
As fast the lady drewe hir heyre,
For here was þer moste care;
Wyth Imayne hard it stode.   8185
Euery man made them redy fast,
And sythen oute of the posturne paste
And to there shippus youde.
The lady sayd wyth sighyng sore,
'Have goodday, Calabere, for euer more!'   8190
She flettys forthe in the flode.

Ipomadon, wythoute any abode,
Agayne to the tente he rode
And off his [h]ors he lyght,   f. 324ᵛ
Caste of his harnes euery deyle,   8195
Went hymselff and coled hym well
And his woundys dyght.
When he had eyton and slept i-nowe,
His harnes agayne to hym he drewe,
Bothe shyld and armowre bright.   8200
Ipomadon leve we thus,
And turne agayne to Cabanus
That was so good a knyght.

8182 woode] K.; MS woo   8188 shippus] Followed by deleted past
8194 hors] K.; MS bors

The tyme Imayne in Cesille was
At Melengere helpe to aske,   8205
Thow sum men better were,
Cabanus, the sothe to saye,
Was an-huntyng all þat day,
And [wist] not of that fare
Tille at evyn that he come home.   8210
Knyghttys told hym when he come
How Imayn had byn thare
After helpe att Melyngere,
To fight for that lady clere
That was of blis full bare.   8215

They told hym all how Imayne sayde
That a sege to here was layde
Vppon a grette araye,
And how Imayne prayed for a knyght
To fyght wyth that cursyd wyght   8220
That wastythe that lady awaye;
'Off all oure knyghttys were there none
Thereto a worde answerde non,
Be God that moste best maye,
But a fole that than come inne   8225
And stonyd all men wyth his dene.
Before vs can he saye

f. 325ʳ   'That he hade gevyn vs all a fall,
Ca[n]an[e]us there wyth all,
And them there levyd on the playne,   8230
Segamus and Manestas,
And trewly ser, that fole is this
Folowyd forthe Imayne.
Hadde ye se how he was arayde,
Ye wold haue byn the better payd,   8235
That is not to layne!'
The knyght stode in a stody still;
He sayd, 'I darre lay my lyff þertill,
It was the Drew-le-rayne!'

8205 aske] *Corr. from* as   8209 wist] *K.; MS om.*   8229 Cananeus] *Kp.;*
MS Cabanus

Cabanus wyth sory chere   8240
He knelys downe to Mellengere
Wyth wrythyng and wyth woo;
'[Th]y nesse off Calabyre, that fre,
Glade ne blythe shall I neuer be
And she be turned soo;   8245
To reskewe hyr I wold be glade.'
Thereoff the kyng grette Ioye hade
And grauntyd hym leve to goo.
That tyme wythinne Cessyle lande
Was sone sembled to his hand   8250
v.c. knyghttys and moo.

Cabanus, the sothe to saye,
Into Calabyr toke the waye,
No lenger bydis he there.
Ryally this knyght roode   8255
Wyth shaftys and wyth shyldys brode,
And bre[n]y burnysshed bare.
This they come be the see;
They sawyn shippus grett plente
And women wepte full sore;   8260
In hertte they hade grette sorowe to s[o]me,   f. 325ᵛ
When they sawe so many come,
All they had muche care.

Downe in sownyng fell the Fere;
Well wend that lady clere   8265
It had byn Lyolyne
That hade hur waytyd on the waye
Here men to sloo, the sothe to saye,
And to [f]ett hyrselff thene.
'Dere God, as thou arte lorde off peas,   8270
Shall neuer this grette sorowe seas
That hathe so long byne myne?
I wende haue lefte all care behynde;
Ille I fle, and worse I fynde!
My lyff now mvste me tyne.   8275

8243 Thy] K.; MS My   8257 breny] K.; MS brevy   8261 some] K.; MS
seme   8269 fett] sett

'I wende haue flede dede fro,
Dethe me folowythe where I goo;
A, lord, what care I fele!
Wyth me take, wyth sempull chere:
Ayens you good God I made no dere;   8280
In you lyethe eueri dell,
Ye nede but byde and it woll bee . . .
My cursyd pryde will me forfare
I am worthy mekyll more,
As I haue happe or sell!'   8285

Cabanus on the banke abode
And harde the mornyng þat they made;
He sayde, 'So mote ye spede,
What are ye, thes schepys wythinne,
That makythe this grette noyse and denne?   8290
It semys ye be in drede.'
The teyres hade made þer chekys wete,

f. 326ʳ   The lady stode vppon her fete
And wepte as she wolde wede;
'I am a sympull woman, syr,   8295
That yesterday owght Calaber:
Today I am in drede,

'For all the lond that there was myne
Is now in hand of Lyolyne,
A, well-a-way the while!'   8300
Cabanus sight and sayd, 'Alas!'
When he wyst what the lady was,
Hym lyst but littill to smylle;
'Dere cosyne of blode,' quod hee,
'Come to land and speke wyth me,   8305
Drede you for no gile!
I am your cosyne Cabanus
That for socoure comythe thus
Oute of the lande of Cesille.'

8279 me] *Followed by* to   wyth] *Followed by* on wyth   8281 eueri dell] *K*.; *MS*
euer Idell   8292 wete] *Preceded by deleted* blake   8300 A] As

Then was the lady fayne i-nowgh,   8310
There bottis to the lande they drowe,
Wyth mekill mone they mette.
Cabanus began to axe;
When she had told hym how it was,
Bothe there chekys was wete.   8315
'Syr, all Calaber, my lande,
Now Lyolyne hathe in his hande,
For no man wille he lette
Where hym lyst to ryde or goo,
A[nd] I am, frend, yflemyd therefro;   8320
Neuer foote there I gette!

'Wythe Imayne heder come a knyght
That for me vndertoke the righte,
As gryme as any bore,   f. 326ᵛ
But whens he was, wot we not;   8325
There was neuer man more worthely wrought
Boore of woman eere.
In battayle was he styf and stronge,
Dweryng wonder well and longe
Wyth sade strokis and sore.   8330
All-way dyd he well i-novgh,
But Lyolyne at the last hym slovgh;
That kyndelyd all my care.'

Cabanus sayd, 'So [b]yd I yole,
I haue herd speke of a fole,   8335
Be God and be my lewte,
That frome vs folowyd Imayne.'
'Syr, as I be sauyd fro payne,
That very same was hee.'
Cabanus sayde, 'Be Godys myght,   8340
In all this world I know no knyght
Vnder heyvyn so hye
That cowthe couer hym so, sertayne,
But yf it were the Drew-le-rayne!'
'In fayth syr, well may be.   8345

8315 was wete] K.; MS wete was   8320 And] K.; MS Am   frend, yflemyd] K.;
MS frendy flemyd   8334 byd] K.; MS kyd

'That thynke I now, be my lewte,
And sertenly, yff it were hee,
Me thynke grette harme it were,
For more worthely than he wrought
Dyd neuer no knyght, as me [th]ought,   8350
Borne of any woman eyre!'
Cabanus sayd, 'Lady dere,
Yourselff shall abyde here,
No forther shall ye fare;
Wheder it turne to good or ille,   8355
In faythe, to the feld go I will

f. 327^r   To here tydyngis thare.

'My folke shall wyth you byde,
To Lyolyne myselff will ryde,
To witt what right he hathe   8360
Here to werke so muche woo!'
Off v.c. knyghtys and moo,
But ten he wyth hym t[as].
Oute of the thyke woode gan he pas;
Into the feld where the battayle was   8365
He come wythin shorte space.
Be thane was Ipomadon
A well good stede lepte vppon,
Awaywarde faste he goothe.

He rode downe thurgh a depe valey   8370
For non shuld know hym, soth to saye,
But yett sa[w] Cabanus.
Till his ten knyght sayd he syne,
'Sorys, younder lyethe Lyolyne,
I wott well it is thus;   8375
Awayward faste hyed hee,
And yf he shall ouertaken be,
Spede vs faste we [b]vs!'
Wyth sporys they stroke there stedis aright,
Cabanus cryed, 'Howe, syr knyght,   8380
Abyde and speke withe [us]!

8350 thought] *K.*; *MS* sought   8363 tas] *K.*; *MS* toke   8372 saw] sayd
8378 bvs] *K.*; *MS* mvste   8381 us] *K.*; *MS* me

'Where were ye borne and in what contre?'
The tother sayd, 'What is that for the?'
He made as he was tene:
'Wett thou well, I am Lyolyne! 8385
I maye ryde here—the londe is myne,
The Fere, and all bedene;
I wanne her wyth my hand right nowe. f. 327ᵛ
But tell me lighttly, what art thou
That spekis this wordys kene, 8390
And of my way dystrobelyst me this?'
'In fayth, my name is Cabanus,
And many a day hathe bene!'

'Arte thou Cabanus?' 'I say the yee.'
'Syr, forthe thy way I rede the goo, 8395
For drede off mornyng more.'
'Nay, be God that made the mone,
Sore shalt thou by that þou hast done
Wyth sade strokys and sore!'
Ipomadon wiste full wele 8400
That Cabanus was bolde vnder stele,
And he was wonder sore;
'And he were as lyght in lythe and lyme,
Or that I were be-knowen wyth hym,
To fight well leuer me were.' 8405

Cabanus sayd, 'Syr, we shall preve here
That thou hade neuer right to the Fere,
Nother be nyght nor day!'
Ipomadon saw that nedys hym mvste;
He made hym redy to Iuste 8410
Wythe all the myght þat he may.
Eythere knyght on othere foyned
Wythe sperys that were sharpe grovnde,
The sertayne sothe to saye.
There shaftes sheverd heyvn wyth that, 8415
But stone stille in there sadyll they satte,
So bygge men were they.

8404 were] *Preceded by deleted* was

Ipomadon was wovndyd sore,
Yett thowȝe he neuer so wery were,
   No thynge that of hym sterde,   8420
In erthe there myght non better be.
Then he hade wyth hym knyghtis thre,
Hymselff was the fovrthe;
Cabanus hade knyghtis x,
The elewenthe was hymself thanne,   8425
And euery man drew his swerd.
Ipomadons knyghttys, wythoute les,
Echone his felowe ches
And bare them to the erthe.

To them presud other moo,   8430
And of Ipomadons knyghttis thoo,
Two was smerttly slayne.
Thanne was hymselff nere-hande woode;
Fowre of Cabanus knyghttis goode
He claffe into the brayne.   8435
The fy[f]te into the forhedde stroke he so,
That to the grounde he made hym goo,
And sithe he ros agayne;
A swerd in hand he grypus than,
And to Ipomadons stede he ranne   8440
Bothe wyth myght and mayne.

He smot his stede that was so wyght,
Ipomadon on his foote he lyght,
Fighttyng wonder faste.
Thow he neuer so wery were,   8445
His strokis were so sade and sore
That blode through mayle itt brast,
That in the stowre before hade ben
So harde bestadde wyth Lyolyne;
Wonder it was that he myght last.   8450
   Ipomadon, wyth hardy herte,
Ouer a dyke fro them he sterte;
To rest hym was his caste.

8421 erthe] r *corr. from* e   8436 fyfte] *K*.; *MS* fyrste

He lenyd his bake till an oke
And gaff many a sory stroke   8455
That all had of hym dowght;
His thre knyghttis were thane slayne;
All they presyd to Ipomadon,
They weryd hym abowte;
And he had not be woundyd so sore   8460
He had them skomfete thore,
All that riall rowte . . .

Helme and shyld he hewis in sounder
And othere harnes that was þer vnder
That right sekyr was [a]re;   8465
Was there neuer knyght sethe this world began,
I trowe, that more worshipe wanne,
Werry yff that he were.
At the laste one away smote
The halfe of his glove of plate   8470
And made his hande all bare;
A ringe on his fyngur shone,
Cabanus lokyd on the stone,
He syghyd wonder sore.

When Cabanus the ring sawe   8475
Hym thought he shuld it knowe,
A littill he drew abake;
He comaundyd his men forthy
They shuld them wythdraw a party
And to the knyght he spake;   8480
He sayd, 'Syr, for thy lewte,
Abyde a while and speke wyth me,
For thow arte not to lake,   f. 329ʳ
As thou be sauyd be heyven kyng,
On what wyse come thou to þat ring?   8485
But to no greffe ye it take.'

When he hard hym speke of the ring,
Ipomadon in a stodeynge

8465 are] *K.*; *MS* before   8470 of his] *K.*; *MS* of the his   8472 ringe] *K.*;
MS ringe of   8473 Cabanus] *Followed by* o

A long while he stode.
Wordis in his hert ranne   8490
That his moder had spokyn before þanne,
To dethe when she youde:
What man dothe this ring know,
He shuld be his brother trowe;
That grettly menchyde his mode.   8495
Cabanus grette hast hadde,
To aske hym more he was glad;
He sayd, 'Syr, for the love of God,

'I aske the not for no reprove,
But for her sake that ye best love,   8500
What so euere she bee,
As where ye had that ring, and howe:
I haue knowen hit or nowe
Be aught that I gan see.'
Ipomadon hard hym all in haste   8505
Speke of that thyng þat he covytte moste
And he was lothe to lye;
The tother sayd [he], 'Be this day,
Synne I shall the sothe saye,
My moder she gaff hit mee.'   8510

'Who was your moder, for your lewte?'
'The quene of Poyl, in faythe!' quod hee,
'I make hit no counsayle.'
'And sayd she you ought, so God you save?'
f. 329ᵛ   'Ye, that I shuld a brother haue;   8515
I trowe that tale be [lele].'
'But sir, be the trought of thyne,
Saye me, arte thou aught Lyolyne?'
'Nay, so haue I happe or selle,
I kepe no lengyr to layne wyth you;   8520
I feld and skoumfett hym right nowe
That wyth hym was moche to dell.'

8497 glad] d *corr. from* ?   8508 he] *K.*; *MS om.*   8516 lele] *K.*; *MS* a lye
8518 Saye] a *written above line*

'Dere syr,' quod Cabanus,
'Tell me muche more ye bus:
In what land was ye borne?   8525
Whens ye come, and whedyr ye shall?
I praye you good syr, tell me all;
Where haue ye dwellyd beforne?'
'Syr, synne all þou the sothe will axe,
The kyngis sone of Poylle I was   8530
That had grett welthe of corne;
Syn come I heder, so haue I sell,
To serve younde worthy damysell,
And there had I many a skorne.

'When me[n] to dede of armus drewe,   8535
I went to the grene wood bovgh,
A huntere as I were.
Lordis and ladyes, lesse and more,
To skorne lowde loughe they me þerfore,
My Ioye was mekill the more.   8540
Off a vowe I hard hyr speke,
That wold I nought she shuld it breke;
That made me fro her fare.
Synne I dwellyd wyth your eyme, þe kyng,
And seruyd the quene, my lady younge,   8545
That tyme I sawe you there.

'Sethe Iust Y here dayes thre,
In white, in rede, in blacke, parde;   f. 330ʳ
I trowe this knowe ye well!
The thryd nyght I went my waye,   8550
And that I wane, the sothe to saye,
I sent you euery deall,
Yf ye be aught avysyd of this?'
'Sertes,' Cabanus sayd, 'Yees,
For me thynkis yet I fele   8555
Your strokis that were bothe sade and sore;
That I myselff that tyme was there,
I know it, so haue I sell!'

8535 men] K.; MS me   8540 more] moree   8550 went] Followed by
crossed-out ma   8551 wane] Corr. from wend

'This twelffe monethe oute wyth spere and lawnse
I haue byn wythe the kyng of Fraunce,   8560
Catryus the k[en]e;
There herde I tell all togedder
How she was bestadde, and I come heder
And haue slayne Lyolyne,
And euer more in my hert I thought,   8565
To hyr vowe I corded nowghte;
Away I wold haue ben.
Now am I spyed right well I se,
And that sore for-thynkys me;
My hertt nere brast for tene.   8570

'A longe tyme haue I louyd the fre,
And so I trowe she hathe done mee.
For no thyng wold she [l]ette,
Syr, younde blythe of blode and bone;
Tille thre yere was comyn and gone,   8575
I was hyr straunge valett,
I kepe no lengur to layne.
Syne I was the Drew-le-rayne—
Ye wott onys when we mett—
f. 330ᵛ   And as a fole now haue I been   8580
For no thyng ellys, wythouten wene,
But the deroye to gette.'

'Telle me syr, what is your name?'
'Ipomadon, wythouten blame,
That no man hathe done wronge [ere].'   8585
'Is this Ipomadon, my brother?'
'I trowe full well it be non nothere,
I kepe hit to layne no lengur.'
'Alas, brother,' quod Cabanus,
'Why haue ye fare wyth vs thus?   8590
In stowre were neuer non strengere
Be grette God that owethe this day;
Had ye this wyse gone awaye,
It wold a wrought grette angure!

8559 monethe] o corr. from e   8561 kene] K.; MS kynge   8571 tyme]
tymee   8573 lette] Ka.;   MS   wette   8579 Ye] K.;   MS   yet
8584 blame] Preceded by crossed-out descender of p   8585 ere] Kp.; MS om.

'Why, dere brother Ipomadon,   8595
That thus prevely wold haue goone
Grettly mervels mee;
Was neuer man borne of woman eyre
Me thynkis that bettur worde were
To haue younde bright of ble!'   8600
Cabanus sayd wyth lawynge chere,
'Welcome be you, brother dere,
Be God and be my lewte!'
Then were they bothe glad and blythe,
Eyther to[ke] other in armys swythe,   8605
Hit was grette Ioye to see.

Be the ring of grette valewe,
For brother ayther oþer knewe,
Her swerdys fell frome tham thane.
More Ioye was neuer eyre sene   8610
Then was the two brethryne betwene
Syn Gode this world began.
This herde and sawe Syr Prynsyus,   f. 331ʳ
One of the knyghttis of Cabanus,
And to a stede he ranne.   8615
Thrugh the thyke wode he [gan] pas
And to the lady there she was
Lyghttly he hym wanne.

The lady was full sore agaste
When she sawe hym come so faste,   8620
She hade mekyll drede.
'Lordyngys, younder comythe a knyght
That semys wele he hath takyn flyght;
He hyes hym a grette spede.
I wotte well trewly it is this: 8625
Slayne is my cosyne Cabanus!'
She wepte as she wo[l]de we[d]e.
'Lordys and knyghttys, armes you
Your mayster to socovre nowe,
As God of hevyne me spede!   8630

8605 toke] *Ka.*; *MS* to   8616 gan pas] *K.*; *MS* paste   8627 wolde wede]
K.; *MS* woode were

'And he be slayne for my sake,
Here to God a vowe I make
That weldythe heyven on hye:
I shall neuer ette of lyues foode,
Ne drynke that shall do me good,   8635
But drowne me in the see!'
Euery man made hym redy thus,
Be then was comyn Syr Pryncyous
And knelys downe on his kne.
'What tydyngis?' quod that lady bright.   8640
He sayd, 'Madame, be Goddis myghte,
There may no better bee!

'Gladder tydyngys, as I trowe,
Was neuer in this world brought you,
Ne to no lady here!'   8645

'Then is dede Syr Lyolyne?'
'Ye lady, be trouthe myne,
He shall noye ye no more.'
'And lyves my cosyn Cabanus?'
'Ye madame,' quod P[ryn]cyvs,   8650
'And ellis grette rewth it were!'
'Now, dere syr, who hathe done þat dede?'
'He was, madame, so God me spede,
Slayne or we come there.'

'Witt any man who hym slo?'   8655
'Yee, madame, well i-nowe,
Be God and be my lewte,
One of the preveyst knyght
That euer was borne be day or nyght:
When he had slayne that sle,   8660
Awaywarde he hyed hym fast!'
Shee thought and trymblyd at þe last,
More prevely done hathe he.
She sayd wyth many a sighyng sore,
'Imayne, and yf that my lemen were,   8665
Lorde God, wele were mee!

8650 Pryncyus] *K.*; *MS* Percyvs   8656 Yee] *K.*; *MS* yee a

'But dere syr,' quod the lady thanne,
'Telle me yf thou can
Whens come he—wot ye aught?'
'He is the kyngis sone of Poyle,   8670
He traveld hathe thorowe many a soyle,
For your love aventurs sought,
For your love he made kytte his heyre,
For your love he made hym fole euerywhere,
For your love grette wonder wrought,   8675
For your love hathe sufferd payne,
And for your love Lyolyne hathe slayne,
And to the grounde hym brought.   f. 332ʳ

'All your frendship myght be glade,
To wyffe and he you weddyd had   8680
For suche on is there none;
The blake baner hathe brought you blis!'
'O what is his name?' 'Madame, i-wis,
He hight Ipomadon.
He was so lothe to knowen be,   8685
That faught wyth vs all hath he,
Fowre of oure knyghttys slayne;
He had made vs all to rewe,
But Cabanus be a ring hym knew
That mendyd bothe there mo[n]e.'   8690

'And as he sayd to Cabanus?'
'Ye madame,' quod Pryncyous,
'Be God and be my lewte,
Was neuer two borne of woman yare,
To my do[m]e, that louyd more,   8695
Gladder thane may non bee.
Brether were they when they mett.
Madame, he [was] your straung valett
Then gonne is yeris thre,
And thanne he was the Drew-le-r[a]yne.'   8700
'Yee, I am loveles,' quod Imayne,
'Be oughte that I can see!

8670 He] *Preceded by deleted* Th   8674 fole] *Followed by* in   8690 mone]
K.; MS mode   8695 dome] *K.; MS* done   8698 was] *K.; MS om.*
8700 Drew-le-rayne] drewleryne

'Ye, no fors, so God me save;
She is more worthy hym to haue
Then euer were ye, Imayne.   8705
For her love he hathe suffyrd woo,
And sertus she for hym also;
Bothe they hadde full mekyll payne.
A full nobull knyght is hee,
Blythe they may now bothe bee,   8710
f. 332ᵛ   The sothe is not to layne.
Imayne, littill to do thou hadde
This endurs day when thou [hym] badde
So frowardely torne agayne;

'All when he folowyd [me],   8715
I cowde neuer wit þat it was he,
Soo wonderly he wrought!
Madame, now dare I savely swere
That mekyll beholdyne to God ye are:
He sendythe you that ye haue sought;   8720
You now right wele may [hym] holde.'
'Ya, Imayne suster, hade I that bolde,
Of no thyng ellys I ravght.
God graunte, if that his will be,
That he will not forsake mee,   8725
Whiche made vs bothe of nought.'

When Ipomadon and Cabanus
There fille togeddyr hade spokyne þis,
Vppon there steddis lepte they;
Togeddur lawȝing f[or]th they rode   8730
To Cander, wytheoute bode,
They toke the redy waye.
When they were come into the citte,
They sent after the bright of ble,
She come in good araye.   8735
He spendithe well his long travayle
That at the laste, wythouten fayle,
His love gette maye!

8713 hym] *MS om.*   8715 me] *K.; MS* hem   8721 hym] you
8730 forth] froth   8738 maye] mayee

The Fere into the citte youde;
Ipomadon when she come toke hede,   8740
And met hyr curtesly;
The lady he full goodely grete,
Wyth kyssynge togeddyr ar they mett,
They tremblyd bothe for [g]ree,
As lovers maners hathe bene   8745 f. 333ʳ
That long while no noþer hathe sene.
Ye maye well witt thereby
Wyth myrthe they ar mett ageyne,
There herttys will quake bothe for fayne,
Be way off drewry.   8750

A long while no worde he spake,
Bott at the last they bothe out brake
Thow3 they were neuer so wrothe:
'God save you, damysell!' quod hee;
She sayd, 'Syr, welcome mot ye be!'   8755
The herttys quakyd bothe.
All the cowrte was full fayne
That Lyolyne was so slayne
That hade theme wrought gret wrothe;
When they had sene Ipomadon,   8760
All they thankyd God alonne
That he skapyd that [ska]the.

Cabanus, wyth good intent,
Letturs to the kyng he sent
And told hym euery deyell,   8765
How hit was the Drew-le-rayne
That had Lyolyne so slayne,
And wonne that lady [lel].
Mellengere wold no lengur abyde
But thedyre he riggud hym to ryde   8770
Wyth styff men vnder stele . . .

The kyng sayd, 'Lordys, wythoute wene,
Long wythoute a kyng haue [y]e bene;

8744 gre]K.; MS yree   8762 skathe] K.; MS dethe   8768 lel] K.; MS gent
8773 ye] we

In sorow that ha[s] you brought.
Now God hathe sent you here a knyght 8775
That will you mayneteyme in your right;
Was there neuer a better wroughte.' . . .
All prayden the kyng, 'For Goddis sake,
Helpe ye that maryage for to make
That it be taryde noughte!' 8780

Ipomadon sayd, 'Securlye,
So mekill of price [have] wo[ld]e I
That I am not k[r]owen[ed] yet.
I love you[r] [nece], so mot I th[ryve],
More thanne al the women of lyve, 8785
I reke nere who it witte:
Will my love asent theretille,
Home into Poyle, ser, wend I will,
And neuer more forther flytte,
Wyth worshipe crownyd for to be, 8790
And there to wedde my lady fre,
And ye will acorde to hitte.'

The kyng sayd, 'So God me save,
Hereof we grette lykyng haue,
Be hym that owethe this daye!' 8795
Euery man made them redy faste,
The waye into Poyle they paste,
To Berlett comyn ar theye.
There hathe he weddyd that lady hynd,
And brought there long love to ende. 8800
They crowyned them bothe I saye,
He for kyng and hur for quene;
The seventhe day they toke there leyve bedene,
Bothe kyng and maye.

Ipomadon gave to Thelamewe, 8805
That to hym was euer good and trewe,

8774 has] *K.*; *MS* haue   8775 hathe] *Followed by* hathe   8782 have wolde]
K.; *MS* wotte   8783 krowened] *K.*; *MS* knowen   8784 your nece] *K.*; *MS*
you   thryve] *K.*; *MS* thee   8788 I will] *K.*; *MS* will I

To his wyff Imayne,
Wyth landys that was long and brode;
Duke of Burgayn he hym made,
The sothe is not to layne;   8810
And to I[aso]ne he gaff the fayre,   f. 334ʳ
The kyngys doughttur of Lorayne and his eyre—
Thereof she was full fayne;
And to his cosyne Egyone . . .
Bothe castell and demayne.   8815

Togeddyr ar this louers two,
Was there neuer non that louyd so
Borne of womon yett.
Betwene them to was neuer no preffe,
So wonder grett delyte of love   8820
In bothe there herttys was sett.
Fro the tyme that they beganne,
Ryght wele they had rekynd tille thanne,
For nothyng wold they lett,
But euer there love alyke was hoote,   8825
Betwene them two was neuer no bate,
Fro the tyme that they were mette.

All that had seruyd the[m] eyre
He warysound, both lesse and more,
Euery man in there degre.   8830
Togedyr gan this louers dwell,
But how long I can not tell,
Be God and be my lewte.
So merely they ledde ther lyff,
Betwene the[m] two was neuer stryff   8835
That man myght here or see.
In hyr tyme she bare hym sonys two,
The fayrest that on ground myȝt goo,
No godelyer myght non been.

Cawnus was the oldest b[ro]there,   8840
Portusalus was the tothere

8810 layne] laynee   8811 Iasone] Iosane   8828 them] the
8831 Togedyr] e corr. from a   8835 them] K.; MS then   8840 brothere]
borthere

That after hym was bryme and bold;
And aftur his fader, wyth oute lesynge,
Of Poyle was Cawnus crownyd kyng
As herytage hit wolde;   8845
And Portusalus of Calabere
Was crownyd, for why it come of hyr,
The modere mylde of mo[l]de.
She toke hit hem be heritage,
For hit was hyr in maryage   8850
And nother hit was bought ne sold.

He was a full nobull kyng,
Lyke to his fader in all thynge,
That was so wonder wighte,
Of kyndnes [and] of curtessye,   8855
Off armvre [and] of chevalrye,
Off semelynes be sight.
Off the fader haue ye now harde,
At the Citte off Tebes how so he farde,
There dyed that nobull knyght;   8860
And when that to the Fere was told,
Neuer aftur ette ne drynke she wold,
For pure love dyed that wight.

Aftur Mellengers dysses,
Cabanus, wythouten lesse,   8865
Off Cessyle crownyd was kyng.
He was a full nobull man,
His burgayes and his barons þanne
Off hym had grette lykyng.
A worthy lady he weddyd to wyff,   8870
Wythe Ioye and blys they led ther lyff,
He and that lady younge.
They were full good at all degre,
But wyth his brothere dyed hee,
They bothe had one endynge.   8875

8848 molde] *K.*; *MS* mode   8849 be] *Written above line, with caret*
8855 and] *K.*; *MS* nor   8856 and] *K.*; *MS* nor   8864 dysses] *Second* s *corr.*
from e

Ipomadon hathe sent his sonde
To lovers that leve in londe;   f. 335ʳ
His mensyngere makythe he me:
He comaundythe on Goddis behalue,
To lovys wounde ye lay no sal[u]e,   8880
But poynttis of grette pette,
Where right loue was in herte brought,
That for a littill lette ye noughte;
Sertes, no more dyd hee.
This endythe Ipomadon, i-wis;   8885
That good lorde bringe vs to his blis
That bought vs on the rode tre.

And that ye shall for louers praye
To hym that made bothe nyght and day
To brynge vs to the blysse that lestis aye   8890
A M E N for charyte.

8880 salue] *K.*; *MS* salle   8882 right] *K.*; *MS* right in   8888 praye] *K.*;
MS prayce

EXPLANATORY NOTES

1–12 The syntax of this first stanza is somewhat obscure, and differing translations have been suggested. If *were* is assumed to be subjunctive, the stanza as a whole could be translated: 'It would be a pleasure and a joy to learn about love for all those who would hear [and] who know what love can be like; but whoever is too hasty in love and cannot attain his goal, *that* condition causes lovers grief. Fair words break no bones; they [the 'fair words'] make each of these lovers think of higher hopes and [thus] exert themselves, whether it be to good effect or not—this has often been observed.'

7 A fuller version of this proverb is cited in James Kelly, *A Complete Collection of Scottish Proverbs* (London, 1818), p. 68: 'Fair words break no bone: but foul words many a one'. See also Whiting, S603. K. saw this line as a variant of a slightly different proverb that appears in Gower's *Confessio Amantis* as: *the harde bon . . . a tunge brekth it al to pieces*, III. 463–5, in *The English Works of John Gower*, ed. G. C. Macaulay, EETS ES 81, 82 (1900–1).

9 *wene* (MS *wone*) Only the rhymes indicate that a scribe has substituted *wone* (apparently ON *ván*) for *wene* (OE *wēn*): both words mean 'hope'.

13–14 *prefe : lefe* (MS *prese : lese*) 'Regarding this point I may well approve of one who was loath to abandon his love': The phrase *lefe of* is well-attested in ME, while the *MED* provides only one example of *lese of* (see *lesen*, 1b.(d)). For the emendation of MS *prese* to *prefe*, cf. l. 2584 where *preysse* is written although rhyme demands *preve*. (The original, or at least an earlier copy, may have been spelt with *f*, which a later copyist consistently mistook for *prese*.) For the sense 'approve of', see *OED prove v.*, 11. The argument against retaining MS *prese*, 'praise', is strengthened by the fact that this word rhymes elsewhere on *ei/ai* (cf. l. 508, *prayse : dayes, alweys*; l. 1807, *preyse : dayes, all-wayes, layes*), while *prese*, 'press, insist', is not recorded as being used with *of*. K. leaves the MS reading without translation. S&J also leave the MS reading and translate 'in respect of this point, I may well commend one who [*that*] was reluctant to fail in his love'.

45 *bus* (MS *mvste*) Rhyme demands the more Northern verb *bus*, a contraction of OE *behōfian* (it appears intact at ll. 5527 and 8524). That the form *mvste* was also used by the poet, however, is indicated by ll. 3978–9, where *mvste* rhymes with *loste*.

79 *yers ten* The number of years varies in the extant AN versions, though the ME *Ipomedon C* also has ten years (the Fere's background is left out of the ME *Ipomydon B* entirely.) See 'The Translator and his Source : The

Translator's Exemplar' on the relationships between this text and the extant AN versions.

99 *Fere* (MS *fayre*) A scribe has mistaken the original *Fere*, 'proud', as required by rhyme for *fayre*, 'fair'. *Fayre* appears for *Fere* again at ll. 177, 647, and 5107.

106–8 I.e. 'If she were the most attractive of women in all other areas, she was labelled proud only in regard to love.'

114 *I'* K. emends to *in*, but *i* occurs again at ll. 843, 987, 3992 in the phrase *i' feythe/faythe*, and is clearly deliberate since the scribe capitalises it. The *OED* notes that in the EML *Ormulum*, *i* is the only form of 'in' to appear before consonants; it also appears in texts of the *Ancrene Riwle*-group and occasionally in other Southern texts. (*Ipomadon* was clearly copied at least once in the South.) The apostrophe is added for the sake of clarity.

121–2 *lowgh / rewe* The rhyme here is *lewe : rewe*, to which S&J emend: this Northern preterite appears several times later in the text (see 'Language of the Text, Part I', (16)).

124–6† These lines remain something of a puzzle. Perhaps: *Than spake as has don other moo/ Some of them; 'saye not so,/ Though it were a skorne!'*; i.e. 'Then [they] said, as many have done [in similar circumstances], "Don't speak thus even in jest!"' This is the essence of Ka.'s suggestion *Some of them said: 'Saye not so . . .'* which S&J also favour. K. emends *Than* to *Thou* and punctuates, '*Thou spake, as has don other moo: / Some of them saye not so, / Though it were a skorne*', translating the latter two lines as 'some say it was well said, and others that it was not right even if it were just in fun'. Kp. objects to the interpretation of *skorne* as 'joke' (he feels it carried a more derogatory sense) and offers the ingenious solution; '*Thou spake as has don other moo: / Some of them to say not so / Thought it were a skorne*', which he translates as 'you spoke as have done many others: some of them thought that to *not* speak thus would have been shameful.' In support of this he points to the scribe's undeniable propensity for omitting the occasional final letter or single-syllable word, and the poet's evident liking for such inverted syntax.

152 *of chasse the chevalrye* (MS *the chasse of chevalrye*) 'the knightly practice of hunting'. Suggested by K. on the model of ll. 986–9 of the version of the tail-rhyme *St. Alexius* found in MS Laud 622: *to be Man of valoure / And lernen chiualrie, / Of huntyng & of Ryuere, / Of chesse pleieyng & of tablere* (in *Adam Davy's Dreams about Edward III; The Life of St. Alexius; Solomon's Book of Wisdom; St Jeremie's 15 Tokens before Doomsday; The Lamentation of Souls*, ed. F. J. Furnivall, EETS os 69, 1878).

165 *sayne* Represents pp. 'seen' rather than 'said'. No emendation has been made, however, since the editorial policy for this text is to emend only substantive variants or errors, and *LALME* (vol. 4) lists three texts in which the spelling *sayn(e)* is a variant of 'seen' (two in Surrey and one in Sussex).The spelling occurs again at l. 378.

177 Fere (MS *fayre*) See note to l. 99.

182 *occyane* (MS *oxylane*) 'the West' The MS spelling is otherwise unrecorded, but it corresponds to *Occident* at AN l. 219, and cf. *Sir Landevale* ll. 93–4, *That ys an ile of the fayré / In occian, full faire to see*, where it refers to the Isle of Avalon, traditionally located in Southwest England: see *Middle English Romances*, ed. S. H. A. Shepherd (New York & London, 1995), p. 354. It is also possible that the original was *occyan* or even *oxian*, cited in the *OED* under sense 1(b) of *ocean*, n..

192 *But* K. notes that this second *but* in as many lines might have been copied from the line above, and the original word was probably *And*.

198 The *he* refers to Ipomadon, who is unaware of Thalamewe's scrutiny.

213 'When his youthful beauty is at its peak.'

219 *mone* Probably the auxiliary 'must' as glossed here, but S&J note that it may also represent a derivative of OE *gemunian*, 'remember'.

221–2 Whiting cites this proverb-like comment under C479: the other citations are ll. 268–70 of this text and a similar statement in *Ipomedon C* (f. 90b). However, he notes that the sentiment is the same as his S90, 'diverse schools make perfect clerks', for which he has two citations from the *Canterbury Tales*.

237 *shulde* (MS *shallde*) The unusual MS form may be the result of a copyist first writing *shall*, perhaps influenced by the *shall* in the line above, and then attempting to correct it by adding *-de*.

260 *ples* K. emends to *pleses*, but a small aside in Mossé's *Handbook* observes that 'in the Northern dialect, in the present indicative (except for the 2nd sg), the verb had no ending when it was immediately preceded or followed by a personal pronoun.' Significantly, he cites examples from Yorkshire texts *The Bee and the Stork* by Rolle (in the Thornton MS) and the *Towneley Plays* (Fernand Mossé, *A Handbook of Middle English*, trans. James Walker (Baltimore, 1952), p. 79).

289 *bekende* (MS *be kynde*) 'granted' This word seems to have been unknown to at least one copyist in the text's history, and it has been rendered as the nonsensical *be kynde* on all three of its appearances (see ll. 6205, 7973).

313 *brodyrd* There are two possible interpretations of this word: the most obvious is 'embroidered' (in the fifteenth century, *broudre/ brouder* was taken as the equivalent of F *bro(u)der*, 'to stitch, embroider'), but the AN here reads *estendent*, 'spread' (l. 344). The ME translator may have translated this literally as *brodyd* (derived from OE adj. *brād*, 'broad') which a copyist later replaced with the more familiar *brodyrd*.

320 *wille* (MS *wolle*) There are no recorded forms of the noun 'will' (OE *willa*) with *o*: the scribe's eye may have skipped to *worthely*.

326–7 I.e. 'I would like to know where the best wine of this country might be.' Cf. the similar construction at l. 1866, *Your will fayne wete wold wee.*

333 *Godys forbode* (MS *Godys forbede*) The phrases *God forbede* and *Godys forbode* were interchangeable in ME, and the MS reading could be emended to either: the choice of *Godys forbode* here is based on the appearance of this variant at l. 8008. (See *MED, forbeden* v. sense 6, and *forbod* n. sense (b).)

345 'Over the preventing of an heir's succession'. See 'The Translator and his Source: The Remodelling Process' for further comment.

349† K. emends to *Ladyes wote that she wille nat*, which fits into the extant version of the text, but could not have been the original line because 'not' in this text is only ever rhymed with other words historically containing [ɣ]+ *t* (e.g. *brought, wrought*), despite the convenience a variant would offer. On the other hand, the MS line makes no sense, and the AN offers no enlightenment since this line is part of a small ME digression on the Fere's virtues. The most imaginative suggestion is from Kp.: *That she will not, ladyes wate, / Abowtte her suffyr no debatte*: he notes that the form *wate* is supported by rhyme at l. 838.

378 *sayne* See note to l. 165.

432–33 This stanza has one line too many, and the rhyme indicates that l. 432 is the odd one out. There are at least two reasonable courses of emendation. Regarding Ipomadon's odd statement that he was *callyd at home by the same name* (i.e. the *stravnge valete*), K. may be right in thinking that the 'Fair Unknown' tradition, to which the AN *Ipomedon* already owes much, lies behind this addition to the ME—specifically, scenes such as that in the ME *Lybeaus Desconus* where the hero explains at court, *I ne wote whate is my name: / . . . But while I was at home, / My moder, on hir game, / Clepped me Bewfice* (*Lybeaus Desconus*, ed. Maldwyn Mills. EETS 261 (1969), Lambeth MS, ll. 62–6). The original stanza here might have read something like, *What ys thy name, þou stravnge valete?' / 'I was callyd at home the same . . .'*. H. Willert offers an emendation that conflates ll. 432–3 as *Anon tell me the same!* in 'Zum ME. *Ipomadon*', *Englische Studien*, 38 (1907), 131–2.

438 K. punctuates this as, *She sayd: 'Sone,–'* but cf. ll. 4957–8, *The burges lowgh and sayd sone, / 'Syr, better myghtte no man haue done'.*

498† *convyence* K. emends to *convenence, iwys*. This is unsatisfactory since the extra *iwys* not only spoils the rhythm but would not have rhymed with *es*, the original text's sole form of the pr.3 sg. in rhyme-position (see

'Language of the Text, Part II: Evidence for the West Riding of Yorkshire'.) Context seems to require a word denoting 'high birth'.

514† K. emends here to *All ladyes to love it lays* to satisfy the requirement for a rhyme on *-ays/eys*, and also suggests *All laythe to love it lays*; he is unhappy with both of these. The ever-inventive Kp. suggests *All layde to love and ays*, which he would translate as 'it all stems from love and complacency'.

540 *cowardise* (MS *cowardenes*) In the corresponding l. 549 of the AN, Holden's MS 'B' reads *Dehez touz jours cuardise*, 'ever cursed be cowardice' (the 'A' and 'D' MSS have *cowardie*).

551 *monys* There are three possible interpretations of this word. The first is that it should be *mornys*: *r* before consonants is the letter most frequently omitted by this (or an earlier) scribe. Without resorting to emendation, it is possible interpret it as 'bewails', from OE *mænan*, or 'thinks about', from ON cp. OI *muna*.

552–4 'Though her heart may be set to love him, it diminishes her pleasure that he does not care for chivalry.'

557–9 *louthe* pa.t. 'laughed', cf. *i-nowthe* 'enough', ll. 2630, 6334, 6682, for this spelling of the fricative. K. emends l. 557 to *Then sum men of his huntyng lowe* and translates these lines as: 'Then some people laughed about his love of hunting; others who heard [the mockery] behind his back were very angry'. Another possibility is that the general discussion of *huntyng* led the scribe to write this word in place of *skorne* here—cf. l. 459 *For that dede* [they] *lovghe hym to skorne*.

567 *of* K. emends here to the expected *on*, observing that *on* and *of* frequently appear in each other's place in MSS. He attributes this to the use in exemplars of the form *o* for one or both words, which later copyists occasionally misinterpret. Mustanoja, however, observes that 'the interchangeability of *of*, *on* and *at* is not uncommon in ME and is also found in later OE', and further that 'it is usually *of* that encroaches upon the other two' (see pp. 350–1 and 400–1). See also the appearance of *on* where *of* is expected at l. 4846.

567 ff. The type of hunt depicted here is evidently the same kind of deer-drive that is described in *SGGK*, although Ipomadon pursues that most prized quarry, the hart or male red deer, while Bertilak, in the winter hunting scenes of *SGGK*, hunts only female deer (harts being out of season). The Fere's men spread through the forest with *brachys* (smaller running hounds that hunt by scent, also called *brachets* or *raches* as at ll. 618 and 615) to flush out the deer (ll. 606–11) which can then be pursued individually. There is no mention of archers in this hunt, although they are usually involved in such 'deer drives' (see *SGGK*); the poet's interest is clearly in Ipomadon's individual feats rather than in the organization of the hunt as a whole. For a useful description of this style of hunting see the chapter 'Bow and Stable' in John Cummins, *The Hound and the Hawk: The Art of Medieval Hunting* (London, 1988).

578–86 The Fere's pavilion has been pitched *be a rennande reuer syde* partly, perhaps, because a river or fountain is one of the standard ingredients of a *locus amoenus*, but also to provide her with a good view when the deer make for the water, which they would do either to mask their scent or to face the hounds 'at bay', as Ipomadon's quarry does later at ll. 632–5. See the observations on this at ll. 1550–2 of the *Boke of St. Albans*, in *English Hawking and Hunting in The Boke of St. Albans*, ed. Rachel Hands (Oxford, 1975).

584–6 'Before any of them were startled into disarray [i.e. flushed out], great harts went to the water to stand at bay.' *Araye* is here left as one word and *oute of araye* glossed as 'in disarray', assuming that it refers to the chaos of splashing water, baying dogs and plunging harts. K., however, translated l. 584 as: 'Or any was disturbed from its way', reading *araye* as *a raye*— 'path, track' of the deer. In support of this he cites the Thornton MS copy of *The Awntyrs off Arthure at the Terne Wathelyn*, l. 58, *And tille thaire riste raches relyes onne thaire raye* (e.g. ed. Ralph Hanna III (Manchester, 1974)). While *raye* [OF *rai*] could mean 'trace of something', such as the scent-trail the dogs are following in the line cited from the *Awntyrs*, it is harder to fit this sense to l. 584.

594 *he* (MS *they*) Sense could just about be made of the MS reading, but the text is tracking the AN very closely in this section and the latter reads: *Comment qu'il seit pruz d'autre riens / Il n'est pas le derein as chiens*, 'although he was not valiant with regard to anything else, he was not the last one with the dogs' (ll. 585–6). The extant ME text has suffered badly from at least one inattentive scribe, and incorrect pronouns in particular are rife throughout.

603 & 609 Medieval hunting manuals stress the importance of blowing horns as a means of communicating the progress of the hunt to others. The ME translation of William Twiti's *Art of Hunting* explains the various horn-signals with engagingly earnest precision: for example, *when* [the hounds are] *fer fro me, Y schall blow in oper maner and pat is pis: trout trout trororout, trout trout trororout, trorerererout, V tymes pis last mote* (*William Twiti: The Art of Hunting*, ed. Bror Danielsson (Stockholm, 1977), p. 48).

604 Before they were released on the chase, hounds were 'coupled', or held together in pairs by a short rope linking their collars.

611 Cf. *The Awntyrs off Arthure at the Terne Wathelyn*, l. 59, *They gaf no gamon no grythe pat on grounde gruwes* (ed. Ralph Hanna III (Manchester, 1974)).

622 The greyhounds would be kept leashed until the deer were actually visible, since they hunt purely by sight (hence their alternative name 'gazehounds').

624–32 There are three lines missing from the middle of this stanza, probably after l. 631, or perhaps after l. 629 as K. suggests.

635 *bone* 'ready to go' K. emends to *bowne* because of the rhyme-pairs *downe* and *browne*, but at l. 3182 *bowne* is linked in the tail-rhyme with *Iasone* (never spelt with *-oun* in the ME text) as well as *presone* and *downe*, and l. 3541 has *bone : Amfyon*: this suggests that the author at least sometimes held words ending in *-on* and *-oun/-own* to be equivalent for the purposes of rhyme.

647 Fere (MS *fayre*) See note to l. 99.

662 *seruyd hym* Marcelle Thiébaux explains this terminology thus: 'Then to end the agony of the animal, the huntsman killed it (*servir le cerf*) by piercing it between the horns and the neck, cutting through the spinal cord to the marrow', in *The Stag of Love: The Chase in Medieval Literature* (Ithaca & London, 1974), p. 35. The fact that this technical term is not employed in the AN indicates that the translator is drawing on his own knowledge of hunting terms.

663 'He undoes the skin [?] to feed the hound.' On *slowche* for MS *sowche*, see the *OED* sb.[2] (2), 'a skin, caul, or membrane, enclosing or covering the body, or some part of it'. In this case it may refer to the deer's skin: it was customary to reward the hounds at the sight of the kill in order to associate the hunt with the reward in their minds, and traditionally the hounds' portion was served to them laid out on the skin of the animal. On the other hand, l. 1808 of the *Boke of St. Albans* reads, *Than shall ye slyt the slough ther as the hert* ['heart'] *lith*, where it seems to refer to the membrane enclosing the body cavity, since the hart's skin has already been slit. Various internal organs are designated as part of the hounds' reward depending on the authority consulted—bowels, liver, paunch, small guts, heart, lungs—so this line may describe the reward of Ipomadon's hound with one of these: see note to l. 1831 of the *Boke of St. Albans* for details (cited in note to ll. 578–86).

668 The 'dyghting', or breaking up, of the deer's carcass was a highly formalized ritual. Detailed descriptions of the technique are given in hunting manuals, and the ability to do it well was evidently seen as a mark of nobility: Tristan, a hero on whom Ipomadon seems to have been partly modelled, was particularly famed for his elegant breaking-up of the deer, and even the much-abbreviated ME version of *Sir Tristrem* retains a gorily detailed description of it (ll. 445–53).

702 It is assumed here that ll. 702–3 are narratorial, although K. begins the Fere's speech with them. The sentiment is echoed later at ll. 3019–20; both statements are listed under Whiting's citations for the proverb 'love has no lack' (L508).

711 *herte* (MS *hete*) K. retains the MS reading without attempting to translate it, but S&J's emendation to *herte* seems preferable in view of the fact that the AN at this point reads *Deus, cum el ad le quer loial*, 'Lord, how she had a faithful heart' (l. 689). Of all the consonants this scribe is inclined to miss out, *r* (before or after another consonant) is by far the most common.

727 *no* Possibly an error for *no(gh)t*, but *LALME* (vol. 4) records this spelling for 'not' in scattered MSS.

729 The AN does not correspond here to allow for any reconstruction of the lost line.

731 In the AN we are never given the number of harts Ipomadon brings in, either here or later when he presents the heads to La Fiere, and all three MS witnesses agree on this (Holden's A, B and D). It is odd therefore that in this text we are first told that he *brought to quary tenne / moo than dyde all other men*, i.e. 'ten more' or 'ten times more than other men', but he then presents the Fere with only *sevyn heddys* from this bounty (l. 743). K. points out that in the AN, 'ten' is the number of hunters whose combined total Ipomadon has single-handedly bested: *Plus ad il sul de granz serfs pris / Ke de trestuz les meillors dis* 'he won more great harts than the best ten of the others' (ll. 701–2). The author of *Ipomedon C* gives the number of heads presented as three (f. 91a)—both ME translators seem to have wanted to be more specific about the extent of Ipomadon's success at hunting. *Ipomydon B*, by contrast, follows the AN's vagueness with *More he toke with howndis thre / Than all þat othyr compaigne* (ll. 395–6).

780 *As* 'Has' Cf. occasional unstressed *ys* for 'his', e.g. ll. 291, 656.

795–6 'That afterwards some regretted deeply, [and were] often disinclined to pleasure.' The AN has the same general sense that something of far-reaching consequence is about to happen: *Tel ovre enprist en my cele eire / Dunt tot dis il avra afere*, 'he undertook such work in that place as he will be involved with forever' (ll. 761–2).

800 *davnte* (MS *dowte*) Cf. AN ll. 764–5, *Tote autre rien puet hom danter, / Mes amour n'ert ja mes dauntee*, 'man may conquer everything else, but love has never been conquered', of which ll. 800 and 802 form an exact translation.

806 *lovys scolys* The translator is fond of this figurative use of 'school'; he uses it three times in reference to 'love's school' (see ll. 1098, 7371) and also in the sense of 'training' or 'teaching' (ll. 6358, 6925, 7371): see *MED*, sense 3(a) of *skole* n. for other ME examples of its figurative use.

831 *Imayne* (MS *aglyne*) Mistakes with proper names and pronouns abound in this text—see 'General Introduction : *Ipomadon A*', note 6.

839 efte 'again' (MS *ofte*) Cf. AN l. 875, *Vers Jason autre foiz s'en turne*, 'She turned once again to Jason'.

840–2† These lines have been punctuated to give the following sense: 'What, fool, do you think that ladies would want to bestow their love on you, to bestow [it] on you for the sake of courtesy?' The same phrasing is used at ll. 846–8. Editors have been divided over these lines. S&J summarise the various proposed solutions thus: '*On the to laye* looks like an attempt to rephrase [l. 841]: it makes no sense. K.'s suggestion *For bewté or for curtesye* gives good sense and is to some extent supported by F 877 f.: *quidez vus, garçon, pur beauté / pussez pur amur estre amé?* Ka. takes *latte* as a noun "appearance", which involves altering MS *be on the* to *be thy* "according to your . . . ."' (Ka. interprets *latte* as 'appearance' on the basis of *Sir Tristrem* l. 2097).

892 *meche yll*† Various emendations have been proposed for this obviously unsatisfactory line. K. emends to *mechyll unsete*; he also suggests *unswete* 'unpleasantness' from a combination of the noun *swete* (e.g. in *SGGK* l. 2518) and the adj. *unswete*, (e.g. in *Sir Tristrem* l. 968). Against the first suggestion, there is no citation of a noun *unsete* in the *MED*, while Kp. objects to both proposals on the grounds that a scribe would be unlikely to misunderstand, and thus attempt to correct, such a common word as *mekyll*, especially when he has evidently felt no need to alter it elsewhere. His not implausible suggestion is *This dyde her meche yll gete*. Another distant possibility is *meche ylet*, based on a single citation in the *MED* of a noun *y-let* meaning 'hindrance' (*Sir Orfeo*, Auchinleck MS copy l. 169; noun derived from OE *gelettan*).

906 bed (MS *sche*) Cf. AN l. 947, *Dit li ad, qe son lit seit prest*, 'she told her that her bed was ready'.

941–3† These difficult lines are partly the result of a misunderstanding on the translator's part of the AN lines, *Mes cil dit bien en reprover: / 'De grant orgoil vient encombrer'* (ll. 971–2)—'but it is often said proverbially: from great pride comes trouble': the translator has rendered *en reprover*, 'prover-bially', as *reprove*, 'setback / reproach' (see further, 'The Translator and his Source : The Translator's Anglo-Norman Competence'). A satisfactory interpretation of the lines is offered by K.: 'It has been said by the wisest men that ever existed that in the matter of love, great reproach comes of pride'. The phrase *lest of love* is assumed to be a variant of *lestes of love*— 'desires of love' (see *MED*, *list* n.[2] sense 1(a) for other examples), and it is used again, clearly meaning 'love's desire', at l. 7344. K. also speculates, rather too imaginatively, that *lest of love* may be an oblique reference to the *Ars Amandi* of Ovid, who would be the 'wisest yet that was' of l. 943, an unlikely reading in view of the far more general nature of the AN lines whose wording the ME poet is trying—albeit unsuccessfully—to follow closely here.

947 *ys* Cf. AN l. 981, *Quant assez vaut plus simpleté,* 'when humility is worth so much more'.

957–8 These lines are a very literal rendering, though in reverse order, of AN ll. 992–3; *Jeo nel devraie pas prier, / Par droit devraie estre prié* : 'I shouldn't ask, I should be invited [to love]'.

962–3 *thys lythe be-lefte I am / of love* A tempting emendation here is to *berefte I am / Of love*, which fits the general sense, but there is a *be-lefte* later on at l. 1011—*in care be-lefte am I*—which suggests that the MS has the correct word here rather than *berefte* or K.'s *belerte*, 'charmed' (though it is not impossible that the scribe's exemplar contained a word unknown to him for which he tried substituting *be-lefte*). The interchangeability in this copy of the spellings *thys* and *thus* allow us to interpret the phrase *thys lythe* as 'so easily' [OE *līþe*]: the whole phrase may then be translated: 'so easily abandoned am I by love'.

1008 *lothe* 'with hostility' The original form must have been *laythe* (rhyming with *faythe*) derived from ON *leiðr*, rather than the OE *lāð* that lies behind the scribe's *lothe*.

1013 *wyll* MS *whye* makes nonsense of the following *I hope naye; / Yes, in fayth he will!*

1026 *no* (MS *a*) K.'s emendation here translates the AN almost exactly: *Ne li mostrei pas tel orgoil,* 'I will not show him such haughtiness' (l. 1094).

1039 *bad* (MS *good*) K's emendation to *bad* has been adopted here in the absence of anything more satisfactory, and it is at least possible to understand how the syntax of these lines might have persuaded a scribe to substitute its opposite *good*. The only other occurrence of *bad(de)* in this text is at l. 1562, where it could be either an adjective or a verb.

1069 *moone* This looks like a derivative of OE *gemunian* 'remember' or OE *mǣnan* 'lament'. See 'Language of the Text, Part I: Rhyming Practice' for other examples of such inexact rhymes.

1076 'Though she showed me [that she knew I loved her] by means of a reproach . . .' This translation takes *wyth* in its instrumental sense, and *gyffe* in its sense of 'show', cf. *Cleanness* l. 1326: *he deuised hade / þat alle goudes com of God, and gef hit hym bi samples.* (ed. J. J. Anderson (Manchester, 1977)). K. instead takes *wyth* as having the adverbial sense 'therewith' (*OED adv.*3, sense B) although the usage is ill-attested.

1103 *hottys* See 'Language of the Text, Part I : Adverbs' on this form of the superlative, and see 'The Translator and his Source: The Translator's

Anglo-Norman Competence' on the relation between ll. 1103–5 and the AN text.

1116 'If she shared a part of it I would not mind at all.'

1118 *We, leef* The interjection *we* or *wi* can be used to denote despair—it is more usually *wei* or *way*—but it can also be used like *why* to introduce a question, as in ll. 2185–6 of *SGGK*: *'We! Lorde,' quoþ þe gentyle knyȝt, / 'Wheþer þis be þe grene chapelle?'* Here it seems to carry both senses. See Mustanoja, pp. 627–8.

1121–3 The interpretation of Ipomadon's comment here rests on the translation of *fallythe*. If it is assumed to be some form of OE *feallan*, 'fall', then he is saying something like: 'He who dedicates his entire life to war fails'. This might explain why he hid the great martial prowess that he goes on to describe in the following lines. This interpretation is slightly different to the AN version, where he says only that he hid his prowess out of pride: *Tant m'en suy par orgoil celé / K'asez i suy vil e blamé*, 'I concealed myself so thoroughly through pride that I am much criticised and blamed here' (AN ll. 1181–2, rendered in ME at ll. 1136–7). Alternatively, *fallythe* could be understood as a form of OE (Anglian) *gefællan*, 'overcome'; the *MED* lists *fall-* as a N and WML form of the more usual *fell-*. Ipomadon would then be saying 'he who dedicates his entire life to war succeeds', which would explain his decision to go off to fight.

1127 ff. Evidently a line is missing, and K. is probably correct in suggesting something like *But prevely go fro them away*.

1136 *love* K. and Ka. here suggest emending to *lorne*, but it is not necessary to emend the MS reading to make sense of the line. The first possibility involves interpreting *love* as the noun 'love': 'But because your only pride is in love'. This sense is compatible with the AN and would pair the ME ll. 1136–7, *But so that love is all thy pryde / Thereffore all men be thy foos* neatly with the AN ll. 1181–2, *Tant m'en suy par orgoil celé / K'asez i suy vil e blamé*, 'I hid myself so thoroughly through pride that I am much criticised and blamed here'. A variation of this reading is to translate *but so that* as 'unless', thus 'unless love is all your pride [i.e. so that he makes himself worthy of love], all men will be your enemies'. For this use of *but so that*, cf. *The Works of Sir Thomas Malory* p. 273, l. 31: *I woll nat take youre yeldyng unto me, but so that ye will yelde you unto thys knyght* (ed. E. Vinaver, 3 vols., 2nd ed., Oxford (1967)).

A different suggestion rests on interpreting *love* as the adj. 'low' [ON *lágr*, eME *lah*], for which the *MED* does list *love* as a variant spelling. The lines could then be read as, 'But so that your pride is [brought] low, all men will be your foos' [i.e. he will now abandon his pride and fight in tournaments]. Unfortunately the ME has diverged from the AN just enough here for the latter text to be no help in interpreting it.

1175 Translating AN l. 1218: *Mal est batu qe plurer n'ose*, 'Sorely beset is he who dares not weep'.

1220 *woll* The *OED* lists *woll(e)* as a possible form for the 2.sg.subj. from the fourteenth to sixteenth centuries.

1223–5 Something has clearly gone wrong in the copying process here. Going purely by rhyme, l. 1224 is the extra line, but it seems to belong to the narrative thread while l. 1223, which does fit into the rhyme-scheme, is otherwise superfluous. In the AN ll. 1269–71, Ipomedon decides to lie to Tholomeu, but there is no mention of feigning illness. Alternatively, ll. 1223–4 may represent an accidental expansion of a single line that read something like *But he fayned hym seke oghte*, 'But he pretended to be somewhat ill'.

1230–4 The root of this curious statement is AN ll. 1277–9: *Mout ay grant poür de ma miere, / Kar songoy qe mon piere / Une des costes out perdue*, 'I had great fear for my mother, for I dreamt that my father lost one of his ribs'. *Costes* can mean 'sides' as the ME poet has, with evident confusion, translated it here, but it also means 'ribs', here employing the metaphor of Adam's rib to indicate that Ipomedon's mother was *prest del murrir*, 'close to death'. See 'The Translator and his Source: The Translator's Anglo-Norman Competence'.

1241 *be God that ys but one* See note to l. 1617.

1250 *lyste* The *MED* cites this line and suggests that *lyste* ('makes himself desolate', from OE *forlēosan*) is an error for the pa.t. form (OE *lēas*), but the *OED* notes that both strong and weak pa.t. forms existed for this verb (*leese* v.[1]). It is also possible that this represents the pr.3 sg., since throughout this section the narrator vacillates between present and past tense.

1253–7 'Although they did not know much about the art [of love], Love is well divided between them, for both drank the same draught [of love]; though it caused great desire for love, either of them had the other's heart'. This translation assumes that *loste* is from OE *lust*. It is also possible that it means 'forfeiture', from the pp. of OE *losian*, *lēosan* 'be deprived', but a similar combination of terms is found in the following example from Gower's *Confessio Amantis* III, ll. 2056–7, where *lust* clearly means 'desire': *How mihtest thou thin herte finde, / For eny lust of loves drawhte* (*The English Works of John Gower*, ed. G. C. Macaulay, EETS ES 81, 82 (1900–1)).

1262–4 The MS reading is defensible here: 'and her [heart] he carries away so that he hardly dares to breathe [although] he didn't know why.' Kp., however, suggests emending *brethen* to *berthen* and *deryþe* to *der ys* to translate these lines as 'and hers he carries away; that burden is hardly dear to him since he is unaware of it'. Neither renders the AN exactly: *Mes* *countre sel un autre en porte,* / *Dont il gueres ne se comforte,* 'but against that [i.e. the fact that he has left his own heart in hostage] he carries another by which he is scarcely comforted' (ll. 1303–4).

1268 *betwene them burgenyd such a bravnche* The metaphor has a proverbial ring to it, although it is not mentioned in Whiting. In *Chevrefoil,* Marie de France uses a similar metaphor to describe Tristram and Iseut: *D'euls deus fu il tut autresi* / *Cume del chevrefoil esteit* / *Ki a la codre se preneit . . . . Mes, ki puis les volt deseuer,* / *Li codres muert hastivement* / *E li chevrefoil ensement* (ll. 68–76): 'the two of them were like the honeysuckle which clings to the hazel . . . but if anyone should then want to separate them, the hazel will quickly die, and the honeysuckle likewise' (*Les Lais de Marie de France,* ed. Jeanne Lods (Paris, 1959)).

1288 I.e. 'For no reason that I can tell [you]'. K. prefers to emend *I* to *you* (although this context would require *þou*).

1302 *a pryce* Kp. observes in a note to a different line (l. 2413) that this is probably the phrase *of pryce,* with *o* (here represented by *a*) appearing for *of* (on which see note to l. 557).

1319–30 S&J observe of this stanza that 'the repeated rhymes . . . suggest corruption rather than an authorial lapse', and that while *fynde* could be *fynne* (cf. ON *finna*), this still leaves a change of tail-rhyme in the second half of the stanza 'against the common practice of the text'. The corruption seems to lie in ll. 1322–4, where the tail-rhyme breaks down and we have two formulaic phrases side by side. The second of these, with its offending rhyme-word, may represent a scribal substitution for an original line that ran something like *Alone now must I wynde,* or perhaps *Wyth me ye may not wynde,* but there is no way to reconstruct it reliably. The passage as a whole corresponds to AN ll. 1361–74.

1362 *chalenge* None of the ME senses of the word *chalenge* seem to fit here and K. is almost certainly right in thinking that some version of AN *eschange* was intended, as in the otherwise almost identical AN l. 1422, *Ja mes n'avrez de ly eschange.* Unfortunately the AN word is itself unclear—while it appears to mean something like 'dealings [with someone]', Holden worries in his note to this line that this sense does not seem to be attested otherwise. As an alternative, he suggests a translation of 'you will never find an adequate replacement'. Kp. is bothered by the lack of a second negative particle and suggests *no chaunge* for the ME.

1411 *Vnto* (MS *And to*) MS *And* may have been imported from the following line. K. emends to *And spake to that damysell,* retaining the inelegant duplication of *And.*

1418 *i-wis* K. emends to *nought wers* to preserve the rhyme with *rehersse,* but admits this is something of a long shot.

1439–40 *va-* (MS *valett*) In the AN, the Fere's attempts to say 'valet' come out like this: *'Ja est,' fet el, 'le estrange va.'* / *En pece aprés si li dist: 'Ha!'*— she explains that she sighed in the middle, then—*'Prenez cel mot ke vus ai dit,* / *Si l'acreisez un petitet,* / *Od ce ke dis metez un let'*: ' "It is," she said, "the strange va-"; a little after then she said "Ha!" . . . "Take the word that I told you and enlarge it a little, put a 'let' with what I said." ' (ll. 1499–1500, 1508–10). The ME as it stands in the MS has the second part intact, indicating that the translator must have been following his source more carefully and deftly than is apparent from the extant version. A tidier reconstruction of l. 1440 is *But syghynge brake the word in twa* (elsewhere in this text *tow* is rhymed with words that could, and clearly sometimes did, rhyme on *a*). The motif of the heroine stuttering the hero's name was popularised by Lavinia's stutter in the OF *Roman d'Eneas* l. 8553 ff.; this was the inspiration for the slightly farcical scene penned by Hue and reproduced here. A stuttering heroine also appears in the OF romances of *Partenopeus* l. 7277 ff, and *Yder* l. 2697.

1442 *that . . . that* The clumsy repetition of *that* is clearly a copying error. K. emends this by altering the second *that* to *a*, but since there are other options (e.g. *the . . . that*), the MS reading has been left to stand here.

1445 *thereto* This line translates almost exactly the AN l. 1510; *'Od ce ke dis metez un let',* 'to that which I said add a "let" '.

1455 Imayne appears to guess correctly the name the Fere is trying to pronounce twice, here and again at l. 1471. The AN indicates, however, that it was probably a scribe rather than Imayne who delivered the punch-line too early. Imayne's original speech must have corresponded almost exactly to the AN, which reads: *Imeine dit: 'Ne sai cument;* / *Va fut vostre cumencement,* / *Apres le va deïstes ha,* / *Le let ovec s'ajustera;* / *Vahalet ad nun, est issi?',* 'Imeine said, "I don't know how; you started with 'va', after the 'va' you said 'ha', the 'let' is added to it—he's called Vahalet, is that it?" ' (ll. 1513–17). The original ME line was probably something like *Then certes it was 'Vahalet'*.

1459 *brynde* (MS *brede*) Cf. a variation on this phrase at l. 1792: *Here hertte for bale wold brenne* (where *brenne* rhymes with *synne, inne, kynne*).

1482 K. notes that *I toke* should probably be emended to *He toke* in line with the AN l. 1532, *Cil trop bien l'entendi e sout,* 'he knew and understood too well', which immediately follows the line translated exactly by ME l. 1481. The English translator has rearranged this whole passage however, and he may have been referring to her distress in recalling her own words now that she understands their full import—a freer rendering of the sentiments contained in the rest of the AN passage: *'Uncor donc ne voil pas saveir* / *K'amur me poüst commoveir,* / *Ore en ai jeo tot le nualz* / *E il s'en* *veit heitez e bauz'*, 'then I still didn't want to know that love could disturb me; now I have the worst of it and he departs hearty and happy' (ll. 1533–6).

1483 *grede* The MS line reads *That made me wayle efte sythe*: this edition adopts K.'s rearrangement and the use of *grede*, but retains MS *efte sythe*, 'again'.

1523 The *lady* here is apparently not Imayne but the Fere, who comforts herself with this resolution—see AN l. 1559, *La Fere auketes se cunforte*, 'The Fere comforted herself somewhat'.

1531 *thryngge* (MS *throngge*) MS *throngge* is a pa.t. form while the original *thryngge* (rhymes *kynge, syghyng, lokynge*) can only be present. Scribal alteration of a present tense to past shows up elsewhere in rhyme-position (eg. l. 1603) and suggests that the poet may have used the historic present much more than is now apparent.

1536 I.e. 'She did not need to boast of her lot.'

1551 *chastenyng* The *MED* does not list this form; it should perhaps be *chasteyng*.

1556–64 These lines remain unclear, and the following translation is a suggestion: 'whoever loves shall take pleasure in winning worship, God save me, and this [i.e. either love or the worship thus won] may be most useful, for often pride in love makes men strive for great honours and to stand their ground in battle; let them be no longer inadequate, but be made knights at once, and put yourself to work'. This translation assumes that *badde* at l. 1562 is the adj., employed in the *MED*'s sense 3. Some support for this interpretation is offered by ll. 1583–4, *Yf he before was neuer not worthe, / Fro tyme he louys, he puttys hymselffe forthe*. The rhyming of short and long *a* (*made*) occurs elsewhere—see 'Language of the Text, Part I : Rhyming Practice'. S&J instead translate *badde* as 'delayed' from the pp. of OE *bīdan*: this makes good sense of the line, but no forms with *-a-* are attested for the pp. of this word or for 'abide'. They also emend *you* at both l. 1564 and l. 1566 to *them*. K. translates this whole section slightly differently as: 'Whoever loves should be happy about this, so as to win honour—so God be merciful to me—and thus love can be very useful, because the pride of the lover [so translated] often prompts men to achieve high honour and to go into battle; it [love] no longer lets them be insignificant, but it demands that they instantly be made knights'.

1573 *That* This must refer to the Fere, although the line has evidently suffered the addition of another metrical stress in transmission, and *that* should perhaps simply be deleted.

1577 *I* (MS *A*) Neither the *MED* nor the *OED* provides examples of *A* for 'I'.

1585 *waxys* (MS *puttys*) MS *puttys* may have been copied from the preceding line. The verb *wax* is the one most commonly used in this text to mean 'to grow, become'.

1594 *tythande* (MS *tydynge*) Although the usual policy of this edition is not to emend purely for rhyme, *tythande*, 'news', has a different root to *tydynge* (ON *tiðendi* as opposed to lOE *tīdung*).

1603 *stande* (MS *stoode*) See note to l. 1531 on the scribal alteration of present tense forms to past.

1610 None of the survivng AN MSS puts the messenger's travels as 'three days' short of a year. Holden's MS A has *vint jurz*; MS B has *owyt jurz* ('eight'—it is possible that the English originally read VIII and the V got lost), and MS D has *dis jurz*.

1617 *for God that is but one* This looks to be a general asseveration of the same order as *Be God that all hathe wroughte*. It reappears at ll. 1241, 2262 and 6092, and the MS reading of *Be that þat is but one* at l. 1916 is probably an error for it as well.

1623–4 Evidently a proverbial expression, though Whiting does not list it, and translated directly from the AN ll. 1671–2, *Asez dit veir li saive autur / Ke aprés un doil venent plusur*, 'wise authors say, truthfully enough, that after one sorrow come many more'.

1652–63 The tail-rhyme of this whole stanza has been spoilt and is virtually impossible to reconstruct. K. suggests *welle* : *ymelle* : *(to witte) welle* : *melle*. This is, however, so far from the MS reading that it has not been included in the present text. l. 1657 seems to be corrupt not only because of its missing third stress, but also in that the AN reads *Nel seit nul hom fors vus e mei*, 'no one knows it except yourself and I' (l. 1705); rhyme aside, the MS reading makes sense and translates the AN adequately, without offering any clue as to how its rhyme might be repaired.

1692 ff. On this author's treatment of knighting ceremonies, see 'The Translator and his Source: The Remodelling Process'.

1718–23 'One would be doing great wrong to one who served a long time if at the end he should lose [the benefits of] his long service; he might think, I suppose, that he was too quick to enter into it.'

1728–9 'But took his leave of king and noble lady in bower, and rode forth.'

1732 *stowre* (MS *stronge*) The phrase *styffe and stowre* occurs again at l. 2957.

1757–65 While apparently following the AN very closely here, the emphasis has been shifted. The English poet retains Hue's avowal of the constancy of Ipomadon's love, *sis quer ja ne partira, / Pur nullui amur de la Fiere, / Tant par l'aime de grant maniere*, 'his heart will never abandon its love for the Fere, he loves her so much' (ll. 1794–6), but omits the more pragmatic addition: *Il out grant dreit, ke ele eime lui*, 'well he might, since she loves him' (l. 1797). He translates the neatly-phrased *Mult par s'entramerent andui, / Chescun pur autre meint dol out / E nul d'eus d'autre rien ne sout*, 'they loved each other greatly; each suffered much pain for the other, and neither of them knew about the other one' (AN ll. 1798–1800; ME ll. 1760–2), but he then inserts his own affirmation of the Fere's unwavering loyalty to Ipomadon (ll. 1763–5). See 'The Translator and his Source : The Remodelling Process' for further comment on this kind of re-working.

1766 Although this large intitial in the MS falls in the middle of a stanza, it does mark a clear break in the narrative and moreover corresponds to a section-capital in the AN manuscripts.

1768 ff. The rhyme indicates that three lines are missing after this, though nothing significant seems to have been lost. The AN has an equally speedy change of subject with *Or repeirum a la matire / Dunc vus me oïstes devant dire; / De Calabre reparlerums, / De la Fiere e de ses baruns,* 'Now let us turn to the matter that you heard me speak of before; let us speak again of Calabria, of the Fiere and of her barons' (ll. 1801–4).

1769–70 'It happened, two years after (the) feast after which Ipomadon left . . .'. The *MED* lists 'occasion for eating, feast' as a possible meaning for *sete* (derived from OE *sǽte* 'seat'), and also of course for *fete*, should the scribe have mistaken an *f* for an *s*. Since Ipomadon did leave immediately after events at a feast, this reading seems tenable, though inserting *the* before *sete* would make it clearer. K.'s emendation here is to *Tow yere felt yt, that after sete*—'To her that remained behind, it felt two years since the strange valet had left; the lady lived quietly' (he takes *sete* as a verb with the sense of 'remain'): this reading strains the syntax severely. Kp. suggests *Tow yere fell yt after yete*: this does not make undue demands on the syntax, but there is no obvious reason why a scribe might have substituted *yete* for *sete*. Regarding the awkward-sounding line *That went was þat straunge valet* (where K. suggests emending the first *that* to *away*), the *OED* observes that it used to be possible to use *that* conjunctively, '(like Fr. *que*) as a substitute instead of repeating a previous conjunction': in this case the previous conjunction is *after*. Mustanoja (p. 191) also records a similar, 'markedly adverbial character' for *that* in such temporal expressions as *þat com þe ilke dæi . . . þat þe king dæd læi* (Layamon's *Brut*, l. 5110, MS Cott. Calig. A IX). As it happens, this would allow the ME to translate exactly the AN *Ke Ipomedon s'en ert turnés* (l. 1806), except that rhyme has necessitated substituting *þat straunge valet* for his name.

1779 *mayneteyme* The *MED* lists variants of 'maintain' with -*me* as possible errors. However, the facts that the 'error' occurs in more than one text, and that this is the only spelling in this text (it reoccurs at ll. 2089 and 8776), suggest rather that the spelling with -*me* was a valid ME variant.

1782 *lordys* Kp. feels that it would be odd for the lords to speak of 'our lords', and would emend this to *londys*, citing the later l. 2092, *On ilke syde her londys ar stroyed*, and the AN *Kar trop i perdent leidement / De lur terres e* *de lur gent,* 'For they are losing, cruelly, far too much of their lands and people' (ll. 1823–4). While this is a plausible emendation, the MS reading (which K. also retains, without comment) also makes sense, and the fact that the English poet has put this section into direct speech means that the correspondence with the AN is inexact in any case.

1808–10 See 'The Translator and His Source: Evidence for the Translator's Exemplar' (point 3) for the varying numbers of days' respite granted in the AN versions. None of the periods mentioned seem to correspond to any recorded medieval law or proverb.

1824 A single line is missing here, though evidently nothing vital for the narrative.

1846–8 'And if they want to have any kind of conclusion, they will have to send messengers to King Malengere.' Three lines are missing after this.

1849† The emendation of MS *svn* to *svm*, suggested by Kp., is supported by the frequency of the rhymes *some* / *come* in this poem; Kp. would emend the line further to *Of the wordyste of the barons svm*—'some of the worthiest of the barons'. This makes good sense of this line, but reconstruction of the section ll. 1848–50 as a whole is impossible: three lines have been lost, probably between ll. 1848–49, and this section does not appear in the AN Ismeine's speech. Given the comparative ease with which the sense of l. 1849 can be understood to follow on from l. 1848 and, conversely, the fact that it seems to be the rhyme-pair of l. 1850, it is possible that the ll. 1849 and 1850 were the first and last lines respectively of two different couplets that rhymed on *-ome*, but whose identical rhyme-sounds (and perhaps actual words) caused the scribe's eye to skip from one to the other (see 'Language of the Text, Part I: Rhyming Practice').

1866 'We wish to know your will.' Cf. the similar construction at l. 327, *Fayne wold I wette where were.*

1869–71 'You know as well [as I do] that I hold all my lands far and near of King Melangere'.

1875 'And whereupon imprison me'. K. instead reads *where* here and at l. 1949 and l. 1997 as the noun 'war'. For the unusual spelling *where*, not recorded in the *OED*, he refers the reader to an occurrence in l. 7937 of the *Gest Historiale of the Destruction of Troy* (eds. G. A. Panton & D. Donaldson, EETS os 39 & 56, (1968)), but the editors of this latter text emend MS *where* to *were* (pa.t. pl. 'were'), as the context clearly requires. A different interpretation of this word is as the N. and Scottish word *were* (*OED were* sb.³), which carried the senses 'danger; distress, confusion, doubt' and could be spelt *where*. However, this word seems to refer mainly to a state of mind or the most general sense of 'danger', and it usually occurs in phrases with *in/out of, with/without*. A third possibility is that *vpon,* following *wer(r)e*, 'war', misled a copyist into writing the adverb *wher-evpon*. Militating against this however is the occurrence at l. 1997, where further emendation is needed in order to read MS *where vpon* as 'war upon', while the adverb 'whereupon' makes sense as it is. In all three cases, good sense can be made of the lines with the adverb 'whereupon', so there is little need to postulate either a copying error or an otherwise unattested spelling of 'war'. In the case of l. 1875, the barons' concern in the AN is more that they will forfeit their lands than that there will be outright war, eg. ll. 2081–3, *Trop avreient vers lui mesfait, / Se feïssent senz lui tel pleit, / Tost serreient desheritez*, 'they would be doing him too great a wrong if they were to conduct this business without him, they would soon be disinherited'.

1878 *Be þe leeffe on the lynde* A formulaic phrase, perhaps chosen solely to fill out the rhyme (*lynde* could simply mean 'tree' in ME), but it is possible the poet was thinking of such phrases as *as light as lef on linde*, 'as light as linden leaves in the breeze', to convey the readiness with which the Fere is claiming she will obey the king.

1891 *awncyente layes* 'ancient laws' The line is a translation of AN *Mut sout des ancïenes lais* (l. 1966). Holden observes that the scribes of MSS A and B misunderstood *lais* as 'songs' since they wrote the masc. *ancïens*, corresponding to masc.pl. *lais* 'songs', rather than *ancïenes*, corresponding to fem.pl. *lais* 'laws', even though the feminine adjective is needed to complete the syllable-count. *Layes* is a legitimate ME form of 'law', but the since the spelling remains unaltered here despite the facts that it is *law-* elsewhere in the text (ll. 935, 1809, 7939), and since this text's copyists have normally been quite willing to spoil the rhyme in favour of a more familiar word, it is possible that the ME scribe also misinterpreted this word.

1894–6 'We may think it poorly-arranged in every way that we are under such obligation at this time to our lady with her pride'. This is almost identical to AN ll. 1970–3: *Mut nus poum irer / Ke nostre dame par orgoil / Nus deit mener a tel tribuil, / El nus ad trop en sa iustise*, 'we may well be angry that our lady leads us into such distress—she has us too much in her power'.

1906 A line is missing either before or after this. Amphion's threat in the AN is that she must either take a lord, *U mun servise e mei perdra*, 'or lose me and my service' (l. 1982).

1916 *By [God] that is but one* (MS *By that þat ys but onee*) For other examples of this formulaic phrase see note to l. 1617.

1929 *nedyste . . . maste* (MS *nedyste . . . mvste*) This looks at first glance like 'needs must', but the rhyme with *chaste* indicates that it must be the N. form *maste*, 'most' (elsewhere rhymed with *waste* l. 2574, *haste* l. 8506) and used in the sense of 'continually': 'I am amazed, Sir Amfyon, as I be saved from pain, that you must interfere continually' (ll. 1927–9).

1933 *old (MS wold)* The *w-* of MS *wold* could illustrate the development of a glide before initial *o-* (see 'Language of the Text, Part I, 20(b)), but as Kp. points out, it is more likely to be a copying error inspired by the *wold* directly above it.

1938–40 'You are of noble lineage, and hold great estates on behalf of the Fere'. Kp. points out that the curious MS form *foys* must be *feys*, a direct translation of the AN *fius*, 'fiefs' of l. 2003, *De li tenez tant riche fius* (Holden's MS D reads *hernez* here, discounting it as a possible exemplar.) K. suggests that *foys* is an error for *foyson*, 'large number', but this is because he has read AN *fius*, 'fiefs', as *fins* and so missed the connection. It is possible, however, that a later helpful scribe had *foyson* in mind when he wrote *foys*.

1944 *eerle* (MS *Eerke*) The MS form is an example of the occasional confusion between the scribe's very similar forms for the letters *l* and *k*— thus MS *erke* for *erle* at l. 1802, and MS *lyng* for *kyng* at l. 3109. The emendation to *eerle* rather than *clerke* (as K. emends) is supported by the AN: *Li barun unt bien entendu / Ke ço q'il dist grant reisun fu*, 'the barons well understood that what he said was very sensible' (ll. 2077–8).

1949 'And in consequence disinherit us', translating *reysse* as 'remove' (see *MED reisen*, sense 7); cf. AN *li reis li eüst toleit / Terre e alez par forfaiture*, 'the king would take away her land and you would be penalised' (ll. 2070–1). On *wherevpon*, see note to l. 1875.

1971–3 'Until then was there never in field such hard battle as I felt under shield, neither by day nor by night!' The emendation of MS *þou* to *þere* at l. 1971 allows one to read these lines as if Dryas is mimicking the boasts of Amfyon, which is precisely what he does in the AN: *A, Deus! quel jeo fui a cel tens, / Cum ere pruz e de grant sens, / Cum ere de grant hardement, / Cum vencqui cel turneement!* 'Lord, such a one I was at that time, how noble and wise I was, how valiant, how I triumphed at the tournament!'. He concludes drily, *Cum purrunt les jofnes saveir / Se il* [boastful old men] *mentent u se il dient veir?*: 'how are young men to know if they lie or if they speak truth?' (ll. 2055–60). Kp. and K. differ with each other and with the present reading of these lines: both believe that the speaker is Dryas throughout, but Kp. suggests emending MS *sete* to *sene*, while K. believes the lines have been irreparably corrupted and leaves the MS reading as is, suggesting in a note that the original might have been something like, *Ne was þou neuer yete in feld / So hardeliche bestad vnder shelde*.

1997 K. emends this instead to *Where vpon the[m] broughte*, reading *where* as 'war' and with the king as the subject. On *where* as 'war' see note to l. 1875.

2000 Evidently three lines are missing from this stanza. The narrative sequence in the AN is that the barons agree the king may well disinherit them if they act without consulting him (cf. ME ll. 1992–6); they decide to send the three messengers Dryas, Amfyon and Madon (AN *Eurimedun*), the worthiest men they could find (here the ME stanza breaks off); they explain to the Fere what they have decided; she agrees to it, and we rejoin the ME narration as the messengers leave (AN ll. 2093–6, ME l. 2001). The AN l. 2095, *El graante ceo qe fait unt*, 'she agrees with what they have done', may have suggested *wroughte* as the tail-rhyme for the third missing line. K. instead locates the missing lines after l. 1997, for which he has a different reading (see above).

2005 *who* A later ME variant of of 'how' (K. emends it to *why*).

2019 *rekkys* (MS *rekkyd*) This is clearly the same expression as l. 6249 *rekkes he nere*, l. 8792 *I reke nere*, and l. 1379 *sche ne rovghte*, meaning 'to not care at all': the apparent weak pa.t. form *rekkyd* probably stems from a misreading of a narrative present form.

2020 The sense of this rather convoluted sentence as it is punctuated it here is 'she cares only to trap him with a ruse'. K. uses different punctuation and emends MS *movȝte* to *scho thovȝte*: this makes sense of the line, but there is no obvious reason for the presumed error *movȝte*. Another possibility is that *come mouȝte* is the result of a mistranscription of *com ouȝte*.

2021 This single line replaces an eleven-line section in the AN in which Hue jokes about the wiles of women before observing smugly that those who think to trick others are often tricked themselves, *de ren si suvent cum d'amur*, 'by nothing so much as love' (AN ll. 2139–50).

2055–66 These innocuous lines of praise for the Fere's beauty replace a much longer and very different description in the Anglo-Norman (ll. 2214–70): see 'The Translator and his Source: The Remodelling Process'.

2079 *To witte* (MS om.) For the sentence that runs from ll. 2076–81 to make sense grammatically, either *place* at l. 2078 must be read as an infinitive, or a new infinitive must be added. According to the *MED*, the verb *place* was used only in the sense of locating or placing physical things, and not in the more figurative sense of 'to learn', as would be required here. ME *plese* 'to please' also has a variant *place*, but none of its senses fit the context here and in any case it rhymes elsewhere on -*e*- (l. 3243–4 *dyssesse* : *please*).

2084 *Trewe in herte he was* (MS . . . *ye is*) While emendation to *he was* turns this statement into apparently undeserved praise for Amfyon, it is, as K. says, indisputably correct: ll. 2082–4 here follow AN ll. 2323–4; *Mut ert rednables e parlers, / En piez salli trestut premers*, 'he was eloquent and a great talker, he jumped to his feet first' . Andersen retains the MS reading and incorporates the line into Amfyon's speech, but this jars somewhat with the querulousness of the rest of the speech, and also forces the tail-rhyme words *face*, *place* and *was* to rhyme on -*e*- (for pr.3.sg. *es*) when they otherwise do not in this text.

2091 *benoyed* While there do not appear to be any other ME examples of *benoyed* (the *MED* lists it but cites only this occurrence), *noyed(e)* occurs at l. 3684 and l. 6117, so the poet may simply have filled out the rhythm of the line by adding the common prefix *be*-. K. reads the MS as *beuoyed*, finds no other examples of either this or *benoyed*, and suggests (with reservations) emending to *anoyed*, while Kp. suggests the more drastic emendation *has ben noyed*.

2104–5, 2109–14 The first two lines as they stand can be interpreted as: 'I am not appallingly disloyal to my lady [as is Amfyon]'. The English word *eratyke*, 'heretic', is a literal translation of the AN *herite* used by Drias, but in the latter text it clearly carried the sense 'homosexual': *Ja ne verrez un sul herite, / Ki en ses garçons se delite . . .*, 'you will never see a single "heretic" who delights in his boys . . . [ever honour a woman]' (ll. 2367–8); Holden glosses it directly as such. That the term *herite* was used to imply homosexuality is evident from its use in these lines from *Li Romans de Witasse Le Moine*: *Wistasces dist, (N'est pas herites, / Ne fout-en-cul, ne sodomites) . . .*, 'Wistasce said, (he was not a heretic, nor a screw-arse, nor a sodomite) . . .': *Li Romans de Witasse le Moine*, ed. Denis Joseph Conlon (Chapel Hill, 1972). The ME, however, clearly does not intend this sense of the word: Dryas's initial protest that he is *no eratyke* is clarified at ll. 2109–14 when he elaborates that 'heretics' are to be despised for their desire to mingle with low-born women—*wyth lassis to loure*—rather than with the noble ladies whose company a Christian gentleman is presumed to prefer (though it is not impossible that *lassis* is a scribe's coy substitution for *laddis*).

2138 *messe* (MS *mercye*) The phrase *so haue I mede of messe/masse* appears again at ll. 3479 and 7458, and with the variation *so haue I nede* [possibly an error for *mede*] *of masse* at l. 1544. (K. emends to *bless* in order to retain the sense of MS *mercye*.)

2152 *ta* (MS *too*) Context requires *ta*, the N. shortened form of 'take'. That the original text had both *ta* and *take* as the infinitive form is shown by the rhymes *goo* : *take* at ll. 235–6 (i.e. *ga* : *ta*, as here), and *sake* (n.) : *take* at ll. 1941–2.

2233 *Love your makys, ser, not so hote* 'do not love your [intended] mistresses so ardently' (MS *Love ser your makys ser not so hote*) This interpretation, one of many possibilities, is suggested by the AN scene in which she snaps that she will never marry him because he presses too hard and is of too little valour: *Kar n'estes pas de tel valur / E pur neent tant me* *hastez, / Jo quit qe ja n'i partirez,* 'because you are not of such valour, and you press me so hard for no reason that I think you will never leave off.' (ll. 2534–6). Other possible emendations are as follows. K. tries *Your love, syr, makes not so hate,* which he translates as 'there is nothing so warming in your love'. Emending the line to *Love, ser, makys [you] not so hote* and translating *make hote* as 'attack, affect severely' (*MED hot* adj. sense 3d) gives the senses, 'you are unassailed by love, sir [unlike me]' or 'love, sir, does not affect you much'. A final possibility is *Love, ser, you makys not so hote*; 'Love, sir, does not make you command thus', i.e. 'you do not push this matter out of love for me' (assuming *hote* is from OE *hātan*).

2253 The preceding line is missing. The corresponding AN couplet is, *Mes se il vus veneit a talent / De assembler un turneiement,* 'but if it would please you to arrange a tournament' (ll. 2549–50), and the English clearly had something similar, whether it borrowed the rhyme with *talent,* e.g. *Yf it be to your talent,* 'if it is to your liking' (the rhyme *talent / turnament* is used at ll. 2827–8), or had something like K.'s suggestion of *And, if ye will perto assent.*

2264 *in-soughte* K. is unhappy with *in* and emends the whole line to *All men [þ]o the kyng [be]soughte.* There is, however, no obvious source for the 'error' of MS *in,* and it has here been treated as a prefix to the following *soughte.* The *MED* observes of the prefix *in-* that, 'perhaps because of its frequent occurrence in L & OF borrowings in which the original sense of the prefix had been forgotten, *in-* is often a semantically empty addition to OE or ON roots (esp. verbs) used for translating foreign words in *in-*.' While there is no foreign word with *in-* to be translated here, the poet may have had in mind such verbs as *injoin,* and he is certainly prone to adding prefixes in order to fill out the metre, such as the varying use of *vowe/avowe, noyed/benoyed* (see note to l. 2091).

2262 *Be God þat is but one* On this formulaic phrase see note to l. 1617.

2267 *her* (MS *your*) As K. observes, it is just too much of a jump to have this line spoken directly to the Fere by the king, as called for by the MS reading, rather than as a continuation of the knights' speech to the king.

2292 *white and clene* 'completely' Cf. l. 7412 with the more common spelling of *quyte and clene.*

2315 *mvste me chese* The MS reading is defensible here in that he might mean he must now decide whether to go back and fight or not. It is also possible, as K. notes, that *me* is an error for *she.*

2330–2† Kp.'s emendation, adopted here, assumes that MS *For* at l. 2332 was mistakenly copied from either l. 2333 or l. 2335. The emendation to *No* allows the reading: 'if I should strive to show myself, I would find no love with her unless I were held worthy of deeds' (*fonde* is taken as the subj. for

'find'). K.'s more awkward emendation to these lines was to reverse *Gyf* and
But and to read *fonde* as 'test' from OE *fandian*, thus: 'but I should hasten to
excel: if I should be thought brave for my deeds, I would strive for her love'.
In the relevant AN passage, the emphasis is not so much on how
Ipomedon's prowess and fame affect the Fiere's regard for him as on his
reputation alone: he says that if he were certain she would marry none other,
he would not hurry to her but would wait until he had accumulated *tant los e
pris, / Ke l'um entende par resun / Pur tut si jo sui pruz u nun*, 'such fame and
honour that people will know, fairly and once and for all, whether I am
valiant or not' (ll. 2614–6).

2334 *laynand* (MS *lovers*) This emendation is a modified version of K.'s *wel
leynand*: the MS has only one spelling of *leyn-/layn-* with *-e-* against
numerous examples with *-a-*.

2335 ff. *prefe* (MS *presse*) Cf. l. 13, and especially l. 2584, where *preysse*
appears for what the rhymes indicate must be *preve*: both words mean
'praise'. In this case, the copyist may also have been misled by *presse* at
l. 2330. Regarding the proverb, Whiting lists several that are similar (B484),
and the image appears twice in Chaucer's *Troilus and Criseyde*: *The yerde is
bet that bowen wole and wynde / Than that that brest* (I, ll. 257–8), and, *And
reed that boweth down for every blast, / Ful lightly, cesse wynd, it wol aryse* (II,
ll. 1387–8). For a comparison of love itself to a branch sprung up between
the lovers see note to l. 1268.

2345 The omission of *no* brings the ME text closer to the AN: *Cil ki mut
parole sovent / Ne se pot astenir neent / Ke aukune feiz folur ne die*, 'he who
speaks constantly cannot be sure that he never speaks nonsense' (ll. 2627–9).
S&J instead emend *fele* ('many') to *few*.

2347–8 These two lines are reversed in the MS.

2348 ff. Perhaps, 'I will go into the battle to win my love without delay,
Master, so quickly, to such degrees of excellence, that it may show I am
most worthy to be master of that creature indeed'.

2379 *reiall* (MS *revill*) The MS reading looks like a garbled version of AN
real, 'royal'. Hawks were occasionally referred to as *real foul(e)*—see *MED
real* adj. sense 1(e)—and in this case they also, of course, belong to a king's
son.

2393 *lest* (MS *best*) It would be odd if the steed Ipomadon used only on the
first day of the tournament were the best of the three, and indeed the
narrator later describes the black steed as *the whyghttys of hem all* (l. 2411).
The emended *lest* translates AN *De treis esteit cestui le meindre*, 'this one was
the least of the three' (l. 3654).

2401 *ycore* (MS *fayre*) K. supplies this word, meaning 'excellent', to fit the
rhymes on *-ore* but wishes there were other examples: Ka. obligingly

supplies one with l. 146 of *Richard Coeur de Lion*: *With a coron off gold icorn* (see *Metrical Romances of the thirteenth, fourteenth and fifteenth centuries: published from ancient manuscripts*, ed. H. Weber, 3 vols., Edinburgh (1810): vol. II).

2406 sterres (MS *sonnes*) This emendation follows AN *reflambeantes cum esteilles*, 'shining like stars' (l. 2678).

2413 *a mykyll make* 'of great stature' It is assumed here that *a* stands for 'of'. For *make* in the sense of 'build, stature', cf. these lines from Gower's *Confessio Amantis*: *Anon he let tuo cofres make / Of o semblance, and of o make* (V, 2295–6, in *The English Works of John Gower*, ed. G. C. Macaulay, EETS ES 81, 82 (1900–1)). K. emends here to *a mykylls make*, though he worries that he cannot find any examples of similar usage.

2462 *clothe of Ynde* This refers to cloth dyed indigo blue. The *MED* cites *inde* as a form of the colour-name 'indigo', and l. 232 of *Sir Launval* describes *kerteles* of *Inde sandel*, confirming the use of *Inde* as the name of a colour.

2466 'No king ever wore better'.

2491 *in dismaye* (MS *this mayde*) The context seems to call for *dismaye*: the MS reading may be the result of a perceived equivalence for one copyist of initial *d* and *th*—see also l. 2982, MS *dether* for *thether*. K. emends half-way to *dismayde*, which does not rhyme, and also suggests *in deray*.

2496 *alone* (MS *and*) K.'s emendation, adopted here, follows AN ll. 2779–80: *Sul sout venir, sul sout aler / E sul sout ses armes porter*, 'he normally comes and goes alone, and carries his arms by himself'. ll. 2495–7 might be translated: 'he who was bold enough to remain [in the country] would normally ride alone, and lead no retinue'.

2501 Cf. AN ll. 2783–5: *En livre ai truvé e veü / Ke Ipomedon li primers fu / Ki unc od lui herneis mena*, 'I have discovered and seen in a book that Ipomedon was the first ever to carry his gear with him'. Unusually, the ME translator has retained one of Hue's references to his imaginary sources, though he has generalized it by removing the narrator's 'I' and referring to plural *bokys*.

2546 This throw-away line fills out the rhyme, but is also probably inspired by AN l. 2813, where Capaneus's *Oïl, amis* is in response to Ipomedon's question as to whether the king he sees is the famous Meleager.

2555–7 'Truly, I would go with you to him if it were not for this maiden who rides by my side.'

2564 ff. The ME translator was evidently delighted with the rhetorical device of the repeated *so fayre* . . . borrowed from the AN, and he expands the original list of six things *si beaus* . . . to eleven.

2573 *Hit semeth he hath no wordys to waste* This comment does not appear in the otherwise closely-translated AN passage. Ipomadon's virtue of being a man of few words—present in both AN and ME versions—is one that the ME poet is at particular pains to stress.

2574 *covyts* (MS *comys*) Cf. l. 8506, *Speke of that thyng þat he covytte moste.*

2581 K. suggests omitting *you* from this over-long line; Kp. thinks the superfluous stress is supplied by the *younde* of *beyounde* (written as two words in the MS), which he suggests was mistakenly copied from the *younder* that follows it; cf. the repetition *forthe for þe* at l. 2648.

2598 *That me deynes* (MS *that at me deyne*) 'Who is worthy for me (to serve)'. Cf. AN ll. 2867–9, *Sachez ke el mund n'ad rei terrestre / Od qi pur servir vodreie estre / Ffors sul od vus ke jo vei ci*, 'know that there is no king on earth whom I would rather be with to serve except you whom I see here'.

2612 *say* This is almost certainly 'test' from OF *assayer*, as Ka. observes: forms without initial *a-* appear also at ll. 2351, 5286, 6429, and *asayd* is written as two words in the MS at l. 8051. *In littill wayes* may be translated 'in minor ways', i.e. 'through little details'.

2631 *mayster* Not 'master' but 'job', from OF *mestier*.

2648 *forthe* This is probably an accidental repetition of the *for þe* that follows it.

2654–7 In addition to being bad at the names of people and places, one of this text's copyists evidently knew little about gemstones. K. and S&J note that MS *tapet* seems to be a mistake for *crapet* or 'toadstone', a semi-precious stone similar to a toad in colour or shape (some were in fact the fossilized teeth of fish) that was believed to have come from the head of a toad and to have possessed talismanic powers (see *OED, toadstone* n.¹). The MS reading may have been occasioned by confusion with a different symbol of luxury—*tapet*, which the *MED* defines as 'decorative fabric bearing a painted, embroidered or woven pattern'. *Sersolette, emeraud* and *ametas* are 'chrysolite', 'emerald' and 'amethyst' respectively. The spellings *sersolette* and *ametas* are otherwise unattested and do not rhyme: the original author probably wrote *cresolyte : amatite*, a rhyme-pair that also appears in a list of gems in *Meditations on the Life and Passion of Christ* (ed. C. D'Evelyn, EETS os 158 (1921), ll. 2149–50). That MS *claspys* should be *jaspys*, as emended here, is demonstrated by the relevant AN couplet ll. 2927–8, *Mut i out grisophas e jaspes, / De quatre parz out quatre haspes*, 'there were many 'grisophas' and gems, on four sides it had four clasps' ('grisophas' may be chrysoprase, an apple-green variety of chalcedony).

2664 *sloo* K. assumes this was OE *slēan* used in the sense of 'be better than'; S&J dismiss this curtly with 'the sense is not attested, and the idea trivial'. They suggest instead that ME ll. 2663–4 originally reproduced AN ll. 2933–5, *Del cuvercle esteit le pomel / De un mut grant safir cler e bel, / La gent del felun garisseit*; 'the knob of the lid was a huge sapphire, bright and beautiful,

that cured people of illness'. The term *felun* in OF seems to have represented various illnesses (S&J define it as 'ulcers' on the basis of *MED feloun*
n.²); they suggest ingeniously that it might have been spelt *fylun* and
subsequently misread as MS *syluer*.

2696–2703 This description of Ipomadon's attire corresponds to AN
ll. 2964–78. The ME poet has retained some of the details of the AN,
but added or omitted others. He takes the *syrket of palle* from AN *un riche
paile*, but adds fur trim. *Bend abowte wyth orfrayes* is a direct translation of
bendé d'orfreis, but he dispenses with the *coife . . . al chef posee / De bonet a
fin or listee*, 'headpiece placed on the head, a cap trimmed with fine gold',
sported by the AN hero. Both authors describe their hero's *stowte and bold*
face (AN *ample . . . e aukes fier*), but Hue goes on to admire his figure, and
makes a point of praising his manly short hair, so appropriate for a modest
tourneying knight: *E out curte la chevelure, / Asez halt estaucez esteit / Kar
de tresces cure n'aveit, / Mut eime plus a turneer / Ke ses chevous aplanier*, 'he
had his hair short, cropped quite high, because he didn't care about tresses,
he much preferred to tourney than to comb his hair' (ll. 2972–6).

2700 *place* On the rhyming of *a* and *ai* see 'Language of the Text, Part I',
(8). K. emends to *pays* and Ka. to *palays*.

2704 Perhaps, 'there was joy of all delight' (K.). Kp. suggests the line
should read *Ther was Ioye of all, [I] wene*, although this adds an undesirable
fourth stress.

2741 *gon* K. and Kp. note scattered examples in ME of an *-n* suffix for a
subj. sing. verb where rhyme requires it: *Torrent of Portyngale* l. 139, *Sertes,
yf I hym slepyng slone* (: *none*) (ed. E. Adam, EETS ES 51 (1887)); the
fifteenth-century *Guy of Warwick* l. 2392, *I schall wene wyth yow, if mystur
bene* (: *kene*) (*The Romance of Guy of Warwick: the second or fifteenth-century
version*, ed. J. Zupitza, EETS ES 25,26 (1866).

2744 *fette* (MS *sette*) Cf. ll. 3000–1, *The quene to hur mete he fett, / And
seruyd hyr when she was sett*.

2764 'There he swore to God', cf. l. 7731, *He was my brothers, I dare lay*.

2779 *We* (MS *he*) Based on AN ll. 3033–4, where the knights realize *Ke lis
reis en serreit huniz, / Se cist vassaus fust si partiz*, 'that the king would be
shamed if this young man departed thus'. For the sake of the court's honour
they ask the king that Ipomadon be granted his request and allowed to stay
(cf. also Cabanus's speech at ME ll. 2774–6).

2793–4 'And if he had asked [to become] something more to her, I believe
he might have been.'

2798 *wottist it* S&J comment that this form appears to be a mixture of pa.t.
wot and pres. *wyst*; they also note that *is* appears in the same line 'where *was*
would be expected', but the historic present was evidently much used by

this poet. The missing half of the couplet makes it impossible to repair this line, although it looks as though the missing line contained an allusion to Ipomadon's real name or status, cf. AN ll. 3068–70, *Ne sout nuls dunt il ert venu, / Ne ne sout hume del regné / Par quel nun i fut apelé*, 'no one knew anything of where he came from, nor did any man in the kingdom know by what name he was called'.

2812 *regyd* The *MED* only gives the definition 'to put the roof ridge on (a house)' for the verb *riggen* (from OE *hrycg*), but it notes the use of the noun *rigge* in phrases concerning clothing and armour. The *OED*'s first citation of the verb in relation to clothing is from 1534. Since the word appears again at l. 8770 (with the more recognisable spelling *riggud*), there are good grounds for presuming that the putting on of clothing is what was intended. It could also be a later copyist's word, perhaps replacing *rayed*.

2814 'In no way did he join them'.

2816 *grede* K. suggests either emending to *spede*, or reading *grede* as the pa.t. of *greithen*, 'make ready'. However, the only pa.t. form cited by the *OED* for both southern and northern texts is *greithed/graithed*: pp. *greyt, graid* does not fit the context here. *Grede* may instead represent OE *grǣdan* 'cry out': if the rhyme-words were also reversed, as Kp. suggests, the lines could be translated, 'when barons in gay apparel cried out, Ipomadon went to the forest'.

2832–3 This edition follows K. in emending MS *sought* to *fett* and regarding l. 2833 as a probable scribal addition.

2853–4 Lit., 'The first time [for hunting there] was not to begin then, for it was there that his pain began,' i.e. this was not the first time he had hunted in that particular forest. This seems to refer to Ipomadon's previous stay in Calabria, when his obsession with hunting aroused the Fere's anger and led to their painful separation. The AN mentions that Ipomedon knew the forest well, *Kar mut suvent chacé i out*, 'for he had hunted very often there' (l. 3162), but the connection the ME poet draws between this fact and the beginning of all Ipomadon's woes, with its implied criticism of the hero, is absent.

2868 *turnament* (MS *turment*) Cf. AN l. 3196, *Ke li turneiz ert pus demain*, '[you know] that the tournament takes place the day after tomorrow'. Cf. the confusion of *turnament* and *turment* at ll. 2876, 4691, 7432.

2869 *in wede* (MS *to wynde*) This emendation (suggested in K.'s notes) is based on the rhyme and on AN *E vos armes tost aprestez*, 'and take up your arms at once' (l. 3200).

2876 *turnament* (MS *turment*) Cf. AN l. 3207, *Quant cil oï parler de juste*, 'when he heard talk of the joust' (l. 3207), and note to l. 2868.

2886 There is a page missing from the MS after this line. With an average of thirty-three lines per side, the approximate tally of missing lines is very

close to the sixty-four lines, roughly, of AN that are skipped before we pick
up the story again (approximately ll. 3227–92). In the missing section, the
angry and disappointed Capaneus leaves Ipomedon and goes to the king
with the answer he has received. The king is astonished and goes to speak
with Ipomedon himself. Ipomedon once again feigns outrage, threatening to
leave and berating the king for breaking his agreement to allow Ipomedon to
serve the queen. The king reports this to the queen; the court in general
laughs at the hero and calls him *le bel malveis,* though they still find him very
courteous. The queen curses destiny that he should have no apparent
prowess, but still wishes to make him her beloved. With appropriate
dramatic irony, her ladies jeer that he will surely win la Fière with all his
hunting in the forest. The king heads off to Candres and the royal tent is put
up. The ME narrative is rejoined in the middle of a description of a
fabulous bell mounted on top of the silken tent. In the AN, it is a model
eagle cleverly constructed so as to cry out when the wind blows: K. observes
drily that the English poet may have thought this either too complicated or
too improbable.

2889 ff. K. quotes several ME descriptions, strikingly similar to the AN, of
tents topped with golden eagles that frequently have glowing carbuncles as
eyes or in their beaks—see for example *Sir Launval* ll. 268 ff. or *Sir
Ferumbras* ll. 78 ff. It is all the more curious then that the ME translator
should have substituted a bell. (*The English Charlemagne Romances, Part I:
Sir Ferumbras,* ed. S. J. Herrtage, EETS ES 34 (1879); *Sir Launfal* in *Middle
English Romances,* ed. S. H. A. Shepherd (New York & London, 1995)).

2914 The *lady clere* that Monestus hopes to have must the Fere in this
context, but it is odd that in order to do so he should serve at Mellyagere's
court rather than her own. This may be the result of a misunderstanding of
the AN, for a woman is mentioned at this point, but it is not la Fière: Hue
says in a smirking aside; *E si vus dirrai une ren: / De la reïne ert aukes ben,*
'and I'll tell you something: he [Monesteus] was well-favoured by the
queen' (ll. 3337–8). The secret lasciviousness of women is one of Hue's
favourite themes; see 'The Translator and his Source : The Remodelling
Process'.

2924 *skore* K. notes that this word puts too much strain on the line's three
stresses, not to mention the audience's credibility, and is probably scribal.
The fifty-five (or fifty-score and five) knights here correspond to fifty in the
AN (l. 3369)—the extra five is evidently for the convenience of the rhyme.

2933 L a skore Fifty-score knights again seems a little excessive. Either the
poet is getting carried away with the exaggeration for which ME romances
are known, or K. is right in assuming that this is the same error as at l. 2924,
and should read L [and] a skore, giving a total close to the sixty of the AN
(l. 3355).

2941 This second mention of participants from *Irelond* may represent a scribal error for *Icelond,* cf. AN *Islande* (l. 3378).

2952 *anes* 'once' (MS *aves*) This emendation of Ka.'s assumes a scribal misreading of *aues* for the exemplar's *anes.* The son of the King of Spain was flatly rejected earlier as a possible suitor on the grounds that he was a heretic (see l. 2097 ff.). K. emends the line more recklessly to *The lady to have, that hathe hym forsakyn.*

2954 *warkyn* (MS *wakyn*) Cf. l. 1234, *That warkys me all this woo.*

2957–66 Emendation is necessary here if any semblance of a tail-rhyme is to be preserved: K.'s emendations to a rhyme on *-e-* have been encorporated here since all of the spellings he proposes are attested elsewhere in Middle English, but a strong case can also be made for a rhyme on *-ou-.* The case for the present emendations is as follows: *Stere* has the same meaning as MS *stowre*; *chambere* is supported by AN *en la chambre a la Fiere / L' out cusu une chambererre,* 'a lady from the Fere's chambers sewed it' (ll. 3415–6); *Calabere* follows the sense of AN ll. 3405–6, *E si quident mut ben cumquere / E la Fiere e tute la terre,* 'and they thought they might well conquer both the Fere and all her land'.

The second possible course of emendation to a rhyme on *-ou-* would give *stowre : bowre : doure : honoure* (with MS *honoure* taking us slightly further away from the sense of the AN lines). The main difficulty with these emendations is the fact that the spelling *doure* for the adv. *dere* is otherwise unattested, whereas the expression *bought full dere* is used—and confirmed by rhyme—several times in this text (eg. ll. 792, 3314, 5549, etc.). However, the *MED* does give *doere* and *dore* as alternative forms for the adv., and *dure, duere* for the adj. There is an example of the adv. spelt *duere* in the WML Harley lyrics: *þat vs so duere bohtes,* l. 18 of lyric 16 (*The Harley Lyrics,* ed. G. L. Brook (Manchester, 1978)), and our author's dialect shares characteristics with the WML dialects (see 'Language of the Text, Part II'). From the above evidence one could postulate the form *doure* (perhaps supported by N. and Scots. adj. *dour* 'hard' from OF *dur*), and indeed the adv. *dere* does appear to rhyme on *-ou-* again at l. 3314.

2958 *Amfyon* As K. observes, this should probably be *Antymore* after AN l. 3413, *Antenor out un penuncel.* Certainly at ME l. 2962 it is the latter knight ('Sir Ottymore') who bears the streamer into tournament. Perhaps the translator intended to make it clear that Antymore obtained the streamer through Amfyon.

2979–80 MS *Semyon* is emended in accordance with AN *Ismenun* (l. 3447), and the occurrence of *Isomyon* at ME l. 3267. MS *the emperours sone* at l. 2980 has likewise been been emended according to both the AN, where Ismenun is the king of Germany himself, and the later ME citation, where *prowde Isomyon off Allmayne* is referred to as an emperor.

2988 *Some . . . wythoute and . . . wythin* It becomes clear later in the text that these terms refer to the two 'teams' into which the tournament participants will be divided, referred to as either *wythoute(n)* and *wythin,* or *the vtter(este) syde* and *the inner syde.* Although the AN does not mention two teams explicitly until part of the way through the first day, they are referred to as *cil dehors* and *cil dedenz* there as well (AN l. 4008 ff.). These terms are also to be found in Chrétien's *Le Conte du Graal: cez de hors* l. 4809; *dedanz* l. 4848; *cil de la* l. 5128; *cil dehors* l. 5129 (*Le Conte du Graal (Perceval),* vols 5–6 of *Les Romans de Chrétien de Troyes,* ed. Félix Lecoy (Paris, 1972)).

2998–9 'He was happy enough with this, for he knew the truth of the matter.' For this sense, and for the emendation in l. 2998 of MS *þey* to *he,* see AN ll. 3471–2, *Mut est escharniz e gabez / E il fet bel semblant asez,* 'he is greatly mocked and teased, and he is cheerful enough'.

3019–20 'Wherever love is drawn, lack [of any desirable qualities] is no hindrance.' See note to l. 702.

3029 *raynedere* That a resident of Apulia, Calabria or Sicily (or even the creation of a resident of England) should *love huntynge at raynedere* is rather surprising, although by now Ipomadon has travelled throughout Europe tourneying, and the reference is not in the AN. The translator may have drawn the idea from a hunting manual such as Gaston de Foix's popular and comprehensive *Livre de Chasse,* where instructions for, and illustrations of, the hunting of reindeer are given.

3046 *foundys* (MS *wendys*) The rhyme *foundes : houndys* also occurs at ll. 3599–3600.

3060 *gert* (MS *gret*) Cf. such lines as ll. 3625–6 *And garte araye hym thare / His stede and hym all in rede.*

3070 *depe* (MS *dede*) See AN *Des l'ermitage out un fossé / Aukettes parfunt e ben lé,* 'from the hermitage there was a ditch, quite deep and very large' (ll. 3557–8).

3072 *couyrd-heddyd* The *MED* gives this expression a separate entry, which it glosses tentatively as '?with covered head', but a simpler explanation is that the ditch was so deep, even the traveller's head would be hidden.

3083 'And often stood by him in the field of battle.' *Stedde* can represent 'field of battle', as the AN l. 3572 indicates it must do here: *Il l'out servi en meinte guerre,* 'he had served him in many battles.'

3096 *He* This refers a single watchman, although the poet had referred to 'watchmen' three lines before. K. notes that this apparent error is the result of poor adaptation of the AN, where at ll. 3576–7, *De corns retentist la cuntree / Des guetes ki cornent le jur,* 'the country resounded with the horns of watchmen who blew [a fanfare for] the day': after this, a single watchman in the tower points out the new white knight to La Fière: *Li guetes ke el dongun esteit . . . A la Fere se escrie en haut*, 'the watchman who was in the tower . . . cried loudly to the Fiere' (ll. 3586–9).

3107–10 This longing for her *straunge valet* is not in AN, where she is merely distressed, *Kar el ne set k'en avendra / Ne ki ert ke a seignur prendra*, 'for she doesn't know what will happen, nor who it is that she will take as [her] lord' (ll. 3607–8).

3109 *kyng* (MS *lyng*) On the occasional confusion of the graphs *k* and *l*, see note to l. 1944.

3131 *blenchyd* 'dodged' (MS *blemesshyd*) The MS reading may be a result of the fact that the spelling *blenchen* is possible variant of the verb *blemishen* (from OF *blesmir*), although not *vice-versa*.

3152 *he sayd* (MS *and sayd*) The emendation makes clear that it is Ipomadon who acts as though he had never seen Jason before. The order of AN ll. 3711–2 has been reversed: *Pus li dit: 'Vadlet, ki est tu?' / Cum se unkes ne l'eüst veü*, 'Then [he] says to him, "Valet, who are you?"', as if he had never seen him before'.

3157 *to* (MS *two*) The preposition is obviously what was intended, and the *OED* does not record *two* as a possible spelling for it.

3192 *fayles* (MS om.) K.'s emendation (though he spells it *failes*) is based on AN l. 3760 *Pruësce i faut, u il est mort*, 'he lacks valour, or he is dead': cf. ll. 363, 6621 for this use of *fayle*. An alternative would be *lakkes*, since both words are equally common in the text.

3206 'He would never need to call a priest again.' This was a popular euphemism for being killed: K. quotes examples from *Beues of Hamtoun* and *Generides*, of which the clearest illustration of meaning is this citation from *Beues*, MO version; *And smote his owne son in the brest, / That he spake neuer wyth clerke no preste* (ll. 2745–6) (*The Romance of Sir Beues of Hamtoun*, ed. E. Kölbing, EETS es 46, 48 & 65 (1885, 1886, 1894)).

3215 'From here till the River Jordan.' Presumably intended to convey the limits of the Christian world: the AN settles more modestly for: *Il n'ad si bon de si k'en Rume*, 'There was none so good from here to Rome' (l. 3825).

3222 'Take him on my authority' or 'with my permission'. The *MED* does not list this particular expression under *might* n., but the meanings 'authority' and 'permission' are well attested.

3227 *gyve* (MS *nym*) The subject of this line is Ipomadon, although a scribe understandably thought Jason (from the previous line) continued to be the subject and substituted *nym*, 'taken', accordingly.

3236 In the AN, this recommendation of Jason's is followed by fourteen lines in which La Fière considers whether or not to give up her *ami* for this splendid new white knight (ll. 3865–78): while the ME Fere is certainly intrigued by the white knight, there is little suggestion that her loyalty to Ipomadon is wavering.

3240 The temple in which Amfyon is buried is an exotic touch not found in the AN: however, at l. 4491 the translator converts the AN's temple of Diana (l. 6077) into a less exotic *churche*.

3246–8 The idea that Amfyon had designs on the Fere appeared earlier at l. 2233 ff., where it was based on the AN, but its reappearance here is only in the ME. It is surprising that he should be described in these glowing terms immediately after we have been told of his opposition to the Fere's wishes, but this pattern too has occurred earlier—see note to l. 2084.

3257 *precys* (MS *specys*) Cf. l. 2078, *They presyd into place.*

3283 Cf. AN ll. 3966–7, *En sun cel heaume l'ad feru / Un coup mut aspre e perillus*, 'On top of the helmet he dealt him a most violent and dangerous blow'.

3300 *skorne* As K. notes, this should probably be *soiorne* after the AN *E vus repoez sujurner, / Beivre clarez e bon vin cler*, 'And you can for your part rest and drink claret and good clear wine' (ll. 4001–2).

3302 Literally, 'you leave evidence of injury': he appears to mean that the emperor leaves behind, in the grisly form of his severed left ear and arm, solid evidence of his defeat by Cabanus.

3304 *cossyn germayn* 'first cousin' (MS *cossyn Elmany*) Based on AN ll. 4047–8, *Pur Ismeun dunt fut mut greins / Kar il fut sis cusins germains*, 'He was furious about Ismeun, because he was his first cousin'. It is conceivable that an earlier scribe understood *germayn* as meaning 'German' (the n.pl. *Germaines* for the Germanic people was known in ME). If this in turn were altered to the more common adj. *almayne*, it might have been the source of MS *Elmany*.

3306–7 *fett : sett* (MS *sett : fett*) Rhyme-pairs are occasionally reversed in this text (e.g. ll. 3108–9), and this offers the most promising solution here. For the sense 'to receive a blow' for *fett* (from OE *(ge)fetian*), the *MED* gives several examples (*fetten*, sense 4a), but all involve a stated direct object, e.g. *The Towneley Plays* 20/392, *Thus am I comen bofettis to fott* (ed. A. C. Cawley and M. Stevens, EETS ss 13,14 (1994)). An even more appropriate sense for the context here is 'attack', which the *MED* lists tentatively as sense 1e, supported by an example from the alliterative *Morte Arthure*: *Fande to fette that freke, and forfette his landez* (l. 557: ed. E. Brock, EETS os 8 (1865)). These lines could be translated either: 'He [the emperor] attacked Cabanus so hard on the helmet that he could hardly remain upright', or 'Cabanus received such a hard [blow] on his helmet that he could hardly remain upright'.

3314 *dere* This looks to be the right word—the expression *bought full dere* is a common one in the text—but the tail-rhymes *emperoure : stoure : succoure* clearly call for a rhyme on *-ou-*. See note to ll. 2957–66 for the distinct, if thus far unprovable, possibility that *doure* existed as a an alternative form of the adv. *dere* in the translator's dialect. K. emends instead to *soure*.

3315 ff. This description of Ipomadon's fight with Dayres is very much watered down from the AN and there is even room for doubt as to whether he has been killed at all (*down he fell as a stone*), whereas the AN version is uncompromisingly direct: Ipomedon puts all his might into the blow to avenge Capaneus and severs Daires's arm at the shoulder, at which *Daires chet mort en mi la pree*, 'Daires falls dead in the middle of the field' (l. 4082). The crowd marvel and say, not the bland statement of the ME that *he was the best / Off knyghtes* (ll. 3339–40), but that they *ne virent tel, / Ne si pesant ne si cruel*, 'never saw one so powerful or harsh' (ll. 4085–6).

3322 *brenniys* (MS *bremmys*) K. offers as support for this emendation *Sir Tristrem* l. 191, *þurch brinies brast þe blod* (ed. E. Kölbing, Heilbronn (1882)), and *Sir Gowther* l. 429, which in the MS Royal 17.B.43 version reads: *Whan blade thorow brenyys brast* (see for example *The Middle English Breton Lays*, eds. Anne Laskaya and Eve Salisbury, Kalamazoo (1995)).

3324–5 *moste : an oste* (MS *a shafte*) The emendation is based on AN ll. 4010–1, *Ke par le cors d'un sul prudume / Est une ost tut aseüree*, 'That an army was saved by one noble man alone'. While the ME does not translate the lengthier AN battle-scenes exactly, the general outline is retained and many individual lines are borrowed: these lines of AN narratorial comment occur in roughly the same position as the ME, just after Capaneus (Cabanus) has bested Ismeun (Isomyon, the 'emperour').

3361 *schosyn* See 'Language of the Text: Part I', (22) on this spelling.

3395 *hight* The rhyme here requires the variant form *het*, although elsewhere *hight* is confirmed by rhyme, eg. at ll. 3147, 4712.

3414–17 The lines as punctuated here may be translated: 'Cursed pride, be ever damned! I may say this of all women, and I believe I shall do again. If he does this [i.e. if Ipomadon really disappears], he does great wrong!'

3435 ff. On the tournament 'teams' *wythoute* and *wythin*, see note to l. 2988.

3439–40 *sett . . . but at a chery stone* A common type of proverb in Middle English: Whiting cites this under C187, 'Not give a cherry-stone'.

3446 *Thre* (MS *The*) While the MS reading would be defensible on its own, the emendation to *thre* is confirmed by l. 3475, *Thre hedys he present her wyth all*. The omission of *r* before or after consonants is one of this scribe's most frequent mistakes.

3475 *present* For the lack of pr.3 sg. suffix, see note to l. 260.

3476 *hathel* (MS *hattred*) K.'s emendation to *hathel*, 'noble', is the best sense that can be made of the MS reading, and it is not dissimilar to the AN l. 4319, *Granz esteient e asez beles*, 'they were large and quite handsome'.

3477 *fone* (MS *foure*) K.'s suggestion of *fone*, 'few', is almost certainly correct here and at l. 3841: the fact that a scribe seems to have substituted non-rhyming *foure* in the first case and *sum* in the second reflects the fact that *fone* is a northern word, and was probably unfamiliar to a southern copyist.

3503 *went neuer* (MS *Ye had gon where þou neuer went*) This reversal of MS *went* and *neuer* does not produce an exact rhyme, but such scribal reversals do occur elsewhere in the text, e.g. ll. 2374, 4205, 5294, 5440, etc.. K. tries to fit the MS reading into the rhyme-scheme by adding *nedur* (presumably 'neither') but is unhappy with the four-stress line thus produced. Kp. notes that the same tail-line rhyme-scheme appears in the stanza at l. 6537 ff., where the fourth rhyme-word is *whedyre*. Based on this, he proposes the more radical emendation of *Haue gon, I wot neuer whedur*.

3507–10 'Madame, since the beginning of the world, [and since] men have been able to tell news, there has never been a fairer tournament by woodland nor field . . .'

3515 Sense can be made of the MS reading, i.e. 'That ever yet could do well' (see *OED* sense 3b. of *wield* v.). Kp., however, finds this explanation too artificial and sees *yet* as a simple mistake for *wit*, cf. l. 2527, *Syn he is witte cowde wyld*. This possibility is strengthened by the fact that the original clearly could spell 'yet' with *i*: it has the rhyme-pairs *witte* (ll. 386, 5622, 6041, 7134, 8783), *yte*, *hitte* 'it' (ll. 4132, 8783), and *flytte* (l. 8783). The line carries the same general sense either way.

3516 *lee* 'meadow' (MS *feld*) MS *feld* may have been copied under the influence of *weld* and *behylde* on either side. K. instead emends *see* at l. 3518 to *behelde*, although he is unhappy with the fact that the resultant stanza repeats both *feld* and *behelde/behylde* in its rhymes.

3537 K. tries to make a case for interpreting *slayn* here as merely 'beaten' to account for the fact that Dayres resurfaces, alive and apparently well, at l. 5663 (see note to this line, and to l. 3315 ff. for his death), but the ME translator is simply reproducing an anomaly in his source.

3541 *bone* (MS *borne*) K. emends here to *done*, but the simpler emendation is *bone*, 'headed for'. See note to l. 635 on this form and the author's willingness to rhyme words normally spelt *-oun* with those normally spelt *-on*.

3543 ff. From this point, about thirty lines of the AN are missing (l. 4390 ff.); i.e. one or possibly two ME stanzas as well as the missing lines from this and the following extant stanza. Thoas describes how the white knight tourneyed magnificently all day to everyone's fascination; the queen asks if this is all true and if he knows the white knight's identity, to which Thoas replies that no one knows, although the king has sought him far and wide and La Fière is especially anxious to find her potential husband. At this point Ipomedon interrupts him by changing the subject, and we rejoin the ME narrative.

3547 K. adds *went* to the end of this line to rhyme with *spent* in l. 3546, but there is no guarantee that these two lines belonged to the same couplet in this badly damaged stanza.

3555 ff. The ME translator has decided to make Ipomadon's game more obvious by giving each day's most successful hound the same colour as Ipomadon's tournament armour. The AN's *Baucan le velu*—'Baucan the hairy'—becomes *the white*, and *Ridel* at AN l. 5474 becomes *Rydell . . . my red hounde* (ME ll. 4243–4). On the third day, however, the hound in the AN is described as black (l. 6513 *men brachet neir Baailemunt*) when Ipomedon innocently remarks on the coincidence that his black hound was most successful at the hunt just as the black knight was victorious at the tournament. The disingenuous comparison is not in the ME, where Ipomadon merely describes the most successful hound as usual (ll. 4831–2), but the AN Ipomedon's sly hint as to his activities presumably provided the inspiration for the less subtle colour-coded hounds of the ME.

3570 *Toke leve* (MS *To he lowe*) The phrase 'take leave', which Ka. proposes as an emendation here, has occurred ten times already in the text, and is a conceivable source for the nonsensical MS *to he lowe*. K. emends to *he gas*.

3623–4 *abyde* n. : *ryde* This should probably be *abode : rode*, although it is just possible that pa.t. *ryde* illustrates rare levelling of the pl. vowel to the sg. form. Cf. *rode : (a)bode* ll. 3276, 6218, 6671, 8193, etc..

3638 ff. ll. 3638–40 can be translated, 'He performs as a worthy knight indeed—the reason he went there then was to help'. After this, the narrator explains that Ipomadon wants to be on the side 'without' because they had suffered under his strokes the day before and were discouraged, and also because he wants to be able to fight the king, who is on the side 'within'. This is the reverse of the AN, where Ipomedon was with *cil dehors* the first day (l. 4008 ff.) and *cil dedenz* the second (l. 4538).

3648 *nold* (MS *wold*) Sense demands this emendation, since Ipomadon has chosen to fight with those *mythoute* (l. 3642), while the king is fighting with those *on the inner syde* (l. 3647). The whereabouts of the king is not a consideration for the AN Ipomedon, who merely feels sorry for the defeated side of the previous day and determines to join them to ensure that *ert li turneiz par equal*, 'the contest was even' (l. 4541).

3685 *enchosone* (MS *echosone*) While the MS form might represent a variant derived from OF *acheson*, the spelling elsewhere in this text is *encheson* or *chesone*. Also, in the surviving MSS of the AN text, the form used is always *ench-* except once in Holden's MS D, which has in any case been ruled out as a possible exemplar for our ME translator.

3686–7† These two lines have been corrupted beyond all hope of emendation. While it may seem amusingly apt that 'wise men' should say something incomprehensible and swear by a non-existent saint, it was clearly not part of the original text. Kp. proposes *Lukas* as the original saint. St. Silas or St. Nicholas might be slightly closer to the nonsensical MS *Sykasbas*. St. Silas, or Silvanus, was a companion of St. Paul: D. H. Farmer notes in the *Oxford Dictionary of Saints* (Oxford, 1978) that he may be identified with the scribe of 1 Peter 5:12.

3690 *chyde* (MS *chastyst*) In support of this emendation, cf. the appearance of this verb elsewhere in the text at ll. 560, 1016, 6629.

3692 *as God wolde pere* The verb *pere* is usually used with *with* or *to*, but as K. observes, it is easy enough to make the jump to *as* if a comparative preposition is called for. Mustanoja writes that, 'in some instances . . . *to* is virtually equivalent to *as*' (p. 410). ll. 3692–4 can be translated: 'because he wanted to be the equal of God, Lucifer fell from heaven to hell for his pride'.

3697–3700 'And now I suffer adversity, to my very great dishonour; now the one whom I have intended to love forsakes me.'

3736 *glade* (MS *brest*) Apart from rhyme, some support for this emendation may be found at ll. 7824–6, *Thorowe all there harnes be pere syde / Euyne bothe her sperys dyd glyde / And brake that sure was fest*, where the verb appears in the same context, if not with precisely the same meaning.

3747 *noble speres* (MS *a noble spere*) Cf. AN l. 4691, *Amis, lances avez asez*, 'friend, you have lances enough'.

3754 *venture* 'braggart' There are no ME (or modern) examples of this noun referring to a person, though the scribe responsible seems to have imagined someone who engaged in *(a)ventures*. The curious occurrence here must stem from AN *Si est un vanteür de dames*, 'he is a braggart regarding ladies' (l. 4697), where an original anglicized version of AN *vanteür* was awkwardly replaced by a scribe to whom it was presumably unfamiliar.

3764–6 'And say a braggart-knight comes to make amends at her will for having trespassed so'. See note to l. 3754 on the process by which *a ventures knyghte* was was arrived at from the original AN *vanteür*, 'braggart'. K.'s suggestion, adopted here, of *wendes* for MS *sendes* brings the passage into line with AN ll. 4701–3, *Amis, se cist est vanteür / Or l'en menez en cele tur / A la Fiere, e a li se rende*, 'friend, if this one is a braggart, lead him now to the tower of the Fiere, and let him give himself up to her'. Ki. would instead leave *sendes* and take *ventures* as a mistake for *aventurous*, which he assumes must refer to Ipomadon. However, this loses the connection with l. 3754's *venture*, which clearly referred to Manastus.

3826 *querte* (MS *grace*) Cf. occurrences of this word at ll. 1159, 4594, 7912.

3828 *metys wyth* (MS *metys was*) K. corrects this by simply omitting the nonsensical *was*, but given the metrical desirability of the extra syllable, it seems more likely that a scribe idly registered a word beginning with *w*, and wrote the wrong one.

3830 ff. The translator has altered Cabanus's motivation for attacking Dryas. Here, it is simply because he is on the opposing team (see l. 3830), but in the AN there is a hint of political power-struggles beyond the tournament when Dryas is described as *uns des baruns de la terre . . . Li plus forcibles del païs, / Despus d'Amfion fut oscis*, 'one of the barons of the land . . . the most powerful in the country since Amfion was killed', and the owner of several strong castles (ll. 4849–54): these qualities are what make him a worthy opponent against whom Capaneus may redeem his own reputation.

3832 Kp. translates the expression *wyth clene love* as 'with great joy'. It is an odd expression, with no counterpart in the AN, but the line can be translated fairly unproblematically as, 'with great joy he made himself ready [to attack]'. K. emends MS *gert* to *gret*, which he translates as 'attacked', but as Kp. points out, it is the MS reading that actually rhymes correctly.

3836 The MS has two independent lines following this one which are not part of this or any neighbouring stanza. K. omits them as here; Andersen retains them and fights to make sense of the resultant fourteen-line stanza. The stray lines in question, *Away ward ledys hym þus / The whiles was Ipomadon* are in fact an exact copy, down to the abbreviations used, of ll. 3784–5 at the foot of f. 252^r.

3841 *fone* (MS *sum*) While the translator does occasionally rely on *n/m* assonance—see 'Language of the Text, Part I: Rhyming Practice'—this emendation is supported by a more obvious instance of the Northern word *fone* being replaced with something presumably more familiar at l. 3477 (see note to this line).

3844 *This day vnder sonne* This line is K.'s creation: in the MS, *vnder sonne* is written at the end of the obviously overstretched l. 3843, and the stanza is lacking its final tail-rhyme line. Detaching the superfluous *vnder sonne* to create the tail-rhyme line seems to be the best solution, although the resultant phrase is not used elsewhere in the text.

3854–5 'No one apart from my love and Cabanus did half so much as this'. There is a crucial difference between this statement and that in the AN, where she says the exact opposite: *Mis amis ne Capaneüs, / Vers cestui ne pot valer nuls*—'Neither my love nor Capaneus is worth a thing next to this one' (ll. 4815–6). Since the difference in the ME is made by the single word *but*, one has to wonder whether it is original, especially given her previous statement *Yesturday, so haue I blis, / Off dede was not a poynte to this* (ll. 3851–2). On the other hand, her private resolution in the AN to take the red knight if her love should fail to appear is ignored by the translator, as is her indecisiveness—she observes to Imayne that *if* it did not involve giving up her love, it would be no shame to take this knight (cf. AN ll. 4804–6, *Se del tut fail a mun ami / Cest chevaler vermail prendrai /, Ja n'ert avant mis en delai*, 'if I fail entirely to get my love, I will take this red knight, there will be no delay').

3866 Cananeus is another sarcastic steward in the tradition of Sir Kay of the Arthurian romances. It is tempting to speculate that the similarity between the names was not accidental. The usual spellings in the AN MSS are Kaenneus, Caemius, Caeninus (the name of one of Jason's companions in the quest for the golden fleece as described in Hyginus—see Holden's note to l. 5017). Since the secondary characters' names seem otherwise to have been chosen at random from various Greek legends, the similarity between this and the Arthurian steward's name may have been intentional: see 'The Translator and his Source: The Anglo-Norman Source'.

3872–4 I.e. 'However worthy anyone was known to be, he would have spoken scornfully of him.' Based loosely on AN ll. 5025–9, *Cele teche aveit cist en sei, / Ke el mund non out si nuble rei, / Si bon vassal en nul empire, / Dunt ja li oïssez bien dire; / De mesdire fut custumers*, 'he had such in his character, that there was not in the world so noble a king nor so noble a knight in any realm of whom you might hear him speak well: to mock was customary [for him]'.

3889 *fet* (MS *feter*) MS *feter*, with the *-er* written as an abbreviation, is clearly a mistake: it is difficult to imagine what Egyon might have been doing with fetters while leading a horse away. (The AN l. 5084 differs slightly here with *Ben set u deit estre menez*, 'he knew well where it should be taken').

3892 *Lyard* is used as a name here, but it is taken from AN l. 5098 where *liarz* is merely the colour of his horse: *sis destrers fut un veirs liarz*, 'his charger was a true dapple-grey'. *Lyard* also appears as a horse's name in *Richard Coeur de Lion* l. 2319 ff.: *Two stedes found the kyng Richard, / That one hight Favel, that other Lyarde* (in *Metrical Romances of the thirteenth, fourteenth and fifteenth centuries: published from ancient manuscripts*, ed. H. Weber, 3 vols., Edinburgh (1810): vol. II).

3893 *wood* (MS *woo*) Cf. l. 1956, *Amphyon waxyd nye wood for wrothe*.

3897 'That he made the spearhead go through [the shield]'.

3899 *lyfi* (MS *lyght*) On the *gh*-spelling for / *f* /, see 'Language of the Text: Part I', (26b).

3908 Cf. AN 5151–4, *Par le costé le fers glaça / Nepurquant la char entama, / Plaie li fist, mes ne fut mie / Trop grant, n'ad dute de sa vie*, 'the steel slid past his side, nevertheless it nicked the flesh; it wounded him, but not very much—there was no danger to his life'.

3911 *Lyard* (MS *hard*) The horse was christened *Lyard* at l. 3892 (see note). The rhymes indicate that a line has been lost before this, though none of the AN narrative is missing.

3912 *sheld* 'child' See 'Language of the Text: Part I', (22) on the spelling *sh-*. The line translates AN l. 5160, *A sun vadlet l'at tost bailli*, 'he quickly handed it to his valet'.

3922–4 These lines, only weakly related to the narrative at hand, seem to be a filler: Dryas (or perhaps a new character, since the MS gives the name as *Deras*) is not mentioned in the AN, where the description of the tournament instead closes with the rescue of the king.

3924 *relyed* (MS *releuyd*) Rhyme indicates that the translator must have written *rely(e)d* in direct translation of AN l. 5106, *E ceus dedenz a sei ralie*, 'and he calls those "within" to his aid', but a later scribe has substituted the semantically similar *releuyd* both here and at l. 4391, where it rhymes with *cryed*. The *MED* records an identical substitution in a version of *Piers Plowman B*, Ps. 20, l. 148: *Thus relyed* [vr. *relyued*] *lyf for a litel fortune And pryked forth with pryde*.

3931 *wyth grett honoure* K. points out that this may be an error for *wyth grett doloure*, a phrase that occurs again at l. 5918 and is also rhymed with *dyscomfetture*. On the other hand it is possible that the poet meant to describe King Mellyagere's side as experiencing an honourable defeat.

3933 *toke þer pavelyons* Cf. AN l. 5173, *Tuit se sunt a lur trefs retrait*, 'everyone retreated to their tents'. Rhyme indicates that the pl. *pavelyons* must have been without suffix in the original, as is occasionally the case with the plurals in this text (see 'Language of the Text, Part I : Nouns' (a)). The expression 'to take one's tent' is listed in the *MED* under sense 50b of *taken*.

3940 The emendation of *be* to *se* and *lewte* to *launce* brings this into line with AN l. 5179, *Amis Jasun, veez ci la lance*, 'Jason, friend, see here the lance'.

3977 A line is missing after this: judging by Jason's response, it might have been an entreaty to 'weep not'.

3991–2 'He is from the land of Fairy—in faith I do believe so!'

4004 K. emends to *thre* based on l. 4031, where Ipomadon presents the queen with *herttys hedis thre*, but is is possible that he killed several deer, three of which he then presented to the queen.

4028 *grette plente* This phrase here means 'very much'; it appears again with this meaning at ll. 4201 and 4847 (though at l. 4878 it has the expected meaning of 'very many').

4044 *put to respyte* The *MED* and the *OED* both list only *put in respyte*. However, Mustanoja notes that *to* could be used 'to indicate position in the sense "at, in"' (p. 409), a sense that would make the MS reading a conceivable variant of *put in respyte*.

4047–8 Cf. AN 5327–8, *Certes, dame, jo ne purreie, / Trop a recreant me tendreie*, 'Indeed madam I could not—I would think myself too much of a coward'.

4050–1 The adverb *non*, 'not', did exist independently in ME, but its presence here is a result of the exact translation of AN 5331–2, *Li quel ke vus chacés u nun, / A fin recreant vus tenum*, 'whether or not you hunt, we think you a true coward!'

4073 *to the Fer holde* Translated here as 'into the Fere's keeping' since the genitive is occasionally found without suffix in this text (see 'Language of the Text, Part I : Nouns' (b)), but it is also possible that *holde* is the adv. 'loyally' from OE *holde*. The AN reads simply *a la Fiere l'enveia*, '[he] sent him to the Fiere' (l. 5373).

4075, 4078 *Dreseus, Dryas* (MS *Dreus, Dares*) MS *Dreus* at l. 4075 looks at first glance to mean Dryas, who was indeed rescued by Ipomadon that day, but the rhyme with *Cabanus* indicates that it should read *Dreseus*, the Earl of Flanders, who was also rescued at l. 3797 ff. After this, Ipomadon rescued Dryas (l. 3836 ff.), and this is who must be meant by MS *Dares* at l. 4078, since Dayres was in fact slain by Ipomadon on the first day (l. 3318, though this does not prevent him from reappearing later on—see note to l. 5663).

4076 'Or else his [Dreseus's] distress would have been acute.' On the spelling *hellys* for 'else', see 'Language of the Text, Part I', (27).

4122–3 The emendations here are a combination of K.'s version, which left MS *strokys ille* at l. 4123 and emended l. 4122 to *folys at will*, and the AN, which at l. 5464 reads: *Ki tut de gré suffrent teus coups*—'who quite willingly suffered such blows'.

4143–4 On the significant colours of Ipomadon's hounds see note to l. 3555.

4164 'And kissed her gently.' Cf. AN l. 5512, *Si la besa de bon' estraine*, 'and kissed her faithfully'.

4189 *for Goddis love* Numerous examples of this phrase support K's addition of *love* here, e.g. ll. 1413, 1509, 2365, 2547, etc.

4201–2 'Who could well interpret a great deal from the stars.' On *grett plente* bearing the sense of 'a great deal', see note to l. 4028.

4214 In medieval astrology, *termes* refer to the divisions of the zodiac which define periods of heightened influence of particular planets (see Chaucer's *Franklin's Tale*, l. 1288 and notes). Anferas has evidently miscalculated them, with unfortunate consequences for the duke.

4221 'The third day, he got up quickly'. In the AN, it is either the seventh (Holden's MS A) or the second day (MSS B and D) when he and his men *Mut unt tost lur punt mis a terre*, 'quickly put their ramp [for disembarking] on the land' (l. 5601).

4238 'He paid for that then, I say!'

4245 *for mannys dede* K. emends to *for Crystys dede*, but there are no strong grounds for rejecting the oath as it stands—'for man's death'.

4263 A missing line before or after l. 4263 makes the narrative lurch awkwardly here, but the knight in red is the newly-arrived Greek duke, and the black knight he attacks is Ipomadon.

4272 Cf. AN ll. 5659–60, *Vers le neir est si pres venuz,/ Ja se entreferent es escuz*, 'so he came close to the black [knight]—soon they fought together with shields'. K. inserts *nyes*, but verbs of action may be omitted where they are implied by context—cf. l. 4377.

4278–82 Cf. AN ll. 5623–6, *Devant le jur un petitet / Out adubbé sun bon vadlet, / Jason, ki esteit sis cusins, / E od lui bien trente meschins*, 'a little before the day, she dubbed her worthy valet Jason, who was her cousin, and with him fully thirty young men'. See 'The Translator and his Source: The Remodelling Process' for the English translator's treatment of knighting ceremonies.

4284–5 'Serve our [knight] with spears as Jason did the other two days forthwith'. The pronoun *oure* could be used as an absolute in ME.

4337–54 Corresponds closely to AN ll. 5774–88 except that in the AN, Ipomedon refers to *sun dru vermail*, 'her darling in red', so he is not necessarily confessing knowledge of La Fière's secret attachment, as he seems to be doing here—he is merely promising to remove all traces of yesterday's champion, whom everyone could reasonably assume she would favour.

4343 *her* (MS *his*) K. takes this emendation from AN l. 5781, *Ne l'avra pas en sa prisun*, 'she will not have him in her prison', where la Fière is the subject.

4359–60 'It is no surprising thing that makes me waste away miserably.'

4370–1 'So intensely she cried and grieved that she is on the point of death.'

4373–5 'If my lover is thus lost, no man shall ever have me as far as I can help it!'

4377 'Ipomadon went into the thickest crowd': the verb is implied by the context.

4385 *for stoneyde* 'stunned' K. omits *for*, but Mustanoja discusses the later ME use of *for* 'with certain semi-substantivised adjectives', e.g. *for feynt, for feble* (pp.381–2). Whether *for* represents a causal preposition (i.e. 'as a result of being—') or the intensifying prefix *for-* (as in l. 633 *for-ron*), the construction is well-attested.

4391 *relyed* (MS *releuyd*) See note to l. 3924.

4411 *grym* (MS *wyʒte*) *Grym(me)* occurs also at ll. 1624, 5826 and 8323, while MS *wyʒte* was probably copied from l. 4416.

4413 *mekill* (MS *littill*) Ipomadon surely meant to praise rather than insult Jason in this speech: K. emends by adding *not* after *thou artte*, but this adds an undesirable fourth stress to the line, while the alliterating phrase *mekill of myghte* occurs elsewhere at ll. 4111 and 6963.

4433–4 The translator has misunderstood, or at least altered, his source here. In the AN it is only Cavder, Dryas's brother, who is knighted by the Irish king, and the only comment Hue makes about both of them is, *Pres de un eage erent andui*, 'they were about the same age' (AN l. 6000).

4435 *vnder stel* (MS *vnder shild*) Cf. l. 4563, *Cabanus was stallworthe vnder stele*, where the rhyme-pair is also *well*.

4436 *The stought* (MS *He thought*) The MS reading on its own might have been emended to *he thought [the] kyng louyd hym wele*, introducing an element of doubt, but in the AN the king's affection is clearly genuine: *Cist reis l'out durement amé*, 'this king loved him greatly' (l. 6001).

4439 *he* I.e. Dryas's brother, Cavder.

4443 *out* K. emends to *out of*, but ME *out* carried the sense 'out of' by itself.

4454 ff. Two lines are missing after this: K. suggests *Doun he fell on the lande* for one of them, which would translate AN l. 6032, *Candor trebucha el sablun*, 'Candor fell on the sandy ground', almost exactly.

4488 *lepe vp* K. emends to *lepe vpon*, but to 'leap up' a horse evidently meant to mount it—cf. *Arthour and Merlin* l. 2891–2, *His hors he lepe vp anon; / To the turnay he com son* (ed. E. Kölbing, Leipzig (1890)).

4512 *in parte* 'somewhat' The MS reading as it stands differs from the AN *La reïne forment amout*, 'he loved the queen deeply' (l. 6093) and it is possible that it should read *in gret parte*—'greatly'. K. emends to *in faythe, parde* in order to satisfy the rhyme, but this is unnecessary since *parte* could retain the accented final *e* of its source, OF *partie*.

4514 *he hym chese* (MS *he chese*) Cf. the identical l. 5718; 'he betook himself to Ipomadon'.

4523 *drawen* The rhyme with *agayne* indicates that the original had the variant pp. form *drayne* (the MS and rhyme forms are derived from OE *dragen* and *drægen* respectively).

4541 'A black knight, madam—that much I know.' This is similar to AN ll. 6141–2, *E il li dist ke il ne saveit, / Mes uns neirs chevalers esteit*, 'and he told him that he did not know, but it was a black knight'.

4581–2 'He thought he would be recognised before he left that place.'

4636 *felows* (MS *felews*) Neither the *MED* nor the *OED* records a spelling with *-ew* for this word, ON-derived lOE *feolaʒa*.

4645 ff. Two lines are missing after this, the sense of which must have been similar to AN ll. 6306–9, *La Fiere saluez, amis, / Dites lui, puis ke la conui / Tuz jurz fui sons e erc e sui / E a tut dis la servirai*, 'greet the Fiere, friend: tell her that since I have known her, I have been, am, and always will be hers, and I will serve her forever'. The mysterious *gyfte* referred to at ME l. 4646 is not in the AN, but the shortness of this line suggests corruption.

4649–50 'All of this may you do, you who spoke to me when I was white, red and black.'

4675 *who has grevyd thee* (MS *who haue gevyd thee man*) K. emends similarly to *who may haue grevyd thee*.

4679–84 It is not always obvious who is speaking in this section. The punctuation here differs from K.'s, whose version is:

> *'Why, cosyn, the knyght in blake?'* (the Fere)
> *'He makyth me all þis mornynge make!'* (Jason)
> *'Why wyste thou, what he be,*
> *He, that will brynge me to my dede?'*
> *'The same, that juste in whyte & rede,*
> *To day in blake was hee!'*

K. evidently felt that it was more appropriate for the Fere to call Ipomadon *he that will brynge me to my dede* (as indeed she does elsewhere), but in this context, Jason's great display of grief (weeping, wringing of hands) makes such a statement seem appropriate.

4688 *in fey* (MS *merey*) This emendation is as speculative as any of those proposed by K. or Kp. Its two virtues are the facts that it has a tenuous link to the MS reading (*in* could have been misread as *m*), and the phrase *in faye* occurs three times elsewhere in the text, each time in rhyme-position (ll. 2362, 5175, 8133), while its more common variant *in feythe/faythe* occurs a total of sixty-one times. Other emendations that have been suggested are as follows: K. emends to *to day*, which S&J accept in the absence of any better alternatives; in his notes K. also offers *I preye* and *to paye*, 'with pleasure'; Kp. more adventurously offers *to my derey*, glossing it as 'to my great distress' and pointing out that a scribe has confused *me* and *my* elsewhere (ll. 710, 2605, 4868). This is an attractive solution initially, since *desrei* is frequent in the AN, but against it, *derey* does not occur elsewhere in the ME text or even in the AN passage corresponding to these lines, and it does not really fit the sense of the passage, since she is evidently welcoming death.

4691 *tvrmente* (MS *ternvmente*) See note to l. 2868 on the occasional scribal confusion of these two words.

4694–5 She is now addressing herself again. This proverb, 'he that will not when he may, may not when he will' (listed in Whiting as W275), replaces the similar AN statment at ll. 6362–3, *Il me amout quant jo ne voleie, / Or revoil jo e il ne volt*, 'he loved me when I didn't want him; now I want [him] and he doesn't want [me]'.

4696 *no fores* 'It doesn't matter' She seems to be expressing the hopelessness of her plight.

4698 *bewte* (MS *bewtenes*) The *MED* does not record any instance of *bewtenes*.

4703–5 'They are rich in their prosperity that may have their love when they will; however, he will never return!'

4723–31 The tail-rhyme words *pere : sore : were : more* were probably intended to rhyme on /a/. For the missing line after l. 4724, K. offers a very plausible *Often tymes he changed his blee*, which various similar lines seem to support, e.g. l. 5702, *That chaungyd all his ble*; l. 6285, *Ladyes chaungyd pere chere*; l. 5118, *she chaungyd colovres*.

4734 *queyre* (MS *queyrted*) The MS reading looks to be an error for *queyre* [OF *quirreie*]—in this case the parts of the deer fed to the hounds as their reward after the hunt. Traditionally, the hunters would blow their horns as the hounds were fed. (On the rewarding of the hounds, see note to l. 663.)

4740 'She did not hold back on account of any lack [in him]'. The sentiment is the same as the proverbial statement at ll. 3019–20, *Whedur that euer love will drawe, / Lake no lettyng mase* (listed as L508 in Whiting).

4755 The policy of this edition is not to emend on purely metrical grounds (see 'Editorial Policy'), but either *Off any*, or *pat euer was*, must be a scribal addition.

4773, 4779 The original must have had the variants *bonne/boune* and *fonne* in these lines.

4774 *A rede* (MS *Mede*) See AN l. 6452, *Uns vermeilz i fut veirement*, 'there was a red one indeed'.

4786 *whas* While this is a valid ME spelling, it more likely represents a simple duplication of *wh-* from the preceding *Who*.

4831–2 On Ipomadon's colour-coded hounds see note to l. 3555.

4837 *well good wonne* (MS *well good onne*) 'a very great quantity' The phrase reappears at l. 7679.

4846 *on sylke* 'of silk' See Mustanoja, pp. 350–1 and pp. 400–1 on the ME interchangeability of *of* and *on*: l. 567 in this text contains an example of the opposite substitution.

4848 *grene* (MS *gore*) Unhealthily pale skin was often decribed as 'green' (as it still is)—cf. Chaucer's *Book of the Duchess* l. 497 ff.: *Hys hewe chaunge and wexe grene / And pale, for ther noo blod ys sene / In no maner lym of hys.*

4868 The sense is clearly intended to be similar to AN l. 6557, *Mis chevaus cesta e chaï*—'my horse stumbled and fell' (throwing his rider onto the sharp tree-trunk). A literal translation of the ME might be 'my horse gave me a cruel injury and a violent fall'. K. emends *stovde* to *store*, 'harsh', without comment, but *stovde* is an attested form of 'stout', and the scribe clearly wanted the latter word, since he had corrected the *v* from an original *n*.

4879 The addition of *he* is perhaps not necessary here since it was acceptable in ME to omit subject-pronouns where they could be easily inferred from context—see Mustanoja, p. 1388 ff.. It has been inserted here for the sake of clarity.

4939 *stedes* (MS *stede*) We know he has his three tourneying steeds with him from ll. 4915–6, and the AN reads: *Ces treis chevaus ke veez ci, / . . . Ces treis jurs les oi al turnei,* 'these three horses that you see here . . . I got from the tournament these three days' (ll. 6626, 6629).

4945–6 'I do not care to boast about this—alas that they ever spoke about me!'

4987 I.e. nothing is too good for her.

4990–5 'You shall give this black steed to Cabanus—and I pray you report my message thus, that [he] did not fall out of any faint-heartedness; and say that by my faith I know of no knight under the heaven so high on whom he [the steed] might be better bestowed.' This translation assumes that *that* at l. 4992 is a conj. and the subject is understood (see note to l. 4879 on omitted subject-pronouns), but it is also possible to read *that* as a rel. pron., i.e. 'give this steed to Cabanus, who did not fall out of any faint-heartedness'.

5002 ff. The bottom right corner of the MS folio has been torn away, affecting ll. 5002–4 and ll. 5024–33. The emendations are K.'s (although at l. 5004 he has *wel clere*) and are based on the similar ll. 5070–73. The page has deteriorated since K. viewed it a century ago, and letters that were evidently visible to him are lost now, e.g. at l. 5027 K reads . . . *well wot*; the MS as it stands now reads . . . *wot*. K.'s emendations are followed throughout except at l. 5029, where *well* is added to K.'s *Grete* (spelt here as *grette*) by analogy with ll. 3548, 4645, 4653 etc..

5018 *bowntes* (MS *bewntenes*) Although the *MED* glosses *bewntenes* as 'goodness, worthiness', this occurrence is the only citation, while the *OED* lists only *bountines, bountenes* with just two citations (dated 1512 and 1650), and adds the cautionary note that 'the standing of the word is insecure: the first instance may be *bouteues;* the second may be an error of the press' (the second citation, from Hanmer's *Ecclesiastical History* 176, is spelt *bountifulnes* in another edition of the text). A possible emendation would be to a variant of *bounteousness*, for which the *OED* has citations from the fifteenth century, although this spoils the rhythm. The present emendation to *bowntes*, 'virtues', is K.'s suggestion.

5024 ff. See note to l. 5002 ff..

5025–7 Cf. AN l. 6681, *A Capaneus refut cist*, 'this one was Capaneus's'; l. 6683 *Tuz sevent ke pas nes emblai, / Mil virent u jos gaaignai*, 'everyone knew that I didn't steal them, a thousand saw where I won'.

5028 Only *here novght says* remains of this line in the MS now, but K. was able to read *he there novght says*. His restoration of this line, including the emendation of the non-rhyming *says* to *gas*, is based on l. 5074, *Wythouten stede may I not goo.*

5030 Cf. l. 5094 and ll. 5194–5.

5039 ff. Cf. AN ll. 6650–2, *De femme aveir ne dei haster; / Le jomble ki trop ço desirent, / Se un en amende, mil empirent*, 'I should not hurry to take a wife: of those young men who desire [marriage] too much, if one benefits from it, a thousand grow worse'.

5043 A variation of the proverb 'marry in haste; repent at leisure', cf. Whiting, M357, R67.

5052 *Candres* (MS *Callabre*) The two speakers are already in Calabria, while those to whom the steeds are to be presented are in Canders. See also AN l. 6653–5, *Le matin vus estot aler . . . A Candres*, 'in the morning you should go . . . to Canders'.

5053 The *MED* records the form *meke* ('make') as a possible error; the *OED* lists it in brackets as a sixteenth-century Scottish variant. Since this text is the result of copyings throughout the fifteenth-century, and through several different dialects, this may be a valid scribal form. There is, however, nothing in the rhymes to indicate such a pronunciation of ME /a:/ in the dialect of composition.

5090 *thyng* (MS *kyng*) This emendation is based on AN l. 6716, *La ren del mund ke il plus ama*, 'the thing in the world that he most loved'.

5092 ff. 'There are but few knights now who had done so much . . . that they would have abandoned such great glory.'

5098–5100 In the corresponding AN l. 6713 ff., no rationalisation of Ipomedon's behaviour is offered: it is presented rather as an extreme example of the extraordinary things that lovers do, and is followed by the dry observation, *mil en sunt ore issi perduz, / E par amer musarz tenuz,* 'thousands are now thus lost, and made fools for love' (ll. 6723–4).

5107 *Fere* (MS *fayre*) For the occasional scribal error of *fayre* for *Fere* see note to l. 99. The AN reads *Li barun sunt la tuz venuz, / Li reis, la reïne e la Fiere, / Ki la nut out fet male chiere,* 'the barons had all come there, the king, the queen and the Fiere, who had been unhappy that night' (ll. 6734–36).

5134–35 'He was not the man he made himself out to be; I believe you experienced how he conducted himself before on these three days!' K.'s emendations, adopted here, allow l. 5134 to translate the AN l. 6763: *Ne fust quel ke il se fist,* 'he was not what he made himself seem'.

5139 'And said, "Lord, was that him?"' *Wheyþer* [OE *hweþer*] could be used as a simple sign of interrogation—see the *OED* sense II *conj.*2 of *whether,* which notes that it was often followed by a subjunctive verb, as it is in the nearly identical l. 5224. K. based the addition of *þat* on this latter line, and noted that *And sayd* should perhaps be omitted to give the line an appropriate length.

5141 *went his weyes* (MS *weye*) The usual expression would be *went his weye*—the plural noun here may be in imitation of the analogous *his gatys goone* (e.g. l. 5304). K. leaves MS *weye* and emends l. 5140 to *gan saye.*

5142 *Cananeus* (MS *Cabanus*) We know that it should be Cananeus's horse from ll. 5065–6 and from the AN ll. 6765–6, *Partiz se sest, n'i volt estre plus, / Sur le destrer Caemius,* 'thus he departed—he did not want to remain any longer—on Caemius's [Cananeus's] charger'. The same mistake occurs at l. 8229.

5143 ff. 'He heartily besought you to testify with him that he did not steal him [the steed], but won him with valorous deeds.'

5160 *vnder this bough* The requirements of the rhyme seem to have inspired this unusual phrase, for which no parallels have been found. Whatever image the translator had in mind, it is evidently intended as a metaphor for the world, and is patterned on such common phrases as *vnder heyven* and *vnder the mone.*

5184 *sowe* 'grieve' (MS *swe*) Cf. l. 7715, *The sorer shalt thou sowe,* where it has the intransitive sense 'suffer'. For this rather rare word, cf. l. 286 of *The Parlement of the Thre Ages,* where the Yorkshire-based Thornton copy has *than sowed myn hert,* but the more southerly Ware version has *sighed* (ed. M. Y. Offord, EETS 246 (1959)). The origin of the word is uncertain, but J. J.

Anderson notes that it was established in Scottish, N and NW writings in Middle English: see his note to l. 391 of *Patience* ((Manchester, 1977), p. 65).

5185–6 It is easy to see how a scribe might have written *borne* for an exemplar's *lorne*, given the similarity of cursive *b* and *l* and the proximity of another *borne*. K. emends further to *we . . . have him lorne*, assuming *lorne* is 'lost'. It can also mean 'forsaken', allowing these lines to be translated 'if we were thus forsaken, he has conducted himself most secretively'. This is close to the AN ll. 6815–6, *Trop nus ad l'ovre esté cuverte, / Perd i avum leide perte*, 'he hid things too well from us—we have suffered a great loss'.

5224 'Good Lord God, was that him?' See note to l. 5139.

5250–1 Cf. AN ll. 6881–2, *Suvent li change sun curage, / Mes el parole cume sage*, 'often her spirit wavered, but she spoke wisely'.

5256 *by my stevyn* (MS *I seyne*) The MS is clearly corrupt here and reconstruction, while necessary, is purely speculative. *By my stevyn*, 'according to my promise', is offered here since she is making the point that she is merely obeying her vow by refusing all but the tournament's champion. In the slightly longer AN speech she reminds the king and barons that they called the tournament, and *Celui ki serreit le plus pruz, / A seignur prendre le devreie; / Ja nen istrai hors de la veie / Ne de vos bons cunseilz pur ren*, 'I should take as lord him who was the most valiant; I will not swerve from this nor from your good counsel [i.e. to marry the champion of the tournament] for anything' (ll. 6886–9). K. suggests the reconstruction *that men may nevyn*.

5265 *graythe* (MS *grathe*) The rhyme *graythe/faythe* appears again at ll. 6373–4.

5289 The 'she' of this line refers to the Fere. The confusion of referents arises from a telescoping of the AN, where the queen's trembling is noted (l. 6873), but is followed by a lengthy description of la Fière colouring, paling, and turning hot and cold (ll. 6874–81) before she makes the gracious speech translated into ME at l. 5289 ff..

5315 K. emends to *And the quene went by his syde* to avoid the repetition of *tyde* in the tail-rhyme sequence, although words are occasionally repeated in the tail-rhymes (see 'Language of the Text, Part I : Rhyming Practice'), and it would be impossible to prove that this was never authorial. The original tail-rhyme line might have been a simpler *wyth the quene þat tyde*.

5326 ff. Six lines are missing here. In the AN, the queen rushes from her chamber to the main hall where the king and barons are; the story pauses for the narrator's comment on the determination of women to have their own way; the queen then addresses the company at l. 5331 ff. (see AN l. 6931 ff.).

5328–30 'Women, to get what they want, will not hold back from doing as they please, whatever the consequences.'

5337 Variations on the formula 'I may say in romance and in rhyme' are used elsewhere in ME literature (K. quotes examples from *Ywain and Gawain* and *Partenope of Blois*), but they are usually in the narrator's voice and sound odd in the queen's mouth here—she appears to be suggesting that she may compose some sort of poem in which to expound her grievances. However, the formula may have been used out of mere habit and convenience—cf. the similarly unexpected line in *King Horn* l. 1461: *Horn sede on his rime* (*King Horn, Floriz and Blauncheflur, The Assumption of Our Lady*, ed. J. R. Lumby, EETS os 14 (1866)).

5392 *her* (MS *he*) It could have been Cananeus who *was woo* that he had left, since Ipomadon has taken his horse with him, but K.'s emendation to *her* has been adopted here on the assumption that the poet was following AN l. 7002, *Ben sout k'el l'aveit cuveité*, 'he knew well enough that she [the queen] had wanted him' (*he* is not a possible form of 'she' in this text).

5437 ff. The MS reading, retained here, might be translated: 'I don't know about other matters regarding this maiden that I lead, but I have often heard said . . .'. However, *lede* should perhaps be emended instead to *misdede* as K. has it—cf. AN ll. 7045–6, *Mes ben quit ke de la meschine / Ai jo mespris vers la reïne*, 'but I do believe that I have done the queen wrong with regard to the girl'.

5439–41 This comment is a politely altered version of the AN ll. 7049–50, *De femmes embler en tapin / Est un mut curteis larecin*, 'to steal a woman secretly is a most courteous theft'.

5443–4 'I will never need to confess that I have done this maiden wrong', i.e. his conscience is clear.

5463–5 '"Why, will you do nothing more than this?" "No, not if you will let me go." "In faith, we will fight here!"' Cf. AN l. 7069, *N'en partirez pas senz medlee*, 'you will not leave without a fight.'

5476 *Eyre* looks to be an otherwise unattested form of 'ire'. It translates *Irez esteit de grant manere*, 'he was extremely angry' (l. 7074), and the expression *with gret ire* occurs elsewhere in ME (see *MED ire* n. sense 2.). On the rhyme with *beyre*, see 'Language of the Text, Part I', (13d, 14).

5490 ff. The sequence of events here is explained more clearly in the AN: Ipomedon charges Caemius; the lance strikes hard and high up on the latter's shield which in turn smacks Caemius in the face, knocking off the nasel of his helmet and crushing his nose. The lance, meanwhile, passes through the shield and Caemius's hauberk to pierce his left shoulder. In the ME, Ipomadon strikes Cananeus so hard that the nasel flies off and his nose is flattened; then the (spear-)head passes through neck-armour (*gorgede*) and hauberk to break his right shoulder bone.

5491 *nasell* (MS *vasell*) Cf. AN l. 7100, *Del heaume ad freit tut le nasel,* 'from the helm he struck off the entire nose-guard'. Nasels were a feature of helmets up until the fourteenth century, but a fifteenth-century copyist seems to have been unfamiliar with the term.

5511 ff. Cf. AN ll. 7110–12, *Vassal, n'alez tant manescant! / Hume ki tant paroles a / Ja mes a bon chef ne vendra,* 'Vassal, do not go threatening so! He who makes such speeches never gains the advantage.'

5520 *of the, broþer* (MS *of thy broþer*) This emendation is based on the fact that there has been no mention of a brother of Cananeus from whom Ipomadon might have won another steed, and that the AN here reads: *Ainz oi de vus un cheval bon,* 'I had a fine horse from you before' (l. 7126).

5534 *ys ouer-hye* 'is too high' (MS *you ouer hye*) A scribe may have mistaken an exemplar *ys* for *ye*, which a later copyist rendered as MS *you*: several medieval scripts have varieties of *s* that closely resemble varieties of *e*. See 'Language of the Text: Part I' (Pronouns) on the alternation of *ye* and *you*. K. cites a couplet from a version of the ballad 'The Cruel Brother': *O, is your saddle set awrye, / Or rides your steed for you owre high?*, which neatly illustrates the sense given by the present emendation. (*English and Scottish Popular Ballads*, ed. F. J. Child, 5 vols. (Boston & New York, 1882–98); I, 70, st.7 of ballad 11, version B.)

5536 *Sheyde,* 'protect', from OE *scēadan* makes the best sense, and this line is cited in the *MED* entry for this verb. No forms with *-i-* listed, so either *ryde* would have to rhyme on *-e-* or alternatively *sheyde* on *-i-*, either of which is possible in this text—see 'Language of the Text, Part I', (13d, 14). Ka. instead proposes an emendation to *chyde,* 'complain'.

5538–51 This speech has no equivalent in the AN, where he simply rides off *pensif, a mal chere e murne,* 'thoughtful, unhappy and mournful' (l. 7152). While it is clear that Cananeus feels hard done by, the missing line and ambiguous pronouns make it difficult to interpret more exactly. The sense of ll. 5445–6 appears to be 'Love for ladies grieves me sore; so it does to him that lays his love on them', but the following two lines do not quite fit: 'They [presumably 'ladies'] love, and unless they are loved again, my great effort has been wasted'. K. reverses these two lines, but this does not clarify matters. Given at least one copyist's extreme carelessness with pronouns, l. 5547 might be emended to: *I love, and but I be louyd ageyne.*

5579 *Fro* K. notes that it should perhaps read *for* in the sense of 'despite' (OED *for*, prep. and conj., sense 23), since *for* is used thus in the next line, and the equivalent AN lines also use *pur* in this sense: *Pur mei en meine il la meschine, / Si fereit il, certes, pur tuz / De ceste curt,* 'despite me he leads away the maiden, and so he would do despite any in this court' (AN ll. 7160–62, and see Holden's note to these lines).

5592 *ne* (MS omitted) Cf. AN ll. 7169–70, *Mut s'en repent, vive s'esrage / Ke el ne li out dit sun curage*, 'greatly she repents, furiously she raves because she did not tell him her feelings'. The end of the ME line looks suspiciously like an amalgamation of the lines on either side of it, and may originally have read something like *that she ne had shewed hym untill*.

5605 *no thyng* (MS *right noughte*) This emendation assumes that the scribe has simply substituted one stock phrase meaning 'not at all' for another, perhaps influenced by the rhyme in the previous line (cf. ll. 908, 1955, 6287, etc.).

5663 This is apparently the same Dayres who competed in the three-day tournament, and the startled reader may recall that the last news we had of him was in this report by the chamberlain to the queen on the anonymous white knight's doings: *The duke of Lorayne has he slayn / In feld* (ll. 3537–8). Any residual doubt that this is indeed the same man resurrected is quelled at ll. 5738–40, where Ipomadon reminds him of their last meeting at this tournament (but not, tactfully, of the fact that he killed him there). This resurrection of Dayres is translated directly from the AN. Holden feels that it is too flagrant to be accidental, and in his opinion it represents 'the impertinent and irreverent attitude of the author with regard to the conventions [of the romance genre] which furnished him with the frame-work of his "roman burlesque"' (see Holden's note to l. 7270). It is, however, equally possible that Hue, in ransacking the story of Thebes for names for his characters, simply forgot that he had borrowed this particular name already. On Hue's possible sources, see 'The Translator and his Source: The Anglo-Norman Source'. There is a Daires at l. 5650 of *Le Roman de Thèbes* (ed. Guy Raynaud de Lage, 2 vols. (Paris, 1968)).

5665 *Dryseus* The AN does not name the duke of Lorraine through whose daughter Dayres inherits the territory: Dryseus is also the name of the duke of Flanders (another participant in the three-day tournament) though they cannot be the same man. Unless the ME translator had invented a new name which fitted the rhymes in *-us* but which later scribes miscopied, he himself would seem to be the source of the confusion.

5679 *stuffud* (MS *stuppud*) Cf. l. 5790, *A castell stovffed in Fraunce þat tyde*.

5688 ff. The referents of the various pronouns are far from clear in this passage. The *knyghttis thre* beheld by the king are the three knights Ipomadon brought with him to France (see l. 5649); the *folke* of l. 5689 are the king's people. The MS reading of the following three lines is virtually nonsensical as it stands: *Many off them he hadde sene before, But he knewe them neuer þe more; / The glader he was to byde.* The first *he* would seem to refer to the king, since he is the subject of the previous clause, but the last *he* must be Ipomadon, and the statement *but he knewe them neuer þe more* is an odd one to apply to either Ipomadon or the king in this context. These lines have been emended so that the subject of these lines continues to be the *folke* of l. 5689, who would have seen Ipomadon before at the tournament but of course do not recognise him now, hence Ipomadon's joy—*the glader he was to hyde.*

5738–40 *that made hym onys vnglad* On this vast understatement, see the note to l. 5663.

5760 *vantoure* (MS *vamsore*) Kp. argues convincingly against K.'s emendation to *many a man sore*: his first point is that *sore* cannot rhyme with *stoure* in this text (see below), and the second is that at least one of the text's copyists did not recognise the word *vantour*; he had previously written *venture* and *ventures* at ll. 3574, 3764 where the corresponding AN word is *vanteür*. (*Stoure* appears five times in rhyme, always with -*oure* words such as *emperoure, honoure, succoure,* while *sore* rhymes either on *a*—*spare, care*— or *o*—*before, therefore*: see 'Language of the Text: Part I', (1a.).)

5764 I.e. 'he met his match.'

5770 Perhaps 'in opposition strategems they were vigorous'. This is an obscure line, of which K. says 'the sense appears to be "They were experienced in all ruses"', but he thinks *thwerte* is wrong and leaves the puzzle for his readers to solve. Kp. attempts to do so with an adventurous *In twente myles they were thyke*: he objects to that fact that *wyke* is repeated, and notes the use of *thyke* elsewhere. Words are, however, repeated in the tail-rhymes occasionally—see 'Language of the Text, Part I : Rhyming Practice'—so this is not a strong objection. Regarding the awkward MS *thwerte*, the *OED* observes of this word (adj., adv. and prep.) that 'the ME material is scanty, and the sense development is not illustrated fully by the extant quotations': in other words, its later development indicates that its medieval usage must have been greater than the extant examples would lead us to believe. The most relevant medieval citations are one adjectival usage from c.1250 (*thwart*, sense C.2.) meaning 'disposed to resist' and used in reference to persons, and one for the verb in the sense of 'oppose' (sense II.5.). When these usages are combined with the occasional medieval citations of the adverbial or prepositional sense of 'across', it seems reasonable to treat this occurrence of the word as another early example of adjectival use, and to read this line as suggested above.

5777 *peryd* (MS *persyd*) An exact translation of AN l. 7402, *Il n'i ad nuls ke vers lui vaille,* 'there was none who would go against him'.

5792 ff. The translator either misunderstood or deliberately telescoped the AN passage from which this is drawn. In the ME, the *nobull knyght* of l. 5795 appears to be Ipomadon, who blows his horn to reassemble his men in the face of the two hundred fresh knights from Dayres's castle; they surround Dayres and eventually unhorse him (l. 5809), although Dayres's men soon recover the animal. In the AN, both Ipomedon and Daires blow their horns at different times. At l. 7390, Ipomedon *a buche met un olifan*, 'puts a horn to his mouth' (clearly the source of l. 5796), but the person who sounds his horn when the two hundred fresh knights appear is Daires (l. 7427), and it is Daires's men who press about him and bring him a new horse.

5812 *worne* There is no convenient AN equivalent to this line through which one might either define *worne* or uncover a different original reading, but there is a ME verb *warne* or *werne*, 'protect', derived from OF *warnir* (*OED warn* v.³). No forms in *-o-* are listed and the expected pp. would be *warned*, but the sense does fit.

5813 *wrothe* 'did' See 'Language of the Text, Part I', (26a) for other examples of such *-th* spellings for the fricative + *t*.

5822 It is Ipomadon who is borne to the ground here.

5823 *wors hap* (MS *worship*) Although the text has been emended here, the MS reading could be taken ironically—'such an honour had never been paid to him before'—and it may be presumptuous to assume that the translator could never be humorously ironic.

5825 Either 'that was nothing to him', or 'that was not at all because of him', i.e. not his fault (see *MED longe* adj.²). It is also possible that it should read *long for hym*, 'that was not at all long-lasting for him', cf. AN l. 7447, *Ipomedon tost en piez saut*, 'Ipomedon immediately leaps to his feet'.

5841 It is assumed here that *defendys* means 'fights defensively', for which no object is needed (see *MED* sense 1), but K. may be right in emending *then* to *them* (or even *hym*) and reading *defendys* as 'beats off' (*MED* sense 10).

5864 Cf. l. 5830, *He fendyd hym well inovghe*, and AN l. 7498, *Defenduz se est cum bon cheval*, 'he defended himself like a good knight'. K. understood *fendys* as the noun 'enemies' and added *assayled. Fresly*, 'boldly', is probably a combination of OF *fers* and ME *fresh*, which could also be written *fersh*: such metathesis with *r* was more frequent in Northern dialects (see Jordan §164).

5865–6 I.e. he was in too much of a hurry to find his stirrups (and athletic enough to be able to leap onto his horse without them).

5895 *relevyd* This should perhaps be *relyed*, 'rallied', a word that never appears in the extant text but whose use in the original is confirmed twice by rhyme where the MS reads *relyued* (ll. 3924, 4391). It is also possible, however, that the translator here used *relevyd* in its sense of 'came to the rescue', so it has not been emended.

5898 Cf. AN l. 7490, *Se il esteit mut febles e las,* 'then he was very weak and exhausted'. The rhyme-pair *gothe : wrothe* would seem at first glance to show the translator using the southern pr.3 sg. *-th* suffix, but this is its only occurrence in rhyme, and in fact probably represents a scribal corruption of an original *wrothe was : he gas.*

5909 *thye* Although the *MED* lists this as a possible spelling for 'they', the length of the line suggests that the word, in whatever form, is a mistaken scribal addition.

5909 ff. This stanza lacks three lines and does not appear to follow the AN except for the first line (AN l. 7517, *Mes rescus l'unt si chevaler,* 'but his knights rescued him'). Indeed, the narrative would be undisturbed if one were to remove this truncated stanza altogether. Evidence of corruption may be found in the rhyme *axe : waxe*: while *ax-* forms are as common as *ask-* in the spelling of the extant text, the word rhymes on *ass-* in all thirteen of its other appearances in rhyme-position. *Socourde to the kyng* may also be an error since the *MED* does not record a usage of this verb with *to*. In the AN, Daires is struck by Ipomedon himself, is rescued by his men, but loses his steed, about which Ipomedon's side is euphoric while Daires' side despairs and takes flight.

5923 '[Who] had never been afraid before that day.'

5929 *bale they brede* 'Brought ruin [onto themselves]' *Brede* could either be 'engender' from OE *brēdan,* or 'cook' from OE *brǣdan,* following the pattern of the expression 'to bake/brew bale' (the *MED* lists several examples under *bale* (n.) sense 2a.). Cf. the similar *hit wold . . . sorow haue brede* at l. 7698.

5941 In the AN, Daires is simply reported as sending messengers (l. 7540): the translator has evidently added his own thoughts on what kind of men make the best war-time messengers.

5963–4 'On that condition, he duly promises her whom he plans to make his heir to you.'

5980 ff. This suspicion of treachery, and the messenger's earnest denials, are not in the AN and they seem incongruous with the rest of Ipomadon's courteous speech.

5995 Cf. AN l. 7580, *Merveille en est Daires heté,* 'Daires was wonderfully delighted'. Three lines are missing after this: in the AN, the joy of the daughter is described, and this is probably what followed here even though it is described again at l. 6011 ff..

6021–2 This proverb, while translated directly from AN ll. 7587–8 in this instance, was widespread in ME literature: see Whiting, B604.

6054 ff. The missing line may have read something like: *But that will do me dere*.

6067 K's addition of *he left* is based on AN l. 7640, *Li rei i lesse od ses barnez*, 'he left the king with his barons'. This results in an extremely clumsy line however, and it might be better if *bedene* were removed and the line written: *The kyng and all his folke lefte he* (: *be*).

6095 *to-yere* On its own, this might simply have meant 'two years', but since Ipomadon actually spent three years in Calabria (see l. 506 in the ME, l. 551 in the AN), this must be the adverbial phrase meaning 'this year'.

6122 The addition of *londys wyde* is K's suggestion, although he retains MS *he wille*. The emendation makes it clear what Lyolyne's options are, i.e. to wait until she gives in and her lands are ruined, or undertake to conquer her land quickly.

6130–1 'One hardly knew whether [he thought this] good or bad, so great a sigh assailed him.'

6156 *Bleche* 'Black dye or ink', from OE *blæc*: the *MED* also cites this word as meaning 'negro'.

6158 *gorget* It is difficult to tell what is being described by this: a *gorget* is a piece of armour for the neck (see the discussion of armour in 'Date of Composition') and the translator may have meant to fit Lyolyne with one of these: alternatively it may be a mistake for *gorge* 'throat', as K. suspects. A third possibility is that the first definition is intended, but as a figurative description of dark hollows or bags under Lyolyne's eyes, i.e. 'he has eyes like two platters, with great grey gorgets [underneath them]'. There is no equivalent in the AN, which gives a shorter, though no less unflattering, description.

6176† *bakkere more abore* K. emends unsatisfactorily to *blakkere more than a bore*—either 'blacker' or 'fiercer than any boar'—but no other possibilities present themselves. ll. 6175–7 are something of a *non sequitur* altogether: clearly one line is superfluous—l. 6177 according to the rhymes—but there is no obvious explanation for its appearance here, and ll. 6175–6 alone still look out of place. The original may well have been something entirely different.

6233 *plowgh gade* 'sharpened stick for goading oxen' Cf. *Havelok* l. 1016, *bondemen with here gades / Als he comen fro þe plow* (in *Middle English Romances*, ed. S. H. A. Shepherd (London & New York, 1995)). This is the only element of Ipomadon's disguise that is not derived from the AN, and it is possible that it was inspired by a Middle English parodic tradition of which the *Tournament of Tottenham* is a later exponent.

6234 *brynie* (MS *brande*) K.'s emendation accords with the rhyme and makes better sense, since Ipomadon's rusty sword (or *brand*) has already been mentioned at l. 6232. K. also notes the frequency of the phrase *brynie bryght* in alliterative poetry.

6235 *ton* (MS *to*) Cf. l. 1265 *tonne . . . tother* and l. 5828, where the scribe has repeated *tother(e)*.

6262 *stere* (MS *sere*) S&J's emendation to *stere*, 'control', is the most plausible emendation here: they note that although the noun is not otherwise recorded as referring to animals, the related verb is (see OED *steer* v.[1] sense 3.). K. emends less convincingly to *lere*, 'cheek' [OE *hlēor*]. Ka. would have retained the MS *sere* and interpreted it anachronistically as 'the touchhole of a pistol'; his elaborate case for this was neatly demolished by Ki. and dismissed by S&J as 'a curiosity of textual scholarship'.

6271 This line is translating, somwhat abruptly, the AN ll. 7803–4, *Mes gueres a gref ne la prist / Ne il unkes semblant n'en fist*, 'but he was hardly disturbed, and he took no notice [of the laughter]'.

6278–9 'Some of them were quite frightened, ladies' faces dropped [i.e. they were taken aback]'. S&J assume that this statement is meant ironically, and there is certainly no mention of fear in the AN, but on the other hand there is no particular reason to assume that the ME translator did not intensify the scene by adding a little alarm on the part of the onlookers.

6281 *fowlie* (MS *fowle*) Cf. l. 6524, *And wordis off foly forthe he caste*.

6283–5 'I am the best knight under shield when anyone comes into the field—you paid dearly for that once' (translating *no man* as 'anyone', a sense similar to that of French *nul(s)*). Cf. ll. 6313–15: *So worthy as I am one, / Vnder heyven I trowe is none / Where freke men fleys awaye*.

6307 This follows K. in inserting *I* and interpreting the line as 'I know of no cause [i.e. for him to have lost his horse]'. (S&J guess that *why* is part of an interrupted question, but find this odd.) The AN differs: Ipomedon claims to have seen Caemius in battle although he cannot quite remember the day, to which the steward replies swiftly, *Par fei, . . . veir avez dit, / Unkes hume cel jur ne vit*', 'In faith, you spoke truth—that day has never been seen!' (ll. 7911–2). This speech is close enough to the ME l. 6308 to suggest that the preceding line may be a garbled version of the end of Ipomadon's speech, to which l. 6308 (rather than l. 6307 as punctuated here) is Cananeus's reply.

6314–5 See ll. 6283–5 for an earlier expression of this sentiment.

6328–9 The shortened form of the emended form *derayne*—*rayne*—appears elsewhere at ll. 6208 and 6329, rhymed with *fayne* and *layne* respectively. S&J also emend to *derayne*, but assume that *fayne* at l. 6328 represents a mistranslation of the AN l. 7867, *Li reis ne pot moveir ne rie*, 'the king could not help laughing'. In fact MS *fayne* translates the AN accurately, since this word can also carry the sense 'refrain from' (*MED feinen* v., sense 8a). K. instead leaves MS *deryne* and emends l. 6328 *fayne* to *fyne*, 'stop'.

6341 *take . . . mythoute* 'exclude' The *MED* does not list this specific usage under *taken* v., but it gives examples of *take with*, 'include', under sense 27 and *take oute*, 'exclude', under sense 30b.

6353 *wrethe* (MS *wrathe*) The rhyme with *myrthe* indicates that this must be *wrethe*, 'anger', from OE *wrǣþu* or ON **wreiði*, rather than the *wrathe* or *wrothe* (from OE *wrāþ*) that appears elsewhere in rhyme.

6358 See note to l. 806 on the semi-figurative use of *skole*.

6363† *pul or pande* Kp. suggests that *pul* is 'St. Paul's Day' and *pande* is 'pond', which is meant to be paired with a punning interpretation of *pul* as 'pool'. The *MED* lists only *pond* or *pound* as variants of 'pond', so if this reading is correct, the rhyme must have been on /o/: *londe/fonde/demonde* (the *MED* lists the latter spelling as a variant of 'demand'). Another interesting possibility is *Yul or maunde*, i.e. 'Christmas or Maundy Thursday': *yole*, 'yule', is used twice in asseverations elsewhere in this text—see note to l. 6840.

6404 *what deell* Probably a form of the asseveration 'what the devil . . .?', of which the longer form *what devill of hell* is used at ll. 7713 and 7729. The AN has *se Deu me saut*, 'as I be saved by God' (l. 7876).

6410 *a ferrome* (MS *frome, ro* corr. from *ar*) Ka. recognised that the MS reading must be a mangled version of the adverbial phrase *a ferrome*, hinted at by the scribe's original copying of *a far-* and confirmed by both the AN l. 7880, *Or sui de vus trop eslunez*, 'now I am too distant from you', and its reappearance here as *on ferom* at l. 8126. The *MED*'s citations for this phrase are all from Northern or Midland texts, so it may have been unfamiliar to a southern copyist.

6422 *Gille* This shortened form of the girl's name Gillian was used as an all-purpose term for women and, apparently, mares. (See *MED, gil* n.(2)). It is used again at l. 6563.

6428 *trenchours* These are either wooden plates, or thick slices of bread used as plates. In the AN, Ipomedon is served even less appetisingly with *de bois, de torchis*, 'wood and straw' (l. 7930): the ME poet may have translated *bois* as *trenchours*, meaning wooden plates, or he may have replaced the bizarre AN fare with the slightly less insulting bread–plates and broken bits of food.

6437–40 Although clearly marked as a proverb, Whiting cites only this occurrence (M197).

6438 'If it were examined closely.'

6468–71 Unusually, the translator has inserted a lewd aside where Hue has been more subtle. The AN reads simply: *Pur lui i out meint trespensé*, 'many had fretted over her' (l. 7972), though admittedly this is after Hue has dwelt lovingly on the white flesh visible through the lacing down the sides of her *bliaut*.

6483 Cf. l. 8221, *That wastythe that lady awaye.*

6485 *helper* 'help her' On such contractions, see 'Language of the Text, Part I', (27).

6486 ff. Three lines are missing here: presumably the maiden finished her request for a man who will defend the Fere against the foreign invader. In this context, the final tail-rhyme line might have been *asaye*.

6487 ff. Although this stanza is perfectly intelligible, its tail-rhyme has been corrupted beyond recovery. ll. 6487–8 follow AN ll. 7990–1, *El n'ad ja en plein ne en forest / Hors de Candres plein pié de terre*, 'outside Canders she has not even a foot of land in plain or forest', so this is clearly not a later insertion, but in general it does not follow the shorter AN speech closely enough to allow for reconstruction.

6503 *ouer* (MS *ou*) The '*-er*' abbreviation has been left off, as at l. 6172 (K. read MS *ou* as *on* and emended to *hom*).

6511 *asorowed* K. observes that this word does not appear in any dictionary, but see *MED a-*, prefix 1 sense 4, where several similar formations, such as *a-angred*, are listed.

6528 *derayne* 'challenge' (MS *denare tynee*) This emendation of Kp.'s is based on AN l. 8063, *Ceste deredne ben ferai*, 'I will gladly take up this challenge'; the word also appears (in its shortened form *rayne*) at ll. 6208 and 7319, rhyming with *fayne* and *layne* respectively.

6541 *'Alas!' sayd Imayne to Melengere* (MS *Alas I maye thow Melengere*) This is Kp.'s emendation, although he has *tho to Melengere* in the belief that the MS read *thow to*. See 'General Introduction' note 6 on scribal miswritings of *Imayne*. K. emends instead to *'Alas, I turne,' sche sayd to Melengere*.

6561 'I see no one stopping you.'

6582 A meaningless rhyme-tag—literally 'as one may witness here in the west'—which is used again at l. 7817. *Weste* appears in such asseverations as *nother (be) este ne weste* (ll. 210, 5016), and characters often arrive from or depart for 'the west' for no discernible reason beyond that of satisfying the rhyme, e.g. ll. 592, 2945, 4430, 4346.

6605–6 'Alas that my lady ever lavished so much attention on King Mellengere.'

6617 *For Goddis love* (MS *For*) The line would be too short if *for* were simply omitted. An asseveration seems to have been intended to follow MS *for*: *for Goddis love* is one of the most common in this text, and fits the rhythym best here.

6620 K. is probably right in suspecting that *sayd the dwarff* should come after *Nay*.

6635 ff. The tail-rhyme of this stanza has been spoilt, but K. offers the very plausible reconstruction adopted in the present text. The apparently mistaken use of *evyn* at l. 6642 offers support for the emendation of l. 6636. The frequency in the text of references to *God in hevyn* (e.g. ll. 1014, 1073, 2872, 3235, etc.) suggests that the equally common *God that sittys above* at MS l. 6639 was an absent-minded substitution for this phrase. The word *nevyn* at l. 6642 does not appear elsewhere in the text, but may have resulted from the scribe's eye skipping up to l. 6636, if the latter's emended reading is the correct one.

6646–8 This speech is entirely different from the AN, where the dwarf beholds the fool-knight with despair; *Ore est aukes desesperez, / Ben quide ke il seit afolez*, 'now he is somewhat despairing; he believes well enough that he [Ipomedon] is mad' (l. 8173–4). In endowing the dwarf with greater powers of perception than the stubborn Imayne or even his own AN counterpart, the ME translator reveals his eagerness to hammer home the moral lesson on deceptive appearances.

6686 Head-shaking was commonly considered to be one of the signs of madness—see for example Trevisa's translation of Bartholomæus's *De Proprietatibus Rerum*, which describes *meuynge & waggynge of heed* (Book 7, Chap. 5 of *On the Properties of Things: John Trevisa's Translation of Bartholomæus Anglicus's De Proprietatibus Rerum*, ed. M. C. Seymour *et al.*, 3 vols. (Oxford, 1975–88), I, 348). It is interesting that this head-shaking, repeated at l. 7055, does not appear anywhere in the AN, where Ipomedon instead resembles a *bricun escapé*, 'escaped madman', because of his long beard and shaven neck (AN ll. 8206–7).

6696 *we* Kp. suggests that this is a mistake for *ye*, which is certainly possible since Imayne is annoyed with the dwarf, but on the other hand she could mean that they are both mad to allow a fool to follow them.

6722 *mard* (MS *mayd*) *Mayd*, 'dismayed', is not recorded as taking the preposition *of*, and K.'s suggestion of *mard*, 'hindered' (A *merran*), has been adopted here.

6727 The image of 'quaking/shaking like an aspen-leaf' was a common one in ME (it is used again at l. 6871) and the *MED* lists several examples under *aspe* n., sense 2(a), including one from this text.

6729 *Angur* is probably used here in the sense of 'anguish', as at l. 900, although it could also carry the modern sense 'anger' since it translates *mut sunt iré e murne andui*, 'they were both very angry and distressed' (l. 8252).

6743 *hande* : *defende* Although 'hand' usually rhymes on -*a*-, this -*e*- rhyme is possible in that it may stem from ON cp. OI *hendi* (dative sg.) and *hendr* (pl.).

6778 *wetly wondyd* 'badly wounded' Although the *OED* does not list the spelling *wetly*, it is clear that it is another variant of the *wyttly* and *wyghttly* used in the same phrase at ll. 6926, 8024, and it appears again at l. 6939. On *i/e* variation, see 'Language of the Text, Part I', (14).

6780 *rouncy* (MS *powyse*) Cf. AN l. 8313, *Amis, cel runcin la pernez*, 'friend, take that packhorse'.

6796–7 'There is no man under the moon who might have acted more valiantly.'

6798 An asseveration used to fill the rhyme, meaning 'may his reward be good'.

6808 The pair to this line is irrecoverable since she does not comment on the dwarf's present in the AN, but *gyfte* is a likely candidate for the rhyme-word.

6821 Cf. AN l. 8378, *Unc cil n'i osa aprocher*, 'he did not dare to approach then'.

6840 *I bede neuer yole* (MS *I bede neuer olde*) *Yole* is 'yule', i.e. Christmas and its attendant festivities: this is evidently some form of asseveration, perhaps 'may I never see Yuletide if . . .': cf. l. 8334. Whiting does not list this expression and nor does the *OED*, although the latter does note the broader use of the word to denote festivities generally, which might have encouraged the development of such an asseveration.

6845 *dalians* (MS *dalentys*) K. writes: '*dalentys* is incomprehensible to me, and with it the entire line'. The emendation to *dalians* adopted here is from Kp., who would also have emended *youre* to *you*, thus 'we drew polite conversation from you', but MS *youre* seems to make equal sense: 'we withdrew from your polite conversation', implying either that he has avoided flirtatious overtures from Imayne in the past, or, more innocently, referring to when he left the Fere's court.

6852 *spekyng alther beste* Perhaps 'speaking eloquently' on the model of 'well-spoken'; the expression is not recorded in the *MED* (*alder*, adv.). Another possibility is 'speaking all their best', which would have much the same meaning.

6854 *syttand* (MS *rydand*) Cf. AN l. 8444, *Mut sist sur un riche cheval*, 'he sat on a rich horse'.

6855–7 Cf. AN ll. 8431–6, *Ismeine le veit, mut se dute, / . . . Mut par suspire de parfund; / Si li membra de l'aventure / Del jur devant*: 'Ismeine sees him, she is very anxious . . . she sighs heavily and remembered the events of the day before'.

6865–6 'For my cousin Lyolyne has given me [you] as a reward'; the 'you' is understood from the preceding line. (On the omission of object-pronouns in ME, see Mustanoja, pp. 144–5).

6867–8 'Maugis had been extremely angry because he [Lyolyne] had given her [Imayne] to them both, a beautiful gift they would lose.' The AN is, as usual, slightly clearer: Leonin grants Ismeine to whichever one of the two knights manages to abduct her first (ll. 8454–8). On the contraction *gyffner*, 'given her', see 'Language of the Text, Part I', (27).

6878 K. and the *MED* assume that 'biting one's beard' is a variation on the more common image of biting one's lips in anger.

6880 *deynely* Although the *MED* lists neither this form nor *disdeynely*, it does list both n. and v. *deyne*, 'contempt', 'hold in contempt', and an adj. *disdeyne*, so *deynely* is an unsurprising formation.

6927–9 I.e. Creon may take holy orders whenever he likes now, since Ipomadon's blow has virtually tonsured him. The joke seems to have been a popular one: K. quotes very similar examples from *Beues of Hamtoun* ll. 1869–72 (ed. E. Kölbing, EETS ES 46, 48 & 65 (1885, 1886, 1894)) and *Guy of Warwick*, Auchinleck version ll. 3651–4 (ed. J. Zupitza, EETS ES 42, 49 & 59 (1883, 1887, 1891)), and it is used again in *Ipomadon* at ll. 8087–92.

6945 *he* (MS *ye*) Cf. the identical statement made to Maugis at l. 6774.

6980 *dereynes* 'fighting' (MS *deueres*) Cf. AN l. 8574, where the verb *deredner*, 'defend in arms', appears in relation to the knights at Meleager's court.

6981 ff. The repeated construction 'as a fool . . .' is copied from AN l. 8575–90, though not nearly so deftly handled as in the latter text.

6986 *he conteynes* 'he behaves' (MS *is his covntenaunse*) Cf. the nearly identical l. 7924.

6992 The inappropriate MS *ofte* has been deleted here, but it could also have been emended to *efte* in the sense of 'promptly' or 'again'.

6995 *fyne* (MS *tyne*) This is, as Kp. observes, the same formulaic phrase as appears at ll. 2707, 3281, 6165: the sense is 'they wasted no time about it'. The MS reading may have arisen from the similarity in meaning between *tyne*, 'lose, fail' and *fyne*, 'cease'.

7008 ff. 'I also know well from her proud words that she will slay me because I struck them [the two knights] down. The devil of hell take you both again for all your trapping and tricks!' Presumably the *trappyng and trayne* refers to their attempt to get him to join them. This differs from AN ll. 8590–2; *La putain me volt fere oscire / Her al disner e ui cest jur, / Andui erent si duneür*, 'the whore wanted to get me killed yesterday at dinner and today this day; both [men] were lovers, certainly!' The translator may have either misunderstood or deliberately altered his source, or indeed he may have done neither: of the extant AN versions, Holden's B is missing the crucial verb *fere* in l. 8590, so that the line translates as 'the whore wants to kill me'. (On the relationship between the extant ME and AN versions, see 'The Translator and his Source : The Translator's Exemplar'.)

7024–8 'You don't recognise what you hear; you don't believe what you see. Men who are wise act like fools, and men without sense appear sensible— such is the case with you, clearly!' The ME makes perfect sense as it is, but it does differ from the AN ll. 8599–8603: *Teus trove l'um vezïez e sagez / Ki tant sunt fol de lur curagez, / Saveir ne volent ço k'il veient / Ne ço ke il sevent pas ne creent; / si est il ore, amis, de vus*; 'there are those whom one thinks to be shrewd and wise who are really foolish-minded—they don't want to know what they see nor believe what they know: so it is with you, my friend'. The odd line out in the ME is l. 7026, which K. accordingly suggests might be emended to *þat are folis, makyth men wyse*, 'men make wise men out of fools', thus echoing the following line. Another possibility is that l. 7027 *witte* is the verb 'blame', i.e. 'men . . . blame those who have no sense'.

7035† This line is impossible to reconstruct, although it is clear that the dwarf is referring to some aspect of the fighting that Ipomadon has done on Imayne's behalf. The AN reads: *Pur vus ad esté pres de mort*, 'for you he has been close to death' (l. 8606). A minor emendation of *orde* to *gorde* might allow the line to be translated as: 'he spurred himself to spear [i.e. fight]', but this assumes that *gorde* is from OE **gyrdan*, *MED girden* v.². The *MED* lists *gorde* only as a pa.t. form, which it cannot be in this context, and there is also only one citation for *spere* as a verb (*MED speren* v.²). Kp. suggests a more ambitious *To speres hymself dyd he shever / Off you he myghte gette a worde neuer*.

7041–3 Cf. AN ll. 8613–4, *Cil ke tuz jurs sert senz eür / De nul grant ben ne seit seür*, 'he who always serves without good fortune will not be sure of any good coming of it'. The same sentiment was expressed at ll. 1718–23.

7048 *þerof ye will not knowe bee* 'and you will not acknowledge it': for this usage see the *OED*, *know*, v., sense 2(d).

7055 On Ipomadon's head-shaking, see note to l. 6686.

7077 *crochett* After his well-wrought shirt, the AN goes on to describe his red hose, so the ME clearly differs at this point. Since a line is missing after this one, however, Ipomadon's *crochett* remains something of a mystery item. The *MED* offers two tentative guesses: '?a hook-like brooch or fastener', for which the only citation is this line, or '?a curl or roll of hair', for which there are other examples (see *MED croket* n. (a)). Some support for taking it as a reference to his hair might be found in AN l. 8643, *De chef, de col out grant beauté*, 'his head and neck were very handsome'.

7088 ff. See 'The Translator and his Source: The Remodelling Process' on the differences between this passage and the corresponding AN ll. 8656–66.

7120 'Thus is she happy to surrender.' The image of bowing to the power of love was used earlier at l. 1444, *it made her low to lowte*, and l. 6957, *Her hertte a littill bowed is*.

7127–8 *it was : I did pase* (MS *waste : she paste*) The apparent contracted form *waste* for 'was it' appears again at l. 7307, *who waste*, where it is clearly scribal since the rhyme demands *wrought*.

7128 *Candres* (MS *the chambyre*) Cf. AN l. 8749–50, *Suvent dit 'Lasse, tant mar mui / Hors de Candre'*; '[she] says often, "Fool, I have left Canders to my detriment." '

7133–5 These lines do not seem to fit where they are, but there is no obvious reason for a scribe to compose a nonsensical extra triplet. Since the following two stanzas are defective (see note to l. 7143 ff.), these lines may represent the mangled remains of the missing parts of the following two stanzas. The puzzle is left to the readers' ingenuity.

7138 'If you come to think of it' is the translation suggested by S&J, though they also contemplate emending *bewitte* to *atwite*, 'reproach'. Kp. favours a more extreme emendation to *But his bewete* ['beauty'], *i-wys*: this is not an unreasonable suggestion, given the obvious corruption in these lines and the fact that the AN does say a little earlier: *De sa beauté est ja suprise*, 'she is quite overcome by his beauty' (l. 8694).

7140–1 As at ll. 6468–71, the ME translator has gone against his usual treatment of female characters and actually increased the sensual element of a scene involving Imayne. The AN reads: *Ne m'enveia pas pur amer / Ne pur aveir mal ne cuntraire, / Ffors sul pur sun message faire* (ll. 8760–2): 'she didn't send me to love, nor to have misfortune or harm, but simply to take her message'.

7143 ff. It is unclear where the division between these two damaged stanzas should lie, since ll. 7142–4 all rhyme (K. begins the new stanza with l. 7144). The matter is further complicated by the fact that the first of these two stanzas is itself preceded by three unattached lines (ll. 7133–5, see note above) which neither match the tail-rhyme of the stanza that follows them, nor belong to the complete stanza that precedes them. Without taking these earlier unattached lines into account, eight lines are missing from somewhere within these two stanzas.

7145 'Wounds without spear.' The image of love wounding without weapons was a popular one. K. points to examples from *Amis and Amiloun*

l. 1562, *Sche brac his hert wiþouten kniif* (ed. E. Kölbing, Heilbronn (1884), based on the Auchinleck MS version) and a related image in Chaucer's *Troilus and Criseyde* III l. 1358, *How koude ye withouten bond me bynde*.

7224 *rose* (MS *say*) Cf. the otherwise identical l. 6825.

7244 *rydyng* With *ryde* appearing in the following line, it is possible that this is an error for the *prykyng* to which K. emends his text.

7251–3 *a farthyng* (MS *a fayre thyng*) 'He granted it easily, and so he might, that thing that never cost him a farthing in forty years!'. Cf. AN l. 8939–40, *Asez fist ben ke li granta / Ce ke gueres ne li custa*, 'he did very well in granting him that which had not cost him anything'.

7265–7 'Sir, you sang [i.e. spoke] wrongly: however generously you give your gifts [i.e. the duchy of Tessayle], you will get nothing here.' K. suggests *fals* by analogy with *Sir Ferumbras* l. 2753 ff.: *Clarioun saide to þe knight: þow syngest an ydel songe: þis day schaltou ben yuele ydyȝt and tomorwe heȝe anhonge* (ed. S. J. Herrtage, EETS ES 34 (1879)).

7304 *wrothe* (MS *wroughte*) Kp.'s emendation to *wrothe* follows AN l. 9034, *Leonins en fet grant dolur*.

7308 ff. Three lines of this stanza are clearly missing, but it is impossible to tell where they might have belonged since none of the sense of the AN seems to have been lost.

7315 *Feres* (MS *fers*) A case could be made for retaining the MS reading *fers*, 'proud', since Imayne has certainly been arrogant, but K.'s emendation is supported by AN ll. 9046–7, *Jo sai . . . / Ke ço est la meschine a la Fiere*, 'I know that she is the Fere's damsel'.

7317 ff. The extant text is not damaged in any way in the following section, so there was clearly a faulty exemplar somewhere in the line of transmission. The preceding stanza is missing three lines; this and the two following stanzas are missing four, six, and nine lines respectively. Since, however, nothing crucial is missing from the narrative until after l. 7330 ff., the missing parts would seem to have consisted mainly of formulaic padding.

7325–6 *come : towne* See 'Language of the Text, Part I : Rhyming Practice' for such use of assonance. Alternatively, the verb *bovne*, 'make ready', would supply an exact rhyme (the pp. form is used several times). It is also possible, given the textual corruption in this passage, that these two lines were not originally a couplet at all.

7330 ff. The surviving ME ll. 7324–39 give snatches of a narrative corresponding to thirty-three lines in the AN (ll. 9057–90): if all of the remaining fragments of stanzas are assumed to represent one stanza each from the original translation, this would make the ME line-count for this section roughly equal to that of the AN. In the AN, Leonin's army returns from Leander's funeral as news spreads through the city that Ismeine is on her way with a valiant knight who has already defeated Leander, Maugis and Creon. The Fere is delighted. Ismeine, Ipomedon and the dwarf leave the main road for fear of being detected by Leonin, and make their way secretly through the forest to the hermitage where Ipomedon once armed himself for the three-day tournament, and where they now find Egeon waiting for them. While they dismount and lodge themselves, Egeon is sent to find Tholomeu, who has made his own way to Calabere with the rest of Ipomadon's armour. From this point (l. 7340 of the ME; l. 9091 of the AN), the two texts run parallel again.

7369 *hoo* Mustanoja notes that this exclamation 'often occurs as an equivalent of "stop"' (p. 626); here it is addressed to the personified Love.

7393 ff. The missing couplet after this must have been based on AN ll. 9147–8: *Aukes murrai plus a delit / Se cist bons chevalers me oscist*, 'I will die with greater pleasure if this good knight slays me'.

7395–7 'And if he should strangle you instantly, no one but yourself need be blamed—honestly Imayne, no!'

7398–7400 'But once he knows it is a woman, I believe we will soon make peace.'

7416 *led ys* (MS *ledys*) Ka.'s emendation here gives the sense 'but Imayne is so ruled by love'. K. emends to *delys*.

7450–1 Either, 'So long as I live (*leve*), I do not want your lady to be frightened so easily', or 'if I leave . . .'.

7455–7 'Seven years on, if you are so bold, you would hold me for a coward whenever you were a little angry with me.'

7469 'For you will only be doing what is reasonable', i.e. it would be only right for Ipomadon to be at the command of two such noble ladies.

7490 The translator seems to use *a bovgh* to mean *forest*, a construction he uses again at l. 8536, *I went to the grene wood bovgh*. Cf. AN l. 9232, *En la forest se est enbuischez*, 'he concealed himself in the forest'.

7520 Ki. translates this line as 'where no man came amiss to me', i.e. in that situation, even a madman was better than none at all. K.'s less convincing interpretation is: 'as long as no evil man was about', implying that the fool's presence became welcome as soon as the evil men did appear.

7545–7 'I would a thousand times rather drown myself in the sea than have that traitor there!'

7587 *wyth the grene woode tre*, 'in the forest'. Cf. l. 7490.

7591 *tyte* (MS *lyght*) The emendation makes little difference to the sense, but the rhyme with *white* indicates that *lyght* must be scribal.

7646 ff. In the MS, the first three tail-rhyme words end in *-ys*, but since the final word *spede* cannot be made to fit this pattern, K.'s emendation of the other three has been adopted here, with a subj. case being assumed where necessary. Ka. less helpfully suggests adding the final three lines to the following stanza, creating one stanza of nine lines and one of fifteen, because *stede* fits the second stanza's tail-rhyme.

7684–5 I.e. 'so that she would not get upset'.

7686–7 It is difficult to determine who the referents are in this sentence, since the three preceding lines are missing and the passage does not appear in the AN. Perhaps, as K. suggested, the ME translator had Ipomadon send Egyon to issue the formal challenge to Lyolyne, ' . . . that he would stop and say that yonder knight comes of his own volition to fight and keep the Fere from harm'.

7698 'It would have caused too much distress'; cf. the note on *bale brede* at l. 5929.

7734–5 *ye : moo* Ye, *ya* and *yo* are all variants of early Modern English 'yea'; this occurrence could have rhymed originally with either *moo* or *ma*.

7767 ff. AN l. 9491 ff. indicates that it is Lyolyne who claims, rather absurdly under the circumstances, that she holds to her famous vow for his sake.

7802 *he* (MS *hym*) Since the reply to l. 7803 translates a speech made by Ipomedon in AN ll. 9511–12, it must be Lyolyne who is preparing to speak here.

7809 'Then every knight took his position on the jousting ground.'

7816 *hedys* This refers to spearheads breaking through the chain mail; cf. l. 5497 and the note to l. 5490 ff..

7817 On this rhyme-tag see the note to l. 6582.

7837 *grene* (MS *ground*) Cf. the opposite scribal substitution of *grene* for *ground* at l. 7812.

7849–51 The *he* in this passage refers to Ipomadon's steed, cf. AN l. 9600, *Li neirs destriers agenuilla*, 'the black steed fell to its knees'.

7875 *hit* (K.; MS *storyde*) On the rhyming of /i/ with /e/, see 'Language of the Text, Part I, (13a, 14).

7882, 7892 *then* (MS *the*) The emendation could equally well have been to the variant *tho*.

7886–7 Cf. AN ll. 9634–5, *Allas, quel dol! si petit faut / Ke le cors ne coupa par mi*: 'Alas, what a shame! it needed so little more to cut the body in half'.

7888 *blow, fyne* (MS *blod, fynde*) The emendation of MS *fynde* to *fyne* is called for by rhyme, but the need to emend MS *blod* also is clear from AN ll. 9639–40, *Bon fut li brancz e cil fort fut,/ A l'arçun pas cil n'arestut*, 'the sword was good and strong, it didn't stop at the saddle'. Another possible emendation would be to *brond*, translating AN *brancz* directly.

7930 *world* The rhyme clearly calls for the N. form *ward*, though both forms derive from OE *weorold*.

7939 *lawys* K. also leaves the MS reading and interprets it as referring to Lyolyne's own personal rules of battle (for example, that Lyolyne always wins). Other possibilities are 'habitual ways', referring to his success in slaying opponents (see *MED laue* n. sense 9), or 'teachings', i.e. the 'lessons' Lyolyne hopes to give Ipomadon on the battlefield (*MED* sense 10): on this last, see the note to l. 806 on the semi-figurative use of *skole*.

7940–1 This emendation of Kp.'s is based on AN ll. 9691–2, *E vus estes plus feble e mendre, / De cors petit, de membres tendre*, 'and you are weaker and littler, smaller bodied, tender-limbed'. The ME may be translated: 'and in addition you are a little man, and receive no lady's love' (see *OED* sense 6b for this used of *understand*). Lyolyne has already boasted of the Fere's supposed love for him, and is magnanimously about to offer Imayne to Ipomadon. Ipomadon's angry retorts at l. 7953, 'I don't want your gift of a wife', and ll. 7955–6, 'I never sent you to woo on my behalf—I could get myself wives enough!', are not present in the AN, though the rest of his speech is: the added emphasis on prowess in the field of love supports the emendation at l. 7941 of Lyolyne's taunting speech to *ladyes love*.

7961–3 'Through the help of him that made the moon [i.e. God], you shall pay dearly for what you have done to that lady!'

7971–2 I.e. 'she would do anything rather than kiss your mouth'.

7973 *bekende* (MS *be kynde*) The same scribal misreading of this word occurs at ll. 289, 6205. For the sense 'consigned [to the Devil]', see *MED bikennen* v., sense 2b.

7992–3 K. suggests emending to *Of the helmus . . . The flowres . .* by analogy with AN ll. 9843–4: *Del brant le fert el heame sus,/ Les flurs abat del heame jus*; 'with the sword he struck him on the helm, and knocked the ornaments (*flurs*) to the ground' (the ME version of this scene does not occur until l. 8078 ff.). It is impossible to know whether the rather different image in the ME was a deliberate choice, or the result of a misunderstanding of the source.

8003 K. observes that *did* could be *kid* [OE *cȳþan*], but *did* can also be used reflexively (see *MED don* v., sense 5d).

8010 Cf. AN l. 9778, *Li branz el poin li est turné*, 'the sword twisted in his hand'.

8027 I.e. 'catch the significance' (of the wound Lyolyne has inflicted).

8081–3 The sword passes first through the great helm, then through the cap (either of steel or padded cloth), and finally through the skull.

8087–92 On the joke of 'tonsuring' one's opponent, see note to ll. 6927–9.

8123–4 'A mile within the Greek Sea, he promptly perishes'. This little touch of poetic justice has been added by the ME translator—in the AN they merely *s'en vunt tut siglant al vent*, 'departed sailing in the wind' (l. 9898).

8126 *on fervm* On this expression see note to l. 6410.

8144 K. notes that this short line would be better filled if *he* were *the knight*, and the AN in fact reads: *N'i targe lunges le vassal*, 'the knight didn't tarry long' (l. 9929).

8160 *corde* (MS *woyde*) The MS reading makes no sense: perhaps a scribe was anticipating the next line with *woyde* [OF *voider*] in its sense of 'withdraw'.

8196 *went* Ka. notes that this is probably *(a)vent* from OF *esventer*, 'to air oneself': see *MED aventen* v..

8218 Perhaps 'with a great show of strength': this is a combination of such definitions for *arrai* as 'army' (*MED arrai* n., sense 4) and *on grette araye*, 'with great splendour' (*MED* sense 6).

8229 *Cananeus* (MS *Cabanus*) The facts that this speech is addressed to Cabanus, and that Ipomadon did banter with Cananeus on his arrival at court as a fool, indicate that *Cananeus* is the correct name here. The same mistake occurs at l. 5142.

8239 ff. Since Cabanus is already convinced that the fool-knight is Ipomadon in disguise, it is odd that he should remain so unhappy in the following stanza. The slight *non sequitur* is the fault of the translator, who has taken Cabanus's misery from the corresponding section of the AN (*mut fut tristes*, l. 9982), where however he will not guess the fool-knight's identity until later when La Fière describes how well the stranger fought (AN ll. 10070–1). Since this scene is also translated into ME at l. 8341 ff., Cabanus confusingly appears to guess Ipomadon's identity twice.

8245 *turned* The MS reading has been retained since the *OED* lists a ME sense of 'to drive mad' for this verb (*OED turn* v., sense 45). However, it is also possible that it should be *turmented*, to which K. emends.

8261–3 The referents of *they* in these lines are ambiguous. They could refer to Cabanus and his men all the way through, or they may change at l. 8262 to the Fere and her entourage. The construction with *to some* (MS *seme*) in this line does not make much sense, but there is no obvious way to improve it. K. considers omitting *to some* from this line and reversing verb and object in the next, so that *sorowe* would rhyme with *sawe*. Kp.'s more extravagant suggestion, *In hertte they hade sorowe all and some*, is equally unsatisfactory.

8269 *thene* The rhyme on *-i-* shows that the original form must have been the adv. *thyne*, 'thence', a northern shortened form of *thethen* (see *MED thine* adv.), rather than OE *þanan*, although the meaning is the same. The awkward MS *sett* is taken to be a mistake for *fett*, 'brought'—an assumption supported by the fact that the two words are reversed at ll. 3306–7, and that the *fett* called for by rhyme has been replaced by other verbs at ll. 2832 and 5810. (K. suggested instead that the line might be similar to l. 910, *Her gerdyll waxit thyn*.)

8279 This garbled line may represent some version of AN ll. 10018–9, *Ei, Deus, tant prenez feble gerre, / Ki vers mei pernez tel estrif*: literally 'Ah, God, you undertake a feeble war when you turn such hostility against me', i.e. 'you needn't use such strength against me', but it is difficult to shape the extant line around this sense. The repetition of *wyth*, and the Fere's contrition, may instead indicate that the phrasal verb *take with*, 'receive' (*OED take* sense 75) lies at the root of the confusion. The present emendation is based on this interpretation and reads, 'Receive me with [my] humble manner; / I did you no harm'. K.'s emendation, which he describes as a 'timid guess', is *Of me take care: wyth sempull chere*.

8281 I.e. 'you are omnipotent'.

8282 Perhaps, *I shall me drown here in the see / That wold I do right well*, based on AN ll. 10021–2, *Ne vus estot fors cumander / Ke jo m'en nie en ceste mer*, 'you have but to command that I drown myself in this sea'.

8284 K. suggests *I am sorowe-worthy more*, though the MS reading could be taken as 'I deserve it all the more'.

8300 This has been emended to the common exclamation *well-a-way the while*, but K.'s emendation to *And I well a way the while*, 'and I will [go] away now', does bring the text into line with the AN l. 10032, *si tenc ma veie*, 'and so I leave'. On reading *well* as the verb 'will', see 'Language of the Text, Part I', (14).

8334 *so byd I yole* See note to l. 6840.

8372 *saw* (MS *sayd*) Cf. AN l. 10093, *Capaneüs l'ad veü ja*, 'Capaneus saw him already'.

8374 It sounds slightly odd for Cabanus to use *yonder lyethe . . .* to describe the galloping Ipomadon, and Kp. may be right in suggesting *flyethe*.

8403–5 'Be he never so agile of body, I would rather fight than be recognised by him.' K. emends *wonder sore* at l. 8402 to *wonded sore*, 'badly wounded' based on AN l. 10140, *Mes la plaie li fist grant mal*, 'but the wound caused him much pain', but *sore* can imply 'wounded' in itself, and this information is conveyed at l. 8418 of the ME in any case.

8412 *foyned* 'thrust at' While MS *foyned* makes the best sense in this context, K.'s emendation to *founde,* 'advanced' (to rhyme with *grovnde*), cannot be discounted.

8423, 8429 *fovrthe : erthe* The more northerly forms *ferde* and *erde* must have been used in the original rhymes, though the MS forms have the same etymological roots (OE *fēorþa, eorþe*).

8436 *fyfte* 'fifth' (MS *fyrste*) Cf. AN ll. 10165–6, *E l'un de sis ke remis sunt / Ad ferru tres par mi le frunt,* 'and he struck one of those remaining [after having slain four of them] right in the middle of the forehead'.

8462 The three missing lines were probably based on the slightly longer AN description of blows resounding, swords clashing and armour sparkling, AN l. 10190 ff..

8465 *are* (MS *before*) While the tail-rhyme partners *sore* and *were* could rhyme on *-o-* or *-a-*, *bare* [OE *bær*] can only rhyme on *-a-*. On *sore, were* see 'Language of the Text, Part I', (1).

8522 K. notes that the line would make better sense if *that* were changed to *though.*

8552 *you* This refers not only to Cabanus but also to the king and others of their company: cf. AN ll. 10270–1, *Par mun oste les enveiai / Al rei, a nos autres amis,* 'I sent them by my landlord to the king, to our other friends'.

8573 *lette* (MS *wette*) Cf. l. 933, *hym to love þou wylt not lette,* and l. 8824, *For nothyng wold they lett.*

8585 'That has wronged no man yet.' The addition of *ere* satisfies rhyme but not meter: no better solution presents itself however.

8601 *Cabanus* K. emends this to *Ipomadon* to remove the clumsiness of Cabanus apparently stopping and starting again (see 'General Introduction' note 6 on scribal carelessness with names). Either way it differs from the AN, where Capaneus concludes that although he and Ipomedon have different fathers, the ring proves they had the same mother (AN ll. 10284–6).

8627 *wold wede* (MS *woode were*) K.'s emendation is based on l. 8294.

8691 Without emendation, this line might be translated: 'And has he spoken to Cabanus?' For *as* as 'has', cf. *a* for 'have' at ll. 4581, 8694 and 'Language of the Text, Part I', (27). K. emends to *And is he saht to Cabanus,* 'And is he reconciled with Cabanus?' (with *saht* from OE *sehtan*); Kp. offers *And is he sib* ['brother'] *to Cabanus?* There is no obvious inspiration for the errors that both these emendations assume, although both make good sense. The AN affords no clues.

8712–4 'Imayne, you had no business doing so when you insolently turned him away the other day.'

8721 *hym* (MS *you*) Cf. AN l. 10402, *Or purrez aveir vostre dru,* 'now you may have your darling'.

8736–8 This narratorial aside is a condensation of a longer, more general, and more plaintive aside by Hue (AN ll. 10413–20), in which he is anxious to make the point that it is a dreadful thing to receive no reward for one's services, and *Ki aime e sert hume felun / Mut avra feble geuredon,* 'he who loves and serves a harsh man will have a poor reward' (ll. 10419–20).

8753 ff. Although this stanza is perfectly intelligible and rhymes correctly as it is, the repetition of *wrothe* in the tail-rhyme led K. to try to emend. He suggests *brathe* 'eager' for the first occurrence, and *lathe* or *wothe* (both meaning 'harm') for the second, although of course only one of the occurrences would need changing to avoid the repetition. However, see 'Language of the Text, Part I : Rhyming Practice' on the occasional repetition of tail-rhyme words.

8770 On this early use of the word *riggud* to mean 'prepared, dressed', see note to l. 2812.

8771 ff. The missing three lines were probably drawn from AN ll. 10464–5, *Unc ne fina si ke il fu; / Assemblez sunt tuit li barun,* 'he did not stop until he was there; the barons were all assembled'.

8773 *ye* (MS *we*) MS *we* makes no sense, since King Melleager can hardly be including himself among those who are without a king.

8777 ff. The three missing lines probably corresponded to AN ll. 10471–2, *Dunt la Fiere pas ne freindra / Sun vu q'el devant vus voa,* 'with whom [i.e. Ipomedon] the Fere will not be breaking the vow that she made before you all'.

8782–4 AN ll. 10482–5 is close enough to the ME that corrections to the latter (as proposed by K.) are relatively easy to make: *Ne sui pas uncor curunez; / Ne voil pas par ma enveiseüre, / En pris aver oi mis ma cure. / Jo ai vostre nece mut amee;* 'I am not yet crowned; I did not want to be for, for my pleasure, I dedicated myself to "pris". I have loved your niece dearly'.

8785 *of lyve* 'alive' On the use of *of* in place of the more familiar *on lyve,* see note to l. 567.

8814 K. reconstructs the missing line convincingly as: *The land that had Syr Amfeon,* a translation of AN l. 10528, *La terre ki fut Amphiun.*

8819 *preffe* 'distress' This is assumed to derive from OF *prove, preuve* (see *MED preve* n., sense 4d), but K. could be right in suspecting that it derives from *reprove* in the same way that *bate* (ll. 2221, 8826) is from *debate.* Either way the sense is the same.

8829 *warysound* Neither the *MED* nor the *OED* records this verb, but it clearly derives from the noun meaning 'reward': see *MED garisoun* n., *OED warison* n..

8837 ff. The following information about Ipomadon's sons and his own fate comes not from the AN *Ipomedon*, but from its sequel *Protheselaus*—see 'The Translator and his Source: *Protheselaus*'.

8876 ff. See 'The Translator and his Source: The Remodelling Process' for a comparison of this ending to the rather less pious conclusion of the AN text.

GLOSSARY

The glossary is selective. Common words used in their modern sense are not glossed unless one of their inflections or spelling variants renders them unfamiliar, or where it is necessary to distinguish the modern sense from the archaic or idiomatic senses that this glossary aims to record. Entries record every spelling of that word occurring in the text, though not every instance of it. In the case of verbs which appear in the glossary only to illustrate a less common variant of spelling or meaning, inflected forms with both the modern spelling and usual meaning may not be listed. Verbs are listed under their infinitive forms where these occur in the text. Cross-references to verbs are labelled *v.* except where that spelling represents only one inflection, in which case this is given instead.

In the definitions of frequently recurring words whose spelling remains the same throughout the text, the first two occurrences of each sense are cited followed by 'etc.'. Where more than one spelling exists, the variant forms are collected at the head of the entry and the first occurrence of each spelling-variant is cited, followed by 'etc.' if there are further examples of any of the listed spellings. Fuller listings of citations are occasionally given where there has been emendation, or in order to avoid confusion between words whose spelling-variants overlap. An asterisk before a citation indicates an emended form, while an 'n' refers readers to the Explanatory Notes.

In the alphabetic sequence, vocalic *y* is treated as *i,* with the semi-vowel *y* listed separately (where it may be unclear which value is intended, a cross-reference is provided); the semi-vowel *I* (modern *j*) is listed separately as I = J; *þ* is treated as *th*; *3* is treated as *gh* except where it occurs initially and is treated as the semi-vowel *y*. In the spelling of this text, *u*, *v* and *w* are used to some extent interchangeably: as far as possible, they have been treated according to whether they represent the vowel *u*, the consonant *v* or the semi-consonant *w*.

Abbreviations used:

adj.	adjective	pp.	past participle
adv.	adverb	ppl.adj.	participial adjective
comp.	comparative	pr.	present
conj.	conjunction	pr.p.	present participle
imp.	imperative	prep.	preposition
impers.	impersonal	pron.	pronoun
inf.	infinitive	refl.	reflexive
interj.	interjection	sg.	singular
n.	noun	sub.	subject (for case of pronoun)
num.	numeral	subj.	subjunctive
obj.	object (for case of pronoun)	sup.	superlative
pa.t.	past tense	v.	verb (inf. unless otherwise indicated)
pl.	plural		
poss.	possessive	vbl.n.	verbal noun

A

a *pron.* he 5922
a *v.* have 4581, 7887, 8594
abbyte *n.* habit 8090
abye *v.* pay for 7273

abyde *n.* delay 3623n
abyde *v.* stay 334, 1688 etc.; stand his ground 2495, 4262 etc.; await 2554; withstand 5775. **abydythe** *pr.3 sg.* 2901. **abydys** *pr.pl.* 3963. **abyde** *subj.*

1025, 1537 etc. **abyde** *imp.sg.* 3349, 4630 etc. **abyde, abydes** *imp.pl.* 3067, 3630, 8381. **abode, abade** *pa.t.* stayed 3730, 7294 etc.; awaited 6934

abode *n.* delay 6217, 6670 etc..

aboughte *adv.* about 2503

above, aboven *adv.* above 1805, 6581 etc.; supreme 798; to prosperity 1428, 3681; in addition 7940n; *bryngys ~ to,* leads to 1193; *com(e)/brouwghte ~,* come/ brought to pass 723, 2321, 5627; *comys ~,* becomes known 1169; *comyste ~,* succeed 862

above *n.* *com(e) to his/here ~,* gain his/her end 5, 103; *att þer ~,* in their prosperity 4703

aboven *adv.* See Above.

aboven, abovyn *prep.* above 6258, *6654

abowne *prep.* from above 4240

acord(e) *n.* agreement 72, 5960, 6005; harmony 1779

acord(e) *v.* *~ to/tille,* agree with 2124, 2181, 8792. **acordys** *pr.3 sg.* 706. **acordyd** *pp.* 1572.

acorde *adj.* in agreement 5619

acordynge *vbl.adj.* compatible 1130

ado *n.* trouble 7746

adrad(e), adred *ppl.adj.* afraid 5055, 5923, 6382

aferd(e) *ppl.adj.* afraid 4612, 6872, 7016

affraye, afraye *n.* *in ~,* dismayed 2488; *made ~,* attacked 4508

agayn(e), ageyne *adv. & prep.* against 140, 1740 etc.; towards 4739, 6084; away 6631, 6799, 7015. *~ the nyght,* around nighttime 3067, 3630; *~ that,* when 3217

agaste, agasste, gaste *adj.* afraid 1969, 4616, 5922, 8619

ay(e) *adv.* ever 211, 268 etc.

ayels, ayl(e)s, aylys, alysse *pr.3 sg.* troubles 1215. *what ~ the/you,* what's wrong with you 833, 1061, 1413, 3375. **ayell** *subj.sg.* trouble 7049

ayre *n.* See Eyre *n.*².

alder, althur, al(l)ther *adv.* *~ beste,* the very best 528, 1460, 6852n; *~ wyseste* the very wisest 7161

alysse *pr.3 sg.* See Ayels.

allsone *adv.* *~ as,* as soon as 338

allther *adv.* See Alder.

allwaye, all-way(e), all-wayes, alwey *adv.* in every way 147, 401, 925, *5208

etc.; every time 985; forever 1163, 1384 etc.

alowe *v.* reward 3149

alse, alce *adv.* too 2415, 2433, 3454 etc. *~ wille,* equally well 1869n

alther, althur *adv.* See Alder.

alwey *adv.* See Allwaye.

am(e) *pr.1 sg.* See Be.

amend *v.* *(refl.)* reform 7101

ametas *n.* amethyst 2655n

amys *adv.* wrongly 712, 2242 etc.; unwelcome 7520n

and *conj.* and 2, 5 etc.; if 470, 967, 1221 etc.

an(e) *pron.* one 1034, *2384

angur *n.* anguish 900, 6729n, 8594; anger 1924, 2101 etc.

angurd *ppl.adj.* angered 6355, 7029

angurlye *adv.* severely 1101, 5432

anon *adv.* soon 1885, 3745, 3999; *~ that,* at once 432, 1563

apayde *pp.* See Payes.

aray(e) *n.* gear 293, 2368 etc.; costume 374, 2036 etc.; manner 2441, 6443. *off grette ~,* very well armed 4218; *on a ryche ~,* in great splendour 4235; *vppon a grette ~,* ?with a great show of strength 8218n; *out of ~,* in disarray 584n; *in good ~,* safe and sound 8735

aray(e) *v.* prepare 3042, 3060 etc. **aryesse** *pr.3 sg.* dresses 4727. **arayde** *pa.t.* prepared 335; dressed 7641. **arayd(e)** *pp.* prepared 1056; equipped 2939, 7589; dressed 4271, 5109 etc.

are, ere, eyre, or, yere, eere, here, yare *adv. & conj.* before 76, 739, 747, *1064, 1425, 5586, 7246, 8327, 8645, 8694 etc.

aryesse *v.* See Aray(e).

aright(e) *adv.* immediately 6423; speedily 8379

armetage *n.* See Ermytage.

armyne *n.* ermine 371

arre *pr.3 pl.* See Be.

art(e) *pr.2 sg.* See Be.

arte *n.* code and principles 1532; *cowde of ~,* understood the principles (of love) *1253n

asay, assaye *n.* *at ~,* under any circumstances 2482; in battle 5202; *see on ~,* test 412

asaye, assaye *v.* test 3116; try 7284. **asayd, assayde** *pp.* tested 120, 8051

asawte *n.* assault 7986

asemble *n.* See SEMBLE.

asethe *n.* *make* ~, give a satisfactory answer 6153

aske, axe, asse *v.* ask 233, 946, 1666 etc. asse *subj.* *4204. axte, axid, askyd, aste, axsyd *pa.t.* 68, 1282, 1945, *3722, 4223 etc.

asounder *adv.* asunder 6290

aspleff, aspenleff *n.* aspen leaf 6727n, 6871

assaye *n.* See ASAY.

assaye *v.* See ASAYE.

assayde *pp.* See ASAYE.

asse *v.* See ASKE.

asslayne *v.* slay 4591

as-tyte, astyte *adv.* immediately *7395, 8107

auntrys *n.pl.* adventures 2498

avayle *v.* be of advantage 11, 1558. avayles *pr.3 sg.* 7866

avyce *n.* *at your owne* ~, as you see fit 3751; *on ther* ~, in their opinion 5232

avysed, avysud, avyssud, avysyd *pp.* advised 5254. *ille* ~, ill-advised 924, 988, 5446 etc.; *be* ~ *(of)*, recall 6372, 8553

awauntys *pr.3 sg.* *(refl.)* ~ *hym of,* glories in 1148

awne *adj.* See OWN(E).

a-wonderd *pp.* See WONDER.

axe, axid, axte, axsyd *v.* See ASKE.

B

babelyng *pr.p.adv.* dangling 6783

badde *adj.* inadequate 1562n

bade *pa.t.* See BYDDE *v.*[1], BYDE *v.*[1].

bay *n.* *byde the* ~, stand at bay 585, 634 etc.; barking of dogs 3457

bakyne, bakone *ppl.adj.* ~ *venyson,* venison baked in dough 6832, 7239

bale *n.* ruin 784, 3101 etc.; torment 1459, 1792 etc.

bande *pa.t.* See BYNDE *subj.*.

bane *n.* slayer 4467, 4477

bankers *n. pl.* cloth bench covers 313

banne *v.* curse 5076, 5147 etc. *bargynne* ~, curse someone's actions 1300, 3883 etc.; arrange an agreement 5429. bannyde *pa.t.* condemned 4182

bare *pa.t.* See BER(E).

barnys *n.pl.* barons 755, 5805

baronage, boronage *n.* body of nobles 86, 5278

barste *v.* See BRASTE.

basnette *n.* pointed helmet 4460

bate *n.* disagreement 2221, 8826

battayle, battayll, battell *n.* battle 1561, 6947, 6966 etc.; distress 7512

batte *n.* blow 5492

be, bec(n), bene, bye *v.* be 21, 237, 372, 907, 6068 etc. am(e) *pr.1 sg.* 962, 7719 etc. art(e), artte *pr.2 sg.* 245, 328, 1142 etc. is, ys, yes *pr.3 sg.* 116, 122, 1364 etc. ar(e), arre, ys, ben(e) *pr.pl.* 887, 935, 1233, 1910, 6514, 7843 etc. be, bene, byne *pr.subj.* 238, 6351, 6352 etc. be *imp.* 1509, 4709 etc. was, whas *pa.t.sg.* 14, 4786n etc. was, wer(e), warre *pa.t.pl.* 174, 175, 558, 4552 etc. *pa.t. subj.* were, wore, ware 1044, 1113, 4222 etc. be, ben(e), byen, byne *pp.* 12, 162, 255, 959, 1937 etc.

be, by *prep.* ~ *that,* when 94, 2907 etc.

bede *subj.* See BYDE *v.*[1].

bedene *adv.* together 299, 915 etc.; indeed 1148, 4605 etc.; forthwith 1085, 8805; completely 2395, 2735 etc. *(all)* ~, every one of them 168, 565 etc.

bedyn *pp.* See BYDE *v.*[1].

bee(n) *v.* See BE.

bees *pr.3 sg.* will be 6732

begge *adj.* big 52

begylede, begillyd *pp.* disappointed 2722, 4818

behove *n.* benefit 868, 5576; situation 5336. *turnyd to no* ~, was of no use 1336

behouythe, behovys *v.impers.* it is necessary for/to 1847, 3965. *nedys* ~, absolutely must 1163

beyre, beyrethe, beyris *v.* See BER(E).

bekende *pa.t.* granted *289n; *the devill* ~, consigned to the Devil *7973. be-kende *pp.* known *6205

be-knowen *pp.* ~ *myth,* known to 8404

belde *n.* happiness *5995n

be-lefte *pp.* abandoned 962n, 1011

beleve *v.* remain 2782

be-lyve *adv.* quickly 3044, 4353 etc.

bell *n.* *berethe/bare the* ~, is/was the best 4782, 5893

ben *v.* See BE.

benche, benke *n.* bench 2640, 4036 etc.

bend *ppl.adj.* ornamented with bands 2699

bene *v.* See BE.

benysone *n.* *yaffe hym thare* ~, called on God to bless him 4507

benke *n.* See BENCHE.

benoyed *pp.* harassed 2091n

bent(e) *n.* open field 583, 634 etc.

ber *v.* See BER(E).

berde *n.*[1] beard 6159, 6878

berde *n.*[2] See BYRDE.

bere, beyre *n.*[1] coffin 1270, 1937 etc.

bere *n.*[2] bear 208, 5845 etc.

ber(e), beyre *v.* bear 297, 2190, 7784 etc. **bereth, berythe, beris, berys, beyrethe, beyris** *pr.3 sg.* 1262, 2256, 3133, 3157, 4782, 5995 etc.; possesses 5914. **beyre** *pr.3 pl.* bear 2510, 6589. **bere** *subj.sg.* 1737. **bare** *pa.t.* 143, 155 etc.

beryall *n.* burial 4492

beryed *pa.t.* buried 3241

beryinge, bereyng *vbl.n.* burial 1686, 3541

berlyde *pp.* served (esp. of drinks) 791

berste *pa.t.* See BRASTE.

besyde, besydys *adv.* nearby 2476, 7231 etc.

besought(e) *pa.t.* asked 2533, 5143 etc.

best *n.* beast 611

bestadde *pp.* beset 8049, 8449 etc.

bestode *pa.t. impers. nede ~*, was in distress *7568

betake *pr.1 sg.* entrust 4812

betyde, betydde *v.* come to pass 5088. *pa.t.* befell 5656, 5823 *subj.*come to pass 5820, *7649

be-tyme *adv.* promptly 8090

bett(e) *pp.* punished 1175, 3592

bewitt *v.* consider 7138n

by *prep.* See BE.

by(e) *v.* pay for 5418, 7963 etc. **bought** *pa.t.* 792, 2963 etc.

bydde, byde *v.*[1] direct 4283; pray 7330; ask 8282. **bydde** *pr.1 sg.* 1463. **byddythe** *pr.3 sg.* 1877. **bydde** *subj.pl.* desire 1845. **bade** *pa.t.* 906, 3175 etc. **byden** *pp.* 4191.

bydde *v.*[2] See BYDE *v.*[1]

byddyng *vbl.n.* command 789, 2519 etc.

byde, bydde *v.*[1] stay 1017, 1155 etc.; wait (for) 585, 2143 etc; face 3841, 3927 etc. **bydythe, bydis** *pr.3 sg.* awaits 2581; puts up with 3470; remains 8254. *~ ouer/on bente*, hold their ground in the field (of battle) 2275, 3494, 3511. **bede** *subj.* anticipate 6840n. **bade, bode** *pa.t.* stayed 5594; awaited 6600. **bedyn** *pp.* awaited 3442.

byde *v.*[2] See BYDDE *v.*[1]

bydyng *vbl.n.* waiting 1442

bye *n.* town 7208

bye *v.* See BE, BY(E).

bye *adv.* nearby 6291

byen *pp.* See BE.

byght *subj.* bite 6878n

bynde *subj.* imprison 1875n. **bonde, bande** *pa.t.* bound 388; joined with 2814n. **bounde, bovnden, bovndyn** *pp.* imprisoned 1197, 4779, 7182; subject 31; bound 1189; *~ wyth*, imprisoned by 6482

byne *pr.subj., pp.* See BE.

byrde, berde *n.* lady of noble birth 1729, 6833 etc. **byrdys** *pl.* 2113

ble *n.* hue 304, 601 etc. *chaungyd his ~*, made him turn pale 5701

bleche *n.* black dye or ink 6156n

blenchyd *pa.t.* See BLENKE.

blenke *v.* flee *7810. **blenchyd** *pa.t.* dodged *3131n

blere *v. there ynne to ~*, delude them 1835

blesse *v.* See BLYSSE.

blynne *subj.sg.* cease 7173

blysse, blys, blesse *v.* bless 436, 5076, 5147. **blessud** *pa.t.* 1517, 1863

blod(e) *n. of bone and ~*, See BON(E).

bo *num.* both *8069

bode, abode *n.* delay 3277, 6217 etc. *wythouten ~*, ceaselessly 7054

bode *pa.t.* See BYDE *v.*[1].

bofetys *n.pl.* blows 6877

bonde *pa.t.* See BYNDE *subj.*.

bon(e), bonne *n. of blod(e) and ~*, of body 52, 763, 997 etc.; *(made of) blode and/ne ~*, living 973, 6028

bone *adj.* See BOVNE.

boore *pp.* born 8327

borde *n.* table 778, 3489 etc.

borderyd *ppl.adj.* with ornamental borders 5935

bore *n.* boar 3652, 6148 etc.

boronage *n.* See BARONAGE.

borowe *n.* guarantor 7109

borowed *pp.* saved 5551, 6450

boteler(e) *n.* See BUTTELER.

bothes *pron. owre ~*, both our 7380

botys, bottis *n.pl.* boats 7548, 8311

botteler *n.* See BUTTELER.

bottry *n.* See BUTTREY.

bovgh *n.* forest 7490n, 8536. **bowes** *pl.* boughs 2446

bought *pa.t.* See BY(E).

bounde, bovnden, bovndyn *v.* See BYNDE *subj.*

bovne, bown(e), bone *adj.* ready, 635, 789, 7357 etc.; eager 5902, 8062; ~ *to,* ready for *4504

bowes *n.pl.* See BOVGH.

bownte, bovnte *n.* virtue 91, 546 etc.; valour 1149, 4782 etc. **bowntes** *pl.* *5018n

bowrdyng *n.* jousting 1133

bowre *n.* (lady's) bedchamber 1537, 1729 etc.

brace *n.* piece of armour protecting the arm *3263

brachet(t), brache *n.* a kind of small scenting hound 618, 641, 675 etc. **brachys, brachettys** *pl.* 609, 2378, 3600

brayd *n.* roast 3008

brayde *n.* outburst 1442

brayde *adj.* broad 4366

braste, barste, breste *v.* break 866, 901, 1394 etc. **brast(e), barste, brest(e), berste** *pa.t.* 2311, 3322, 3906, 4160, 4458, 5838 etc.

brathe *adj.* eager *4184

bravnche *n.* branch 1268n; form 7385

braune *n.* muscle 4604

brede *pa.t. bale* ~, brought on ruin 5929n. *pp.* brought 7698

breme *adj.* See BRYME.

brenne *v.* burn 1792. **brynde** *pa.t.* *1459n

breny *n.* coat of mail *8257. **brenniys** *pl.* *3322

breste *v.* See BRASTE.

brethellys, brothels *n.pl.* wretches 857, 1086

brether *n.pl.* brothers 8697

brym *n.* shore 1987

bryme, breme *adj.* fierce 3652, 6432 etc.

brynde *pa.t.* See BRENNE.

brodyrd *pp.* embroidered 313n

broke *n.* stream 7058

brond(e), bronnde *n.* sword 1693, 3282, 4608. **brondys** *pl.* 4366

brothels *n.pl.* See BRETHELLYS.

browe *n. kest downe wyth the* ~, lowered the eyebrows 7114. **browys** *pl.* brows 6149

burgays, burgayes, burges(se), burgas *n.* citizen 319, 4919, 5057, 5140, 5225 etc. **burges, burgayes** *pl.* 8180, 8868

bus, bvs *v.* must *45n, *3993, 5527, *5668, *8378, 8524

but *conj. & adv.* however 4, 19 etc.; unless 2987, 6198 etc.; apart from 3854n; *(adv.)* simply 6327

butteler, butelere, boteler(e), botteler *n.* man in charge of wine cellar 443, 449, 456, 467, 473, 492

buttrey, buttery, bottry *n.* wine cellar 446, 465, 776

C

C *num.* hundred 2916, 2950 etc.

cayre *v.* go *336

can, con(n) *v.*[1] **couthe, covthe, cowth(e), cowde** *pa.t & subj.* (1) be capable of *inf.* 212, 222 etc. *pr.1 sg.* 43 etc. *pr.2 sg.* 1306 etc. *pr.3 sg.* 50 etc. *subj.* 149 etc. *pa.t.* 59, 613 etc.
(2) ~ *of,* know about *pr.3 sg.* 270, 1133 etc. *subj.* 1253 etc. *pa.t.* 127, 319 etc.

can *v.*[2] See GAN.

cantell, cavntell *n. kyst in* ~, carried to one side 6751, 6896

care *n.* distress 280, 1011 etc.; hardship 1065, 4084 etc.

carefull *adj.* wretched 3682, 4687

carpynge *vbl.n.* gossiping 384

carpud *pa.t.* See KARPE.

cassadouns *n.pl.* chalcedony 2650

cast(e) *n.* intention 2302, 2967 etc.; doing 5389; hurling (of spears) 7988

cast(e), keste *subj.* plan 2230. *2imp.pl.* 1858; *(refl.)* arrange 2871. **caste, keste, kyst(e)** *pa.t.* planned 2143; set 3554, 6751; *(refl.)* acted 3244. ~ *of,* cast off 604; *(refl.)* contrive 6212; *colovre* ~, turned pale 1679, 5248, 7610; ~ *forthe,* proclaimed 6524

cawce, cause *n.* reason 3793, 4635 etc.; matter 6745

cecurly *adv.* See SECURLY(E).

certenly *adv.* See SERTENLY.

certes, certys, certus *adv.* See SERTYS.

charebokyll *n.* carbuncle (gemstone) 2896

chasse *v.* hurry 8066

chase *pa.t.* See CHESE.

chaste *adj.* chaste 62, 102 etc.; faithful 1930

chastenyng *vbl.n.* criticism 1551

chastyce, schastys *v.* chastise 826, 828

chaunce, chaunse *n.* exploit 4425; adventure in arms 5656; situation 6439. *þorow*

~, by chance 818. *tede hym a sely* ~, fortunately it so happened 6081

cheldorne *n.pl.* See CHYLD.

chere *n.* manner 62, 102 etc.; cheer 2017, 5933; mood 3376, 3977 etc.

chese *v.* choose 1824, 6193; *(refl.)* decide 2315. **chesse** *subj.* 2115, 2119 etc. **chosse** *2 imp.pl.* 3751. **chase, ches(s)e, ches** *pa.t.* 630, 8428; *(refl.)* betook himself *4514n, 5718. **chosyne, schosyn** *pp.* chosen 2132, 2157, 3361

chesone *n.* See ENCHESON.

chesour *n.* hunter (horse) 2429

chyd(e) *v.* scold 560, 6629. *subj.* complain 1837. **chyde** *pa.t.* scolded 1016

chyld, sheld, shyld *n.* youth of noble birth 164, 2412, 3912 etc. **chyldern, chyldorne, chyldur, cheldorne** *pl.* 770, 1697, 2524, 2566, 5108

chyne *n.* backbone 7891

chosse *2 imp.pl.* See CHESE.

claffe, clave *pa.t.* See CLEVE.

clene *adv.* entirely 4929, 5428. *white/quyte and* ~, completely 2292n, 7412

clenly *adv.* completely 5715

cleve, clave, claffe *pa.t.* split *4399, 8081, 8435. **clovyn** *pp.* 7889

clowgh *n.* steep hillside 5833

clovyn *pp.* See CLEVE.

cold *adj.* acute 4076n

comente *n.* See COMYNTE.

comynalte *n.* people 4561

comynte, comente *n.* community 1953, 2085

comnaunte, comnaunde *n.* agreement 2610, 6010 etc. *hold* ~, keep (this) promise 3122

con *v.* See CAN *v.*[1].

conyng *ppl.adj.* ~ *of craftys*, well-versed in (fighting) skills 6903

conysaunce, conisaunce, conusaunce *n.* knight's badge *2417, 3654, 3941, *4419

conn *v.* See CAN *v.*[1].

constreyne *v.* control 7142. **constrayns** *subj.pl.* force 2117. **constrenede** *pa.t.* arranged 5251

conteynes *pr.2 & 3 sg.* behave(s) *6986n, 7924

cope *n.*[1] fault 1481

cope *n.*[2] mantle 5201

copled *pp.* See COVPLED.

corde *v.* agree 2096, 3195. *pr.1 sg.* 2232. **cordys** *pr.3 sg.* ~ *to*, agrees with 549.

corded(e) *pa.t.* was compatible with 1502, 5099, 8566

coryous *adj.* skilful 3274

coste *n.* manner 617. *pl.* qualities 716. *nedys* ~, necessarily 6416

coste *v.* pay 1908. *pa.t.* cost 7252. *pp.* spent *4319

cotte, kytte *v.* cut 6226, 8673

covde *pa.t.* See CAN *v.*[1].

covncell, covnsell, counsell, counsayle *n.* judgement 1030; wisdom 1420; secret 1647, 4921 etc.; advice 1826, 1862 etc.; suggestion 2182

counten(n)aunce, countenavnce, covntenavnce *n.* conduct 515, 819 etc.; outward appearance 376, 894 etc.

covntre *v.* fight 5465

couthe, covthe, cowth(e) *pa.t.* See CAN *v.*[1].

cowenaunte *n.* agreement 6893

coueryd *pa.t.* recovered 4424

covytte *pa.t.* desired 8506

cowpe *pr.1 sg.* accuse 6745

cowpell *n. on* ~ *keste*, leashed together 3554

covpled, cowpled, copled *pp.* leashed together 3045, 3601, 4173

crabbyd *adv.* cantankerously 7919

crafte *n.* power 1306; work 5405. **craftys** *pl.* skills 6903

crapet *n.* toadstone *2654n

crasse *pa.t.* shattered 7988

crave *v.* ask for *2180

creante *n. yeld the* ~, acknowledge yourself vanquished 8031

crochett *n.* ?a curl of hair 7077n

crokand *pr.p.* hunched over 6259

crokyd *adj.* decrepit 6240, 6255

crownyd(e) *pp.* tonsured 8089; crowned 8790, 8844 etc.

currure *n.* courier 296

curte *n.* court 771

D

dalians *n.* polite or flirtatious conversation *6845n

dame *n.* mother 6567

dang *pa.t.* battered 4550, 6265

daungerus *adj.* haughty 2058

davnte *v.* overcome *800n, 802, 7347. *pa.t.* *386

daved *pa.t.* See DAWE.

dawe *v.* dawn 3089. **daved** *pa.t.* 1208

deale, deall *n.* See DEYLE.

deale *v.* See DEYLE.

debat(t)e *n.* dispute 344, 347 etc.; quarrel 5947

dede *n.* death 1423, 1477 etc.

defawte *n.* lack 703

defende *v.* ward off 5668; protect 6497, 6742 etc. **defendys** *pr.3 sg.* fights defensively *5841n. **defende** *subj.sg.* protect 6198

degre *n.* social level 116, 961 etc.; state 939. *in/at all ~,* in every way 92, 179 etc.

deyle, deyell, deale, deall, dell *n.* part 685, 1469, 5271 etc. *euery ~,* completely 1074, 1469 etc. (see also under ILK(E)); *neuer a ~,* not at all 6018, 6365; *sum ~,* somewhat 2407

deyle, deale, dell *v.* cope 7925, 8522; deal 7283

deynes *pr.3 sg.* seems worthy of *2598n

deynely *adv.* disdainfully 6880n

deynere *n.* See DYNER(E).

deyre *n., adj., adv.* See DERE.

deyred, deyris *v.* See DERE.

deysse *n.* dais 3574

dell *n.* See DEYLE.

dell *v.* See DEYLE.

demenyste *pr.2 sg.* conducts 7921. **demeynes** *pr.3 sg. (refl.)* conducts himself 6983

denne, dene *n.* noise 7626, 8290; clamour 8226

dent *n.* blow 3285, 3900 etc. *pl.* 4551. *~ off hand,* armed assault 3534

derayne *n.* challenge to single combat *6329n, *6528n. **dereynes** *pl.* fighting *698on (see also RAYNE)

dere, deyre *n.*[1] harm 1120, 1535 etc. *made no ~ ayens,* did no harm to 8280

dere *n.pl.*[2] deer 581, 607 etc.

dere *v.* harm 5422, 8115. **deyris** *pr.3 sg.* 5917. **deyred** *pa.t.* 5697

dere *adj.* noble 33, 2050 etc.; beloved 205, 244 etc.

dere, deyre *adv.* at great cost 792, 1115, 2963n, 3314n etc.

dereynes *n.pl.* See DERAYNE.

dereworthy *adj.* honoured 248, 394 etc.

deroye *n.* judicial combat 8582

deskrye *v.* See DYSCRYE.

destaunce n. makythe ~, cause trouble 6338

devyce *n. at his owne ~,* at his discretion 357; *at ~,* obediently 4143

devyce *v.* arrange 827

dether *adv.* thither 2982

derne *adj.* secret or profound 797; hidden 3088, 3634 etc.

devynyte *n.* divination 4205

dyd *pa.t. ~ to,* made to 4215; *~ vpone,* put on 6566

dyght(e) *v.* dress (a carcass) 668; *(refl.)* make ready 8147. **dyght** *pa.t.* dressed 3451, 5766, 8197; built 7335. **dyght(e)** *pp.* dressed 2430, 3849 etc.

dyner(e), deynere *n.* dinner 2632, 6954, 7229 etc.

dyscomfettour, dyscomfetture *n.* defeat 3932, 5919

dysconfyte, dyscomfett *pp.* defeated 3643, 4226

dyscrye, dyscryve, deskrye *v.* describe 2062, 4058, 7833. **dyscryede** *pa.t.* 6128

dyscure *v.* discover 2342

dyssece, dysses *n.* decease 7204, 8864

dyssesse *n. done grette ~,* caused much trouble 3243

dystresse *n. of ~,* of violence 7860

dystrobelyst *pr.2 sg.* disturbs 8391

dystrowys, dystrwes *pr.3 sg.* cures 703; destroys 7967

dyueres, dyueresse, dyvers *adj.* different 606, 2908, 4941 etc.

dobelers *n.pl.* platters 6157

dole *n.* See DULL(E).

dome *adj.* unable to speak *1072

doome *n. be my ~,* in my opinion *6961

doser *n.* decorative cloth used as wall hanging or seat cover 314

doter *n.* feeble-minded person 1984

dotyste, dottyst *pr.2 sg.* grow feeble-minded 1968; rave 7745; **dotte** *pr.1 pl.* are mad 6696

doway *interj.* enough! 3707, 7742

dowte, dovte *n.* fear 4551; respect 5938. *in ~,* anxious 2494, 5707

dowtly *adv.* doughtily 6797

draught *n.* drink 1255n

draw *pa.t.* See DRYVE.

draw(e) *v.* go 734, 3019 etc.; draw 936, 1477 etc.; come 2439. **drawythe, drawethe, drawys** *pr.3 sg.* draws 653, 4474; goes 3343, 3930, 5858. **drawes** *pr.3 pl.* draw 5799. **drew(e), drowgh, drawen** *pa.t.* drew 3674, 3790, 3812 etc.; pulled out 4473, 4686 etc.; came 5542; went 8535. **drawen** *pp.* drawn 4523

drede *pa.t.* feared 818, 865. *imp.sg. (refl.)* 2754.

dred(d)e *n.* dread 1351, 1843 etc.; distress 2287. *wythoute(n)* ~, without doubt 4996, 7558

dreve, drevyn(e) *v.* See DRYVE.

drew(e) *n.* darling 2739, 3013 etc.

drew(e) *pa.t.* See DRAW(E).

drewry *n.* love courtship 702, 8750

dryve *v.* suffer 1114; force 1897; draw (*for* drave), dreve *pa.t.* passed 2043, 2145, 2687. **drevyn(e)** *pp.* driven 3932, 6799

drowgh *pa.t.* See DRAW(E).

dulfuly *adv.* terribly *4304

dull(e), dole *n.* sorrow 7605, 7626; lament 6611

dure *v.* continue 7117. **dweryng** *pr.p.* enduring 8329

dweryng *pr.p.* See DURE.

E

eere *adv. & conj.* See ARE.

eft(e), heft *adv.* again *839n, 1443 etc.; still 2260, 3184 etc.; likewise 472; back 1389; after 2396. ~ *agayne*, once again 4585. ~ *synes*, again 3367. ~ *sythe*, ever since 1483. ~ *sonys/sones*, immediately 5908, 6805 etc.; again *4664

eye, iȝe *n.* eye 898, 2665 etc. **eyne, ynne, yȝen** *pl.* 1627, 1835, 4315 etc.

eyme *n.* See EME.

eyne *n.pl.* See EYE.

eyre *n.*[1] ear 1574, 3295 etc.

eyre, ayre *n.*[2] heir 34, 82, 345n etc.

eyre *n.*[3] manner 5476

eyre *adv. & conj.* See ARE.

eyrste *adv.* first 7808

eysythe *pr.3 sg. (refl.)* be reassured 7107

eyton *pp.* See ETE.

elde, eolde *n.* age 94, maturity 114. *to* ~, of age 58

elde *adj.* See OLD.

eldythe *pr.3 sg.* See YELD(E).

eme, eyme *n.* uncle 1840, 2356 etc.

emydys, emyddis *prep.* in the middle of 3896, 6427

encheson, enchosone, chesone *n.* cause 2778; reason 3640, *3685

endure, indewre *v.* withstand 6966, 7914

endurs, endyrs *adj.* this ~ *day*, the other day 3216, 8713

entent(e), intent(e), tente *n.* intention 464, 2885. *did his* ~, carried out his intention 2994. *take* ~, take heed 519, 3292 etc. *wyth goode* ~, with good will 47, 8763

envye *n.* malice 6113; *have* ~ *(at/of)* be angered (by) 718, 5666, 7733 etc.

eratyke, eretyke *n.* heretic 2104n, 2109n

erber(e) *n.* garden 2046, 2213

ere *adv. & conj.* See ARE.

ermytage, armetage *n.* hermitage 3058, 3624 etc.

essu *v.* come 5932

essuynge *vbl.n.* departing 6082

estate *n.* social standing 844, 2232

ete, ette *v.* eat 194, 8634 etc. **ettys** *pr.3 sg.* 7051. **ette** *subj.sg.* 3668. **etand** *pr.p.* 6451. **ete** *pa.t.* 783. **ettyn, etton, eyton** *pp.* 199, 780, 7192 etc.

F

facyon(e) *n.* appearance 644, 7604

fade *v.* waste away 4360

faye *n.* faith 4094, 4922 etc. *in* ~, truly 2362, 5175 etc.

faye *adj.* enchanting 6366

faylard *n.* delinquent 2102

fayle *v.* disappoint 1717; end 3323; lack 4894; fail 7290, 7816. **fayl(e)s** *pr.3 sg.* fails 2977, 2984; lacks *3192. *subj.sg.* lack 6621; ~ *of*, fail at 1466. **faylyd** *pa.t.* failed 2968, 4295 etc. ~ of, lacked 363

fayne *v.* refrain from 6328n. **faynes** *pr.3 sg.* pretends 6989. **faynyd, feynde** *pa.t. (refl.)* pretended to be 1224; restrained herself *5250n

fayne *adj.* pleased 450, 1117 etc. *for* ~, for joy 6085, 8749

fayne *adv.* eagerly 327, 1316 etc.

fayre *n.* land of fairy 3991

fayre, feyre *adj.* fair 7, 2444 etc. **fayre, fayrer** *comp.* 972, 2526 etc. **feyrest** *sup.* 63, 3098

fayre *adv.* duly 5963, 6005 etc.; well 339, 686 etc.

fayrehedde *n.* beauty 848, 1403

fayrenes *n.* beauty 536, 693

fayreth *pr.3 sg.* See FARE.

fande *pa.t.* See FYNDE.

fande *pp.* striven 4941

farand(e) *adj. ille* ~, unseemly 6249, 6581

farde *pa.t.* See FARE.

fare *n.* fuss 4662, 4974 etc.; demeanour

6979, 7380; business 8209. *freshe* ~, bold
doings 4342

fare *v.* go 246, 281 etc.; do 7898. **farithe,
faris, fayreth** *pr.3 sg.* fares 6098;
behaves 6969, 7002; ~ *be/of,* is the case
with 2337, 7023, 7028, 7044; *so* ~ *of,*
such is the case with 7028n. **fare** *subj.sg.*
get on 324, 5513. **faryd, farde** *pa.t.*
behaved 6334; fared 8859. **fard, fare**
pp. dealt 7933, 8590

fare, farre, fer(r)e *adj.* far 171, 1750 etc.;
distant 405, 434 etc.

fare, farre, fer(r)e *adv.* far 281, 654, 4718
etc. *puttys hymselfe so* ~, pushes himself
so hard 1121

faringlye *adv. ille* ~, unattractively 6228

faris, farithe *pr.3 sg.* See FARE.

farre *adj. & adv.* See FARE.

fast(e) *adv.* quickly 356, 575 etc.; intently
999, 6739 etc.; severely 1399, 3791 etc.;
intensely 3321, 4370 etc.; soundly 4176,
6712; firmly 1189; hard 8183

favght(e) *v.* See FYGHT(E).

favnde *pa.t.* See FYND(E).

favelard *n.* pretender 1966

febly *adv.* poorly 5513

fee *n. of* ~, by heritable right 1707

feelle *pr.3 sg.* See FELLE.

feynde *pa.t.* See FAYNE.

feyntys *n.* weakness 638; faint-heartedness
4992n

feyre *n.* fear 7004

feyre, feyrest *adj.* See FAYRE.

feys *n.pl.* estates *1940n

feelle *v.* experience 1985. **felle, fele** *pr.1
sg.* experience 475; feel 2881, 5183; think
7387. **feld, felte** *pa.t.* experienced 1972,
5175

feld(e) *v.* See FELL *v.*[1], FELLE, v.

fele *pr.1 sg.* See FEELLE.

fele *adj.* many 2345

fell *v.*[1] strike down 4093, 4115. **feld(e)**
pa.t. 3265, 3516 etc. **feld(e)** *pp.* 3161,
3753 etc.

fell *v.*[2] *pa.t.* happened *1769n, 6441, 6530

fell *adj.* bold 4785, 5896 etc.

felle *pr.1 sg.* See FEELLE.

fellt *ppl.adj.* felled 4386

felow(e) *n.* comrade 2865, 3390; good
fellow 1386n; match 4350, 5764 etc.
felow(e)s *pl.* comrades 1419, 1951 etc.

feltred *ppl.adj.* tangled 6147

ferd *ppl.adj.* afraid 6278

ferde *n.* fear 7453

fere *n.*[1] companion 3190; spouse 4964; *to
his* ~, as his wife 2978; *fendys* ~, devil's
accomplice 6482, 7612

fere *n.*[2] *in* ~, together *5974

fere *adj. & adv.* See FARE.

ferlye *adv.* wonderfully 2075

ferre *adj. & adv.* See FARE.

ferrome, fervm *adv. a/on* ~, far away
*6410n; in the distance 8126

fers *adj.* proud 948, 959; fierce 4785, 5896

feste *pa.t. forward* ~, pledged 5013, 5292

fest(e) *pp.* fixed *207, 599 etc.

fet(e) *n.* feat of arms 652; manner *3889

fete, fett *n.pl.* feet 5801, 7235 etc.

fetowre, fetter *n.* build, figure (of body)
166, 363

fett *n.pl.* See FETE.

fett(e) *v.* conduct *2744n; take *8269n.
fett(e) *pa.t.* went *2832n; struck
*3306n; conducted 3000. **fette** *pp.*
brought *5810

fetter *n.* See FETOWRE.

fewte *n.* fealty 5616

feuter, fewter *n.* lance-rest 4568, 7811

fyght(e), fyghtte *v.* fight 1941, 1970, 4273
etc. **favght(e)** *pa.t.* 5837, 7794. **faught**
pp. 8686

fyle *v.* sully 2440. **fylyd** *pp.* 1403

fynde *v.* find 257, 724 etc. **fyndys** *pr.3 sg.*
maintains 6975. **fonde** *subj.* 2332n.
fonde, fande, favnde *pa.t.* found 266,
1119, 4216 etc. **fonne, fovne, fovnden**
pp. found 5310, 6862; thought of 6674

fyne *n.* recompense 7001

fyne *v.* cease 2707, 3281 etc.; stop *7888.
pr.3 pl. delay *6995n

fyne *adv.* satisfactorily 7240

fyr(e) *n.* sparks *7836, 7983

fyrste *ord.num. at the* ~, forthwith 6420

fyrthe *n.* See FRITHE.

flem *n.* ~ *Iurdanne,* River Jordan 3215

fletyn *pp.* ~ *wyth,* disputed with 3873n

flettys *pr.3 sg.* sails 8191

flytand *pr.p.* quarrelling *6671.

flyte *pp.* See FLYTTE.

flytte *v.* move 8789. **flyte** *pp.* removed
6410

flode *n.* sea 4219, 7551 etc.

floure, flowre *n.*[1] flower 111; the best
1735. **flovrys, flouris, flowres** *pl.* flow-
ers 564, 2447, 7993 etc.

floure, flore *n.*[2] floor 788, 6427, etc.

foyned *pa.t.* ~ *on*, thrust at 8412n

fole, foole, foll(e), foule *n.* fool 840, 980, 1017, 1097, 3580 etc.

foley *adj.* foolish 7274

folelyche *adj.* mad 7311

foly(e), folly, fowlie *n.* foolishness 709, 2241 etc.; imprudence 811; madness *6281n, 6524, 6624 etc.; *makyth* ~, causes harm 1781

foll(e) *n.* See FOLE.

fonde *pa.t.* See FYNDE.

fone *num.* few *3477n, *3841

fonge, fonnge *v.* take 2674, 2984

fonne *v.* make a fool of him 7279

fonne *pp.* See FYNDE.

fonnge *v.* See FONGE.

foors *v.* strive 6742. **forses** *pr.3 sg.* 4273. *pr.3 pl.* 4382. **forsyd** *pa.t.* (*refl.*) 5749

for *prep.* for 48, 57 etc.; because of 435, 540 etc.; ~ *to* + *inf.*, to 22, 65 etc.

for *conj.* because 666, 697 etc.; so that 600

forbode *n. Godys* ~, God forbid *333n, 8008

fore-dede *n.* favour 6690

fores *n.* See FORS.

foresoke *pa.t.* See FORSAKE.

forfare *v.* destroy 8283

forfete *pp.* See FORFYTTE.

forfettynge *vbl.n.* offence 7111

forfytte *v.* lose 1854. **forfete** *pp.* confiscated *1987

forgett *v.* forget 2830. **forgettys** *pr.3 sg.* 2450. **forgat(t)e, forȝete** *pa.t.* 775, 864 etc.; omitted 693. **forgetton, forgotton** *pp.* forgotten 200, 8061 etc.

formeste *adj.* greatest 2055

for-rwne, for-ron, for-renne *pp.* exhausted with running 582, 633, 645

fors, fores *n.* force 5853. *no* ~, it doesn't matter 4696, 6788, 8703; *gaff no* ~, do not care 2362; *made no* ~, wouldn't care 7971

forsake *v.* refuse 6401, 8725. **forsakys** *pr.3 sg.* abandons 3680, 3699. **foresoke** *pa.t.* refused 450. **forsake, forsakyn** *pp.* 2080, 2163, 2952, 4692

forses, forsyd *v.* See FOORS.

fortenyght(e) *n.* two weeks 1493, 6505

forthy(e), forthe *adv.* therefore 494, 1084, 1508 etc.

for-þynkys *pr.3 sg.* (*impers.*) regret 3298, 3401 etc. **for-thought** *pa.t.* 3053, 4597, etc.

forward *n.* contract 2791; ~ *feste*, pledged 5013, 5292

for-wery *adj.* exhausted 5374

foule *n.*[1] See FOLE.

fowle *n.*[2] bird 315. **foulys, fovlys, fowlys** *pl.* 565, 2445, 2807 etc.

fowle *n.*[3] evil 5171, 6694

fovle *adj.* horrible 6161, 6163. **fowler** *comp.* 6145

fowle *adv.* miserably 4360, 5171

fowlie *n.* See FOLY(E).

foundes, foundys *pr.3 sg.* rushes *3046; sets off 3599; hastens 4174. *pr.3 pl.* rush 605. **fovnde, foundyd** *pa.t.* set out 2811, 5792; hastened 5992. **fowndyn** *pp.* undertaken 7987

fowndyn *pp.* See FOUNDES.

fovne *pp.* See FYNDE.

frayne *v.* ask 6045

fre(e) *n.* lady 132, 1315 etc.; gracious one 5276, 6914

fre(e) *adj.* gracious 231, 4881 etc.

frely *adv.* beautifully 2692

freyght *n.* charge 4588

freke *n.* man 722

freke *adj.* bold 6315

frendship *n.* friends 8679

freshe *adj.* ~ *fare*, bold doings 4342

freshely *adv.* boldly 7994

fresly *adv.* fiercely 5864n

frethe *n.* See FRITHE.

frette *ppl.adj.* decorated 6458

frithe, frythe, fyrthe, frethe *n.* woodland 605, 2447, 2471, 6672 etc.

fro *conj.* from (when) 103, 764 etc.; when 6661

frowardely *adv.* insolently 8714

ful, full *adv.* very 222, 3801 etc. ~ *longe*, the whole time 199

G

ga *v.* See GO.

gade *n. plowgh* ~, sharpened stick to goad oxen 6233n

gadyrd, gadurd *pa.t.* See GEDYRS *pr.3 sg.*

gaye *n.* jay 6312

gay(e) *adj.* bright 153, 1185 etc.

gayne *adj.* quick 6219

gayne *prep.* towards 744

game(n) *n.* pleasure 75, 4820; hunting 530

gamen *v.* play 796n

gan, can *pa.t. aux. verb:* 'did + (*inf.*)' 60, 306 etc.

gang(e) *v.* go 214, 1150 etc. *pr.3 pl.* *7917. *subj.* 8168

gar(re) *v.* cause 2143, 2183. **gars** *pr.3 sg.* 1228. **gart(t)e, gert(t)e** *pa.t.* 1023, 1256, *3042 etc.; made 1480, 3882 etc.; prepared 3832. **gerte** *pp.* made 3696

gart(t)e *v.* See GAR(RE).

gas *pr.3 sg.* See GO.

gaste *adj.* See AGASTE.

gate *n.* way 6628. **gatys** *pl.* 6219; *his* ~ *goone*, gone on his way 5304, 5317

gate *pa.t.* See GETT.

gatys *n.pl.* See YATE.

gatte *pa.t.* See GETT.

gedyrs *pr.3 pl. (refl.)* assemble 1775. **gadyrd, gadurd** gained 4281, 5671

geyre *n.* armour 2400, 2499 etc.

gent(e) *adj.* noble 1523, 2269 etc.

gentryse *n.* nobility of birth 539

gerdyll *n.* belt 910

germayn *adj. cossyn* ~, first cousin *3304n

gert(t)e *pa.t.* See GAR(RE).

gett *v.* get 2978, 6209 etc. **gate, gatte, gett** *pa.t.* got 34, 4138 etc.; had 80; took 6229, 7191; went 7874n

gydyde *pa.t. (refl.)* behaved 511

gile, gille *n.* trickery 2434, 8306 **gylyde** *pp.* deceived 1404

gille *n.* See GILE.

gyrdythe *pr.3 sg.* puts on 1693; attires 4280

gyte *n.* gown 6460

glade *pa.t.* See GLYDE.

glas *pr.3 sg.* glances *3908n. **glasyd** *pa.t.* 4579

glyde *v.* glide 7819. **glade** *pa.t.* flew *3736n

glyttrand *pr.p.adj.* glittering 6317

go, ga *v.* go 224, 638 etc. **goos** *pr.2 sg.* 1159 **go(o)s, go(o)the, gas** *pr.3 sg.* 630, 1347, 1695, 2394, 2423 etc. **goothe** *pr.3 pl.* 1036. **gon** *subj.sg.* 2741. **went(e)** *pa.t.* 16, 744 etc. **gon(e), gonne, goone** *pp.* 506, 887, 1050, 3423 etc.

godely *adj.* excellent 918, 2703. **godelyer** *comp.* 8839

godely *adv.* well 889, 2073 etc.

gon(e), gonne *pp.* See GO.

good *n.* good man 6104

goone, goos, goothe *pp., pr.3 sg.* See GO.

gore *n.* robe 4860

gorgede, gorget *n.* piece of armour protecting neck 5496n, 6158n

gos, gothe *pr.3 sg.* See GO.

grace *n. sory* ~, misfortune 5542

graythe *adj.* clear *5265, 6373

graunt(e) *v.* grant 1690, 2265 etc.; concede 8030. **graunte, gravntyd** *pa.t.* granted 283, 895 etc.; agreed (with) 2144, 2781. **graunte, grauntyd** *pp.* yielded 808; granted 3722

gre *n.* victor's prize 3341, 4349 etc.

grede *v.*[1] lament *1483n

grede *v.*[2] *pa.t.* called out 2816n

gree *n.* pleasure *8744

greffe *n., v.* See GREVE *n.*[1], *v.*

gremly *adj.* ferocious 4611, 4796

gresly *adj.* terrible 1217

gresse *n.*[1] *of* ~, well fattened 3571

gresse *n.*[2] grass 7837. **gresses** *n.pl.* 4666

grete *n.* ground 5802

grete *pp.* afflicted 1468

greve, greffe *n.*[1] sorrow 1468, 4484 etc.; offence 8486. *pl.* sorrows 1801

greve *n.*[2] grove 2581

greve, greue, greffe *v.* upset 232, 1053, 5410 etc. **grevythe, greuythe** *pr.3 sg.* 5545, 5584 etc. **greve** *imp.2 sg.* 874. *subj. what* ~ *vs*, what is it to us (if . . .) 6627. **grevyd, greuyd** *pa.t.* upset 1923; was upset 7429. **grevyd, greuyd** *pp.* upset 2763, 6804

grevo(u)s *adj.* harsh 1642, 8030

grewo(u)sly, grevessly *adv.* violently 5503, 7189, 7874

gryethe *n.* See GRYTHE.

grym(e), grymme *adj.* fierce *4411, 5826, 8324; intense 1624

grythe, gryethe *n.* mercy 234; *haue* ~, be spared 611

groande *pr.p.* growing 4666

groche *v.* deny 2265. **groge** *pr.2 sg.* 2733. **grochyees** *pr.pl.* grumble 1799. **grogyd(de)** *pa.t.* grumbled 1879, 7064

gurdovn *n.* reward (or punishment) 804

H

hackeney *n.* small saddle horse 5529, 5533

hade *pa.t.* took 4491

hale *adj.* healthy 1187

halff-dele, haundell *n.* half as much 3855, 4067

hals(s)e *n.* neck 591, 2414 etc.

hame *n.* See HOME.

hand(e), hond *n.* hand 1600, 2469 etc.; might 6743; fighting ability 1566, 1731 etc. *in* ~, under control 6587, 8299 etc. *on* ~, in his hand(s) 457, 2647 etc. *take in* ~, undertake 6123; *to* ~, assiduously 1315, 6822. *to his* ~, under his command 31, 8250. **handys, hande** *pl.* hands 1815, 4672 etc.

hange, hangyth *subj., pp.* See HYNGYTH.

hap(p)e *n.* prosperity 131, 469 etc.; fate 3900, 4578 etc. *if me be* ~, if it be my fortune 6688

happy *adj.* prosperous 160

harburage *n.* lodgings 7060

harbured, harboryd *pa.t. (refl.)* lodged 2947; 6820

hard(e) *v.* See HERE.

harde, herde *adv.* firmly 883; fiercely 4384, 5859 etc.

hardely *adv.* assuredly 3679, 7384

hardenes, hardynes *n.* boldness 516, 545 etc.

hardy, herdy *adj.* brave 544, 3829 etc.

hare *adv.* at this time 1896

harnes, harneys, harnays, harnys, hernes *n.* belongings 1280, 1376, 6599 etc.; fighting equipment 2364, 2493, 2510 etc.

harnessyd *pp.* armed 7634

hartte *n.* See HERT(E) *n.*[1]

haspis *n.pl.* fastenings *2658n

hathel *adj.* noble *3476n

hat, hat(t)e *pr.1 sg.* am called 1125, 3950 etc. *pr.3 sg.* is called 1467, 5189, 6038 etc. **hight(e)** *pa.t.* 762, 1999 etc.; promised 3147, 3216, 3359 etc. *pp.* promised 2833, 6053 etc.

hate, hatte *n.* cap (cloth or steel) 4522, 8082 etc.

hawbreke, haubreke, hawbrake, hawberke *n.* coat of mail 3906, 5497, 5726, 5817. **haubrakys, hawberkys** *pl.* 3262, 5804

haundell *n.* See HALFF-DELE.

havoke *n.* ruin 7565

hede, hedde, heede *n.* heed 774, 1348, 4055 etc.

hedeowes *adj.* See HEDOVS.

hedde *n.*[1] head 684, 754 etc.; spearhead 5497, 7289. **heddys, hedys** *pl.* heads 743, 3475 etc.; spearheads 7816n

hedde *n.*[2] See HEDE.

hedovs, hedeowes *adj.* tremendous 4175; frightful 7606, 7627

heed *pa.t.* See HYE.

heede *n.* See HEDE.

heft *adv.* See EFT(E).

heyes *pr.3 sg.* raises 3653

heyld *pa.t.* See HOLD.

heyr(e) *n.* hair 4473, 4686 etc.

held(e), heldyn, heldythe *v.* See HOLD(E).

hele *n.* health 395

hem *pron.* them 346, 500 etc.; him 1196, 2804 etc.

hende, hynde *n.* noble one 4712, 5641

hend(e), hynde *adj.* noble 160, 2925, *7106 etc.

hent(e) *pa.t.* took hold of 2215, 3275, 4741; pulled 5384

her *poss.pron.* See THEY.

herbowre *n.* lodgings 309

herde *v.* See HERE.

herde *adv.* See HARDE.

herdy *adj.* See HARDY.

here *v.* hear 2, 524 etc. **herde, hard(e)** *pa.t.* heard 185, 247, 417 etc. *pp.* 20, 739 etc.

here *adv. & conj.* See ARE.

heryne *n.* ~ *pan*, cranium 8082

herytage, heritage *n.* right of inheritance 8845, 8849

herke *imp.2 sg.* See HERKYNE.

herkyne *v.* listen for 2071; ~ *aftur*, seek word of 5641. **herkyns, herke, herkyn** *imp.2 sg.* 2668, 6321, 6480

hernes *n.* See HARNES.

hert(e), hertt(e), hartte, hurt *n.*[1] heart 188, 284, 287, 561, 4737, 7559 etc.; spirit 2319, 2084 etc.; resolution 5728, 5826. **herttys** *pl.* 3280, 6290 etc.

hert(e) hertte *n.*[2] hart 573, 630 etc. **herttys** *pl.* 585, 733 etc.

herttly *adv.* heartily 1807, 2580 etc.

hethen *adv.* here 3215

hete, hette *n.* heat 2459, 6816

hevyn *adv.* directly 8415

hy(e) *adj.* See HIGH.

hyde *n. chaungynge hewe and* ~, changing colour 3374

hye, hy *v.* hurry 523, 5388 etc. **hyes, hyeth** *pr.3 sg.* 621, 1342 etc. **hygh** *subj.sg.* 7410. **hye, high** *imp.pl.* 2325, 4190. **hyed, hyde, heed** *pa.t.* 735, 3253, 4617 etc.

hye *interj.* hey! 7920

high *n.* exalted one 366.

high *imp.pl.* See HYE.

high, hy(e), hygh *adj.* high 3476, 4994,

7957 etc. *on* ~, soon 3790, 4049, 6385; aloft 4609; on high 8633

hight(e), hyghte *n. on* ~, on top 3283n; on high *3694, *7407, 8146; aloud 5020, 7852

highte, hyghte *v.* See HAT.

hyly *adv.* earnestly 4121

hynde *n., adj.* See HENDE.

hyngyth *pr.3 sg.* hangs 6152. **hynge** *pr.3 pl.* 6149. **hange** *subj.sg.* 1964, 7271. **hangyng** *pr.p.* 6237. **hyng(e)** *pa.t.* 5567, 6783. **hange, hangyd** *pp.* 1901, 6231 etc.

hyrone *n.* corner 6275

his, is, ys *detached genitive marker* 57, 3237, 5066, 5142, 7902

hit, hytte *pron.* it 445, 803 etc.

hode, hoode *n.* hood 6572. *be my* ~, 'by my hood' 2599, 7562. **hode** *pl.* 5138

hold(e) *n.* castle 2849, 5931; keeping 4073; ~ *at*, help from 7529

hold(e) *v.* hold 117, 1016 etc.; *(refl.)* stand firm 1561, 2343; consider 508, 6574 etc.; maintain 2833, 6010 etc. ~ *of* rule as vassal of 71, 1871. **hold(e)** *pr.1 sg.* consider 3009, 3158 etc.; maintain 3122, 3359 etc. **holdest(e)** *pr.2 sg.* consider 2758, 7714. **holdys, holdythe, heldythe** *pr.3 sg.* maintains 181; considers 1097; stays 4406, *(refl.)* 5751. **hold(ys)** *pr.3 pl.* consider 6973, 6978. **hold(en)** *subj.* maintain 5012, 7768; hold back 6561; ~ *wyth*, support 2226. **hold** *imp.pl. (refl.)* stay 7798. **held(e), heyld** *pa.t.* maintained 128, 135; held 484, 881 etc.; considered 688, 3579 etc.;*(refl.)* stood firm 4519. **heldyn** *pa.t.pl.* held 6769. **hold(e), holden, holdyn** *pp.* considered 26, 157 etc.; obliged 254; maintained 312, 402 etc.; held 5291; ~ *hoote*, vigorously pursued 640

holdynge *vbl.n.* ~ *of*, preventing 345n

hole *adv.* wholly 1205

holyne *n.* holly 7596

home, whome, hame *n.* home 211, 2596, 3564 etc.

home *pron.* See WHOME.

hond(e) *n.* See HAND(E).

hoo *interj.* stop! 7369

hoode *n.* See HODE.

hoope *v.* See HOPE.

hoote *adj.* ardent 8825. **hottys** *super.* hottest 1103

hoote, hote *adv.* ardently 640, 835, 2233n; hot 6673

hope, hoope *v.* ~ *of,* expect 9. *pr.1 sg.* believe 20, 1157 etc. **hopys** *pr.2 sg.* 981

hopyng *vbl.n.* expectation 1501

hose *n.* stocking 6236. *pl.* hose 2462

hote *adv.* See HOOTE.

hottys *adj.* See HOOTE.

howse *n.* household 128, 135 etc.

hove *v.* ride 3094, 3103 etc. **houythe, hovis, houys, hoves** *pr.3 sg.* rides 2557, 2605, 4243 etc.; halts 3090, 7284 etc. **hov(e)and** *pr.p.* waiting 3963, *7779.* **hovyd, houyd** *pa.t.* stopped 3518, 3730, 7984 etc.; rode 4239, 8126

how(e), who *adv.* how 43, 2005, 8502 etc.

huncouthe *adj.* See VNCOVTH(E).

hurt *n.* See HERT(E).

I

I *interj.* exclamation of frustration 1109

ibete *ppl.adj.* decorated 368

ycore *ppl.adj.* excellent *2401n

idyght *ppl.adj.* dressed 7078

yflemyd *pp.* exiled 8320

i3e, y3en *n., n.pl.* See EYE.

ilk(e), ylk, ilk(e) a *adj.* each 1894, 2092 etc. ~ *a dell/de(y)le/dealle,* a great deal 192; all 1405, 1541, 2825, 3575, 3847

ilkone, ilke one *pron.* each one 8, 352 etc.

ill(e), yll(e) *n.* harm 892n, 1761 etc.; wrong 7100, 7175. *take it at/to/for* ~, feel insulted 870, 1874, 1948 etc. *gaff her* ~, grieved 4370, 6518. *wyth* ~, causing harm 5555, 6120, 7197

ill(e), yll(e) *adj.* difficult 1332; sinful 2111; mad 4122; sorry 7297; bad 7497; ~ *chere,* lamenting 7297

ill(e), yll(e) *adv.* bitterly 896, 5043; badly 924, 988 etc.; wrong 1021, 1777 etc.; little 2093, 2103 etc.

in *n.* See INNE.

indewre *v.* See ENDURE.

ynge *adj.* See YONG(E).

inne, in *n.* lodging 321, 2621 etc.; guest chamber 1004, 1050 etc. **innys, innes** *pl.* 887, 2627

ynne *n.pl.* See EYE.

inner *adj. the* ~ *syde,* the 'inside' team at the tournament 3647, 3931 etc.

insamble *n.* ~ *take,* interpret 4202

in-soughte *pa.t.* asked 2264n

intent(e) *n.* See ENTENT(E).
yrkys *pr.2.sg.* ~ *of,* are weary of 1934
is, ys *pron.* his 291, 656 etc.
is, ys *genitive marker* See HIS.
issue *n.* exit 3037
yt(e) *adv.* See YET(E).
iwroughte *pp.* See WERKE.

I = J

Iaggys *n.pl.* slashes 6572
Ianglys *pr.3 pl.* chatter 6312
Iape *v.* joke 6536
Iaspys *n.pl.* precious stones *2657n
Ioye *v.* make merry 2113

K

karpe *pr.subj.pl.* speak 3528. **carpud** *pa.t.* recited 6612
kele *v.* diminish 3995
ken *adj.* See KENE.
kenne *pr.1 sg.* know 3353. **kend(e)** *subj./ pa.t.* *1003, 6201. *pp.* known 1914
kene *n.* boldness 6699
kene, ken *adj.* bold 166, 2047 etc.; acute 6447; sharp 7406
kepe *n.* *take (in)* ~, pay attention (to) 1174, 1482 etc.
kepe *v.* look after 49, 50 etc.; keep 2831, 3011 etc.; protect 2813, 6185; keep secret 4937; guard 5931; stop 7686n. *pr.1 sg.* desire 2727, 4945 etc. *imp.2 sg.* keep 1650; defend 7736; protect 7855. **kepes, kepythe** *pr.3 sg.* keeps 1695; looks after 6598. *subj. sg.* **kepe** keep 395; ~ *of,* care about 4311, 6635 etc. *pa.t.* **keppyd** looked after 145. **kept(e)** *pp.* kept 4269, 7710 etc.
keste *pa.t.* See CAST(E).
kyde *pp.* See KYTHE.
kynd(e) *adj.* generous 158, 5209 etc. **kyndere** *comp.* 974
kynde *ppl.adj.* famous 6496
kyne, kynne *n.* kind 1789; family 318, 7174 etc.; *all* ~ *þinge,* in every way 3568
kynrede *n.* high rank 7716
kyrtell, kyrtyll *n.* tunic 660, 7077
kyst(e) *pa.t.* See CASTE.
kyth *n.* area frequented by wild animal 616
kythe *v.* reveal 716. **kythes** *pr.2 sg.* speak 1974. **kyde** *pa.t.* performed *6016. **kyde** *pp.* displayed 5332; ~ *for,* known to be 1142
kytte *v.* See COTTE.

knett *pp.* established 6893
know(e) *v.* know 1332, 8168 etc. **knew(e)** *pa.t.* 98, 1703 etc. **knowe(n), knoven** *pp.* known 4581, 6699, 7467 etc.; ~ *for,* known to be 22, 6699; *bee* ~ *of,* acknowledge 7048n

L

L *num.* fifty 2933
lachettes *n.pl.* leather fastenings 4458
lacys *pr.3 sg.* loosens 663
lad(d)e *pa.t.* See LEDE.
lafte *pa.t.* See LEVE *v.*[1]
lay(e) *v.* bestow 842n, 847, 3106; stake 2168, 3428; swear 7731. **layes** *pr.3 sg.* lays 1816; bestows 5546n. **layde, leyd(e)** *pa.t.* brought down 3467, 5794; attacked 4384; swore 2764n; staked 7592. **layd(e)** *pp.* attributed 514n; laid 1937, 7439 etc.; ~ *on,* rained blows 3791, 4384 etc.
lay(e) *pa.t.* See LY(E).
layes *n.pl.* laws 1891n
layde *pa.t.* See LAYE.
layne *n.* *wythout(en)* ~, truly 44
layne, leyne *v.* conceal 677, 4830 etc.
lake, leke *v.* diminish 553. *to* ~, be disparaged 4199, 4502 etc. **lakyd** *pp.* ~ *for,* disparaged as 7156
lange *adv.* longer 1151, 7639
langeare, langeyre, lang-e(y)re, lanyere *adv.* long since 249, 2155, 4711, 5510, 6799 etc.
lare, lore *n.* wisdom 7090; *wyse off* ~, learned 736, 5279
largely *adv.* generously 555; presumptuously 2761
lasse *adj., adv.* See LES.
lassis *n.pl.* young women 2112n
last(e) *v.* last 1190, 2305 etc. **lestis** *pr.3 sg.* lasts 8890. **lastynge** *pr.p.* 2187. **lastyd, laste** *pa.t.* 2855, 3928
latte *pp.* See LETT(E) *v.*[1]
laughand *ppl.adj.* See LAWȜING.
laughe, lowȝe *v.* laugh 259, 2249 etc. **lawghis** *pr.3 sg.* 6984. **laughynge, lawȝing, lauȝhyng** *pr.p.* laughing 2311, 2319, 8730 etc. **lawȝed, lewȝ, lowȝe, lough(e), louȝth** *pa.t. 3 sg.* 437, 651, 2205, 2759, 3569, 3579 etc. **lewȝe, lewgh, lowȝ(e), louȝgh, lough(e), lovghe, lowgh, louȝhen,**

louthe *pl.* 121, 459, 557n, 2822, 2997, 3012, 3460, 3557, 3582, 6309, 6423 etc.

lawȝinge *vbl.n.* amusement 4092, 6271; laughing 5174.

lawȝing, lawynge, laughand, lawghyng, laughyng *ppl.adj.* *wyth* ~ *chere/herte*, cheerfully 1022, 2531, 2679, 5212, 8601 etc.

lawe, lave *n.* law 1809; good manners 6331; *be* ~, duly 935. **lawys** *pl.* laws 7939n

leasse *n.* See LES.

leche *n.* physician 8094

leddurs *n.pl.* *storoppus* ~, stirrup-leathers 6256

lede *v.* lead 1981, 2495 etc. **ledys, leydys** *pr.3 sg.* 927, 2691 etc.; takes 3570. **lede** *imp.sg.* take 4825. **ledand** *pr.p.* 2529. **led(e), ledde, lad(d)e** *pa.t.* led 74, 622, 1048, 2371, 2805 etc.

lee *n.* meadow *3516n

leef *n.* *we* ~, alas 1118n

leeff *n.* See LEFF(E).

leeff *v.* See LEVE *v.*[2]

leeffe *n.* leaf 1878n

leeffe *v.* See LEVE *v.*[1]

leeffe *adj.* See LEVE.

lefe *v.* See LEVE *v.*[1]

leff(e), leeff *n.* dear one 3187, 4036, 4341

leff(e) *adj.* See LEVE.

leffe *n.* See LEVE.

leffe, lefte *v.* See LEVE *v.*[1]

leyd(e) *pa.t.* See LAY(E).

leyne *v.* See LAYNE.

leyser *n.* leisure 4656; opportunity 5286, 7216

leyve *n.* See LEVE.

leke *v.* See LAKE.

lekyng *n.* See LYKYNGE.

lel(e) *adj.* true *8516, *8768

leman, lemon, lemen *n.* sweetheart 2451, 7153, 8665 etc.

leme *n.*[1] See LYM(E).

leme *n.*[2] radiance 2406

lemys *pr.3 sg.* flashes 7836

lemon *n.* See LEMAN.

lende *v.* remain 227

lene *n.* leanness 6239

lere *v.* teach 653; learn 7090; ~ *of* learn about 1, 108. *pa.t.* **leryd** taught 151

leryd *ppl.adj.* ~ *and lewede*, clergy and laity 7996

les, lesse, leasse *n.* *wythout(en)* ~, without lying 2349, 3370, 5717 etc.

les, lesse, lasse *adj., adv.* less *(adj.)* 460, 1683, 1793, 2804 etc. *(adv.)* 893, 917, 3213, 7459 etc.

lese, lesse *n.* leash 622, 3577

lese, lesse, lose *v.* lose 1909, 2170 etc.; waste 1721; forgo 3032. **lesis** *pr.2 sg.* waste 7373. **lesythe** *pr.3 sg.* wastes 2928. **lesse, losse** *subj.* lose 3197; waste 7438. **lorn(e)** *pp.* lost 3378, 4677 etc.; wasted 5339

lesyng(e) *vbl.n.* lie 1626, 2155. *wythout(e)* ~, in truth 84, 2882 etc.

lesis, lesythe *pr.3 sg.* See LESE.

lesse *n.* See LESE; LES.

lesse *v.* See LESE.

lest *n.* See LYSTE.

lestis *pr.3 sg.* See LAST(E).

lete *v.* See LETT(E) *v.*[1]

lethe *n.* See LYTHE.

lett(e), lete *v.*[1] allow to 235, 272 etc. *imp.* 855, 955 etc. **lete, lett** *pa.t.* 2460, 2706 etc.; ~ *as*, pretended as if 1379, 2018 etc. **latte** *pp.* bestowed 841

lett(e) *v.*[2] refrain 727, 933 etc.; refuse 2270; deny 5600; stop 7116, 7286; hold back 8824, 8883; ~ *of*, impede 6628. *pr.3 pl.* refrain from 5329. **lett** *imp.* refrain 4697. *pa.t.* **lettyd, lett, lete** refrained 4740, 5229; lessened 4496; held back 6824

lette *n.* *wythoute(n)* ~, without delay 886, 2280 etc.

lette *v.* See LETE, LETT(E).

letter *n.* sign 8027n. **letturs** *pl.* letters 8764

lettyng *vbl.n.* hindrance 3020

levand, lewand, leuynge *ppl.adj.* living 24, 548, 1426 etc.

leve, leffe, leyve *n.* leave 233, 283, 8803 etc.

leve, leff(e), leeffe *adj.* dear 1430, 6925; pleasing 1052. ~ *or lothe*, willing or not 1839, 6115. **leuer, levere** *comp.* *had/were* ~, would rather 1113, 2112 etc.; *(refl.)* 1706, 2151 etc.

leve, leeffe, lefe, leffe *v.*[1] (1) abandon 1080; leave 2578, 5416 etc.; lose 2772; cease 4400. ~ *of*, abandon *14n. **levythe** *pr.2 sg.* leave 3302. **levys, leves** *pr.3 sg.* leaves 1260, 4494 etc. **leve** *pr.1 pl.* leave 1766, 2285 etc. **imp.sg.** leave out 1464; leave 7450, 8118. **lafte, lefte, levyd** *pa.t.* left 3535, 5222, 8230 etc.; abandoned 5402. **lefte** *pp.* left 1473; abandoned 3480

(2) remain 262, 1024, 1199, 5047. **levythe** *pr.3 sg.* 1327, 2287. **levys** *pr.2 pl.* 332. **levythe** *pr.3 pl.* 2025. **leve** *subj.pl.* 256. **levyd** *pa.t.* 1771

leve *v.²* live 272, 1716 etc. **leeff** *pr.1 sg.* 4647. **lyves** *pr.3 sg.* 1639, 8649. **leve** *pr.3 pl.* 1832, 8877. **leve** *subj.sg.* 1825. **levyd** *pa.t.* 79, 2827

leve *v.³ imp.pl.* believe 5264

leuer, levere *comp. adj.* See LEVE.

leuynge *ppl.adj.* See LEVAND.

lewede *n.* laity 7996

lewgh, lew3e *pa.t.* See LOW3E.

lewte, levte *n. be my* ~, upon my honour 496, 547, 2582 etc.

lyand(e) *pr.p.* See LY(E).

lycande *adj.* pleased 2329

ly(e) *v.* lie 3798, 3920 etc. *pr.1 sg.* 208. **lythe, lyethe, lysse, lyes** *pr.3 sg.* lies 351, 1180, *1196, 3621, *5235 etc. **lythe** *pr.3 pl.* 6479, 7089. **lyand(e)** *pr.p.* 3287, 5222 etc. **lay(e)** *pa.t.* 648, 1641 etc.

lyethe *n.* See LYTHE *n.¹*

lyff(e), lyve *n.* life 143, 1089, 1495 etc.; *on/of* ~, alive 548, 2061, 8785n etc.; **lyues** ~ *foode,* nourishing food 8634. **lyves, lyvys** *pl.* 1269, 5803 etc.

lyfte *adj.* left 3296, 4577 etc.

lygaunce *n.* relief 7430

lyght *n.* light 3074, 7983. *be pus* ~, by this light *(asseveration)* 6326

lyght *v.* settle 7163. *pr.1 sg.* ~ *full lowe,* suffer adversity 3697. **lyght(t), lyghte** *pa.t.* dismounted 659, 1630 etc.; struck 4398; landed 7846; ~ *to,* halted before 6474. **lyght, ly3te** *pp.* dismounted 308, 2628 etc.; settled 7119

lyght(e) *adj.* light 1208, 2044 etc.; agile 608, 7931 etc.; valiant 1979, 6326 etc.

lyght *adv.* readily 3480, 7450

lyght(t)ly *adv.* readily 1153, 2200 etc.; lightly 2456, 3137 etc.

lyke *v.* like 425, 6747; be satisfied 2103; *(impers.)* please 2093, 8170. **lykys, lykythe** *pr.3 sg. (impers.)* 6325, 6527 etc. **lykys** *pr.2 pl.* like 8023. **lyke** *subj.* like 5417, 6725 etc. **lykyd, lyked, likyd** *pa.t.* liked 416, 3166, 4408 etc.; *(impers.)* liked 2851, 3536 etc. ; pleased 628, 3242

lykynge, lekyng *n.* pleasure 1n, 75, 553n etc.

lykynge *adj.* pleasant 882

lykkely *adj.* suitable 1911

lym(e), lymme, leme *n.* limb 40, 361, 1621, 2409 etc. **lymmes** *pl.* 7931 (see also LYTHE *n.¹*)

lynde *n.* (linden) tree 1878n, *7295

lyne *v.* cease 6179

lysse *pr.3 sg.* See LY(E).

lyste, lest *n.* ~ *of love,* desire of love 941n, 7344

lyst(e) *v.¹ pr.2 sg.* wish 1970, *(impers.)* 7217; *subj. (impers.)* 2360; 2448 etc. *pa.t.* 3078, 7223, 8303. *pa.t subj.* 3471

lyste *v.² pr.3 sg.* makes himself desolate *(refl.)* 1250n

lythe, lyethe, lethe *n.¹ lyme/leme and* ~, all the body 40, 361, 1621 etc.

lythe *n.²* estate 7554

lythe *pr.3 sg. & pl.* See LY(E).

lythe *adv.* easily 962n

lyve *n.* See LYFF(E).

lyuerlye *adv.* nimbly 5382

lyves *pr.3 sg.* See LEVE *v.²*

lofte *n. on* ~, in the sky 3114. *a/on* ~, upright *3307, 3333

logge *n.* shelter 7335. **logys** *pl.* 587

logys *pr.3 sg.* conceals *(refl.)* 7490

loke *v.* appear 4611, 4796 etc.; ~ *on,* look at 316, 753 etc.; see 4810, 5695 etc. **lokys** *pr.2 sg.* look 831, 8027. **lokys, lokythe** *pr.3 sg.* looks (at) 984, 2615 etc.; watches 6730. **lokys** *pr.3 pl.* look 359. **loke** *imp.* ensure 324, 1653 etc.; preserve 2588, 6282 etc.; search out 3409; find out 6992. **lokyd** *pa.t.* looked 380, 820 etc.; seemed 2877

long *adj.* ~ *on,* because of 5825n

longys *pr.3 sg.* ~ *to,* is fitting for 407

looffe *n.* See LOVE.

loos *n.* See LOS(E).

lordyng *n.* nobleman 5602. **lordyngys** *pl.* 5264, 7302

lore *n.* See LARE.

lorn(e) *pp.* See LESE.

los(e), loos, losse *n.* renown 29, 1566, 1731, 3480 etc.

lose, losse *v.* See LESE.

lossyd *pp.* released 3577

loste *n.* See LUSTE.

lothe *adj.* reluctant 14, 1008 etc. *(impers. with 'to be'),* not wish 232, 2065 etc. *leeffe/leff or* ~, willing or not 1839, 6115. **lother** *comp.* 22

lothe *adv.* with hostility 1008n
lowde *adv.* *on* ~, aloud 393; loudly 6128
lowe *n.* fire 7836
low3(e), lou3gh, lovghe, lough(e), lowgh, loughen, lou3hen, lou3th, louthe *v.* See LAUGHE.
loure *v.* lurk 2112. lowryd *pa.t.* ~ *vnder þere hode,* sorrowful beneath their hoods 5138
lowryd *pa.t.* See LOURE.
lowte *v.* *low to* ~, be defeated 1444
love, loue, looffe *n.* love 1, 847, 7369 etc.
love, luffe *v.* love 4, 926, 2131 etc.
luste, loste *n.* desire 753, 1256

M

M¹ *num.* thousand 2834, 3402 etc.
may(e) *n.* woman 85, 1381 etc.
may(e), moo, mowe *pr. sg.* may 3, 1152, 1856, 7739 etc. myght(e), might, mow3te, mov3te, movghte, mowthe *pa.t.* might 63, 93, 1187, 2020, 3110, 7251 etc.; could be 7304
mayde, maydon *pa.t.* See MAKE.
mayll, mayle *n.* piece of chain mail 3320; chain mail armour 6950, 7046 etc. mayles *pl.* 7988
maynde *n.* *haue no* ~ *on,* have no thought of 1200
mayn(e), meyne *n.* strength 1632, 2024, 8108 etc.
mayn(e)teyme *v.* preserve 1779n; rule 2089; uphold 8776
maynere *n.* See MANER(E).
mayster *n.* job 2631n
maystrye, mastry *n.* *make* ~, perform a great deed 8000. *made grette* ~, behaved most high-handedly 6786. maystr(y)es *pl.* deeds 6016. *make* ~, perform deeds of war 4196, 6400
make *n.* companion 2413. makys *pl.* mistresses 2233n
make *v.* make 37, 60 etc.; prepare 5634; perform 4196, 6400 etc. makys, makyste *pr.2 sg.* make 1071, 4674 etc. makyth(e), makys, makes, mas(s)e *pr.3 sg.* makes 8, 218, 553, 1822, 3020, 6982 etc. makythe *pr.2 pl.* 6338. make, makys, makythe *pr.3 pl.* 5234, 6647, 7026. makys *imp.pl.* 6059. made, mayde *pa.t.sg.* 21, 4369 etc. maydon *pa.t.pl.* 7810. made *pp.* 346, 748 etc.
manasand *pr.p.* threatening *5511

maner(e), maynere *n.* way of life 240, 252 etc.; manner 2516, 2532. maners *pl.* ways 8745
many, mony(e), mone, money *adj.* many 32, 1801, 1913, 2080, 2486 etc.
mard *pp.* hindered *6722n
mase *pr.3 sg.* See MAKE.
massage *n.* See MESSAGE.
masse, messe *n.* mass 1544, *2138n, 3479 etc.
masse *pr.3 sg.* See MAKE.
maste *adv.* See MOSTE.
mastry *n.* See MAYSTRYE.
matter *n.* subject 2239, 4043; grounds 5353; problem 6051. *pl.* business 6982, 7923
meane, mene *v.* mean 3, 1093 etc. mene *pr.1 sg.* ~ *off,* refer to 6618. meanys *pr.3 sg.* 891 mend, ment *pa.t.* meant 1488, 7181
meche *adj.* See MEKYLL.
mede *n.¹* meadow 2278
mede *n.²* benefit 2138n, 3479 etc.; *to* ~, for your/my/his benefit 4880, 5063, 5275 etc.
medull *v.* interfere 1929, 7374
meyne, meyny, meny(e), meneye, mene *n.¹* retinue 172, 295, *352, 396, 741, 4511 etc.
meyne *n.²* See MAYNE.
meyny *n.* See MEYNE *n.¹*
meyre *n.* See MERE.
mek(e)ley *adv.* readily 4970; gently 7446
mekyll, moche *pron.* much 2760, 4204, 8522 etc.
mekyll, mekill, mekell, meche, muche *adj.* great 89, 280 etc.; much 536, 892n, 6544 etc.; many 2841, 3268. *ouer* ~, too much 1545, 3698 etc.
mekyll, mekill, mekell, muche, moche *adv.* much 195, 219, 2801, 4081, 8524 etc.; greatly 202, 255 etc. *ouer* ~, too much 1478, 4048
mekley *adv.* See MEK(E)LEY.
mell *prep.* *in* ~, between two things 1182
melle *v.refl.* concern (himself) 517; exert (himself) 5887; ~ *of,* meddle with 1098
menchyde *pa.t.* See MENGYS.
mend *pa.t.* See MEANE.
mend *v.* better 2677. *subj.sg.* cure 1554. mendyd *pa.t.* cured 8690. mendyd *pp.* bettered 471
mende *v. subj. (refl.)* remember 5242
mene *n.* See MEYNE *n.¹*

mene *v.*[1] mourn for *5560; *(refl.)* complain 258
mene *v.*[2] See MEANE.
meneye *n.* See MEYNE *n.*[1]
mengys, myngys *pr.3 sg.* ~ *my mode*, confuses me 994; upsets me 1218.
menchyde *pa.t.* 8495
meny(e) *n.* See MEYNE *n.*[1]
mensyngere *n.* See MESSYNGERE.
ment *pa.t.* See MEANE.
mere, meyre *n.* mare 6240, 6255 etc.
merely *adv.* merrily 7226, 8834
merthes *n.pl.* See MYRTHE.
message, messavge, massage *n.* message 2004, 2787 etc. *in* ~ / *on* ~ / *of* ~, bearing a message 1990, 6707, 7317 etc.; *do a* ~, carry message 4970, 5277 etc.
messe *n.* See MASSE.
messyngere, mensyngere *n.* messenger 1598, 8878. **messengers** *pl.* 1847, 2013
mesure *n.* *be* ~, prudently 6967
mete, mett(e) *n.* meal 193, 3000 etc.; food 325, 783, 7050 etc. **mettys** *pl.* 2642
met(t), mette *pa.t.* met 1278, 5793, 8312 etc.; dealt with 2839. **mett(e)** *pp.* united 8748, 8827; met 1601, 1614 etc.
meve *v.* discuss 2239. **mevis** *pr.3 sg.* ~ *my mode*, disturbs my mind 3871
mewsus *pr.3 sg.* hesitates 1182
myde *prep.* middle 1464; in the middle of 4420
myddys(t) *prep. in* / *the* ~, in the middle (of) 637, 5478, 5816.
myght(e) *n.* power 715, 1177 etc. *off my* ~, on my authority 3222n
myght(e), might *pa.t.* See MAY(E).
myngys *pr.3 sg.* See MENGYS.
myrthe *n.* pleasure 2038, 2043 etc. **merthes** *pl.* 4894
myrthe *v.* delight 6380
myster *adj.* *what* ~ *man*, what kind of man 2762
mystur *n.* need 6215
mo(o) *n.* more 269, 270 etc. *other(e)* ~, many others 124, 5884; *wythowten* ~, without exaggeration 1697, 2663; *wythoute* ~, without further ado 3241 etc.
mo(o) *adj.* more 66, 295 etc.
moche *pron.* & *adv.* See MEKYLL.
mode, moode *n.* disposition 772, 3709; mind 994, 1218 etc.; mien 3219; spirit 4590; distress *8023

mold(e) *n.*[1] earth 285, 748 etc.
molde *n.*[2] character *8848
mon, mone, mvn *pr.1 sg.* must 724, 1198. *pr.3 sg.* 219n, 1199
mone *n.*[1] moon 1296, 2897 etc.
mone, moone *n.*[2] lament 976, 5316; remonstrance 6724; lamenting *6544, 7177 etc.; distress *8690
mone(y), mony(e) *adj.* See MANY.
monys *pr.3 sg.* See MOONE.
moo *n., adj.* See MO(O).
moo *pr.3 sg.* See MAY(E).
moode *n.* See MODE.
moone *n.* See MONE *n.*[2]
moone *v.* mourn 1069. **monys** *pr.3 sg.* 551
morne *v.* mourn 1046, 4880 etc. **mornys, morny(e)the** *pr.3 sg.* 691, 1060, 1526. **mornyng(e), mornand** *pr.p.* 1177, 5594, 6597 etc. **mornyd(e), mvrnyd** *pa.t.* mourned 1381, 4850, 5080 etc.
moserd *n.* dolt 6881
moste, maste *adv.* to the greatest degree 598, 600; continually *1929n
mot, mut *subj.* may 938, 1375 etc.
mowe *pr.3 sg.* See MAY(E).
mow3te, mov3te, movghte, mowthe *pa.t.* See MAY(E).
muche *adj.* & *adv.* See MEKYLL.
mvn *pr.3 sg.* See MON.
mvrnyd *pa.t.* See MORNE.

N
nat *pr.1 sg.* See NOT.
naturall *adj.* ~ *fole*, congenital fool 6610
nebe *n.* face 6162
nede *adv.* necessarily 4322; *mvst* ~, absolutely must 1310
nedys *adv.* *mvste*/*bus*/*behovys* ~ *(with sub. or obj. pron.)*, absolutely must 926, 1163, 5527 etc.
nedyste *pr.2 sg.* must 1929. **nedys, nedis** *pr.3 sg.* *it* ~ *no(t)*, it is not necessary 946, 6724. **nede** *pr.2 pl.* need 2229, 8282. **nede** *subj.* would require *(impers.)*3043; need 3206, 6899; *(impers.)*7568. **nedyd** *pa.t.* needed 968
nere, neyre *adv.*[1] not at all 1116, 6243, 8786
nere *adv.*[2] nearer 7886
nere-hande *prep.* nearby 1857; close to 5163
nerehande, nere-hand(e), ny-hand *adv.*

almost 1233, 3286, 4293, 4396 etc.;
hardly 6130

nevyn v. tell *6642n

newov n. nephew 36

next adv. after 3271

nyce adj. foolish 855, 1102 etc.

nycely adv. foolishly 7270

nygh adv. nearly 3284, 4016

nyghe v. deny 2210

ny-hand adv. See NEREHANDE.

nyte v. deny *4978

no adj. ~ man, anyone 6284n

noyce n. See NOYSE n.²

noye n. ? noise 627

noye v. persecute 8648. **noyed(e)** pp.
harmed 3684, 6111

noyese n. See NOYSE n.²

noyse n.¹ harm 1881

noyse, noyese, noyce n.² noise 3608,
4175, 6713 etc.

noke n. corner 4861

nold(e) pa.t. would not 2637, 2724 etc.

nome pa.t. took 2035, 3129 etc. **nom(m)e,
nomyn** pp. chosen 3738, 7573; taken
5730

non adv. not 4050

nonys n.pl. for the ~, for the occasion 2648

norture, nvrture n. good breeding 5235,
5402

nortouryd pp. well brought-up 5161

not, nat pr.1 sg. do not know 257, 1433 etc.

noþer(e), noþure pron. neither 646, 1266
etc.; no ~, no other 1653, 4945 etc.

nother(e) adj. no ~, no other 502, 2820,
7540 etc.

nother conj. neither 194, 210 etc.

noune adj. See OWN(E).

nvrture n. See NORTURE.

O

o, oo adj. one 1796, 4485 etc.

occyane n. Occident *182n

old, elde adj. old 26, 3562 etc.

olywhantys n. elephant's 5796

omage n. acknowledgement of allegiance
76, 1788 etc.

oncowpelyd pa.t. unleashed 604

onyes, onys adv. ever 1986, 6169, 7556;
once 3954, 4636 etc.; ~ for aye, once and
for all 8047

onskylle n. want of reason 1408

onwyse, vnwyse adj. ignorant 4212, 7281,
7514

oo adj. See O.

or adv. & conj. See ARE.

ordayned pa.t. arranged 3142. pp. ordered
3154

ordayned ppl.adj. well ~, well made 6457

orderde pp. put in holy orders 6927

orfrayes n.pl. gold embroidery 2699

ostage n. hostage 1260

ost(e) n. host 316, 5079; army *3325n,
4258

other conj. either 6184; or 5085

ought(e), owght pron. anything 476, 934,
1367 etc.

oughte, owght, ovght, oghte, owte adv.
at all 1223, 1349, *1365 etc.; somewhat
7467. or ~ long, before very long 5449

oure n. divine office for a canonical hour
8091

oure pron. our man 4284

outeraye n. injury 4868n

outerage, owterage n. mishap 6594;
wrongdoing 6721, 7140

ovthere pron. either 1761

ouercome pp. defeated 4555, 6951 etc.;
passed by 6816

ouer-hye adj. too high 3696, 5534

ouer-mekyll, ouer-mekill adj. too much
3698, 6199 etc.

ouer(-)provde adj. over-proud 948, 3695

ouertane, ouertaken pp. overtaken 6596,
8377

oweth(e), owth(e) pr.3 sg. owns 477, 1291,
1311 etc.; impers. ought 5182. **owght**
pa.t. owned 8296

own(e), owen, awne, noune adj. own 357,
4037, 4477, 4984, 4997 etc.

owght pa.t. See OWETH(E).

owte adv. See OUGHT(E).

P

paye n. to ~, satisfactorily 150, 2751; to his
~, to his satisfaction 2431

payes, pays pr.3 sg. satisfies 1955, 5543.
payd(e), apayde pp. satisfied 1490,
1882, 2209 etc.

payne n. pain 1114, 1388 etc. do/dothe ~,
cause(s) suffering 1549, 2344 etc. done
my/his ~, done my/his best 4836, 7248

payne v. (refl.) strive 1560, 6700

pays pr.3 sg. See PAYES.

palfray, palffraye, palfreye, palffrey n.
riding horse 292, 4985, 6676, 6716 etc.
palffreys, palfrayes pl. 2376, 2522 etc.

palle *n.* luxurious cloth 2697, 4118

panyd *ppl.adj.* lined 2457

pappe *n.* side of chest 3899, 4577 etc.

paramowers *n.* *pryde of* ~, pride in love 1559

paramowers, paramowres *adv.* *loue* ~, love romantically 2131, 2448

parte *n.* (a) share 1116, 1533; lot 1536. *in* ~, somewhat *4512n

parte *v.* part 2773; ~ *awey*, leave 1013. *imp.* part 1661. **partyd** *pa.t.* parted 5311. **parte** *pp.* divided 1254

party *n.* *a* ~, somewhat 8479

pase *n.* pace 355

peche *v.* accuse 5401, 5447

pensell *n.* streamer identifying individual knight 2392, 2404 etc.

pere *n.* equal 27, 105. **perys** *pl.* 960

pere *v.* ~ *as*, be the equal of 3692. **peryd** *pa.t.* ~ *to*, was comparable to *5777n

pette *n.* See PITTE.

petteweslye *adv.* piteously 8166

pyght(e), py3tte *pa.t.* pitched 587, 4227, 5930 etc. *pp.* 6118

pyment *n.* sweetened spiced wine 2645, 3290

pyne, pynne *n.* pain 830, 1928, *7689. *done hym* ~, injured him 3284

pitte, pette *n.* compassion 3958, 8881 etc.

playne *adv.* clearly 7028

playns *pr.3 sg.* *(refl.)* complains 8166

plenere *adj.* full 340; *ful* ~, completely full 5104

plenerly *adv.* thoroughly 5053

plyde *pa.t.* yielded 5722

poynte *n.* condition 6; subject 13, 2344; point 274, 1796 etc.; quality 694, 949, 1026; opportunity 6530. *in* ~ *(to)*, about to 2174, 4371, 7630 etc. *in* ~ *of,* on the verge of 7032. *not a* ~, nothing 3852, 4066 etc. **poynt(t)ys, poynttis** *pl.* virtues 27; qualities 107, 2351, 8881; points 2559

pomell *n.* ornamental knob on lid 2663

porveyde *pp.* ordained 6495

posturne *n.* side gate 8187

precande *pr.p.* See PRYKE.

prece *n.* See PRESE.

prefe *v.* See PREVE.

preffe *n.* distress 8819

prekand, prekyd, prekys, prekkythe *v.* See PRYKE.

presand *n.* See PRESENT.

prese, pres(se), prece *n.* crowd 621; the thick of the battle 2348, 3200, 3369 etc.; hoard of combatants 5831, 5876 etc.

prese, presse *v.* strive 2330. **presus, precys** *pr.3 sg.* strives 803, *3257n. **presyd, preste, presud** *pa.t.* crowded 2078, 5807; *(refl.)* rushed 8430, 8458

present, presand *n.* gift 3337, 5613 etc.

presse *v. & n.* See PRESE.

prest *n.* priest 3206n

preste *pa.t.* See PRESE.

preste *adj.* eager 4333

preve, prefe *v.* praise *13n, *2335n, *2584; prove 8406

preveyste *adj. sup.* See PREVY.

prevely(e) *adv.* secretly 1126, 3635 etc.; secretively 5186

prevy *adj.* imperceptible 2661. **preveyst** *sup.* most secretive 8658

prevyd *ppl.adj.* morally excellent 1742

prevyte, preuyte *n.* privacy 488; *in* ~, privately 4538, 4920

price, pryce, pryse *n.* (recognition of) pre-eminence 18, 29 etc.; *of* ~, excellent 89, 354 etc.; *holdyn a* ~ *wyth*, thought highly of by 1302

pryde *n.* pride 938, 942 etc.*wyth* ~, splendidly 2457; *of* ~, splendid 5930

pryke *v.* gallop 5767. **prekys, prekkythe** *pr.3 sg.* 3922, 4478, 4601. **precande, prekand** *pr.p.* galloping 5386, 5391. **prykyd, prekyd** *pa.t.* 3369, 5910, 7123

pryme *n.* the canonical office of prime 8091; *hye* ~, approx. 9 a.m. 6828

pryse *n.* See PRICE.

prove *n.* general experience 1018

proves, prowes *n.* valour 537, *694 etc.

prowe *n.* *for her* ~, to her advantage 1569

purfelyed *ppl.adj.* trimmed with fur 2698

purpos(se) *n.* intention 279, 2313 etc.; narrative 1553; *toke his* ~, resolved to 1205

purposyde *pp.* resolved 245, 3052

put *pa.t.* ~ *of,* took off 7068

Q

quary, queyre *n.* game killed in chase 731; hounds' reward (of meat) *4734n

quarte, querte *n.* health 1159, *3826 etc.; *in* ~, untroubled 1199; healthy 6105

queynte *adj.* ingenious 2659

queyre *n.* See QUARY.

querte *n.* See QUARTE.

queste *v.* hunt 619. questyd(e) *pa.t.* bayed 649, 4028

quyke *adj.* alive 5877

quyte *v.* renounce 5973; repay 6689. quyt(t)e *pp.* repaid 478, 1907, 8047; granted 804; *make me* ~, relinquish my claim 8101

quyte, white *adv.* ~*and clene,* completely 2292n, 7412

R

rache *n.* dog that hunts by scent 615; racchis *pl.* 2568

rafte *pa.t.* See REWYS *pr.3 sg.*[1]

raggis *n.pl.* torn strips 6571

raye *n.* armour 5839

raye *pr.2 pl.* See RAYS.

raynd *pa.t.* tethered 6684, 6836

rayne, reyne *n.* challenge to single combat 6208, 6559 etc. (see also DERAYNE)

raynes *pr.3 sg.* exists 7927

rays *pr.3 sg.* dresses 4007. raye *pr.2 pl.* 2869

ran(e) *pa.t.* See RENNE.

ranke *n.* jousting ground 7809n

ranne *pa.t.* See RENNE.

rapokys *n.pl.* wretches 7006

raste *n.* sharebeam of a plough 6578

rathe *adv.* at once 4190

ravght *pa.t.* See REKE.

reason(e) *n.* See RESON(E).

recreaunte *adj.* cowardly 4048

red, redde *v.* See REDE *v.*[1]

redden *pp.* See RYDE *v.*[1]

reddoure *n.* fear 3644

rede *n.* advice 1831, 2314. *toke there* ~, made their decision 87

rede, red(de), ryde *v.*[1] decide 1844. *pr.1 sg.* advise 271, 1150, 6347, 7232 etc.

rede *v.*[2] See RYDE *v.*[1]

rede *v.*[3] *imp.* read 8027

reden *pp.* See RYDE *v.*[1]

redy(e) *adj.* ready 570, 4911 etc.; direct 8732

regyd, riggud *pa.t. (refl.)* dressed 2812n, 8770n

reiall *adj.* See RYALL.

reyne *n.* See RAYNE.

reyse, reysse *v.* rouse 607; remove 1949n. reysyd, reysud *pa.t.* startled 584n; erected 2904

reysone *n.* See RESON(E).

reke *pr.1 sg.* care 7713; 8786. rekkys,

rekkes *pr.3 sg.* *2019n, 6243. rovght(e), roughte, ravght *pa.t.sg.* 1116, 2795, 5362, 8723

rekynne *v.* reckon 2986. rekynd *pa.t.* determined 8823

relevyd *pa.t.* came to the rescue 5895n

relyed *pa.t.* rallied *3924n, *4391n

reme *n.* realm 1841

rennand(e) *ppl.adj.* running 579

renne *v.* run 529, 642 etc. rennethe *pr.3 sg.* 7896. rennythe, rennes *pr.3 pl.* 4124, 4730. rennand(e) *pr.p.* 1597, 5377. ran(e), ranne *pa.t.* 624, 4143, 4859 etc. ronne, renne *pp.* 3552, 4141 etc.

rent(e) *pa.t.* tore 3262, 4473

rente *ppl.adj.* torn 6236

repeyre, repayre *n.* retinue 342; throng 5807

reprove, reproffe *n.* reproach 865, 950; disgrace 942; harm 1041; insult 1339, 5342; shame 3858, 7391; dishonour 8499

reson(e), reason(e), reysone *n.* capacity for reason 145; explanation 1450; a reasonable thing 1945, 2258 etc.; argument 1993; tale 3581, 4841 etc.; right 5414; sanity 7351. ~ *wold,* it would be proper 957. *all þat* ~ *wille,* all that is fitting 2721. *be* ~, rightly 1758, 6056; it stands to reason 2345

respyte, respytte, ryspyte *n.* postponement 1797, 1810, 2140; *put to* ~, abandon 4044

retenaunce *n.* retinue *5650

reued *pp.* See REWYS *pr.3 sg.*[1]

revyn *ppl.adj.* torn 6572

rewde *adj.* barbarous 6110

rewe *n.* pity 122

rewe *v.* regret 5205, 7051, have pity 7608, 8034; grieve 8688; *(impers.)* regret 5578, 6063. rewys, rewes, rewis *pr.3 sg.* regrets 6782; *(impers.)* 513, 3398, 5550 etc. rewyde *pa.t.* 795

rewell *n.* ~ *bone,* walrus ivory 6456

rewes *pr.3 sg.* See REWYS *pr.3 sg.*[1]; REWE *v.*

rewyde *pa.t.* See REWE *v.*

rewys, rewes *pr.3 sg.*[1] deprives of 216, 940. rafte *pa.t.* 5399. reued *pp.* 882

rewys, rewis *pr.3 sg.*[2] See REWE. *v.*

rewthe *n.* compassion 5731, 7461; pity 8651

ryall, riall, reiall *adj.* royal 64, *2379n, 8462 etc.

ryally *adv.* royally 335, 2560 etc.
ryches *n.* wealth 4697
ryde *v.*[1] ride 59, 335 etc. rydythe,
    rydethe, rydis, rydys, ryd(d)es,
    rides *pr.3 sg.* 3176, 3878, 3895, 4008,
    4263, 4569, 7623 etc. ryde *subj.sg.* 6627,
    7803. *subj.pl.* 3805. *imp.* 4412, 6943.
    rydyng, rydand *pr.p.* 2486, 6710 etc.
    ryd(d)e, rede *pa.t.* 3624, 3807, 5474 etc.
    rydden, red(d)en *pp.* 3441, 4132, 4192
ryde *v.*[2] See REDE *v.*[1]
ryff *adj.* numerous 2807
riggud *pa.t.* See REGYD.
righte *n.* truth 752; power 1301, 2512 etc.;
    what is right 1367, 8325; virtuous 7959;
    right 8360, 8407. righttis *pl. att all* ~, in
    the best manner 5703
rightewos *adj.* just 5959
ryse *v.* rebel 140; rise 424, 818 etc. rysis,
    ryses *pr.3 sg.* 6985, 7149. ryse, rose
    pa.t. rose 744, 4221 etc.
ryspyte *n.* See RESPYTE.
rode *n.* ~ *tre,* cross 8887
ro, roo, rowe *n.* peace 216, 940, 986 etc.
ronne *pp.* See RENNE.
roo *n.* See RO.
roos *n.pl.* roe deer 3029
rose, rows *n.* boast 1536. *make* ~, boast
    4945. *made* ~ *of,* boasted 3755
rose *n.pl.* See ROWE.
rose *v.* praise 1144. ~ *of, (refl.)* boast of
    3759
rose *pa.t.* See RYSE.
roughte, rovght(e) *pa.t.* See REKE.
rouncy *n.* riding or pack horse *6780
row *adj.* bristling 6147
rowe *n.*[1] *on a* ~, all together 5800, 7510.
    rose *pl. in* ~, one after the other 2424
rowe *n.*[2] See RO.
rows *n.* See ROSE.
rowte *n.* entourage 2438, 2497 etc.; com-
    pany 5793, 5879 etc.

S

sad(e), sadde *adj.* heavy 793; powerful
    3646, 3915, 4552 etc. sadder *comp.* 6883
sade, sadde, sadely *adv.* heavily 909,
    1741, 4451 etc.
sayd *pa.t.* See SAYE *v.*[1]
say(e) *v.*[1] prove 2351; test 2612n, 5286,
    7581, 7932. sayd *pa.t.* assailed 6429
saye, sayne *v.*[2] See SE.
salue *n.* healing ointment *8880

sare *adj.* See SORE *adj.*[2]
sare *adv.* See SORE.
sartayne *adj.* See SERTAYNE.
savely *adv. dare* ~ *saye/swere,* expect
    confidently 979, 1123 etc.
sauerly *adv.* confidently 6153, 6164
saw(e) *n.* saying 1385, 3018; speech 6332,
    7720, 8167
saw(e), sawyn *pa.t.* See SE.
sawters *n.pl.* psalters 5984
schastys *v.* See CHASTYCE.
schawes *n.pl.* groves 571
sche *pron.* See SHE(E).
scheld(e) *n.* See SHELD(E) *n.*[1]
schene *adj.* See SHENE.
schepys *n.pl.* See SHIPPUS.
scherovde *n.* See SCHROVDE.
schyld(e) *n.* See SHELD(E) *n.*[1]
schosyn *pp.* See CHESE.
schrovde, scherovde *n.* clothing 106, 387
scole, scolys *n.* See SKOLE.
se, see *v.* see 240, 252 etc. sees, sythe *pr.2
    sg.* 3848, 4246. sees *pr.2 pl.* 3666. saw(e)
    pa.t.sg. 197, 491 etc. saw, sawyn, saye
    pa.t.pl. 1596, 8259 etc. sene, seene,
    sayne *pp.* 12, 165n, 378, 2386, 4100 etc.
seall *n.* See SELE.
secur, sekyr, seker *adj.* strong 3878, 5471,
    6953 etc. sekyrer *comp.* 5202
securly(e), sekerlye, sekyrlye, seker,
    cecurly(e), *adv.* indeed 440, 717, 1939,
    4781, 5261, 6241, 7540 etc.
see, seene, sees *v.* See SE.
sege *n.* seat 6456
sege *v.* besiege *5928
sehyde *pa.t.* See SIGH(E).
seyle *n.* See SELE.
seke *v.* undertake 214; look for 1065, 1613
    etc.; investigate 1119; search 2383, 2464
    etc. sekyth *pr.3 sg.* looks for 3432.
    sought(e), sowght(t)e *pa.t.* went *201,
    366 etc.; came 1723, 3868 etc.; searched
    266; looked for 3996, 8672 etc. ~ *on,*
    assailed 6131. *pp.* come 404, 2603;
    sought 966, 2880 etc.; pursued 7093;
    deserved 6438
seke *adj.* ill 1224n, 1620, 1641
sekyr, seker *adj.* See SECUR.
seker, sekerlye, sekyrlye *adv.* See SECUR-
    LY(E).
sele, sell(e), seyle, seall *n.* happiness 131,
    469, 4140, 3556, 7280 etc.
sely *adj.* lucky 6081

sell(e) *n.* See SELE.

semande *pp.* See SEMYS *pr.3 sg.*

semblant, semblande, semblaunte, sembleant, semblent *n.* appearance 2995, 3729, 5571, 6271, 7569 etc.

semble, asemble *n.* gathering 2274, 4211, 4808 etc.

semble *v.* congregate 742; muster (a fighting force) 4220. **sembled** *pp.* mustered 8250

sembleant, semblent *n.* See SEMBLANT.

semely *adj.* attractive 250, 770 etc. **semelyeste** *sup.* 106

semelynes *n.* beauty 8857

semys *n.pl.* seams 2458

semys, semes, semythe, semeth *pr.3 sg.* appears to be 546, 2515 etc.; seems 2511, 2573 etc.; *(impers.)* 1149, 7673. **semyd, semed** *pa.t.* seemed 1598, *2053; appeared to be *(impers.)* 515. **semande** *pp.* appropriate 462

sempylte *n.* humility 947

sempull *adj.* See SYMPULL.

sendell *n.* type of costly fabric 373, 6463

sene *pp.* See SE.

ser(e) *n.* See SYR.

serke *n.* shirt *7074, *8004

sersolette *n.* chrysolite 2654n

sertayne, serten, sartayne *adj.* certain 156, 4576, 6183 etc.

sertenly, certenly, sertayne *adv.* certainly 801, 2748, 3189 etc.

sertys, serttys, sertes, sertus, certes, certys, certus *adv.* certainly 253, 837, 923, 972, 3519, 5538, 8554 etc.

seruyd *pp.* deserved 6033

sesyn *n. take* ~, take possession of freehold 110

set *pa.t.* See SETT(E) *v.*

sete *n.*[1] seat 2216, 6427

sete *n.*[2] feast 1769n

sete *v.* See SIT.

sethe *adv.* See SYTH(E).

sethe *conj.* See SYN(E).

setheed *pa.t.* See SIGH(E).

sethen, sethyn(e) *adv.* See SYTH(E).

sett(e) *v.* arrange 2253, 2266; ~ *be,* care for 7006. **sett** *subj.* 1454. **set** *imp.pl.* set 1446, 1465. **set, sett(e)** *pa.t.* set 580, 601, 2074 etc.; struck 1741, 3204; ~ *at,* valued as 3439; ~ *be,* cared about 531, 554 etc. *pp.* set 175, 193, 2458 etc.; fixed 694, 721, 883 etc.; arranged 1894; chosen

2023, 2176; *was* ~, took place 1971; ~ *of,* made of 385; ~ *on,* bestowed on 4995

sett(e), settynge, settis *v.* See SIT.

sewrance, sewrance, suravns *n.* guarantee 7112. *his* ~ *nome/nomyn,* accepted his surrender 3738, 5730

shamyd *pa.t.* ~ *off,* was ashamed of 3558. **shamyd, shamed** *pp.* ashamed 878, 4134

share *pa.t.* sheared 7837

she(e), sche, sho(o) *pron.* she 83, 811, 4116, 6946, 8662 etc.

sheld(e), shyld(e), shild(e), scheld, schyld *n.*[1] shield 120, 1128, 2390, 2399, 2414, 3905, 4383, 6751 etc. **sheldys, shyldys** *pl.* 4671, 7991 etc.

sheld *n.*[2] See CHYLD.

shend(e) *v.* harm 4660, 7454 etc. **shent** *pp.* wounded 3794; ruined 4016, 5962

shene, schene *adj.* beautiful 381, 571 etc.

shent *pp.* See SHEND(E).

sheverd, shevyrd *pa.t.* shattered 4499, 7991 etc.

shevers *n.pl.* little pieces 4422, 6904

shew(e) *v.* show 1026, 5040 etc. **shew** *pr.2 pl.* 1806. **shew(e)** *imp.pl.* 2547, 4108. **shewyd** *pa.t.* appeared 3655. **shewyd(e), shewed** *pp.* shown 1139, 5343, 5592

shyld *n.*[1] See CHYLD.

shyld(e), shild(e) *n.*[2] See SHELD(E) *n.*[1]

shippus, schepys *n.pl.* ships 8122, 8289 etc.

sho(o) *pron.* See SHE(E).

shrewed *adj.* dreadful *7999

shryfte *n.* confession 5444

shure *v.* See SURE.

syde *n.* side 1230n

sigh(e) *v.* sigh 2452, 8171. **syghyng(e), sykynge, syghand, sighand(e)** *pr.p.* 713, 1516, 4465, 5319, 7126 etc. **setheed, sighed, syghed, syghyd, sy3hed, sight, syghte, sehyde, syhyde, syte** *pa.t.* 300, 909, 1633, 1669, 3412, 3622, 4717, 6073, 6512, 8301

syghyng(e), sighyng, sighand, sykyng(e) *vbl.n.* sighing 189, 793, 1051, 5785, 7184, 7853 etc.

sight, syghte, syhyde *pa.t.* See SIGH(E).

syke *pron.* such 2421

sykynge *vbl.n.* See SYGHYNG(E).

sykynge *pr.p.* See SIGH(E).

sympull, symple, sempull *adj.* humble

470, 7495, 8279n etc.; sad 3673, 6052.
sympelyste *superl.* humblest 2053
syn(e), synne, synes *adv.* See SYTH(E).
syn(e), synne, sethe *conj.* since 245, 3620, 3761, 6993 etc.
synne *n.* shame 538; wrong 3417, 8035; harm 7131; *thynke* ~, think ill 1783
syr, sir, ser(e) *n.* sir 78, 1214, 1547, 8517 etc. **sorys** *pl.* 8374
syrket, syrkote *n.* overtunic 2697n, 6461
sit, sitt(e), sete *v.* sit 3259, 3333, 6991 etc.; remain 1899. **syttys, sittys, sittis, sittythe, sitteth, settis** *pr.3 sg.* sits 1805, 4813, 5345, 6654, 7741 etc.; ~ *sore*, causes distress 6501. **sitt** *imp.sg.* 6741, 7271. **sett** *imp.pl.* 788. **sittande, syttand, settynge** *pr.p.* 992, 2402, *6854. **sitt, sett(e), satt(e), sat(e)** *pa.t.* sat 203, 415, *(refl.)*1925, 2127, 3574, 3759, 7367 etc. **sett** *pp.* 2640
syte *pa.t.* See SIGH(E).
sythe *pr.2 sg.* See SE.
syth(e), sythen, sythes, sythyn, sethe(n), sethyn(e), sothen also **syn(e), synne, synes** *adv.* then 152, 299, 503, 713, 792, 1272, 1446, 1585, 2424, 4238, 4586 etc.; since 896, 2561 etc. *eft(e)* ~, ever since 1483
sythe(s) *n.* *efte* ~, again 3367; *ofte* ~, frequently 12, 1418 etc. *a thousand* ~, a thousand times over 7555
sitt, sittande, syttand, syttys, sittys, sittis, sittythe, sitteth *v.* See SIT.
skapyd *pa.t.* escaped 8762
skarlett *n.* a kind of rich cloth 370
skath(e) *n.* misfortune 1830, 2754; harm 3299, 7877, *8762
skyll(e), skille *n.* good sense 277, 1018 etc.; (faculty of) reason 1070; reason 5040. *agayne* ~, against reason 7755. *be* ~, rightly 487; in truth 785, 2114 etc.; *be that* ~, for that reason 5411. **skille** *pl.* reasons 5354
skole, scole *n.* teaching *(figurative)* 1098, 6925, 7371. *att my* ~, when in my hands 6358n. *of* ~, of learning 6436, 6972, 7159. **scolys** *pl.* teachings 806n
skomfyght, skomfete, sko(u)mfett *pa.t.* defeated 7282, 7323, 7521, 8521. **skomfete** *pp.* 8461
skorne *n.* scorn 459, 2249 etc.; slight 1166, 8534; laughable thing 126n, 1085.

thowght ~, scorned 482; felt ashamed 5231. **skornys** *pl.* gibes 4033
skornynge *vbl.n.* derision *3299; mockery 5234, 7999
skoumfett *pa.t.* See SKOMFYGHT.
slaye, slayne *pp.* See SLOO.
slake *v.* cease 1637. *pr.3 pl.* end 6353
slave *pa.t.* split 8083
sle *n.* sly one 8660
sle *v.* See SLOO.
slye, sle *adj.* clever 1170, 8094
sloo, sle *v.* slay 2664n, 7753 etc. **slow(e)** *pa.t.* slew 5783, 7524. **slon(e), slayne, slaye** *pp.* slain 671, 3250, 3446, 4689 etc.
slowche *n.* skin *663n
smake *n.* stink 6160
smarte *adj.* heavy 7876, 7915
smyte, smytte *v.* strike 6916, 7411. **smythe** *pr.3 sg.* 6922. **smot(e)** *pa.t.* 3295, 3894 etc.
smythe *pr.3 sg.* See SMYTE.
smytte, smot(e) *pa.t.* See SMYTE.
socoure, socur(e), succoure, succure *n.* help 3311, 3737, 5729, 6215, 6477 etc.
socoure, socovre *v.* secure 4459; rescue 8629. **socurryd, socourde** *pa.t.* ~ *(to)*, rescued 3916, 5916
sodenly, sodaynly *adv.* rashly 1110, 7611; quickly 912, 5056, 7393
sodyoure *n.* soldier 5652
sogarende *pa.t.* See SOIOYRNE.
soget *adj.* conquered 3774
soioyrne *v.* rest 2845. **soioyrons** *pr.3 sg.* 268. **sogarende** *pa.t.* 2294
soket *n.* spearhead 3897, 3908 etc.
solas *n.* pleasure 600
somere *n.* packhorse 6932. **somers, somors** *pl.* 293, 1247
sonde *n.*[1] land 2028
sonde *n.*[2] grace 4947; message 8876
sonder *adv.* See SUNDER(E).
sondurde *pa.t.* split 7991
sone *n.* son 143, 202 etc.
sone, soon *adv.* soon 264, 4628 etc.; immediately 885, 2050 etc.; easily 1899
sonyd *pa.t.*[1] declared 3676
sonyd(e) *pa.t.*[2] See SOWUNE.
sonyng(e) *vbl.n.* See SOWUNYNGE.
sonys, sones *adv.* *efte/heft* ~, immediately 5908, 6805, 7827; again *4664
soon *adv.* See SONE.
sore, soure *adj.*[1] chestnut 2398, 4980

sore, sare *adj.*[2] grievous 1051, 1059 etc.;
aching 5370, 8402
sore, sare *adv.* grievously 300, *1741 etc.;
zealously 7093. *sittys* ~, causes distress
6501. sorer *comp.* worse 7715
sory(e) *adj.* unfortunate 538, 708 etc.; sad
1065, 1181 etc.; sorry 1371, 1671 etc.
sorys *n.pl.* See SYR.
sorow *v.* cause to suffer 1152; regret 7709
sorowe *adj.* gloomy 6948, 8133
sot *n.* villain 6495
sotell *adj.* fine 2659
soth(e) *n.* truth 156, 857 etc. *for* ~, truly
2242, 3097 etc.
sothe *adj.* true 1587, 1794 etc. sother
comp. 1915.
sothely *adv.* truly 2556, 5459
sothen *adv.* See SYTH(E).
soty(e) *adj.* filthy 6229, 6577
sought(e), sowght(t)e *v.* See SEKE.
sounder *adv.* See SUNDER(E).
soure *adj.* See SORE *adj.*[1]
soveryd *pp.* left alone 574
sowe *v.* grieve *5184n; suffer 7715
sowen *n.* swoon 3286
sowyde *ppl.adj.* sewn 7076
sownyng *vbl.n.* See SOWUNYNGE.
sowune *v.* swoon 1635; sonyd(e),
swonyd, swovned *pa.t.* 1407, 5906,
6917, 8107
sowunynge, sownyng, sonyng(e), swounyng *vbl.n.* a faint 1628, 3814, 4254,
4301, 8163 etc.
space *n.* space of time 8366
sparkels *n.pl.* sparks 7835
spede *v.* hasten 2015, 3005 etc.; prosper
6687, 7442 etc. spede *pa.t.* hastened 902.
spede *subj.* succeed 2942, 2955. *God* ~,
God help 486, 2622 etc.
spere, spyre, spyrre *v.* ask 45, 251, 2516
etc. speryd, spyrd *pa.t.* 304, 1390 etc.
speryd *pa.t.*[2] barred 5927
spetowsly *adv.* See SPETTUESLY.
spetuous, spytuos *adj.* cruel 4457, 4602;
violent 4869
spettuesly, spetowsly *adv.* harshly 5395;
savagely 5911
spille, spyll *v.* die 4371, 8173; kill 7352
spyrd, spyr(r)e *v.* See SPERE.
spytuos *adj.* See SPETUOUS.
sporys, sporres, sporris, spurrys *n.pl.*
spurs 2465, 5911, 6263, 7488 etc.
spousayle *n.* wedding 6773

spousehode *n.* wedlock 7727
spryng *n.* dawn 3594, 6066
sprynge *v.* dawn 3041
spurrys *n.pl.* See SPORYS.
squate *n.* heavy fall 4352, 6371
stabull *v.* bring order to 2090, 3221.
stabuld *pa.t.* calmed 5670
stade, stadde *pp.* See STEDE.
stage *n.* space of time 4721, 6591
stakyre *v.* stagger 7828. stakyrd *pa.t.*
7848. stakerand *pp.* staggering 4385
stale *pa.t.* See STELE.
stalworthy, stalleworthy, stall(e)-
worthe, stalworthe *adj.* valiant 2042,
2927, 4291, 4435, 4563, 4968
starte, startte *v.* See STERTE.
stede, stedde *n.*[1] place 96, 2323 etc.; field
of battle 3083n. *in that* ~, in my place
3627. *stoode in no* ~, was of no advantage
3877
stede, stedde, steede *n.*[2] war horse 2042,
4187, 5467 etc. stedys, steddis, stedes
pl. 2381, *4939, 8729 etc.
stede, steede *v.* stop 1407, 3801. stade,
stadde, stede *pp.* beset 1042, 1768, 3914
etc.; stuck 5850
steede *v.* See STEDE *n.*[2]
steffly *adv.* staunchly 5846
steynyd *pa.t.* decorated 314
stele *v.* sneak 5407. stale *pa.t.* stole 3885,
5026 etc.
stelyne *adj.* steel 4522
stere *n.* control *6262n
stere *v.* provoke 6002; move 6267. *pr.2 pl.*
bring up 6043. sterd, sterryd *pa.t.*
fought 5845; moved 8420; *(refl.)* exerted
himself 4069
stere *adj.* hardy *2957n
steropus, storoppus *n.pl.* stirrups 5865,
6256
sterres *n.pl.* stars 4201, 4208 etc.
stert(e), stertte, start(t)e *pa.t.* lept 1802,
2100, 2481, 4590, 7515 etc.(*refl.*) 3279
stevyn(e) *n.* promise *5256n; voice 6633
sty(e) *n.* path 3088, *3634, 7331
styf, styff(e) *adj.* staunch 1732, 2957, 8328
etc.
stille, stylle *adj.* calm 869, 5348 etc.;
quiet 1343, 6311; *wyth mowthe* ~,
gently 4164n
stodeynge *n. in a* ~, in thought 8488
stody(e) *n. in a* ~, lost in thought 749, 821
etc.

stoke *n.* tree-trunk 4870
stonde *n.* See STOVNDE.
stonyde *pa.t.* astonished 8226. stonyd, stonyed(e) *pp.* 3309, 6919, 7850. *ill ~ off,* badly stunned by 6941
stonyede *ppl.adj.* stunned 4385n
storde *pp.* attacked 1782
storoppus *n.pl.* See STEROPUS.
stovde *adj.* See STOWTE.
stovffed *pp.* See STUFFUD.
stought *adj.* See STOWTE.
stouȝte *n.* bold one 4227
stovnde, stounde, stonde *n.* time 1184, 1530; while 2805. *that ~/ in the ~,* then 603, 664, 3797 etc.
stoure, stowre *n.* battle 3294, 4497 etc. stowrys *pl.* 3947
stowre *adj.* stalwart *1732
stowte, stovte, stought, stovde *adj.* bold 2500, 2702, 5713, *4436n; cruel 4868n
strafe *pa.t.* See STRYVE.
strayned *pa.t.* stretched 4859
strayte *adv.* ~ *stade,* sore beset 7699
strange, straung(e), stravng(e), *adj.* curious 19, 5604; foreign 217; unknown 431, 3354, 8698 etc.; great 5880; reluctant 6790; aloof *7084, 7091
strangely, stravngely, stravngly(e) *adv.* greatly 1526, 1768, 5107, 5481 etc.
strave *pa.t.* See STRYVE.
streyte *adj.* cramped 7062
streytly, stretlye, strettly *adv.* sorely 5821. ~ *(be)stadde/stede,* sore beset 1042, 3914, 8049
strenghe *adj.* mighty 1959. strengere *comp.* 8591. strengythe *sup.* 1808
stretlye, strettly *adv.* See STREYTLY.
strewed *pp.* See STROWED.
stryve, stryff *v.* strive 2927, 4968 etc. strave, strafe *pa.t.* strove 1037, 7695
stroyed(e) *pp.* destroyed 2092, 6112
strong(e) *adj.* strong 2323, 2981 etc.; influential 5424
strowed *pa.t.* scattered 7993. strowyd, strewed *pp.* 5798, 5870
stuffud, stuffyd *pa.t.* garrisoned *5679; provisioned 7567. stovffed *pp.* garrisoned 5790
stuppyd *pa.t.* treated 4726
succoure, succure *n.* See SOCOURE.
suerly *adv.* firmly 6114
sum, some *pron.* some 125, 558 etc. ~ *off,* one of 3991

sunder(e), sundyr, sonder, sounder, sovnder *adv.* *in/on ~,* asunder 1458, 3264, 3736, 4458, 5806, 5871 etc.
suravns *n.* See SEWRANCE.
sure, shure *v.* promise 4527, 4922, 5299
sure *adj.* private 2343
swayne *n.* retainer 5620
swang *pa.t.* ~ *togeddyrs,* exchanged blows 7831
sweltys *pr.3 sg.* perishes 8124n
swete, swette *adj.* sweet 564, 1192 etc.; dear 3349
swettely *adv.* tenderly 993
swettnes *n.* tenderness 7392
swime *n.* *in ~,* unconscious *5906
swythe *adv.* promptly 1628, 4258 etc.; *as ~,* at once 3464
swythely *adv.* promptly 2790, 8124
swonyd *pa.t.* See SOWUNE.
swoughe *n.* faint *5836
swovned *pa.t.* See SOWUNE.
swounyng *vbl.n.* See SOWUNYNGE.
swtte *n.* *in a ~,* dressed alike 767

T

ta, taas *v.* See TAKE.
tabard *n.* sleeveless overcoat 6571
take, ta *v.* give 51; take 113, *2152 etc.; ~ *in hand,* undertake 6123; ~ *wyth,* receive 8279n. take *pr.1 sg.* commend 5077; ~ *wythoute,* exclude 6341n. tas, taas, takys, takyth *pr.3 sg.* takes 1694, 3777, 4608, 6750 etc. takys *pr.3 pl.* 5042. take *subj.sg.* 870, 1174 etc. take *imp.* take 1649, 2676 etc.; put 8090. toke *pa.t.* took 87, 95 etc.; gave 8016; brought 8849; ~ *þer pavelyons,* retired to their tents 3933n. tane, take, taked, takyn(e), takynne *pp.* 678, 817, 1162, 1621, 2953, 7155 etc.
talent *n.* habit 2827
tame *adj.* makys ~, overcomes 7861
tane *pp.* See TAKE.
tare *pa.t.* tore 4686
tarye *v.* delay 4811. taryande *pr.p.* 1860. taryd *pa.t.* 3595, 7577. taryd(e) *pp.* 6377, 8780
tarying, tar(r)ynge, tareynge *vbl.n.* delay 265, 288, 1674, 1880 etc.
tas *pr.3 sg.* See TAKE.
tatrys *n.pl.* torn strips 6237
tede *pa.t.* happened 6081. tydde *pp. has byn ~,* has happened 6019

tene *n.* misery 866, 3406 etc.; anger 3781, 3893 etc.; distress 5115. *gave* ~, showed anger 1082. *do/dothe* ~ , cause(s) suffering 7409, 8052

tene *v.*[1] vex 6. **tened** *pp.* became angry 7457

tene *v.*[2] See TYNE.

tene *adj.* angry 2223, 2996 etc.

tente *n.* See ENTENT(E).

þay, tham *pron.* See THEY.

than, thanne, þan(ne), þen, then(ne) *conj.* than 23, 401, 732, 996, 1707, 2893, 4560 etc.

þan(ne), than(ne) *adv.* See THEN.

thanke-worthy *adj.* praiseworthy 4052, 6959

thar, thar(r)e *v.impers.* need 1466, *1536n, 1666 etc.

thar(e), þare *adv.* See THERE.

thare *poss.pron.* See THEY.

that *conj.* since 5304

the *pron.* that one 5166

they, þey, þay, thye *pron.* they 79, 199, 5909, 6469 etc. **them(e), þem, theym, tham, hem** *obj.* them 50, 69, 346, 2438, 5365, 7838 etc. **there, þere, þer, thare, her** *poss.* their 87, 1269, 2440, 3238, 4507 etc.

then, thenne, þen, þan(ne), than(ne) *adv.* then 24, 80, 267, 309, 1129, 2964, 3468 etc.

then *conj.* when 1987

then(e) *adv. (fro)* ~, from that place 3069, 8269n

there, þere, þer *poss.pron.* See THEY.

there, þere, þer, thar(e), þare, thore *adv.* there 41, 338, 681, 899, 1260, 2198, 3625 etc.; where 3759

thye *pron.* See THEY.

thye *v.* cause to prosper *1087

thyy *n.* thigh 6908

thyke *adv.* numerous 5840. *so* ~, in such numbers 4115, 8065. *lay on* ~, strike heavily and often 6886

thynke, thynkys, thynkythe *pr.3 sg. (impers.)* it seems to (+ *obj. pron.*) 215, 920, 1931 etc. **thought(e), þouȝte** *pa.t.* 105, 188, 199 etc.

þo, tho *rel.pron.* those 2492, 2559, 4367, *4716

tho, thoo *adv.* then 5811, 8431; when 4734

thore *adv.* See THERE.

thought(e) *v.impers.* See THYNKE.

thrawe *n.* a little while 672

thryfte *n.* prosperity 471, 479 etc.

thryngge *v.* crowd *1531n. **thronge** *pa.t.* 1519, 5083

thryve, thryue *v.* prosper 1088, 3230 etc.

thro *adj.* bold 2916, 2951

thronge *pa.t.* See THRYNGGE.

thwerte *adj.* ~ *wyles*, opposition stratagems 5770n

tydandys, tydandis *n.pl.* See TYTHANDE.

tydde *pp.* See TEDE.

tyde *n.* time 561, 566 etc.

tydynge *n.* news 3964. **tydyngys, tydyngis** *pl.* 1355, 8357 etc.

tyȝte *pp.* determined 3700

tyne *n.* a *littill* ~, a little bit 3909

tyne, tene *v.* lose 6738, *7690; *(refl.)* 8275. *subj.* *6869

tyt(e) *adv.* quickly 3060, *7591n; immediately *7410

tythande, tythandys, tydandys, tydandis *n.pl.* news 297, *1594n, 3493, 5700

to *num.* See TWO.

toke *pa.t.* See TAKE.

tome *n.* opportunity 4822, 6075

tone *adj.* one *5828

tonne *pron.* one 1265

too *num.* See TWO.

to-rente *ppl.adj.* torn apart 5804

torne, tornyþe, tornyde *v.* See TURNE.

tother(e) *pron.* other 1265, 3351 etc.

tother(e) *adj.* other 4285, 4750 etc.

tow *num.* See TWO.

to-yere *adv.* this year 6095n

trayne *n.* ruse 2021, 5980, 6225, 7011

trapoure *n.* cloth covering for horse 6457

tras *n.* track 5369

travayle, travell *n.* labour 10, 2928 etc. *in* ~, to work 1564

travayllyd *pa.t.* See TRAVELLYD.

travasyd *ppl.adj.* across 1277

travell *n.* See TRAVAYLE.

travellyd, travayllyd *pa.t.* travelled 301, 1730. **traveld, travelyd** *pp.* 1608, 8671

trenchours *n.pl.* wooden plates or slices of bread used as plates 6428n

trestyer *comp.* See TRUSTY.

trew(e), trowe *adj.* true 206, 5149, 8494 etc.

trewgh(t) *n.* See TROUTH(E).

trymblyd *pa.t.* trembled 8662

tryste *pa.t.* See TRUSTE.

trobelyng *pr.p.* tossing 7124

trouthe, trovthe, trowth(e), trough(e), trought, trewgh(t) *n.* truth 4082, 4783, 6604, 6620 etc.; troth 1906, 4313, 4325, 4527, 5524, 6744, 6928, 8176, 8647 etc.

trowe *v.* believe 3155, 5149 etc. *pr.1 sg.* 224, 723 etc. **trow(e)s, trowyst(e), trowest** *pr.2 sg.* 846, 921, 1496, 6181, 6810 etc. **trow(e)** *pl.* 2222, 3990 etc. *imp.pl.* 1258. **trowed** *pa.t.* 4856

trowe *adj.* See TREW(E).

trowthe *n.* See TROUTHE.

truse *v.* ~ *of,* leave 6651

trussyd, trussud *pp.* packed 1280, 1376

truste *pr.1 sg.* trust 6175, 7470 etc. *subj.* 6126. **tryste** *pa.t.* 3079

trusty *adj.* trusty 206, 1713. **trestyer** *comp.* 1710

turne, torne *v.* turn 522, 8714; leave 7486; ~ *to,* lead to 1830, 6199. **turnys** *pr.2 sg.* turn 1161. **turnys, turnethe, turnythe, tornyþe** *pr.3 sg.* 690, 701, 1527, 3330 etc. **turnes** *pr.3 pl.* 5611. **turne** *subj.* 6327; ~ *to,* lead to 2202, 7164 etc. **turne** *imp.* 1304, 1313 etc. **turned, turnyd, tornyde** *pa.t.* 839, 4557 etc.; ~ *to no behove,* was of no use 1336; ~ *hym the bake,* fled 4797. **turnyd, turned** *pp.* driven mad 8245n; ~ *to,* changed to 5919, 7148

turnay *n.* tournament 3006

turnayeng, turnaynge *vbl.n.* engaging in tournament(s) 854, 3050 etc.

turneyed, turneyd *pa.t.* fought (in tournament) 3321, *4819

twayn, tweyne *adj.* two 2660

twyn *v.* break up 3342. **twyned** *pa.t.* parted 7531

two, tow, to(o) *num.* two 69, 2806, 4399, 4750 etc.

U, V = U

vmbrayde *n.* See VPBRAYDE.

vnblythe *adj.* unhappy 707, 1629

vnbrayde *n.* See VPBRAYDE.

vncell, vncele, vnsyle, vnsele *n.* unhappiness 189, 1476, 5785, 7184

vncomely *adj.* unlovely 6146, 6241

vncovth(e), huncouthe *adj.* strange 239, 2306, 5233

vnderstond(e) *v.* understand 2307, 2714 etc. *pr.1 sg.* 109, 2194 etc. **vnderston-**

dythe *pr.2 sg.* receive 7941n. **vndersto(o)de** *pa.t.* 813, 1514 etc.; knew 1000

vndertake *pr.1 sg.* undertake 5976. *subj.* understand 752. **vndertoke** *pa.t.* understood 317, 816, 1538; undertook 8323

vnderyode *pa.t.* found out 1225

vnglad *adj.* unhappy 1791, 5740

vnglad(e) *adv.* unhappily 1228, 7760

vnhape *n.* misfortune 5527

vnnethe *adv.* hardly 3307, 6239

vnresnable *adj.* irrational 7157

vnryde *adj.* violent 5725, 5762 etc.

vnsele, vnsyle *n.* See VNCELL.

vnsought(e) *ppl.adj.* easily 6519; unbidden 6658

vnwyse *adj.* See ONWYSE.

vpbrayde, vmbrayde, vnbrayde *n.* reproach 872, 1076, 3470

vtter, vttereste *adj.* the ~ *syde,* the 'outside' team at the tournament 3919, 4506

V = V

valet(e), valett(e) *n.* young man 431, 758, 780, 1359 etc. **valettys** *pl.* attendants 2379

vantoure, venture *n.* braggart 3754n, *5760n

velage *n.* village 7059

velony(e), velanye *n.* shame 4759; shameful conduct 5435; *do* ~, give insult 5344, 5398

venarye *n.* the practice of hunting beasts 598

vencust *pa.t.* defeated 4077

ventayle *n.* neck-armour *or* lower movable part of front of helmet 3317

venture *n.* See VANTOURE.

ventures *adj.* boastful 3764n

veralye, verely(e) *adv.* in truth 610, 5270, 6304 etc.

vertu *n.* inherent power 8020

vertuous, vertuyus *adj.* virtuous 100; possessing inherent powers 2652

vesnamy *n.* physiognomy 6161

vetaylle *n.* food 7567

visage *n.* face 2702, 3285 etc.

vyse *pr.2 sg.* ~ *off,* (*refl.*) remember 3388

visibyll *adj.* pleasing to look at 100

vysse *n.* vice 3677

W

waginge *pr.p.* dangling 5567

way(e), wey(e) *n.* way 251, 502, 3972 etc;

path 2481, 3071 etc. *a littill* ~, a short distance 2425. *be no* ~, by no means 801. *be* ~ *off,* because of 8750. **way(e)s, wey(e)s** *pl.* way 1611, 1952, *5595 etc.; ways 606, 2612. *in þe* ~, along the way 6598

waykyr *n.* See **WEKER.**

waylond *pr.p.* lamenting 1989

wayte *n.* watchman 4240, 4245. **wayt(t)ys** *pl.* 2891, 3092 etc.

wayte *pr.2 pl.* delay 2867. **waytyd, watyd** *pa.t.* espied 5952; lay in wait for 6709. **waytyd** *pp.* lain in wait for 8267

waltrand, waltryng *pr.p.* sprawling 3135, 7125

wan *pa.t.* See **WYNNE.**

wan *adj.* See **WANNE.**

wand(e) *n.* slender branch 2335, 6263

wane, wanne *pa.t.* See **WYNNE.**

wanne, wan *adj.* pallid 196, 4848 etc.

warde *adv.* *to hym* ~, towards him 5858

ware *n.* See **WERRE.**

ware, warre, were *adj.* prudent 28, 154 etc.; aware 3130, 5564

ware *pa.t. subj.* See **BE.**

warely *adv.* cautiously 1267

warysound *pa.t.* rewarded 8829n

warkyn, warkys *v.* See **WERKE.**

warkys *n.pl.* See **WERKE.**

warnyngys *n.pl.* signs 2824

warre *n.* See **WERRE.**

warre *v.* fight 1122n. **weryd** *pa.t.* attacked 8459

warre *pa.t.* See **BE.**

warre *adj.* See **WARE.**

was *pa.t.* See **BE.**

waste *v.* waste 2573. **wastythe, wastys** *pr.3 sg.* wastes 7777; ~ *awaye,* ruins 6483, 8221. **waste** *pp.* laid waste 6122

wat *pr.3 sg.* See **WITT(E)** *v.*²

wathe *n.* harm *3302n

watyd *pa.t.* See **WAYTE.**

waxys *pr.3 sg.* grows *1585n. **wex, wexyd, wax(e), waxed, waxid, waxyd, wax(i)t** *pa.t.* 41, 104, 154, 836, 910, 1330, 2771, 3261, 3893 etc.

we *interj.* why 1118n, 6812

wedde *n.* object left as evidence 3302n

weddows, wedovs *n.pl.* widows 7608, 8181

wede *n.* armour *2869, 3135 etc.

wede *v.* go mad 8294, *8627n

wedovs *n.pl.* See **WEDDOWS.**

wey(e), weyes *n., n.pl.* See **WAY(E).**

weynde *v.* See **WEND(E).**

weys *n.pl.* See **WAY(E).**

weker, waykyr *n.* wicker object 6242; wicker bridle 6424

weld(e), wyld(e) *v.* wield 59, 153, 1893 etc. **weldys, weldyþe, weldyth** *pr.3 sg.* takes 2930; wields 3138; conducts *(refl.)* 6921; rules 7407, 8633. **weldythe** *pr.3 pl.* wear 7992. **weldande** *pr.p.* busying themselves 4365. **wolde** *pa.t.* 1696

well(e), wele, wille, wylle, wile *adv.* well 13, 39, 247, 1794, 1869, 1977, 5593, 8088

welthe *n.* wealth 129, 8531. **welthes** *n.pl.* riches 2643

wend(e), weynde, wynd(e) *v.* go 239, 276, 331, 1290, 1711 etc.. **wendys, wyndythe, wendyth(e), wyndys** *pr.3 sg.* 673, 3373, 3474, 5645, 6630 etc.; *(refl.)* *3764. **wende, wynde** *subj.sg.* 226, 411. **wend** *subj.pl.* 1239. **wende** *pa.t.* *5953

wend(e) *pa.t.* See **WENE, WEND(E).**

wendyng *vbl.n.* departure 1242

wen(e) *v.* believe 1979. *pr.1 sg.* 945, 1083 etc. **wene, wenyste** *pr.2 sg.* 840, 3288. **wenys** *pr.3 sg.* 7279. **wend(e), went** *pa.t.* 1244, *2268, 4302 etc.

wene *n.* hope *9n. *wythoute(n)* ~, without doubt 261, 4932 etc.

wenys, wenyste *v.* See **WEN(E).**

went *pa.t.*¹ See **GO.**

went *pa.t.*² See **WENE.**

went *pa.t.*³ *(refl.)* aired himself 8196n

were *n.* See **WERRE.**

were *v.* defend 6569. **weryd** *pp.* 6875

were *pa.t.* See **BE.**

were *adj.*¹ See **WARE.**

were *adj.*² See **WERY.**

wery *v.* grow weary 1612

wery, werry, were *adj.* exhausted 582, 4845, 8468 etc.

weryd *pa.t.*¹ See **WARRE.**

weryd *pa.t.*² wore 2466

weryd *pp.* See **WERE.**

werke, worke *n.* business 8003; workmanship 7075. ~ *wrought,* caused trouble 7971. **warkys, werkes, werkys** *n.pl.* 1714, 2888, *5033 etc.

werke, worke, warkyn *v.* do 1798, 1932, 2324 etc.; ~ *woo,* inflict suffering (on) *2954n, 8361. **worke** *pr.1 sg.* do 7638. **werkys, workys, workis, warkys** *pr.3 sg.* inflicts on 1234, 7388; acts 3638,

3767; causes 6109. **werke** *pr.1 pl.* act 7378. **werke** *subj.* act 1873. **wrought(e), wroght(e), wro(u)ȝte, wrothe** *pa.t.* did 712, 1020, 4505, 5813 etc.; behaved 1267, 3585 etc.; made 2234. **wrought(e), wroughtte, wrovghte, wrouȝte, wroght(e), iwroughte** *pp.* done 781, 1714 etc.; made 369, 423, 1328, 7073 etc.; created 996, 1656, 2106, 2959, 3980 etc.; caused 8594

werre, were, war(r)e *n.* battle 1736, 1972n etc.; war 1772, 1845 etc.; manner of fighting 5780. *of ~,* of martial prowess 3269, 3527 etc. *on ~,* in battle 3780, 3895 etc.

werry *adj.* See WERY.

werryng *vbl.n.* making war 2809

west, wet, wete, wetyn *v.* See WITT(E) *v.*[2]

wetles *adj.* foolish 955

wetly *adv.* See WYGHTTLY.

wette *v.* See WITT(E) *v.*[2]

wettly *adv.* SEE WYGHTTLY.

wettnes *pr.3 sg.* See WYTTNES.

wex, wexyd *pa.t.* See WAXYS.

whas *v.* See BE.

what-sum, what-sum-euer *pron.* whatever 4936, 5330

wheder, whedyr *conj.* See WHETHER.

whedyr *adj.* which 4222, 7697

whedur, whedyr(e) *adv.*[1] See WHETHER.

whedur *adv.*[2] for all that 3055; however 4705

whedur, wheyþer *conj.* See WHETHER.

wheref(f)ore *adv.* for what reason 911, 1112 etc.; for which reason 1863, 3183 etc.

whether, whedur, whedyr(e) *adv.* wherever 3019; whither 1283, 3400, 4108, 6543, 8526. *no ~,* nowhere 23

whether, whethur, whethere, wheyþer, whedur, wheder, whedyr *conj.* whether 115, 238, 410, 1839, 2019, 2202 etc.; *(as interrogative conj.)* 5139n, 5224n. *~ . . . other,* whether . . . or 5084

whyce *adj.* See WYSE.

whyȝte, whyghttys *adj.* See WYGHTE.

while *n.* See WYLE.

white *adv.* See QUYTE.

whittly *adv.* See WYGHTTLY.

who *adv.* See HOW(E).

whome *n.* See HOME.

whome, home *pron.* whom 258, 963 etc.

wyce *n.* See WYSE.

wyfe, wyff(e) *n.* wife 5049, 5669 etc. *to/ till ~,* as wife 117, 6494, 7953 etc.

wyffys *pl.* wives 5042, 5869 etc.

wyff(e) *v.* marry 4962, 5039, 7968

wyght *pr.1 sg.* See WITT *v.*[1]

wyght(e), wight, wyȝte *n.* person 142, 2244, 6185, 8863 etc.

wyght(e), wighte, whyȝte *adj.* valiant 1699, 3042, 3266, 4761, 8854 etc. **wyghter** *comp.(as n.)* 6875. **whyghttys** *sup.* 2411

wyghttly, wet(t)ly, wyttly, whittly *adv.* fiercely 6921; badly 6778n, 6926, 6939, 8024; quickly 8109

wyke *adj.* vigorous 5770n, 5776

wylde *n.* dyne of the ~, dine on game 6999

wyld(e) *v.* See WELD(E).

wyle, wile, while *n.* trick 825, 6674. *caste a ~,* devise a stategem 1858, 2143, 6212.

wyles *pl.* tricks 2230, 5770n

wile *adv.* See WELL(E).

wille *n.* is in ~, intends 1183, 1529. *to ~,* at his disposal 1725

wille, wylle *adv.* See WELL(E).

wynd(e), wyndys, wyndythe *v.* See WEND(E).

wyne *n.* delight 2704n

wynne *v.* gain 535, 851 etc.; win 6194; go 4379. **wynnes** *pr.3 sg.* wins 3231, 5655.

wan(ne), wane, won *pa.t.* won 18, 581, 1099 etc.; came 3209, 3838 etc.; went 4586, 5815 etc. *~ vp,* rose 3175; *~ on/ vpon,* mounted 6564, 6752, *6817 etc.

won(n)e *pp.* won 3466, 7659 etc.

wyse, wysse, wyce *n.* way 852, 6736 etc. *all ~,* in every way *3620. be ~ of,* with respect to 7788. *off what ~,* in what way 7589. *on all ~,* in any way 4906. *this ~,* thus 8593

wyse, wyce, whyce, wysse *adj.* wise 28, 348, 1096, 1506 etc. **wyser** *comp.* 1243, 1586. **wysest(e)** *sup.* 807, 943 etc.

wysely *adv.* cleverly 2890

wyshe *pa.t.* washed 773

wysse *n.* See WYSE.

wysse *adj.* See WYSE.

wiste, wyst(e), wit *v.* See WITT(E) *v.*[2]

wyte, witte *n.* good sense 385, 6479 etc.; sanity 7005, 7373; skill 8098. *syn he is ~ cowde wyld,* since he could remember 2527. *wastythe ~ away,* drives mad 6483. *be ~,* skillfully 6967

wyte *pr.1 sg.*[1] See WITT *v.*[1]

wite *pr.1 sg.*[2] See WITT(E) *v.*[2]

wyth(e) *prep.* in the opinion of 159, 1302; on behalf of 1940n

wythhold *v.* retain 6320, 6347, 6398. wythholdon *pr.2 sg.* hold 1939n. wythhold *imp.* 6354

wythin *n. & adv.* the 'inside' team at the tournament 2988n, 3436 etc.

wythoute(n) *n. & adv.* the 'outside' team at the tournament 2988n, 3435 etc.

wythoute *prep.* outside of 2944

witnes *imp.pl.* See WITTNES.

witt *v.*[1] blame on 7396. wyte, wyght *pr.1 sg.* blame 5526, 5538, 8098; blame for 7152

witt(e), wit, wytte, wet(t)e, wotte *v.*[2] know 44, 327, 1467, 5458, 8038, 8360 etc.; *to* ~, to be sure 261, 375 etc. wot, wott(e), wit(t)e *pr.1 sg.* know 498, 838, 963, 1794, 1933 etc. wot, wott(e), wottys *pr.2 sg.* 1405, 2756, 3030, 6640 etc. wot, wott(e), wit(te), wet, wat, wottist *pr.3 sg.* 490, 1124, 1655, 2358, 2798, 3950, 6246, 7398 etc. wot(e), wott(e), witte, wytte *pr.pl.* 3, 435, 1869, 3426, 5290, 6386 etc. woste, wyste *subj.* 1043, 4633 etc. wete, wette *imp.* 1434, 8150 etc. wiste, wyst(e), west *pa.t.sg.* 282, 875, 4562, 8400 etc. wiste, wyst(e) *pa.t.pl.* 1221, 3352, 5915 etc. witten, wetyn, wyst *pp.* 3872n, 5207, 5541

witte *n.*[1] See WYTE.

witte *n.*[2] reproach 5621

witten *pp.* See WITT(E) *v.*[2]

wyttenesse *n.* See WYTTNES.

witte-saff *pr.1 sg.* See WOVCHE-SAFFE.

witty, witte *adj.* sensible 2068, *5379 etc.

wyttly *adv.* See WYGHTTLY.

wyttnes, wyttenesse, wettnes *n.* testimony 5173. *as* ~, standing as testimony 5662, 6582, 7817

wittnes *v.* testify 39. witnes *imp.pl.* 5144

wo, woo *n.* misfortune 115, 1813 etc.; anguish 904, 1212 etc.

wo, woo *adj.* grieved 698, 2148 etc.

wo, woo *adv.* ~ *worthe*, a curse upon 541, 5528 etc. ~ *mot thou be*, a curse upon you 938

wode *adj.* See WOOD(E).

wolde *n. in* ~, in his possession 6007

wolde *pa.t.* See WELD(E).

womanhoode *n.* womanliness 90

won, wonne *v.* stay 211, 1384. wonnand

pr.p. living 5341, 7930. wonyd, wonnyde *pa.t.* lived 25, 4195

won *pa.t.* See WYNNE.

wonder, wondur, wondyr *n.* surprise 1009, 2864, 7914 etc. ~ *thynke/þought*, be/were astonished 1220, 5772; ~ *hadde*, was astonished 8048

wonder *v.* marvel 362. wondyrs *pr.3 sg. (impers.)* 1927. wonders *pr.3 pl.* 4766. wonder *imp.sg.* 1019. wondyrd, wonderd *pa.t.* 3319, 4404. wonderd, a-wonderd *pp.* astonished 1281, 5742

wonder, wondyr *adj.* marvellous 1227, 7075 etc.

wonder(e), wondyr, wondur *adv.* exceedingly 41, 730, 2283, 2792 etc.

wonderd *v.* See WONDER.

wonderly *adv.* marvellously 8717

wondyr *n., adj., adv.* See WONDER.

wondyrd, wondyrs *v.* See WONDER.

wondur *n., adv.* See WONDER.

wone *pp.* See WYNNE.

wonyd *pa.t.* See WON.

wonis *n.pl.* dwelling-place 6270

wonnand *pr.p.* See WON.

wonne, woone *n. good* ~, a large quantity *4837n, 7679

wonne *v.* See WON.

wonne *pp.* See WYNNE.

wonnyde *pa.t.* See WON.

wont(e) *pp. was* ~, was accustomed 2496, 2499, 2861

woo *n., adj., adv.* See WO.

wood(e), wode *adj.* crazed 1956, 1965, 8013 etc.

woone *n.* See WONNE.

worde *adj.* See WORTHY(E).

wordynes *n.* See WORTHYNES.

wore *pa.t. subj.* See BE.

worke *n.* See WERKE.

worke, workis, workys *v.* See WERKE.

worove *subj.* strangle 7395

worthe *subj. well/woo* ~, blessed/cursed be 541, 6798 etc.

worthe *adj.* valuable 947; worth 1583, 2331 etc.

wortheer, wortheeste *comp. & sup. adj.* See WORTHY(E).

worthely *adj.* worthy 88, 154

worthenes *n.* See WORTHYNES.

worthy *n.* worthy one 4061. *pl.* 2094

worthy(e), worde *adj.* worthy 28, 4874, 8599 etc.; sufficiently good 3872n.

worthyer, wortheer *comp.* 1586, 5200 etc. worthyeste, wortheeste *sup.* 1576, 5019
worthy *adv.* excellently 423
worthynes, worthenes, wordynes *n.* worthiness 1581, 1975 etc. ~ *(of hand, of warre)*, feats of arms 2315, 2326, 2545, 6756 etc.
woste, wot, wott(e), wottys, wottist *v.* See WITT(E) *v.*²
wovche-saffe, wovche-save *v.* bestow 4988, 5168. witte-saff *pr.1 sg.* 3223
wowe *v.* woo 65, 7955 etc.
wrange *n.* See WRONG(E).
wrange *pa.t.* See WRYNGE.
wrathe *adj.* See WROTHE.
wreke *v.* avenge 719. wrokyn *pp.* 3789
wrethe *n.*¹ twisted band 6242
wrethe *n.*² See WROTHE.
wrynge *v.* twist 710. wrynggyng *pr.p.* 1180. wrange *pa.t.* 1815, 4672
wroght(e), wro3te *v.* See WERKE.
wrokyn *pp.* See WREKE.
wrong(e), wrange *n.* wrong 343, 1485 etc. *worke* ~, act unjustly 7638
wrothe, wrethe *n.* anger 1956, 3293, *6353n etc.; act done in anger 8759
wrothe *pa.t.* See WERKE.
wrothe, wrathe *adj.* angry 558, 7292 etc.
wrothely *adv.* angrily 7030
wrought(e), wrovghte, wroughtte, wrou3te *v.* See WERKE.

Y

yard *n.* staff 6475
yare *adv.*¹ quickly 466, 4221; soon 573, 2195; indeed 3638, 4513
yare *adv.*² & *conj.* See ARE.
yate *n.* gate 4732. gatys, yattis *pl.* 3459, 4026, 5927
yede, 3ede *pa.t.* see YOUDE.
yeld(e) *v.* surrender 4306, 8099; *(refl.)* 4530, 4598 etc.; repay 4397; render 5998. yeldis, yeldys, eldythe *pr.3 sg.* surrenders 4526, *(refl.)* 3139, 5733. yolde *pa.t.* surrendered *(refl.)* 3792. yeldun, yeldone, youlden *pp.* surrendered *(refl.)* 3776; repaid 5350, 8057
yemyde *pa.t.* cared for 516
yene *adj.* See YON.
yenge *adj.* See YONG(E).
yere *adv.* & *conj.* See ARE.
yet(e), yett(e), 3et, yt(e) *adv.* yet 386, 782, 812, 917, 1971, 5183, 7702 etc.
ynge *adj.* See YONG(E).
yolde *pa.t.* See YELD(E).
yole *n.* yuletide *6840n, 8334n
yon, yene *adj.* that 4875, 4881, 7545
yong(e), young(e), yenge, ynge *adj.* young 26, 65, 81, 809, 2025, 2261 etc.
yonne *pron.* those 7783
youde, yede, 3ede *pa.t.* went 76, 456, 2815 etc.
youlden *pp.* See YELD(E).
yte *adv.* See YET(E).

INDEX OF PROPER NAMES

An asterisk before a citation indicates an emended form, while an 'n' refers readers to the Explanatory Notes.

People and Animals

The names given in brackets are the Anglo-Norman counterparts. The Anglo-Norman titles of characters have been given only where they differ from those in the Middle English version.

Places

The modern English name is given in brackets.